British Qualifications 2013

British Qualifications 2013

43RD EDITION

A Complete Guide to Professional, Vocational & Academic Qualifications in the United Kingdom

LONDON PHILADELPHIA NEW DELHI

Publisher's note

Every possible effort has been made to ensure that the information contained in this book is accurate at the time of going to press, and the publishers and authors cannot accept responsibility for any errors or omissions, however caused. No responsibility for loss or damage occasioned to any person acting, or refraining from action, as a result of the material in this publication can be accepted by the editor, the publisher or any of the authors.

First published in Great Britain in 1966

Forty-third edition published in Great Britain and the United States in 2013 by Kogan Page Limited

Apart from any fair dealing for the purposes of research or private study, or criticism or review, as permitted under the Copyright, Designs and Patents Act 1988, this publication may only be reproduced, stored or transmitted, in any form or by any means, with the prior permission in writing of the publishers, or in the case of reprographic reproduction in accordance with the terms and licences issued by the CLA. Enquiries concerning reproduction outside these terms should be sent to the publishers at the undermentioned addresses:

120 Pentonville Road	1518 Walnut Street, Suite 1100	4737/23 Ansari Road
London N1 9JN	Philadelphia PA 19102	Daryaganj
United Kingdom	USA	New Delhi 110002
www.koganpage.com		India

© Kogan Page, 2013

British Library Cataloguing-in-Publication Data

A CIP record for this book is available from the British Library.

ISBN 978 0 7494 6743 2
E-ISBN 978 0 7494 6744 9
ISSN 0141-5972

Typeset by AMA DataSet Ltd, Preston
Production managed by Jellyfish
Printed and bound by CPI Group (UK) Ltd, Croydon, CR0 4YY

PUBLISHER'S NOTE

This 43rd edition of *British Qualifications* has been considerably revised and updated to reflect the many changes in degree, diploma and certificate courses and to take account of legislative reforms affecting the structure of higher and further education over the past year.

The editor and compilers are most grateful to the academic registrars and the secretaries of the many bodies they have contacted for information and advice. Without their cooperation, the revision and updating of *British Qualifications* would not have been possible.

CONTENTS

References		*xvii*
How to Use this Book		*xviii*
Index of Abbreviations and Designatory Letters		*xix*
PART 1	INTRODUCTION	1
	Education Reform	3
	Foundation Degrees	4
	Policy and Regulation	4
	Quality Assurance	5
	Qualification Frameworks	5
PART 2	TEACHING ESTABLISHMENTS	9
	Further and Higher Education	11
	Further and Higher Education Institutions	12
	England and Wales	12
	Scotland	12
	Northern Ireland	12
	Universities and HE Colleges	13
	Institutions receiving funding from Higher Education Funding Council for England	13
	Universities receiving funding from the Department for Employment and Learning in Northern Ireland	14
	Higher Education Institutions receiving funding from the Scottish Further and Higher Education Funding Council for Scotland	14
	Institutions receiving funding from the Higher Education Funding Council for Wales	14
	Other HE Organizations	15
PART 3	QUALIFICATIONS	17
	Introduction	19
	Definition of Common Terms	19
	Accrediting Regulatory Bodies	20
	England	20
	Scotland	23
	Validating, Examining and Awarding Bodies/Organizations	24
	ABC Awards	24
	AQA	25
	ASDAN	25
	City & Guilds	25
	Edexcel Foundation	26
	EDI plc	26
	NCFE	26
	OCR	27
	WJEC	27

Contents

PART 4		QUALIFICATIONS AWARDED IN UNIVERSITIES	29
		Admission to Degree Courses	31
		Higher Education Institutes (HEIs)	31
		The Open University	31
		Business Schools	31
		Awards	31
		First degrees	31
		Higher degrees	33
		Foundation degrees	33
		Honorary degrees	33
		Diplomas and certificates of higher education	33
		Postgraduate diplomas and certificates	33
		Postgraduate courses	34
		Business schools	34
		First awards	34
		Higher awards	35
		University of Aberdeen	35
		University of Abertay, Dundee	37
		Aberystwyth University	37
		Anglia Ruskin University	38
		Colchester Institute	40
		Ashridge	40
		Aston University	40
		Bangor University	42
		University Centre Barnsley	44
		University of Bath	44
		Bath Spa University	45
		University of Bedfordshire	46
		The Queen's University of Belfast	47
		University of Birmingham	49
		School of Education, Selly Oak	52
		University College Birmingham	52
		Birmingham City University	52
		Bishop Grosseteste University College	54
		East Lancashire Institute of Higher Education at Blackburn College	54
		Bournemouth University	54
		University of Bradford	55
		Bradford College	56
		University of Brighton	56
		University of Bristol	58
		University of the West of England, Bristol	60
		Brunel University	62
		University of Buckingham	63
		Buckinghamshire New University	64
		University of Cambridge	64
		Cambridge International College	67
		Canterbury Christ Church University	67

Cardiff University	69
Cardiff Metropolitan University	71
University of Central Lancashire	73
University of Chester	74
University of Chichester	76
City University London	76
Guildhall School of Music & Drama	78
Laban	78
School of Psychotherapy & Counselling Psychology at Regent's College	78
The Nordoff-Robbins Music Therapy Centre	78
Coventry University	79
Cranfield University	80
University for the Creative Arts	81
University of Cumbria	81
De Montford University	82
University of Derby	83
University Centre Doncaster	84
University of Dundee	84
Durham University	87
Cranmer Hall, St John's College	88
New College Durham	88
Royal Academy of Dance	89
Ushaw College	89
University of East Anglia	89
City College Norwich	91
Otley College	91
The University of Edinburgh	91
Edinburgh Napier University	94
Edinburgh College of Art	95
University of Essex	95
Writtle College	97
University of Exeter	97
UCP Marjon-University College Plymouth St Mark & St John	98
University College Falmouth (Inc Dartington College of Arts)	99
University of Glamorgan	99
University of Glasgow	100
Glasgow Caledonian University	102
The Glasgow School of Art	103
University of Gloucestershire	103
University of Greenwich	104
Grimsby Institute/University Centre	105
Harper Adams University College	106
Heriot-Watt University	106
Edinburgh College of Art	107
University of Hertfordshire	107
Hertfordshire Regional College	109
North Hertfordshire College	109

Contents

Oaklands College	109
West Herts College	109
The University of Huddersfield	109
University of Hull	110
Bishop Burton College	112
Doncaster College	112
Imperial College, London	112
Keele University	113
University of Kent	114
Kingston University	116
Lancaster University	117
Blackpool and The Fylde College	119
Edge Hill University	119
University of Leeds	120
Askham Bryan College	123
College of the Resurrection	123
Leeds College of Art	123
Leeds College of Music	123
Leeds Trinity University College	123
Northern School of Contemporary Dance	124
York St John University	124
Leeds Metropolitan University	124
University of Leicester	126
Newman University College	127
University of Lincoln	128
East Riding College	129
Hull College	129
North Lindsey College	129
University of Liverpool	130
Liverpool Hope University	132
Liverpool John Moores University	132
University of the Arts London	134
London Contemporary Dance School	134
London Metropolitan University	135
The London School of Osteopathy	136
London South Bank University	137
University of East London	138
University of West London	139
University of London; Birkbeck	140
University of London; Courtauld Institute of Art	141
University of London; Goldsmiths	141
University of London; Heythrop College	142
University of London; Institute in Paris	142
University of London; Institute of Education	142
University of London; King's College London	143
University of London; London School of Economics & Political Science	145
University of London; London School of Jewish Studies	145

University of London; Queen Mary	145
University of London; Royal Holloway	147
University of London; Royal Veterinary College	148
University of London; School of Oriental and African Studies	149
University of London; The School of Pharmacy	149
University of London; University College London (UCL)	150
University of Loughborough	153
University of Manchester	155
Manchester Metropolitan University	158
Middlesex University	160
University of Newcastle upon Tyne	162
University of Northampton	165
University of Northumbria at Newcastle	167
University of Nottingham	169
Nottingham Trent University	173
Southampton Solent University	175
The Open University	177
University of Oxford	178
Oxford Brookes University	182
University of Plymouth	184
South Devon College	186
Truro & Penwith College	186
University of Portsmouth	186
Queen Margaret University College	189
University of Reading	189
Robert Gordon University	191
Roehampton University	192
The Royal Academy of Dance	193
Royal Academy of Dramatic Art	193
Royal Agricultural College	194
Royal Ballet School	194
Royal College of Art	194
Royal College of Music	194
The Royal College of Organists	195
Royal Conservatoire of Scotland	195
Royal Northern College of Music	195
University of St Andrews	195
University of Salford	197
Riverside College, Halton	198
University of Sheffield	199
Sheffield Hallam University	203
University of Southampton	206
Staffordshire University	209
University of Stirling	210
Stockport College	212
University of Strathclyde	212
University Campus Suffolk	214

Contents

	University of Sunderland	215
	City of Sunderland College	216
	University of Surrey	216
	Farnborough College of Technology	218
	NESCOT (North East Surrey College of Technology)	219
	St Mary's College	219
	University of Sussex	219
	Swansea University	222
	University of Teesside	223
	Trinity College London	224
	University of Ulster	225
	University of Wales: Glyndwr University	227
	University of Wales: Newport	229
	University of Wales: Swansea Metropolitan University	230
	University of Wales: Trinity Saint David	231
	University of Warwick	233
	University of West of Scotland	235
	The University of Westminster	236
	The University of Winchester	237
	University of Wolverhampton	238
	University College Worcester	240
	University of York	241
	Yorkshire Coast College	243
PART 5	**QUALIFICATIONS AWARDED BY PROFESSIONAL AND TRADE ASSOCIATIONS**	**245**
	The Functions of Professional Associations	247
	Qualifications	247
	Study	247
	Protection of Members' Interests	247
	Membership of Professional Associations	248
	Qualifying Associations	248
	Examinations and Requirements	248
	Gaining Professional Qualifications	248
	Accountancy	249
	Acoustics	255
	Advertising and Public Relations	256
	Agriculture and Horticulture	258
	Ambulance Service	260
	Arbitration	260
	Archaeology	261
	Architecture	261
	Art and Design	263
	Astronomy and Space Science	265
	Aviation	266
	Banking	267
	Beauty Therapy and Beauty Culture	268

Biological Sciences	270
Brewing	271
Building	272
Business Studies	274
Catering and Institutional Management	277
Chemistry	279
Chiropody	281
Chiropractic	282
The Churches	284
Cinema, Film and Television	291
Cleaning, Laundry and Dry Cleaning	292
Colour Technology	293
Communications and Media	294
Computing and Information Technology	295
Counselling	297
Credit Management	298
Dancing	299
Dentistry	301
Dietetics	303
Distribution	303
Diving	304
Dramatic and Performing Arts	304
Driving Instructors	305
Embalming	306
Employment and Careers Services	307
Engineering	
Aeronautical	308
Agricultural	308
Automobile	309
Building Services	311
Chemical	311
Civil	312
Electrical, Electronic and Manufacturing	312
Energy	313
Environmental	314
Fire	315
Gas	317
General	317
Marine	320
Mechanical	321
Mining	322
Nuclear	323
Production	324
Refractories	324
Refrigeration	325
Road, Rail and Transport	325
Sheet Metal	327

Structural	328
Water	328
Engineering Design	329
Environmental Sciences	329
Export	330
Fisheries Management	330
Floristry	331
Food Science and Nutrition	331
Forestry and Arboriculture	332
Foundry Technology and Pattern Making	333
Freight Forwarding	334
Fundraising	334
Funeral Directing, Burial and Cremation Administration	335
Furnishing and Furniture	336
Gemmology and Jewellery	337
Genealogy	338
Geography	340
Geology	340
Glass Technology	341
Hairdressing	342
Health and Health Services	343
Horses and Horse Riding	347
Housing	348
Indexing	348
Industrial Safety	349
Insurance and Actuarial Work	352
Journalism	354
Land and Property	355
Landscape Architecture	358
Languages, Linguistics and Translation	358
Law	360
Leisure and Recreation Management	368
Librarianship and Information Work	370
Management	370
Manufacturing	381
Marketing and Sales	382
Martial Arts	386
Massage and Allied Therapies	386
Mathematics	388
Medical Herbalism	390
Medical Secretaries	391
Medicine	391
Metallurgy	401
Meteorology and Climatology	402
Microscopy	403
Museum and Related Work	404
Music	404

Musical Instrument Technology	405
Naval Architecture	406
Navigation, Seamanship and Marine Qualifications	407
Non-destructive Testing	408
Nursery Nursing	408
Nursing and Midwifery	409
Occupational Therapy	409
Opticians (Dispensing)	409
Optometry	411
Orthoptics	412
Osteopathy and Naturopathy	413
Patent Agency	413
Pension Management	414
Personnel Management	414
Pharmacy	416
Photography	417
Physics	419
Physiotherapy	420
Plastics and Rubber	421
Plumbing	421
Printing	422
Professional Investigation	423
Psychoanalysis	423
Psychology	424
Psychotherapy	424
Public Administration	429
Purchasing and Supply	429
Quality Assurance	430
Radiography	430
Retail	431
Secretarial and Office Work	434
Security	434
Social Work and Probation	435
Sociology	436
Speech and Language Therapy	436
Sports Science	437
Statistics	437
Stockbroking and Securities	438
Surgical, Dental and Cardiological Technicians	439
Surveying	439
Swimming Instruction	440
Taxation	440
Taxi Drivers	442
Teaching/Education	442
Technical Communications	444
Textiles	444
Timber Technology	445

Contents

	Town and Country Planning	445
	Trading Standards	446
	Transport	447
	Travel and Tourism	448
	Veterinary Science	450
	Wastes Management	451
	Watch and Clock Making and Repairing	452
	Welding	453
	Welfare	453
PART 6	**BODIES ACCREDITING INDEPENDENT INSTITUTIONS**	455
	The British Accrediation Council for Independent Further and Higher Education (BAC)	457
	The British Council	457
	The Open and Distance Learning Quality Council (ODLQC)	458
	The Council for Independent Further Education (CIFE)	458
PART 7	**STUDY ASSOCIATIONS AND THE 'LEARNED SOCIETIES'**	461
	Occupational Associations	463
	List of Study Associations and Learned Societies	463
Index		*471*

REFERENCES

Association of MBAs (AMBA) (annual) *AMBA – Financial Times Guide to Business Schools*, AMBA, London

Committee of Vice-Chancellors and Principals (CVCP) (annual) *University Entrance: The official guide*, CVCP, London

Department for Education and Skills (DfES) (2003) *The Future of Higher Education*, The Stationery Office, London [online] http://www.dfes.gov.uk/hegateway/strategy/hestrategy/foreword.shtml

DfES (2004) *Five-Year Strategy for Children and Learners*, DfES, London

Qualifications and Curriculum Authority (QCA) (2004) *New Thinking for Reform: A framework for achievement*, QCA, London (July)

HOW TO USE THIS BOOK

You may find these notes helpful when using the book.

Part 1 presents an overview of the further and higher educational systems currently in operation in the United Kingdom, including a discussion of the major reforms that have taken place over the past year and their impact.

Part 2 takes a look at the teaching establishments whose qualifications are listed in Part 4 of the book, offering an explanation of the different types of institution, their place in the overall system and the levels of qualification that they award.

Part 3 presents a detailed description of vocational qualifications awarded by many of the professional associations included in Part 5, including an explanation of validating, examining and awarding bodies.

Part 4 is a directory of qualifications awarded by universities in the United Kingdom (ordered by university name). There is a brief introduction detailing admission to degree courses, degree structure and the various categories of degree available.

Part 5 is a directory of qualifications awarded by professional, trade and specialist associations in the United Kingdom (ordered by profession/discipline), including certificates, diplomas, NVQs and SVQs. A short introduction explains the functions of professional associations and how to gain membership.

Part 6 describes various bodies involved in the accreditation of colleges in the independent sector of further and higher education.

Part 7 is a list of study associations and learned societies.

Also included (at the beginning of the book) is a list of all abbreviations and designatory letters used throughout *British Qualifications*.

INDEX OF ABBREVIATIONS AND DESIGNATORY LETTERS

AAB	Associate of the Association of Book-keepers
AACB	Associate of the Association of Certified Bookkeepers
AACP	Associate of the Association of Computer Professionals
AAFC	Associate of the Association of Financial Controllers and Administrators
AAIA	Associate of the Association of International Accountants
AAMS	Associate of the Association of Medical Secretaries, Practice Managers, Administrators and Receptionists
AASI	Associate of the Ambulance Service Institute
AASW	Advanced Award in Social Work
AAT	Association of Accounting Technicians
ABC	Awarding Body Consortium
ABDO	Associate of the British Dispensing Opticians
ABE	Association of Business Executives
ABEng	Associate Member of the Association of Building Engineers
ABHA	Associate of the British Hypnotherapy Association
ABIAT	Associate Member of the British Institute of Architectural Technologists
ABIPP	Associate of the British Institute of Professional Photography
ABMA	Associate of the Business Management Association
ABPR	Association of British Picture Restorers
ABRSM	Associated Board of the Royal Schools of Music
ABS	Association of Business Schools
ABSSG	Associate of the British Society of Scientific Glassblowers
ACA	Associate of the Institute of Chartered Accountants in England and Wales
ACA	Associate of the Institute of Chartered Accountants in Ireland
ACB	Association of Certified Bookkeepers
ACC	Accredited Clinical Coders
ACCA	Associate of the Association of Chartered Certified Accountants
ACCA	Association of Chartered Certified Accountants
ACE	Association for Conferences and Events
ACEA	Associate of the Institute of Cost and Executive Accountants
ACertCM	Archbishop of Canterbury's Certificate in Church Music
ACGI	Associate of City and Guilds of London Institute
ACIArb	Associate of the Chartered Institute of Arbitrators
ACIB	Associate of the Chartered Institute of Bankers
ACIBS	Associate of the Chartered Institute of Bankers in Scotland
ACIBSE	Associate of the Chartered Institution of Building Services Engineers
ACIH	Associate of the Chartered Institute of Housing
ACII	Associate of the Chartered Insurance Institute
ACILA	Associate of the Chartered Institute of Loss Adjusters
ACIM	Associate of the Chartered Institute of Marketing
ACIOB	Associate of the Chartered Institute of Building
ACIS	Associate of the Institute of Chartered Secretaries and Administrators
ACIT	Advanced Certificate in International Trade
ACLIP	Certified Affiliate of CILIP
ACMA	Associate of the Chartered Institute of Management Accountants
ACP	Association of Child Psychotherapists
ACP	Associate of the College of Preceptors

Index of Abbreviations and Designatory Letters

ACP	Association of Computer Professionals
ACPM	Associate of the Confederation of Professional Management
ACPP	Associate of the College of Pharmacy Practice
ACT	Associate of the College of Teachers
ACYW	Associate of the Community and Youth Work Association
ADCE	Advanced Diploma in Childcare and Education
ADCM	Archbishop of Canterbury's Diploma in Church Music
AdDipEd	Advanced Diploma in Education
ADI	Approved Driving Instructor
AECI	Association Member of the Institute of Employment Consultants
AEWVH	Association for the Education and Welfare of the Visually Handicapped
AFA	Associate of the Faculty of Actuaries
AFA	Associate of the Institute of Financial Accountants
AFBPsS	Associate Fellow of the British Psychological Society
AFCI	Associate of the Faculty of Commerce and Industry Ltd
AffBMA	Affiliate of the Business Management Association
AffIManf	Affiliate of the Institute of Manufacturing
AffIMI	Affiliate of the Institute of the Motor Industry
AffIMS	Affiliate of the Institute of Management Specialists
AffInstM	Affiliate of the Meat Training Council
AffIP	Affiliate of the Institute of Plumbing
AffProfBTM	Affiliate of Professional Business and Technical Management
AFIMA	Associate Fellow of the Institute of Mathematics and its Applications
AFISOL	Aerodrome Flight Information Service Officer's Licence
AFPC	Advanced Financial Planning Certificate
AFRCSEd	Associate Fellow of Royal College of Surgeons of Edinburgh
AGCL	Associate of the Guild of Cleaners and Launderers
AGI	Associate of the Greek Institute
AGSM	Associate of the Guildhall School of Music and Drama
AHCIMA	Associate of the Hotel and Catering International Management Association
AHFS	Associate of the Council of Health Fitness and Sports Therapists
AHRIM	Associate of the Institute of Health Record Information and Management
AIA	Associate of the Institute of Actuaries
AIA	Association of International Accountants
AIAgrE	Associate of the Institution of Agricultural Engineers
AIAT	Associate of the Institute of Asphalt Technology
AIBCM	Associate of the Institute of British Carriage and Automobile Manufacturers
AIBMS	Associate of the Institute of Biomedical Science
AICB	Associate of the Institute of Certified Book-Keepers
AIChor	Associate of the Benesh Institute of Choreology
AICHT	Associate of the International Council of Holistic Therapists
AICM(Cert)	Associate Member of the Institute of Credit Management
AICS	Associate of the Institution of Chartered Shipbrokers
AICSc	Associate of the Institute of Consumer Sciences Incorporating Home Economics
AIDTA	Associate of the International Dance Teachers' Association
AIE	Associate of the Institute of Electrolysis
AIEM	Associate of the Institute of Executives and Managers
AIExpE	Associate of the Institute of Explosive Engineers
AIFA	Associate of the Institute of Field Archaeologists
AIFBQ	Associate of the International Faculty of Business Qualifications
AIFireE	Associate of the Institution of Fire Engineers
AIFP	Associate of the British International Freight Association

Index of Abbreviations and Designatory Letters

AIGD	Associate of the Institute of Grocery Distribution
AIHort	Associate Member of the Institute of Horticulture
AIIMR	Associate of the Institute of Investment Management and Research
AIIRSM	Associate of the International Institute of Risk and Safety Management
AIL	Associate of the Institute of Linguists
AILAM	Associate of the Institute of Leisure and Amenity Management
AIMBM	Associate of the Institute of Maintenance and Building Management
AIMC	Associate of the Institute of Management Consultancy
AIMgt	Associate of the Institute of Management
AIMIS	Associate of the Institute for the Management of Information Systems
AIMM	Associate of the Institute of Massage and Movement
AInstAM	Associate of the Institute of Administrative Management
AInstBA	Associate of the Institute of Business Administration
AInstBCA	Associate of the Institute of Burial and Cremation Administration
AInstBM	Associate of the Institute of Builders' Merchants
AInstCM	Associate of the Institute of Commercial Management
AInstM	Associate of the Meat Training Council
AInstPkg	Associate of the Institute of Packaging
AInstPM	Associate of the Institute of Professional Managers and Administrators
AInstSMM	Associate of the Institute of Sales and Marketing Management
AInstTA	Associate of the Institute of Transport Administration
AInstTT	Associate Member of the Institute of Travel and Tourism
AIOC	Associate of the Institute of Carpenters
AIOFMS	Associate of the Institute of Financial and Management Studies
AIP	Associate of the Institute of Plumbing
AIQA	Associate of the Institute of Quality Assurance
AIS	Accredited Imaging Scientist
AISOB	Associate of the Incorporated Society of Organ Builders
AISTD	Associate of the Imperial Society of Teachers of Dancing
AISTDDip	Associate Diploma of the Imperial Society of Teachers of Dancing
AITSA	Associate of the Institute of Trading Standards Administration
AIVehE	Associate of the Institute of Vehicle Engineers
AIWSc	Associate Member of the Institute of Wood Science
ALCM	Associate of the London College of Music
ALI	Associate of the Landscape Institute
ALS	Associate of the Linnean Society of London
AMA	Associate of the Museums Association
AMABE	Associate Member of the Association of Business Executives
AMAE	Associate Member of the Academy of Experts
AMASI	Associate Member of the Architecture and Surveying Institute
AMBA	Association of MBAs
AMBA	Non-Teacher Associate Member of the British (Theatrical) Arts
AMBCS	Associate Member of the British Computer Society
AMBII	Associate Member of the British Institute of Innkeeping
AmCAM	Associate of the Communication Advertising and Marketing Education Foundation
AMCT	Associate of the Association of Corporate Treasurers
AMCTHCM	Associate Member of the Confederation of Tourism, Hotel and Catering Management
AMI	Association Montessori Internationale
AMIA	Affiliated Member of the Association of International Accountants
AMIAgrE	Associate Member of the Institution of Agricultural Engineers
AMIAP	Associate Member of the Institution of Analysts and Programmers

Index of Abbreviations and Designatory Letters

AMIAT	Associate Member of the Institute of Asphalt Technology
AMIBC	Associate Member of the Institute of Building Control
AMIBCM	Associate Member of the Institute of British Carriage and Automobile Manufacturers
AMIBE	Associate Member of the Institution of British Engineers
AMIBF	Associate Member of the Institute of British Foundrymen
AMICE	Associate Member of the Institution of Civil Engineers
AMIChemE	Associate Member of the Institution of Chemical Engineers
AMIED	Associate Member of the Institution of Engineering Designers
AMIEE	Associate Member of the Institution of Electrical Engineers
AMIEx	Associate Member of the Institute of Export
AMIHIE	Associate Member of the Institute of Highway Incorporated Engineers
AMIHT	Associate Member of the Institution of Highways and Transportation
AMIIE	Associate Member of the Institution of Incorporated Engineers
AMIIExE	Associate Member of the Institution of Incorporated Executive Engineers
AMIIHTM	Associate Member of the International Institute of Hospitality Tourism & Management
AMIISE	Associate Member of the International Institute of Social Economics
AMIM	Associate Member of the Institute of Materials
AMIManf	Member of the Institute of Manufacturing
AMIMechE	Associate Member of the Institution of Mechanical Engineers
AMIMechIE	Associate Member of the Institution of Mechanical Incorporated Engineers
AMIMI	Associate Member of the Institute of the Motor Industry
AMIMinE	Associate of the Institute of Mining Engineers
AMIMM	Associate Member of the Institution of Mining and Metallurgy
AMIMS	Associate Member of the Institute of Management Specialists
AMInstAEA	Associate Member of the Institute of Automotive Engineer Assessors
AMInstBE	Associate Member of the Institution of British Engineers
AMInstE	Associate Member of the Institute of Energy
AMInstR	Associate Member of the Institute of Refrigeration
AMInstTA	Associate Member of the Institute of Transport Administration
AMIPlantE	Associate Member of the Institution of Plant Engineers
AMIPR	Associate Member of the Institute of Public Relations
AMIPRE	Associate Member of the Incorporated Practitioners in Radio and Electronics
AMIQ	Associate Member of the Institute of Quarrying
AMIQA	Associate Member of the Institute of Quality Assurance
AMIRTE	Associate Member of the Institute of Road Transport Engineers
AMISM	Associate Member of the Institute for Supervision & Management
AMIStrutE	Associate Member of the Institution of Structural Engineers
AMITD	Associate Member of the Institute of Training and Development
AMIVehE	Associate Member of the Institute of Vehicle Engineers
AMNI	Associate Member of the Nautical Institute
AMPA	Associate Member of the Master Photographers Association
AMProfBTM	Associate Member of Professional Business and Technical Management
AMRAeS	Associate Member of the Royal Aeronautical Society
AMRSH	Associate Member of the Royal Society for the Promotion of Health
AMS	Associate of the Institute of Management Services
AMS(Aff)	Affiliate of the Association of Medical Secretaries, Practice Managers, Administrators and Receptionists
AMSE	Associate Member of the Society of Engineers (Inc)
AMSPAR	Association of Medical Secretaries, Practice Managers, Administrators and Receptionists

Index of Abbreviations and Designatory Letters

AMusEd	Associate Diploma in Music Education
AMusLCM	Associate in Music of the London College of Music
AMusTCL	Associate in Music of Trinity College of Music
AMWES	Associate Member of the Women's Engineering Society
ANAEA	Associate of the National Association of Estate Agents
ANCA	Advanced National Certificate in Agriculture
AOP	Association of Photographers
AOR	Association of Reflexologists
APA	Accreditation of Prior Experience
APC	Assessment of Professional Competence
APCS	Associate of the Property Consultants Society
APMI	Associate of the Pensions Management Institute
APMP	Association for Project Management Professional
AQA	Assessment & Qualifications Alliance
ARAD	Associate of the Royal Academy of Dancing
ARAM	Associate of the Royal Academy of Music
ARB	Architects Registration Board
ARCM	Associate of Royal College of Music
ARCO	Associate of the Royal College of Organists
ARCS	Associate of the Royal College of Science
AREC	Associate of the Recruitment and Employment Confederation
ARELS	Association of Recognised English Language Services
ARELS-FELCO	Association of Recognised English Language Teaching Establishments in Britain
ARIBA	Associate of the Royal Institute of British Architects
ARICS	Associate of the Royal Institution of Chartered Surveyors
ARIPHH	Associate of the Royal Institute of Public Health and Hygiene
ARPS	Associate of the Royal Photographic Society
ARSC	Associate of the Royal Society of Chemistry
ARSCM	Associate of the Royal School of Church Music
ARSM	Associate of the Royal School of Mines
AS	Advanced Supplementary level
ASCA	Associate of the Institute of Company Accountants
ASCT	Associate of the Society of Claims Technicians
ASDC	Associate of the Society of Dyers and Colourists
ASE	Associate of the Society of Engineers (Inc)
ASI	Ambulance Service Institute
ASI	Architecture and Surveying Institute
ASIAffil	Affiliate of the Ambulance Service Institute
ASIS	Accredited Senior Imaging Scientist
ASLC	Advanced Secretarial Language Certificate
ASMA	Associate of the Society of Sales Management Administrators Ltd
ASNN	Associate of the Society of Nursery Nursing
AssCI	Associate of the Institute of Commerce
AssociateCIPD	Associate of the Chartered Institute of Personnel and Development
AssociateIEEE	Associate of the Institution of Electrical and Electronics Engineers Incorporated
AssociateIIE	Associate of the Institution of Incorporated Engineers
AssocIMechIE	Associate of the Institution of Mechanical Incorporated Engineers
AssocIPD	Associate of the Institute of Personnel & Development
AssocIPHE	Associate of the Institution of Public Health Engineers
AssocMIWM	Associate Member of the Institute of Wastes Management
AssocTechIIE	Associate Technician of the Institution of Incorporated Engineers
ASTA	Associate of the Swimming Teachers' Association

ASVA	Associate of the Incorporated Society of Valuers and Auctioneers
ATC	Art Teacher's Certificate
ATCL	Associate of Trinity College of Music
ATCLicence	Air Traffic Controller's Licence
ATCLTESOL	Associate Diploma in the Teaching of English to Speakers of Other Languages, Trinity College
ATD	Art Teacher's Diploma
ATI	Associate of the Textile Industry
ATII	Associate of the Chartered Institute of Taxation
ATPL	Airline Transport Pilot's Licence
ATSC	Associate of the Oil and Colour Chemists' Association
ATSC	Associate in the Technology of Surface Coatings
ATT	Association of Taxation Technicians
ATT	Member of the Association of Taxation Technicians
ATTA	Association of Therapy Teachers Associate
ATTF	Association of Therapy Teachers Fellow
ATTM	Association of Therapy Teachers Member
AWeldI	Associate of the Welding Institute
BA	Bachelor of Arts
BA(Econ)	Bachelor of Arts in Economics & Social Studies
BA(Ed)	Bachelor of Arts (Education)
BA(Lan)	Bachelor of Languages
BA(Law)	Bachelor of Arts in Law
BA(Music)	Bachelor of Music
BABTAC	British Association of Beauty Therapy and Cosmetology Ltd
BAC	British Accreditation Council for Independent Further and Higher Education
BAC	British Association for Counselling
BAcc	Bachelor of Accountancy
BACP	British Association for Counselling Psychotherapy
BADA	British Antique Dealers' Association
BADN	British Association of Dental Nurses
BAE	British Association of Electrolysists Ltd
BAGMA	British Agricultural and Garden Machinery Association
BAgr	Bachelor of Agriculture
BAO	Bachelor of Obstetrics
BAP	British Association of Psychotherapists
BArch	Bachelor of Architecture
BASELT	British Association in State English Language Teaching
BBO	British Ballet Organisation
BChD	Bachelor of Dental Surgery
BChir	Bachelor of Surgery
BCL	Bachelor of Civil Law
BCom	Bachelor of Commerce
BCombStuds	Bachelor of Combined Studies
BComm	Bachelor of Communications
BCS	Bachelor of Combined Studies
BCS	British Computer Society
BD	Bachelor of Divinity
BDA	British Dietetic Association
BDes	Bachelor of Design
BDS	Bachelor of Dental Surgery
BEconSc	Bachelor of Economics

BECTU	Broadcasting, Entertainment, Cinematograph and Theatre Union
BEd	Bachelor of Education
BEng	Bachelor of Engineering
BEng and Man	Bachelor of Mechanical Engineering, Manufacture and Management
BER	Board for Engineers' Regulation
BFA	Bachelor of Fine Arts
BFin	Bachelor of Finance
BHA	British Hypnotherapy Association
BHI	British Horological Institute Ltd
BHS	British Horse Society
BHSAI	British Horse Society's Assistant Instructor's Certificate
BHSI	British Horse Society's Instructor's Certificate
BHSII	British Horse Society's Intermediate Instructor's Certificate
BHSIntSM	British Horse Society's Intermediate Stable Manager's Certificate
BHSSM	British Horse Society's Stable Manager's Certificate
BIA	Beauty Industry Authority
BIAT	British Institute of Architectural Technologists
BIBA	Bachelor of International Business Administration
BIE	British Institute of Embalmers
BIFA	British International Freight Association
BIPP	British Institute of Professional Photography
BIS	British Interplanetary Society
BKSTS	British Kinematograph Sound and Television Society
BLD	Bachelor of Landscape Design
BLE	Bachelor of Land Economy
BLEng	Bi-Lingual Engineer
BLib	Bachelor of Librarianship
BLing	Bachelor of Linguistics
BLitt	Bachelor of Letters
BLS	Bachelor of Library Studies
BM	Bachelor of Medicine
BMA	British Medical Association
BM, BCh	Conjoint degree of Bachelor of Medicine, Bachelor of Surgery
BM, BS	Conjoint degree of Bachelor of Medicine, Bachelor of Surgery
BMedBiol	Bachelor of Medical Biology
BMedSci	Bachelor of Medical Sciences
BMedSci(Speech)	Bachelor of Medical Sciences (Speech)
BMet	Bachelor of Metallurgy
BMid	Bachelor of Midwifery
BMidwif	Bachelor of Midwifery
BMSc	Bachelor of Medical Sciences
BMus	Bachelor of Music
BN	Bachelor of Nursing
BNNursing	Bachelor of Nursing, Nursing Studies
BNSc	Bachelor of Nursing
BNurs	Bachelor of Nursing
BOptom	Bachelor of Optometry
BPA	Bachelor of Performing Arts
BPharm	Bachelor of Pharmacy
BPhil	Bachelor of Philosophy
BPhil(Ed)	Bachelor of Philosophy (Education)
BPL	Bachelor of Planning

Index of Abbreviations and Designatory Letters

BSc	Bachelor of Science
BSc(Archit)	Bachelor of Science (Architecture)
BSc(DentSci)	Bachelor of Science in Dental Science
BSc(Econ)	Bachelor of Science in Economics
BSc(MedSci)	Bachelor of Science (Medical Science)
BSc(Social Science)	Bachelor of Science (Social Science)
BSc(Town & Regional Planning)	Bachelor of Science (Town & Regional Planning)
BSc(VetSc)	Bachelor of Science (Veterinary Science)
BScAgr	Bachelor of Science in Agriculture
BScEng	Bachelor of Science in Engineering
BScFor	Bachelor of Science in Forestry
BScTech	Bachelor of Technical Science
BSocSc	Bachelor of Social Science
BSSc	Bachelor of Social Science
BSSG	Member of the British Society of Scientific Glassblowers
BTEC	Business and Technology Education Council
BTech	Bachelor of Technology
BTechEd	Bachelor of Technological Education
BTEC HC	Business and Technology Education Council Higher Certificate
BTEC HD	Business and Technology Education Council Higher Diploma
BTEC HNC	Business and Technology Education Council Higher National Certificate
BTEC HND	Business and Technology Education Council Higher National Diploma
BTechS	Bachelor of Technology Studies
BTh	Bachelor of Theology
BTheol	Bachelor of Theology
BTP	Bachelor of Town Planning
BVC	Bar Vocational Course
BVetMed	Bachelor of Veterinary Medicine
BVMS	Bachelor of Veterinary Medicine
BVM&S	Bachelor of Veterinary Medicine
BVSc	Bachelor of Veterinary Science
C&G	City and Guilds
CA	Member of the Institute of Chartered Accountants of Scotland
CAA	Civil Aviation Authority
CABE	Companion of the Association of Business Executives
CACHE	Council for Awards in Children's Care and Education
CAE	Certificated Automotive Engineer
CAE	Companion of the Academy of Experts
CAM	Communication Advertising and Marketing Education Foundation
CAS	Certification of Accountancy Studies
CASS	Certificate of Applied Social Studies
CAT	Certificate for Accounting Technicians
CAT	College of Advanced Technology
CATS	Postgraduate Qualification by Credit Accumulation and Transfer
CBA	Companion of the British (Theatrical) Arts
CBAE	Companion of the British Academy of Experts
CBIM	Companion of the British Institute of Management
CBiol	Chartered Biologist
CBLC	Certificate in Business Language Competence
CBSSG	Craft Member of the British Society of Scientific Glassblowers
CCETSW	Central Council for Education and Training in Social Work

Index of Abbreviations and Designatory Letters

CChem	Chartered Chemist
CCol	Chartered Colourist
CCST	Certificate of Completion of Specialist Training
CDBA	Certified Doctor of Business Administration
CDipAF	Certified Diploma in Accounting and Finance
CEE	Extended European Command Endorsement
CeFA	Certificate for Financial Advisers
CEM	Certificate in Executive Management
CeMAP	Certificate in Mortgage Advice and Practice
CEng	Chartered Engineer
CertAMed	Certificate in Aviation Medicine
CertArb	Certificate in Arboriculture
CertBibKnowl	Certificate of Bible Knowledge
CertCIH	Chartered Institute of Housing recognised Housing Qualification
CertCM	Certificate of Cash Management
CertDesRCA	Certificate of Designer of the Royal College of Art
CertEd	Certificate in Education
CertEPK	Certificate of Essential Pensions Knowledge
CertHE	Certificate of Higher Education
CertHSAP	Certificate in Health Services Administration Practice
CertHSM	Certificate in Health Services Management
CertMFS	Certificate in the Marketing of Financial Services
CertOccHyg	Certificate in Operational Competence in Comprehensive Occupational Hygiene
CertRP	Certificate in Recruitment Practice
CertTEL	Certificate in the Teaching of European Languages
CertTESOL	Certificate of Teaching of English to Speakers of Other Languages
CertTEYL	Certificate of Teaching of English to Young Learners
CertYCW	Certificate in Youth and Community Work
CETHV	Certificate of Education in Training as Health Visitor
CEYA	Council for Early Years Awards
CFS	Certificate in Financial Services
CFSP	Certificate in Financial Services Practice
CGeol	Chartered Geologist
CGLI	City & Guilds of London Institute
CHARM	Centre for Hazard and Risk Management
ChB	Bachelor of Surgery
CHD	Choral-Training Diploma
ChM	Master of Surgery
CHP	Certificate in Hypnosis and Psychology
CHRIM	Certified Member of the Institute of Health Record Information and Management
CIAgrE	Companion of the Institution of Agricultural Engineers
CIArb	Chartered Institute of Arbitrators
CIB	Chartered Institute of Bankers
CIBM	Corporate Member of the Institute of Builders' Merchants
CIBS	Chartered Institute of Bankers in Scotland
CIBSE	Chartered Institution of Building Services Engineers
CIC	Construction Industry Council
CIEx	Companion of the Institute of Export
CIFE	Conference for Independent Further Education
CIH	Chartered Institute of Housing
CII	Chartered Insurance Institute
CILA	Chartered Institute of Loss Adjusters

Index of Abbreviations and Designatory Letters

CILIP	Chartered Institute of Library and Information Professionals
CIM	Chartered Institute of Marketing
CIMA	Chartered Institute of Management Accountants
CIMediE	Companion of the Institution of Mechanical Engineers
CIMgt	Companion of the Institute of Management
CIOB	Chartered Institute of Building
CIP	Certificate of Institute Practice
CIPD	Chartered Institute of Personnel and Development
CIPFA	Chartered Institute of Public Finance & Accounting
CIPS	Chartered Institute of Purchasing and Supply
CISOB	Counsellor of the Incorporated Society of Organ Builders
CIT	Certificate in Information Technology
CIWEM	Chartered Institution of Water and Environmental Management
CL(ABDO)	Diploma in Contact Lens Practice of the Association of British Dispensing Opticians
CLAC	Commercial Language Assistant Certificate
CLAIT	Computer Literacy & Information Technology
CLC	Council for Licensed Conveyancers
CLE	Limited European Command Endorsement
ClinPsyD	Doctorate in Clinical Psychology
CMA	Certificate in Management Accountancy
CMathFIMA	Fellow of the Institute of Mathematics and its Applications
CMBA	Certified Master of Business Administration
CMBHI	Craft Member of the British Horological Institute
CMC	Certified Management Consultants
CMet	Chartered Meteorologist
CMIWSc	Certified Member of the Institute of Wood Science
CMS	Certificate in Management Studies
CNAA	Council for National Academic Awards
COA	Certificate of Accreditation
COBC	Certificate of Basic Competence
CoEA	Certificate of Educational Achievement
COES	Certificate of Educational Studies
CofE	Church of England
CofS	Church of Scotland
CompBCS	Companion of the British Computer Society
CompIAP	Companion of the Institution of Analysts and Programmers
CompIEE	Companion of the Institution of Electrical Engineers
CompIGasE	Companion of the Institution of Gas Engineers
CompIManf	Companion of the Institute of Manufacturing
CompIMS	Companion of the Institute of Management Specialists
CompIP	Companion of the Institute of Plumbing
CorporateIRRV	Corporate Member of the Institute of Revenues, Rating and Valuation
COSCA	Confederation of Scottish Counselling Agencies
CPA	Chartered Patent Agents
CPC	Certificate of Professional Competence, the Institute of Transport Administration
CPD	Continuing Professional Development
CPE	Common Professional Exam
CPEA	Certificate of Practice in Estate Agency
CPFA	Member of Chartered Institute of Public Finance and Accountancy
CPhys	Chartered Physicist of the Institute of Physics
CPIM	Certificate in Production and Inventory Management

Index of Abbreviations and Designatory Letters

CPL	Commercial Pilot's Licence
CPM	Certified Professional Manager
CPP	Certificate of Pre-school Practice
CPR	Chartered Professional Review
CProfBTM	Companion of Professional Business and Technical Management
CPS	Certificate in Pastoral Studies and Applied Theology
CPSC	Certificate of Proficiency in Survival Craft
CPsychol	Chartered Psychologist, British Psychological Society
CPT	Continuing Professional Training
CPVE	Certificate of Pre-Vocational Training
CRAeS	Companion of the Royal Aeronautical Society
CRAH	Central Register of Advanced Hypnotherapists
CRCW	Church Related Community Workers
CRNCM	Companion of the Royal Northern College of Music
CSCT	Central School for Counselling Training
CSD	Chartered Society of Designers
CSE	Certificate of Secondary Education
CSM	Certificate in Safety Management
CSMGSM	Certificate in Stage Management (Guildhall School of Music and Drama)
CStat	Chartered Statistician
CSYS	Certificate of Sixth Year Studies
CTABRSM	Certificate of Teaching of the Associated Board of the Royal School of Music
CTextATI	Associate of the Textile Institute
CTextFTI	Fellow of the Textile Institute
CTHCM	Confederation of Tourism, Hotel and Catering Management
CVA	Certificated Value Analyst
CVM	Certificated Value Manager
CVT	Certified Vehicle Technologist
DA	Diploma in Anaesthetics
DAdmin	Doctor of Administration
DAES	Diploma in Advanced Educational Studies
DArch	Doctor of Architecture
DAvMed	Diploma in Aviation Medicine
DBA	Doctor of Business Administration
DBE	Diploma in Business Engineering
DBO	Diploma of the British Orthoptic Society
DBS	Diploma in Business Studies
DCC	Diploma of Chelsea College
DCDH	Diploma in Child Dental Health
DCE	Dangerous Cargo Endorsements
DCE	Diploma in Childcare and Education
DCG	Diploma in Careers Guidance
DCH	Diploma in Child Health
DChD	Diploma of Dental Surgery
DChM	Diploma in Chiropodial Medicine, Institute of Chiropodists and Podiatrists
DCHT	Diploma in Community Health in Tropical Countries
DCL	Doctor of Civil Law
DCLF	Diploma in Contact Lens Fitting
DClinPsych	Doctor of Clinical Psychiatry
DCLP	Diploma in Contact Lens Practice
DCR(R)or(T)	Diploma of the College of Radiographers
DD	Doctor of Divinity

DDH(Birm)	Diploma in Dental Health, University of Birmingham
DDOrthRCPSGlas	Diploma in Dental Orthopaedics of the Royal College of Physicians and Surgeons of Glasgow
DDPHRCS(Eng)	Diploma in Dental Public Health, Royal College of Surgeons of England
DDS	Doctor of Dental Surgery
DDSc	Doctor of Dental Science
DEBA	Diploma in European Business Administration
DEdPsy	Doctor of Educational Psychiatry
DEM	Diploma in Executive Management
DEng	Doctor of Engineering
DES	Department of Education and Science (now the Department for Education)
DETR	Department of the Environment, Transport and the Regions
DFin	Doctor of Finance
DFSM	Diploma in Financial Services Management
DGA	Diamond Member of the Gemmological Association and Gem Testing Laboratory of Great Britain
DGDPRCSEng	Diploma in General Dental Practice, Royal College of Surgeons of England
DGM	Diploma in Geriatric Medicine
DGO	Diploma in Obstetrics and Gynaecology
DHC	Doctorate in Healthcare
DHE	Diploma in Horticulture, Royal Botanic Garden, Edinburgh
DHMSA	Diploma in the History of Medicine, Society of Apothecaries of London
DHP	Diploma in Hypnosis and Psychotherapy
DIA	Diploma of Industrial Administration
DIB	Diploma in International Business
DIC	Diploma of Membership of Imperial College of Science and Technology, University of London
DIH	Diploma in Industrial Health
DipABRSM	Diploma of the Associated Board of the Royal Schools of Music
DipAD	Diploma in Art and Design
DipAdvHYP	Diploma in Advanced Hypnotherapy
DipAE	Diploma in Adult Education
DipAgrComm	Diploma in Agricultural Communication
DipArb	Diploma in Arbitration
DipArb	Diploma in Arboriculture
DipArch	Diploma in Architecture
DipASE(CofP)	Graduate Level Specialist Diploma in Advanced Study in Education, College of Preceptors
DipASSc	Diploma in Arts and Social Sciences
DipAT	Diploma in Accounting Technology
DipAvMed	Diploma in Aviation Medicine
DipBA	Diploma in Business Administration
DipBldgCons	Diploma in Building Conservation
DipBMA	Diploma in Business Management
DipCAM	Diploma in the Communication Advertising and Marketing Education Foundation
DipCD	Diploma in Community Development
DipCHM	Diploma in Choir Training, Royal College of Organists
DipClinPath	Diploma in Clinical Pathology
DipCOT	Diploma of the College of Occupational Therapists
DipCP	Diploma of the College of Teachers
DipCT	Diploma in Corporate Treasury Management
DipDerm	Diploma in Dermatology

Index of Abbreviations and Designatory Letters

DipEd	Diploma in Education
DipEF	Diploma in Executive Finance
DipEH	Diploma in Environmental Health
DipEM	Diploma in Environmental Management
DipEMA	Diploma in Executive and Management Accountancy
DipEngLit	Diploma in English Literature
DipFD	Diploma in Funeral Directing, National Association of Funeral Directors
DipFS	Diploma in Financial Services
DipGAI	Diploma of the Guild of Architectural Ironmongers
DipGrTrans	Diploma in Greek Translation
DipGSM	Diploma of the Guildhall School of Music and Drama
DipHE	Diploma of Higher Education
DipHS	Diploma of the Heraldry Society
DipIEB	Diploma of the International Employee Benefits
DipISW	Diploma of the Institute of Social Welfare
DipLE	Diploma in Land Economy
DipLP	Diploma in Legal Practice
DipM	Postgraduate Diploma in Marketing
DipMedAc	Diploma in Medical Acupuncture
DipMetEng	Diploma in Meteorological Engineering
DipMFS	Diploma in the Marketing of Financial Services
DipMth	Diploma in Music Therapy
DipOccH	Diploma in Occupational Health
DipOccHyg	Diploma of Professional Competence in Comprehensive Occupational Hygiene
DipPDTC	Diploma in Professional Dancers Teaching Course
DipPharmMed	Diploma in Pharmaceutical Medicine
DipPhil	Diploma in Philosophy
DipProjMan	Diploma in Project Management
DipPropInv	Diploma in Property Investment
DipRAM	Diploma of the Royal Academy of Music
DipRCM	Diploma of the Royal College of Music
DipRMS	Diploma of the Royal Microscopical Society
DipSc	Diploma in Science
DipSM	Diploma in Safety Management
DipSurv	Diploma in Surveying
DipSW	Diploma in Social Work
DipTCL	Diploma of the Trinity College of Music, London
DipTCR	Diploma in Organ Teaching
DipTESOL	Diploma in Teaching of English to Speakers of Other Languages
DipTHP	Diploma in Therapeutic Hypnosis and Psychotherapy
DipTM	Diploma in Training Management, Institute of Personnel and Development
DipTransIoL	Diploma in Translation, Institute of Linguists
DipUniv	Diploma of the University
DipVen	Diploma in Venereology, Society of Apothecaries of London
DipWCF	Diploma of the Worshipful Company of Farriers
DIS	Diploma in Industrial Studies
DLang	Doctor of Language
DLit(t)	Doctor of Letters or Literature
DLO	Diploma of Laryngology and Otology
DLORCSEng	Diploma in Laryngology and Otology, Royal College of Surgeons of England
DLP	Diploma in Legal Practice
DM	Doctor of Medicine

Index of Abbreviations and Designatory Letters

DMedRehab	Diploma in Medical Rehabilitation
DMedSc	Doctor in Medical Science
DMet	Doctor of Metallurgy
DMJ(Clin) or DMJ(Path)	Diploma in Medical Jurisprudence (Clinical or Pathological), Society of Apothecaries of London
DMRD	Diploma in Medical Radio-Diagnosis
DMRT	Diploma in Radiotherapy
DMS	Diploma in Management Studies
DMU	Diploma in Medical Ultrasound
DMus	Doctor of Music
DMusCantuar	Archbishop of Canterbury's Doctorate in Music
DNSc	Doctor in Nursing Science
DO	Diploma in Ophthalmology
DO	Diploma in Osteopathy
DocEdPsy	Doctorate in Educational Psychology
DOpt	Diploma in Ophthalmic Optics
DOrth	Diploma in Orthoptics
DOrthRCSEdin	Diploma in Orthodontics, Royal College of Surgeons of Edinburgh
DOrthRCSEng	Diplomate in Orthodontics, Royal College of Surgeons of England
DP	Diploma in Psychotherapy
DPA	Diploma in Public Administration
DpBact	Diploma in Bacteriology
DPD(Dund)	Diploma in Public Dentistry, University of Dundee
DPH	Diploma in Public Health
DPharm	Diploma in Pharmacy
DPhil	Diploma in Philosophy
DPHRCSEng	Diploma in Dental Public Health, Royal College of Surgeons of England
DPM	Diploma in Psychological Medicine
DPodM	Diploma in Podiatric Medicine
DProf	Doctor of Professional Studies
DPS	Diploma in Professional Studies
DPSE	Diploma in Pastoral Studies and Applied Theology
DPsychol	Doctor of Psychology
DrAc	Doctor of Acupuncture
Dr(RCA)	Doctor of the Royal College of Art
DRCOG	Diploma of the Royal College of Obstetricians and Gynaecologists
DRDRCSEd	Diploma in Restorative Dentistry, Royal College of Surgeons of Edinburgh
DRE	Diploma in Remedial Electrolysis, Institute of Electrolysis
DRI	Diploma in Radionuclide Imaging
DRSAMD	Diploma in the Royal Scottish Academy of Music and Drama
DSA	Diploma in Secretarial Administration
DSc	Doctor of Science
DSc(Econ)	Doctor of Science (Economics) or in Economics
DSc(Eng)	Doctor of Science (Engineering)
DSc(Social)	Doctor of Science in the Social Sciences
DScEcon	Doctor in the Faculty of Economics and Social Studies
DSCh(Ox)	Diploma in Surgical Chiropody (Oxon), Oxford School of Chiropody and Podiatry
DScTech	Doctor of Technical Science
DSocSc	Doctor of Social Science
DSSc	Doctor of Social Science
DSTA	Diploma Member of the Swimming Teachers' Association
DTCD	Diploma in Tuberculosis and Chest Diseases

DTech	Doctor of Technology
DTI	Department of Trade and Industry
DTMH	Diploma in Tropical Medicine and Hygiene
DTM&H	Diploma in Tropical Medicine and Hygiene
DTp	Department of Transport
DUniv	Doctor of the University
DVetMed	Doctor of Veterinary Medicine
DVM	Doctor of Veterinary Medicine
DVM&S	Doctor of Veterinary Medicine and Surgery
DVS	Doctor of Veterinary Surgery
DVSc	Doctor of Veterinary Science
ECBL	European Certification Board for Logistics
ECDL	European Computer Driving Licence
ECG	Executive Group Committees (of the Board for Engineers Registration)
EDBA	Executive Diploma in Business Accounting
EdD	Doctor of Education
EDH	Efficient Deck Hand
EdPsyD	Doctor of Educational Psychology
EEAC	European Executive Assistant Certificate
EFB	English for Business
EFL	English as a Foreign Language
EHO	Environmental Health Officer
EIS	Educational Institute of Scotland
EITB	Engineering Industry Training Board
EMBA	European Master of Business Administration
EMBS	European Master of Business Sciences
EMFEC	East Midland Further Education Council
EN	Enrolled Nurse
EN(G)	Enrolled Nurse (General)
EN(M)	Enrolled Nurse (Mental)
EN(MH)	Enrolled Nurse (Mental Handicap)
ENB	English National Board
EngC	Engineering Council
EngD	Doctor of Engineering
EngTech	Engineering Technician
ENS	Electronic Navigational System
ESD	Executive Secretary's Diploma
ESOL	English for Speakers of Other Languages
ESSTL	Engineering Services Training Trust Ltd
EurIng	European Engineer
EuroBiol	European Biologist
FABE	Fellow of the Association of Business Executives
FACB	Fellow of the Association of Certified Bookkeepers
FACP	Fellow of the Association of Computer Professionals
FAE	Fellow of the Academy of Experts
FAFC	Fellow of the Association of Financial Controllers and Administrators
FAIA	Fellow of the Association of International Accountants
FAMS	Fellow of the Association of Medical Secretaries, Practice Managers, Administrators and Receptionists
FAPM	Fellow of the Association for Project Management
FASI	Fellow of the Ambulance Service Institute
FASI	Fellow of the Architecture and Surveying Institute

Index of Abbreviations and Designatory Letters

FASP	Fellow of the Association of Sales Personnel
FBA	Fellow of the British Academy
FBA	Fellow of the British (Theatrical) Arts
FBCS	Fellow of the British Computer Society
FBDO	Fellow of the Association of British Dispensing Opticians
FBDO(Hons)	Fellow of the Association of British Dispensing Opticians with Honours Diploma
FBDO(Hons)CL	Fellow of the Association of British Dispensing Opticians with Honours Diploma and Diploma in Contact Lens Practice
FBEI	Fellow of the Institution of Body Engineers
FBEng	Fellow of the Association of Building Engineers
FBHA	Fellow of the British Hypnotherapy Association
FBHI	Fellow of the British Horological Institute
FBHS	Fellow of the British Horse Society
FBID	Fellow of the British Institute of Interior Design
FBIDST	Fellow of the British Institute of Dental and Surgical Technologists
FBIE	Fellow of the British Institute of Embalmers
FBIPP	Fellow of the British Institute of Professional Photography
FBIS	Fellow of the British Interplanetary Society
FBMA	Fellow of the Business Management Association
FBPsS	Fellow of the British Psychological Society
FCA	Fellow of the Institute of Chartered Accountants in England and Wales
FCAM	Fellow of the Communication Advertising and Marketing Education Foundation
FCB	Fellow of the British Association of Communicators in Business Ltd
FCBSI	Fellow of the Chartered Building Societies Institute
FCCA	Fellow of the Association of Chartered Certified Accountants
FCEA	Fellow of the Institute of Cost and Executive Accountants
FCGI	Fellowship, City & Guilds
FChS	Fellow of the Society of Chiropodists and Podiatrists
FCI	Faculty of Commerce and Industry
FCI	Fellow of the Institute of Commerce
FCIArb	Fellow of the Chartered Institute of Arbitrators
FCIB	Fellow of the Chartered Institute of Bankers
FCIBS	Fellow of the Chartered Institute of Bankers in Scotland
FCIBSE	Fellow of the Chartered Institute of Building Services Engineers
FCIH	Fellow of the Chartered Institute of Housing
FCII	Fellow of the Chartered Insurance Institute
FCIJ	Fellow of the Chartered Institute of Journalists
FCILA	Fellow of the Chartered Institute of Loss Adjusters
FCIM	Fellow of the Chartered Institute of Marketing
FCIOB	Fellow of the Chartered Institute of Building
FCIPD	Fellow of the Chartered Institute of Personnel and Development
FCIPS	Fellow of the Chartered Institute of Purchasing and Supply
FCIS	Fellow of the Institute of Chartered Secretaries and Administrators
FCIT	Fellow of the Chartered Institute of Transport
FCLIP	Chartered Fellow of CILIP
FCLS	First Certificate for Legal Secretaries
FCMA	Fellow of the Chartered Institute of Management Accountants
FCMA	Fellow of the Institute of Cost and Management Accountants
FCMC	Fellow Grade Certified Management Consultants
FCOphth	Fellow of the College of Ophthalmology
FCOptom	Fellow of the College of Optometrists
FCoT	Ordinary Fellow of the College of Teachers

Index of Abbreviations and Designatory Letters

FCPM	Fellow of the Confederation of Professional Management
FCPP	Fellow of the College of Pharmacy Practice
FCSP	Fellow of the Chartered Society of Physiotherapy
FCT	Fellow of the Association of Corporate Treasurers
FCoT	Fellow of the College of Teachers
FCTHCM	Fellow of the Confederation of Tourism, Hotel and Catering Management
FCYW	Fellow of the Community and Youth Work Association
FDSRCPSGlas	Fellow in Dental Surgery of the Royal College of Surgeons of Glasgow
FDSRCSEd	Fellow in Dental Surgery of the Royal College of Physicians and Surgeons of Edinburgh
FDSRCSEng	Fellow in Dental Surgery of the Royal College of Surgeons of England
FE	Further Education
FEANI	Fédération Européene d'Associations Nationales d'Ingénieurs
FECI	Fellow of the Institute of Employment Consultants
FEFC	Further Education Funding Council
FEIS	Fellow of the Educational Institute of Scotland
FFA	Fellow of the Faculty of Actuaries
FFA	Fellow of the Institute of Financial Accountants
FFARCSEng	Fellow of the Faculty of Anaesthetists of the Royal College of Surgeons in England
FFARCSIrel	Fellow of the Faculty of Anaesthetists of the Royal College of Surgeons in Ireland
FFAS	Fellow of the Faculty of Architects and Surveyors (Architects)
FFCA	Fellow of the Association of Financial Controllers and Administrators
FFCI	Fellow of the Faculty of Commerce and Industry
FFCS	Fellow of the Faculty of Secretaries
FFHom	Fellow of the Faculty of Homeopathy
FFPHM	Fellow of the Faculty of Public Health Medicine, Royal College of Physicians of London and Edinburgh and Royal College of Physicians and Surgeons of Glasgow
FFPHMIrel	Fellow of the Faculty of Public Health Medicine, Royal College of Physicians of Ireland
FFRRCSIrel	Fellow of the Faculty of Radiologists, Royal College of Surgeons in Ireland
FFS	Fellow of the Faculty of Architects and Surveyors (Surveyors)
FGA	Fellow of the Gemmological Association and Gem Testing Laboratory of Great Britain
FGCL	Fellow of the Guild of Cleaners and Launderers
FGI	Fellow of the Greek Institute
FGSM	Fellow of the Guildhall School of Music and Drama
FHCIMA	Fellow of the Hotel and Catering International Management Association
FHFS	Fellow of the Council of Health, Fitness and Sports Therapists
FHG	Fellow of the Institute of Heraldic and Genealogical Studies
FHRIM	Fellow of the Institute of Health Record Information and Management
FHS	Fellow of the Heraldry Society
FHSM	Fellow of the Institute of Health Services Management
FHT	Federation of Holistic Therapies
FIA	Fellow of the Institute of Actuaries
FIAB	Fellow of the International Association of Book-keepers
FIAEA	Fellow of the Institute of Automotive Engineer Assessors
FIAgrE	Fellow of the Institution of Agricultural Engineers
FIAP	Fellow of the Institution of Analysts and Programmers
FIAT	Fellow of the Institute of Asphalt Technology
FIBA	Fellow of the Institution of Business Agents
FIBC	Fellow of the Institute of Building Control

Index of Abbreviations and Designatory Letters

FIBCM	Fellow of the Institute of British Carriage and Automobile Manufacturers
FIBCO	Fellow of the Institute of Building Control Officers
FIBE	Fellow of the Institution of British Engineers
FIBF	Fellow of the Institute of British Foundrymen
FIBiol	Fellow of the Institute of Biology
FIBM	Fellow of the Institute of Builders' Merchants
FIBMS	Fellow of the Institute of Biomedical Science
FIBMS	Fellow of the Institute of Medical Laboratory Sciences
FICA	Fellow of the Institute of Company Accountants
FICB	Fellow of the Institute of Certified Book-Keepers
FICE	Fellow of the Institution of Civil Engineers
FIChemE	Fellow of the Institution of Chemical Engineers
FIChor	Fellow of the Benesh Institute of Choreology
FICHT	Fellow of the International Council of Holistic Therapies
FICM	Fellow of the Institute of Credit Management
FICorr	Fellow of the Institute of Corrosion
FICS	Fellow of the Institute of Chartered Shipbrokers
FICW	Fellow of the Institute of Clerks of Works of Great Britain Incorporated
FIDTA	Fellow of the International Dance Teachers' Association
FIED	Fellow of the Institution of Engineering Designers
FIEE	Fellow of the Institution of Electrical Engineers
FIEM	Fellow of the Institute of Executives and Managers
FIEx	Fellow of the Institute of Export
FIExpE	Fellow of the Institute of Explosives Engineers
FIFBQ	Fellow of the International Faculty of Business Qualifications
FIFireE	Fellow of the Institution of Fire Engineers
FIFM	Fellow of the Institute of Fisheries Management
FIFST	Fellow of the Institute of Food Science and Technology
FIGasE	Fellow of the Institution of Gas Engineers
FIGD	Fellow of the Institute of Grocery Distribution
FIGeol	Fellow of the Institute of Geologists
FIHEc	Fellow of the Institute of Home Economics Ltd
FIHIE	Fellow of the Institute of Highway Incorporated Engineers
FIHort	Fellow of the Institute of Horticulture
FIHT	Fellow of the Institution of Highways and Transportation
FIIE	Fellow of the Institution of Incorporated Engineers
FIIHTM	Fellow of the International Institute of Hospitality Tourism & Management
FIIM	Fellow of the International Institute of Management
FIIMR	Fellow of the Institute of Investment Management and Research
FIIRSM	Fellow of the International Institute of Risk and Safety Management
FIISE	Fellow of the International Institute of Social Economics
FIISec	Fellow of the International Institute of Security
FIL	Fellow of the Institute of Linguists
FILAM	Fellow of the Institute of Leisure and Amenity Management
FILT	Fellow of the Institute of Logistics and Transport
FIM	Fellow of the Institute of Materials
FIMA	Fellow of the Institute of Mathematics and its Applications
FIManf	Fellow of the Institute of Manufacturing
FIMarE	Fellow of the Institute of Marine Engineers
FIMatM	Fellow of the Institute of Materials Management
FIMBM	Fellow of the Institute of Maintenance and Building Management
FIMechE	Fellow of the Institute of Mechanical Engineers

FIMechIE	Fellow of the Institute of Mechanical Incorporated Engineers
FIMF	Fellow of the Institute of Metal Finishing
FIMgt	Fellow of the Institute of Management
FIMI	Fellow of the Institute of the Motor Industry
FIMIS	Fellow of the Institute for the Management of Information Systems
FIMM	Fellow of the Institute of Massage and Movement
FIMM	Fellow of the Institution of Mining and Metallurgy
FIMM	International Federation of Manual Medicine
FIMS	Fellow of the Institute of Management Specialists
FIMunE	Fellow of the Institution of Municipal Engineers
FInstAEA	Fellow of the Institute of Automotive Engineer Assessors
FInstAM	Fellow of the Institute of Administrative Management
FInstBA	Fellow of the Institute of Business Administration
FInstBCA	Fellow of the Institute of Burial and Cremation Administration
FInstBM	Fellow of the Institute of Builders' Merchants
FInstBRM	Fellow of the Institute of Baths and Recreation Management
FInstCh	Fellow of the Institute of Chiropodists
FInstCM	Fellow of the Institute of Commercial Management
FInstD	Fellow of the Institute of Directors
FInstE	Fellow of the Institute of Energy
FInstLEx	Fellow of the Institute of Legal Executives
FInstMC	Fellow of the Institute of Measurement and Control
FInstNDT	Fellow of the British Institute of Non-Destructive Testing
FInstP	Fellow of the Institute of Physics
FInstPet	Fellow of the Institute of Petroleum
FInstPkg	Fellow of the Institute of Packaging
FInstPM	Fellow of the Institute of Professional Managers and Administrators
FInstPS	Fellow of the Institute of Purchasing and Supply
FInstR	Fellow of the Institute of Refrigeration
FInstSMM	Fellow of the Institute of Sales and Marketing Management
FInstTA	Fellow of the Institute of Transport Administration
FInstTT	Fellow of the Institute of Travel and Tourism
FInstWM	Fellow of the Institute of Wastes Management
FInstWM	Fellowship of the Institute of Wastes Management
FIntMC	Fellow of International Management Centre
FIOC	Fellow of the Institute of Carpenters
FIOM	Fellow of the Institute of Operations Management
FIOP	Fellow of the Institute of Plumbing
FIOP	Fellow of the Institute of Printing
FIOSH	Fellow of the Institution of Occupational Safety and Health
FIPA	Fellow of the Institute of Practitioners in Advertising
FIPD	Fellow of the Institute of Personnel Development
FIPI	Fellow of the Institute of Professional Investigators
FIPlantE	Fellow of the Institution of Plant Engineers
FIPR	Fellow of the Institute of Public Relations
FIQ	Fellow of the Institute of Quarrying
FIQA	Fellow of the Institute of Quality Assurance
FIR	Fellow of the Institute of Population Registration
FIRSE	Fellow of the Institution of Railway Signal Engineers
FIRTE	Fellow of the Institute of Road Transport Engineers
FIS	Fellow of the Institute of Statisticians
FISM	Fellow of the Institute for Supervision & Management

Index of Abbreviations and Designatory Letters

FISOB	Fellow of the Incorporated Society of Organ Builders
FISTC	Fellow of the Institute of Scientific and Technical Communicators
FISTD	Fellow of the Imperial Society of Teachers of Dancing
FIStrucE	Fellow of the Institution of Structural Engineers
FISW	Fellow of the Institute of Social Welfare
FIT	Foundation Insurance Test
FITD	Fellow of the Institute of Training and Development
FITSA	Fellow of the Institute of Trading Standards Administration
FIVehE	Fellow of the Institute of Vehicle Engineers
FIWM	Fellow of the Institute of Wastes Management
FLAW	Foreign Languages at Work
FLCM	Fellow of the London College of Music
FLCSP	Fellow of the London and Counties Society of Physiologists
FLI	Fellow of the Landscape Institute
FLIC	Foreign Languages for Industry and Commerce
FLS	Fellow of the Linnean Society of London
FMA	Fellow of the Museums Association
FMAAT	Fellow Member of the Association of Accounting Technicians
FMPA	Fellow of the Master Photographers Association
FMR	Fellow of the Association of Health Care Information and Medical Records Officers
FMS	Fellow of the Institute of Management Services
FMusEd	Fellowship in Music Education
FN	Fellow of the Nautical Society
FNAEA	Fellow of the National Association of Estate Agents
FNAEAHon	Honoured Fellow of the National Association of Estate Agents
FNCP	Fellow of the National Council of Psychotherapists
FNI	Fellow of the Nautical Institute
FNIMH	Fellow of the National Institute of Medical Herbalists
FPC	Financial Planning Certificate
FPC	Foundation for Psychotherapy and Counselling
FPCS	Fellow of the Property Consultants Society
FPMI	Fellow of the Pensions Management Institute
FPodS	Fellow of the Surgical Faculty of the College of Podiatrists
FProfBTM	Fellow of Professional Business and Technical Management
FRAeS	Fellow of the Royal Aeronautical Society
FRAS	Fellow of the Royal Astronomical Society
FRCA	Fellow of the Royal College of Anaesthetists
FRCGP	Fellow of the Royal College of General Practitioners
FRCM	Fellow of the Royal College of Music
FRCO	Fellow of the Royal College of Organists
FRCO(CHM)	Fellow of the Royal College of Organists (Choir-training Diploma)
FRCOG	Fellow of the Royal College of Obstetricians and Gynaecologists
FRCP	Fellow of the Royal College of Physicians of London
FRCPath	Fellow of the Royal College of Pathologists
FRCPEdin	Fellow of the Royal College of Physicians of Edinburgh
FRCPsych	Fellow of the Royal College of Psychiatrists
FRCR	Fellow of the Royal College of Radiologists
FRCS(Irel)	Fellow of the Royal College of Surgeons in Ireland
FRCSEd	Fellow of the Royal College of Surgeons of Edinburgh
FRCSEd(C/TH)	Fellow of the Royal College of Surgeons of Edinburgh, specialising in Cardiothoracic Surgery

FRCSEd(Orth)	Fellow of the Royal College of Surgeons of Edinburgh, specialising in Orthopaedic Surgery
FRCSEd(SN)	Fellow of the Royal College of Surgeons of Edinburgh, specialising in Surgical Neurology
FRCSEng	Fellow of the Royal College of Surgeons of England
FRCSEng(Oto)	Fellow of the Royal College of Surgeons of England, with Otolaryngology
FRCSGlasg	Fellow of the Royal College of Physicians and Surgeons of Glasgow
FRCVS	Fellow of the Royal College of Veterinary Surgeons
FREC	Fellow of the Recruitment and Employment Confederation
FRHS	Fellow of the Royal Horticultural Society
FRIBA	Fellow of the Royal Institute of British Architects
FRICS	Fellow of the Royal Institution of Chartered Surveyors
FRIN	Fellow of the Royal Institute of Navigation
FRINA	Fellow of the Royal Institution of Naval Architects
FRIPHH	Fellow of the Royal Institution of Public Health and Hygiene
FRNCM	Fellow of the Royal Northern College of Music
FRPharmS	Fellow of the Royal Pharmaceutical Society of Great Britain
FRPS	Fellow of the Royal Photographic Society
FRS	Fellow of the Royal Society
FRSC	Fellow of the Royal Society of Chemistry
FRSCM	Fellow of the Royal School of Church Music
FRSH	Fellow of the Royal Society for the Promotion of Health
FRTPI	Fellow of the Royal Town Planning Institute
FSAPP	Fellow of the Society of Advanced Psychotherapy Practitioners
FSBP	Fellow of the Society of Business Practitioners
FSBT	Fellow of the Society of Teachers in Business Education
FSCT	Fellow of the Society of Claims Technicians
FSDC	Fellow of the Society of Dyers and Colourists
FSE	Fellow of the Society of Engineers (Inc)
FSElec	Fellow of the Society of Electroscience
FSG	Fellow of the Society of Genealogists
FSG(Hon)	Honorary Fellow of the Society of Genealogists
FSGT	Fellow of the Society of Glass Technology
FSIAD	Fellow of the Society of Industrial Artists and Designers
FSMA	Fellow of the Society of Martial Arts
FSMA	Fellow of the Society of Sales Management Administrators Ltd
FSNN	Fellow of the Society of Nursery Nursing
FSS	Fellow of the Royal Statistical Society
FSSCh	Fellow of the British Chiropody and Podiatry Association
FSSF	Fellow of the Society of Shoe Fitters
FSTA	Fellow of the Swimming Teachers' Association
FSVA	Fellow of the Incorporated Society of Valuers and Auctioneers
FTCL	Fellow of the Trinity College of Music
FTI	Fellow of the Textile Institute
FTII	Fellow of the Chartered Institute of Taxation
FTSC	Fellow of the Oil and Colour Chemists' Association
FTSC	Fellow in the Technology of Surface Coatings
FWeldI	Fellow of the Welding Institute
FYDA	Associate Fellowship of the Youth Development Association
GAGTL	Gemmological Association and Gem Testing Laboratory of Great Britain
GAI	Guild of Architectural Ironmongers
GASI	Graduate Member of the Ambulance Service Institute

GBSM	Graduate of the Birmingham School of Music
GCE	General Certificate of Education
GCE A	General Certificate of Education Advanced Level
GCE O	General Certificate of Education Ordinary Level
GCGI	Graduateship, City & Guilds
GCL	Guild of Cleaners and Launderers
GCSE	General Certificate of Secondary Education
GDC	General Dental Council
GIBCM	Graduate of the Institute of British Carriage and Automobile Manufacturers
GIBiol	Graduate of the Institute of Biology
GIEM	Graduate of the Institute of Executives and Managers
GIMA	Graduate of the Institute of Mathematics and its Applications
GIMI	Graduate of the Institute of the Motor Industry
GInstP	Graduate of the Institute of Physics
GIntMC	Graduate of the International Management Centre
GIS	Graduate Imaging Scientist
GLCM	Graduate Diploma of the London College of Music
GMAT	Graduate Management Admissions Test
GMC	General Medical Council
GMDSS	Global Maritime Distress & Safety System
GMInstM	Graduate Member of the Meat Training Council
GMus	Graduate Diploma in Music
GMusRNCM	Graduate in Music of the Royal Northern College of Music
GNSM	Graduate of the Northern School of Music
GNVQ	General National Vocational Qualifications
GradAES	Graduate of the Royal Aeronautical Society
GradBEng	Graduate Member of the Association of Building Engineers
GradBHI	Graduate of the British Horological Institute
GradDip	Graduate Diploma
GradIAP	Graduate of the Institution of Analysts and Programmers
GradIBE	Graduate of the Institution of British Engineers
GradIElecIE	Graduate of the Institution of Electrical and Electronics Incorporated Engineers
GradIIE	Graduate of the Institution of Incorporated Engineers
GradIISec	Graduate of the International Institute of Security
GradIManf	Graduate of the Institute Manufacturing
GradIMF	Graduate of the Institute of Metal Finishing
GradIMS	Graduate of the Institute of Management Specialists
GradInstNDT	Graduate of the British Institute of Non-Destructive Testing
GradInstP	Graduate of the Institute of Physics
GradInstPS	Graduate of the Institute of Purchasing and Supply
GradIOP	Graduate of the Institute of Printing
GradIPD	Graduate of the Institute of Personnel and Development
GradIS	Graduate of the Institute of Statisticians
GradISCA	Graduate of the Institute of Chartered Secretaries and Administrators
GradMechE	Graduate of the Institution of Mechanical Engineers
GradMIWM	Graduate Member of the Institute of Wastes Management
GradRNCM	Graduate of the Royal Northern College of Music
GradRSC	Graduate of the Royal Society of Chemistry
GradSMA	Graduate of the Society of Martial Arts
GradStat	Graduate Statistician
GraduateCIPD	Graduate of the Chartered Institute of Personnel and Development
GraduateIEIE	Graduate of the Institution of Electrical and Electronics Incorporated Engineers

Index of Abbreviations and Designatory Letters

GradWeldI	Graduate of the Welding Institute
GRC	General Readers Certificate
GRC	Grade Related Criteria
GRIC	Graduate Membership of the Royal Institute of Chemistry
GRSC	Graduate of the Royal Society of Chemistry
GRSM	Graduate Diploma of the Royal Manchester School of Music
GRSM(Hons)	Graduate of the Royal Schools of Music
GSMA	Graduate of the Society of Sales Management Administrators Ltd
GSNN	Graduate of the Society of Nursery Nursing
GTC	General Teaching Council
HABIA	Hairdressing and Beauty Industry Authority
HC	Higher Certificate
HCIMA	Hotel and Catering International Management Association
HD	Higher Diploma
HDCR (R) or (T)	Higher Award in Radiodiagnosis or Radiotherapy, College of Radiographers
HEFCE	Higher Education Funding Council for England
HFInstE	Honorary Fellow of the Institute of Energy
HNC	Higher National Certificate
HND	Higher National Diploma
HonASTA	Honorary Associate of the Swimming Teachers' Association
HonDrRCA	Honorary Doctorate of the Royal College of Art
HonFAE	Honorary Fellow of the Academy of Experts
HonFBID	Honorary Fellow of the British Institute of Interior Design
HonFBIPP	Honorary Fellow of the British Institute of Professional Photography
HonFCP	Charter Fellow of the College of Preceptors
HonFEIS	Honorary Fellow of the Educational Institute of Scotland
HonFHCIMA	Honorary Fellow of the Hotel, Catering and Institutional Management Association
HonFHS	Honorary Fellow of the Heraldry Society
HonFIEE	Honorary Fellow of the Institution of Electrical Engineers
HonFIExpE	Honorary Fellow of the Institute of Explosives Engineers
HonFIGasE	Honorary Fellow of the Institution of Gas Engineers
HonFIMarE	Honorary Fellow of the Institute of Marine Engineers
HonFIMechE	Honorary Fellow of the Institution of Mechanical Engineers
HonFIMM	Honorary Fellow of the Institution of Mining and Metallurgy
HonFInstE	Honorary Fellow of the Institute of Energy
HonFInstMC	Honorary Fellow of the Institute of Measurement and Control
HonFInstNDT	Honorary Fellow of the British Institute of Non-Destructive Testing
HonFIQA	Honorary Fellow of the Institute of Quality Assurance
HonFIRSE	Honorary Fellow of the Institution of Railway Signal Engineers
HonFIRTE	Honorary Fellow of the Institute of Road Transport Engineers
HonFPRI	Honorary Fellow of the Plastics and Rubber Institute
HonFRIN	Honorary Fellow of the Royal Institute of Navigation
HonFRINA	Honorary Fellow of the Royal Institution of Naval Architects
HonFRPS	Honorary Fellow of the Royal Photographic Society
HonFSE	Honorary Fellow of the Society of Engineers (Inc)
HonFSGT	Honorary Fellow of the Society of Glass Technology
HonFWeldI	Honorary Fellow of the Welding Institute
HonGSM	Honorary Member of the Guildhall School of Music and Drama
HonMIFM	Honorary Member of the Institute of Fisheries Management
HonMInstNDT	Honorary Member of the British Institute of Non-Destructive Testing
HonMRIN	Honorary Member of the Royal Institute of Navigation
HonMWES	Honorary Member of the Women's Engineering Society

Index of Abbreviations and Designatory Letters

HonRAM	Honorary Member of the Royal Academy of Music
HonRCM	Honorary Member of the Royal College of Music
HonRNCM	Honorary Member of the Royal Northern College of Music
HonRSCM	Honorary Member of the Royal School of Church Music
HSC	Higher School Certificate
HSE	Health & Safety Executive
HTB	Hairdressing Training Board
HTC	Higher Technical Certificate
IAAP	International Association for Analytic Psychology
IAB	International Association of Book-Keepers
IABC	International Association of Business Computing
IAC	Investment Advice Certificate
IAgrE	Institution of Agricultural Engineers
IAP	Institution of Analysts and Programmers
IAQ	Investment Administration Qualification
IAT	Institute of Asphalt Technology
IBA	Institute of Business Administration
IBC	Institute of Building Control
IBE	Institution of British Engineers
IBF	Institute of British Foundrymen
IBMS	Institute of Biomedical Science
ICAEW	Institute of Chartered Accountants in England and Wales
ICAI	Institute of Chartered Accountants in Ireland
ICAS	Institute of Chartered Accountants of Scotland
ICB	Institute of Certified Book-Keepers
ICE	Institution of Civil Engineers
ICEA	Institute of Cost and Executive Accountants
ICG	Institute of Careers Guidance
IChemE	Institution of Chemical Engineers
ICIOB	Incorporated Member of the Chartered Institute of Building
ICM	Institute of Commercial Management
ICM	Institute of Complementary Medicine
ICM	Institute of Credit Management
ICMQ	International Capital Markets Qualification
ICSA	Institute of Chartered Secretaries and Administrators
ICSF	Intermediate Certificate of the Society of Floristry
IDA	Improvement and Development Agency
IDTA	International Dance Teachers' Association Ltd
IED	Institution of Engineering Designers
IEE	Institution of Electrical Engineers
IEM	Institute of Executives and Managers
IEng	Incorporated Engineer
IETTL	Insulation and Environmental Training Trust Ltd
IEx	Institute of Export
IExpE	Institute of Explosives Engineers
IFA	Institute of Field Archaeologists
IFA	Institute of Financial Accountants
IFA	Insurance Foundation Certificate
IFBQ	International Faculty of Business Qualifications
IFM	Institute of Fisheries Management
IFST	Institute of Food Science and Technology (UK)
IHBC	International Health & Beauty Council

Index of Abbreviations and Designatory Letters

IHIE	Institute of Highway Incorporated Engineers
IHort	Institute of Horticulture
IHT	Institute of Highways and Transportation
IIA	Institute of Internal Auditors
IIE	Institution of Incorporated Engineers
IIExE	Institution of Incorporated Executive Engineers
IIHHT	International Institute of Health & Holistic Therapies
IIHTM	International Institute of Hospitality Tourism & Management
IIRSM	International Institute of Risk and Safety Management
ILAM	Institute of Leisure and Amenity Management
ILE	Institution of Lighting Engineers
ILEX	Institute of Legal Executives
ILT	Institute of Logistics and Transport
IMarE	Institute of Marine Engineers
IMBM	Institute of Maintenance and Building Management
IMC	Institute of Management Consultancy
IMechE	Institution of Mechanical Engineers
IMF	Institute of Metal Finishing
IMI	Institute of the Motor Industry
IMIBC	Incorporated Member of the Institute of Building Control
IMInstAEA	Incorporated Member of the Institute of Automotive Engineer Assessors
IMIS	Institute for the Management of Information Systems
IMM	Institution of Mining and Metallurgy
IMS	Institute of Management Specialists
IncMWeldI	Incorporated Member of the Welding Institute
InstAEA	Institute of Automotive Engineer Assessors
InstAM	Institute of Administrative Management
InstBCA	Institute of Burial and Cremation Administration
InstE	Institute of Energy
InstPet	Institute of Petroleum
IOB	Institute of Brewing
IOC	Institute of Carpenters
IoD	Institute of Directors
IOM	Institute of Operations Management
IOP	Institute of Packaging
IOSH	Institution of Occupational Safety and Health
IOTA	Institute of Transport Administration
IPA	Institute of Practitioners in Advertising
IPD	Initial Professional Development
IPD	Institute of Personnel and Development
IPFA	Member of the Chartered Institute of Public Finance and Accountancy
IPlantE	Institution of Plant Engineers
IPR	Incorporated Professional Review
IPR	Institute of Public Relations
IPSM	Institute of Public Service Management
IQ	Institute of Quarrying
IQA	Institute of Quality Assurance
IRMT	International Register of Massage Therapists
IRRV	Corporate Member of the Institute of Revenues, Rating and Valuation
IRRV	Institute of Revenues, Rating and Valuation
IRSE	Institution of Railway Signal Engineers
IRTE	Institute of Road Transport Engineers

Index of Abbreviations and Designatory Letters

ISEB	Information Systems Examinations Board
ISM	Incorporated Society of Musicians
ISM	Institute for Supervision & Management
ISMM	Institute of Sales and Marketing Management
ISRM	Institute of Sport and Recreation Management
ISTD	Imperial Society of Teachers of Dancing
IStructE	Institution of Structural Engineers
ITEC	International Therapy Examination Council
ITIL	IT Infrastructure Library
ITSA	Institute of Trading Standards Administration
IVehE	Institute of the Vehicle Engineers
IVM	Institute of Value Management
IWSc	Institute of Wood Science
JEB	Joint Examination Board
JET	Jewellery, Education and Training
JP	Justice of the Peace
LA	Library Association
LABAC	Licentiate Member of the Association of Business and Administrative Computing
LAE	Licentiate Automotive Engineer
LAEx	Legal Accounts Executive
LAMDA	London Academy of Music and Dramatic Art
LAMRTPI	Legal Associate Member of the Royal Town Planning Institute
LASI	Licentiate of the Ambulance Service Institute
LASI	Licentiate of the Architecture and Surveying Institute
LBEI	Licentiate of the Institution of Body Engineers
LBIDST	Licentiate of the British Institute of Dental and Surgical Technologists
LBIPP	Licentiate of the British Institute of Professional Photography
LCCI	London Chamber of Commerce and Industry
LCCIEB	London Chamber of Commerce and Industry Examinations Board
LCEA	Licentiate of the Association of Cost and Executive Accountants
LCFI	Licentiate of CFI International (Clothing and Footwear Institute)
LCGI	Licentiate, City & Guilds
LCIBSE	Licentiate of the Chartered Institution of Building Services Engineers
LCP	Licentiate of the College of Preceptors
LCSP	London and Counties Society of Physiologists
LCSP(Assoc)	Associate of the London and Counties Society of Physiologists
LCSP(BTh)	Member of the London and Counties Society of Physiologists (Beauty Therapy)
LCSP(Chir)	Member of the London and Counties Society of Physiologists (Chiropody)
LCSP(Phys)	Member of the London and Counties Society of Physiologists (Physical and Manipulative Therapy)
LCT	Licentiate of the College of Teachers
LDS	Licentiate in Dental Surgery
LDSRCPSGlas	Licentiate in Dental Surgery of the Royal College of Physicians and Surgeons of Glasgow
LDSRCSEd	Licentiate in Dental Surgery of the Royal College of Surgeons of Edinburgh
LDSRCSEng	Licentiate in Dental Surgery of the Royal College of Surgeons of England
LFA	Licentiate of the Institute of Financial Accountants
LFCI	Licentiate of the Faculty of Commerce and Industry
LFCS	Licentiate of the Faculty of Secretaries
LFS	Licentiate of the Faculty of Architects and Surveyors (Surveyors)
LGCL	Licentiate of the Guild of Cleaners and Launderers
LGSM	Licentiate of the Guildhall School of Music and Drama

Index of Abbreviations and Designatory Letters

LHCIMA	Licentiate of the Hotel and Catering International Management Association
LHG	Licentiate of the Institute of Heraldic and Genealogical Studies
LI	Landscape Institute
LicentiateCIPD	Licentiate of the Chartered Institute of Personnel and Development
LicIPD	Licentiate of the Institute of Personnel & Development
LicIQA	Licentiate of the Institute of Quality Assurance
LICW	Licentiate of the Institute of Clerks of Works of Great Britain Incorporated
LIDPM	Licentiate of the Institute of Data Processing Management
LIEM	Licentiate of the Institute of Executives and Managers
LIIST	Licentiate of the International Institute of Sports Therapy
LILAM	Licentiate of the Institute of Leisure and Amenity Management
LIM	Licentiate of the Institute of Materials
LIMA	Licentiate of the Institute of Mathematics and its Applications
LIMF	Licentiate of the Institute of Metal Finishing
LIMIS	Licentiate of the Institute for the Management of Information Systems
LInstBCA	Licentiate of the Institute of Burial and Cremation Administration
LInstBM	Licentiate of the Institute of Builders' Merchants
LIOC	Licentiate of the Institute of Carpenters
LIR	Licentiate of the Institute of Population Registration
LISTD	Licentiate of the Imperial Society of Teachers of Dancing
LISTD(Dip)	Licentiate Diploma of the Imperial Society of Teachers of Dancing
LittD	Doctor of Letters
LIWM	Licentiate of the Institute of Wastes Management
LLB	Bachelor of Law
LLCM	Performers Diploma of Licentiateship in Speech, Drama and Public Speaking
LLCM(TD)	Licentiate of the London College of Music and Media (Teachers' Diploma)
LLD	Doctor of Law
LLM	Master of Law
LM	Licentiate in Midwifery
LMIFM	Licentiate Member of the Institute of Fisheries Management
LMInstE	Licentiate Member of the Institute of Energy
LMPA	Licentiate Member of the Master Photographers Association
LMRTPI	Legal Member of the Royal Town Planning Institute
LMSSALond	Licentiate in Medicine, Surgery and Obstetrics & Gynaecology, Society of Apothecaries of London
LMusEd	Licentiate Diploma in Music Education
LMusLCM	Licentiate in Music of the London College of Music
LMusTCL	Licentiate in Music, Trinity College of Music
LNCP	Licentiate of the National Council of Psychotherapists
LPC	Legal Practice Course
LRAD	Licentiate of the Royal Academy of Dancing
LRAM	Licentiate of the Royal Academy of Music
LRCPEdin	Conjoint Diplomas Licentiate of the Royal College of Physicians of Edinburgh
LRCPSGlasg	Conjoint Diplomas Licentiate of the Royal College of Physicians and Surgeons of Glasgow
LRCSEdin	Conjoint Diplomas Licentiate of the Royal College of Surgeons of Edinburgh
LRCSEng	Licentiate of the Royal College of Surgeons in England
LRPS	Licentiate of the Royal Photographic Society
LRSC	Licentiate of the Royal Society of Chemistry
LRSM	Licentiate Diploma of the Royal Schools of Music
LSBP	Licentiate of the Society of Business Practitioners
LSCP(Assoc)	Associate of the London and Counties Society of Physiologists

Index of Abbreviations and Designatory Letters

LTCL	Licentiate of Trinity College of Music
LTh	Licentiate in Theology
LTI	Licentiate of the Textile Industry
LTSC	Licentiate of the Oil and Colour Chemists' Association
LVT	Licentiate Vehicle Technologist
MA	Master of Arts
MA(Architectural)	Master of Arts (Architectural Studies)
MA(Econ)	Master of Arts in Economic and Social Studies
MA(Ed)	Master of Arts in Education
MA(LD)	Master of Arts (Landscape Design)
MA(MUS)	Master of Arts (Music)
MA(RCA)	Master of Arts, Royal College of Art
MA(SocSci)	Master of Arts (Social Science)
MA(Theol)	Master of Arts in Theology
MAAT	Member of the Association of Accounting Technicians
MABAC	Member of the Association of Business and Administrative Computing
MABE	Member of the Association of Business Executives
MAcc	Master of Accountancy
MACP	Member of the Association of Computer Professionals
MAE	Member of the Academy of Experts
MAgr	Master of Agriculture
MAgrSc	Master of Agricultural Science
MAMS	Member of the Association of Medical Secretaries, Practice Managers, Administrators and Receptionists
MAMSA	Managing & Marketing Sales Association Examination Board
MAnimSc	Master of Animal Science
MAO	Master of Obstetrics
MAP	Membership by Assessment of Performance
MAPM	Member of the Association for Project Management
MAppSci	Master of Applied Science
MAQ	Mortgage Advice Qualification
MArAd	Master of Archive Administration
MArb	Master of Arboriculture
MArch	Master of Architecture
MArt/RCA	Master of Arts, Royal College of Art
MasFCI	Master of the Faculty of Commerce and Industry
MASHAM	Management and Administration of Safety and Health at Mines
MASI	Member of the Architecture and Surveying Institute
MBA	Master of Business Administration
MBAE	Member of the British Association of Electrolysists
MB, BCh	Conjoint Degree of Bachelor of Medicine, Bachelor of Surgery
MB, BChir	Conjoint Degree of Bachelor of Medicine, Bachelor of Surgery
MB, BS	Conjoint Degree of Bachelor of Medicine, Bachelor of Surgery
MB, ChB	Conjoint Degree of Bachelor of Medicine, Bachelor of Surgery
MBChA	Member of the British Chiropody and Podiatry Association
MBCO	Member of the British College of Ophthalmic Opticians
MBCS	Member of the British Computer Society
MBEng	Member of the Association of Building Engineers
MBHA	Member of the British Hypnotherapy Association
MBHI	Member of the British Horological Institute
MBIAT	Member of the British Institute of Architectural Technologists
MBID	Member of the British Institute of Interior Design

Index of Abbreviations and Designatory Letters

MBIE	Member of the British Institute of Embalmers
MBII	Member of the British Institute of Innkeeping
MBioc	Master of Biochemistry
MBKS	Member of the British Kinematograph, Sound and Television Society
MBM	Master of Business Management
MBMA	Member of the Business Management Association
MBSc	Master in Business Science
MBSSG	Master of the British Society of Scientific Glassblowers
MCAM	Member of the Communication Advertising and Marketing Education Foundation
MCB	Mastership in Clinical Biochemistry
MCB	Member of the British Association of Communicators in Business
MCBDip	Member of the British Association of Communicators in Business who hold the Association's Certificate and Diploma
MCC	Master of Community Care
MCCDRCS(Eng)	Member of the Royal College of Surgeons of England, Clinical Community Dentistry
MCD	Master of Civic Design
MCDH	Master of Community Dental Health
MCGI	Membership, City & Guilds
MCGPIrel	Member of the Irish College of General Practitioners
MCh	Master of Surgery
MChD	Master of Dental Surgery
MChem	Master of Chemistry
MChemA	Master of Chemical Analysis
MChemPhys	Master of Chemical Physics
MChemPST	Master of Chemistry Polymer Science and Technology
MChir	Master of Surgery
MChOrth	Master of Orthopaedic Surgery
MChS	Member of the Society of Chiropodists and Podiatrists
MCIArb	Member of the Chartered Institute of Arbitrators
MCIBS	Member of the Chartered Institute of Bankers in Scotland
MCIBSE	Member of the Chartered Institution of Building Services Engineers
MCIH	Corporate Member of the Chartered Institute of Housing
MCIJ	Member of the Chartered Institute of Journalists
MCIM	Member of the Chartered Institute of Marketing
MCIOB	Member of the Chartered Institute of Building
MCIPD	Member of the Chartered Institute of Personnel and Development
MCIPS	Member of the Chartered Institute of Purchasing and Supply
MCIT	Member of the Chartered Institute of Transport
MCIWEM	Member of the Chartered Institution of Water and Environmental Management
MCLIP	Chartered Member of CILIP
MCom	Master of Commerce
MCommH	Master of Community Health
MComp	Master of Computer Science
MCOptom	Member of the College of Optometrists
MCoT	Member of the College of Teachers
MCPM	Member of the Confederation of Professional Management
MCPP	Member of the College of Pharmacy Practice
MCQ	Multiple Choice Question paper
MCSD	Member of the Chartered Society of Designers
MCSP	Member of the Chartered Society of Physiotherapy
MCT	Member of the Association of Corporate Treasurers

xlvii

Index of Abbreviations and Designatory Letters

MCTHCM	Member of the Confederation of Tourism, Hotel and Catering Management
MCYW	Member of the Community and Youth Work Association
MD	Doctor of Medicine
MDA	Master of Defence Administration
MD; ChM	Conjoint Doctorate in Medicine, Doctorate in Surgery
MDCR	Management Diploma of the College of Radiographers
MDent	Master of Dental Science
MDes	Master of Design
MDes(RCA)	Master of Design, Royal College of Art
MDORCPSGlas	Membership of Dental Orthopaedics, Royal College of Physicians and Surgeons of Glasgow
MDra	Master of Drama
MDS	Master of Dental Surgery
MDSc	Master of Dental Science
MEBA	Master of European Business Administration
MECI	Member of the Institute of Employment Consultants
MEd	Master of Education
MEd(EdPsych)	Master of Education (Educational Psychology)
MEdStud	Master of Educational Studies
MEng	Master of Engineering
MEnv	Master of Environmental Studies
MEnvSci	Master of Environmental Science
MESc	Master of Earth Sciences
MFA	Master of Fine Art
MFC	Mastership in Food Control
MFCM	Member of the Faculty of Community Medicine
MFDO	Member of the Faculty of Dispensing Opticians
MFDS	Member of the Faculty of Dental Surgery
MFGDPEng	Membership in General Dental Practice, Royal College of Surgeons of England
MFHom	Member of the Faculty of Homeopathy
MFM	Master of Forensic Medicine
MFPHM	Member of the Faculty of Public Health Medicine, Royal College of Physicians of London and Edinburgh and Royal College of Physicians and Surgeons of Glasgow
MFPHMIrel	Member of the Faculty of Public Health Medicine, Royal College of Physicians of Ireland
MFTCom	Member of the Faculty of Teachers in Commerce
MGDSRCSEd	Membership in General Dental Surgery, Royal College of Surgeons of Edinburgh
MGDSRCSEng	Membership in General Dental Surgery, Royal College of Surgeons of England
MGeog	Master of Geography
MGeol	Master of Geology
MGeophys	Master of Geophysical Sciences
MHCIMA	Member of the Hotel and Catering International Management Association
MHM	Master of Health Management
MHort(RHS)	Master of Horticulture, Royal Horticultural Society
MHSM	Member of the Institute of Health Services Management
MIAB	Member of the International Association of Book-keepers
MIAEA	Member of the Institute of Automotive Engineer Assessors
MIAgrE	Member of the Institution of Agricultural Engineers
MIAP	Member of the Institution of Analysts and Programmers
MIAT	Member of the Institute of Asphalt Technology
MIBC	Member of the Institute of Building Control

MIBCM	Member of the Institute British Carriage and Automobile Manufacturers
MIBCO	Member of the Institution of Building Control Officers
MIBE	Member of the Institution of British Engineers
MIBF	Member of the Institute of British Foundrymen
MIBiol	Member of the Institute of Biology
MIBM	Member of the Institute of Builders' Merchants
MICB	Member of the Institute of Certified Book-Keepers
MICE	Member of the Institute of Civil Engineers
MIChemE	Member of the Institution of Chemical Engineers
MICHT	Member of the International Council for Holistic Therapies
MICM	Member of the Institute of Credit Management
MICM(Grad)	Graduate Member of the Institute of Credit Management
MICorr	Member of the Institute of Corrosion
MICS	Member of the Institute of Chartered Shipbrokers
MICSc	Corporate Member of the Institute of Consumer Sciences Incorporating Home Economics
MICW	Member of the Institute of Clerks of Works of Great Britain Incorporated
MIDTA	Member of the International Dance Teachers' Association
MIED	Member of the Institution of Engineering Designers
MIEE	Member of the Institution of Electrical Engineers
MIEM	Member of the Institute of Executives and Managers
MIEx	Member of the Institute of Export
MIEx(Grad)	Graduate Member of the Institute of Export
MIExpE	Member of the Institute of Explosives Engineers
MIFA	Member of the Institute of Field Archaeologists
MIFireE	Member of the Institution of Fire Engineers
MIFM	Registered Member of the Institute of Fisheries Management
MIFST	Member of the Institute of Food Science and Technology
MIGasE	Member of the Institution of Gas Engineers
MIGD	Member of the Institute of Grocery Distribution
MIHEc	Member of the Institute of Home Economics
MIHIE	Member of the Institute of Highway Incorporated Engineers
MIHM	Member of the Institute of Healthcare Management
MIHort	Member of the Institute of Horticulture
MIHT	Member of the Institution of Highways and Transportation
MIIA	Member of the Institute of Internal Auditors
MIIE	Member of the Institution of Incorporated Engineers
MIIExE	Member of the Institution of Incorporated Executive Engineers
MIIHTM	Member of the International Institute of Hospitality Tourism & Management
MIIM	Member of the Institute of Industrial Managers
MIIM	Member of the International Institute of Management
MIIRSM	Member of the International Institute of Risk and Safety Management
MIISE	Member of the International Institute of Social Economics
MIISec	Member of the International Institute of Security
MIL	Member of the Institute of Linguists
MILAM	Member of the Institute of Leisure and Amenity Management
MILT	Member of the Institute of Logistics and Transport
MIM	Professional Member of the Institute of Materials
MIMA	Member of the Institute of Mathematics and its Applications
MIManf	Member of the Institute of Manufacturing
MIMarE	Member of the Institute of Marine Engineers
MIMatM	Member of the Institute of Materials Management

Index of Abbreviations and Designatory Letters

MIMBM	Member of the Institute of Maintenance and Building Management
MIMC	Member of the Institute of Management Consultancy
MIMechE	Member of the Institution of Mechanical Engineers
MIMechIE	Member of the Institution of Mechanical Incorporated Engineers
MIMF	Member of the Institute of Metal Finishing
MIMI	Member of the Institute of the Motor Industry
MIMinE	Member of the Institution of Mining Engineers
MIMIS	Member of the Institute for the Management of Information Systems
MIMM	Member of the Institute of Massage and Movement
MIMM	Member of the Institution of Mining and Metallurgy
MIMS	Member of the Institute of Management Specialists
MInstAEA	Member of the Institute of Automotive Engineer Assessors
MInstAM	Member of the Institute of Administrative Management
MInstBA	Member of the Institute of Business Administration
MInstBCA	Member of the Institute of Burial and Cremation Administration
MInstBE	Member of the Institution of British Engineers
MInstBM	Member of the Institute of Builders' Merchants
MInstCF	Master Fitter of the National Institute of Carpet and Floorlayers
MInstChP	Member of the Institute of Chiropodists & Podiatrists
MInstCM	Member of the Institute of Commercial Management
MInstD	Member of the Institute of Directors
MInstE	Member of the Institute of Energy
MInstLEx	Member of the Institute of Legal Executives
MInstMC	Member of the Institute of Measurement and Control
MInstNDT	Member of the British Institute of Non-Destructive Testing
MInstP	Member of the Institute of Physics
MInstPet	Member of the Institute of Petroleum
MInstPkg	Member of the Institute of Packaging
MInstPkg(Dip)	Diploma Member of the Institute of Packaging
MInstPM	Member of the Institute of Professional Managers and Administrators
MInstPS	Corporate Member of the Institute of Purchasing and Supply
MInstPSA	Member of the Institute of Public Service Administrators
MInstR	Member of the Institute of Refrigeration
MInstSMM	Member of the Institute of Sales and Marketing Management
MInstTA	Member of the Institute of Transport Administration
MInstTT	Full Member of the Institute of Travel and Tourism
MInstWM	Member of the Institute of Wastes Management
MIOC	Member of the Institute of Carpenters
MIOFMS	Member of the Institute of Financial and Management Studies
MIOM	Member of the Institute of Operations Management
MIOP	Member of the Institute of Printing
MIOSH	Member of the Institution of Occupational Safety and Health
MIP	Member of the Institute of Plumbing
MIPA	Member of the Institute of Practitioners in Advertising
MIPD	Member of the Institute of Personnel and Development
MIPI	Member of the Institute of Professional Investigators
MIPlantE	Member of the Institution of Plant Engineers
MIPR	Member of the Institute of Public Relations
MIPRE	Member of the Incorporated Practitioners in Radio & Electronics
MIQ	Member of the Institute of Quarrying
MIQA	Member of the Institute of Quality Assurance
MIR	Member of the Institute of Population Registration

MIRRV	Member of the Institute of Revenue, Rating and Valuation
MIRSE	Member of the Institution of Railway Signal Engineers
MIRTE	Member of the Institute of Road Transport Engineering
MISM	Member of the Institute for Supervision & Management
MISOB	Member of the Incorporated Society of Organ Builders
MISTC	Member of the Institute of Scientific and Technical Communicators
MIStrucE	Member of the Institution of Structural Engineers
MISW	Member of the Institute of Social Welfare
MITAI	Member of the Institute of Traffic Accident Investigators
MITSA	Member of the Institute of Trading Standards Administration
MIVehE	Member of the Institute of Vehicle Engineers
MIWM	Member of the Institute of Wastes Management
MIWPC	Member of the Institute of Water Pollution Control
MJur	Master of Jurisprudence
MLA	Master of Landscape Architecture
MLang	Master of Languages
MLangEng	Master of Language Engineering
MLD	Master of Landscape Design
MLE	Master of Land Economy
MLI	Member of the Landscape Institute
MLing	Master of Languages
MLitt	Master of Letters
MLPM	Master of Landscape Planning and Management
MLS	Master of Library Science
MM	Master of Midwifery
MMA	Master of Management and Administration
MMAS	Master of Minimal Access Surgery
MMath	Master of Mathematics
MMedE	Master of Medical Education
MMedSci	Master of Medical Science
MMet	Master of Metallurgy
MML	Master of Modern Languages
MMS	Member of the Institute of Management Services
MMSc	Master of Medical Sciences
MMus	Master of Music
MMus(Comp)	Master of Music (Composition)
MMus(Perf)	Master of Music (Performance)
MMus, RCM	Master of Music, Royal College of Music
MMusArt	Master of Musical Arts
MN	Master of Nursing
MNAEA	Member of the National Association of Estate Agents
MNatSc	Master of Natural Science
MNCP	Member of the National Council of Psychotherapists
MNeuro	Master of Neuroscience
MNI	Member of the Nautical Institute
MNIMH	Member of the National Institute of Medical Herbalists
MNRHP	Full Member of the National Register of Hypnotherapists and Psychotherapists
MNRHP(Eqv)	Full Member (Equivalent) of the National Register of Hypnotherapists and Psychotherapists
MNTB	Merchant Navy Training Board
MObstG	Master of Obstetrics and Gynaecology
MOptom	Master of Optometry

Index of Abbreviations and Designatory Letters

MOrthRCSEng	Membership in Orthodontics, Royal College of Surgeons of England
MPA	Master of Public Administration
MPaedDenRCSEng	Membership in Paediatric Dentistry, Royal College of Surgeons of England
MPC	Master of Palliative Care
MPH	Master of Public Health
MPharm	Master of Pharmacy
MPharmSci	Master of Pharmaceutical Science
MPhil	Master of Philosophy
MPhil(Eng)	Master of Philosophy in Engineering
MPhys	Master of Physics
MPhysGeog	Master of Physical Geography
MPlan	Master of Planning
MPPS	Master of Public Policy Studies
MPRI	Member of the Plastics and Rubber Institute
MProf	Master of Professional Studies
MProfBTM	Member of the Professional Business and Technical Management
MPS	Member of the Pharmaceutical Society of Northern Ireland
MPsychMed	Master of Psychological Medicine
MPsychol	Master of Psychology
MQB	Mining Qualifications Board
MRad	Master of Radiology
MRad; MRad(D)	Master of Radiology (Radiodiagnosis) or (Radiotherapy)
MRAeS	Member of the Royal Aeronautical Society
MRCGP	Member of the Royal College of General Practitioners
MRCOG	Member of the Royal College of Obstetricians and Gynaecologists
MRCP	Member of the Royal College of Physicians of London
MRCP(UK)	Member of the Royal College of Physicians of the United Kingdom
MRCPath	Member of the Royal College of Pathologists
MRCPEdin	Member of the Royal College of Physicians of Edinburgh (superceded by MRCP(UK))
MRCPGlasg	Member of the Royal College of Physicians of Glasgow (superceded by MRCP(UK))
MRCPIrel	Member of the Royal College of Physicians of Ireland
MRCPsych	Member of the Royal College of Psychiatrists
MRCSEd	Member of the Royal College of Surgeons of Edinburgh
MRCSEng	Member of the Royal College of Surgeons of England
MRCVS	Member of the Royal College of Veterinary Surgeons
MRDRCS	Membership in Restorative Dentistry, Royal College of Surgeons of England
MREC	Member of the Recruitment and Employment Confederation
MREHIS	Member of the Royal Environmental Health Institute of Scotland
MRes	Master of Research
MRIN	Member of the Royal Institute of Navigation
MRINA	Member of the Royal Institution of Naval Architects
MRIPHH	Member of the Royal Institute of Public Health and Hygiene
MRPharmS	Member of the Pharmaceutical Society of Great Britain
MRSC	Member of the Royal Society of Chemistry
MRSH	Member of the Royal Society for the Promotion of Health
MRSS	Member of the Royal Statistical Society
MRTPI	Member of the Royal Town Planning Institute
MS	Master of Surgery
MSA	Marine Safety Agency
MSAPP	Member of the Society of Advanced Psychotherapy Practitioners

Index of Abbreviations and Designatory Letters

MSBP	Member of the Society of Business Practitioners
MSBT	Member of the Society of Teachers in Business Education
MSc	Master of Science
MSc(Econ)	Master of Science in Economics
MSc(Ed)	Master of Science in Education
MSc(Eng)	Master of Science in Engineering
MSc(Entr)	Master of Entrepreneurship
MSc(Mgt)	Master of Science in Management
MScD	Master of Dental Science
MScEcon	Master in Faculty of Economic and Social Studies
MSCi	Master of Natural Sciences
MScTech	Master of Technical Science
MSE	Member of Society of Engineers (Inc)
MSF	Member of the SMAE Institute
MSFA	Advanced Financial Planning Certificate
MSIAD	Member of the Society of Industrial Artists and Designers
MSMA	Member of the Society of Martial Arts
MSocSc	Master of Social Science
MSSc	Master of Social Science
MSSc	Master of Surgical Science
MSSCh	Member of the British Chiropody and Podiatry Association
MSSF	Member of the Society of Shoe Fitters
MSt	Master of Studies
MSTA	Member of the Swimming Teachers' Association
MSTI	Certificate of Insurance Work
MSurgDentRCSEng	Membership in Surgical Dentistry, Royal College of Surgeons of England
MSW	Master of Social Work
MTCP	Master of Town and Country Planning
MTD	Master of Transport Design
MTech	Master of Technology
MTh	Master of Theology
MTheol	Master of Theology
MTP	Master of Town Planning
MTPI	Master of Town Planning
MTropMed	Master of Tropical Medicine
MTropPaediatrics	Master of Tropical Paediatrics
MUniv	Master of University (Honorary)
MURP	Master of Urban and Regional Planning
MusB	Bachelor of Music
MusD	Doctor of Music
MVC	Management Verification Consortium
MVM	Master of Veterinary Medicine
MVSc	Master of Veterinary Science
MWeldI	Member of the Welding Institute
MWES	Member of the Women's Engineering Society
MYD	Member of the Youth Development Association
NACOS	National Approval Council for Security Systems
NAEA	National Association of Estate Agents
NAG	National Association of Goldsmiths
NAMCW	National Association for Maternal and Child Welfare
NC	National Certificate
NCA	National Certificate in Agriculture

Index of Abbreviations and Designatory Letters

NCC	National Computing Centre
NCC	Navigational Control Course
NCDT	National Council for Drama Training
NCTJ	National Council for the Training of Journalists
NCVQ	National Council for Vocational Qualifications
ND	Diploma in Naturopathy
NDD	National Diploma in Design
NDF	National Diploma in Forestry
NDH	National Diploma in Horticulture
NDSF	National Diploma of the Society of Floristry
NDT	National Diploma in the Science and Practice of Turfculture and Sports Ground Management
NEBOSH	National Examination Board in Occupational Safety and Health
NEBS	National Examining Board for Supervision & Management
NFTS	National Film and Television School
NICCEA	Northern Ireland Council for the Curriculum, Examinations and Assessment
NID	National Intermediate Diploma
NIM	Northern Institute of Massage
NNEB	National Nursery Examination Board
NRHP	National Register of Hypnotherapists and Psychotherapists
NRHP(Affil)	Affiliate of the National Register of Hypnotherapists and Psychotherapists
NRHP(Assoc)	Associate of the National Register of Hypnotherapists and Psychotherapists
N-SHAP	National School of Hypnosis and Psychotherapy
NTTG	National Textile Training Group
NUJ	National Union of Journalists
NVQ	National Vocational Qualifications
NWRAC	North Western Regional Advisory Council for Further Education
OCR	Oxford, Cambridge & RSA Examinations
ODLQC	Open & Distance Learning Quality Council, formerly CACC, Council for Accreditation of Correspondence Colleges
ONC	Ordinary National Certificate
OND	Ordinary National Diploma
OSCE	Objective Structured Clinical Exam
PBTM	Professional Business and Technical Management
PCN	Personnel Certification in Non-Destructive Testing Ltd
PDP	Professional Development Programme
PESD	Private and Executive Secretary's Diploma, London Chamber of Commerce and Industry
PgC	Postgraduate Certificate
PGCE	Postgraduate Certificate in Education
PGCert	Postgraduate Certificate
PgD	Postgraduate Diploma
PGDip	Postgraduate Diploma
PGDip(Comp)	Postgraduate Diploma in Composition
PGDip(LCM)	Postgraduate Diploma of the London College of Music
PGDip(Perf)	Postgraduate Diploma in Performance
PGDip(RCM)	Postgraduate Diploma of the Royal College of Music
PGDipMin	Postgraduate Diploma in Ministry
PGDipMus	Postgraduate Diploma in Music
PhD	Doctor of Philosophy
PhD(RCA)	Doctor of Philosophy (Royal College of Art)
PIC	Professional Investment Certificate

Index of Abbreviations and Designatory Letters

PIFA	Practitioner of the Institute of Field Archaeologists
PIIA	Practitioner of the Institute of Internal Auditors
PInstNDT	Practitioner of the British Institute of Non-Destructive Testing
PJDip	Professional Jewellers' Diploma
PJGemDip	Professional Jewellers' Gemstone Diploma
PJManDip	Professional Jewellers' Management Diploma
PJValDip	Professional Jewellers' Valuation Diploma
PPL	Private Pilot's Licence
PPRNCM	Professional Performance Diploma of the Royal Northern College of Music
PQS	Professional Qualification Structure
PQSW	Post-Qualifying Award in Social Work
PRCA	Public Relations Consultants Association
PSC	Private Secretary's Certificate
PSD	Private Secretary's Diploma
PTA	Pianoforte Tuners' Association
PVM	Professional in Value Management
QC	Queen's Counsel
QCA	Qualifications and Curriculum Authority
QCG	Qualification in Careers Guidance
QDR	Qualified Dispute Resolver
QICA	Qualification in Computer Auditing
QIS	Qualified Imaging Scientist
QPA	Qualification in Pensions Administration
QPSPA	Qualification in Public Sector Pensions Administration
RA	Royal Academician
RAD	Royal Academy of Dancing
RADA	Royal Academy of Dramatic Art
RAM	Royal Academy of Music
RANA	Royal Animal Nursing Auxiliary
RAS	Royal Astronomical Society
RBS	Royal Ballet School
RC	Roman Catholic
RCM	Royal College of Midwives
RCN	Royal College of Nursing
RCSLT	Royal College of Speech and Language Therapists
RCVS	Royal College of Veterinary Surgeons
REA	Regional Examining Body
REC	Recruitment and Employment Confederation
Ret'dABID	Retired Associate of the British Institute of Interior Design
Ret'dFBID	Retired Fellow of the British Institute of Interior Design
Ret'dMBID	Retired Member of the British Institute of Interior Design
RGN	Registered General Nurse
RHS	Royal Horticultural Society
RHV	Registered Health Visitor
RIBA	Royal Institute of British Architects
RICS	Royal Institution of Chartered Surveyors
RINA	Royal Institution of Naval Architects
RJDip	Diploma for Retail Jewellers
RJGemDip	National Association of Goldsmiths Gemstone Diploma
RM	Registered Midwife
RMN	Registered Mental Nurse
RMS	Royal Microscopical Society

Index of Abbreviations and Designatory Letters

RNMH	Registered Nurse for the Mentally Handicapped
RP	Registered Plumber
RPS	Royal Photographic Society
RSA	Royal Society of Arts
RSBEI	Registered Student of the Institution of Body Engineers
RSC	Royal Society of Chemistry
RSCN	Registered Sick Children's Nurse
RSP	Registered Safety Practitioner
RTO	Recognised Training Organisation
RTPI	Royal Town Planning Institute
SA	Salvation Army Management
SBP	Society of Business Practitioners
SCAA	School Curriculum and Assessment Authority
ScD	Doctor of Science
SCE	Scottish Certificate of Education
SCLS	Second Certificate for Legal Secretaries
SCMT	Ship Captain's Medical Training
SCOTVEC	Scottish Vocational Education Council
SCPL	Senior Commercial Pilot's Licence
SE	Society of Engineers
SEE	Society of Environmental Engineers
SEFIC	Spoken English for Industry and Commerce
SenAWeldI	Senior Associate of the Welding Institute
SEng	Qualified Sales Engineer
SenMWeldI	Senior Member of the Welding Institute
SF	Society of Floristry Ltd
SFA	Securities and Futures Authority
SFInstE	Senior Fellow of the Institute of Energy
SG	Society of Genealogists
SGT	Society of Glass Technology
SHNC	Scottish Higher National Certificate
SHND	Scottish Higher National Diploma
SIEDip	Securities Industry Examination Diploma
SInstPet	Student of the Institute of Petroleum
SITO	Security Industry Training Organisation Ltd
SLC	Secretarial Language Certificate
SLD	Secretarial Language Diploma
SNC	Scottish National Certificate
SND	Scottish National Diploma
SNNEB	Scottish Nursery Nurses Examination Board
SPA	Screen Printing Association
SPRINT	Sport Play and Recreation Industries National Training Executive
SQA	Scottish Qualifications Authority
SRD	State Registered Dietician
SRN	State Registered Nurse
SSC	Secretarial Studies Certificate, London Chamber of Commerce and Industry
STA	Specialist Teacher Assistant (CACHE)
STA	Swimming Teachers' Association
STAT	Society of Teachers of the Alexander Technique
StudentIEE	Student of the Institution of Electrical Engineers
StudentIIE	Student of the Institution of Incorporated Engineers
StudentIMechE	Student of the Institution of Mechanical Engineers

Index of Abbreviations and Designatory Letters

StudIAP	Student of the Institution of Analysts and Programmers
StudIManf	Student Member of the Institute of Manufacturing
StudIMS	Student of the Institute of Management Specialists
StudProfBTM	Student of the Professional Business and Technical Management
StudSE	Student of the Society of Engineers (Inc)
StudSElec	Student of the Society of Electroscience
StudWeldI	Student of the Welding Institute
SVQ	Scottish Vocational Qualification
TC	Technician Certificate
TCA	Technician in Costing and Accounting
TCA	Technician of the Institute of Cost and Executive Accountants
TCert	Teacher's Certificate
TD	Technician Diploma
TDCR	Teacher's Diploma of the College of Radiographers
TechICorr	Technician of the Institute of Corrosion
TechMIWM	Technician Member of the Institute of Wastes Management
TechRICS	Technical Surveyor of the Royal Institution of Chartered Surveyors
TechRMS	Technological Qualification in Microscopy, Royal Microscopical Society
TechRTPI	Technical Member of the Royal Town Planning Institute
TechSP	Technician Safety Practitioner
TechWeldI	Technician of the Welding Institute
TEMOL	Training in Energy Management through Open Learning
TI	Textile Institute
TIMBM	Technician of the Institute of Maintenance and Building Management
TMBA	Teacher Member of the British (Theatrical) Arts
TnIMBM	Technicians of the Institute of Maintenance and Building Management
TOEFL	Test of English as a Foreign Language
TPP	Test of Professional Practice
TVM	Trainer in Value Management
UCAS	Universities and Colleges Admissions Service
UCL	University College London
UEB	United Examining Board
UKCC	United Kingdom Central Council
UKCP	United Kingdom Council for Psychotherapy
UMIST	University of Manchester Institute of Science and Technology
URC	United Reformed Church
VetMB	Bachelor of Veterinary Medicine
VTCT	Vocational Training Charitable Trust
WCMD	Welsh College of Music and Drama
WES	Women's Engineering Society
WJEC	Welsh Joint Education Committee
WMAC	West Midlands Advisory Council for Further Education
WSA	West of Scotland Agricultural College
YHAFHE	Yorkshire and Humberside Association for Further and Higher Education
ZSL	Zoological Society of London

Part 1

Introduction

Since its first publication in 1970, *British Qualifications* has charted a number of fundamental changes in further and higher education provision in the UK. Major advances in technology and more flexible delivery and attendance patterns have created different types of learning opportunity, encouraging an ever more diverse student population to access education at all levels. The range of subjects delivered has grown beyond all recognition. New areas of research have been established and developed into major subject specialisms. Employers and professional bodies have collaborated to develop subject areas aligned to changing industry requirements. Flexibility and choice are the hallmarks of today's system, and anyone new to higher education may well be bewildered by the sheer variety of degree pathways available. The capacity to combine and mix modules and subjects has in fact grown beyond anything that could have been imagined in 1970.

Traditional boundaries between academic and vocational pathways continue to break down, and today most degrees have a vocational slant. Extended industry and professional placements, sponsored research projects, practitioner input and field-based assignments are common features in many degrees, and provide an important link into practice at the early stages of learning. Overall, in 20 years universities have doubled in size and the responsibilities they have taken on have expanded considerably. Collaboration between further education (FE) and higher education (HE) institutions has enabled a substantial amount of HE-level provision to be delivered in FE institutions. Clear progression routes have been established for some time. Considerable breadth of provision is now available in FE: not only has the sector grown to accommodate sub-degree provision, it has also continued to deliver a wide range of pre- and post-18 vocational qualifications, which include technical, occupational and professional awards.

Today, certain types of external qualification cross the boundaries between further and higher education. Several higher education institutions (HEIs) – particularly those that gained university status in the 1990s and in 2005 – deliver advanced professional qualifications and higher national diplomas or certificates from awarding bodies like Edexcel, OCR and SQA. At the same time there has been a significant shift towards FE's involvement in delivery of these types of qualification, and a greater input from private sector colleges.

EDUCATION REFORM

The Higher Education Act 2004 introduced in 2006/07 brought new student support and tuition fee arrangements. Following the Browne Review of 2010, universities are able to charge full-time UK and EU undergraduate students up to £9,000 a year as part of a reorganization of HE funding and student finance. You will find further authoritative, official information about universities and colleges in the UK at the Unistats website: http://unistats.direct.gov.uk/. Information on student finance can be found at www.direct.gov.uk.

As well as implementing reforms, the further and higher education sectors contribute to UK economic performance and the delivery of the government's policies on HE. As part of this shared responsibility a great deal of effort is being made to increase access to and participation in education, particularly among individuals who have not had much involvement in the past. The general availability of modular study programmes and related credit recognition of units, and greater use of ICT and e-learning resources, have done a lot to create more flexible methods of delivery and attendance requirements in further and higher education.

Introduction

FOUNDATION DEGREES

Foundation degrees (FDs) were established to give people the intermediate technical and professional skills that are in demand from employers, and to provide more flexible and accessible ways of studying. They are a higher level qualification awarded by universities. The qualification can be 'built up' from a range of relevant learning experiences, to allow for extremely flexible and adaptable qualifications that can be 'tailored' by employers to support their workforce and business development needs. They offer opportunities for employment and career advancement. Progression routes include links with associated professional qualifications and/or direct entry to the final year of a relevant Honours-level degree. FDs are offered by universities, colleges and other providers.

The first FDs in 2001 were studied by 4,000 students. In 2010, there were just over 99,700 enrolled on FDs. There are now hundreds of FD courses available, both full- and part-time. Foundation degree forward (fdf) was established in the 2003 Higher Education White Paper, but closed on 31 July 2011; however:

- fdf's Employer Based Training Accreditation (EBTA) service is now hosted by QAA; details can be found at www.fdfebta.co.uk.
- fdf's information, advice and guidance resources for work-based learners and their advisers are now hosted by unionlearn at www.higherlearningatwork.org.
- fdf e-learning resources that support delivery of work-based higher education in sectors such as retail, travel and low carbon energy remain available at www.workforcedevelopment.fdf.ac.uk.

POLICY AND REGULATION

National priorities for further and higher education are set by the UK and Scottish parliaments and the Welsh and Northern Ireland assemblies. Policy development, planning and implementation rest with the government departments responsible for each national education brief – the Department for Business, Innovation and Skills (BIS) (www.bis.gov.uk), the Department for Employment and Learning Northern Ireland (DELNI) (www.delni.gov.uk), the Scottish Government (www.scotland.gov.uk), and The Department for Education and Skills (DfES) (www.learning.wales.gov.uk) in Wales.

In England, delivery of FE is subject to external audit and public reporting by the Office for Standards in Education, Children's Services and Schools (Ofsted). In Scotland, the Scottish Funding Council (SFC) (www.sfc.ac.uk) has overall responsibility for planning, funding and quality assurance of FE through its work with Her Majesty's Inspectorate of Education (HMIE).

DfES is responsible for planning, funding and promotion of all post-16 education in Wales. Estyn (the Welsh-language acronym for Her Majesty's Inspectorate for Education and Training in Wales, website: www.estyn.gov.uk) is the appointed authority for audit of the quality of provision and related areas.

The Department for Employment and Learning (DELNI) is responsible for planning and funding of further education provision in Northern Ireland. Inspection and audit are undertaken by the Education and Training Inspectorate on behalf of the Department (www.delni.gov.uk, www.etini.gov.uk).

QUALITY ASSURANCE

A degree of convergence exists in the area of quality assurance of qualifications at Level 3 and below. England, Wales and Northern Ireland share a common qualifications system, and the regulators in each country (listed below) work together in regulating qualifications for use across the three countries. Scotland has a separate qualifications system, although there is close correlation across all four countries, particularly in the area of vocational qualifications.

The following four bodies are responsible for the accreditation and standards of external qualifications and for curriculum and assessment for ages 3–16:

- *England*: Office of the Qualifications and Examinations Regulator (Ofqual);
- *Northern Ireland*: Council for Curriculum, Examinations and Assessment (CCEA*);
- *Scotland*: Scottish Qualifications Authority (SQA*);
- *Wales*: Department for Education and Skills (DfES).

*CCEA is also an Awarding Body for qualifications in Northern Ireland, which include National Qualifications to A level. SQA is also an Awarding Body that develops and validates SQA-branded qualifications including National Qualifications (Access, Intermediate, Higher and Advanced Higher Levels), Higher National Certificates and Diplomas, Scottish Vocational Qualifications and Scottish Professional Development Awards.

In HE the responsibility for standards and quality rests firmly with each institution. All institutions work with the independent Quality Assurance Agency for Higher Education (QAA) for England, Northern Ireland, Scotland and Wales. Institutional audits and subject-level reviews have been undertaken by QAA since 2001. It publishes its findings on its website as publicly accessible information; see www.qaa.ac.uk.

Given the current scale and diversity of degree provision in the HE sector, there has been a need to clarify what can reasonably be expected from undergraduate and postgraduate programmes. QAA has responded to this requirement and developed a quality code for HE providers, and subject benchmark statements indicating the expected standards of degrees across a range of subjects.

QUALIFICATION FRAMEWORKS

In further response to the breadth and diversity of qualifications available, a number of national qualification frameworks have been introduced. The framework concept is closely associated with greater transparency and comparability between types of qualification, particularly between those that were traditionally classified as academic or vocational. Common characteristics of all frameworks include universal adoption and understanding of qualification titles, and national tariffs of credits that recognize relevant levels of achievement.

The framework for Higher Education Qualifications in England, Wales and Northern Ireland (FHEQ) applies to degrees, diplomas, certificates and other academic awards by higher education providers (see Figure 1.1). The Scottish Credit and Qualification Framework (SCQF) was

Introduction

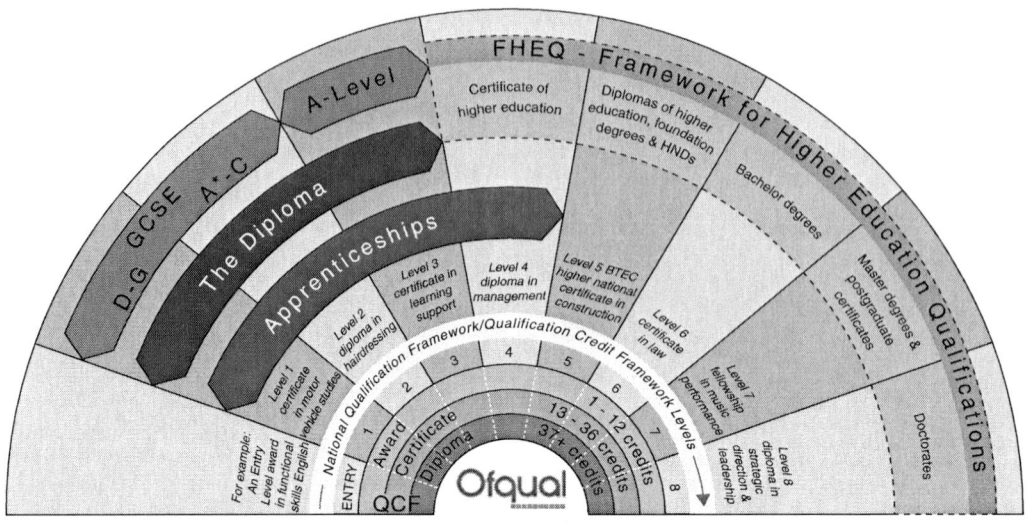

Figure 1.1 Framework for Higher Education Qualifications in England, Wales and Northern Ireland
Source: www.qaa.ac.uk

developed by SQA, the Scottish Executive, QAA (Scottish Office) and Universities for Scotland. It provides an overview of all levels of national and higher qualifications provision in Scotland (see Figure 1.2).

The Qualifications and Credit Framework (QCF) is a new framework for recognizing and accrediting qualifications in England, Wales and Northern Ireland. The intention behind the reform was to make the system and qualifications offered far more relevant to the needs of employers, with more flexibility for learners. Every unit and qualification in the framework has a credit value (where one credit represents 10 hours) and a level between Entry level and level 8. There are three sizes of qualification in the QCF:

Awards: 1–12 credits
Certificates: 13–36 credits
Diplomas: 37 credits or more

This means that each qualification title contains the level (from Entry to level 8), the size (Award/Certificate/Diploma) and the details of the content of the qualification. For a full list of accredited qualifications please visit the National Database of Accredited Qualifications at www.accreditedqualifications.org.uk. This is a fully searchable database of qualifications that are accredited by Ofqual, DCELLS and CCEA.

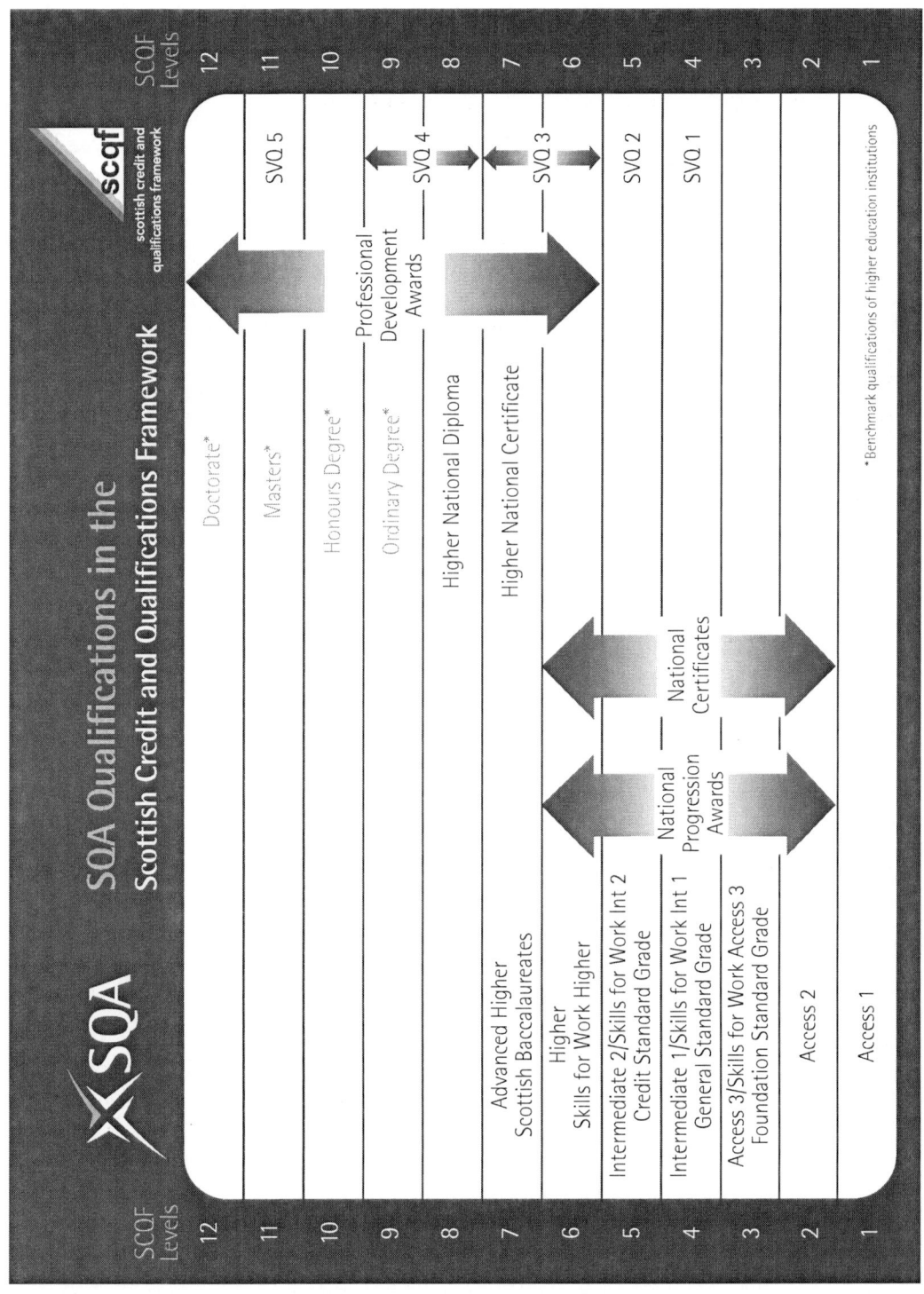

Figure 1.2 Framework for Higher Education Qualifications in Scotland

Part 2

Teaching Establishments

INTRODUCTION

The statutory responsibility for the provision of education in the United Kingdom lies with the Department for Education and the Department for Business, Innovation and Skills (BIS) in England, the Welsh Assembly Government's Department for Education and Skills (DfES), the Education Department of the Scottish Government and the Department of Education and Department for Employment and Learning in Northern Ireland. In the United Kingdom the statutory system of public education has three progressive stages: primary education (up to the age of 11 or 12), secondary education (up to age 16), and further education (post-16).

This section briefly describes further and higher provision and the main types of institution.

FURTHER AND HIGHER EDUCATION

'Higher education' (HE) is a term that broadly defines any course of study leading to a qualification at level 4 and above in the Qualifications and Credit Framework (QCF)/National Qualifications Framework (NQF) for England, Wales and Northern Ireland, and level 6 and above in the Scottish Credit and Qualifications Framework.

HE incorporates study towards a wide range of qualifications including Foundation, undergraduate and postgraduate degrees, certificates and diplomas awarded by individual universities and other higher education institutions (HEIs) with degree-awarding powers.

It can also include study towards general, technical or occupationally-related diplomas and certificates awarded by the large unitary awarding bodies. Unitary awarding bodies are characterized by their breadth of provision, from GNVQ and A levels through to qualifications at level 5 and above in the national frameworks.

The other category that can be characterized as HE includes post-experience education above level 4 (and level 7 in Scotland). This includes qualifications available from awarding bodies that represent a particular sector, occupation or technical/craft area, and professional institutions that are also approved as awarding bodies.

HE can take place in universities and HE colleges (which continue to provide the majority of undergraduate and postgraduate courses). It can also take place in colleges of further education (FE). A significant number of colleges deliver parts of, and in some cases entire, Foundation and undergraduate degree courses in agreement with a selected university partner that is responsible for quality assurance and final awards.

In general terms, FE is available for students who are over the age of 16 and still in full-time education, and for adults aged 19 and over. FE provision includes GCSEs, A levels and other types of general and vocational qualifications below level 4 (and level 6 in Scotland) in the National Qualifications Frameworks.

All qualifications are awarded by approved external awarding bodies that include AQA, City & Guilds, Edexcel, LCCI, OCR, OCN and SQA in Scotland. This also includes qualifications below level 4 (level 6 in Scotland) that have a craft or technical focus or are related to an occupation/sector. At the time of writing, readers who want to find out more about approved qualifications below level 4 will find The Register of Regulated Qualifications website informative (http://register.ofqual.gov.uk/). It contains details of all those qualifications that are accredited by the regulators of external qualifications in England (Ofqual), Wales (DfES) and Northern Ireland (CCEA).

FURTHER AND HIGHER EDUCATION INSTITUTIONS

England and Wales

There is a wide range of further and higher education establishments, including colleges with various titles. There are also a number of independent specialist establishments, like secretarial and correspondence colleges.

According to latest UK figures available, there were 116 universities, 165 HE institutions in 2011, and 411 further education colleges (of which 94 were sixth-form colleges in England) in 2012. Of the universities, 89 are in England (including The Open University), 10 are in Wales, 15 are in Scotland and two are in Northern Ireland. Courses include those for first and second degrees, certain graduate-equivalent qualifications, and the examinations of the principal professional associations. These institutions also provide courses leading to important qualifications below degree level, such as Foundation degrees, Higher National Diplomas and Certificates, and Diplomas of Higher Education.

Most FE colleges specialize in providing courses that lead to qualifications below degree level, such as A levels and BTEC qualifications. Some offer degree courses, including in many cases Foundation degrees.

Students aged 16–18 who have been ordinarily resident in the UK for three years and European Economic Area nationals normally have the right to attend a full-time course without paying tuition fees. More detailed information on tuition fees can be found at www.ukcisa.org.uk. Colleges are free to determine fee levels for students who do not qualify for 'home fees'.

Scotland

There are 41 FE colleges in Scotland which provide a broad mix of courses, many awarded by the Scottish Qualifications Authority (SQA). Most HE courses at or near degree level and beyond are provided by the 18 universities/HE institutions and The Open University in Scotland. These institutions offer a range of vocationally-oriented courses ranging from science, engineering and computing to health care, art and design, music and drama, and teacher training, as well as the more traditional 'academic' courses. All the universities and HE institutions are funded by the Scottish Funding Council.

Northern Ireland

Responsibility for the FE sector in Northern Ireland rests with the Department for Employment and Learning (DELNI) which directly funds colleges. There are six further and higher education colleges, offering a wide range of vocational and non-vocational courses for both full- and part-time students. Details can be found at www.anic.ac.uk.

Queen's University Belfast and the University of Ulster receive funding from the Department for Employment and Learning, Northern Ireland. Many of the courses in both universities are designed to suit the needs of industry, commerce and the professions. Agricultural, horticultural and food colleges in Northern Ireland are administered through the Department of Agriculture and Rural Development (DARD). DARD offers a range of further and higher education courses at the College of Agriculture, Food and Rural Enterprise (CAFRE).

UNIVERSITIES AND HE COLLEGES

Universities are self-governing bodies, largely financed by the government through the Higher Education Funding Councils in the UK. They generally derive their rights and privileges from Royal Charter or Act of Parliament, and any amendment of their charters or statutes is made by the Crown acting through the Privy Council on the application of the universities themselves. The universities alone decide what degrees they award and the conditions on which they are awarded; they alone decide which students to admit and which staff to appoint. However, government policies have started to influence admission criteria, particularly in terms of widening access and participation in HE. Student fees set by universities are also subject to strict guidelines set by the government.

The Higher Education Funding Council funds HE, research and related activities in English HE institutions and FE colleges. It funds 130 HE institutions (including University Campus Suffolk, a connected institution of the Universities of East Anglia and Essex) and 122 FE colleges.

Institutions receiving funding from Higher Education Funding Council for England

(*Source*: Higher Education Funding Council for England)

The 19 schools and institutes of the University of London which receive funds directly from the HEFCE are marked *.

Anglia Ruskin University; Aston University; University of Bath; Bath Spa University; University of Bedfordshire; Birkbeck College*; University of Birmingham; University College Birmingham; Birmingham City University; Bishop Grosseteste University College Lincoln; University of Bolton; Arts University College at Bournemouth; Bournemouth University; University of Bradford; University of Brighton; University of Bristol; Brunel University; Buckinghamshire New University; University of Cambridge; Institute of Cancer Research*; Canterbury Christ Church University; University of Central Lancashire; Central School of Speech and Drama*; University of Chester; University of Chichester; City University, London; Conservatoire for Dance and Drama; Courtauld Institute of Art*; Coventry University; Cranfield University; University for the Creative Arts; University of Cumbria; De Montfort University; University of Derby; Durham University; University of East Anglia; University of East London; Edge Hill University; Institute of Education*; University of Essex; University of Exeter; University College Falmouth; University of Gloucestershire; Goldsmiths, University of London*; University of Greenwich; Guildhall School of Music and Drama; Harper Adams University College; University of Hertfordshire; Heythrop College, University of London*; University of Huddersfield; University of Hull; Imperial College London; Keele University; University of Kent; King's College London*; Kingston University; Lancaster University; University of Leeds; Leeds College of Art; Leeds Metropolitan University; Leeds Trinity University College; University of Leicester; University of Lincoln; University of Liverpool; Liverpool Hope University; Liverpool Institute for Performing Arts; Liverpool John Moores University; University of London; University of the Arts, London; London Business School*; London School of Economics and Political Science*; London School of Hygiene and Tropical Medicine*; London Metropolitan University; London South Bank University; Loughborough University; University of Manchester; Manchester Metropolitan University; Middlesex University, London; Newcastle University; Newman University College; University of Northampton; Northumbria University; Norwich University College of the Arts; University of Nottingham; Nottingham Trent University; The Open University; School of Oriental and African

Teaching Establishments

Studies*; University of Oxford; Oxford Brookes University; School of Pharmacy*; University of Plymouth; University College Plymouth Marjon; University of Portsmouth; Queen Mary, University of London*; Ravensbourne; University of Reading; Roehampton University; Rose Bruford College; Royal Academy of Music*; Royal Agricultural College; Royal College of Art; Royal College of Music; Royal Holloway, University of London*; Royal Northern College of Music; Royal Veterinary College*; St George's, University of London*; St Mary's University College; University of Salford; University of Sheffield; Sheffield Hallam University; University of Southampton; Southampton Solent University; Staffordshire University; University Campus Suffolk; University of Sunderland; University of Surrey; University of Sussex; Teesside University; Trinity Laban Conservatoire of Music and Dance; UCL*; University of Warwick; University of the West of England, Bristol; University of West London; University of Westminster; University of Winchester; University of Wolverhampton; University of Worcester; Writtle College; University of York; York St John University.

In 2012–13 The Higher Education Funding Council will be providing direct funding to 65 FE colleges as a result of the bidding exercise for a share from the 'margin' of up to 20,000 places for 2012–13.

Universities receiving funding from the Department for Employment and Learning in Northern Ireland

(*Source*: Higher Education Funding Council for England)
  Queen's University Belfast; University of Ulster.

Higher Education Institutions receiving funding from the Scottish Funding Council

(*Source*: Scottish Further and Higher Education Funding Council)
  University of Aberdeen; University of Abertay Dundee; University of Dundee; Edinburgh Napier University; University of Edinburgh; Glasgow Caledonian University; Glasgow School of Art; University of Glasgow; Heriot-Watt University; The Open University in Scotland; Queen Margaret University, Edinburgh; Robert Gordon University; Royal Conservatoire of Scotland; Scottish Agricultural College; University of St Andrews; University of Stirling; University of Strathclyde; University of the Highlands and Islands; University of the West of Scotland.

Institutions receiving funding from the Higher Education Funding Council for Wales

(*Source*: Higher Education Funding Council for Wales)
  Aberystwyth University; Bangor University; Cardiff University; Cardiff Metropolitan University (formerly UWIC); University of Glamorgan; Glyndwr University; University of Wales, Trinity Saint David (Lampeter campus); University of Wales, Newport; The Open University in Wales; Swansea Metropolitan University; Swansea University; University of Wales Trinity Saint David (Carmarthen campus).

OTHER HE ORGANIZATIONS

There are a number of other organizations involved in shaping the HE sector, for example the British Academy, the General Medical Council and Research Councils UK. You can find a full list of these organizations on the Universities UK website, www.universitiesuk.ac.uk (UK HE Sector, Useful links).

Part 3

Qualifications

INTRODUCTION

Definition of Common Terms

A number of terms are commonly used as synonyms for qualifications, for example 'examinations' and 'courses'. This can hide important differences of meaning and lead to confusion and misunderstanding. In some contexts it may be important to make these differences explicit in order to guard against exaggerating or diminishing the level of achievement, which is an essential core of the concept of qualification. It is especially important to clarify the difference in meaning between 'examination', 'course' and 'qualification'.

Examination

An examination is a formal test or assessment. It can focus on one or more of the following: knowledge, understanding, skill or competence. An examination may be set as a written test, an oral test, an aural and oral test (eg a foreign language test) or a practical test. In the past, most forms of external assessment in FE were based on a model of examination dominated by the psychometric model, designed to discriminate between individuals – normative referencing – and took the form of written tests. There was considerable variation in different kinds of written examination, ranging through essays, question and answer, and 'multiple response'. Today, largely as a result of the introduction of National Vocational Qualifications (NVQs), the purpose and format of many examinations have been reappraised, and criterion-referenced examinations that focus on achievement (and in the case of NVQs, competence) are increasingly common. Many forms of assessment are now an integral part of the learning process, with a formative as well as a summative function rather than a separate, terminal, summative function.

Course

A course implies an ordered sequence of teaching or learning over a period of time. A course is governed by regulations or requirements, frequently imposed by an external awarding body and sometimes by the institution providing the course. An important distinguishing feature between different courses is the length of time allocated to study: it can vary from a few days to several years. Some courses offer a terminal award on the basis of course completion, and these courses are set for a given period of time. Other 'set period' courses may prescribe examinations; these can include continuous assessment, terminal testing or a combination of both. In other courses, the programme of study may be accomplished at a faster or slower rate; such courses normally enjoin continuous assessment or a terminal examination, or both. Many courses require attendance at an institution, while distance learning, correspondence courses, and various forms of flexible-learning courses are usually free of these requirements, although some of these courses may require occasional attendance for residential components or face-to-face tutoring. A successful examination result usually confers a qualification or an award.

Qualification

A qualification is normally a certificated endorsement, from a recognized awarding body, that a level or quality of accomplishment has been achieved by an individual. Qualifications are usually conferred on successful completion of an examination, although not all examinations necessarily offer qualifications. An examination may offer an award that is a part-qualification. For example, an NVQ candidate may acquire a unit of competence that is a part-qualification building towards a full statement of competence – an NVQ. A first-year student on an HND course may be required to pass all first-year examinations to be permitted to continue into the second year; in a sense, that student is 'qualified' to continue the course but no qualification is awarded. Some award-bearing examinations may be fully recognized and certificated qualifications in themselves (eg a BTEC HNC) but only part-qualifications for a profession (eg chartered engineer).

Apparent anomalies do exist. Some professional bodies and trade associations award qualifications that are recognized within the profession or association but are not obtained by examination. They are usually awarded on the basis of experience, and payment of a fee, and denote membership or acceptance. When the body also offers an examination route to the same qualification, successful examinees are usually known as 'graduate members'.

There are a number of accreditation authorities that approve qualifications. There are also many specialist and general validating, examining and awarding bodies that are responsible for the design and assessment of qualifications.

ACCREDITING REGULATORY BODIES

England

Sector Skills Councils

The Alliance of Sector Skills Councils, launched in April 2008, is an organization that supports the network of licensed UK Sector Skills Councils (SSCs). These are employer-led, independent organizations that cover specific work sectors across the UK (currently accounting for approximately 90 per cent of the UK workforce). With the influence granted by licences from the governments of England, Scotland, Wales and Northern Ireland, and with private and public funding, this independent network engages with the education and training supply-side such as universities, colleges, funders and qualifications bodies to increase productivity at all levels in the workforce. Details are listed below.

Table 3.1   Sector Skill Councils

Asset Skills
Sector: Property and planning, housing, cleaning sectors and facilities management
Tel: 01392 423 399
E-mail: enquiries@assetskills.org
Website: www.assetskills.org

Cogent
Sector: Chemicals, pharmaceuticals, nuclear, oil and gas, petroleum and polymer industries
Tel: 01925 515 200
E-mail: info@cogent-ssc.com
Website: www.cogent-ssc.com

ConstructionSkills
Sector: Construction
Tel: 0344 994 4400
E-mail: call.centre@cskills.org
Website: www.cskills.org

Creative & Cultural Skills
Sector: Crafts, cultural heritage, design, literature, music, performing and visual arts
Tel: 020 7015 1800
E-mail: info@ccskills.org.uk
Website: www.ccskills.org.uk

Creative Skillset
Sector: TV, film, radio, interactive media, animation, computer games, facilities, photo imaging, publishing, advertising and fashion and textiles
Tel: 020 7015 1800
E-mail: info@creativeskillset.org
Website: www.creativeskillset.org

continued

Table 3.1 *Continued*

e-skills UK
Sector: Software, internet and web, IT services, telecommunications and business change
Tel: 020 7963 8920
E-mail: info@e-skills.com
Website: www.e-skills.com

Energy & Utility Skills
Sector: Gas, power, waste management and water industries
Tel: 0845 077 9922
E-mail: enquiries@euskills.co.uk
Website: www.euskills.co.uk

Financial Skills Partnership
Sector: Finance, accountancy and financial services
Tel: 0845 257 3772
E-mail: info@financialskillspartnership.org.uk
Website: www.financialskillspartnership.org.uk

Improve Ltd
Sector: Food and drinks manufacturing and processing
Tel: 08456 440448
E-mail: info@improveltd.co.uk
Website: www.improveltd.co.uk

IMI The Institute of the Motor Industry
Sector: Retail motor industries
Tel: 01992 511 521
E-mail: imi@motor.org.uk
Website: www.motor.org.uk

Lantra
Sector: Land management and production, animal health and welfare and environmental industries
Tel: 024 7669 6996
E-mail: connect@lantra.co.uk
Website: www.lantra.co.uk

People 1st
Sector: Hospitality, leisure, passenger transport, travel and tourism
Tel: 01895 817 000
E-mail: info@people1st.co.uk
Website: www.people1st.co.uk

Proskills UK
Sector: Process and manufacturing
Tel: 01235 833 844
E-mail: info@proskills.co.uk
Website: www.proskills.co.uk

SEMTA
Sector: Science, engineering and manufacturing technologies
Tel: 0845 643 9001
E-mail: customerservices@semta.org.uk
Website: www.semta.org.uk

Skills Active
Sector: Sport and recreation, health and fitness, outdoors, play-work and caravanning industry
Tel: 020 7632 2000
E-mail: skills@skillsactive.com
Website: www.skillsactive.com

Skills for Care & Development
Sector: Social care, children, early years and young people's workforces in the UK
Tel: 01133 907 666
E-mail: sscinfo@skillsforcareanddevelopment.org.uk
Website: www.skillsforcareanddevelopment.org.uk

Skills for Health
Sector: UK Health
Tel: 01179 221 155
E-mail: office@skillsforhealth.org.uk
Website: www.skillsforhealth.org.uk

continued

Table 3.1 *Continued*

Skills for Justice
Sector: Community justice, courts services, custodial care, fire and rescue, forensic science, policing and law enforcement and prosecution services
Tel: 0114 261 1499
E-mail: info@skillsforjustice.com
Website: www.skillsforjustice.com

Skills for Logistics
Sector: Freight logistics and wholesaling industry
Tel: 01908 313 360
E-mail: info@skillsforlogistics.org
Website: www.skillsforlogistics.org

Skillsmart Retail
Sector: Retail
Tel: 0207 462 5060
E-mail: contactus@skillsmartretail.com
Website: www.skillsmartretail.com

SummitSkills
Sector: Building services engineering
Tel: 01908 303 960
E-mail: enquiries@summitskills.org.uk
Website: www.summitskills.org.uk

The Alliance of Sector Skills Councils (ASSC)
Tel: 0845 072 5600
E-mail: info@sscalliance.org
Website: www.sscalliance.org

The Qualifications and Curriculum Development Agency (QCDA)

The QCDA was the public body responsible for the development of the National Curriculum, qualifications and delivery of assessment. The QCDA closed on 31 March 2012 as part of the government's wider education reforms. The exams administration function is now performed by the Teaching Agency. The National Curriculum assessments function is now performed by the Standards and Testing Agency (STA).

The Teaching Agency

The Exams Delivery Support Unit (EDSU) Helpline supports exams office staff, helping them to manage and administer exams; Tel: 0300 100 0100; e-mail: edsu@education.gov.uk; website: www.education.gov.uk

Standards and Testing Agency (STA)

Tel: Public enquiries 0370 000 2288; National Curriculum assessments helpline: 0300 303 3013; e-mail: assessments@education.gov.uk; website: www.education.gov.uk

Ofqual: Office of the Qualifications and Examinations Regulator

Tel: 0300 303 3344; Helpline: 0300 303 3346; e-mail: info@ofqual.gov.uk; website: www.ofqual.gov.uk

In 2009, the government passed the Apprenticeship, Skills, Children and Learning Act, which established Ofqual as the regulator of qualifications, examinations and tests in England. Ofqual commenced work as a fully independent non-ministerial government department on 1 April 2010. Ofqual is now accountable to parliament rather than to government ministers.

Ofqual's role is to ensure all learners get the results they deserve, standards are maintained, and qualifications are correctly valued and understood, now and in the future. It regulates exams, qualifications and tests in England and vocational qualifications in Northern Ireland.

Scotland

Scottish Qualifications Authority (SQA)

Customer Contact Centre, Tel: 0845 279 1000; Fax: 0845 213 5000; e-mail: customer@sqa.org.uk

The Scottish Qualifications Authority (SQA) is the national accreditation and awarding body in Scotland. It is an executive non-departmental public body (NDPB) sponsored by the Scottish Government's Learning Directorate.

SQA works in partnership with schools, colleges, universities and industry to provide high-quality, flexible and relevant qualifications and assessments – embedding industry standards where appropriate. It strives to ensure that SQA qualifications are inclusive and accessible to all, that they provide clear progression pathways, facilitate lifelong learning and recognize candidate achievement.

People take SQA qualifications at all stages of their lives – at school, at college, at work, and in their leisure time. There are qualifications at all levels of attainment. SQA is responsible for three main types of qualification: units, courses and group awards. Most SQA-awarded qualifications are made up of a combination of units, which can also be used in their own right. Each unit represents approximately 40 hours of teaching with additional study. Units are achieved by passing an assessment.

Courses consist of Standard Grades and six National Courses levels – Access 2 & 3, Intermediate 1 & 2, Higher, Advanced Higher and the Scottish Baccalaureate. They are mainly taken at school but some colleges may also offer provision at some levels.

National Qualification Group Awards – National Certificates (NCs), Higher National Certificates and Diplomas (HNCs and HNDs) and National Progression Awards (NPAs) – are designed to be taken at college; Scottish Vocational Qualifications (SVQs), Professional Development Awards (PDAs) and Customized Awards in the workplace. A private company or training provider must become an 'approved centre' to deliver SQA qualifications, or work in partnership with a college or training provider.

Standard Grades and National Courses. Standard Grades are generally taken over two years in the third and fourth years of secondary school. The courses are made up of different parts, called elements, usually with an exam at the end of fourth year. National Courses, with the exception of Access level, are made up of three units plus an external assessment usually an examination. These can be taken in the fourth, fifth and sixth years at school. There is a comprehensive appeals system for those who do not perform as well as expected.

Higher National Qualifications. Higher National Certificates (HNCs) and Higher National Diplomas (HNDs) are developed by SQA in partnership with FE colleges, universities, and industry and commerce. They are credible, flexible qualifications that are designed to deliver skills and knowledge to meet the needs of today's businesses.

National Progression Awards (NPAs). NPAs are designed to assess a defined set of skills and knowledge in specialist vocational areas. They are mainly used by colleges for short programmes of study.

National Certificates. National Certificates are primarily aimed at 16–18-year-olds and adults in full-time education, normally at a college. They prepare candidates for employment or further study, by developing a range of knowledge and skills.

Scottish Vocational Qualifications (SVQs). SVQs are based on job competence, and recognize the skills and knowledge people need in employment. SVQs can be attained in most occupations and are available for all types and levels of job. They are primarily delivered to candidates in full-time employment and in the workplace.

Professional Development Awards (PDAs). PDAs are qualifications for people who are already in a career and who wish to extend or broaden their skills. In some cases they are designed for people wishing to enter employment. PDAs can be taken at college or the workplace.

Customized Awards. Though these qualifications meet the needs of the majority of organizations, SQA also offers specially designed vocational qualifications at any level to meet an organization's need for skills and expertise and provide recognition and development opportunities for individuals. They can also help a company meet regulatory requirements and to demonstrate the competence of its employees to external parties.

New Awards. As well as developing new National Qualifications, SQA has developed a number of new Awards. Some of the new Awards cover work from across different subject areas, are shorter than traditional Courses and recognize success across different levels of difficulty, meaning they're suitable for young people of all abilities. The new Awards are available to deliver from August 2012. They are marked and assessed by schools and colleges and do not have any external assessment or exams.

Scottish Credit and Qualifications Framework

The SQA is a partner in a 'credit' system called the Scottish Credit and Qualifications Framework (SCQF), which sets out the Scottish qualifications and how they relate to one another by making clear the credit value of each type of qualification available in Scotland. The framework has 12 levels: from Level 1 for very basic education to Level 12 for doctoral degrees.

More information about SQA and its qualifications can be found at its website: www.sqa.org.uk.

Validating, examining and awarding bodies/organizations

A large number of external bodies provide qualifications recognized by accrediting and regulatory bodies. Not all qualifications are available across the entire FE sector: some colleges specialize in particular vocational areas while others are involved in more general adult education provision.

The Federation of Awarding Bodies (FAB) is a trade federation and membership organization for vocational awarding bodies. At the time of writing there are over 120 Ofqual-recognized awarding bodies that are full members of FAB. It also has associate members. Find more information at www.awarding.org.uk.

It is important to contact the examining or awarding bodies directly to find which colleges deliver the qualifications desired. However, most colleges deliver courses leading to qualifications awarded by the sample selection of organizations listed below.

ABC Awards

Robins Wood House, Robins Wood Road, Aspley, Nottingham NG8 3NH, Tel: 0115 854 1616; Fax: 0115 854 1617; e-mail: enquiries@abcawards.co.uk; website: www.abcawards.co.uk

ABC Awards is a vocational awarding organization with accredited QCF qualifications in all sectors. Many of ABC's qualifications are included in the Foundation Learning Catalogue and are recognized as being eligible for apprenticeships and additional and specialist learning for diplomas. ABC Awards is dedicated to working with centres to deliver exceptional and flexible qualifications.

AQA

Stag Hill House, Guildford, Surrey GU2 7XJ, Tel: 01483 506 506 or 0161 953 1180; Fax: 01483 300 152; e-mail: mailbox@aqa.org.uk; website: www.aqa.org.uk

AQA is the largest of the English exam boards currently awarding around 49 per cent of full-course GCSEs and 42 per cent of A-Levels nationally. As an awarding body AQA offers a broad range of qualifications available through academic or vocational pathways including GCEs, GCSEs, AQA Certificates (iGCSE), Entry Level Certificates, Basic and Key Skills, Functional Skills, Vocationally Related Qualifications and others such as the Diploma, the Extended Project Qualification, and the AQA Baccalaureate.

ASDAN

Wainbrook House, Hudds Vale Road, St George, Bristol BS5 7HY, Tel: 0117 941 1126, e-mail: info@asdan.org.uk; website: www.asdan.org.uk

ASDAN is established as a registered charity for 'The advancement of education, by providing opportunities for all learners to develop their personal and social attributes and levels of achievement through ASDAN awards and resources, and the relief of poverty, where poverty inhibits such opportunities for learners.'

The following ASDAN qualifications are available at Entry Level:
- Qualifications in Personal Progress: Entry 1
- Personal and Social Development (PSD): Entry 1–3
- Certificate of Personal Effectiveness (CoPE): Entry 1–3
- Employability: Entry 2 and 3
- Entry Level Diplomas in Life Skills: Entry 1–3
- Volunteering: Entry 1–3

The following ASDAN qualifications are available at Level 3:
- Wider Key Skills
- Certificate of Personal Effectiveness (CoPE)
- Employability Qualifications
- Volunteering Qualifications
- Award of Personal Effectiveness (AoPE)

To find out more about ASDAN visit www.asdan.org.uk.

City & Guilds

1 Giltspur Street, London EC1A 9DD, Tel: 0844 543 0000; e-mail: learnersupport@cityandguilds.com, website: www.cityandguilds.com

City & Guilds is a leading vocational educational organization, offering 500 work-related qualifications worldwide. Around 2 million people every year start City & Guilds qualifications, which span from basic skills to the highest level of professional achievement.

With over 130 years of experience, City & Guilds offers a wide range of qualifications from agriculture to engineering; hairdressing to health and social care; IT to tourism; and photography to catering. They are developed with the help of industry experts and are workplace-relevant, so these qualifications equip people for doing a real job – benefiting them and their employer.

City & Guilds qualifications develop both knowledge and practical skills. They are available at nine levels and are suitable for anyone, whether they are beginners or advanced in their career or area of study. Assessment is based on any combination of examination, projects or coursework. The organizations that offer City & Guilds qualifications include schools, colleges, training organizations, companies and adult education institutes. Depending on the organization, it is possible to study full time, part time or through distance learning.

Edexcel Foundation

190 High Holborn, London WC1V 7BH, Tel. 0845 618 0440; website: www.edexcel.org.uk

Edexcel is the UK's largest awarding body, operating in over 90 countries and offering a range of international qualifications including GCEs, GCSEs, vocational and business learning and adult literacy and numeracy qualifications that are offered in schools and colleges, through training providers or in the workplace. Edexcel's BTEC qualifications provide a range of widely accessible, high-quality education programmes of study directly related to employment. Edexcel approves nationally recognized qualifications and Certificates of Achievement that equip students both for employment and for further study. These include adult learning qualifications and NVQs. They are delivered through a network of approved centres around the world. It collaborates closely with industry, government and others to ensure that Edexcel programmes serve the interests of individuals, employers and the nations they are taken in.

EDI plc

International House, Siskin Parkway, Middlemarch Business Park, Coventry CV3 4PE,
Tel: 08707 202 909; Fax: 024 7651 6505; e-mail: enquiries@ediplc.com; website: www.ediplc.com

Education Development International plc (EDI) is a leading provider of education and training qualifications and assessment services. In the UK, EDI is accredited by the government to award a wide range of vocational qualifications, including apprenticeships and diplomas. EDI's expertise is in quality assuring work-based training programmes working closely with employers and over 1,500 private training providers and FE colleges. Internationally, EDI trades under the London Chamber of Commerce and Industry brand and offers a range of business and English language qualifications that have a history that can be traced back to 1887. LCCI International Qualifications are widely used in South East Asia and over 100 countries around the world.

The EDI website has a search facility: www.ediplc.com/Qualifications_Search.asp

NCFE

Citygate, St James' Boulevard, Newcastle upon Tyne NE1 4JE, Tel: 0191 239 8000; Fax: 0191 239 8001; e-mail: info@ncfe.org.uk; website: www.ncfe.org.uk

NCFE is a national awarding organization and registered educational charity. It currently offers over 420 nationally accredited qualifications from Entry level up to and including Level 4 as well as NVQs, Functional Skills, Diplomas, Apprenticeships and Key Skills. Further qualifications are in development. The NCFE website has a qualifications finder search facility at www.ncfe.org.uk/QualificationFinder.aspx

OCR

1 Hills Road, Cambridge, CB1 2EU, Fax: 01223 552627; 14-19 qualifications: Tel: 01223 553998, e-mail: general.qualifications@ocr.org.uk; Post-19 qualifications: Tel: 02476 851 509, e-mail vocational.qualifications@ocr.org.uk; website: www.ocr.org.uk

OCR is a leading UK awarding body, committed to providing qualifications that engage learners of all ages at school, college, in work or through part-time learning programmes to achieve their full potential. It offers a wide range of general and vocational qualifications, from GCSEs, A levels and Diplomas to OCR Nationals, NVQs and specialist qualifications. You can find a full index of OCR qualifications at: www.ocr.org.uk/qualifications/index.aspx

WJEC

245 Western Avenue, Cardiff CF5 2YX, Tel: 02920 265000; e-mail: info@wjec.co.uk; website: www.wjec.co.uk

WJEC is an examining board offering the following major qualifications: General Certificate of Secondary Education (GCSE); Entry Level (EL) and Advanced (A)/Advanced Supplementary (AS) levels and the Welsh Baccalaureate, a new overriding qualification for Wales available at different levels and incorporating GCSEs, A Levels, GNVQs or NVQs. In addition, WJEC provides Key/Essential Skills, Functional Skills (in England), Project and Extended Project and Principal Learning qualifications.

Part 4

Qualifications Awarded or Validated by Universities

ADMISSION TO DEGREE COURSES

Higher Education Institutions (HEIs)

Most institutions have a general requirement for admission to a degree course; special requirements may be in force for particular courses. Requirements are usually expressed in terms of subjects passed at GCE A level and the Higher Grade of the SCE. The universities have a clearing-house to handle applications for university courses: UCAS, www.ucas.ac.uk.

All intending students who live in the UK may obtain information on application procedures from their schools or colleges, or directly from UCAS. The scheme covers all universities and all medical schools. UCAS also has specialist services: the Graduate Teacher Training Registry (GTTR), the UK Postgraduate Application and Statistical Service (UKPASS) and the Conservatoires UK Admissions Service (CUKAS). HEIs have specific schemes to encourage access and participation in higher education. These can include partnerships with further education colleges that run access to higher education courses.

The Open University

All intending students who live in the UK may obtain information on application procedures from their schools or colleges, or directly from UCAS. The scheme covers all universities and all medical schools. UCAS also has specialist services: the Graduate Teacher Training Registry (GTTR), the UK Postgraduate Application and Statistical Service (UKPASS) and the Conservatoires UK Admissions Service (CUKAS). HEIs have specific schemes to encourage access and participation in higher education. These can include partnerships with further education colleges that run access to higher education courses.

Business schools

The degrees awarded by the various university business schools are postgraduate and therefore normally require an honours degree as part of their entrance qualification.

AWARDS

The awards made by the universities may be separated into the following categories: first degrees; higher degrees; honorary degrees; first diplomas and certificates; higher diplomas and certificates.

First degrees

Nomenclature

Various names are given to first degrees at British universities. At most universities the first degree in Arts is the BA (Bachelor of Arts) and the first degree in Science is the BSc (Bachelor of Science). But at the universities of Oxford and Cambridge and at several new universities, the BA is the first degree gained by students in both arts and science. In Scotland the first arts degree at three of the four old universities is Master of Arts (MA). There are numerous variations on the bachelor theme, eg BSc (Econ) (Bachelor of Science in Economics), BCom (Bachelor of Commerce), BSocSc (Bachelor of Social Science), BEng (Bachelor of Engineering) and BTech (Bachelor of Technology). The first award in medicine is the joint degrees of MB, ChB (Bachelor of Medicine, Bachelor of Surgery), the designatory letters of which vary from university to university.

Structure of courses

First-degree courses vary considerably in structure, not only between one university and another but also between faculties in a single university. The degree examination is usually in two sections, Part I coming after one or two years of the course and Part II, 'finals', at the end of the course. The first-degree system at some Scottish universities differs substantially from that in English and Welsh universities (see below).

Bachelor degrees

These degrees, sometimes known as 'ordinary' or 'first' degrees, lead to qualifications such as Bachelor of Arts (BA), Bachelor of Science (BSc) or Bachelor of Medicine (MB). Each university decides the form and content of its own degree examinations. These vary from university to university.

The first-degree structure in all British universities is based on the honours degree. Successful candidates in honours degree examinations are placed in different classes according to their performance, first class being the highest. The other classes given vary from university to university, but the classification most often used is: Class I; Class II (Division 1); Class II (Division 2); Class III. Most graduates who go on to higher academic qualifications and those entering, for example, the higher grades in the Civil Service or research, normally have a good class honours degree.

You can find out more about recognized UK degrees at the BIS website; www.bis.gov.uk.

Number of subjects studied

Excluding medicine and dentistry, the broad subject areas are Arts (or Humanities), Social Science, Pure Science and Applied Science. Most students study one main subject selected from one of these areas. It is possible to distinguish many types of degree course according to the number of subjects studied; these types are a variation on three main categories:

1. Honours course in one to three subjects with or without examinable subsidiary subjects;
2. Pass or ordinary courses in one to three subjects with or without examinable subsidiary subjects;
3. Common studies for pass and honours in one to three subjects, with or without examinable subsidiary subjects.

Length of degree course

First-degree courses may be preceded by a preliminary year, from which students with the appropriate entry qualifications may be exempted. At most universities honours and pass courses in arts, social science, pure and applied science last three or four years, but courses in architecture, dentistry and veterinary medicine usually last five years, and complete qualifying courses in medicine up to six years. Courses in fine arts and pharmacy may last four years; four-year courses exist mainly in double honours schools, especially when they involve foreign languages and a period of study abroad, and in the technological universities where some courses include a period of integrated industrial training (sandwich courses).

The Scottish first degree

The distinctive feature of first degrees at some Scottish universities is the Ordinary MA course, which has no counterpart in England and Wales, and the Ordinary BSc course. The function of the Ordinary MA is to provide a broad, general education. Scottish undergraduates are required to show during their first two years of study, over a range of subjects, that they are fit to go on to an honours degree course, which takes a further two years to complete.

Aegrotat degrees

Candidates who have followed a course for a degree but have been prevented from taking the examinations by illness may be awarded a degree certificate indicating that they were likely to have obtained the degree had they taken the examinations.

Higher degrees

These comprise:
- some Bachelor's degrees: BPhil, BLitt, etc;
- Master's degrees: MA, MSc, etc;
- Doctor of Philosophy: PhD or DPhil;
- Higher Doctorates: DLitt, DSc, etc.

At Oxford and Cambridge the degree of MA is conferred on any BA of the university without any further course of study or examination after a specified number of years and on payment of a fee.

Candidates for a Master's degree at other universities (and at some for the degrees of BPhil, BLitt and BD, which are of equivalent standing) are normally required to have a first degree, although it need not have been obtained in the same university. Master's degrees are taken after one or two years' full-time study. The PhD requires at least two or more – usually three – years of full-time study.

In some universities and faculties students may be selected for a PhD course after an initial year's study or research common to both a PhD and a Master's degree. Candidates for a Master's degree are required either to prepare a thesis for presentation to examiners, who may afterwards question candidates on it orally, or to take written examination papers; they may be required to do both. All PhD students present a thesis; some may be required to take an examination paper as well. MPhil, MSc and similar degrees are usually awarded at the end of a one- or two-year course in a special topic on the results of a written examination or a thesis. Higher doctorates are designated on a faculty basis, eg DLitt (Doctor of Letters) and DSc (Doctor of Science). Candidates are usually required to have at least a Master's degree of the awarding university. Senior doctorates are conferred on more mature and established people, usually on the basis of published contributions to knowledge.

Foundation degrees

Foundation degrees were established to give people the intermediate technical and professional skills that are in demand from employers and to provide more flexible and accessible ways of studying. Increasing opportunities for employment and career advancement are priorities; foundation degree content and assessment are therefore designed in consultation with employers. Additional progression routes include links with associated professional qualifications and/or direct entry to the final year of a relevant honours-level degree. Provision is available across a range of FE colleges and a number of HEIs.

Honorary degrees

Most universities confer honorary degrees on people of distinction in academic and public life, and on others who have rendered service to the university or to the local community. Normally degrees awarded are at least Foundation level.

Diplomas and certificates of higher education

Courses for first diplomas and certificates are relatively simple in structure; they usually reach a level lower than that required for the award of a degree. There is usually a carefully defined course in a specialized or vocational subject, lasting one or two years, followed by all candidates. Most courses are full time.

Postgraduate diplomas and certificates

Diplomas (eg in public health, social administration, medicine and technology) are awarded either on a full-time or, less often, part-time basis according to the subject and the university. Candidates must usually be graduates or hold equivalent qualifications. Diplomas are awarded after formal courses of instruction and success in written examinations. A Certificate or Diploma in Education is awarded to graduates training to become teachers after one year's full-time study and teaching practice.

Qualifications

Postgraduate courses

A number of courses for graduates or people with equivalent qualifications are offered in FE establishments. They include short specialist courses in management and business studies and secretarial courses for graduates.

Business schools

A Master of Business Administration (MBA) is an internationally recognized postgraduate qualification intended to prepare individuals for middle to senior general managerial positions. Most programmes contain as their core a number of subjects considered essential for understanding the operations of any enterprise. These are: accounting and finance, operations management, business policy, economics, human resource management, marketing, information systems and strategic planning.

Unlike any other Master's programme, the MBA is not only postgraduate, it is also strongly post-experience. A minimum of three years' (often more) work experience at an appropriate level of responsibility is generally expected of applicants. The requirement for a first degree (or equivalent) is sometimes waived for those holding an impressive track record of over five years at managerial level. Approximately one-third of MBA students have an engineering or information technology background. Many undertake the qualification to facilitate change from technical or specialist positions to more general ones.

The MBA was conceived originally in the United States at the beginning of the 20th century. Introduced in the United Kingdom in the late 1960s, it did not grow in popularity until the late 1980s. The popularity of this degree in the United Kingdom can be seen in the rapid expansion in the number of providers.

The Association of MBAs (AMBA) operates a system of accreditation. The accreditation process, which is internationally recognized for all MBA, DBA and Masters in Business and Management (MBM) programmes, measures individual MBA programmes against specific accreditation criteria.

Further information, including a list of accredited MBA programmes, can be obtained from the Association of MBAs, 25 Hosier Lane, London EC1A 9LQ; Tel: 0207 246 2686; e-mail: info@mbaworld.com; website: www.mbaworld.com.

The Association of Business Schools (ABS)

137 Euston Road, London NW1 2AA; Tel: 020 7388 0007; Fax: 020 7388 0009; website: www.associationofbusinessschools.org

The ABS is the representative body for management and business education and all the United Kingdom's leading business schools. The ABS works broadly in three main areas: policy development, promotion and representation, and training and development.

The ABS is able to provide general information about the wide range of courses and programmes provided by the United Kingdom's business schools.

First awards

- **BA, BEd, BEng, LLB, BSc:** with 1st Class, 2nd Class (Divisions 1 and 2), 3rd Class Honours or Pass; or unclassified with or without Distinction.
- **MEng:** awarded to students who successfully complete a course of study that is longer and more demanding than the BEng first degree course in Engineering.
- **GMus (Graduate Diploma in Music):** awarded to those students who complete three years' approved full-time study (or equivalent) in Music and who demonstrate competence in musical performance.
- **DipHE (Diploma of Higher Education):** equivalent in standard and often similar in content to the first two years of an Honours degree course.
- **Certificates of Higher Education:** equivalent to the first year of an Honours degree course.

Higher awards

- **MA, MBA, Med, MSc:** for successful completion of an approved postgraduate course of study of 48 weeks' duration (or the part-time equivalent).
- **MPhil, PhD:** for successful completion of approved programmes of supervised research.
- **DSc, DLitt, DTech:** for original and important contributions to knowledge and/or its applications.
- **Postgraduate Diploma:** awarded for the successful completion of an approved postgraduate course of study of 25 weeks' duration (or the part-time equivalent).
- **Postgraduate Certificate:** awarded for the successful completion of postgraduate/post-experience courses of 15 weeks' duration (or the part-time equivalent).
- **Postgraduate Certificate in Education (PGCE):** awarded on completion of a one-year full-time course; candidates must be British graduates or hold another recognized qualification.
- **Diploma in Professional Studies:** available in the fields of education and nursing, health visiting, midwifery and sports coaching. Students normally hold an initial professional qualification. A minimum of two years' experience is normally expected.

UNIVERSITY OF ABERDEEN
www.abdn.ac.uk

College of Arts and Social Sciences; www.abdn.ac.uk/about/social-sciences/php

Aberdeen Business School; www.abdn.ac.uk/business
accountancy, coaching, economics, energy/health economics, enterprise, entrepreneurship, finance, innovation, management studies, petroleum economics, real estate management, MBA programmes; MA(Hons), MBA, MRes, MSc, MPhil, PgCert, PhD

School of Divinity, History & Philosophy; www.abdn.ac.uk/sdhp
biblical studies, cultural history, divinity, history, history of art, Jewish studies, pastural studies, philosophy, religious studies, theoethics, theology, ministry, biblical/practical/systematic theology, church history, visual culture; BD, BTh, DMin, LicTh, MA(Hons), MLitt, MTh, PgDip, PhD,DPS

School of Education; www.abdn.ac.uk/education
childhood practice, continuous learning & development, primary education, professional development, TQFE, secondary education, tertiary education, autism, adult literacy, inclusive practice, social pedagology; BA(Hons), BEd(Hons), MEd, MPhil, MRes, MSc, Mus(Hons), PGCert, PGDE, PGDip, PhD,EdD,

School of Language & Literature; www.abdn.ac.uk/sll
Celtic, comparative literature, creative writing, English/literature/language, early modern studies, film & visual culture, French, German & Hispanic studies, Irish–Scottish studies, linguistics the novel, literature in world context, sociolinguistics, language & linguistics; MA, MA(Designated), MA(Hons), MLitt, PhD

School of Law; www.abdn.ac.uk/law
law, European, French/Belgian/Spanish/German law, international commercial/business/private/oil & gas law, criminal justice, human rights, climate change; LlB(Hons), LlM, MPhil, PhD

School of Social Science; www.abdn.ac.uk/socsc
anthropology, gender studies, politics & international relations, social anthropology, cultural/sociology, religion & society, Europolitics & society, sex, gender & violence, strategic studies, transitional justice; MA(Hons), MA, MLitt, MPhil, MRes, MSc, PGDip, PhD

College of Life Sciences and Medicine; www.abdn.ac.uk/clsm

School of Biological Sciences; www.abdn.ac.uk/biologicalsci
animal ecology, biology, biological science, conservation biology, environmental science/sustainability/

microbiology, forestry, global health, medical physics, marine biology, nursing/midwifery/health,wildlife management, zoology; BSc(Hons), MPhil, MSc, MSc/PGDip, MRes, PhD

School of Medical Science;
www.abdn.ac.uk/sms
applied sports science, biochemistry, biomedical sciences, biotechnology, genetics, health economics, human embryology & development, immunology, medical education, microbiology, molecular biology, neuroscience, pharmacology, physiology, sport & exercise science, sports studies; BSc(Hons), MPhil, MSc, MSc, PGDip/Cert, PhD, MD, MRes

School of Medicine & Dentistry;
www.abdn.ac.uk/medicine-dentistry
dentistry, health science/studies, medicine, primary care, rural health, chronic disability, epidemiology, immunology, psychiatry, respiratory, muscoskeletal; BDS, BSc, MA, MBChB, MMedSci, MPhil, MSc, PhD, PGDip

School of Psychology; www.abdn.ac.uk/ psychology
psychology, social perception/cognition; BSc(Hons), MA, MRes, MSc, PhD

Rowlet Institute of Nutrition and Health Studies; www.rowletac.uk
impacts on human health; BSc(Hons), MSc, MSc/ PgDip, PhD

College of Physical Sciences; www.abdn.ac.uk/about/physical-sciences.php

School of Engineering; www.abdn.ac.uk/ engineering
chemical engineering, civil engineering, electrical & electronic engineering, mechanical engineering, project management, safety engineering, renewable energy subsea engineering, oil & gas engineering/ structures, petroleum engineering; BEng(Hons), BScEng, EngD, MEng, MSc

School of Geosciences; www.abdn.ac.uk/ geosciences

Dept of Archaeology; www.abdn.ac.uk/ archaeology
archaeology, with Celtic civilization/history/geography, archaeology of the north; BSc(Hons), MA(Hons), MPhil, PhD, MSc

Dept of Geography & the Environment; www.abdn.ac.uk/geography
geography, geospatial information science, marine & coastal resource management, urban/rural planning, property, rural surveying, spatial planning, sustainable rural development, environmental management; BSc(Hons), MA(Hons), MSc, PgDip/Cert, PhD, MLE, DiplE

Dept of Geology & Petroleum Geology; www.abdn.ac.uk/geology
oil & gas enterprise management, geology, geoscience, integrated petroleum geoscience, petroleum geology; BSc(Hons), MA(Hons), MRes, MSc, PgDip/Cert, PhD, MGeol

Centre for Planning & Environmental Management; www.abdn.ac.uk/cpem
geographical & spatial planning, property, urban planning, real estate, rural planning & environmental management, sustainable rural development, land economy; BSc(Hons), MA(Hons), MSc, PhD

School of Natural & Computing Sciences; www.abdn.ac.uk/sncs

Chemistry; www.abdn.ac.uk/chemistry
chemistry, biomedical materials, chemical science, environmental chemistry, materials, medicinal chemistry; BSc(Hons), MChem, MSc, PgDip, PhD

Computing Science; www.csd.abdn.ac.uk
artificial intelligence, business information systems, computing science, business computing systems, cloud computing, computing & e-business, software project management, information systems/technology/science, electronic commerce technology, informatics, natural language generation, software project management; BSc(Hons), MA(Hons), MSc, MSci, PhD, PGDip

Mathematics; www.maths.statistics;
BSc(Hons), MA(Hons), MSc, PhD, MPhil

Physics; www.abdn.ac.uk/physics
physical sciences, physics, physics with chemistry/ geology/philosophy/engineering/mathematics/education; BSc(Hons), MSc(Hons)

UNIVERSITY OF ABERTAY, DUNDEE
www.abertay.ac.uk

School of Arts, Media & Computer Games
www.abertay.ac.uk/studying/schools/amg;
computer arts, computer games/technology/design/production/applications, creative sound production, visual communication & media design; BA(Hons), BSc(Hons), DipHE, MProf, MSc/PGDip

School of Computing & Engineering Systems; www.abertay.ac.uk/ces
computing, countermeasures, web design/development; BSc(Hons), MSc, DipHE, PGDip

Dundee Business School;
www.abertay.ac.uk/studying/schools/dbe
accounting, business administration/studies, enterprise, Europe (economy, business law, management), entrepreneurship, finance, HRM, international management, law, marketing, management accounting, oil & gas accounting, retail marketing, tourism, golf management, biotechnology; BA (Hons), GradCert, MBA, MSc, PGDip, DipHE

The School of Contemporary Sciences;
www.abertay.ac.uk/studying/schools/cs
bioinformatics, biomedical science, food nutrition & health, medical biotechnology, civil engineering, energy & environmental management, environment & business industrial environment, food biotechnology/product design, nutrition, consumer science, forensic sciences, industrial environment, policing & security, renewable energy, urban water, water pollution control; BSc(Hons), DipHE, MSc, MTech, PGDip

The School of Social & Health Sciences;
www.abertay.ac.uk/studying/schools/shs
behavioural science, coaching, cognitive behavioural therapy, counselling, criminological studies, forensic psychobiology, media, culture and society, mental health/nursing, psychology, public administration, social & health science, sociology, sports/coaching, golf, physical activity sport & exercise/management/nutrition/psychology, sports development; BA(Hons), BSc(Hons), GradCert, MSc, PGDip, DipHE

ABERYSTWYTH UNIVERSITY
www.aber.ac.uk

School of Art; www.aber.ac.uk/en/art
art/history, fine art, museum & gallery studies; BA(Hons), MA, MPhil, PhD

Institute of Biological, Environmental & Rural Sciences; www.aber.ac.uk/en/ers
agriculture, animal science/zoology, biochemistry, biology, conservation/countryside/environmental management, environmental bioscience & ecology, microbiology, equine science, food & water security, genetics, livestock science, marine & freshwater biology, tourism & recreation; BSc(Hons), MPhil, MSc, PhD

Dept of Computer Science;
www.aber.ac.uk/en/cs
business IT, computer graphics, internet engineering, mobile wearable computing, open source computing, robotics, software engineering, artificial intelligence, ubiquitous computing, 3D imaging; BEng, BSc(Hons), HND, MEng, MSc, PhD

School of Education & Lifelong Learning;
www.aber.ac.uk/en/sell
childhood studies, lifelong learning, education; BA(Hons), BSc(Hons), MPhil, PGCE, PGDip, PhD

Dept of English & Creative Writing;
www.aber.ac.uk/en/english
creative writing, English literature, literary/classical studies, American studies; BA(Hons), MA, PhD

Dept of European Languages;
www.aber.ac.uk/en/eurolangs
French, German, Italian, European culture, Romance languages, Spanish; BA(Hons), MA, PhD

Institute of Geography & Earth Sciences;
www.ies.aber.ac.uk/en/ges
environmental earth/science, geography, GIS and remote sensing, glaciology, human/physical geography, local and regional economic development,

quaternary environmental change; BSc(Hons), MPhil, MRes, MSc, PhD

Dept of History & Welsh History;
www.aber.ac.uk/en/history
economic/social/European/medieval & modern history, contemporary politics, Welsh history, history & media, early British/18th-century history, history of medicine, Celtic history; BA(Hons), MA, PhD

Dept of Information Studies;
www.dis.aber.ac.uk/en/dis
business information, historical & archival/information & library studies, records management, information management/systems; BA(Hons), BSc(Econ), Dip/Cert, MPhil, MSc(Econ), PhD

Dept of International Politics;
www.aber.ac.uk/en/interpol
European studies, intelligence & strategic studies, international history/strategic studies/third world/military history, international relations, military history, political studies, intelligence studies, peace conflict & security, international politics & the third world; BSc(Econ), MA, MSc, MSc(Econ), PhD

Dept of Law and Criminology;
www.aber.ac.uk/en/law-criminology
business law, criminal law, criminology with applied psychology/law, European law, human rights, law; BA(Hons), BSc(Econ), LlB, LlM, PhD

School of Management and Business;
www.aber.ac.uk/en/smb
accounting & finance, business, business economics/finance, economics, entrepreneurship, marketing, international business/finance, management; BSc(Econ), MBA, MSc(Econ), PhD

Institute of Mathematical & Physical Sciences; www.aber.ac.uk/en/maps
applied mathematics, statistics, computer science, pure mathematics, physics, planetary and space physics, space science, theoretical physics, astrophysics, robotics; BSc(Hons), MMath, MPhys, PhD

Dept of Psychology; www.aber.ac.uk/en/psychology
psychology, BSc(Econ), BSc(Hons), PhD

Dept of Sport & Exercise Science;
www.aber.ac.uk/sport/exercise
sport & exercise science, equine & human sport exercise, exercise psychology/physiology/biomedicine; BSc(Hons), PhD

Dept of Theatre, Film & Television Studies;
www.aber.ac.uk/en/tfts
drama & theatre, film & television, film studies, media & communication, performance, scenography/theatre design, scriptwriting, Welsh medium courses; BA(Hons), MA, MPhil, PhD

Dept of Welsh; www.aber.ac.uk/cymraeg-welsh
Breton, Welsh & Celtic languages, Celtic studies, Irish, Welsh 1st language, medieval Welsh literature; BA(Hons), MA

ANGLIA RUSKIN UNIVERSITY
www.anglia.ac.uk

Faculty of Arts, Law and Social Sciences; www.anglia ac.uk/en/home/faculties/alss.html

Dept of English, Communication, Film & Media; anglia.ac.uk/ruskin/en/home/faculties/alss/deps/english_media
English language/literature/teaching, TESOL, film/media studies, creative writing, applied linguistics, intercultural communication, international business writing, publishing; BA(Hons), MPhil, PhD

Anglia Law School; www.anglia.ac.uk/ruskin/en/home/faculties/alss/deps/law
criminology, international business/ law, law, legal practice, professional legal studies; BA(Hons), LlB, LlD, LlM, PGDip, MPhil,PhD

Cambridge School of Art;
www.anglia.ac.uk/ruskin/en/home/faculties/alss/deps/csoa
children's book illustration, computer games, fashion/interior design, film, TV, fine art, illustration, photography, professional typography, graphic design, visual effects; BA(Hons), FdA, MA, MFA

Dept of Humanities & Social Sciences;
www.anglia.ac.uk/ruskin/en/home/
faculties/alss/deps/hss
criminology, forensic science, history, English, philosophy, psychosocial studies, public service, sociology, transnational crime; BA(Hons), FdA, MPhil, PhD

Dept of Music & Performing Arts;
www.anglia.ac.uk/ruskin/en/home/
faculties/alss/deps/music
creative music technology, drama/music/therapy, performing arts, pop music, film studies; BA(Hons), FdADip, MA, MPhil, PhD

Lord Ashcroft International Business School; www.anglia.ac.uk/ruskin/en/home/faculties/aibs
accounting, business/economics/corporate management, finance, enterprise & international/entrepreneurship, HRM, innovation, international business/economics/entrepreneurship/logistics, tourism management, leadership, marketing; BA(Hons), BSc(Hons), MA, MBA, MSc, CertHE, HNC, HND

Faculty of Health, Social Care & Education; www.anglia.ac.uk/ruskin/en/home/faculties/thse
early acute care, adv practice, care of newborn, childhood studies, children & young people, community public health nursing, disability equality, early childhood/education studies, early years, ESOL, EYPS, FE/HE, learning through technology, PGCE primary and primary education/with modern foreign languages, teaching and learning, teaching English (literacy), teaching mathematics (numeracy, children & young people's nursing, children and family, community public health nursing, health care/management, hospital administration, international nursing studies, learning support, management and leadership in social care, midwifery, palliative care, perioperative care, psycho social intervention, physiotherapy, primary care, magnetoresonance imaging, nursing (adult, child, learning disabilities), medical & healthcare education, mental health, public health, teaching in lifelong learning sector, young people, social work/policy; BSc(Hons), FdSc, FdA, Cert HE, Dip HE, MSc, PGDip/Cert, BA(Hons), Dips, Professional Practice

Faculty of Science and Technology; www.anglia.ac.uk/ruskin/en/home/faculties/fst

Dept of Built Environment;
www.anglia.ac.uk/ruskin/en/home/
faculties/fst/departs/builtenv
architecture/technology, building surveying, civil engineering, construction management, environmental planning, project management in built environment, quantity surveying, real estate management, structural engineering, sustainable construction, town planning; BSc(Hons), FdSc, MSc, PGCert, PGDip,FSc

Dept of Computing & Technology;
www.anglia.ac.uk/ruskin/en/home/
faculties/fst/departments/comptech
audio & video, music technology, business information systems, computer games/networking, computing & information systems, music technology, electrical engineering, electronics, engineering management, forensic computing, computing, information security, engineering, mechanical engineering, media & internet technology, mobile telecommunication, multimedia, network security/management; BEng(Hons), BSc(Hons), HND

Dept of Vision and Hearing Science;
www.anglia.ac.uk/ruskin/en/home/
departments/vision-hearing
ophthalmics, optometry, hearing aid technology; BOptom(Hons), BSc(Hons), FdSc, UnivCert

Dept of Psychology; www.anglia.ac.uk/ruskin/enhome/departments/psychology
cognitive neuroscience, abnormal/clinical/child psychology, criminology; BSc(Hons), MSc

Dept of Life Sciences; www.anglia.ac.uk/ruskin/en/home/faculties/fst/deps/lifesciences
animal behaviour/welfare, biodiversity & conservation, biomedical sciences, conservation, ecology, crimininal & investigative studies, equine studies, forensic science, marine biology, microbiology, sports coaching & PE/science, zoology; BSc(Hons), FdSc, MSc, PGDip

Degrees validated by Anglia Ruskin University offered at:

COLCHESTER INSTITUTE
www.colchester.ac.uk

School of Art
art & design, 3D design & craft, fashion textiles, fine art, photography, design & the book, contemporary art, sculptural practice; BA(Hons), FdA, HNC, MA

Business, Management & Computing
business, hospitality, sport management, tourism, computing solutions (internet/networking), business administration, financial reporting, management/& leadership, managing information, organizational development, project management, systems development; BSc(Hons), BA(Hons) BTEC, Dipl Man, HNC/D, FdSc, PgDip/Cert

Construction
construction management (commercial/site), construction in built environment, building service engineering; BSc(Hons), FD, HNC

Education
early years, lifelong learning, teaching literacy & ESOL/numeracy, TESOL teacher training; BA(Hons), Cert Cont Ed, EFT, FD, PGCE

Engineering
electrical engineering (power), electronics engineering, mechanical engineering; HNC/D

Recreation & Welfare
counselling, health, social care, person-centred counselling, public services, sport (coaching & development); BA(Hons), FD, DipHE

Hospitality & Food Studies
hospitality supervision; HND

Music & Performing Arts
creative performance (acting) film, creative media production, popular music, music, musical/technical theatre; BA(Hons), FD, MA

ASHRIDGE
www.ashridge.ac.uk

executive coaching, management, organizational change, sustainability & responsibility, organizational development supervision; Doc Orgn Change, ExecMBA, MBA, MSc

ASTON UNIVERSITY
www.aston.ac.uk

Aston Business School;
www.aston.ac.uk/aston-business-school
accounting, business/economics & management, business & marketing analytics, business computing & IT, economics, finance/& investments, financial regulation, HRM, international business & management/economic investments/commercial law, information systems management, IT project management, investment analysis, Islamic finance, law, strategy, administration, marketing, mathematics with economics, management/& strategy, operational research, organisational behaviour/psychology & business, social responsibility & sustainability, supply chain management, work psychology & business; BSc(Hons), DBA, LlB, LlM, MBA, PhD, FD

Centre for Learning, Innovation and Professional Practice; clipp/
www.aston.uk.ac
curriculum & learning development, teaching, media & learning technologies; MA, PG Cert

Aston University

School of Engineering and Applied Science; www.aston.uk.ac/eas

Chemical Engineering & Applied Chemistry; www1.aston.ac.uk/eas/about-eas/academic-groups/ceac/

applied/biological chemistry, chemical engineering, chemistry; BEng, MEng, MChem

Computer Science; www1.aston.ac.uk/eas/about-eas/academic-groups/computer-science/

computing science, computing for business, multimedia computing, IT project management, software engineering, professional engineering, BSc, MSc

Electrical, Electronic & Power Engineering; www1.aston.ac.uk/eas/about-eas/academic-groups/electronic-engineering/

communications engineering, data communications systems, electronic & electrical engineering, sensors & sensing systems, electrical & electronic engineering/computer secience, telecommunications technology, professional engineering; BEng, MEng, MSc

Engineering Systems & Management; www1.aston.ac.uk/eas/about-eas/academic-groups/esm/

construction project management, engineering management, industrial enterprise management, supply chain management, professional engineering, logistics management, transport management; BSc, MSc

Mathematics; www1.aston.ac.uk/eas/about-eas/academic-groups/mathematics/

mathematics, mathematics with computing/business/economics, mathematics in complex systems; BSc, MSc

Mechanical Engineering & Design; www1.aston.ac.uk/eas/about-eas/academic-groups/med/

electromechanical engineering, mechanical engineering, design engineering, transport product design, product design/& management/enterprise/innovation, professional engineering; BEng, MEng, MSc

School of Life and Health Sciences; www.aston.ac.uk/life-health-sciences

human biology, audiology, biological sciences, cell & molecular biology, microbiology & immunology, biomedical science, clinical health management/science, health psychology, healthcare science, molecular toxic drug design, psychiatric pharmacy/therapeutics, hearing aid audiology, optometry, pharmacy, psychiatric pharmacy/ therapeutics, psychology; BSc(Hons), GradDip, FD, MPharm, MRes, MSc, PGCert/Dip, PhD

School of Languages and Social Sciences; www.aston.ac.uk/lss

Languages & Translation Studies

French, German, Spanish, translation studies, international business & modern languages studies, TESOL, applied linguistics, forensic/corpus linguistics, literary linguistics, sociolinguistics

English Language

English language, number of joint honours degrees with English language, ELT, TESOL, TESP, TEYL, EMT, applied linguistics, international business

Politics & International Relations

sociology, politics, global governance, international relations & business/politics/policy/sociology, social change, public policy & management/sociology

Sociology & Public Policy

sociology & business/social policy/international relations/politics/psychology/social change, social policy, politics, international relations/policy, public policy, business & management; BA(Hons), BSc(Hons), MA, MPhil, MRes, MSc, PhD

BANGOR UNIVERSITY
www.bangor.ac.uk

College of Arts and Humanities; www.bangor.ac.uk/cah

Creative Studies & Media; www.bangor.ac.uk/creative_industries
creative/film studies, digital media, film-making, creative practice, film & visual culture, journalism, media studies, theatre, professional writing, creative writing, digital media, film; BA (Hons), MA, MRes, MSc, PhD/MPhil

English; www.bangor.ac.uk/english
creative writing, English literature/language, journalism, publishing, theatre/film studies, Arthurian legend, medieval & early modern literature, songwriting; BA (Hons), MA/Diploma, PhD/MPhil

History, Welsh History & Archaeology; www.bangor.ac.uk/history
archaeology, contemporary/medieval & early modern/Welsh history, heritage, Celtic archaeology, political & social sciences; BA (Hons), MA/Diploma, PhD/MPhil

School of Linguistics & English Language, history, film studies; www.bangor.ac.uk/linguistics
creative writing, English language/literature, applied/cognitive/forensic linguistics, bilingualism, media studies, film studies, ELT, early development; BA (Hons), MA, MSc, PhD/MPhil

School of Modern Languages; www.bangor.ac.uk/ml
French, German, Italian, Spanish, European languages & cultures, translation studies; BA (Hons), MA, PhD/MPhil

School of Music; www.bangor.ac.uk/music
music/technology/electronics, composition, elecroacoustics, early music, 20/21st century music, sonic arts; BA, BMus, BSc, MA/Diploma/Certificate, MMus/Dip

Theology & Religious Studies; www.bangor.ac.uk/spar/
religious studies, theology, study of religion; BA, MA

School of Welsh; www.bangor.ac.uk/ysgolygymraeg;
details of courses provided in Welsh language, Welsh, bilingualism, Welsh for beginners

BA(Hons), BD, BMus, Dip, MA, MMus, MPhil, MTh, PgDip, PhD, MSc

College of Business, Social Sciences & Law; www.bangor.ac.uk/cbss

Bangor Business School; www.bangor.ac.uk/business
accounting, banking, business studies, consumer psychology, international banking & development finance, economics, environmental management, finance, financial economics, marketing, administration, ICT, social authority law, Islamic banking, information management; BA, BSc(Hons), MA, MSc, MBA

School of Social Sciences; www.bangor.ac.uk/so
criminology & criminal justice, health & social care, language policy, policy/social research, social policy/work/studies/research, sociology; BA(Hons), MA, DipPG, PhD, MPhil

School of Law; www.bangor.ac.uk/law
law, criminology, public procurement, international UIP law, European law, global trade, internatioanl crime/human rights, criminal justice, law & devolved government, company/commercial/family & welfare/media, international law/ intellectual property; BA(Hons), DBA, HND, LlB, LlM, MA, MBA, MSc, MPhil, PGDip, PhD

School of Education and Lifelong Learning; www.bangor.ac.uk/sell
childhood studies, community development, design & technology, education studies, secondary education, early childhood & learning support studies, fine art, primary education, PGCE primary/secondary, lifelong learning, women's studies; BA Cert, Dipl, FdA, HNC/HND, MA, MEd

Academic Development Unit; www.bangor.ac.uk/adu
Welsh for adults; PGCertHE, BSc(Hons), EdMed, FdA, MA, MEd, MMusD, MPhil, MTh, PGCE, PhD

College of Natural Sciences; www.bangor.ac.uk/cns

CNS School of Biological Sciences; www.bangor.ac.uk/biology

medical biology, biology, biomedical science, biotechnology, ecology, zoology with animal behaviour/conservation/marine zoology, genetics, medical biology, molecular zoology, ecology; BSc(Hons), Dipl, MA, MBiol, MPhil, MRes, MSc, MZool, PhD

School of Environment, Natural Resources, & Geography; www.bangor.ac.uk/senrgy

agriculture, agroforestry, conservation management/science, environmental conservation/management/forestry, environmental science, forest ecosystems, forestry, geography, land management, sustainable development/forestry, terrestrial and marine ecology; tropical forestry, BA/BSc(Hons), BSc(Hons), MA, MBA, MPhil, MSc, PhD

School of Ocean Sciences; www.bangor.ac.uk/sos

applied marine biosciences, coastal & marine environment geological oceanography, marine biology/& geology, environmental studies/science/vertebrate zoology, oceanography, marine biology & zoology, ocean science, physical oceanography; BSc(Hons), MMBiol, MMSci, MOcean, MPhil, MSc, PhD

Welsh Institute for Natural Resources; www.bangor.ac.uk/wnr

College of Health & Behavioural Sciences; www.bangor.ac.uk/cohabs

School of Healthcare Sciences; www.bangor.ac.uk/healthcaresciences

adv clinical practice, health studies/science, critical care, risk management, health & social care leadership, midwifery, nursing, occupational therapy, pharmacology, operating department practice, public health, radiography, social care; BN(Hons), BSc(Hons), BMidw, DipHE, GradCert/Dip, MPhil, PhD

School of Medical Sciences; www.bangor.ac.uk/sms

medical education/science, behavioural neurology, clinical & functional brain imaging, exercise physiology, sport science, molecular science for medicine; MSc, PGDip/Cert(HE), BMed Sci, BSc PhD

School of Psychology; www.bangor.ac.uk/psychology

child & language development, clinical & health psychology/neuropsychology, applied behavioural analysis, consumer psychology, neuroimaging, BSc(Hons), MSc, PhD, MRes, MA

School of Sport, Health & Exercise Science; www.bangor.ac.uk/sport

sport science, sport, health & exercise, physical education, exercise science, physiology, exercise psychology, outdoor activities, rehabilitation; BSc(Hons), MPhil, MSc, PhD

Institute of Medical & Social Research; www.bangor.ac.uk/imscar

dementia & ageing, health economics, health services; PhD

College of Physical and Applied Sciences; www.bangor.ac.uk/copas

School of Chemistry; www.chemistry.bangor.ac.uk/

analytical chemistry, chemistry, biomolecular sciences, environmental/marine/experimental chemistry, molecular science for medicine; BSc, MChem, MSc, PGDip, PhD, MPhil

School of Electronics; www.eng.bangor.ac.uk/

bioelectronics, critical safety engineering, computer systems engineering, control & instrument engineering, electronic engineering, microtechnology, microwave dev, music technology, broadband communications, optoelectronics, nanotechnology; BEng (Hons), BSc(Hons), MEng (Hons), MSc, PhD

School of Computer Science; www.cs.bangor.ac.uk

adv visualisation, AI, communication networks, computer science for business, internet systems and e-commerce, creative technologies, information & communications technology, computer systems engineering, electronic engineering, medical visualisation, oceanography & business, pattern recognition; BA(Hons), BEng(Hons), MEng(Hons), MPhil, MRes, MSc, PhD

UNIVERSITY CENTRE BARNSLEY
www.hud.ac.uk/barnsley

Art & Design
interdisciplnary art & design; BA(Hons)

Construction
construction, project management; BSc(Hons), FdSc, HNC

Computing
animation, & visual effects; BA(Hons), FdSc

Early Years & Childhood Studies
early years; FdA, BA(Hons)

Education & Training
early years, professional development, teacher training, lifelong learning, action research for education, leadership in public service & education, children's workforce; BA(Hons), CertEd, FdA, MA/PGDip/PGCert, PGCE

Film
digital film & visual effects, film, animation, music; BA(Hons)

Music
music production & sound recording, popular music & promotion; BA(Hons)

Professional Development for Staff in Education
professional development; BA, MA, PGDip/Cert

Teaching
teacher training (lifelong learning)/pre/in/service, professional development; CertEd, PGCE, BA(Hons), BSc(Hons)

UNIVERSITY OF BATH
www.bath.ac.uk

Faculty of Engineering and Design; www.bath.ac.uk/engineering

Architecture & Civil Engineering; www.bath.ac.uk/ace
architectural engineering: environmental design, architecture, civil engineering, conservation of historic innovative structural materials/buildings/gardens, facade engineering, international construction management; BEng, BSc, EngD, MArch, MEng, MPhil, MSc, PGCert, PhD

Chemical Engineering; www.bath.ac.uk/chem-eng
biochemical/chemical/biomedical engineering; BEng, EngD, MEng, MPhil, MSc, PhD

Electronic & Electrical Engineering; www.bath.ac.uk/elec-eng
communication/computer systems engineering, digital communications, electrical & electronic/electrical power engineering, mechanical engineering, mechatronics, wireless systems; BEng, EngD, MEng, MPhil, MSc, PhD

Mechanical Engineering; www.bath.ac.uk/mech-eng
aerospace/automotive engineering, innovation/& engineering design, fluid power engineering, mechanical/manufacturing engineering, mechatronics, technology management, adv design & innovation; EngD, MEng, MPhil, MSc, PhD

Faculty of Humanities and Social Science; www.bath.ac.uk/hss

Dept of Economics; www.bath.ac.uk/economics
economics/& finance, international development, politics, international money & banking, economics (development); BSc(Hons), MPhil, MRes, PhD

Dept of Education; www.bath.ac.uk/education
childhood, youth & education studies, coach education, initial teacher training,, TESOL, sports performance; BA(Hons), EdD, FdSc, MA, MPhil, MRes, PGCE, PhD, ProfPGCE

Dept of Politics, Languages & International Studies; www.bath.ac.uk/polis
European politics, contemporary European studies, international relations/studies, interpreting, translating, international management/security, modern languages, language & politics, economics, professional language studies; BA(Hons), BSc(Hons), MA, MPhil, PGDip, PhD

Dept of Psychology; www.bath.ac.uk/psychology
health/psychology, science, risk & health communication, applied cognition, social processes; BSc(Hons), MPhil, MSc, PhD

Department for Health; www.bath.ac.uk/health;
health, primary care, sport & exercise science/medicine, sports physiology; BSc, MPhil, MRes, MSc, PhD, Prof Doc

Faculty of Science; www.bath.ac.uk/science

Dept of Biology & Biochemistry; www.bath.ac.uk/bio-sci
biology, biochemistry, biosciences, molecular & cellular biology, developmental biology, evolution & population biology, medical bioscience, molecular plant science, protein structure & function; BSc(Hons), MPhil, MRes, PhD

Dept of Chemistry; www.bath.ac.uk/chemistry
chemistry/for drug discovery, natural sciences, management, education; BSc(Hons), MChem, MSci, PhD

Dept of Computer Science; www.bath.ac.uk/comp-sci
computer information systems/business, computer science, software/internet systems & security, human-computer interaction; BSc(Hons), EngD, MComp, MSc, PhD

Dept of Mathematics; www.bath.ac.uk/math-sci
mathematical biology/sciences, mathematics, modern applics of mathematics, statistics; BSc(Hons), MMath, MSc, PhD

Dept of Natural Sciences; www.bath.ac.uk/nat-sci
multidisciplinary studies include biology, chemistry, pharmacology, physics; BSc(Hons), MSci

Dept of Pharmacy & Pharmacology; www.bath.ac.uk/pharmacy
advanced & specialist/clinical pharmaceutical practice & therapeutics, pharmacology, pharmaceutical prescribing, medicine management, pharmacy; MPharm, MPharmacol, PhD

Dept of Physics; www.bath.ac.uk/physics
mathematics and physics, physics/with computing, nanoscience, medical physics, photonics; BSc, MSc, MPhil, MPhys, PhD

School of Management; www.bath.ac.uk/management
accounting & finance, business administration, international management, management, marketing, innovation & technology management, sustainability, HR; BSc(Hons), DBA, EngD, MBA, MPhil, MRes, MSc, PhD

School for Health; www.bath.ac.uk/health
health care/informatics, information governance, primary care, lifelong health & wellbeing, child & adolescent mental health, sport & exercise science/medicine, sports physiotherapy; BSc(Hons), MD, MPhil, MS, PGDip, PhD

BATH SPA UNIVERSITY
www.bathspa.ac.uk

Bath School of Art & Design; www.artbathspa.com
art/design, ceramics, contemporary arts practice, fine art, graphic communication, fashion/textile design, ceramics, digital/3D design, photography & digital media, visual design/communication, graphic des, curatorial practice, brand development; BA(Hons), FdA, MFA, MPhil, PhD

School of Education; www.bathspa.ac.uk/schools/education
early years/education, teaching assistants, PGCE (primary (3–11)/middle years (7–14)/ secondary (11–16); range of subjects), TESOL, international

education; FD, GradCert, MA/MTeach, PGCE, PGCert/Dip

School of Humanities & Creative Industries; www.bath-spa.ac.uk/schools/humanities-and cultural-industries

creative media practice/writing/arts, film & screen studies, media communications, music production, pop, English literature, heritage, contemporary circus, publishing, study of religions, philosophy & ethics, history; BA(Hons), MPhil, PhD, MA

Music & the Performing Arts; www.bathspampa.com

commercial music, creative arts, music technology, dance, drama, performing arts, music, theatre

production, arts management; BA(Hons), FdA, FdMus, MA, PhD

School of Science, Society & Management; www.ssmbathspa.com

biology, business & management, applied geography/science, development/geography, counselling, HRM, environmental science, food & nutrition, GIS, health studies, health & social care management, human nutrition, marketing, tourism, psychology, sociology; BA(Hons), BSc (Hons), MPhil, MSc, PhD, FDA, DipHE

UNIVERSITY OF BEDFORDSHIRE
www.beds.ac.uk

Faculty of Creative Arts, Technologies & Science; www.beds.ac.uk/departments/cats

Bedfordshire Institute of Media and the Creative & Performing Arts; www.beds.ac.uk/departments/bim

Div of Art & Design

advertising design, animation, art & design, fine art, advertising/craft/graphic/interior/fashion design, illustration, interior design, photography & video art, contemporary fine arts practice, art design & internet technologies

Div of Journalism & Communication

creative writing/photography, sports/magazine/international broadcast/journalism, media performance/practice, mass communication arts/practices/performances, PR, international cinema, professional writing

Div of Media Arts & Production

media production (moving image, new media, radio, scriptwriting), documentary, music technology, internet technologies, TV production, digital imaging

Div of Performing Arts & English

dance & professional practice, education studies, English studies, performing arts, theatre & professional practice, international cinema, media performance/practice, professional writing, creative writing; BA(Hons), FdA, MA, MRes, PhD

Dept of Computer Science & Technology; www.beds.ac.uk/departments/computing

computer science/networking/software/applications/systems/science & applied/internet/mobile computing, robotics, business information systems, computer games development, AI and robotics, applied computing & IT, computer animation, computer & internet applications, information systems, software engineering, network management; BSc(Hons), FdSc, MSc

Div of Science

biomedical science, biological sciences, bioscience, environmental management, mechanical engineering, forensic science, medical science, nutritional sciences, pharmacology; BSc(Hons), FdSc, MSc, PgCert, PgDip, MPhil, PhD

Faculty of Health and Social Sciences; www.beds.ac.uk/departments/healthsciences

Dept of Acute Health Care; Dept of Community Services; Dept of Midwifery & Child Health

accident & emergency, antenatal education, applied/psychology, sicial studies, long-term/temporary care, midwifery, neonatal care, operating dept practice, palliative care, perioperative care, postnatal care, criminology, counselling, respiratory care, social work, sports therapy, surgical care, youth & community/child & adolescent studies, complementary therapies, coronary care, diabetes, environmental health, health and social care, health psychology, intensive care, nursing (adult, children, mental health, learning disabilities, mental health, osteopathy, care management, complementary therapy, management & leadership in health & social care, dental nursing/practice management, clinical science, health studies, leadership, medical education/simulation, public health nursing; BSc(Hons), FdA, FdSc, MSc, PGDip/Cert, Adv/DipHE, FdA/Sc, MOst

Dept of Applied Social Studies; www.beds.ac.uk/departments/ appliedsocialstudies

applied social studies, criminology, early years/child and adolescent studies, counselling health and social care, social work, sociology, young people's services, youth & community studies, public policy; BSc(Hons), FdA, FdSc, MSc, ProfDoc

Div of Psychology; www.beds.ac.uk/departments/ psychology

applied/health psychology, counselling and therapies, criminal behaviour, criminal behaviour, forensics; BSc(Hons), CertHE, FdA, MSc, PhD

Div of Sports Therapy; www.beds.ac.uk/departments/ spoth

sports therapy/& exercise rehabilitation; BSc(Hons)

Bedfordshire & Hertfordshire Postgraduate Medical School; www.beds.ac.uk/ departments/bhpms

diabetes, dental/medical education, public health, sexual health, medical simulation; MA, MSc, PGDip, PGCert

Institute for Health Research; www.beds.ac.uk/researchir

psychological approach to health & management, public health, research & evaluation; MSc, PhD

Institute of Applied Social Research; www.beds.ac.uk/research/lasr

applied social studies, Europerspectives, leadership; ProfDoc, MA

University of Bedfordshire Business School; www.beds.ac.uk/departments/ ubbs

Depts of Accounting & Finance, Marketing, Strategy & HRM, Business Systems, Law (School of), Language & Communication

accounting, international/finance, banking investment; advertising, marketing, PR, retail management, engineering/ business management, hospitality & hotel bus management, information systems, logistics & supply chain management, marketing communications; international/HRM, business administration, business studies, business decison making/strategy, e-business, creativity & innovation; project management; corporate/international commercial law, Islamic finance and banking; applied linguistics, (ETL), intercultural communication, English for business, TESOL; BA(Hons), BSc(Hons), DBA, FdA, LlB, LlM, MA, MBA, MSc, PGCErt, LLM

Faculty of Education, Sport & Tourism; www.beds.ac.uk/es

primary education/QTS, early years, primary languages, ESOL, specialist maths, post-compulsory education, lifelong learning, PGCE secondary education (range of subjects), applied/special education, childhood & youth/disability studies, footbal studies, PE, sports management/studies, event management, sport/international tourism management; PGCE, BA(Hons), BEd(Hons), MA, FdA, PGCSMT

THE QUEEN'S UNIVERSITY OF BELFAST
www.qub.ac.uk

School of Biological Sciences; www.qub.ac.uk/schools/ schoolofbiologicalsciences

agricultural biotechnology, adv food safety, animal behaviour, biological sciences, environmental biology, ecological management, food quality, safety & nutrition, genetics, land use & environmental management, land environmental sustainability, marine biology, microbiology, molecular biology, rural sustainability, sustainable/rural development/aquaculture, zoology; BSc(Hons), MSc, PGDip, PhD

School of Chemistry and Chemical Engineering; www.ch.qub.ac.uk

chemistry, medicinal chemistry, chemistry with forensic analysis, chemical engineering, chemical biology, process engineering; BSc(Hons), MSci, BEng, MEng, MSc, PGDip, PhD

School of Creative Arts; www.qub.ac.uk/schools/SchoolofCreativeArts

music, music technology, composition, sonic arts, film studies, film & drama, visual studies, arts management; BA, MA, BMus, BSc, MPhil, PhD

School of Education; www.qub.ac.uk/schools/schoolofeducation

autism spectrum disorders, coaching & mentoring, education studies, inclusion, counselling, initial teacher education (range of subjects), leadership in education, inclusion/education & special education needs, lifelong learning, professional development, work-based learning, TESOL; AdvCertEd, DASE, EdD, MA, MEd, MSc, MSSc, PGCE, PGDip/Cert, UnivCert, BA(Hons)

School of Electronics, Electrical Engineering and Computer Science; www.qub.ac.uk/schools/eeecs

business IT, computing and IT, computer games design & development, computer science, creative multimedia, educational multimedia, electrical & electronic engineering, electronics, telecommunications, software/development & electronic systems engineering, advanced wireless communication, web technology, sustainable electrical energy systems; BEng, BSc, MEng, MSc, MPhil, PhD

School of English; www.qub.ac.uk/schools/SchoolofEnglish

creative writing, English literature & linguistics, Irish writing, linguistics, medieval studies, modern literary studies, modern poetry, reconceiving the Renaissance, broadcast literacy; BA(Hons), MA, PhD

School of Geography, Archaeology and Palaeoecology; www.qub.ac.uk/schools/gap

professional/archaeology, dating & chronology, geography, landscape, heritage, social space & culture, palaeoecology, geography; BA(Hons), BSc(Hons), MSc, PhD

School of History and Anthropology; www.qub.ac.uk/schools/SchoolofHistoryandAnthropology

ancient history, archaeology, history, ethnomusicology, Irish history, modern history, social anthropology, cognition & culture; BA(Hons), GradDip, MA, MPhil, PhD

School of Modern Languages; www.qub.ac.uk/schools/SchoolofModernLanguages

French/German/Irish & Celtic/ Spanish & Portugese studies; BA(Hons), MA, PhD

School of Law; www.law.qub.ac.uk/law/ with politics

law/with politics, common & civil law, environmental law, criminal justice, legal science, criminology, governance, international commerce, human rights; LlB, LlM, MSSc, MLSc, PGdip, MPhil, PhD

Queen's University Management School; www.qub.ac.uk/schools/QueensUniversityManagementSchool

accounting, finance, actuarial science & risk, organisation & business economics/management, economics, management, international business, environmental management, financial regulation, sustainabilty & corporate responsibility, HRM; BSc(Hons), MSc, MScs, MBA, PhD

School of Mathematics and Physics; www.qub.ac.uk/schools/SchoolofMathematicsandPhysics

applied/pure mathematics, computer science & physics, operational research, statistics, astrophysics, physics with medical applications, theoretical/plasma physics, vacuum technology; BSc(Hons), GradDip, MSc, MSci, PhD, GradDip

School of Mechanical and Aerospace Engineering; www.qub.ac.uk/schools/SchoolofMechanicalandAerospaceEngineering

aerospace engineering, mechanical/manufacturing engineering, product design & development, polymers engineering; BEng, MEng, MSc, PhD

School of Medicine, Dentistry and Biomedical Sciences; www.qub.ac.uk/schools/mdbs

medicine, biomedical science, clinical education, dentistry, surgery, human/computational biology, molecular medicine, mental health, obstetrics, public health, pain science, health & social care; BCh, BAO, BSc(Hons), BDS, DAO, Diploma, MB, MD, MSc

School of Music and Sonic Arts; www.mu.qub.ac.uk

music, composition, creative practice, ethnomusicology, jazz, pop, Irish traditional music, musicology, music technology, performance, sonic arts, sound design/engineering; BMus, BSc(Hons), MA, PhD

School of Nursing and Midwifery; www.qub.ac.uk/schools/ SchoolofNursingandMidwifery

nursing – adult/children's/learning disability/mental health, maternal and child health, midwifery, continuing professional development, clinical practice; BSc(Hons), Diploma, MPhil, PhD, DNursingPractice

School of Pharmacy; www.qub.ac.uk/ schools/SchoolofPharmacy

clinical pharmacy, community pharmacy, pharmacist prescribing, pharmacy practice; MPharm, MSc, PGCert/Dip

School of Planning, Architecture and Civil Engineering; www.qub.ac.uk/schools/ SchoolofPlanningArchitectureand CivilEngineering

architecture, civil engineering, construction & project management, durability of structures, environmental engineering/planning, management, spatial regeneration, urban & rural design, water resource mgt, structural engineering, sustainable design; BSc(Hons), MSc, MArch, MPhil, PhD

School of Politics, International Studies and Philosophy; www.qub.ac.uk/schools/ SchoolofPoliticsInternationalStudies andPhilosophy

comparative ethnic conflict, gender & society, European Union politics, international relations/studies, Irish politics, law with politics, legislative studies & practice, philosophy, politics & economics, international politics & conflict studies, violence, terrorism and security; BA(Hons), LlB, MA, MRes, MPhil, PhD

School of Psychology; www.psych.qub.ac.uk

atypical child development, educational child & adolescent psychology, political psychology, applied/clinical psychology, performance in sport & health; BSc(Hons), MSc, DocClinPsych, PhD DocEducational

School of Sociology, Social Policy and Social work; www.qub.ac.uk/schools/ SchoolofSociologySocialPolicy SocialWork

applied social studies, criminology, childhood studies, social work, social policy, social research methods, sociology; BA(Hons), BSW, MA, MSc, DChild Stud

UNIVERSITY OF BIRMINGHAM
www.bham.ac.uk

College of Arts and Law; www.colleges.bham.ac.uk/artslaw

Institute of Archaeology and Antiquity; www.iaa.bham.ac.uk

antiquity, archaeology (classical/conflict/European/ Greek/practical), ancient history, heritage management, Egyptology, Byzantine, Ottoman & modern Greek studies, classics, classical literature & civilization, cuneiform & ancient near eastern studies, Egyptology, historical environmental conservation, Roman history, E Mediterranean history, Ottoman studies; BA(Hons), MA, MPhil, diploma, PhD

Birmingham Law School; www.law.bham.ac.uk

law, commercial law, criminal law & criminal justice, European law, international commercial law; GradDip; LlB, LlM, MPhil/MJur/PhD

English, Drama and American & Canadian Studies; www.bham.ac.uk/schools/edacs

American & Canadian studies, English & American literature, creative writing, directing & dramaturgy, playwriting studies, drama & theatre arts, English language/literature, literary linguistics, medieval studies, modernity, Shakespeare studies, film & TV; BA(Hons), BSc(Hons), MPhil, PhD

School of History and Cultures; www.historycultures.bham.ac.uk

African studies, history (ancient & medieval/economic & social/modern, contemporary) archaeology & anthropology, Caribbean literature, cultural heritage of Shakespeare's England, early modern history, history of Christianity, modern European history, Reformation & early modern studies, medieval studies, 20th-century British history, war studies, West Midlands history, air power, 1st/2nd world war studies; BA(Hons), MA, MPhil, PGDip, PhD

School of Languages, Cultures, Art History and Music; www.bham.ac.uk/schools/cahm

modern languages, film studies, cultural enquiry, European studies, French, gender studies, German, Hispanic, Italian, translation studies, modern European culture, Japanese history of art, music, composition, editing, musicology, performance/practice, electroacoustic composition, British music, choral conducting; BA, MA, BMus, MA, MPhil,PhD

The School of Philosophy, Theology and Religion; www.about.bham.ac.uk/schools/ptr

electronic scholarly editing, global ethics, history of Christianity, inter-religious relations, cognitive science, Islam and Christian–Muslim relations, Islamic studies, philosophy, philosophy of language and linguistics/of mind & cognition/of religion and ethics/health & happiness, pentecostal & charismatic studies, human rights & values, Quaker studies, religion & culture, Sikh studies, theology & religion, ethics; BA(Hons), BMus, MA, MPhil, PhD,MRes,Dip/Cert

College of Engineering and Physical Sciences; www.about.bham.ac.uk/colleges/eps

School of Chemistry; www.chem.bham.ac.uk

chemical biology, chemistry/with analytical science/bioorganic chemistry/pharmacology, materials chemistry, molecular processes & theory, molecular synthesis; BSc, MSci, Msc, PhD/MPhil

School of Chemical Engineering; www.eng.bham.ac.uk/chemical

chemical engineering, biochemical engineering, energy engineering, food safety, hygiene & management, industrial project management; BEng, MEng, Masters/MSc/Diploma/PG Certificate

School of Civil Engineering; www.eng.bham.ac.uk/civil

civil engineering, energy engineering, geotechnical engineering, railway systems engineering & integration, road management & engineering, transport technology, construction management, water resources technology & management; BEng, MEng, Masters/MSC/Diploma/Certificate

School of Computer Science; www.cs.bham.ac.uk

artificial intelligence, computer science, software engineering, computer security, electronic & software engineering, intelligent systems engineering, internet software systems, natural computation, multidisciplinary optimisation, human/computer interaction, robotic/cognitive psychology; BSc, MEng, MSc, MRes, PhD

School of Electrical, Electronic and Computer Engineering; www.eece.bham.ac.uk

communications engineering/networks, software engineering, digital entrepreneurship, electromagnetic sensor networks, RF engineering, computer engineering, embedded systems, computer systems, RF & satellite engineering; BEng, MEng, MSc, MRes, PhD

School of Mathematics; www.mat.bham.ac.uk

pure/applied mathematics, mathematics/with engineering, operational research, statistics/& economics, mathematics in computing & biology, financial engineering, OR, econometrics; BA, BSc, MSci, MSc, MRes, PhD

School of Mechanical Engineering; www.eng.bham.ac.uk/mechanical

mechanical/automotive engineering, engineering/operations/project management; BEng, MEng, Masters/MSc, PhD/MSc

School of Metallurgy and Materials; www.eng.bham.ac.uk/metallurgy

materials/for sustainable energy technologies, metallurgy, biomaterials, nuclear engineering, science & engineering of materials, materials engineering, energy engineering, metallurgy & materials, sports & materials science; BSc, BEng, MEng, MRes, PhD/MSc

School of Physics and Astronomy; www.ph.bham.ac.uk

physics, physics & astrophysics/technology of nuclear reactors/nanoscale physics/particle physics & cosmology, theoretical physics, & applied mathematics, nanotechnology, radioactive waste management & decommissioning; BEng, BNatSci, BSc(Hons), DEng, MEng, MPhil, MRes, MSc, MSci, PGDip/Cert, PhD

College of Life and Environmental Sciences; www.about.bham.ac.uk/colleges/les

School of Biosciences; www.biosciences.bham.ac.uk

biochemistry, biological sciences, genetics, molecular biotechnology, microbiology, molecular cell biology, environmental/human/medical biology, ornithology, toxicology, plant biology, zoology, human/medical biology, natural sciences; BSc, MSci, MSc

School of Geography, Earth and Environmental Sciences; www.gees.bham.ac.uk

geography, geology, air pollution management & control, applied meteorology & climatology, enterprise, environment & place, micropalaeontology, environmental science/geoscience/health/management/planning, hydrotechnology, nuclear decommissioning & waste management, nanoscience & nanotechnology, public & environmental health science, safety & the environment, resource & applied geology, river environmental management, palaeobiology & palaeoenvironment, resilience & urban living, urban & regional planning/studies/regeneration; BA, BSc/MSci, MSci, MSc, MRes

School of Psychology; www.psychology.bham.ac.uk

psychology, brain injury/rehabilitation/imaging, clinical criminology/psychology, cognition & computational neuroscience, cognitive behaviour therapy/neuropsychology & rehabilitation, forensic psychology, neuroscience, psychological practice; BSc, MSci, MSc/Diploma/Certificate

School of Sport and Exercise Sciences; www.sportex.bham.ac.uk

sport & exercise science, sports science/& materials technology/mathematics; BSc(Hons), Clin, ForenPsyD, MPhil, MRes, MSc, PhD, PsyD, PGDip, PhD, PGDips

College of Medical and Dental Sciences; www.about.bham.ac.uk/colleges/mds

The Five Schools of the College are: Cancer Sciences, Clinical & Experimental Medicine, Dentistry, Health & Population Sciences, Immunity & Infection

biomedical materials science, cancer, cardiovascular sciences, clinical & experimental medicine, dental hygiene & therapy, dental surgery, dentistry, health sciences, hormones & genes, immunity & infection, medical science, medicine, surgery, neuroscience, nursing, physiotherapy; BDS, BMedSci, BSc(Hons), BNurs, DDS, MBChB, MD

College of Social Sciences; www.about.bham.ac.uk/colleges/socialsciences

Birmingham Business School; www.business.bham.ac.uk

accounting & finance, banking, business management/with communications, business administration, corporate governance, development economics, economic policy/& international business, economics, environmental & natural resource economics, global business & finance, HRM, international accounting & finance, international business/economics/marketing/money & banking, investments, land & regional economic development, management, marketing/communications, mathematical economics & statistics/ finance, money, planning with economics, political science, social policy, spatial planning, strategy & procurement management, strategic marketing & consulting, urban & regional studies; BSc Economics, BSc(Hons), Dip, MSc, MBA, DBA, MPhil, PhD PGCert, PGDip, UCert

School of Education; www.education.bham.ac.uk

autism/spectrum disorders, bilingualism in education, childhood, culture & education, English language & literature/international studies in education, IT and education, leadership in education, learning and learning contexts,speech/learning difficulties/disabilities, multisensory impairment (deafblindness), school improvement & educational leadership, sport, physical education & coaching science, social, emotional and behavioural difficulties, sports coaching, teacher training (early years, primary, secondary subject courses) – (English, geography, history and citizenship, mathematics, modern foreign languages, PE, RE, biology, chemistry, physics), TEFL, visual impairment; AdCert, BA(Hons), BPhil, ChildPsyD, EdD, EdPsychD, MEd, MPhil, PGCE, PGCert/Dip, PhD

School of Government and Society; www.about.bham.ac.uk/colleges/socialsciences/governmentsociety

political science, African studies, Russian studies, sociology, social & political theory, political economy/science/theory, international relations, European politics/studies, society & economics, Central & East European studies, international development (conflict/security/poverty/inequality), aid management, HR & development management (competence/gender/education), global economy, international peace & security, terrorism, urban development, development/aid management, public service, poverty reduction, local government, social & political theory; BA(Hons), BSc(Hons), GradDip/Cert, MA, MPhil, MSc, PhD

The School of Social Policy (The Health Services Management Centre; Institute of Applied Social Studies);
www.hsmc.bham.ac.uk;
www.iass.bham.ac.uk
community justice, health care policy management, policy into practice, planning, leadership for health service improvement, health service management, leading public service change and organizational development, managing integrated health & wellbeing, new migration, public service commissioning, management for social care/work, social policy, social work; BAMA, MSc, PGDip

Degrees validated at the University of Birmingham offered at:

SCHOOL OF EDUCATION, SELLY OAK
www.education.bham.ac.uk

applied golf management studies, autism, bilingualism in education, childhood, culture & education, dyslexia studies, education for health professionals, English language and literature in education, educational psychology, hearing impairment, inclusion & special educational needs, international studies in education, IT & education, leaders & leadership in education, learning & learning contexts, learning difficulties/ multisensory impairment, sports coaching, teacher training – primary courses; early years, general primary/secondary subject courses (English, geography, history & citizenship, mathematics, modern foreign languages, PE, professional development, RE, biology, chemistry, physics), TEFL, visual impairment; AppEd, BA, ChildPsyD, EdPsychD, MPhil, PhD, PGCE

UNIVERSITY COLLEGE BIRMINGHAM
www.ucb.ac.uk

business & marketing, childhood & education, hospitality, food & events management, recreation sport & tourism, sports therapy, salon management; BA(Hons), BSc(Hons), FdA Dip HE, FdSc, MA, MSc, PGCE, PGDip/Cert

BIRMINGHAM CITY UNIVERSITY
www.bcu.ac.uk

Birmingham Institute of Art and Design;
www.bcu.ac.uk/bid
animation, architecture, art/& design/education, curatorial practice, fashion promotion/styling, interior design, design, fashion design/retail management/promotion, fine art, horology, jewellery & silversmithing, history of art & design, landscape architecture, theatre, performance & event, product/urban/textile/graphic design, visual communication; BA(Hons), BTEC, CertHE/DipHE, HND, MA, MPhil, PgCert/PgDip, PhD

Birmingham City Business School;
www.bcu.ac.uk/business-school
accountancy, advertising, business & management/administration, management, internal audit practice, risk management, business studies, economics, consultancy, finance & consultancy, marketing/practice, international/business, international/HRM, PR; BA(Hons), DBA, HND, MBA, MPhil, MSc, PhD

Faculty of Education, Law and Social Sciences; www.bcu.ac.uk/elss

School of Education; www.bcu.ac.uk/els
children & integrated professional care, cont prof development/teachers, early childhood/education studies, early years, international education, post-compulsory education & training, secondary/art & design/drama/education, mathematics, music, primary education/with QTS, subject enhancement in mathematics, teaching & learning; BA(Hons), FD, FC, CA, MPhil, PGDip/Cert, PGCE, PhD, PGCE

The School of Law; www.bcu.ac.uk/law
corporate & business law, international human rights, legal studies, law, law with American legal studies/criminology/business law/human rights, legal practice; GradDip, MPhil/PhD, HND, LlB(Hons), PGCert/PGDip/LLM

School of Social Sciences; www.cu.ac.uk/socialsciences
forensic/social sciences, public sociology, integrative/forensic psychology, crime & policing/pyschology/security studies; BA(Hons), BSc(Hons), CertHE, FdA, MA, MPhil, MSc, PGCert, PGDip, PhD

Faculty of Health; www.bcu.ac.uk/health
advanced health care/practice, health and social care/wellbeing (exercise science/nutrition science/individuals and communities), public health, midwifery, nursing (adult, child learning disability), operating dept practice, perioperative specialist practice, diagnostic/radiography, paramedic science, leadership, medical ultrasound, pain management, social work, speech & language therapy, strategic leadership; BSc(Hons), DipHE, FdA, MPhil, MSc, PgCert, PGDip, PQ, PhjD

Faculty of Performance, Media and English; www.bcu.ac.uk/pme

Birmingham Conservatoire; www.conservatoire.bcu.ac.uk
jazz, performance/& pedagogy, composition, conducting, digital arts in performance, orchestral performance, pop music, vocal performance; AdvPGDip, BMus(Hons), HND, MA, MMus, MPhil, PGCert, PhD

Birmingham School of Media; www.bcu.ac.uk/mediacourses
journalism, freelance photography/media, creative/future media, PR, international/radio/production, broadcast/online journalism, freelance photography, media & communication, TV musical heritage, screen studies, social media, web & new media; BA(Hons), PGDip, MA, MPhil, PhD, HND

Birmingham School of Acting; www.bsa.bcu.ac.uk
community & applied theatre/dance theatre, physical theatre, professional voice practice acting, stage management; BA(Hons), MA, PgDip

School of English; www.lmds.bcu.ac.uk/English
English/ & media/drama/creative writing, English literature/language, linguistics, writing, philosophy; BA(Hons), Diploma, MA, MPhil, PhD

Faculty of Technology, Engineering and the Environment; www.bcu.ac.uk/tee-landing
business information & communication technology, computer networks/& security, computer science/technology/games technology, computing & sound & multimedia technology, data networks & security, film production & technology, forensic computing, music technology, TV technology & production, telecommunication networks, web technology; automotive engineering, electronic engineering, mechanical engineering, architectural technology, building surveying/services engineering, construction/management & economics, construction quantity surveying, international logistics & supply chain management, project/quality management, real estate management, planning & development, environmental spacial planning/sustainability; BSc, HNC, FdSc, MSc, PgCert, PgDip

BISHOP GROSSETESTE UNIVERSITY COLLEGE
www.bgc.ac.uk

early childhood/children & youth work, learning support, drama in the community, education, primary education with QTS, heritage studies, education studies in art & design/drama/English/geography/history/mathematics/music PGCE (primary/secondary), graduate teacher education, community archaeology, English literature, theology & society; BA(Hons), FdA, GradDip, MA, PGCE

EAST LANCASHIRE INSTITUTE OF HIGHER EDUCATION AT BLACKBURN COLLEGE
www.blackburn.ac.uk

Vocation qualifications (BTEC, City & Guilds etc) applied psychology, business accounting/studies/administration, design (contemporary textiles/graphic communication/illustration and animation/interiors/moving image/new media), early childhood, educational studies, civil/electrical/electronic/mechanical engineering, computing (business information, networks, forensic, software), English language & literature, financial services, fine art (integrated media), fire & rescue services, hospitality management, housing studies, criminology, HRM, journalism, law/with psychology, legal studies, leadership, marketing, mechanical engineering, photographic media, public service management, social care, sociology, sports coaching, sustainable construction, teacher training, working with children & young people; BA(Hons, Ord), BEng(Hons, Ord), BSc(Hons, Ord), DMS (validated externally), FD, HNC, HND, LlB (validated by Lancaster), LlM, MBA, MSc

BOURNEMOUTH UNIVERSITY
www.bournemouth.ac.uk

The School of Applied Sciences; www.bournemouth.ac.uk/applied-sciences
prehistoric & Roman archaeology, archaeology & geography, archaeological, anthropological & forensic sciences, biological/forensic/environmental science, animal and landbased studies, biological/forensic anthropology, forensic osteology, anthropology & heritage, conservation, ecology & environmental change, toxicology; BSc(Hons), BA(Hons), MSc, PhD

The Business School; www.business.bournemouth.ac.uk
accounting, business studies, corporate governance, operations & project management, economics, finance, HRM, risk management, professional development, international business finance/management/commercial law, intellectual property, law and taxation, management, marketing; BA(Hons), LlB(Hons), LlM, MA, MBA, MPhil, MSc, PhD

School of Design, Engineering & Computing; www.dec.bournemouth.ac.uk
design business management, engineering design innovation, engineering project management, sustainable/product design/management, design engineering, industrial/product design, games/music & audio technology, computer games, psychology, clinical psychology, ageing neuropsychology, cognitive neuropsychology, business computing, computer animation, information technology management, internet/multimedia comunication systems, software engineering/product design, forensic computing & security, digital media/music & audio production, network systems management, smart systems, software systems engineering, sustainable network/web systems; BA(Hons), BSc(Hons), FD, HNC, HND, MA, MPhil, MSc, PhD

School of Health and Social Care; www.bournemouth.ac.uk/hsc
nutrition, early years care, emergency care, operating dept practice, paramedic science, adult/child health

nursing, learning disability, mental health, children & family studies, adv nurse practitioner, midwifery, exercise science, occupational therapy, professional practitioner, physiotherapy, psychosocial intervention, social work, sociology, social policy; AdvDip, BA(Hons), BSc(Hons), DipHE, FdA, FdSc, MPhil, PGDip/Cert, PhD, Dr Prof Practice

The Media School; www.media.bournemouth.ac.uk
advertising, marketing/communications, communication & media, 3D computer animation & visual effects, animation, games & effects, digital cinematography, English, cinematography, global computer animation practice, media design/production/effects, multimedia journalism, journalism & new media, politics and media, photography, PR, radio production, sound production, software design for games, scriptwriting for film and TV, TV & film production, politics & media, screenwriting; BA(Hons), BSc(Hons), FdA, MA, MBA, MPhil, MSc, PhD, DProfD

School of Tourism; www.bournemouth.ac.uk/tourism
events management, leisure marketing, destination marketing & management, e-tourism, retail management, tourism & hospitality, tourism management & marketing/planning; FDA, FDSc, BA(Hons), BSc(Hons), MA, MSc, PhD

UNIVERSITY OF BRADFORD
www.bradford.ac.uk

School of Computing, Informatics and Media; www.scim.brad.ac.uk
Computing: advanced computer science, AI for games computing, business computing, computational mathematics, computer science/for games, forensic computing, ICT with business/law/marketing, intelligent systems & robotics, internet computing & systems security, mobile computing applications, computing networks & performance engineering, software development applications/engineering

Media: digital media, digital & creative enterprise, digital arts/media/film-making, film studies, informatics, media studies with cinematics/computer animation/digital imaging/TV, music video production, photography for digital media, TV production, web design & technologies

Mathematics; www.maths.brad.ac.uk; computational mathematics; informatics

Creative technology: advanced computer animation and effects, computer animation, graphics for games, informatics, interactive systems & video games design, visual computing effects/production; BA(Hons), BSc(Hons), MA, MSc, FdSc, BEng(Hons)

School of Engineering, Design and Technology; www.eng.brad.ac.uk
applied physics, automotive design technology/engineering quality improvement, chemical & petroleum engineering, civil & structural engineering, clinical technology, electrical & electronic engineering, health science, telecommunications & internet computing, power electronics, IT management, industrial engineering, manufacturing engineering/management, mechanical/& automotive engineering, medical engineering, personal, mobile & satellite communications, polymer engineering, product design, technology management, wireless sensor & embedded systems; BEng, BSc, FD, MEng, MPhil, MSc, PhD

School of Health Studies; www.brad.ac.uk/acad/health
acute & critical care, adult/child/mental health, nursing, cancer care, dementia care & older people, diversity management, health & social care, leadership & management, midwifery, occupational therapy, physiotherapy, public health & well being, diagnostic radiography, reproductive & child health; AdvDip, BSc(Hons), CertHE, DipHE, FD, MSc, MPhil, PGDip/Cert, PhD

School of Life Sciences; www.brad.ac.uk/acad/lifesci

Div of Archaeological Geographical & Environmental Sciences
archaeological prospection/sciences, analytical science, archaeology, environmental management/science, forensic archaeology & crime scene investigation, human osteology & palaeopathology; BA, BSc, CertHE, MA, MSc, MPhil, PhD

Div of Biomedical Sciences
biomedical science, cellular pathology, chemical & forensic science, drug toxicology, medical biochemistry, medical microbiology, pharmacology, medicine development; BSc(Hons), MSC, PgD

55

University of Bradford

Bradford School of Pharmacy
clinical pharmacy, pharmacy, pharmaceutical services/management, and medicines control, prescribing, drug discovery; DPharm, MSC, MPharm

Dept of Chemical and Forensic Sciences
chemistry/with pharmacy for forensic science/for analysis, forensic & bimolecular science/medical science, medical chemistry & anti-cancer drug development; BSc(Hons), MPhil, PhD

Div of Optometry
optometry; BSc, MPhil, PhD

The School of Lifelong Education and Development; www.brad.ac.uk/admin/conted/cfa
coaching & mentoring, combined studies, community justice/regeneration, HE practice, TESOL/applied linguistics, public sector, training & development; FD, Certs, MA, MSc, PGDip/Cert

The School of Management (inc Law); www.brad.ac.uk/acad/management
accounting, business studies, finance, financial planning, business & management studies, HRM, international business & management, law, financial management, marketing, operational & information management; BA(Hons), BSc(Hons), DBA,LlB,GradDip(Law), MBA, MRes, PhD

The School of Social and International Studies; www.brad.ac.uk/acad/ssis
counselling, conflict resolution/security, creative writing, criminal justice studies, international/financial/business economics, English, mod European/history, interdisciplinary human studies, human trafficking, international development/relations, mental health studies/practice, peace studies, philosophy, politics, law, psychology, social policy, social work, sociology, working with children, young people & families; BA(Hons), BSc(Hons), MA, MPhil, PhD, PGDip

Degrees validated by University of Bradford offered at:

BRADFORD COLLEGE
www.bradfordcollege.ac.uk

accountancy, business administration, international business/financial management, business computing/studies, community & social care, computing & ICT, civil engineering, counselling & psychology, early years practice/studies, education, construction management, English & communication, fashion & textiles, fashion design, financial services, HRM, project management, health & nutrition, health & social welfare, illustration, interior design, law/international & comparative, lifelong learning, mechanical engineering, marketing, mathematics, metallurgy & materials, media & creative writing, music, ophthalmic dispensing, PCET, performing arts, pharmacy, photography, public services, quantity surveying, science, social work/care, sport & leisure, sports coaching, teaching, ESOL, ELTS, EFL, PGCE(primary/secondary/vocational) TU studies, travel & tourism, visual culture/arts, youth & community studies; BSc(Hons), CertHE, DipHE, FD, HNC, HND, BA(Hons), LlB(Hons), MA, MEd, PGDipCert,MSc

UNIVERSITY OF BRIGHTON
www.brighton.ac.uk

Faculty of Arts; www.arts.brighton.ac.uk

School of Architecture and Design, School of Arts and Media, School of Humanities
3D design, applied ethics, sustainable design, materials & craft, architecture, interior architecture & urban studies, fashion design, graphic design, illustration, digital arts, history of art & design, humanities, history, philosophy, culture & politics, language & linguistics, literature, media, performance & visual arts/practice, photography, sustainable design, fine art, inclusive arts practice, digital media, sequential design, English language teacher development, media-assisted language teaching, TESOL/TEFL; broadcast/creative media, philosophy of language, culture, politics, war, conflict & modernity, applied ethics, cultural & critical theory, media studies, radio/TV production, broadcast media/journalism; BA (Hons), FdSA, Grad Dip, MA, MDes, MFA, MPhil, PGDip/Cert, PhD

Faculty of Education and Sport; www.brighton.ac.uk/fes

Chelsea School; www.brighton.ac.uk/chelsea

physical education, sport and exercise science/leisure management, sport coaching, sport journalism studies, physiological studies, health science; BA(Hons), BSc(Hons)

School of Education; www.brighton.ac.uk/education

key stage 2/3 English/mathematics/education, secondary design & technology/mathematics/science, education studies, PGCE primary education, secondary (numerous subjects), HE, knowledge enhancement courses, post-compulsory education, professional education studies, professional studies in learning and development/primary education, RE, teacher education, working with young people, youth work; BA(Hons), PGCE, FD, CertED, PhD, EdD

School of Service Management; www.brighton.ac.uk/ssm

food & culinary arts, food services wellbeing, hospitality & event management, international event management, tourism/travel management, retail management/enterprise/marketing, tourism & international development/social anthropology, travel & tourism marketing; BA(Hons), FdA, MA, MSc, PhD

Centre for Learning and Teaching; www.brighton.ac.uk/clt

higher education, learning & teaching in HE; BA(Hons), BSc(Hons), CertEd, EdD, FdA, MA, MPhil, MPhil/PhD, MSc, PGCert, PGCE, PhD

Faculty of Health and Social Science; www.brighton.ac.uk/fhss

School of Applied Social Science; www.brighton.ac.uk/sass

applied psychology/social science, community psychology/research, counselling & psychotherapy, criminology, mental health/social work, politics, psychology, public admin, social policy, sociology, substance misuse, therapeutic counselling, public adm; BA(Hons), MA, MPhil, MSc, PGDip/Cert, PhD, MPA, FD, Prof Doc

School of Health Professions; www.brighton.ac.uk/sohs

clinical education/practice, diabetes, clinical biomechanics, complementary healthcare, health through occupation, occupational therapy, physiotherapy/and education/management, podiatry/surgery, sports injury management; BS (Hons), MSc, PGDip/Cert, PhD, Prof Doc

School of Nursing and Midwifery; www.brighton.ac.uk/snm

acute clinical practice, adult/child/mental health nursing, clinical studies, community specialist practice, health & social care, health studies, nurse practitioner, midwifery, paramedic practice, professional practice, specialist community public health nursing/promotion; BSc(Hons), FdSc, MPhil, MRes, MSc, PGDip/Cert, PhD

Brighton Business School; www.brighton.ac.uk/bbs

accounting, business administration/management, economics, finance, international business, investment, knowledge & innovation, law with business, leadership, logistics & supply chain management, marketing (branding, international, social), personnel & development, HRM, retail management; ACCA, BA(Hons), LlB, MBA, MSc

Faculty of Science and Engineering; www.brighton.ac.uk/scieng

School of Computing, Engineering & Mathematics; www.brighton.ac.uk/cem

business computer/information systems, computer science/games, digital media/production, digital games production, European computing, internet/computing, software engineering, computing, information systems, internet & distributed systems, electrical & electronic engineering, digital electronics, communications, automotive electronic engineering, mathematics/with business/finance, aeronautical engineering, mechanical/manufacturing/automobile engineering, product innovation & design, product design technology, sports/ sustainable product design, user experience; BSc(Hons), FdSc, MA, MComp, MPhil, MSc, PGDip/Cert, MEng

School of Environment and Technology; www.brighton.ac.uk/set

architectural technology, building studies, building surveying, construction management, environmental assessment & management, facilities management,

University of Brighton

project management for construction, town planning; civil engineering, environmental engineering; environmental/hazards/management & assessment/sciences, GIS & sustainability of the built environment, water & environmental management; geography, earth & ocean science, environmental geology, geology; BA/BSc(Hons), BEng(Hons), BSc(Hons), FdSc, FdEng, MEng, MPhil, PGDip/Cert, PhD

School of Pharmacy and Biomolecular Sciences; www.brighton.ac.uk/pharmacy

analytical chemistry with business, biochemical materials, biomedical/biological sciences, clinical pharmacy practice, disease improvement, medical devices, pharmacology, ecology, industrial pharmaceutical studies, biomedical sciences, chemical sciences; BSc(Hons), MSc, MPharmHons, MPhil, MRes, PGDip, PhD

Brighton and Sussex Medical School; www.bsms.ac.uk

cardiology, medical education, diabetes, health or social care, global health, oncology, infectious disease, primary care, psychiatry, medicine, nephrology, public health, surgery, trauma & orthopaedics; BM, BS, MD, MPhil, MSc, PGDip/Cert, PhD

UNIVERSITY OF BRISTOL
www.bris.ac.uk

Faculty of Arts; www.bris.ac.uk/arts

School of Arts; www.bris.ac.uk/arts

Dept of Archaeology & Anthropology; www.bris.ac.uk/archanth;
archaeology, anthropology, archaeological & anthropological sciences, conflict/landscape/maritime archaeology, social anthropology, ancient history, archaeology for screen media, historical archaeology of the modern world

Dept of Drama, Theatre, Film, Television; www.bris.ac.uk/drama
screen & performance, documentary practice, cinema studies, drama, film & TV studies, performance research, music for film & TV

Dept of Music; www.bris.ac.uk/music
British music, composition/for film, TV, medieval music, music/theory, musicology, performance, Russian music

Dept of Philosophy; www.bris.ac.uk/philosophy
philosophy, philosophy & history of science/law/biology & logic, philosophy of mathematics/psychology; BA(Hons), BSc(Hons), MA, Mlitt, MMus, MSci, PGDip, PhD

School of Humanities; www.bris.ac.uk/humanities

Dept of Classics & Ancient History; www.bris.ac.uk/classics
ancient history, ancient history & archaeology, classical studies, classics, history, Greece, Rome

Dept of English; www.bris.ac.uk/english
English, English & philosophy/classical studies/drama, English literature/& community engagement, modern poetry, romanticism, Shakespeare & English literature, late medieval & early modern literature

Dept of History; www.bris.ac.uk/history
empires, contemporary history, medieval and early modern history, Russian history, ancient history, medieval studies

Dept of Art History; www.bris.ac.uk/arthistory
art histories and interpretations, history of art/& languge

Dept of Theology and Religious Studies; www.bris.ac.uk/thrs
biblical studies, theology & religious studies, Buddhist studies, philosophy & ethics, reception of the bible: tradition, theology, & culture, medieval studies

School of Modern Languages; www.bris.ac.uk/sml
French, German, Hispanic, Portuguese & Latin American studies/history, Italian, Russian, Russian studies (includes Czech); European literatures, screen studies, medieval, Renaissance & early modern studies, literary & cultural studies, linguistics; BA(Hons), MA, MLitt, MPhil, PGDip, PhD

Faculty of Engineering; www.bris.ac.uk/engineering

Dept of Aerospace Engineering; www.bris.ac.uk/aerospace
integrated aerospace systems design aeronautical engineering

Dept of Civil Engineering; www.bris.ac.uk/civilengineering
civil engineering, water & environmental management

Dept of Computer Science; www.cs.bris.ac.uk
computer science/& electronic/mathematics, internet technologies with security, machine learning & data mining & high performance computing, creative technologies, adv microelectronic systems

Dept of Electrical and Electronic Engineering; www.bris.ac.uk/eeng
optical communications, communication networks & signal processing, computer science & electronics, electrical & electronic engineering, communications engineering, wireless communication systems & signal processing

Dept of Engineering Mathematics; www.enm.bris.ac.uk
complexity studies, systems engineering, adv engineering robotics/neurodynamics engineering mathematics

Dept of Mechanical Engineering; www.bris.ac.uk/mecheng
mechanical engineering, adv engineering robotics BSc(Hons), BEng, EngD, PGCert, MEng, MSc, PhD

Faculty of Medical and Veterinary Science; www.bris.ac.uk/mvs

Dept of Biochemistry; www.bris.ac.uk/biochemistry
biochemistry/with molecular biology & biotechnology, medical biochemistry, biomedical sciences

Dept of Cellular and Molecular Medicine; www.bris.ac.uk/cellmolmed
cancer biology, immunology, medical /microbiology, pathology, transfusion & transplantation science, virology, cellular & molecular medicine

Bristol Veterinary School; www.bris.ac.uk/vetscience
animal behaviour & welfare, meat science & technology, veterinary cellular & molecular science, veterinary nursing & bioveterinary science, veterinary science, systems neuroscience, transfusion & transplant science

Dept of Physiology & Pharmacology; www.bris.ac.uk/phys-pharm
cardiovascular science, cell signalling & cell biology, neuroscience, pharmacology, physiological science; BSc(Hons), BVS, MD, MSc, MSci, PhD

Faculty of Medicine and Dentistry; www.bris.ac.uk/fmd

medicine, surgery, dentistry, dental implantology, health care ethics & the law, molecular neuroscience, orthodontics, palliative medicine, reproduction & development, stem cells and regeneration, health professionals; MB, BDS, BSc(Hons), ChB, ChM, DDS, Diploma, DPDS, MClinDent, MD, MMedEd, MSci, PhD

Faculty of Science; www.bris.ac.uk/science

School of Biological Sciences; www.bris.ac.uk/biology
biology, botany, ecology and management of the natural environment, geology, psychology, zoology

School of Chemistry; www.chm.bris.ac.uk/
chemistry, chemical physics, inorganic & materials chemistry, organic & biological chemistry, physical & theoretical chemistry, chemical synthesis

School of Earth Sciences; www.bris.ac.uk/earthsiences
earth sciences, biology, environmental geoscience, geology, palaeobiology & evolution,, science of natural hazards

Dept of Experimental Psychology; www.psychology.psy.bris.ac.uk/
biological psychology, cognition, computational/clinical/applied neuroscience, neuropsychology, psychology & philosophy/zoology, vision sciences

School of Geographical Sciences; www.ggy.bris.ac.uk/
geography, human/physical geography, society & space, science of natural hazards, environmental policy, climate change science & policy

Dept of Mathematics; www.maths.bris.ac.uk/
applied/pure mathematics, economics & mathematics, mathematics, mathematics & philosophy/physics/statistics, statistics, mathematical science, applied/pure mathematics

Dept of Physics; www.bris.ac.uk/physics
astrophysics, astronomy, mathematics and physics, nanoscience & functional nanomaterial particle physics, physics/& philosophy, quantum photonics, theoretical physics; BSc(Hons), DSc, LlB, MRes, MSci, MSc, PhD, UGCert

University of Bristol

Faculty of Social Science and Law; www.bris.ac.uk/fss

Bristol Institute for Public Affairs; www.bris.ac.uk/bipa

Graduate School of Education; www.bris.ac.uk/education

education, education, technology & society, science & education, TESOL, PGCE in range of subjects, special & inclusive education

School for Policy Studies; www.bristol.ac.uk/sps

early/childhood studies, international health, social policy & politics, disability studies, inclusion policy & practice, public policy, social work, sociology

School of Applied Community and Health Studies; www.bris.ac.uk/sachs

Centre for Deaf Studies; Centre for Hearing & Balance Studies; Centre for Personal & Professional Development

audiology, deaf/deafhood studies, counselling, audiological audiological rehabilitation adv clinical audiology

Norah Fry Research Centre

educational psychology, inclusive theory and practice: empowering people with learning disabilities

School of Economics, Finance & Management; www.bristol.ac.uk/efm

accounting, finance, management, econometrics, public policy, investment, strategic management, economics & mathematics/politics/philosophy

School of Law; www.bris.ac.uk/law

law, law and French/ German, socio-legal studies, adv studies legal system

School of Sociology, Politics & international relations; www.bristol.ac.uk/spais

sociology, politics, social policy, philosophy, theology & sociology, contemporary identities, ethnicity & multiculturalism, social & cultural theory, European governance, gender, international relations, international security, development & security, E Asian development & global economy, international development; BA(Hons), BSc(Hons), DSocSci, EdD, LlB, LlD, LlM, MEd, MPhil, MSc, MSci, PCGE, PhD, Dip

UNIVERSITY OF THE WEST OF ENGLAND, BRISTOL
www.uwe.ac.uk

Faculty of Business & Law; www.uwe.ac.uk/bl

Bristol Business School; www.uwe.ac.uk/bbs

business enterprise/management/finance/practice, business studies/with management & finance/economics/HRM/marketing/tourism, coaching & mentoring, international business, professional accounting, banking & finance, applied economics, family business admin, marketing/communications, business & law/management, leadership & management in health & social care, international HRM/business/tourism, coaching & mentoring, social marketing, tourism management; BA(Hons), BSc(Hons), MA, MBA, MSc, PhD

Bristol Law School; www1.uwe.ac.uk/bl/bls

adv legal practice, commercial law, criminology, environmental law & sustainability, European & international law, international banking & financial/trade law, law; LlB, LlM, PhD

Faculty of Arts, Creative Industries & Education; www.uwe.ac.uk/cahe;

Dept of Creative Industries; www,uwe.ac.uk/cahe/creative industries;

animation, art & visual culture, art, media & design by project, creative practices/media, design, drawing & applied art, craft, fashion/textile design, film studies/making & creative media, illustration, media practice & art, fine art, graphic arts, journalism, PR, wildlife filming, photography, printmaking; BA(Hons), FdA, MA, MPhil, PhD

Dept of Education; www1.uwe.ac.uk/cahe/edu

applied social research, careers education, early childhood studies, early years education, education in professional practice, initial teacher education, PGCE primary – early years (3–7)/7–11/ secondary/post-16 training, educational support, inclusive practice, lifelong learning, post-compulsory education, learning & skills; ASR, BA(Hons), CertEd, DipHE, MA, MPhil, MSc, PGCert/Dip, PhD, FD

University of the West of England, Bristol

Dept of Arts; www.uwe.ac.uk/cahe/arts

drama, English, creative writing, English language, history, journalism, philosophy, linguistics, film studies, screenwriting, politics, international relations, media & cultural studies, European philosophy, human rights, intercultural conflict; BA(Hons), MA, Phd

Faculty of Environment and Technology; www.uwe.ac.uk/et

Dept of Computer Science & Creative Technologies; www.uwe.ac.uk/et/cst

audio music tehnology, computer science for games/security/systems integration, computing, creative music technology, digital media, enterprise/forensic computing, IT management for business, information & library management, network system, software engineering, web design; BSc(Hons), MSc, MPhil, PhD

Dept of Construction & Property; www.uwe.ac.uk/et/cp

applied social research, building/quantity surveying, business in property, building services engineering, built & natural environment, commercial/property management, conserving historic environments, construction/project management, housing developments & management, property development & planning/investment, real estate/management,construction law/project management; traffic engineering FDA BA(Hons), BSc(Hons) MSc, MPhil, PhD

Dept of Engineering, Design & Mathematics; www.uwe.ac.uk/et/edm

aerospace engineering/manufacture, computer systems, creative product design, design for smart products, electrical & electronic engineering, engineering, electronics & communications, manufacturing process improvement, mathematics, mechanical engineering, motor sport engineering, product design technology, adv technology in electronics, adv engineering/robotics, machine vision, statistics; BEng, MEng, BSc(Hons), MPhil, PhD

Dept of Geography & Environmental Management; www.uwe.acf.uk/et/gem

civil engineering, geography, environmental management/engineering, tourism/management, planning, climate change & environment management, garden history, river & coastal engineering; BA(Hons), BSc(Hons), GradDip, MPhil, PhD

Dept of Planning & Architecture; www.uwe.ac.uk/et/pa

architecture, architectural technology & design, environment engineering, geography, town & country planning, spatial/transport planning, urban design; BA(Hons), BSc(Hons), BArch, MA, MSc, MPlan, MPhil, PhD

Faculty of Health & Life Sciences; www.uwe.ac.uk/hls

Dept of Allied Health Professions; www.uwe.ac.uk/hls/ahp

diagnostic imaging, paramedic science, veterinary/physiotherapy, health professions, occupational therapy, radiotherapy & oncology, sports therapy & rehabilitation, medical ultrasound, nuclear medicine; FdSc, BSc(Hons), MSc, PGDip/Cert, MPhil, PhD

Dept of Applied Sciences; www.uwe.ac.uk/hls/as

applied/biomedical sciences/(clinical), biological science, cellular pathology, conservation biology, environmental health/science, forensic science/biology/chemistry/photography, healthcare sci, human biology, integrated wildlife conservation, life sciences, physiological science, sport science, biosensing technologies, science communication, medical microbiology, molecular biotechnology, haematology, immunology, cellular pathology, clinical chemistry; FdSc, BSc(Hons), MSc, MRes, ProfDoc, PGCert, MPhil, PhD

Dept of Health & Applied Social Sciences; www.uwe.ac.uk/hls/hass

criminology, criminal justice, sociology, early childhood studies, environmental health, psychology, public health, social work/with adults, working with children, young people & their families, substance misuse, psychosocial studies, leadership & management in health & social services, social work with adults, specialist community public health; FdA, BSc(Hons), BA(Hons), MSc, PGDip/Cert, GradDip, MPhil, PhD

Dept of Nursing & Midwifery; www.uwe.ac.uk/hls/nm

adult/children's/mental health/learning disability nursing, adv practice, community practice, midwifery, health & social care practice, health professions, child & adolescent mental health, clinical research, psychosocial interventions, specialist practice; FdSc, BSc(Hons), MSc, PGDip/Cert, ProfDoc, MPhil, PhD

Dept of Psychology; www.uwe.ac.uk/hls/psychology
psychology, psychology & criminology, law/sociology, health psychology, pscho-social studies, psychological therapy, research methods, counselling, sport & exercise psychology; BA(Hons), BSc(Hons), MSc, DPS, ProfDoc, MPhil, PhD

Hartpury College (Associate Faculty); www.hartpury.ac.uk
agricultural business management, animal behaviour & veterinary science/welfare, animal science, bioveterinary science, conservation & countryside management; equine/business management/dental science/performance/sports science; coaching science, sport & exercise management, sport/events/management/studies/business management/coaching performance, equine veterinary nursing, veterinary nursing science/physiotherapy; BA(Hons), BSc(Hons), FdSc, FdA, MA, MSc, PGDip/Cert

BRUNEL UNIVERSITY
www.brunel.ac.uk

School of Arts; www.brunel.ac.uk/about/acad/sa
contemporary performance making, contemporary literature & culture, performance making, creative writing, digital games theory & design documentary practice, drama, cult film & TV, English/literature/& contemporary drama, games design, campaigning & journalism, international/journalism, performance studies; BA(Hons), BMus, MA, MMus, MPhil, PhD

Brunel Law School; www.brunel.ac.uk/about/acad/bls
law, legal practice, European & international commercial law/financial regulation, & corporate law, intellectual property/economic/international economic & trade, international human rights law, international & comparative criminal justice; CPE, European Masters, GradDip, LlM, LLB, MPhil, PhD

School of Engineering and Design; www.brunel.ac.uk /about/acad/sed
advanced manufacturing systems/engineering design, engineering management, design & innovation/& branding strategy, industrial design & technology, integrated product design, media design, multimedia technology, packing technology, product design/engineering, multimedia design & 3D technologies, computer systems engineering, electrical/electronic/computer engineering & communications, distributed computer systems, renewable energy systems, sustainable electrical power, wireless communication systems, advanced engineering design/mechanical engineering, aerospace/aviation/engineering, aeronautics, automotive & motorsport engineering, biomedical engineering, building services engineering/management, automatic design building services, engineering/management, civil engineering, project & infrastructure studs, sustainable energy/technologies, water engineering; BA(Hons), BEng, BSc(Hons), EngD, MEng, MPhil, MSc, PhD

Brunel Business School; www.brunel.ac.uk/about/acad/bbs
business & management, accounting, aviation management, marketing, international business, corporate brand management, global supply chain management, healthcare management, HRM, HR and employment relations; BSc, MSc, MBA, PhD

School of Health Sciences and Social Care; www.brunel.ac.uk/about/acad/health
biomedical sciences, biochemistry/forensics/genetics/human health/immunology, occupational therapy, physiotherapy, social work, specialist community social work, health promotion and public health, neurorehabilitation, occupational therapy, molecular medicine, hand therapy, youth & community work; BSc, BA, MSc, MA, PGDip, PGCert

School of Information Systems, Computing and Mathematics; www.brunel.ac.uk/about/acad/siscm
artificial intelligence, adv business systems integration, computational mathematics with modelling, computer science, computing, digital media & games, financial computing/maths, information & communication technology in business, mathematics, modelling and management of risk, network computing, software engineering, statistics; BSc, MSc, MTech, PhD

**School of Social Sciences;
www.brunel.ac.uk/about/acad/sss**

accounting, economics, finance, social/anthropology, psychology, sociology, business economics, history, cross cultural evolution/psychology, globalisation & governance, intelligence & security, psychoanalysis, international money/politics/relations, investment, media & communications/studies, modern political theory, public affairs & lobbying, war & conflict, politics, anthropology of childhood, psychology & psychiatry; BA, BSc, MRes, MSc, PhD

**School of Sport and Education;
www.brunel.ac.uk/about/acad/sse**

sport sciences (coaching/human performance/sport development/PE & youth sport), sport psychology, contemporary education, PE, education, PGCE(in range of secondary subjects) information & communication technology, sport & exercise psychology; BA, BSc, MSc, MA, PGCert, EdD, MPhil, PhD

University Specialist Research Institutes offer postgraduate degree opportunities

UNIVERSITY OF BUCKINGHAM
www.buckingham.ac.uk

**Buckingham School of Business;
www.buckingham.ac.uk/business**

accounting, business, business enterprise/administration, communication studies, economics, finance, financial management, investment, international financial services, management, marketing, media communications; BSc(Econ)(Hons), BSc(Hons), CMS, MBA, MSc/Diploma

*School of Humanities;
www.buckingham.ac.uk/humanities*

Dept of Education; www.beds.ac.uk/departments/schoolofeducation/education

Teacher Training: PGCE with QTS, educational leadership, English studies for education; MEd, BA(Hons), MPhil, DPhil

Dept of Economics & International Studies; www.beds.ac.uk/international

biography, business, business/economics, contemporary art & collecting, EFL, English literature, global affairs, heritage management, history, international studies, journalism, law, military history, politics, security & intelligence studies; BA(Hons), BSc(Econ)-Hons, DPhil, MA, MPhil, MSc

Dept of Modern Foreign Languages; www.buckingham.ac.uk/mfl

range of languages taught for part of joint degrees

Dept of English; www.buckingham.ac.uk/english

foundation English, English language/literature, communication studies, media, journalism, biography, English studies for teaching; BA(Hons), MA

**London Programmes;
www.buckingham.ac.uk/london**

biography, decorative arts & historic interiors, garden histories, military history, war studies

*Buckingham Law School;
www.buckingham.ac.uk/law*

law, common law, international & commercial law, joint degrees; Cert/Dip, LlB, LlM

*School of Sciences & Medicine;
www.buckingham.ac.uk/sciences*

School of Medicine; www.buckingham.ac.uk/medicine

graduate entry, PG medical school, general internal medicine, clinical science; Clinical MD, MBBS, MSc

Dept of Applied Computing; www.buckingham.ac.uk/applied computing

applied computing, computing, innovative computing; BSc, Cert Comp, MSc, PGDip, PhD

Dept of Psychology; www.buckingham.ac.uk/psychology

psychology, adult dyslexia; BSc(Hons), MPhil, MSc, PhD

Clore Laboratory; www.buckingham,ac.uk/clore

diabetes, obesity & metabolic research, molecular genetics, biochemistry, bioinformatics, nutrition; DPhil, MPhil, MSc

BUCKINGHAMSHIRE NEW UNIVERSITY
www.bucks.ac.uk

Faculty of Design, Media & Management;
www.bucks.ac.uk/about/structure/academic/faculties/design-media-management
School of Applied Management & Law; www.bucks.ac.uk/about/structure/academic-schools/applied-management-law
School of Design, Craft & Visual Arts; www.bucks.ac.uk/about/structure/academic_schools/design-craft-visual-arts
www.bucks.ac.uk/about/structure/academic_schools/music-entertainment-image

Faculty of Society and Health;
www.bucks.ac.uk/about/structure/faculties/society-and-health
School of Social Sciences, Primary Care & Education; www.bucks.ac.uk/about/structure/academic_schools/social-care-education
School of Advanced and Continuing Practice; www.bucks.ac.uk/about/structure/academic_schools/advanced-continuing-practice
School of Pre-qualifying Nursing; www.bucks.ac.uk/about/structure/academic_schools/pre-registration-nursing

first and postgraduate degrees are offered in the following academic areas of study: audio music production, art & design, business & management, children & young people, computing technology & new media, drama & performance, education, furniture, health & nursing, law, media production, music & event management, security & safety, social science, social work, sport & fitness, travel & aviation

BA(Hons), BSc(Hons), Certs, DMS, GradDip, FD, HNC, HND, LlB(Hons), LlM, MA, MBA, MCommunMan, MSc, PhD, FD

UNIVERSITY OF CAMBRIDGE
www.cam.ac.uk

Arts and Humanities;
www.csah.cam.ac.uk

Faculty of Architecture and History of Art; www.aha.cam.ac.uk
architecture, British architecture, building history, history of art, medieval art & architecture, Renaissance art & architecture, sustainable building, conflict in the city, 20th-century art & theory, western & non-western cultural exchange; BA, MPhil, MSt, PhD

Faculty of Asian & Middle Eastern Studies; www.ames.cam.ac.uk
Chinese studies, Hebrew and Semitic studies, Japanese studies, Korean studies, Arabic & Persian studies, East Asia, Southern Asia studies, Assyriology, Egyptology; BA, MPhil, PhD

Faculty of Classics; www.classics.cam.ac.uk;
classics & Latin literature, history, philology and linguistics, philosophy; BA, MPhil, PGCE

Faculty of Divinity; www.divinity.cam.ac.uk
biblical studies, church history, historical & systematic theology, religious studies & the philosophy of religion, the Christian tradition, world religions, New Testament, patristics; BA, MPhil, PhD, PGDip

Faculty of English; www.english.cam.ac.uk
American literature, Anglo-Saxon, Norse & Celtic, English & applied linguistics, medieval/English literature, European languages & literatures, English studies: criticism & culture/18th-century & romantic

studies; language for literature; BA, MLitt, MPhil, PhD

Faculty of Modern and Medieval Languages; www.mml.cam.ac.uk
Depts of French, German & Dutch, Italian, Spanish & Portuguese, European literature, linguistics, modern Greek, neo-Latin, Polish, Russian studies, screen & media cultures, Slavonic studies, Ukrainian; BA, MPhil, PhDE

Faculty of Music; www.mus.cam.ac.uk
ethnomusicology, music studies, music/with education studies, analysis, jazz & pop music, performance studies, recitals, tonal compositions & analysis & repertoire, musical composition, choral studies; BA, MPhil, PhD, MMusD

Faculty of Philosophy; www.phil.cam.ac
ethics, experimental psychology, history of philosophy, logic, metaphysics, philosophy of science, political philosophy, aesthetics, mathematical logic, ancient philosophy; BA, MPhil, PhD

Humanities & Social Sciences; www.cshss.cam.ac.uk

Faculty of Human, Social & Political Science
Dept of Archaeology and Anthropology; www.hsps.cam.ac.uk
archaeological heritage & museum/science, Aegean prehistory, archaeology, archaeology of the Americas, biological anthropology, Egyptian archaeology, Egyptology, Assyriology, European prehistory, human evolutionary studies, medieval archaeology/Britain, Mesopotamian studies, palaeolithic & mesolithic archaeology, social anthropology, south Asian archaeology; BA, MPhil, PhD

Dept of Politics & International Studies; www.hsps.cam.ac.uk

Centre of Latin American Studies; www.latin-america.cam.ac.uk
economic issues in contemporary Latin America, history of South American external relations, Latin American literary culture/film and visual arts, race & ethnicity/anthropology/sociology & politics in Latin America; MPhil, PhD

Centre of African Studies; www.africa.cam.ac.uk
African studies; MPhil

Centre of South Asian Studies
modern South Asian studies; MPhil

Centre of Development Studies; www.devstudies.cam.ac.uk
development studies; MPhil

Dept of Social Sciences

Sociology; www.sociology.cam.ac.uk
sociology, modern society & global transformations; BA, MPhil, PhD

Social and Developmental Psychology; www.sdp.cam.ac.uk
psychology, social and developmental psychology

Centre for Family Research; www.cfr.cam.ac.uk
bioethics & the family, early social development & the family, genetics, health & families, non-traditional families, parent, children & family relationships; MPhil, PhD

The Pyschometrics Centre; www.psychometrics.cam.ac.uk MPhil, PhD

Faculty of Economics; www.econ.cam.ac.uk
asset pricing, behavioural economics, economic theory, finance, microeconomics, quantitative methods, microeconomics, macroeconomics, macroeconometrics, economics; BA, Diploma, MPhil, PhD

Faculty of Education; www.educ.cam.ac.uk
arts culture & education, counselling, children & literature, education, educational leadership & school improvement, educational diversity & inclusion, language communication & literacy, mathematics education, PGCE; early years, primary, secondary; BA, MEd, PGCE, PGDip/Cert, PhD

Faculty of History; www.hist.cam.ac.uk
American history, British/early modern history, economic, social & cultural history, European history, ancient & medieval history, political thought & intellectual history, world history; BA, MPhil, PhD

History and Philosophy of Science; www.hps.cam.ac.uk
philosophy of science, history of ancient & medieval/early modern science, technology & medicine, history, philosophy & sociology of the lifesciences/physical & mathematical sciences/social & psychological sciences/medicine, ethics & politics of science; BA, MPhil, PhD

Faculty of Law; www.law.cam.ac.uk
criminological research, criminology, international law, law, legal studies, large range of legal topics at Master level; BA, Diploma, LLD, LLM, MLitt, MPhil, PhD

Institute of Criminology; www.crim.cam.ac
applied/criminology, penology & management, applied criminology & police management; MPhil, MSt, PhD

School of Biological Sciences;
www.cam.ac.uk/sbs

Faculty of Biology; www.cam.ac.uk

Biochemistry; www.bio.cam.ac.uk
biology of cells, evolution & behaviour, biochemistry & molecular biology

Experimental Psychology; www.psych.cam.ac.uk
psychology & human behaviour, experimental psychology, neurobiology/science

Genetics; www.gen.cam.ac.uk
mathematical biology, molecules in medical science, cells & developmental biology, genetics, ecology, systems biology

Pathology; www.path.cam.ac.uk
graduate clinical course in medicine

Pharmacology; www.pha.ca.ac.uk
pharmacology, medicinal chemistry

Physiology, Development & Neuroscience; www.pdn.cam.ac.uk
biological & biomedical sciences, physiology, neuroscience, neurobiology, developmental biology, stem cell biology

Plant Science; www/pplant.cam.ac.uk
plant science, cell & developmental biology, ecology, plant & microbiogical science

Zoology; www.zoo.cam.ac.uk
animal biology, cell & developmental biology, ecology, zoology; BA, MPhil, PhD

Faculty of Veterinary Medicine

Department of Veterinary Medicine; www.vet.cam.ac.uk
Clinical Course: veterinary science, preclinical course; MPhil, VetMB

Wellcome Trust Centre for Stem Cell Research; www.cscr.cam.ac.uk
stem cell biology; PhD

Wellcome Trust/Cancer Research UK Gurdon InstituteTechnology; www.gurdon.cam.ac.uk
cellular & molecular biology, developmental, cell & cancer biology; PhD

School of Technology; www.tech.ac.uk

Faculty of Engineering; www.eng.cam.ac.uk
energy, fluid mechanics & turbomechanics, materials design, civil, structural and environmental engineering, manufacture & management, information engineering, engineering for life sciences; BA(Hons), MEng, MPhil, PhD

Faculty of Business & Management (Judge Business School); www.jbs.cam.ac.uk
courses include: finance & accounting, management science, operations, information, marketing; MBA, MFin

Computer Laboratory; www.clcam.ac.uk
adv/computer science, network architecture, internet user interface, forensic signal analysis, language processing, embedded systems, programming logic etc; BA, MPhil, PhD

Department of Chemical Engineering & Biotechnology; www.ceb.cam.ac.uk
advanced chemical engineering, biotechnology, measurement, microstructure engineering, modelling, processes; BA/MEng, MPhil, PhD

Cambridge Programme for Sustainability Leadership; www.cpi.cam.ac.uk
sustainable business, sustainability leadership, health care services, built environment; MSt, PGCert

School of Physical Sciences;
www.physci.cam.ac.uk

Faculty of Earth Sciences & Geography; www.physci.cam.ac.uk

Dept of Earth Sciences; www.esc.cam.ac.uk
earth sciences, environment, environmental science, palaeontology, geological sciences, climate change, tectonics, minerals physics/science, palaeobiology, volcanic studies, petrology; BA, MPhil, PhD

Dept of Geography; www.geog.cam.ac.uk (inc Scott Polar Research Institute)
geography, earth's atmosphere, glacial environments, volcanology, physical geography, polar science, environmental science, environment & development; BA, MPhil, PhD

Faculty of Mathematics; wwwmaths.cam.ac.uk

Dept of Applied Mathematics & Theoretical Physics; www.physci.cam.ac.uk/about the school/dampt
mathematical science, quantum mechanics, relativity, fluid dynamics, numerical analysis

Dept of Pure Mathematics & Mathematical Statistics;
pure mathematics & mathematical statistics, statistical science; BA, MPhil, PhD, MMath, MAdvStud

Faculty of Physics & Chemistry;
www.cam.ac.uk/physchemfaculty

Institute of Astronomy; www.ast.cam.ac.uk
theoretical & observational astronomy

Dept of Chemistry; www.ch.cam.ac.uk
physical, theoretical, organic, inorganic biochemistry, synthesis, materials chemistry, chemistry

Dept of Material Science & Metallurgy; www.physci.cam.ac.uk/aboutthe school/materialsscience
materials science, metals, alloys, ceramics, polymers, semiconducting/magenetic/superconducting/ferro-electric/biomedical materials, composites

Dept of Physics; www.phyi.cam.ac.uk
experimental & theoretical physics, astrophysics, scientific computing, nanoscience & technology, atomic/high energy/quantum & condensed matter/thin film magnetism; BA, MPhil, MSci, PhD

School of Clinical Medicine; www.medschl.cam.ac.uk

Dept of Clinical Biochemistry (Metabolic Research Laboratories); www.clbc.cam.ac.uk
biomedical research, diabetes, molecular cell biology of membrane traffic pathways, obesity & other related endocrine and metabolic disorders; PhD

Dept of Clinical Neurosciences (Cambridge Centre for Brain Repair; Neurology Unit; Neurosurgery; Wolfson Brain Imaging Centre);
www.neurosciences.medschl.am.ac.uk
brain repair, neurology, neurosurgery, brain imaging; MB/PhD

Dept of Haematology; www.haem.cam.ac.uk
transfusion medicine diagnostics development; PhD

Dept of Medical Genetics; www.cimr.cam.ac.uk/medgen
genetics of inflammatory disorders, juvenile diabetes, autoimmune liver disease; BChir, MB, MD, PhD

Dept of Medicine; www.med.cam.ac.uk
anasthesia, clinical pharmacology
Obstetrics & Gynaecology
Oncology
Paediatrics
Psychiatry
brain mapping, developmental psychiatry
Public Health & Primary Care
general practice & primary care research, clinical gerentology
Radiology
Surgery
orthopaedic research

CAMBRIDGE INTERNATIONAL COLLEGE
www.cambridgecollege.ac.uk

business/financial/project/HR/logistics administration, commerce, hospitality (many courses at non-graduate level), BA, Diplomas, AMBA

CANTERBURY CHRIST CHURCH UNIVERSITY
www.canterbury.ac.uk

Faculty of Arts and Humanities; www.canterbury.ac.uk/arts-humanities

English & Language Studies;
www.canterbury.ac.uk/arts-humanities/english-language-studies/
English/literature/language & communication, children's literature, creative writing, Victorian & modern literature, TESOL, TEAL, applied linguistics

History & American Studies;
www.canterbury.ac.uk/arts-humanities/history-and-american-studies/Home.aspx
American studies, Canadian studies, archaeology, history

Media, Art & Design;
www.canterbury.ac.uk/arts-humanities/
MediaArtAndDesign/home.aspx

digital media, film, radio & TV, multimedia journalism, graphic design, web design, fine & applied arts, fine arts/ceramics, media & communication, cultural studies, PR, media marketing, photography, multimedia design, video production

Music; www.canterbury.ac.uk/arts-humanities/Music/departmenthome/Home.aspx

access to music, commercial music production, creative music technology, performing arts, church music

Theology & Religious Studies;
www.canterbury.ac.uk/arts-humanities/
theology-and-religious-studies/
Home.aspx

theology, religious studies;
BA, BSC, MA, MPhil, PhD, PGDip, FD, MMus

Faculty of Education;
www.canterbury.ac.uk/ education

early/childhood studies, careers guidance, early years/professional status/studies, educational studies, enabling learning, leadership & management for learning, lifelong learning, literacy & learning, religion in education, teaching skills for life – numeracy, literacy/ESOL, PGCE, primary teaching, post-compulsory primary education, teaching & learning, modular (primary/secondary), PE, RE, post-primary education, professional development, supervision studies, sport & exercise science; BA(Hons), EdD, EYPS, FDA, MA, MPhil/PhD

Faculty of Health and Social Care;
www.canterbury.ac.uk/health/home

Department of Allied Health Professions;
www.canterbury.ac.uk/health/allied-health-professions

advanced/occupational therapy, clinical reporting, diagnostic radiography, interprofessional health & social care, medical imaging, operating dept practice, ophthamic dispensing, paramedic science, speech & language therapy

Centre for Health and Social Care Research; www.canterbury.ac.uk/health/health-social-care-research

Dementia Services Development Centre South East; www.dementiacentre.canterbury.ac.uk

mental health, public health

Dept of Health, Well-being & the Family;
www.canterbury.ac.uk/health

midwifery, advanced practice, child nursing, health studies, (health promotion, public health, mental health/practice/nursing), interprofessional health & social care, play therapy, dance movement therapy, social work, children & families

Department of Nursing and Applied Clinical Studies; www.canterbury.ac.uk/health/nursing-applied-clinical-studies

adult nursing, acute care, advanced nursing practice, cancer care, practice development/education, interprofessional health & social care, public health nursing, workforce analysis & development, optical dispensing

Sidney De Haan Research Centre;
www.canterbury.ac.uk/research/centre/SDHR

singing & mental health, singing & dementia projects, arts & health

Faculty of Social and Applied Sciences;
www.canterbury.ac.uk/social applied-science

Dept of Applied Psychology;
www.canterbury.ac.uk/social-applied-sciences/aspd

cognitive behavioural therapy and psychological wellbeing practice, psychology/arts & health

Dept of Applied Social Science;
www.canterbury.ac.uk/social-applied-sciences

global governance, politics & governance/ international relations, sociology & social science, psychology

Faculty of Business and Management;
www.canterbury.ac.uk/business-management

The Business School;
www.canterbury.ac.uk/business-management/business-school

accounting & finance, advertising management, arts management, business management/administration, education/health & social care leadership & management, economics, entrepreneurship, HRM, management studies, marketing, organisational behaviour, strategy management

Centre for Leadership & Management; www.canterbury.ac.uk/business-management/CLMD

coaching, leadership development, organizational development, personal effectiveness, project management, recruitment and selection, team dev, strategic leadership; BSc(Hons), MA, MBA, MPhil/PhD, MSc, PGDip/Cert

Centre for Entrepreneurship & Innovation; www.canterbury.ac.uk/business-management/CEI

Dept of Computing; www.canterbury.ac.uk/social-applied-sciences/computing

business computing, computing, cybercrime forensics, forensic computing, internet computing

The Department of Law and Criminal Justice Studies; www.canterbury.ac.uk/social-applied-sciences/crime-and-policing

law & legal studies, applied criminology, crime & policing/policing studies, forensic investigation

Dept of Geographical and Life Sciences; www.canterbury.ac.uk/social-applied-sciences/geographical-and-life-sciences

conservation, environmental biology/science, geography, integrated science, urban and regional studies, GIS

Dept of Sports Science, Tourism and Leisure; www.canterbury.ac.uk/social-applied-sciences/sport-science-tourism-and-leisure

sport & exercise science/exercise psychology, leisure management, tourism and leisure studies, tourism management, physical education & sport; BA/BSc, MBA, MSc, MA, Adv Dip, Grad Cert, PGDip, FD

CARDIFF UNIVERSITY
www.cardiff.ac.uk

Welsh School of Architecture; www.cardiff.ac.uk/archi

architectural studies, environmental design of buildings, sustainable energy & environment, urban design, sustainable design, professional studies, building, energy & environment, performance modelling; BSc, DipProfStudies, MA, MArch, MPhil, MSc, PhD

School of Biosciences; www.cardiff.ac.uk/bios

biochemistry, biology, biomedical science – anatomy/neuroscience/physiology, biotechnology, ecology, dental hygiene/therapy, medical pharmacy, biophotonics, genetics, microbiology, medicine, medical pharmacology, molecular biology, tissue engineering, zoology; BSc(Hons), MRes, MSc, PhD, BDS, MBBCh

Cardiff Business School; www.cardiff.ac.uk/carbs

accounting, banking, business administration, economics, business management – HR, international/logistics & operations management, marketing, economics, finance, financial economics, HRM, international transport, lean operations, marine policy, marketing, port and shipping administration, public /policy/administration, strategic marketing; BSc, BScEcon, MBA, MPA, MSc, PhD

School of Chemistry; www.cardiff.ac.uk/chemy

chemical biology, chemistry, chemistry with physics/industrial experience, catalytic science, inorganic chemistry, organic synthesis, physical organic chemistry, solid state and materials chemistry, molecular modelling, sustainable chemistry, theoretical and computational chemistry; BSc, MChem, MPhil, PhD

School of City & Regional Planning; www.cardiff.ac.uk/c/plan

city & regional planning, geography (human) & planning, geology, international planning, regeneration studies, sustainability, planning/practice, planning & development transport planning, urban design, housing, regeneration studies; BSc, MSc, PhD

School of Computer Science & Information; www.cardiff.cs.cf.ac.uk

computer science/with high performance/security & forensics, information business systems, computer systems engineering, visual computing, software engineering, information security & privacy, strategic information systems, IT management; BSc, MSc, PhD

School of Dentistry; www.cardiff.ac.uk/denti

dental surgery, conscious sedation, dental therapy & hygiene, implantology, orthodontics, tissue engineering; BDS, BSc(Hons), MClinDent, MD, MPhil, MSc, PhD

School of Earth and Ocean Sciences; www.cardiff.ac.uk/earth

applied environmental geology, earth sciences, environmental geoscience/hydrogeology, exploration & resource geology, geobiology, geology, marine geography; BSc, MESc, MPhil, MSc, PhD

School of Engineering; www.cardiff.ac.uk/engin

architectural/civil/environmental/clinical engineering, computer systems, electrical and electronic engineering, electrical energy systems, electronic and geoenvironmental/integrated engineering, mechanical/medical/orthopaedic/structural engineering, sustainable energy & environment, electroenergy engineering, hydroenvironmental engineering, wireless & microwave communications; BEng, EngD, MEng, MPhil, MSc, PhD

School of English, Communication & Philosophy; www.cardiff.ac.uk/encap

applied linguistics, creative writing, critical & cultural theory, analytic & modern mid-European philosophy, English language/literature, ethics & social philosophy, forensic linguistics, language & communication, philosophy, analytic mid-European philosophy; BA, Diploma, MA/Dip, MPhil, PhD

School of European Studies; www.cardiff.ac.uk/euros

French, German, Spanish, Italian, European/European Union studies, European governanace & public policy, international relations, political theory, law, politics, translation studies, politics & public policy, Welsh politics & government; BA, BScEcon, LlB, MA, MScEcon, MPhil, PhD

School of Healthcare Studies; www.cardiff.ac.uk/sohcs

healthcare science, intra & perioperative practice, medical illustration, image appreciation, neuro-musculoskeletal physiotherapy, occupation & health, occupational therapy, operating department practice, physiotherapy, radiography & imaging, diagnostic/radiotherapy & oncology, sports physiotherapy, surgical care practice; CertHE, DipHE, MPhil, MSc, PGDip/Cert, PhD

School of History, Archaeology & Religion; www.cardiff.ac.uk/share

ancient/& medieval history, archaeology, conservation, history & archaeology of the Greek and Roman world, Byzantine studies, late antique & history of the Crusades, medieval British studies/history, political & modern history, Welsh history, religious & theological studies, Christian doctrine/ethics, Islamic contemporary Britain, church history, chaplaincy studies; BA, BSc, MA, MPhil, MSc, PhD

Journalism, Media and Cultural Studies; www.cardiff.ac.uk/jomec

international journalism, PR/political/global communication, science, media & communication, media management, journalism, media & cultural studies; BA, MA, MPhil, MSc, PGDip, PhD

School of Law; www.law.cf.ac.uk

canon law, commercial law, European legal studies, governance & devolution, law & governance of European legal & political aspects of international affairs, medical practice, social care law, human rights, medical practice, international commercial law, law & social care, governance development, law; LlB, LlM, MPhil, PhD

Centre for Lifelong Learning; www.cardiff.ac.uk/learn/

languages, business & management, computer studies, law, science & environment, social studies

School of Mathematics; www.cardiff.ac.uk/maths

applied statistics, mathematics/& its applications, numerical analysis, operational research & statistics and risk; BSc, MMath, MPhil, MSc, PhD

School of Medicine; www.cardiff.ac.uk/medic

advanced surgical practice, geriatric medicine, intensive care medicine, public health, genetics, medical pharmacology, medicine, obstetrics & gynaecology, occupational health, oncology, paediatrics, pain management, palliative medicine, pharmacology, psychiatric medicine, public health, ultrasound, therapeutics & toxology, psychiatry, therapeutics, wound healing; MBBCh, MD, MPH, MPhil, MSc/PGDip/Cert, PhD

School of Music; www.cardiff.ac.uk/music

composition, ethnomusicology, music, musicology, music, culture & politics, performance studies; BA/BMus, MA, MMus, PhD

School of Nursing & Midwifery Studies;
www.cardiff.ac.uk/sonims
adult/child/community public health nursing, advanced/clinical/community practice, health studies, independent prescribing, mental health, midwifery, non-medical prescribing, nursing children and young people with cancer; BMid, BN, BSc(Hons), DipHE, DNurs, DocProf, MPhil, MSc, PGDip/Cert, PhD

School of Optometry & Vision Sciences;
www.cardiff.ac.uk/optom
clinical optometry, vision sciences, optometry, visual neuroscience & molecular biology, structural biophysics; BSc, MPhil, PhD

School of Pharmacy; www.cardiff.ac.uk/phring
clinical pharmacy, clinical research/practice, community pharmacy, health economics, non-medical prescribing, pharmaceutical medicine, pharmacy, pharmacology, international pharmacological economics; Dipl, MPharm, MPhil, MSc, PhD

School of Physics and Astronomy;
www.astro.cardiff.ac.uk
astrophysics, biophotonics, physics, medical physics, astronomy, theoretical and computational physics; BSc, MPhil, MPhys, PhD

Postgraduate Medical and Dental Education; www.cardiff.ac.uk/pgmde
paediatric/emergency medication, paediatric intensive care, obstetrics & gynaecology

School of Psychology; www.cardiff.ac.uk/psych
clinical/educational psychology, neuroimaging, cognitive behavioural theory, psychology; BSc, DEdPsych, DClinPsych, GradDip, PhD

School of Social Sciences;
www.cardiff.ac.uk/socsci
criminal justice, criminology, education, equality and diversity, science, media & communications, social policy/work, sociology; BA, BSc, DHS, DSW, EdD, MA, MSc, PGCE

School of Welsh; www.cardiff.ac.uk/welsh
into to/Welsh, Welsh history/literature, early Celtic studies, medieval British studies, Wales & its culture; BA, MA, PhD

CARDIFF METROPOLITAN UNIVERSITY
www.cardiffmet.ac.uk

Cardiff School of Art & Design;
www.csad.cardiffmet.uwic.ac.uk
advanced/product design, architectural design & technology, art & design/communication, ceramics, design, environmental change & practice: building, fine art, textiles, graphic communication, illustration, maker: artist designer, product design/management; BA, BSc, HNC, HND, MA, MFA, MPhil, MSc, MDes, PGCert, PhD

Cardiff School of Education;
www3.cardiffmet.ac.uk/English/education

Dept of Humanities;
www3.cardiffmet.ac.uk/English/education/humanities
educational studies with early childhood studies/English/psychology/sport & physical activity/Welsh, English & contemporary media/drama/creative writing; BA, MA, PGCert, PGDip

Dept of Professional Development;
www3.cardiffmet.ac.uk/English/education/profdevelopment
education, management in the community professions, youth & community work, CPD framework, learning support; BA, MA, MPhil, MSc, PhD, CertEd, FdD, PGCE

Dept of Teacher Education & Training; PGCE (primary, secondary), secondary music/Welsh; BA, PGCE

Cardiff School of Health Sciences;
www3.cardiffmet.ac.uk/English/health

Centre for Applied Social Sciences;
www3.cardiffmet.ac.uk/English/health/ass
health & social care, housing: policy & practice/supported housing, youth & community, management in the community professions, health & social science res, social work; BA, BSc, FdSc, GradCert, GradDip, HNC, HND, MRes, MSc PGCert, PGDip

Institute of Biomedical Science;
www3.cardiffmet.ac.uk/English/
StudyAtUWIC/Courses/Pages/
CareerBiomedical

applied/biomedical sciences, healthcare science, sports biomedicine & nutrition; BSc, FdSc, HNC, HND, MSc, PGCert/Dip

Centre for Complementary Therapies;
www3.cardiffmet.ac.uk/English/health/
cct

complementary therapies, aromatherapy, reflexology, holistic massage; BSc, Dip/Cert

Centre for Dental Technology;
www3.cardiffmet.ac.uk/English/health/
cdt

dental technology; BSc, FdSc, MSc, PGCert, PGDip

Centre for Nutrition, Dietetics & Food Sciences; www3.cardiffmet.ac.uk/English/
health/cnfc

applied public health, dietetics, food science & technology, human nutrition, public health nutrition, sports biomedicine & management/nutrition, food science & technology/safety management; BSc, FdSc, HNC, MSc, PGDip

Dept of Applied Psychology;
www3.cardiffmet.ac.uk/English/health/cp

forensic/health psychology, psychology; BSc, FdSc, MSc

Centre for Environmental Health & Public Protection; www3.cardiffmet.ac.uk/
English/health/cpp

applied public health, environmental health/risk management, health science, occupational health, safety, & wellbeing, waste management; BSc, FdSc, HNC, MSc, PGDip

Centre for Speech & Language Therapy;
www3.cardiffmet.ac.uk/English/health/
cslt

speech & language therapy; BSc

Wales Centre for Podiatric Studies;
www3.cardiffmet.ac.uk/English/health/
wcps

musculoskeletal studies, podiatry, adv/therapeutic footware; BSc, MSc, PGCert, PGDip

Cardiff School of Management;
www3.cardiffmet.ac.uk/English/
management

Business & Management;
www3.cardiffmet.ac.uk/English/Cardiff-
School-of-Management/Business-and-
Management/Pages/Home.aspx

business administration/studies, business & management, management, health sector management, international business management/administration, marketing, project development management; BA, HND, MBA, MSc

Accounting, Economics & Finance;
www3.cardiffmet.ac.uk/English/Cardiff-
School-of-Management/Accounting-
Economics-Finance/Pages/Home.aspx

accounting, finance, business economics, economics, financial management, finance & information management, international economics & finance; BA, BSc, FdA, MSc

Computing & Information Systems

business information systems/technology, computing, software development, information & communication project technology management, computing, management & technology, mobile technology, software development, technology project management, international business management/adminstration; BSc, HNC, HND, MSc

Tourism, Hospitality & Events Management;
www3.cardiffmet.ac.uk/English/Cardiff-
School-of-Management/Tourism-
Hospitality-Events-Management/Pages/
Home.aspx

events management/marketing management, international tourism/events hospitality marketing/sports tourism management; BA, FdA, HNC, HND, MSc, PGCert, PGDip

Cardiff School of Sport;
www3.cardiffmet.ac.uk/English/sport

applied sports coaching, dance, performance analysis, physical activity & health, sports coaching/development, sport & exercise science, sport psychology, sport & PE/conditioning/leadership, rehabilitation & massage, sport, body & society; BA(Hons), BSc(Hons), MA, MSc, PGDip/Cert

UNIVERSITY OF CENTRAL LANCASHIRE
www.uclan.ac.uk

School of Art, Design & Performance; www.uclan.ac.uk/schools/adp
acting, animation, antiques, arts health, art & design, ceramics, computer games, contemporary theatre & performance/crafts, creative thinking, dance, performance, & teaching, fine art/studio practice, consumer product design, contemporary visual arts, drawing, design enterprise, digital design for fashion/graphics, Eastern/fashion design, drawing, fashion brand management/promotion, games design, children's/ books/illustration, interior design, music production/ theatre, performance, product design, surface pattern, textiles; MA, MBA, MPhil, PGCert/Dip, PhD, UniCert

School of Built & Natural Environment; www.uclan.ac.uk/schools/built_natural_environment
architecture/technology, building conservation & regeneration, building services & sustainable engineering, building/quantity surveying, construction law, construction/project management, construction economics/facilities management, environment hazards/management, project management, geography, sustainable energy/waste management; BSc(Hons), BA(Hons), FdSc, PGDip/Cert, MSc

School of Computing, Engineering & Physical Sciences; www.uclan.ac.uk/schools/computing_engineering_physical
computing: computer games/networks, computing, database systems, forensic computing, information systems, IT security, mobile interactive technology, multimedia/games development, network computing, renewable/wind energy engineering, software engineering
engineering: electronic computing, robotics & mechatronics, digital computing/signal & image processing, electronic design automation, engineering development, computer-aided engineering; motorsports/ engineering, mechanical maintenance engineering, renewable energy engineering; nuclear engineering
physics & mathematics: mathematics, physics, astrophysics, astronomy; BSc(Hons), BEng(Hons), MPhys, MSc, FdSc, MPhil, PhD

School of Dentistry, & Institute for Postgraduate Dental Education; www.uclan.ac.uk/health/schools/dentistry_at_uclan/
dental surgery, dentistry, endodontology, oral surgery, orthodontic therapy, continuous professional development; BDS, CertHE, MSc, PGDip, Adv Cert

School of Education and Social Sciences; www.uclan.ac.uk/schools/education_social_sciences
lifelong learning, adult literacy, British sign language, ESOL, children, schools & families, community leadership/safety, criminal justice, criminology, deaf studies, ethnicity & human rights, education studies, history, museums & heritage, history, Islamic studies, modern world history, philosophy, public services, religion, culture & society, sociology, volunteering & community action, professional practice in education/ children & young people, promoting equality & managing diversity;
BA(Hons), BSc(Hons),MA, MSc, PGcert/Dip, DipHE, UnivCert

School of Forensic & investigative Sciences; www.uclan.ac.uk/schools/forensic.investigative
archaeology of death, osteoarchaeology, chemistry, toxicology, instrumented analysis, synthorganic chemistry, fire & disaster studies/rescue services, fire engineering/investigation, scene investigation, safety engineering, forensic science/anthropology, policing, airport security, counter-terrorism, DNA profiling; BA(Hons), BEng, BSc(Hons), FdSc, MPhil, PhD

School of Health; www.uclan.ac.uk/schools/school of health
nursing, mental health, paramedic practice, operating dept practice, physiotherapy, complementary medicine, counselling, health information, occupational therapy, sexual health, professional practice, midwifery; BA(Hons), BSc(Hons), MA, MPhil, PGDip/ Cert, PhD

School of Journalism, Media and Communication; www.uclan.ac.uk/schools/journalism_media_communication
journalism (international, magazine, newspaper), communication, film/production/studies, film &

media, web & multimedia, screenwriting, scriptwriting, digital, media management/technology, photography, English language/literature & linguistics, creative writing, play writing, publishing, rhetorics, TV production, web & multimedia, writing for children; BSc(Hons), BA(Hons), MA, MPhil, PGDip, PGCert, PhD

Lancashire Business School; www.uclan.ac.uk/schools/lbs

accounting, advertising, finance, business/administration, management/studies, business project management, economics, economic management, financial management/analysis, global business, HRM, international business, investment, logistics & supply chain management/operations, marketing management/communications, strategic communications/marketing, oil & gas operations management, PR & communications, retail management; BA(Hons), DBA, MA, MBA, MSC, PGDip/Cert

Lancashire Law School; www.uclan.ac.uk/schools/lancashire_law_school

advanced legal practice, employment/European business law, forensic & legal medicine, human rights law, criminology, senior status, legal practice, medical law & bioethics; BA(Hons), BA/BSc, LlB, LLM, MA, MPhil, PGDip

School of Languages and International Studies; www.uclan.ac.uk/schools/languages_and_international

business English, Arabic, French, German, Japanese, international business English, English for foreigners, modern foreign languages, interpretation & translation, TESOL; BA(Hons), MPhil, PhD

School of Pharmacy and Biomedical Sciences; www.uclan.ac.uk/schools/pharmacy

appl biomolecular sciences – biotechnology/clinical sciences/medicinal chemistry, pharmaceutics, biological sciences, healthcare science, pharmacy, physiology, cancer biology & therapy, clinical pharmacy practice, industrial pharmaceutics; BSc(Hons), MPharm, MSc, PGDip/Cert, PhD

School of Psychology; www.uclan.ac.uk/schools/psychology

applied/psychology, criminology, forensic psychology, child development, social psychology, sport & exercise psychology, health psychology, neuropsychology; BSc(Hons), GradDip, MSc

School of Social Work; www.uclan.ac.uk/health/schools/school_of_social_work/

child health & welfare/practice, safeguarding children, social policy/work, social work practice (adults); BA(Hons), MA, PGCert

School of Sport, Tourism and the Outdoors; www.uclan.ac.uk/management/ssto

adventure sports coaching, event management, exercise & fitness management, hospitality/international hospitality management, nutrition & food science, PE & school sport, international tourism management, nutrition & exercise science (human nutrition/personal fitness training) outDoor leadership, physiotherapy, sport & exercise physiology, sport development/coaching/development/studies/business management/therapy/marketing, strength & conditioning, elite performance, food quality & safety management, hazard analysis, international festivals & tourism management, sport & exercise biomechanics, management of long-term conditions; BSc(Hons), FdA, BA(Hons), Cert, MSc, PGDip/Cert, MA

UNIVERSITY OF CHESTER
www.chester.ac.uk

Faculty of Applied Sciences; www.chester.ac.uk/faculties#A

Dept of Biological Sciences; www.chester.ac.uk/biology

animal behaviour, animal/zoo management, biomedical sciences, biology, conservation & ecology, wildlife conservation, forensic biology; BSc, MSc, PhD

Computer Science and Information Systems; www.chester.ac.uk/csis

computer science, computing, digital technology/media, e-business, internet, information systems/management, multimedia technology, programming, information systems, web-based technology; BSc(Hons), MPhil, PhD, FD

Dept of Mathematics; www.chester.ac.uk/maths; mathematics

Dept of Clinical Science; www.chester.ac.uk/cens; cardiovascular rehabilitation, exercise & nutrition science, weight management, human nutrition, nutrition & dietetics, osteopathy, public health; MSc, PhD, MPhil

Centre for Public Health Research; www.chester.ac.uk/cphr public health, research methods; MSc

Centre for Science Communication

Centre for Research into Sport & Society; www.chester.ac.uk/scicom; sociology of sport & exercise; MSc, PhD

Dept of Sport & Exercise Science; www.chester.ac.uk/sport sport science/development, sport coaching, fitness health, sport & exercise science; BA, BSc, MSc

Faculty of Arts & Media; www.chester.ac.uk/faculties#B

Dept of Art & Design; www.chester.ac.uk/art & design; fine art, graphic design, design, photography; BA(Hons), MA, MSc

Dept of Media; www.chester.ac.uk/media advertising, commercial music production, digital photography, radio/TV production, film studies, sports/journalism, media studies; BA(Hons)

Dept of Performing Arts; www.chester.ac.uk/departments/performing-arts drama, dance & music, pop music, performance practice; BA(Hons), MA

Faculty of Business, Enterprise & Lifelong Learning; www.chester.ac.uk/faculties#C

Chester Business School; www.chester.ac.uk/chester-business-school business administration/management/studies, business & management development, accounting, entrepreneurship, information systems, international business, finance, HRM, management, marketing, PR, tourism & events management, tourism management, strategy; BA(Hons), BA/BSc, FdA, MBA, MPhil, PhD

Centre for Work Related Studies; Professional Development Unit; Work Based Learning Office; www.chester.ac.uk/pdu work-based & integrated studies; FD, BA, MA

Faculty of Education & Children's Services; www.chester.ac.uk/education

children & young people, coaching, families, early childhood studies, continuing professional development, early years practice, education/studies, PGCE secondary/primary/early years, teaching assistance; teacher trg/primary & early years, QTS, teaching & learning, coaching; BA(Hons), BEd, EdD, FdA, MA, MEd, PGCE

Faculty of Health and Social Care; www.chester.ac.uk/health

midwifery, nursing, health & social care, children, non-medical prescribing, social work, young people & families, public health nursing, community health studies, advanced practice, mental health practice, art therapy, communicable diseases, endontology, health improvement & well-being, infection prevention, psychotherapy, method therapy, neonatal clinical practice, occupational health, oncology, paediatrics, sexual & reproductive health, teaching & learning in clinical practice, youth matters; FD, BA(Hons), BSc(Hons), MA, MSc, PGCert, PhD

Faculty of Humanities; www.chester.ac.uk/faculties#F

English; www.chester.ac.uk/english creative writing, English/ language & literature, 19th-century literature and culture, modern & contemporary fiction; BA, MA, PhD

History and Archaeology; www.chester.ac.uk/departments/history-archaeology American, British, Irish, world history, military history, archaeology; BA(Hons), MA, MPhil, PhD

Dept of Modern Languages; www.chester.ac.uk/languages European languages & cultures, French, German & Spanish; BA(Hons), MA, PGCert/Dip

Theology & Religious Studies;
www.chester.ac.uk/trs
religious studies, theology, faith & public policy, practical & contextual theology; BA(Hons), BTh, Dip HE, FdA, MA, MPhil, MTh, PhD

Faculty of Social Sciences;
www.chester.ac.uk/faculties#G

Geography and Development Studies;
www.chester.ac.uk/geography
geography, international development studies, natural hazard/environmental management, housing practice, regeneration; BA(Hons), MA, MSc, PhD, PGDip/Cert

Dept of Psychology; www.chester.ac.uk/psychology
psychology cognitive & behavioural approches, cognitive behavioural therapy, family & child psychology; BA(Hons), BSc(Hons), PhD, MPhil, MSc

Dept of Social Science & Counselling;
www.chester.ac.uk/scc
criminology, sociology, politics, psychological trauma, counselling; BA, BSc, MA, MSc

Law School; www.chester.ac.uk/law
law, family law, criminal justice, human rights & discrimination

UNIVERSITY OF CHICHESTER
www.chiuni.ac.uk

adventure education, dance, English, creative writing, performance, early childhood, mathematics learning, PGCE (primary, secondary), teacher education, TESOL, fine art, history, media production/studies, choral studies, music (performance/composition/business/theatre), instrumental/vocal teaching, musical theatre, theatre performance, commercial music, performing arts, theology, psychology, counselling, accounting, finance, business studies, event management, finance, HRM, IT management for business, marketing, management, tourism management, international business, social work, social care, sport & exercise science/psychology, coaching science, biomechanics, physiology, sport development/studies, sport & fitness, community sport coaching, theology & religion; BA(Hons), BSc(Hons), FD, GradDip/Cert, MA, PGCE, MSc, MSW, PhD

CITY UNIVERSITY LONDON
www.city.ac.uk

School of of Arts; www.city.ac.uk/arts

Dept of Journalism; www.city.ac.uk/journalism
broadcast/TV/investigative/magazine/newspaper/science/international/financial/interactive/political journalism, creative writing, electronic publishing, publishing studies; BA(Hons), MA, MSc, PhD

Dept of Creative Practice & Enterprise;
www.city.ac.uk/creative-practice-and-enterprise

Centre for Music Studies
music, music composition (electroacoustic/instrumental and vocal), music performance, musicology/ethnomusicology, culture studies

Centre for Cultural Policy & Management
cultural & creative industries, cultural policy & management

Centre for Creative Writing, Translation & Publishing Studies
creative writing, electronic publishing, publishing studies, audiovisual translation, legal translation, translating popular culture

Centre for Language Studies
BMus, DMA, MA, MMA, MPhil, PhD
Dip, MA, PGCert

Cass Business School;
www.cass.city.ac.uk

Faculty of Actuarial Science and Insurance; www.cass.city.ac.uk/facact

actuarial management, actuarial science, insurance; BSc(Hons), MSc, Dip, PhD, MPhil

Faculty of Finance; www.cass.city.ac.uk/facfin

accounting, finance, investment & financial risk management, actuarial science, banking, business studies, insurance & risk management, quantitative analysis, real estate, shipping, supply chain & energy, charity accounts, charity marketing & fund-raising, voluntary sector management; BSc, MSc, PGDip

Faculty of Management; www.cass.city.ac.uk/facmana

accounting, finance, banking & international insurance, actuarial management/science, banking & international finance, business studies, energy, trade & finance, European business, finance and investment, financial mathematics, investment & financial risk management, management, mathematical trading, quantitative finance, real estate, voluntary sector management, charity accounting/marketing/fundraising, NGO management; BSc(Hons), MBA, MEb, MPhil, MSc, PGDip, PhD

School of Engineering and Mathematical Sciences; www.city.ac.uk/sems

aeronautical engineering, air safety management/transport engineering/transport operations/management, aircraft maintenance management, analysis and design of structures for fire, blast & earthquakes, automotive & motorsport engineering, biomedical engineering, civil engineering/structures with architecture/surveying, construction management, clinical engineering with healthcare technology management, computer systems engineering, engineering with management & entrepreneurship, electrical/electronic engineering, energy engineering, energy & environmental technology & economics, maritime operations & management, mathematical science with statistics/computer science, mathematics & finance, mechanical engineering, media communication systems, power systems and energy management, project management with finance & risk, statistics, signals & sensor systems, systems & control engineering, telecommunications/& networks, transport strategy & systems; BEng, BSc(Hons), MEng, MMath, MPhil, MSc, PgDip, PhD

Centre for Mathematical Science; www.city.ac.uk/sems/mathematics;

mathematics, finance, mathematical science with statistics/computer science/finance/economics; BSc, MMath, PhD

School of Health Sciences;
www.city.ac.uk/communityandhealth

human communication, midwifery, nursing (adult/child/mental health), clinical/optometry, radiography (diagnostic imaging/oncology), speech & language therapy, health sciences, health services e-learning, primary care (practice nursing), professional practice (child & youth studies, policing of public services, language & communication, public health (school nursing, health visiting, district nursing), food policy/food & nutrition policy, health management in strategic management & leadership, health policy, health services research, medical ultrasound, nuclear medicine technology, ophthalmic dispensing, public service management, speech & language therapy, working with children & young people; FD, BSc(Hons), MSc, DipHE, PGDip, MPhil, PhD, Grad Dip, Cert

School of Informatics; www.soi.city.ac.uk

business computing systems, computer science, artificial intelligence, games technology, information systems, software engineering, business systems analysis, computer games technology, e-business systems, electronic publishing, health informatics, human-centred systems, information management in culture sector, information science/security & management, information systems & technology, information, creativity & leadership, library science, social media; MSc, PhD, MPhil, BSc(Hons), MA, MScMIl, MInnov

City Law School; www.city.ac.uk/law

law, city litigation & dispute rsolution, int banking & finance/commercial/competition law/energy litigation. maritime law, energy law, competition law, criminal litigation, dispute resolution, EU commercial law, innovation, creativity & leadership, legal practice, professional legal practice/study, public international law; LlB, LlM, MPhil, PhD, MJur, Grad Dip

School of Social Sciences; www.city.ac.uk/social

Department of Economics; www.city.ac.uk/economics

accountancy, int business economics, economics, economic evaluation in health care, economic regulation & competition, development/financial/health economics; BSc, MSc, PhD

Department of International Politics; www.city.ac.uk/intpol

international politics/& sociology, human rights, global political economy; BSc, MA, PhD

Department of Psychology; www.city.ac.uk/psychology

counselling psychology, clinical supervision, health psychology, organizational psychology/organizational behaviour, psychology, international business psychology; BSc, MSc, PhD, DPsych

Dept of Sociology; www.city.ac.uk/sociology

criminology, criminal justice, global migration, human rights, international communications & development, media studies, international politics, social research methods, sociology, political communication, transnational media & communication; BEng, BSc(Hons), DPsych, GradDip/Cert, MA, MSc, PhD, ProfDoc

Degrees validated by City University offered at:

GUILDHALL SCHOOL OF MUSIC & DRAMA
www.gsmd.ac.uk

acting, training actors, design realisation, music, music composition, music therapy, leadership, performance, singing, electronic music, theatre technology, stage management; BA(Hons), BMus, MA, MMA/DMA, MMP, MMus, MPerf, PGDip

LABAN
www.laban.org

choreography, dance, dance studies/theatre/performance/science, music, music theatre, jazz composition, performance, composition, design creative practice; PGCE; BA(Hons), MA, MPhil, MSc, PGDipls, PhD

SCHOOL OF PSYCHOTHERAPY & COUNSELLING PSYCHOLOGY AT REGENT'S COLLEGE
www.spc.ac.uk

counselling, psychology, psychotherapy, creative leadership; DCounsPsy, MA, MPhil/PhD, PGDip

THE NORDOFF-ROBBINS MUSIC THERAPY CENTRE
www.nordoff-robbins.org.uk

music therapy, music, health, society; MMusTherapy, PGDip, MPhil, PhD

COVENTRY UNIVERSITY
www.coventry.ac.uk

Coventry School of Art & Design; www.coventry.ac.uk/artanddesign

Dept of Design & Visual Arts; wwwm.coventry.ac.uk/csad/ Designandvisualarts/Pages/ DesignandVisualArts.aspx
fashion, art, graphic design; BA(Hons)

Dept of Industrial Design; wwwm.coventry.ac.uk/csad/ industrialdesign/Pages/ IndustrialDesign.aspx
automotive/& transport design, industrial product design, interior design, product/industrial product design, design & transport, vehicle interiors; BA (Hons), BSc(Hons), MA, MDes, MSc

Dept of Media & Communication; wwwm.coventry.ac.uk/csad/ mediaandcommunication/Pages/ Media_home.aspx
advertising, applied/communications, culture & media, digital media & culture, film & visual culture, journalism & media, media/production, photography, communication; BA(Hons), MA, PGDip/Cert

Dept of Performing Arts; wwwm.coventry.ac.uk/csad/ performingarts/Pages/Performingarts.aspx
animation, dance making, illustration, music performance/technology/composition, music production online, theatre, performance, performing arts innovation & enterprise, professional practice; BA(Hons), BSc(Hons), MA

Faculty of Business, Environment & Society; www.coventry.ac.uk/bes

Coventry University Business School; www.coventry.ac.uk/bes/cubs
accounting, advertising, banking & finance, business administration/economics/management/studies, design & ergonomics, economics, finance, financial/international business economics, European business management, event management, financial management, general management, institutional/investment, international economics & business, international/HRM, international business/management, international sports management/marketing, labour markets (skills), marketing, sport business management, sport & exercise therapy, strategic marketing; BSc(Hons), MA, MSc, MBA, LlM, BA(Hons), PGDip/Cert, MPhil, PhD

Coventry University Law School; www.coventry.ac.uk/bes/law
law, commercial law, international law, legal practice; LlB, LlM, MSc

Department of Geography, Environment & Disaster Management; www.coventry.ac.uk/bes/ged
climate/& environmental management, disaster management & emergency planning, food security management, petroleum & environmental technology, geography, global sustainability, natural hazards, international tourism management, oil & gas energy management; Prof Dip, PGCert, BA, BSc, MA, MSc, MBA, MPhil, PhD

School of International Studies & Social Science; www.coventry.ac.uk/bes/isss
community & social action, criminology, history, international crime & global security, peacebuilding, peace & reconciliation, terrorism, international relations, politics, sociology, diplomacy, law & social change; MA, PhD, MPhil

Faculty of Engineering & Computing; www.coventry.ac.uk/ engineeringandcomputing
aerospace systems/technology/electronics, air transport management, applied mathematics & theoretical physics, architecture, architectural technology, automotive engineering, aviation management, business information technology, business management (engineering), building services engineering/surveying, civil/& structural engineering, communications engineering, computing/science, computer hardware & software engineering, computers, networking & communications technology, construction management/project & cost management, control engineering, electrical systems, embedded microelectronics & wireless systems, engineering & management, engineering management/business management/project management, ethical hacking & network security, forensic computing, information technology, lean manufacturing & engineering management, logistics,

management for construction, management information systems/technology, manufacturing systems engineering, mechanical engineering, network computing, software development, supply chain management, systems & control, vehicle dynamics; BEng, BSc(Hons), MEng, MSc, MPhil, PhD, DEng

Faculty of Health & Life Sciences;
www.coventry.ac.uk/hls

Depts of: Biomolecular & Sports Science, Health Professions, Nursing & Health Studies, Psychology & Behavioural Science, Social, Therapeutic & Community Studies
biological sciences, leadership & management, occupational therapy, sport & exercise science, analytical sciences, career guidance, dietetics, environmental health, forensic & investigative studies, health, midwifery, nursing, operating dept practice, paramedic science, physiotherapy, psychology, social work & community, youth work; BSc(Hons), DipHE, FdSc, MSc, PGDip/Cert,Dip, HND, PhD

CRANFIELD UNIVERSITY
www.cranfield.ac.uk

School of Applied Sciences;
www.cranfield.ac.uk/sas

manufacturing, materials & nanotechnology design, motorsport, business & IS, economics & management, engineering, environment & water, energy & offshore, ultraprecise techniques, welding; EngD, MPhil, MSc, MTech, PhD

Cranfield Defence and Security;
www.cranfield.ac.uk/cds

cyber defence & information assurance, defence acquisition management, defence/leadership/sensors & data/simulation & modelling, enhanced engineering, explosives ordnance eng, forensic archaeology & anthropology/ballistics/computing/engineering & science/investigation, global security, guided weapons, gun systems design, information capability management/operations, international defence & security/marketing, military aerospace & airworthiness/electronic systems/OR/vehicle technology, programme & project management, resilience, scientific computation, security sector management, systems engineering for defence capability, through-life system sustainment; EngD, MSc, PGDip/Cert, PhD

School of Engineering;
www.cranfield.ac.uk/soe

aircraft engineering, airport planning & management, air transport management, airworthiness, astronautics & space engineering, automotive technology mgt, autonomous vehicle dynamics & control, computational fluid dynamics, computational & software techniques, design of rotating machinery, driver behaviour, energy systems & thermal processes, flow assurance, human factors & safety in aeronautics, process systems engineering, thermal power; EngD, MSc, PhD, PGCert/Dip

Cranfield Health; www.cranfield.ac.uk/health

applied bioinformatics, analytical biotechnology, clinical research/information/management, health operations, medical diagnostics/technology, nanomedicine, translational medicine, environment & health, food chain systems, molecular medicine, quality management, toxicology & epidemiology; DM, MSc

Cranfield School of Management;
www.cranfield.ac.uk/som

finance & management, international HRM, managing organizational performance, logistics & supply chain management, management development, programme & project management, strategic marketing; DBA, MBA, MSc, PhD

UNIVERSITY FOR THE CREATIVE ARTS
www.ucreative.ac.uk (at Canterbury, Epsom, Farnham, Maidstone and Rochester)

broadcast media, hand embroidery, graphic design, film production, fashion/promotion/design/journalism/atelier/textiles, print, music/sports journalism, fine art, contemporary jewellery, animation, illustration, interior achitecture & design, textiles for fashion & interiors, product design/& interaction, advertising & brand communication, computer games arts, silversmithing, goldsmithing & jewellery, CG arts & animation, photography (contemporary practice), digital film & screen arts, creative arts for theatre & film, 3D design (ceramics or glass or metalwork & jewellery), architecture, graphic media, art & design; BA(Hons), FD, Grad Dip, MA, MPhil, PGCert, PhD

UNIVERSITY OF CUMBRIA
www.cumbria.ac.uk

Faculty of the Arts, Business & Science; www.cumbria.ac.uk/about us/faculties/ABS

Arts & Humanities; art of games des, drama/performance, religious studies, children's ministry, relations in ministry, practical theology, creative writing, English, event management, film & TV production, TESOL, fine art, graphic design, illustration, journalism, mass communications, musical theatre, performance, festivals & events, photography, performing arts, stage management

Business & Computing: applied business computing, applied business management, management/studies, sustainability, leadership, professional practice

Science, Natural Resources & Outdoor: adventure media, animal conservation science, conservation biology, forensic science, forest & woodland mgt, forestry, wildlife & media, outdoor studies, sustainable energy technology; BA(Hons), BSc(Hons), MBA, FdA, MA, PGDip/Cert

Faculty of Education; www.cumbria.ac.uk/about us/faculties/FacultyEducation

early years/QTS, early childhood studies, primary ed(QTS), inclusive ed/special needs, teaching, learning support, working with children & families, PGCE; general/lower primary(QTS), secondary with QTS in range of subjects, TESOL, QTS Direct, assessment, academic practice, education, graduate teacher programme; BA(Hons), MA, PGDip/Cert, PGCE

Faculty of Health, Wellbeing, Social Work & Sport; www.cumbria.ac.uk/about us/facultyofHealthWellbeing

adv nurse practitioner, coaching & sport development, adv practice/cognitive behaviour therapy, community special practice (district nursing/general practice nursing), counselling, developing paramedic practice, management & leadership/adv practice in health & social care, midwifery, non-medical prescribing, nursing (adult/child/learning disabilities/mental health), nursing practice, occupational health, children's & young people's psychological well being & mental health, counselling & psychotherapy, evidence-based psychological approaches, higher specialist social work (mental health), international health, medical imaging: magnetic resonance, physical activity & health development, sport rehabilitation, sport massage therapy, sport/coaching & sport development, sport & exercise science/therapy, PE; BA, BSc(Hons), GradDip, MA, MSc, PgC,UC, UAD, DipHE, FdA, MPhil, PhD

DE MONTFORD UNIVERSITY
www.dmu.ac.uk

Leicester Business School;
www.dmu.ac.uk/about-dmu/schools-and-departments/leicester-business-school
business man/studies/information systems, international marketing/busines & global enterprise/corporate social responsibility/PR, politics & public policy, project management public finance, risk management, strategic marketing & management, accounting, economics, finance, HRM, marketing, retail; BA(Hons), BSc(Hons), DipHE, GDL/CPE, HND, MA, MPhil, MBA, MSc, PGDip/Cert, PhD

Leicester De Montfort School of Law;
www.dmu.ac.uk/about-dmu/schools-and-departments/leicester-de-montfort-law-school/leicester-de-montfort-law-school
law, criminology/law & criminal justice, HR & social justice, business law, environmental law, sports law, medical law, food law; LlB(Hons), LlM, LPC, DCCJ, MA, PGDip/Cert

Leicester School of Architecture;
www.dmu.ac.uk/about-dmu/schools-and-departments/leicester-school-of-architecture/leicester-school-of-architecture
architecture, architectural design/practice; BA, BArch, PGDip, MA

School of Arts; www.dmu.ac.uk/about-dmu/schools-and-departments/school-of-arts
art & design, arts & festival management, dance, drama studies, fine art, music, technology & innovation/performance, performing arts, cultural events management, independent study in art & design/humanities; BA(Hons), MA, MSc

School of Design; www.dmu.ac.uk/about-dmu/schools-and-departments/school-of-design
design crafts/production, furniture/interior/product design, multimedia design, design entrepreneurship/innovation/management; BA(Hons), MDes, MA

School of Fashion & Textiles;
www.dmu.ac.uk/about-dmu/schools-and-departments/school-of-fashion-and-textiles
contour fashion, fashion design/buying/fabrics & accessories, footwear design, textile design, fashion & bodywear; BA(Hons), MA

School of Humanities; www.dmu.ac.uk/about-dmu/schools-and-departments/school-of-humanities
creative writing, English/language, history, adaptations, English language teaching, sports history & culture, management, law and humanities of sport; BA(Hons), MA, PGDip

School of Media & Communication;
www.dmu.ac.uk/about-dmu/schools-and-departments/school-of-media-and-communication
animation design, film studies, game art design, graphic design, illustration, e-media, journalism, media & communication, photography, creative technologies, independent study/art & design/humanities, international journalism/PR, TV scriptwriting, visual journalism & documentary photography; BA(Hons), FdA, MA, MSc

Institute of Creative Technologies;
www.ioct.ac.uk
e-science, technology, digital arts, design, humanities; Masters, PhD

Dept of Computer Technology;
www.dmu.ac.uk/about-dmu/schools-and-departments/department-of-computer-technology
computer science, computing, software engineering, forensic computing; BSc(Hons), MSc

Dept of Engineering; www.dmu.ac.uk/about-dmu/schools-and-departments/department-of-engineering
mechanical engineering, mechatronics, green energy technology, communications engineering, microelectonics & nanotechnology, rapid production development; BSc(Hons), BEng(Hons), MSc

Dept of Informatics; www.dmu.ac.uk/about-dmu/schools-and-departments/department-of-informatics

business informatics/information systems, computing for business, information & communications technology, artificial intelligence, robotics, computer games programming, data mining, information technology, intelligent systems; BSc(Hons), MSc

Dept of Media Technology; www.dmu.ac.uk/about-dmu/schools-and-departments/department-of-media-technology

audio recording/creative sound/music technology, radio production & technology, games technology, multimedia computing, media production/technology, digital video & broadcast production; BSc(Hons), MSc

Institute of Energy & Sustainable Development; www.iesd.dme.ac.uk

climate change & sustainable development, energy & sustainable building design, energy & industrial sustainability; MSc

School of Allied Health Sciences; www.dmu.ac.uk/about-dmu/schools-and-departments/school-of-allied-health-sciences

speech & language therapy (human communication), biomedical science, healthcare science (audiology), cardiovascular, respiratory, sleep science, medical science, speech & language therapy; BSc(Hons), PGDip/Cert, MSc

School of Applied Social Sciences; www.dmu.ac.uk/about-dmu/schools-and-departments/school-of-applied-social-sciences

children, families & community health, criminology & criminal justice, education studies, health studies, policing studies, psychology, sociology, social work, communities & young people, youth & community development; BA(Hons), BSc(Hons), FD, MSc, PGDip/Cert

School of Nursing & Midwifery; www.dmu.ac.uk/about-dmu/schools-and-departments/school-of-nursing-and-midwifery

nursing, midwifery, palliative care; BSc(Hons), RSHDip

School of Pharmacy; www.dmu.ac.uk/about-dmu/schools-and-departments/school-of-pharmacy

pharmacy, forensic science, pharmaceutical & cosmetic science, pharmaceutical technology/quality by design; BSc(Hons), MPharm, MSc

UNIVERSITY OF DERBY
www.derby.ac.uk

Faculty of Art, Design, and Technology; www.derby.ac.uk/adt

Art & Design: animation, fashion, fine art, film & TV production, photography, textiles, visual communication, graphic design, illustration; Humanities: American studies, creative writing, English, film & TV, horror & transgression, history, media, theatre; Technology: architecture & built environment/healthy buildings, control & instrumentation, construction project management, electrical/electronic/mechanical/civil/manufacturing engineering, construction, product design, professional engineering, music/production & media technology, motorsport, sustainable design & innovation; BA(Hons), MDes, PhD, Univ Cert/Dip, BEng, FdSc/Eng

Faculty of Business, Computing and Law; www.derby.ac.uk/bcl

Derbyshire Business School; www.derby.ac.uk/dbs

accountancy & finance, business, coaching, enterprise, HRM, leadership, marketing, purchasing & supply, management, strategy, payroll management, international business

Law & Criminology; www.derby.ac.uk/law

law, commercial/corporate & financial law, international/protection of human rights/intellectual property & information technology/comparative law, transnational criminal law; criminology, crime & justice, legal practice

University of Derby

Computing & Mathematics; www.derby.ac.uk/computing
computer forensics, computer games modelling & animation/programming, computer science/networks, information technology/security, networks & security, mobile device software development, computer graphics production, games, mathematics; BA(Hons), BSc(Hons), FD, LlBHons, LlM, MA, MPhil/PhD, MSc, PGDip/Cert

Faculty of Education, Health and Sciences; www.derby.ac.uk/ehs

Education & Social Sciences; www.derby.ac.uk/education
applied community & youth work, child & youth work, education studies/guidance, CPD, teacher education, early childhood/years, children's & young people's services, sociology, social studies

Health & Social Care; www.derby.ac.uk/health
advanced practice, mentoring, nursing studies (adult/mental health/public health), nursing & healthcare practice, mental health & therapeutic practice, community specialist practitioner, long term conditions, non-medical prescribing, LBR modules, occupational therapy, health & social care practice, radiography

Science; www.derby.ac.uk/science
biological science, geography, geology, environmental science, forensic science, psychology, sport & exercise science; Adv Dip, BA(Hons), BEd, BSc(Hons), EdD, FdA, HNC/HND, jtHons, MA, MSC, PGCert/Dip, PGCE, PhD, Univ Cert/Dip, MPhil, PhD

UNIVERSITY CENTRE DONCASTER
www.don.ac.uk/dbs

Undergraduate subject areas: animation & games/illustration, applied social science, building services, business, construction, counselling, criminal justice, dance & theatre, early years/working with children & young people, education, fashion & textiles, fim & TV, fine art, graphic design, music technology, sport & exercise science; Postgraduate topics: business administration, HRM, relationship therapy, psychosexual therapy, education, innovation & enterprise; BA(Hons), BSc(hons), MBA, MSc, PGDip/Cert, MA, PGCE

UNIVERSITY OF DUNDEE
www.dundee.ac.uk

College of Art, Sciences and Engineering; www.dundee.ac.uk/case

School of Computing; www.computing.dundee.ac.uk
applied computing, artificial intelligence, business computer intelligence, computing/science, information technology, human-computer interaction, vision & imaging computing

Duncan of Jordanstone College of Art and Design; www.dundee.ac.uk/djcad
animation & bivisual art, art & digital film, art philosophy, graphic design/interior & environmental/interactive media/jewellery & metal/textiles design, digital interaction, exhibitions, fine art, illustration, media arts & imaging, forensic/media/medical art, product design, time-based art – digital film, design ethnology

School of Engineering, Physics and Mathematics; www.dundee.ac.uk/eps
biomedical engineering, civil engineering, concrete engineering & environmental management, construction enterprise management, design for medical technology, electronic & electrical engineering, physics, electronic circuit design & manufacture, earthquake & offshore geotechnical engineering, mathematics, mathematical biology, motion analysis, mechanical engineering & mechatronics, product design, renewable energy & environmental modelling, structural engineering; BEng, BSc, CertHE, DipHE, MArch, MEng, MA, MSc, MSci, PhD, PGDE, PGDip

College of Arts and Social Sciences; www.dundee.ac.uk/artsoc

School of Business; www.dundee.ac.uk/business
accountancy, finance, business management, international/accounting/HRM/marketing finance/business, financial/economics, strategic financial management; BSc, BAcc, BFin, MA, MSc, PGDip

Continuing Education; www.dundee.ac.uk/conted;
CPD, communication & languages, community outreach; MACert, Dip

School of Education, Social Work and Community Education; www.dundee.ac.uk/eswce
childhood practice, community learning & development, education (primary), HE (adult literacies)/teaching in, professional development (community regeneration, leadership & management, healthcare/integrated services, volunteering, social work, adult care & protection, applied professional studies: adult care & protection, child care & protection, community learning & development, community planning, equality & social inclusion, leadership & organisational development, policing studies, practice learning, tertiary education, education: leading learning & teaching, inclusion & learner support, nursery/early education, pupil care & support, adult literacies, primary, science (maths/sciences), educational psychology, teaching qualification (FE); BA/BA(Hons), Dip, Cert, PGCert, Masters, PGDE, MSc, PhD, MPhil, ProfDoc

Interdisciplinary Disability Research Institute (IDRIS)

Institute for Research and Innovation in Social Services (IRISS)

School of the Environment; www.dundee.ac.uk/socialsciences;
Architecture: architecture, architectural humanity, technology, communication, macro/micro, urbanism, rationalism, material
Environmental Science: environmental science, geography
Geography: geography, environmental science/sustenance/management, American studies, applied population & welfare geography, remote ensing, sustainable catchment areas
Town & Regional Planning; environmental sustenance, geography & planning, community geography, spatial planning, sustainable urban design, maritime spatial planning & design; BSc, MA, BArch, MArch

School of Humanities; www.dundee.ac.uk/humanities

American Studies
American studies

Centre for Archive and Information Studies; www.dundee.ac.uk/cias
archives & records management/information rights, family & local history, digital records appl

Languages; www.dundee.ac.uk/languagesstudies;
French, German, Spanish

English; www.dundee.ac.uk/English
English, English and film studies, women, comic & graphic novels, comics studies, theatre studies, writing practice, culture & society, creative writing

European Studies
interdisciplinary courses

History; www.dundee.ac.uk/history
early America, European history, Greater Britain in the twentieth century, history, Scottish/church history, urban and cultural history, church history

Philosophy; www.dundee.ac.uk/philosophy
European philosophy, philosophy/& literature, continental/recent analytic philosophy, women, culture & society

Politics; www.dundee.ac.uk/politics
European politics, international relations & politics/geopolitics, international politics & security; MA(Hons), MLitt, MSc

School of Law; www.dundee.ac.uk/law
commercial & international commercial law, corporate & commercial law, international criminal justice & human rights, environmental law & sustainable development, family law, European law, law & governance, public law, Scottish law, international dispute resolution; LlB, LlM, PhD

Graduate School of Natural Resources Law, Policy and Management; www.dundee.ac.uk/postgradschool
mineral resource management, international oil & gas management

UNESCO Centre for Water Law, Policy and Science
water law; PGCert, LlM, PhD

School of Psychology; www.dundee.ac.uk/psychology
visual/cognition, eye movements, language & communication, psychological therapy, abnormal & clinical psychology; BA(Hons), MA(Hons), PhD

College of Life Sciences; www.lifesci.dundee.ac.uk

anatomical sciences, anatomy & adv forensic anthropology biochemistry, biomedical/biological sciences, drug discovery, cancer biology, crops for the future, environmental biology, forensic anthropology/facial identification, human anatomy, medical art, microbiology, molecular biology, molecular genetics, neuroscience, pharmacology, physiological sciences, sports biomedicine; BSc(Hons), MRes, MSc, PhD

Schools of Research

Centre for Anatomy and Human Identification; www.lifesci.dundee.ac.uk/cahid
Biological Chemistry & Drug Discovery (CLS); www.lifesci.dundee.ac.uk/bcdd
Div of Cell and Developmental Biology; www.lifesci.dundee.ac.uk/cdb
Div of Cell Signalling & Immunology; www.lifesci.dundee.ac.uk/csi
Drug Discovery Unit; www.drugdiscovery.ac.uk
Gene Regulation & Expression; www.lifescience.dundee.ac.uk/gre
Molecular Microbiology; www.lifesci.dundee.ac.uk/mmb
Div of Molecular Medicine; www.lifesci.dundee.ac.uk/mm
CRUK Nucleic Acid Structure Research Group; www.lifesci.dundee.ac.uk/nasg
MRC Protein Phosphorylation Unit
Div of Plant Sciences; www.lifesci.dundee.ac.uk/pl
Scottish Institute of Cell signalling
Div of Signal Transduction Therapy; www.lifesci.dundee.ac.uk/dstt
Wellcome Trust Centre for Gene Regulation & Expression

College of Medicine, Dentistry and Nursing; www.dundee.ac.uk/cmdn

Graduate School; www.dundee.ac.uk/cmdn/graduate

Postgraduate degrees offered in the following subject areas: cancer biology, global health, medical education, surgery, nursing & midwifery, nursing & palliative care, orthopaedic & trauma surgery, psychiatry, public health, health & social care, sports & biomechanical medicine, dentistry; MSc, MRes, Masters, Dip, Cert, MCHOrth, MNurs, MDSc

School of Dentistry; www.dundee.ac.uk/dentalschool

oral health science, prosthodontics, dental surgery, cancer biology

School of Nursing and Midwifery; www.dundee.ac.uk/medden

advanced practice, nursing, palliative care, midwifery, global health & well-being, infection prevention & control, health studies, community health nursing, mental health, physiotherapeutics, quality management, clinical assessment governance

School of Medicine; www.dundee.ac.uk/medschool

anaesthesia, cardiovascular disease & diabetes, health skills, immunology, medical science, medicine, molecular medicine, neuroscience, oncology, orthopaedic & trauma surgery, orthopaedic and rehabilitation technology, palliative care, population science, primary care, psychiatry cognitive behavioural psychotherapy, psychological therapy in primary care, public health, skin disease, surgery; BDS, BHealthN, BM, BMSc, BN, BSc, DDSc, DipCert, MA, MBChB, MChOrth, MD, MDSc, MFM, MMAS, MMSc, MNurs, MPH, MPhil, MSc, MSSc

School of Medicine Institutes

Centre for Biomedical Science & Public Health; Centre for Medical Education; Centre for Undergraduate Medicine; Clinical Skills Centre; CLS/MRI Molecular Medicine; Cuschieri Skills Centre; Division of Cancer Research; Division of Cardiovascular & Diabetes Medicine; Division of Neuroscience; Division of Population Health Sciences; Division of Imaging & Technology; Medical Education Institute; Medical Research Institute

DURHAM UNIVERSITY
www.dur.ac.uk

Faculty of Arts and Humanities; www.dur.ac.uk /arts.humanities

Dept of Classics and Ancient History; www.dur.ac.uk/classics

ancient history & archaeology, ancient history, classics, ancient, medieval & modern history, ancient epic/histiography/philosophy, classical tradition, Greece, Rome & the Near East

Dept of English Studies; www.dur.ac.uk/english.studies

English literature, medieval & Renaissance literary studies, poetry, 20th-century literary studies, the novel, drama, Victorian & romantic literary studies

English Language Centre; www.dur.ac.uk/englishlanguage

English past & present, English language teaching, English & its social context, TESOL, applied language studies

Dept of History; www.dur.ac.uk/history

history, medieval history, early modern/modern history, research methods (economic and social history)

Dept of Music; www.dur.ac.uk/music

music, ethnomusicology, composition, electroacoustic studies, performance, musicology

School of Modern Languages and Cultures; www.dur.ac.uk/mlac

Arabic/English translation & interpreting, medieval and Renaissance studies, French, German, Hispanic studies, Italian, Russian, Chinese, 17th century studies, translation studies, culture & difference

Dept of Philosophy; www.dur.ac.uk/philosophy

philosophy, history & philosophy of science & medicine, metaphysics, ethics, aesthetics

Dept of Theology and Religion; www.dur.ac.uk/theology.religion

biblical studies, Christian theology (Anglican, Catholic studies), religion and society, theology & philosophy/European studies, spirituality, theology & health; BA(Hons), GDip, MA, MLitt, MMus, MTh, PhD

Faculty of Science; www.dur.ac.uk/science.faculty

School of Biological and Biomedical Sciences; www.dur.ac.uk/biological.sciences

biology, biomedical sciences, biosciences, cell biology, ecology, molecular biology & biochemistry

Dept of Chemistry; www.dur.ac.uk/chemistry

chemistry, biochemistry, materials/adv computational, catalysis, organometallic, inorganic materials, optical & molecular chemistry, physical/organic/polymer chemistry, structural chemistry, natural science

Dept of Engineering and Computer Science; www.dur.ac.uk/ecs/computing.science

advanced software engineering, aeronautics, civil/electronic/mechanical/electrical engineering, communications/computer engineering, computer science, design, general engineering, internet and distributed systems technologies, internet systems and e-business, new and renewable energy, design & operations engineering, software engineering management

Dept of Earth Sciences; www.dur.ac.uk/earth.sciences

earth sciences, geology, natural sciences, geophysics, environmental/geosciences

Dept of Mathematical Sciences; www.dur.ac.uk/mathematical.sciences

mathematics, mathematical sciences, particles, strings & cosmology

Dept of Physics; www.dur.ac.uk/physics

physics, astronomy, theoretical physics, particles, strings & cosmology, natural science

Dept of Psychology; www.dur.ac.uk/psychology

cognitive neuroscience, developmental psychopathology, applied/psychology, research methods; BA(Hons), BEng, BSc(Hons), MA, MChem, MEng, MMath, MPhil, MPhys, MSc, MSci, PhD

Faculty of Social Science and Health; www.dur.ac.uk /science.health

School of Applied Social Sciences; www.dur.ac.uk/sass
criminology & criminal justice, social policy, social work, society & politics, social research, managing community practice/youth work practice, community and youth work, sociology/with law, sport, exercise & physical activity

Dept of Anthropology; www.dur.ac.uk/anthropology
anthropology, development/evolutionary anthropology, health and human sciences, medical anthropology, well-being, sustainability, culture & development anthropology, sociocultural anthropology

Dept of Archaeology; www.dur.ac.uk/archaeology
archaeology/& ancient civilizations/history, conservation of archaeological & museum objects, museums & artefacts, palaeopathology, archaeological science, natural science

Durham Business School; www.dur.ac.uk/dbs
accounting & finance, business finance/economics, client management, corporate & international finance, economics, enterprise management, financial accounting, investment, Islamic finance, leadership & management, management accounting, sponsorship, strategy and organization, strategic marketing, philosophy, politics & economics

School of Education; www.dur.ac.uk/education
educational assessment, education studies, initial training PGCE primary/secondary, intercultural education, history of art, maths/science education, practice of education, technically enhanced education

Dept of Geography; www.dur.ac.uk/geo
risk & environmental hazards, geography, contemporary human geography, research methods, natural science

School of Government and International Affairs; www.dur.ac.uk/sgia
Arab world studies, defence, development, diplomacy, conflict prevention & security, international relations/studies, Islamic finance, economics, philosophy & politics; BA(Hons), DBA, EdD, MA, MA(Ed), MBA, MAnth, MSc, MScW, PGCE, PGCert/Dip, PhD

Durham Law School; www.dur.ac.uk
European trade/international trade & commercial law, law, society & law, legal studies

School of Medicine & Health; www.dur.ac.uk/school.health
clinical management, health research methods, history & philosophy of science, interdisciplinary mental health, medical education, pharmacy, public policy and health, spirituality theology & health; BA(Hons), BA(Ed), BSc(Ed), BSc(Hons), Cert Leg Stud, LlB, LlM, MA, MBBS, MPhil, PGCert, PGCert/Dip, PGCE, PhD, MA, MPharm

Degrees validated by Durham University offered at:

CRANMER HALL, ST JOHN'S COLLEGE
www.cranmerhall.com

theology and ministry; BA, MA, diploma/certificate, Doc

NEW COLLEGE DURHAM
www.newdur.ac.uk

accountancy, business management, construction, education, electronic/civil engineering, graphic design, housing, information technology management, complementary healthcare, counselling, social work, sport & exercise, travel & tourism; BA(Hons), BSc(Hons), FD, HND, HNC

ROYAL ACADEMY OF DANCE
www.rad.org.uk

ballet education, ballet teaching studies, Benesh, dance education, movement notation; BA(Hons), Dip/CertHE, MTeach(Dance), licenciate

USHAW COLLEGE
www.ushaw.ac.uk

theology & ministry; BA, Certs, Dipls, MA, PGCert/Dip

UNIVERSITY OF EAST ANGLIA
www.uea.ac.uk

Faculty of Arts and Humanities; www.uea.ac.uk/hum

American Studies; www.uea.ac.uk/ams

American studies/literature, & American history/English history/politics, & creative writing

School of World Art & Museum Studies; www.uea.ac.uk/art

archaeology, anthropology & art history, arts of Africa, Oceana & the Americas, creative entrepreneurship, film studies & art history, history of art & literature, gallery & museum studies, history of art, cultural heritage & international development/museum studies

School of Film & Television Studies; www.uea.ac.uk/ftv

film & TV studies, film & English/American studies, media studies, TV & creative practice, film archives

School of History; www.uea.ac.uk/his

modern history, history, modern British history, history & politics/languages/landscape, medieval/mod European history, environmental science & humanities

School of Literature, Drama & Creative Writing; www.uea.ac.uk/lit

biography & creative non-fiction, creative entrepreneurship, creative writing – poetry/prose/scriptwriting, culture & modernity, drama, scriptwriting & performance, English & American literature, critical writing, literary translation, literature & history, medieval & early modern textual cultures, theatre direction, writing the modern world

School of Language and Communication Studies; www.uea.ac.uk/lcs

cross-cultural communication/business & management, language studies, international development, film & TV, French, media, Spanish, Japanese, applied translation studies, language & conflict in intercultural communication

School of Music; www.uea.ac.uk/mus

music, music & technology, creative entrepreneurship, performance, conducting

School of Political, Social and International Studies; www.uea.ac.uk/psi

culture, literature, broadcast journalism, European studies/politics, international relations & politics/European politics/modern history, media & cultural /culture & society, philosophy & politics, politics & economics of public choice, international/public policy & management, social & political theory, society, culture & media; BA(Hons), MA, MMus, MPhil, PGDip, PhD, MRes

Faculty of Health; www.uea.ac.uk/foh

School of Allied Health Professions; www.uea.ac.uk/ahp

occupational therapy, physiotherapy, speech & language therapy, clinical education, musculoskeletal research & practice, stroke recovery

School of Medicine, Health Policy & Practice; www.uea.ac.uk/med

medicine, surgery, clinical science/research, cognitive behavioural therapy, onoplastic breast surgery, health economics/research, CPD

School of Nursing and Midwifery; www.uea.ac.uk/nam

acute, children's palliative care, critical and emergency practice, midwifery, nursing (adult, children's, learning disabilities), medicine management/mental health, nurse practitioner, operating department practice, HE community healthcare, sport & exercise injuries

Institute of Biomedical and Clinical Science; www.uea.ac.uk/foh/research/Institutes/biomed

infection & immunity, nutrition & healthy ageing

Health and Social Science Research Institute; www.uea.ac.uk/foh/research/Institutes/hss

health economics, medical statistics, mental health & psychological sciences, public health & health services research, stroke & rehabilitation, shared decision making

Education in Health Institute; www.uea.ac.uk/foh/research/Institutes/educationinhealth

medical education, interprofessional education, educational theory; BA(Hons), BSc(Hons), ClinPsyD, DipHE, FD, MBBS, MClinEd, MD, MHeaRes, MPhil, MSc, PGDip, PhD

Faculty of Science; www.uea.ac.uk/sci

School of Biological Science; www.uea.ac.uk/bio

applied ecology & conservation, biochemistry, ecology, biological sciences, biomedicine, cell biology, plant science, biotechnology for a sustainable future, plant genetics & crop improvement, molecular biology/biochemistry/medicine, sustainable agriculture & food security

School of Chemical Science; www.uea.ac.uk/che

chemistry, adv organic chemistry, analytical science, biological and medicinal chemistry, chemical & forensic physics, forensic chemistry/science, pharmaceutical chemistry, forensic & investigational chemistry

School of Computing Science; www.uea.ac.uk/cmp

actuarial sciences, computing science, business information systems, business statistics, computational biology, computer graphics/systems engineering/science, computing for business, games development, knowledge discovery & data mining, software engineering, statistics

School of Environmental Sciences; www.uea.ac.uk/env

applied ecology, environmental social science, atmospheric sciences, climate change/science, environmental assessment & management/chemistry/earth sciences, environmental geography & international development/geophysics, geophysical sciences, meteorology & oceanography

School of Natural Science; www.uea.ac.uk/sci/natsci; natural science

School of Mathematics; www.uea.ac.uk/mth

mathematics, business statistics, energy engineering & enviromental management

School of Pharmacy; www.uea.ac.uk/pha

general pharmacy practice, pharmacy; BSc(Hons), GradDip, MPhil, MSc, MSci, PGDip, PhD

Faculty of Social Sciences; www.uea.ac.uk/ssf

School of Economics; www.uea.ac.uk/eco

economics & accountancy, business economics, business finance & economics, environmental/experimental/industrial economics, international business finance & economics, media economics, politics, international relations

School of Education and Lifelong Learning; www.uea.ac.uk/edu

adult literacy, advanced educational practice, counselling/ focusing-orientated psychotherapy, early childhood studies, education studies, lifelong learning & development

School of International Development; www.uea.ac.uk/dev

agriculture & rural development, international development with economics/overseas experience/sociology/social anthropology & politics/environment & society, agriculture & rural development, development economics/practice/politics, education & development, globalisation/gender studies/media & international development, international relations & development studies, international social development, climate change/environmental/impact /valuation/water security & international development, conflict, governance & international development

Norwich Law School; www.uea.ac.uk/law
law, employment law, European legal systems, information technology & intellectual property law, international commercial & business law/competition law & policy/trade law, law with American law/French law & language, legal studies, media law, policy and practice

Norwich Business School; www.uea.ac.uk/nbs
accounting & finance/management, brand leadership, international business management/accounting & financial/HRM, management consultancy, marketing, strategic information systems, strategic supply chain management, strategic carbon management

School of Social Work and Psychology; www.uea.ac.uk/swp
child & family psychology, psychology, social work; BA(Hons), BSc(Hons), CPE/Dip, DEd, GradDip, LlBHons, LLM, MA, MA/DipSW, MBA, MPhil, MRes, MSc, MScEd, PGCert, PGDip, PhD

Degrees validated by University of East Anglia offered by:

CITY COLLEGE NORWICH
www.ccn.ac.uk

applied social work, business computing, business management, care management, child care & education, construction & the built environment, culinary arts, early childhood studies/years, engineering (civil, electrical, electronic, mechanical), English, & cultural studies, financial services/retail, finance & accountancy, health & exercise, health studies, hospitality management interactive media, HRM, journalism, leisure management, leadership & management, retail, psychology/& sociology, public sector management, social work, teaching assistants, travel & tourism; BA(Hons), BSc(Hons), FdA, FdSc, HNC, HND

OTLEY COLLEGE
www.otleycollege.ac.uk

agriculture, animal studies, arboriculture, business conservation, construction, engineering, fishery studies, floristry, food skills, horse studies, horticulture, land & countryside, leisure learning, management, sport, teacher training

THE UNIVERSITY OF EDINBURGH
www.ed.ac.uk

College of Humanities and Social Sciences; www.hss.ed.ac.uk

The Edinburgh College of Art; www.ed.ac.uk/schools-departments/edinburgh-college-art
School of Fine Art: fine art, painting, photography, sculpture, contemporary art – painting/photography/practice/sculpture/theory
School of Design: animation, fashion, film & TV, glass, graphic design, illustration, interior design, jewellery & silversmithing, performance costume, product design, film direction
Architecture & Landscape: architecture, landscape architecture, architecture in the creative environment, architectural history, advanced sustainability design, architectural & urban design, design & digital media, art, space & nature, sound design, cultural studies, architectural conservation
History of Art: history of art, architectural history, art in the global middle east, theory & display, Renaissance & early modern studies, modern & contemporary art, Scottish art & visual culture
Music: music, music technology/acoustics, early keyboard studies, instrument studies, digital composition & performance, musicology

The Business School; www.business-school.ed.ac.uk
analysis, accounting & finance, banking & risk, business studies, carbon finance/management, economics, finance & investment, international business & emerging markets, management science, marketing

School of Divinity; www.div.ed.ac.uk
divinity, biblical studies, ethics, ministry, philosophy & theology, religious studies, science & religion, theology in religion, world Christianity

School of Economics; www.ed.ac.uk/schools-departments/economics
asset pricing, corporate finance, economics, international money & finance, economics analysis, econometrics/finance, macroeconomics, microeconomics

School of Health in Social Science; www.ed.ac.uk/schools-departments/health
advancing nursing practice, applied psychology for children & young people, children & young people mental health, clinical psychology, counselling, dementia, integrated serivvce improvement, nursing studies/adult, psychotherapy, social science in health

School of History, Classics and Archaeology; www.shc.ed.ac.uk
American history, classical studies, diaspora & migration studies, ancient philosophy, contemporary/medieval/intellectual/ Scottish history, 18th century culture, 1st millennium history, Renaissance to enlightenment, landscape, environment & history, modern British & Irish history, social & cultural history, classical art & archaeology, Celtic, Scottish studies, Greek/Latin studies. classics, gender history, late antique, Islamic & Byzantine studies, archaeology (European/forensic/Mediterranean), osteoarchaeology, social anthropology

School of Law; www.law.ed.ac.uk
law (English, family, criminal, European, public health, international private, competition/innovation, international economic), trusts, international tax law, criminal & global crime

School of Literatures, Languages and Cultures; www.ed.ac.uk/schools-departments/literatures-languages-cultures
Asian studies, Celtic & Scottish studies, comparative literature, European languages & cultures, English literature, European theatre, film studies, Islamic & Middle Eastern studies, literature & transtlanticism, material cultures & study of the book, medieval studies, theatre studies, translation, word & music studies

Moray House School of Education; www.education.ed.ac.uk
academic practice, additional support for learning, childhood practice, applied sport science, community education, dance science & education, e-learning, leadership, headship, inclusive & special education, language teaching, management of training & development, outdoor education, performance psychology, PE, primary education, sport & recreation business management, TESOL, strength & conditioning, swimming science, theory & practice of literacy

School of Philosophy, Psychology and Language Science; www.ppls.ed.ac.uk
ancient philosophy, artificial intelligence, psychology/of language, cognitive science, cognition in science & society, developmental linguistics, evolution of language & cognition, English language, epistemology, ethics, history & theory of psychology, human cognitive neuropsychology, language & embodied cognition, linguistics, philosophy, aesthetics, knowledge, epistemology, logistics, Hellenistic philosophy, metaethics, psychology/of individual differences, mind & language/cognition

School of Social & Political Science; www.sps.ed.ac.uk
politics & international relations, science, innovation & technology, social anthropology, social policy, social work, sociology adult protection, African studies/international development, comparative public policy, European Union politics & law. global social change/crime, justice & security, global health & anthropology/public policy, health inequalities/systems & public policy, international & European politics, internationa political theory, international Relations/of the Middle East/with Arabic management of bioeconomy, innovation & governance, medical anthropology, multi-level and regional politics, policy studies, science & technology in society/& international development, social anthropology, social research; BA(Arch), BD, BEd(Hons), BMedSci, BMus, BN, BSc(Hons), DD, DLitt, DMus, DClin-Pyschol, EdD, LlM, MA, MA(Hons), MBA, MLA, MPhil/PhD, MSc, MTeach, MTh/Sc, PGDipCert, PGDE

College of Medicine and Veterinary Medicine; www.ed.ac.uk/schools-departments/medicine-vet-medicine

animal biology, biomedical & clinical sciences, clinical skills, dental primary care, diagnosis, medicine, oral health science/surgery, orthodontics, paediatric dentistry, pharmacology, therapeutics, posthodontics, public health, psychological medicine, surgery, transfusion, transplantation and tissue banking, veterinary medicine & surgery

School of Clinical Sciences and Community Health; www.ed.ac.uk/schools-departments/clinical-sciences

clinical & surgical sciences, community health sciences, medical and radiological sciences, reproductive and developmental sciences, postgraduate dental education

School of Biomedical Sciences; www.ed.ac.uk/schools-departments/biomedical-sciences

biomedical sciences, translational medicine, international animal health, biodiversity, wildlife, global health

School of Molecular and Clinical Medicine; www.mcm.ed.ac.uk

clinical brain services, neuroimaging, molecular medicine, transfusion, transplantation & tissue banking

The Royal (Dick) School of Veterinary Studies; www.ed.ac.uk/schools-departments/vet

veterinary medicine & surgery, population medicine & veterinary public health; BSc(Hons), MBChB, MSC, BVMS, DipCert, MPhil,PhD

College of Science and Engineering; www.scieng.ed.ac.uk

School of Biological Sciences; www.ed.ac.uk/schools-departments/biology

biochemistry, biodiversity & taxonomy of plants, bioinformatics, biological sciences, biotechnology, cell biology, developmental/evolutionary/medical/molecular/reproductive biology, drug discovery & translational biology, ecology, plant science, pharmacology, zoology, quantitative genetics & genome analysis, molecular genetics, physiology, neuroscience

School of Chemistry; www.chem.ed.ac.uk

chemical physics, chemistry/with environmental & sustainable chemistry/materials chemistry, medicinal & biological chemistry

School of Engineering; www.see.ed.ac.uk

Chemical Engineering with environmental engineering/management, materials & processes, energy systems

Civil and Environmental Engineering: civil engineering, civil and environmental engineering/construction management, structural engineering with architecture, structural & fire safety engineering

Electronics and Electrical Engineering: electrical engineering, renewable energy, electronics, computer science, bioelectronics, communications, software engineering, mechanical engineering, energy systems, integrated micro and nano systems, digital communications

Mechanical Engineering: advanced materials applications, electrical & mechanical engineering, fluid and particle dynamics, manufacturing & process optimization, materials & processes, mechanical engineering with management/structural mechanics

Institute for Energy Systems: environmental mitigation, energy delivery, renewable energy, restructuring and regulation

General Engineering

School for Informatics; www.inf.ed.ac.uk

informatics, artificial intelligence, cognitive science, computational linguistics/physics, computer science, software engineering/computer science, analytical & scientific databases, bioinformatics, systems & synthetic biology, informatics & economics, intelligent robotics, knowledge management, representation & reasoning, learning from data, music informatics, natural languages & language engineering, neural computation & neuroinformatics

School of Geosciences; www.geos.ed.ac.uk

Ecological Sciences,Geography,Earth Science: geography, physical geography, geology, geophysics, archaeology, GIS, meteorology, conservation & eco-management, environmental studies, earth sciences, ecological economics, forestry, ecology & environmental science, integrated resource management, environment & development, carbon capture & storage/management

School of Mathematics; www.maths.ed.ac.uk

pure/applied mathematics, financial mathematics/& modelling mathematical physics, mathematics &

statistics/management/physics/artificial intelligence/ computer science/philosophy operational research, scientific computing

School of Physics and Astronomy;
www.ph.ed.ac.uk

astrophysics, physics, chemical physics, computational physics, mathematical physics, theoretical physics, physics and computer sci/mathematics/ meteorology/music, high performance computing; BEng, BSc, MChem, MChemPhys, MEarthSci, MEng, MInf, MPhil, MPhys, MS, MSc, MSci, PGDip, PhD

EDINBURGH NAPIER UNIVERSITY
www.napier.ac.uk

The Business School; www.napier.ac.uk/business-school

School of Accountancy, Financial Services & Law; www.napier.ac.uk/business-school/ SchoolsandCentres/Pages/ SchoolofAccountingFinancialLaw.aspx

School of Management; www.napier.ac.uk/ business-school/SchoolsandCentres/ Pages/SchoolofManagement.aspx

School of Marketing, Tourism & Languages; www.napier.ac.uk/business-school/ SchoolsandCentres/Pages/ SchoolofMarketingTourismLanguages.aspx

Accounting, Economics and Statistics;
accounting/for corporate finance, advertising, advanced networking/leadership, business management/studies, business & entrepreneurship, business information systems, consumer studies, corporate strategy & law/finance, economics, ecotourism, facilities management, finance, financial services, global investment banking/languages, heritage & cultural tourism management, hospitality & tourism management, HRM, international business languages, international tourism management, international finance/ marketing, investment, law, festival & event management, management, marketing, promotion & economic development, property management, PR, tourist marketing, marketing management/with consumer studies; BA, BA(Hons), MSc, MBA, MPhil, LlB, LlM

Faculty of Engineering, Computing and Creative Industries; www.napier.ac.uk/fecci

School of Computing; www.napier.ac.uk/ soc/Pages/Home.aspx

advanced networking, applied informatics, business information systems/technology, computer network systems, computing security & forensics, computing, digital media/networking, mobile & embedded computer systems, interactive media design/systems/ entertainment & games development, mobile/network computing, web-based systems, adv/security & digital forensics, adv/software engineering, web technologies, strategic ITC leadership; BEng, BSc, MPhil, MSc, PhD

Arts & Creative Industries;
www.napier.ac.uk/sci/Pages/ SchoolOfArtsCreativeIndustries.aspx

adv film practice, acting for stage & screen, advertising, PR, creative advertising/writing, communication, design (international/lighting/sustainable/urban digital arts), English, film, graphic design, interaction/ interdisciplinary design, interior architecture, journalism, music (pop), photography, product design, magazine/publishing, screen project development, screenwriting; BA/BA(Hons), BDes, BDes(Hons), BMus, BMus(Hons), MDes, MFA, MSc, PGCert/Dip

Engineering & the Built Environment; www.napier.ac.uk/sebe/Pages/ default.aspx

architectural technology & building performance, automation & control, building surveying, built environment, timber engineering, computer-aided design, construction project management, electronic/ computer/electrical engineering, digital systems, energy & environmental engineering, engineering design, engineering with management, environmental sustainability, facilities management, adv materials engineering, mechanical engineering, mechatronics, polymer engineering, product design engineering, project management, property development & valuation/investment, quantity surveying, safety & environmental management, structural engineering, timber industry management/engineering, transport management/planning and engineering, transportation engineering; BSc/BSc(Hons), BEng, BEng/Hons, MEng, MSc, MSci, PGCert/Dip

Faculty of Health, Life & Social Science; www.napier.ac.uk/fhlss

Life, Sport & Social Sciences; www.napier.ac.uk/FHLSS/SLSSS/Pages/Home.aspx

animal biology, biomedical science, biotechnology, career guidance, complementary healthcare (aromatherapy/reflexology), criminology, drug design & biomedical science, psychology, sociology, social science, social research; biological science, biotechnology, biomedical science, conservation & management of protected areas, ecotourism, environmental biology, forensic biology, pharmaceutical science, sports & exercise science, sport performance enhancement/coaching, wildlife biology & conservation, youth work; BSc(Hons), MSc, BA(Hons), PGCert/Dip

School of Nursing, Midwifery and Social Care; www.napier.ac.uk/fhlss/NMSC/Pages/SchoolofNursing.aspx

nursing – child health/adult/mental health/intellectual disabilities, adv/profession practice, clinical research, complementary therapy practice, neonatal nursing/child protection/diabetes nursing, counselling, health admin/& social work care, midwifery, physiology, social care, veterinary nursing, CPD; BMid, BN, DipHE, MSc, PGDip/Cert

EDINBURGH COLLEGE OF ART
www.eca.ac.uk

fine art, intermedia art, painting, photography, sculpture, animation, fashion, film & TV, glass, graphic design, illustration, interior design, jewellery & silversmithing, performance costume, product design, textiles, architecture/in creative & cultural environments, landscape architecture, architectural history, music, music technology, sound design, digital composition & media/performance, acoustics, adv sustainable design, architectural & urban design/conservation/project management/art in the global middle ages, art, space & nature, composition for screen, contemporary art painting/photography/practice/sculpture/theory, cultural studies, design and digital dedia, digital composition & performance, early keyboard performance studies, film directing, interior architectural design, landscape architecture, modern & contemporary art, history, curating & criticism, music in the community, musical instrument research, musicology, performance costume, Renaissance early modern studies, Scottish art & visual culture, sound design

UNIVERSITY OF ESSEX
www.essex.ac.uk

Faculty of Humanities and Comparative Studies; www.essex.ac.uk/hcs

History; www.essex.ac.uk/depts/history.aspx

history (modern, social & cultural, American), film studies, joint honours in range of subjects, cultural & social, digital, local, community & family/history in Britain

Department of Literature, Film, and Theatre Studies; www.essex.ac.uk/depts/lifts.aspx

comparative literature, creative writing, drama/& literature, English language/literature, English & United States literature, literature & film studies/history of art/sociology/philosophy/history, myth, literature and the unconscious, wild writing, literature, science & the environment, theatre studies

Dept of Philosophy & Art History; www.essex.ac.uk/depts/spah

philosophy/religion & ethics, continental philosophy, philosophy & psychoanalysis, theory & practice of human rights, numerous joint hons degrees, history of art/with theory, with mod langs/literature/film studies/history, gallery studies, curating contemporary art, curating Latin American art

Centre for Interdisciplinary Studies in the Humanities; www.essex.ac.uk/depts/centres-and-institutes/cish

Latin American Studies
Latin American studies with human rights or business

European Studies
European studies/with politics or modern languages

American studies
American (US) studies with politics/criminology

Humanities
BA(Hons), CertHE, Dip/MA, FdA, MA, MFA, MPhil, PGCert, PhD

Faculty of Social Sciences; www.essex.ac.uk/ss

Dept of Economics; www.essex.ac.uk/economics

accounting & financial economics, applied economics & data analysis, business economics, econometrics, economics, economics with mathematics/history; numerous jt courses, financial/international/management economics

Dept of Government; www.essex.ac.uk/government

European integration/politics, global & comparative politics, ideology & discourse analysis, international development/relations/& media, philosophy, politics & economics, political behaviour/economy, political science, conflict resolution, public opinion and polling

Dept of Languages and Linguistics; www.essex.ac.uk/linguistics

applied/experiential/linguistics, English language/literature, language acquisition, translation, interpretation & subediting, sociolinguistics, teaching English, language disorders, psycholinguistics & neurolinguistics, TEFL, phonology, syntax, literature & mod languages

Dept of Sociology; www.essex.ac.uk/sociology

advertising, culture & the media, media, culture & society, sociology & humanities/politics, criminology & media/social legislation, social psychology, social neurology, psychosocial studies, organized crime, terrorism & security; BA(Hons), BSc(Hons), Diploma, GradDip, MA, MPhil, MRes, MSc, PGDip, PhD, ProcDoc

Faculty of Law and Management; www.essex.ac.uk/lm

Essex Business School; www.essex.ac.uk/ebs
Centre for Global Accountability; Centre for Entrepreneurship Research; Essex Finance Centre; Essex Management Centre

accounting, economics, entrepreneurship & innovation, finance, financial management, banking, brand management, business management/administration, marketing, HRM, financial engineering, international enterprise & entrepreneurship/accounting/finance, social enterprise, global project & innovation management, management & organizational dynamics

Human Rights Centre; www.essex.ac.uk/humanrightscentre

human rights & Latin American studies/law/philosophy/politics/sociology, human rights & cultural diversity, human rights theory & practice

School of Law; www.essex.ac.uk/law

law/philosophy/politics/human rights, criminology & socio-legal research, English & French laws, European business law/governance, EU law, international law, health care law, human rights law, information technology, international human rights & humanitarian law, media and e-commerce, humanitarian law, international trade law/internet law, public law, environmental governance, UK human rights & public law; BA(Hons), BSc(Hons), DocProg, LlM, LLB, MPhil, MSc, PhD

Faculty of Science and Engineering; www.essex.ac.uk/se

Dept of Biological Sciences; www.essex.ac.uk/bs

biochemistry, biological sciences, biology, biomedical science, biotechnology, cardiac rehabilitation, ecology, environment & society, environmental governance, natural world, environmental resource management, genetics, marine biology, molecular medicine, sports & exercise science, plant biotechnology, wild writing

School of Computer Science and Electronic Engineering; www.essex.ac.uk/csee
computer games/networks/science/systems engineering, computational finance, data communication, electronics engineering, telecommunications engineering, telecommunications & data communications

School of Health and Human Sciences; www.essex.ac.uk/hss
adult/mental health nursing, health studies, health & organisational research, public health, midwifery, clinical psychology, social psychology & sociology, speech & language/occupational therapy, physiotherapy, healthcare practice, CPD

Department of Mathematical Sciences; www.essex.ac.uk/maths
mathematics & computing/economics/biology/finance, cryptography & network security, discrete mathematics & its applications, econometrics, operational research, statistics & data analysis, mathematics for secondary teaching

Dept of Psychology; www.essex.ac.uk/psychology
psychology, cognitive psychology/neuropsychology/neuroscience, research methods in psychology; BA(Hons), BEng, BSc(Hons), GradDip, MA, MPhil, MRes, MSc, PGDip, PhD, ProfDoc

Degrees validated by the University of Essex offered at:

WRITTLE COLLEGE
www.writtle.ac.uk

agriculture, animal science & management, business management, conservation wild life/management, design, equine, floristry, horticulture, post-harvest technology, sport & exercise performance; BA(Hons), BSc(Hons), CertMS, Certs, DipMS, FDAs, Higher Certs, MA, MBA, MSc

UNIVERSITY OF EXETER
www.exeter.ac.uk

University of Exeter Business School; www.business-school.exeter.ac.uk
accounting, finance, business, economics, econometrics, management, marketing, leadership, politics, tourism, employability; BA(Hons), MBA, MPhil, MSc, PGDip/Cert, PhD

Cambourne School of Mines; emps.exeter.ac.uk/mining-minerals-engineering/
renewable energy, sustainable use of national resources

College of Engineering, Mathematics & Physical Sciences; www.emps.exeter.ac.uk/engineering
Computer Science: bioinformation & systems biology, IT management for business, computer science, networking, electronics, applied artificial intelligence, electronic engineering
Engineering: civil/environmental/electronic/mechanical/materials engineering, engineering and management, adv/mathematics, computer science, biosystems engineering, urban water systems, international supply chain management, renewable energy, mining engineering
Geology: applied geology, mining geotechnology, engineering geology, mining geology, engineering technology, applied geotechnics
Mathematics: mathematics (applied climate science, mathematical biology), mathematics with computer science/accounting/economics/finance, bioinformatics & systems biology, biosystems engineering, financial management, natural science
Medical Imaging: diagnostic radiography
Minerals & Mining Engineering: minerals/mining engineering, mining geology, surveying & land/environment management, applied geotechnics
Physics & Astronomy: physics, astrophysics, medical imaging, biomedical physics, quantum systems, electromagnetic materials, nanomaterials, natural science

Renewable Energy: renewable energy; BSc(Hons), BEng, MEng, MSc, MPhil, PhD, MPhys

College of Humanities; www.humanities.exeter.ac.uk

Archaeology: archaeology & forensic science, anthropology, ancient history, heritage management, bioarchaeology, experimental/landscape archaeology, material culture studies

Classics & Ancient History: ancient history, classical studies, classics, art history/art & archaeology, ancient drama & society, Hellenistic culture, Roman myth & history, food & culture

Drama: drama, theatre practice – appl theatre, directing, physical performance, actor training, playwriting, dramaturgy, staging Shakespeare

English: English/studies, film, creative writing, criticism & theory, the 20th century, Victorian studies

Film Studies: film studies/with English, modern languages

History: ancient/modern/maritime/medieval/naval history, Arabic/M East studies, comb degs

Modern Languages: French, German, Italian, Hispanic studies, Russian, literature, linguistics, literary & applied translation

College of Life & Environmental Sciences; www.lifesciences.exeter.ac.uk

Biosciences: biology & animal behaviour, human bioscience, clinical/environmental science, biocatalysis, medical/bioinformatics, systems biology, food security & sustainability, applied ecology, conservation & diversity

Geography: geography, environmental science/management, conservation biology, climate change, critical human geography, sustainable development, energy policy

Psychology: psychology, animal behaviour, social & organizational psychology, psychological/cognitive therapies, sports exercise science

Sport and Health Sciences: sport & health science paediatric exercise, sport & exercise medicine/science/psychology, exercise, human biosciences, sports science; BSc(Hons), MPhil, BA(Hons), DocCiniPsychology, MSc, PhD, PGCert/Dip, MRes, BClinSci

College of Social Science & International Studies; www.social sciences.exeter.ac.uk

Arab & Islamic studies: Arab/Islamic studies, Kurdish/East/Persian/Palestine/Gulf/Iranian studies, ethnopolitics, Middle East history, north African politics

Graduate School of Education

creative art, special educational needs, TESOL, technology, creativity training, educational psychology, childhood & youth studies, English & education, sport science

PGCE: primary art/music/science/modern foreign languages, early years, secondary sciences/design & technology/English with media/drama/modern foreign languages/geography/information, communication technologies

School of Law

law, European (German/French) law, European studies, international business/international & comparative public law, international human rights law

Politics & International Relations: politics, international relations/studies

Sociology & Philosophy: sociology, philosophy, archaeology & anthropology, political economy, genetics & society, history & philosophy of biology, philosophy & sociology of science; BA(Hons), MA, PhD, MPhil, MA, PhD, LlB, LlM, MRes, DEdPsych, EdD, MEd

Peninsula College of Medicine and Dentistry; www.pms.exeter.ac.uk

clinical sciences, infection prevention & control, remote healthcare, clinical education, dentistry, clinical education, environmental & human health, medicine, surgery; BClinM, BDS, BMMS, MPhil, MD/MS, PhD, MSc

Degrees validated by University of Exeter offered at:

UCP MARJON-UNIVERSITY COLLEGE PLYMOUTH ST MARK & ST JOHN
www.ucpmarjon.ac.uk

acting, children, youth & community, drama, education & teacher training, English language, literature/teachng/creative writing, leadership, live music, media, journalism, speech, language, linguistics, sport, outdoor, coaching & PE; BA(Hons), BA/BSc, BEd, FdA church college certs; GTP, MA, MEd, MPhil, PGCE

UNIVERSITY COLLEGE FALMOUTH (INC DARTINGTON COLLEGE OF ARTS)
www.falmouth.ac.uk

3D design, advertising, applied art, ceramics, performance, choreography, contemporary crafts, creative music technology/computing, curatorial practice, dance, digital animation, drawing, English with creative writing/media, fashion design, film, fine art, game design, glass, graphic design, illustration, interactive design, interior design, jewellery, journalism, persuasive media, mobile apps, fashion/photography, radio production, screen & media performance, textile design, theatre (design and production, directing, writing); BA(Hons), FdA, MA, MPhil, PGDip, PhD

UNIVERSITY OF GLAMORGAN
www.glam.ac.uk

Cardiff School of Creative and Cultural Industries; www.ccc.glam.ac.uk
computer animation, culture & communication, drama, theatre, fashion/interior design, film studies/producing, video, games art, graphic communication, media culture & journalism, music/sound technology, performance & moving image, pop, photography, media production technology, radio, sound technology, scriptwriting, TV & film set design, visual effect & motion graphics; BA(Hons), FdA, MA, MPhil

Faculty of Health, Sport and Science; www.hesas.glam.ac.uk
Health & Social Care: chiropractic, clinical physiology(cardiology/respiratory), systemic counselling, diagnostic clinical ultrasound, nursing (children, adult, mental health, learning disability), midwifery, pharmacology & prescribing, social work & social care
Science: astronomy, chemistry, pharmaceutical science, biology, geology, geography, natural history, forensic & police science, environment & sustainability
Sport & Coaching: coaching sports & exercise science, coaching & performance, conditioning, sports development/management/psychology/studies, youth sport, nutrition, physical activity, rugby, football; BA(Hons), BSc(Hons), BN, FoundCerts, HEDip, HNC, HND, MA, MPhil, MSC/PGD/, PGC, PhD

Faculty of Advanced Technology; www.fat.glam.ac.uk
built environment, building information modelling, civil engineering, construction & surveying, quantity surveying & commercial management, construction project management, structural engineering management, computer science, computing, embedded systems design, GIS, mobile applications development/computing/telecommunications, communications engineering, computer games development, software engineering, intelligent computer systems, electrical & electronic engineering, computer forensics/security/systems security/systems engineering, information technology/mgt in business, mechanical/manufacturing engineering, energy systems engineering, renewable energy, lighting design & tech, live events technology, aeronautical engineering/systems, aircraft maintenance, avionics, mathematics, computing/financial mathematics, mathematical science; BEng(Hons), BSc, BSc(Hons), CertHE, DipHE, HNC, HND, MEng

Faculty of Business & Society; fbs.glam.ac.uk

Glamorgan Business School; www.bus.glam.ac.uk/business
finance, accounting, business, forensic/international accounting, Islamic banking & finance, management & development of international financial systems, HRM, logistics & supply chain management, strategic procurement management, marketing, international fashion marketing, PR, sports management/development, psychology

School of Humanities & Social Sciences; fbs.glam.ac.uk/humanities
art & design, fine art, art practice, art & health, wellbeing, criminology, criminology & law/psychology/sociology criminal justice, English/literature, creative & professional writing, Gothic studies, language, culture, & society, history, social & cultural

history, professional Welsh/TESOL/education/history/law, Welsh courses, public services, public/emergency services, health/& public service management, public leadership, community regeneration, health/& public service management, sociology & criminology/education/history/law/psychology

School of Law, accountancy & finance; fbs.glam.ac.uk/law

law, accounting, finance, forensic/international accounting, business, forensic/audit, Islamic banking & finance, management & development, international financial sytems, law, legal practice, international/commercial law, criminology/sociology, legal practice

School of Psychology; fbs.glam.ac.uk/psychology

psychology, applied/developmental/sport/health psychology, behavioural analysis, supervisory practice & therapy, play & therapeutic play, play therapy, supervisory practice in sport psychology, clinical & abnormal psychology; BA(Hons), BA/BSc, BSc(Hons), DocPublServ, FCert, FdA, GradDip Law, LlB(Hons), LlM/PhD/PgD, MA/PDip/Cert, MSc, PGD/PGC

The Centre for Lifelong Learning; www.cell.glam.ac.uk

astronomy, business courses, community courses/regeneration, communication technology, craft and design, creative industries, environmental studies, information, languages, social sciences

UNIVERSITY OF GLASGOW
www.gla.ac.uk

College of Arts; www.gla.ac.uk/colleges/arts

American studies, battlefield & conflict Mediterranean/archaeology, archaeological studies, art, style & design, arts of China/Europe, art history (transgression: 20th century avant-gardes/dress & textiles history), Celtic & Viking archaeology, American studies, Scottish/& Celtic studies, classics, composition, computer/forensics & e-discovery/& music, creative writing, English/English literature, early modern/modern/medieval history, European studies, film & TV studies, film journalism, historically informed performance practice, information management & forensics/preservation, international cinemas, media management, medieval & renaissance studies, modern & contemporary art, modernities(modernism/modernity & postmodernism), museum studies, musicology, music, philosophy, Scottish literature/history, social & cultural history, textile conservation, theatre studies, Victorian literature, war studies; BD(Min), BMus, DLitt, MA, MAHons, MLitt, MPhil, MTh, PhD

College of Medical Veterinary & Life Sciences; www.gla.ac.uk/colleges/mvls

Institutes: Biodiversity, Animal Health & Comparative Medicine; Cancer Sciences; Cardiovascular & Medical Sciences; Health & Wellbeing; Infection, Immunity & Inflammation, Molecular, Cell & Systems Biology, Neuroscience & Psychology;
Postgraduate degrees in: ecology & environmental biology, environmental biology & systematics, marine & freshwater ecology & environmental management, molecular medicine, cardiovascular sciences, clinical pharmacology, sport & exercise science/medicine, translational medicine, clinical/applied neuropsychology, clinical psychology, global health, primary care, public health, health technology, biomedical sciences, plant science, crop/biotechnology, behavioural sleep medicine, brain science

School of Life Sciences; www.gla.ac.uk/schools/lifesciences

anatomy, biochemistry, bioinformatics, biomedical/biological sciences, biotechnology, ecological & environmental biology/management, computing/& physiology, exercise science, genetics, immunology, marine & freshwater biology/ecology & environmental management, medical/& veterinary microbiology, microbiology, molecular/medicine & cellular biology, molecular/parasitology, pharmacology, physiology, plant science, sports medicine/science, veterinary bioscience, virology, zoology

School of Medicine; www.gla.ac.uk/medicine,

applied medical sciences, dentistry, medicine, health care, immunology, nursing (community, adult, surgical, children, public health), cardiovascular, child health, clinical nutrition/pharmacology/physics/psychology/neuroscience, critical care, evidence-based informatics, health profession education, human nutrition, forensic toxicology, medical visualisation, primary dentistry, oral surgery, endo/orthodontics, primary healthcare, paediatric science, medical genetics, public health, physiology, reproductive & maternal science, sport science & nutrition, sports/ & exercise medicine, surgical oncology, translational medicine

School of Veterinary Medicine; www.gla.ac.uk/schools/vet
veterinary biosciences, animal reproduction, veterinary medicine/surgery/public health
BSc, BSc(Vet Sci), BVMS, MVPH, PhD B(MedSci), MBChB, MD, MML, MMLE, MPC, MPH, PhD, BDS, BSc(Dent Sc), DDS, MSc

College of Science & Engineering; www.gla.ac.uk/colleges/scienceengineering

School of Chemistry; www.gla.ac.uk/schools/chemistry
chemistry, chemical physics, medical chemistry, sustainable energy

School of Engineering; www.gla.ac.uk/schools/engineering
aerospace engineering/systems & management, aeronautical engineering, aeronautics, architecture, automotive engineering, biomedical engineering, civil engineering, computer systems engineering, electronics & software engineering/music, electronic design, engineering & management, mechanical design/engineering, mechatronics, microcomputer systems engineering, nanosystems & nanotechnology, product design engineering, embedded systems engineering, structural engineering & mechanics, sustainable energy/world resources, telecommunications electronics

School of Computing Science; www.gla.ac.uk/schools/computing
computing, neuroinformatics, electronic & software engineering/development, software engineering, information retrieval/security/technology, mobile & ubiquitous sytems

School of Geographical & Earth Sciences; www.gla.ac.uk/schools/ges
earth science, geography, freshwater/marine/aquatic systems science, geoinformation technology & cartography, geomatics & management, geospatial & mapping science, human geography, landscape monitoring, marine systems science, international development

School of Mathematics & Statistics; www.gla.ac.uk/schools/mathematicsstatistics;
applied/pure mathematics, finance/accounting & mathematics, mathematical science, adv/statistics, environmental/social statistics, financial modelling/finance

School of Physics & Astronomy; www.gla.ac.uk/schools/physics
astronomy, physics, chemical/theoretical physics, astrophysics, advanced materials, energy & the environment, global security, life sciences

School of Psychology; www.gla.ac.uk/schools/psychology
psychology, brain imaging/sciences, psychological science; BEng, BSc, EngD, MEng, MSc, PGDip, PhD, EngD, PGDip

College of Social Sciences; www.gla.ac.uk/schools/social sciences

Adam Smith Business School; www.gla.ac.uk/schools/business
accountancy, finance, economics, banking & financial services, business & management, corporate governance & accountability, development studies, economic & financial sector policies, environmental & sustainable/Europe & international/finance & economic development, financial economics/forecasting & investment/modelling/risk management, international accounting & financial management/investment/banking & finance/business & economic development/entrepreneurship/corporate finance & banking/finance & economic policy/financial analysis, economics/management & design innovation/leadership/, management for China/strategic marketing/trade & finance/local economic development, management/with enterprise & business growth, HR, international finance, international real estate, quantitative finance, HR, public admin; BA, BSc, MA, MAQ(SocSci), MAcc, MBA, MFin, MSc, PhD

University of Glasgow

School of Education; www.gla.ac.uk/schools/education
academic practice, adult & continuous education, childhood practice, drug & alcohol studies, education (primary, secondary), literature & literacy, community learning/& development, music, RE, English language teaching/studies, inclusive education, learning & teaching in HE, organizational leadership, primary PE, professional learning & enquiry, psychological studies, religious & philosophical education, religion, education & culture, school strategic leadership, teaching adults, technological education, TESOL, young people, social inclusion & change; BA(Hons), BTechEd, BTechS, EdD, MA, MA(Hons), MEd, MLitt, MSc, MusicBEd, PhD

School of Interdisciplinary Studies; www.gla.ac.uk/schools/interdisciplinary
environmental stewardship, health & social studies, health & wellbeing, tourism, heritage & development, environment, culture & community, environmental science, technology & society; BSc, MA, MLitt, PGCert/Dip

School of Law; www.gla.ac.uk/schools/law
law, contemporary law & practice, corporate & financial/medical law, intellectual property & digital economy, international competition/commercial law, international law, law & security, professional legal practice, socio-legal studies; MRes, LlB, LlM, MRes, PgDip/Cert, PhD

School of Social & Political Science; www.ac.uk/schools/socialpolitical
Central & East European studies, Chinese studies, economic & social history, politics, public policy, sociology, city/regional planning & real estate planning, criminology, criminal justice, equality & human rights, Euro politics/law, global health/economy/security, housing studies, international politics/relations, international management for China, landscape/integrated research & practice, political communication, public policy, real estate regeneration, Russian, Central & East European studies, social science, social & cultural history, sociology, spatial planning, transnational crime, urban policy/practice/regeneration; MA, MA(SocSci), MSc, MRes, CPD, MLitt, EdD, PhD

GLASGOW CALEDONIAN UNIVERSITY
www.gcu.ac.uk/ebe

School of Engineering & the Built Environment; www.caledonian.ac.uk/ebe
3D computer animation, 3D design for virtual environments, adv computer networking, applied instrumentation & control, audio technology with electronics, building services engineering/surveying, computer aided mechanical engineering, computer games (art & animation/design/software development), computing (information/web systs development), construction management/economics, cyber security & networks, design practice & methods, digital security, forensics & ethical hacking, digital systems engineering, engineering: computing or creative industries, electrical power engineering, energy & environmental management, environmental civil engineering/management & planning, fire risk engineering, foundation (built environment/computing.engineering), graphic design for digital media, instrumentation & robotic/systems engineering, interior design, international project design/management, maintenance management, mechanical & power plant systs engineering, mechanical electronic systs engineering, mechanical engineering design/manufacture, network & communication engineering, network security/systems engineering, NET web systs development, particulate solids handling, quantity surveying, real estate management, robotic & mechatronic systems engineering, sustainable energy technology, telecomunication engineering, waste management, wireless communication technologies/networks; BA/BA(Hons), BEng/BEng(Hons), BSc/BSc(Hons), DipHE, MA/PGD, MSc/PGD, PhD, FD, Dips

Glasgow School of Business & Sociology; www.caledonian.ac.uk/cbs
accountancy, banking finance & risk management, business/studies/management/law, fashion buying, finance, financial investment & management/services, risk & operations, HRM, innovation & enterprise marketing, investment, international business/hospitality management/event management/tourism management, international brand management/fashion branding & marketing, international HR,

international trade, international retailing, law, business law, operations & business management, management, technology & enterprise, marketing, multimedia journalism, railway operations management, risk management, social enterprise, social sciences, TV writing (fiction); BA (Hons), MRes, PhD, LlB, LlM, MSc, PGD/C, PhD

School of Health & Life Sciences; www.caledonian.ac.uk/hls

diagnostic imaging sci, health studies, human nutrition & dietetics, human bioscience, nursing (adult/child/mental health/learning disabilities), nursing studies, oncology, operating dept practices, optometry, orthoptics, professional development specialist practice, physiotherapy, radiography, social work, biological & biomedical sciences, cell & molecular biology, food bioscience, forensic investigation, human biology, sociology, psychology, microbiology, pharmacology, psychology, BSc, BSc(Hons), DipHE, DPsych, MSc, OpthDisp, PGCert/Dip, PhD, MResBSc(Hons), BA(Hons), GradCert, MPhil, MSc, PgCert/Dip, PhD, ProfDoc, BMidwifery, BN

THE GLASGOW SCHOOL OF ART
www.gsa.ac.uk

animation, architecture, communication design, creative practices, design innovation, media/ceramics/interior/silversmithing & jewellery/fashion & textiles/product design, product design engineering, fine art, graphics, illustration & photography, medical visualisation & human anatomy, product engineering, sound for the moving media, visual communication; BA(Hons), BEng, BArch, DipArch, MA, MArch, MDes, MEng, MPhil, MRes, PhD

UNIVERSITY OF GLOUCESTERSHIRE
www.glos.ac.uk

School of Accounting & Law; insight.glos.ac.uk/academicschools/dal/Pages/default.aspx

accounting, law, financial management

School of Art & Design; insight.glos.ac.uk/academicschools/dad/Pages/default.aspx

advanced graphic design, fine art, photography, illustration, landscape architecture

School of Business & Management; insight.glos.ac.uk/academicschools/dbm/Pages/default.aspx

business & management, economics, enterprise, international business, strategy, marketing, management & branding/advertising, management studies, hospitality management, HRM, marketing management, tourism management

School of Media; insight.glos.ac.uk/academicschools/dcmp/Pages/default.aspx

creative media, film/production, journalism, mass communication, media practice, pop music, radio/TV production, film & screen enterprise, media film communication

School of Computing & Technology; insight.glos.ac.uk/academicschools/dc/Pages/default.aspx

forensic/computing. multimedia web design, interactive games design, information & communication technology, information technology

School of Humanities; insight.glos.ac.uk/academicschools/dh/Pages/default.aspx

creative writing, English literature/language, history, religion, philosophy, ethics, theology & religious study

School of Leisure; insight.glos.ac.uk/academicschools/delth/Pages/default.aspx

performing arts, strategic events hospitality/tourism management, sports management, play & playwork

School of Natural & Social Sciences; insight.glos.ac.uk/academicschools/NSS/Pages/default.aspx

animal biology, biology, counselling, community engagement & governance, criminology, geography, psychology, sociology, business/criminal/forensic/occupational psychology, environmental policy & management

University of Gloucestershire

Sport & Exercise; insight.glos.ac.uk/academicschools/dse/Pages/default.aspx
applied/sport & exercise science, sports science/coaching/development/education/strength & conditioning/therapy, sports chaplaincy/ministry

Institute of Education & Public Service; insight.glos.ac.uk/academicschools/education/Pages/default.aspx
applied health study, child care/community practice, health community & social care, integrated youth practice, social work/with adults, youth work; BA/BA(Hons), BSc/BSc(Hons), DipSW, HND, BEd, LlB MA, MPhil, MRes, MSc, PGCert, PGDip, MBA, CMS, DMS

UNIVERSITY OF GREENWICH
www.gre.ac.uk

School of Architecture and Construction; www.gre.ac.uk/schools/arc
architecture, advanced architectural design, building surveying/rehabilitation/engineering, built environment studies, construction surveying/management & economics, design & construction management, 3D digital design & animation, graphic & digital design, housing management & policy, facilities management, project management, real estate, estate management, fine art, garden design/history, landscape architecture/design/planning & assessment, occupational safety, health & environment, photography, project management, quantity surveying, web design & content planning; BA(Hons), BSc(Hons), Certs, Dip, HNC, HND, MA, MSc, MPhil, PGDip, PhD

The Business School; www.gre.ac.uk/schools/business
accounting, advertising, international/banking, business administration/entrepreneurship & innovation/psychology/studies/economics, business technology/law/technology, business logistics & transport management, business management/studies, economics, events management, finance, financial information systems, HRM, investment, international business/banking, international tourism management, marketing, marketing/communications, multimedia, personnel & development, PR & communication, project management for logistics, public services, purchasing & supply chain management/e-logistics, tourism management, strategic marketing/communications, transport & logistics management; BA(Hons), BSc(Hons), Certs, DBA, FD, HNC, HND, MA, MBA, MSc, PGDip, PhD

School of Computing & Mathematical Science; www.gre.ac.uk/schools/cms
applicable mathematics, business computing/information systems/information technology, computer science, computer security & forensics/& the law, computer systems & networking, computing (with games development, digital multimedia), computing & information systems, data warehousing & data mining, digital media technologies, film production/TV & interactive media, film & TV production, enterprise systems, financial mathematics, games & multimedia techniques, information systems management, IT with ebusiness/esecurity/systems & digital media, mathematics & computing, mathematics, statistics, software engineering, web technologies; BSc(Hons), FDSc, MA, MEng/BEng, MPhil, MSc, PhD

School of Education; www.gre.ac.uk/education
childhood studies, early years, education studies, ESOL, lifelong learning, primary education with QTS, PGCE, secondary education, numerous subject courses, physical education & sport, primary education, design & technology, learning, teaching & training with digital techn, youth & community work; BA(Hons), BELT, Cert, DipHE, EdD, FD, MA, MPhil, MSc, PGCert/Dip, PhD, PGCE

School of Engineering; www.gre.ac.uk/schools/engineering
business admin, accounting & financial management, business technology management, civil engineering/project management, communications systems & software engineering, computer networking/& server administration, computing & electronic systems, computer forensics/network security/networking/systems & software eng, electrical & electronic/

communications engineering, electrical power engineering, engineering business management, engineering management/projects & programming, embedded systems, extended engineering, highway structures, information & communication technology, IT management for business, manufacturing systems engineering, mechanical/& sustainable electrical power engineering, telecommunications systems engineering, waste environmental management engineering, wireless mobile communications systems engineering; BEng(Hons), BSc(Hons), HNC, HND, MEng, MSc

Greenwich Maritime Institute; www.gre.ac.uk/schools/gmi
maritime history/management/security studies, international maritime policy; MA, MBA, MPhil, PhD

School of Health and Social Care; www.gre.ac.uk/schools/health
health & wellbeing/social care, health visiting & school nursing, nursing (adult, child, mental health), occupational therapy, osteopathy, paramedic science, professional practice health & social care, public health, safeguarding children & young people, social work & social care, speech & language therapy, special community public health nursing; BA(Hons), BSc(Hons), DipHE, FD, GradDips, MA, MPhil, PGCert, PhD

School of Humanities and Social Sciences; www.gre.ac.uk/schools/humanities
creative writing, criminal psychology, criminology, drama, English literature/language/literature, London, film studies, financial & ecommerce/international & commercial law, history, international studies/justice, Japanese language teaching, language learning, law, media & communication/philosophy, media arts production/writing, professional acting, French, German, Italian, Spanish, politics, theatre practice, ELT; BSc(Hons), BA(Hons), FD, LlB, MA, MPhil, MSc, PGCert, PGDip, PhD

Medway School of Pharmacy; www.gre.ac.uk/schools/study/pa
medicines management, general/pharmacy practice, independent/supplementary prescribing, pharmacotherapy & services development; BSc(Hons), FdMM, FdPP, MPharm, MSc, PGCert/Dip

Natural Resources Institute; www.gre.ac.uk/schools/nri
agriculture for sustainable development, sustainable environmental management, rural development dynamic, food safety & quality management; BSc(Hons), MPhil, MSc, PhD

School of Science; www.gre.ac.uk/schools/science
app/biomedical sciences, biosciences, biotechnology, chemistry, forensic science, formulation science, environmental & earth sciences/conservation, geography, GIS, remote sensing, human nutrition, landscape economics, natural resources, pharmaceutical science/technology/analysis, professional football coaching, sport science, strength & conditioning; BSc(Hons), HNC, HND, MPhil, MSc, PGDip, PhD

GRIMSBY INSTITUTE/UNIVERSITY CENTRE
www.grimsby.ac.uk

accounting, animal care, business mgt, children/parenting, community development, creative music, criminality & youth work, computing, construction, creative arts, early childhood studies, digital film & TV production, electrical/electronics engineering, events/hospitality management, fine arts, food management, hair & beauty, health & child care, learning support, marketing, mechanical engineering, operations management, make-up/design, performance, photography, professional writing, refrigeration, sports & fitness, travel & tourism; BA(Hons), BSc(Hons), FdA, FdEd, FdSc, HEdDip, HNC, HND, MA, MBA, MSc, PGCE

HARPER ADAMS UNIVERSITY COLLEGE
www.harper-adams.ac.uk

agriculture, agricultural engineering/food marketing/science, animal health/welfare/wellbeing/science, bioveterinary science, business management, conservation & forest protection, countryside management/& environment, crop management, entomology, environmental management, farm business management, food marketing/& consumer studies, food, nutrition & wellbeing, meat business management, off-road vehicle design, production management, rural affairs estate management, management, marketing, soil & water management, veterinary/nursing, physiotherapy/pharmacy, wildlife conservation & resource management, sustainable agriculture; BSc(Hons), FdSc, MBA, MSc, PGDip/Cert

HERIOT-WATT UNIVERSITY
www.hw.ac.uk

School of the Built Environment; www.sbe.hw.ac.uk
architectural engineering/project management, carbon management in the built environment, civil & structural engineering, housing & real estate, quantity surveying, construction project management, structural & foundation engineering & water resources, built environment research, real estate & planning/investment & finance/management & development, building conservation, sustainable urban management, community design, urban and regional planning, planning & property development, water resources and catchment development, safety & risk management, urban studies; BSc(Hons, Ord), BEng, MEng, MRes, MSc, PGDip/Cert, PhD

School of Mathematical and Computer Sciences; www.macs.hw.ac.uk
actuarial mathematics/science, advanced internet applications, applied mathematical sciences, artificial intelligence, computational biology, computer science (interactive design/internet systems technology), computer systems management, creative software systems, financial mathematics, information systems/technology (business/software systems), mathematics, probabilty & statistics, software engineering, statistical modelling, statistics; BSc(Hons), MEng, MMath, MRes, MSc, PGDip/Cert, PhD

School of Engineering and Physical Sciences; www.eps.hw.ac.uk
biochemistry, bioprocessing, biochemical engineering, chemistry/with forensic materials, chemical/biochemical management, chemical engineering/physics, combined science, computational chemistry/engineering, forensic science/materials, pharmaceutical chemistry, bioprocessing, chemical engineering with pharmaceutical chemistry/nanotechnology & microsystems, oil & gas technology, pharmacological chemistry, sustainability engineering, automobile & energy engineering, electrical power engineering, petroleum/pipeline engineering, energy engineering, physics/with electronics/environmental science, mathematical engineering physics, microengineering, nano-technology and microsystems, ocean systems, photonics, optoelectronic devices, robotics, computing & electronics, electrical & electronic engineering (computer & internet engineering/microwaves & electronics information technology (embedded systems/mobile communications, applied systems), microsystems, nanoscience, photonics & optoelectronic devices, renewable energy, sustainability engineering, mechanical engineering, creative 3D digital technologies, materials for sustainable & renewable energies, renewable/energy engineering, robotics & cybertronics, sustainability, super conductivity, gravitation & vacuum engineering; BEng, BSc(Ord,Hons), EngD, MChem, MEng, MPhil, MPhys, PhD

School of Life Sciences; www.hw.ac.uk/sls
applied psychology (forensic science), engineering psychology with ergonomics, psychology with human health, biological sciences (cell and molecular biology/food science/human health/microbiology), bioprocesses, biotechnology, brewing and distilling, food science/safety & health/nutrition, food & beverage science, applied marine biology, climate change: managing the marine environment, environmental analysis & assessment, marine biodiversity & biotechnology, marine resource development & protection,; BSc(Hons), MSc/Cert/Dip, PGDip, PhD

School of Management and Languages; www.hw.ac.uk/sml

accountancy & business law/finance, business/adminstration, business management with HRM/marketing/business law/enterprise/economics, economics, finance & management, international fashion marketing/management, international business management with accountancy/finance/HRM/logistics/sustainable management, investment management, logistics & supply chain management, management with business law/enterprise/HRM/marketing/operations management, maritime logistics & supply chain management, retail, Arabic–English translating & conference interpreting, applied languages & translating (French/German) (French/Spanish) (German/Spanish), Chinese–English translating and conference interpreting/computer-assisted translation tools, international management & languages, interpreting studies & skills, British sign language; BA(Hons, Ord), GradDip, MA(Hons), MSc

Heriot-Watt Institute of Petroleum Engineering; www.pet.hw.ac.uk

geoscience, marine resource management, marine renewable energy, petroleum engineering, renewable energy development, reservoir evaluation & management; MPhil, MSc, PhD

School of Textiles and Design; www.tex.hw.ac.uk

design for textiles/fashion/interior/art, fashion technology/communication/marketing & retailing/menswear/womenswear, interior design, practice-based design, textile design & clothing manufacture, textile science & technology; BA, BSc(Hons,Ord), MA, MSc, MPhil,PhD

Edinburgh Business School; www.ebsglobal.net

financial management, HRM, marketing, strategic planning; DBA, MBA, MSc

Degrees validated by Heriot-Watt University offered at:

EDINBURGH COLLEGE OF ART
www.eca.ac.uk

architectural/conservation/project management, animation,, fashion, film directing, glass, graphic design, illustration, interior design, fine art, jewellery, landscape architecture, media art, painting, performance costume, photographic science, product design, textiles, urban design; BAArch, BA(Comb), BSc(Hons, Ord), MAHons, MPhil, MSc, PhD

UNIVERSITY OF HERTFORDSHIRE
www.herts.ac.uk

Business School; www.herts.ac.uk/schools-of-study/courses/business

applied/accounting with financial management, business adminstration/economics/studies, corporate governance, economics, events management, finance, financial management/modelling, global business, hospitality, HRM, information systems, international/management tourist & hospitality management, investment management, IT for business, marketing, tourism, project mnagement; BA/BSc, BA(Hons), BSc, DBA, DMan, MA, MBA, MPhil, MSc, PGCert/Dip, PhD

School of Computer Science; www.herts.ac.uk/courses/schools-of-study/computer-science

artificial intelligence/robotics, business computing, computer science/networking, distributed data measurement/systems & networks, e-learning technology, business/entertainment systems, information technology (networks/software engineering), mobile computing, multimedia technology, networks, robotics, secure computing systems, software eng, web-based systems; BSc(Hons), MEng, MPhil, MSc, PGCert/Dip, PhD

School of Creative Arts; www.herts.ac.uk/courses/schools-of-study/creative-arts

audio recording & production, digital/animation, games art, character creation, contemporary applied arts, engineering product design, fashion, film & TV documentary/entertainment/fiction, fine art, graphic design, illustration, interactive media software/design, industrial/engineering product/product/multimedia design, model design/effects, music composition/technology/entertainment industry management/technology, photography/& media, screen cultures & media production, songwriting, sound design, special/visual effects; BA(Hons), MA, PgCert/Dip, MSc, MPhil, PhD

School of Education; www.herts.ac.uk/courses/schools-of-study/education

deaf children education, early years, graduate teaching, mentoring & coaching, primary/secondary education; BA(Hons), BEd, EdD, FdA, MA, MPhil, PGCert/Dip, PGCE, PhD

School of Engineering & Technology; www.herts.ac.uk/courses/schools-of-study/engineering-and-technology

aerospace engineering/systems/management, pilot studies, space technology, automotive engineering, motorsport technology, computer & network technology, digital film & TV technology, data communication networks, embedded intelligent systems, film & TV production, mechanical engineering, multimedia technology, digital communications & electronics, digital systems & computer engineering, electronics/electrical engineering, adv digital systems, biometrics & cybersecurity, radio mobile communication, manufacturing management, operations & supply chain management, internet technology; BSc(Hons), BEng, MEng, MSc, PgDip/Cert, MPhil, PhD

School of Health and Emergency Professions; www.herts.ac.uk/courses/schools-of-study/health-and-emergency-professions

diagnostic imaging/radiography, dietetics, medical imaging, oncology, paramedic science, physiotherapy, radiation sciences, radiotherapy, sports therapy/science, sport, health & exercise wellbeing, ultrasound; BSc(Hons), DHRes, FD, MPhil, MSc, PG/ert/Dip, PhD

School of Humanities; www.herts.ac.uk/courses/schools-of-study/humanities

acting & screen performance, American studies, creative writing, English language & communication/literature/teaching, ELT, film & TV aesthetics, history, journalism/& media communications, media cultures, mass communication, modern literary cultures, new media publishing, philosophy; BA(Hons), MA, MPhil, PGCert/Dip, PhD

School of Law; www.herts.ac.uk/courses/schools-of-study/law

commercial law, e-commerce law, international law, telecomm law, legal practice, maritime law, corporate practice, dispute resolution, private client, goverment & politics; BSc(Hons), Diploma, LlB(Hons), LlM, MPhil, PGDip, PhD, Univ Cert

School of Life Sciences; www.herts.ac.uk/courses/schools-of-study/life-sciences

biochemistry, bioinformatics, biological/biomedical/science, biotechnology, environmental management, exercise science, genetics, geography, molecular biology, pharmaceutical science, pharmacology, pharmacovigilance, physiology, sports studies/therapy, sport & exercise science/rehabilitation, sustainable planning/transport, water & environmental management; BSc/BSc(Hons), MSc, PgCert/Dip

School of Nursing, Midwifery & Social Work; www.herts.ac.uk/courses/schools-of-study/nursing-and-midwifery/

nursing (pre & postqual, adult, child, mental health, learning disabilities), health visiting, social work/intervention midwifery (pre & postqual) and women's health, nursing (learning disability), social work, specialist community nursing; BSc/BSc(Hons), DipHE, DipHE Nursing, MSc, NVQs, PGDip/PGCert

School of Pharmacy; www.herts.ac.uk/courses/schools-of-study/pharmacy

advancing pharmacy practice, medicinal chemistry, pharmacy, pharmaceutical science/analysis; MPharm, MPhil, MSc, PGCert/Dip, PhD

School of Physics, Astronomy and Mathematics; www.herts.ac.uk/courses/schools-of-study/physics-astronomy-and-mathematics

astrophysics, financial market analysis, financial maths, mathematics, physics; BSc(Hons), MPhil, MSc, PhD

School of Post Graduate Medicine;
www.herts.ac.uk/courses/schools-of-study/postgraduate-medicine
clinical medicine, dermatology skills & treatment, health & medical education, medical healthcare & stimulation, mental health practice, psychiatric practice, western medical acupuncture, skin integrity skills & practice; MD, MSc, PGCert/Dip

School of Psychology; www.herts.ac.uk/courses/schools-of-study/psychology
psychology, behavioural therapy/neuropsychology, clinical/health psychology, therapeutic counselling, occupational/organizational psychology; BSc(Hons), DClinPsy, MSc, PGDip

Degrees validated by the University of Hertfordshire offered at:

HERTFORDSHIRE REGIONAL COLLEGE
www.hrc.ac.uk

3D dimensional design, art & design, business, early years, engineering, fine art practice, graphic design, IT, multimedia; FD

NORTH HERTFORDSHIRE COLLEGE
www.nhc.ac.uk

bioscience, business (with marketing/HRM/ IT/multimedia/finance), computer technology, early years, education, leisure management, sports studies, management studies, fashion & textiles; BSc, FD, PGCE

OAKLANDS COLLEGE
www.oaklands.ac.uk

animal management, teacher training, numerous non-degree courses in range of subjects, work-based learning; FD, Dips, HNC, HND, Nat Dips NVQs, BSc(Hons)

WEST HERTS COLLEGE
www.westherts.ac.uk

accounting, advertising, art & design, beauty, business & management, care & early years, construction, counselling, ESOL, forensic science, holistic therapies, hospitality & catering, information technology, legal executive, management studies, marketing, media & photography, performing arts & music, personal development, public services, retail, sport, teaching & training, travel; BA(Hons), BTEC, C&G, College Cert/Dips, Nat Dips, PGDip

THE UNIVERSITY OF HUDDERSFIELD
www2.hud.ac.uk

School of Applied Sciences;
www2.hud.ac.uk/sas
Chemical & Biological Sciences: analytical/chemistry, biochemistry, bioscience, chemical engineering/science, nutrition & health, forensic & analytical science, medical biochemistry/biology/genetics, pharmacy, pharmaceuticals, public health

Logistics & Hospitality Management: business & logistics management, transport & logistics management, logistics & supply chain management, global logistics, hospitality management, events management, travel & tourism; BA(Hons), BSc(Hons), HND, MA, MChem, MPharm, MSc, MSci, PhD

School of Art, Design and Architecture; www2.hud.ac.uk/ada

3D digital design, advertising design, animation, architectural technology, architecture, construction/& project management, contemporary arts, construction, costume/with textiles, digital arts practice (games art/media art/multimedia design), exhibition & retail design, fashion, fashion and textiles buying/management/retailing/design with marketing/production/textiles, fine art, graphic design, illustration, interdisciplinary art & design, international design marketing & communication/fashion design/graphic design practice motion graphics, multimedia design, photography, product design, spatial design, surface design for fashion & interiors, transport design, textiles, textile/crafts design for fashion & interiors,; BA(Hons), BSc(Hons), CerHE, DipHE, FdA, FdSc, MA, MArch, MSc

University of Huddersfield Business School; www2.hud.ac.uk/uhbs

accountancy, advertising, banking & finance, business administration/information management/law & management/project management/operational management/studies, commercial law, entrepreneurship, environmental management, European business, events management, financial services, finance, global business, hospitality management, HRM, international business/marketing/hospitality management/HRM, legal executive/practice, marketing, journalism, law, legal practice, management studies, marketing communications, international/marketing, media relations, PR, retail, risk, disaster & environmental management, small business, travel & tourism; BA(Hons), FdA, GradDipLaw, HND, LlB(Hons), LlM, MBA, MSc, PGCE, PGDip, PGDip/Cert

School of Computing and Engineering; www2.hud.ac.uk/ce

automotive design/engineering, motorsport engineering, computer games programming/technology, computing science/systems engineering, computer games production/technology, communications/electronic/electrical engineering, engineering control systems & instrumentation, engineering management, information & communication technology, information systems management, intrrnet security, network technology & management, software development/engineering, engineering & technology management, web technology; BEng(Hons), HNC, HND, MEng, MSc, PhD, UniFdCert

School of Education and Professional Development; www2.hud.ac.uk/edu

teacher training (PGCE in numerous subjects; primary, secondary, lifelong learning), education, early/childhood studies, early years, guidance, leadership in education & public service, learning & development, learning support, multimedia & e-learning, religion & education, TESOL, vocational education; BA(Hons), CertEd, FdA, MA, PGradDip/Cert, PGCE

Human and Health Sciences; www2.hud.ac.uk/hhs

adv healthcare/nursing practice, childcare welfare & safeguarding, criminology/& international politics, community nursing, diabetes/end of life palliative care, health & social care, health visiting/schools, operating dept practice, public health nursing, sociology, behavioural sciences, district nursing, midwifery, occupational therapy, physiotherapy, podiatry, psychology, social work, nursing (adult, child, learning disability, mental health), perioperative practice, child/welfare, safeguarding, health & community studies; DipHE, MA, MSc, PGDip/Cert, PhD, ProfDoc

Music, Humanities and Media; www2.hud.ac.uk/mhm

drama, English/literature, creative writing, broadcast/sports, history/& politics, literary studies, modern languages, music technology/audio/production & sound recording/technology, pop music; BA(Hons), FdA, MA, PdF, PhD

UNIVERSITY OF HULL
www.hull.ac.uk

Faculty of Arts and Social Sciences; www.hull.ac.uk/fass

American studies, archaeology, arts & new media,- creative writing, digital media, drama, English, EFL, EU governance, film studies, French, German, Spanish, Italian, translation studies, TESOL, gender studies, geography, globalization & governance, history (20th century, cultural, medieval, maritime, military, European, social), history of art, music/technology, jazz and pop music, internet computing, media culture & society, theatre & performance, philosophy, international/politics, globalization & governance, psychology, social policy/work, social science, sociology, Spanish law, religion, theatre & performance, theology, travel studies, war & security studies

School of Law

law (commercial, international, business, human rights, environmental, French, Spanish, German, European public), legislative studies, criminology, international law & restorative justice/politics; BA(Hons), BMus, BSc(Hons), LlB, LLM, MA, MEd, MMus, MPhil, MR/MRes, PGDip/Cert, PhD

The Hull University Business School; www.hull.ac.uk/hubs

accounting, advertising, business, business/economics/technology management/analytics, economics, financial management, HRM, international business, investment, IT/management, logistics, marketing management, money, banking, finance, sport, leisure, tourism, supply chain management; BA(Hons), BSc(Hons), MBA, MPhil, MRes, MSc, PhD

Faculty of Health and Social Care; www.hull.ac.uk/fhsc

autonomous practice, community care, colonoscopy, cconsultation, clinical leadership, critical care, dental nursing, nursing (adult, children's, knowledge transfer, practice teaching, learning disabilities, acute/mental health, community), gastroenterology, leadership in health & social care, midwifery, non-medical prescribing, operating dept practice, critical/emergency/neonatal care, public health, sexual health & well being; Adv Diploma, BSc(Hons), FD, MPhil, MRes, PhD,Univ Cert,PGDip/Cert

The Hull York Medical School; www.hyms.ac.uk

anatomical science, biomedical science, cancer, cardiovascular medicine, child health, clinical sciences, clinical techniques & skills, cognitive behavioural therapy, dermatology, evidence-based decision making, gastrointestinal medicine, human evolution, immunology, medicine, medical education, mental health, metabolic & renal medicine, pathology, person-centred care, population health & medicine, reproduction, respiration, sport & exercise educscience, surgery; BSc, MBBS, MPhil, MA, MRes, MSc/Dip/Cert, PGCert/Dip, PhD

Faculty of Education; www.2.hull.ac.uk/ifl

childhood education & care, children's interpersonal studies, early childhood studies/years, education & learning/society, primary education (QTS), e-learning, EYPS, HE, inclusive education, integrative counselling, learning & support/teaching, lifelong learning, TESOL, inclusive education, learning support, mentoring in education, PGCE primary/secondary, primary teaching, social inclusion, special needs; BA, EdD, FD, GradCert, MA, MEd, MPhil, MSc, PGCE, PhD

Postgraduate Medical Institute; www2.hull.ac.uk/pgmi

cancer, cardiovascular respiratory, community/rehabilitation studies; MD, MPhil, PhD

Faculty of Science; www.hull.ac.uk/science

Biological Sciences: aquatic zoology, biology, biomedical science, coastal marine biology, ecology, human biology, marine & freshwater biology, molecular medicine, zoology

Chemistry: biological chemistry, chemistry, analytical chemistry, forensic science, pharmaceutical science, molecular medicine, nanotechnology, toxicology

Computer Science: computer science/engineering games development/programming, computer software/systems engineering, information systems, computer graphics/games programming, NET distribution systems/development

Engineering: chemical engineering, electrical & electronic engineering, electrical product design, mechanical engineering, medical engineering, medical product design, product innovation, embedded systems, automatic control, wireless systems engineering

Geography: human/physical geography, environmental management/technology

Physics: applied/physics, astrophysics, nanotechnology, philosophy

Sports Science, Health & Exercise: coaching, sports & exercise science, rehabilitation

Psychology: psychology, clinical psychology, health psychology; BA, BEng, BSc, BSc/MEng, MPhil, MPhys, MPhysGeog, MRes, MSc, PhD

Degrees validated by the University of Hull offered at:

BISHOP BURTON COLLEGE
www.bishopburton.ac.uk

agriculture, animal management, applied science, art, design & fashion, business & management, countryside, environmental sustainability, equine, floristry, food, garden design & horticulture, public services, sport, teacher training, tourism; BA(Hons), BSc(Hons), BSc(Ord), BTECExtel, FD, FdSc, HNC, MSc, PGCE

DONCASTER COLLEGE
www.don.ac.uk

animation & games/illustration, applied social science, business/& management, building services, criminal justice, construction, counselling, dance & theatre, early years, education, engineering, English, film & TV, fine art, fashion & textiles, graphic design, HRM, music technology, sport & exercise science; BA(Hons), BSc, BSc(Hons), FD, HNC, HND, MA, MSc, NVQs, PCE, PGCert

IMPERIAL COLLEGE, LONDON
www3.imperial.ac.uk

Faculty of Engineering;
www3.engineering.imperial.ac.uk

adv composites for aeronautics, aeronatical engineering, aerospace materials, adv computational methods, bioengineering, biomedical engineering, biochemistry, biotechnology, composites in science, technology, & engineering, chemical technology, chemical engineering, process systems engineering; civil/structural engineering, structural steel design, concrete structures, earthquake engineering, engineering geology, environmental eng, geotechnics, hydrology, soil mechanics, transport, water resources management; computing & artificial intelligence/in biology & medicine/games/vison & interactivity/software engineering, computer science (games, vision, software engineering, biology, medicine), computing (biomedical applications/architecture/creative industries/distributed systems/machine learning/performance modelling/visual information processing), pure mathematics & computational logic, computational statistics, earth science & engineering, geology, geophysics, environmental/petroleum geoscience/geophysics, materials & energy finance, petroleum science engineering, electronic/electrical engineering, analogue & digital integrated circuit design, information systems engineering, communications & signal processing, control systems; material science & engineering management, biomaterials & tissue engineering, nuclear engineering, advanced materials, composites; adv/mechanical engineering, nuclear engineering, innovation design engineering; BEng, MA, MEng, MSc, MSci, PhD

Faculty of Medicine;
www1.medicine.imperial.ac.uk

medicine, allergy, bioinformation & theoretical systems, biomedical research, cardiorespiratory nursing, epidemology, haematology, human molecular genetics, immunology, infection management for pharmacists, medical ultrasound, molecular biology & pathology of viruses, molecular medicine, neuroscience, paediatrics, preventative cardiology, public health, quality & safety in healthcare, reproductive biology, surgery/technology/science, BSc, CAS, MB BS, MEd, MPH, MRes, MSc, MSci, PhD

Imperial College Business School;
www3.imperial.ac.uk/business-school

accounting/management analysis, actuarial finance, business economics, finance, innovation, international health management, management, managerial economics, marketing/management, people & organisational behaviour, project management, risk management and financial engineering, strategic marketing; BSc, MBA, MSc, PhD

Faculty of Natural Sciences; www3.imperial.ac.uk/naturalsciences

chemical biology, chemistry and management/medicinal chemistry/molecular physics, green chemistry, nanomaterials, plastic electronics, drug discovery,
Life Sciences: applied biosciences, biochemistry, biology, bioimaging sciences, bioinformatics & genomics, biomedical science, biotechnology, cell & molecular biology, conservation/science & forest protection, ecological applications, ecology, environment & conservation, microbiology, plant science & biotechnics, taxonomy & biomedicine, zoology
Mathematics: applied/pure mathematics, mathematical finance, mathematical physics, statistics
Physics: physics, optics and photonics, plastic electronics, plasmonics & metamaterials, quantum fields and fundamental forces, shock physics, theoretical physics, theory and simulation of materials; BSc, MRes, MSci, PhD

KEELE UNIVERSITY
www.keele.ac.uk

Faculty of Health; www.keele.ac.uk/facs/health

School of Medicine; www.keele.ac.uk/depts/schoolofmedicine
biomedical engineering, cell and tissue engineering, clinical audit/practice/pathology, end of life care, primary care, parasitology, vector biology, foundation medical practice, geriatric medicine, leadership & management, medical education, medical science, medicine, obstetrics & gynaecology, stroke treatment, surgery

School of Pharmacy; www.keele.ac.uk/schools/pharm
clinical (hospital) pharmacy, public health/community pharmacist, prescribing adviser, medical/non medical/practice-based prescribing, medicines management

Nursing and Midwifery; www.keele.ac.uk/depts/ns
acute care, adult/children's nursing/mental health/learning disabilities, adv professional practice, clinical practice, critical care, end of life care, independent practice development, midwifery, operating dept practice, pain science & management, post-registration rheumatology nursing

School of Health and Rehabilitation; www.keele.ac.uk/depts/pt
applied clinical anatomy, health science, individual health, neurological rehabilitation, neuromusculoskeletal healthcare, osteopathy, pain science management, physiotherapy; MBChB, BSc, MSc, MSci, MPharm, PGCert, MMedSci, MPhil, PhD, MD

Faculty of Humanities and Social Sciences; www.keele.ac.uk/facs/humass

Keele Management School; www.keele.ac.uk/schools/ems
accounting, finance, actuarial science, business management/economics, economics, European industrial relations, employment law, finance & IT/management, HRM, international business, leadership, management, management & IT, marketing; MA, MBA, MSc, PGCert, PGDip, UnivCert

School of Humanities; www.keele.ac.uk/schools/hums
American studies/literature and culture, English, creative writing, film studies, English and American literatures, humanities, Victorian studies, early modern history, history, local and public history, medieval cultural history, film studies/theory, media communication/global media & culture, medical humanities, music/technology, popular music, performance, composition

Keele Law School; www.keele.ac.uk/depts/law
child care law & practice, gender, sexuality & human rights, globalization & justice, medical ethics & law, law, law with politics/criminology, law & society, safeguarding adults

School of Politics, International Relations and Philosophy; www.keele.ac.uk/spire
diplomatic studies, environmental politics, European politics & culture, global security, human rights, international relations, parties & politics, philosophy, politics, climate change

School of Public Policy and Professional Practice; www.keele.ac.uk/schools/pppp
Education: ADP, creative and critical practice, developing educational practice, educational leadership/studies/management/learning, mathematics development, PGCE (subject enhancement, pre-teaching training), teaching & learning, social work, education, health executive/systems/policy, public policy, gerontology, health services management, HE teaching & learning, communiity health, geriatric medicine, mentoring management, professional leadership & management; GradDip Law, EdD, LlB, LLM, MA, MBA, MRes, MSc, PGCE, PGDip/Cert, PhD

Faculty of Natural Sciences; www.keele.ac.uk/facs/sci/

School of Computing and Mathematics; www.scm.keele.ac.uk
actuarial science, computer science, creative computing, finance/management and IT, information systems, IT management for business, mathematics (pure, applied, statistics), project management, smart systems, web & internet technologies

School of Life Sciences; www. keele.ac.uk/depts/bi
biochemistry, biology, biomedical blood/science, human biology, molecular parasitology and vector biology, neuroscience

School of Physical and Geographical Sciences; www.keele.ac.uk/schools/dps/
chemistry, chemicals sciences, medicinal chemistry, analytical, materials & surface chemistry, spectroscopy, bioinorganic chemistry, chemical ecology, green chemistry and clean energy, organic chemistry, photochemistry, applied environmental science, earth science, environment and sustainability, green technology, geography, geology, geoscience, human/physical geography: forensic science; astrophysics, physics

School of Psychology; www.keele.ac.uk/depts/ps
psychology, child social development, clinical psychology, counselling psychology/supervision, psychology/of health & wellbeing; BA, BSc, DClinPsy, DSc, MGeoscience, MRes, MSc, PGCert, PGDip, PhD

UNIVERSITY OF KENT
www.kent.ac.uk

Faculty of Humanities; www.kent.ac.uk/humanities

Kent School of Architecture; www.kent.ac.uk/architecture
architecture, architectural visualisation, arhitecture & cities/sustainable development

School of Arts; www.kent.ac.uk/arts
drama & theatre studies, European theatre, film studies, fine art, history & philosophy of art/aesthetics, music technology/composition, performance arts/practice, event & experience design, music & audio arts, theatre dramaturgy

School of English; www.kent.ac.uk/english
English/American literature, post-colonial studies, creative writing, critical theory, Dickens & Victorian culture, medieval & early modern studies, 18th century studies, jt degrees

School of European Culture & Languages; www.kent.ac.uk/secl
classical & archaeological studies/history, archaeology of the late transmarche, Hellenic & Hellenic middle east, comparative literature, drama, English language & linguistics, English & American literature, history, French, German, Hispanic studies, history of archaeology, Italian, language & linguistic studies, modern European literature, philosophy, religious studies, Roman history & art, history & philosophy of art

School of History; www.kent.ac.uk/history
American studies, history, European history, history of science, modern history, technology & medicine, medieval & modern studies, propaganda & war, war studies, war, media & society, science, community & society; BA(Hons), BSc(Hons), MA, MArch, MDram, MPhil, PhD

Faculty of Science; www.kent.ac.uk/stms

Dept of Bioscience; www.kent.ac.uk/bio
biology, biomedical imaging, biochemistry, bioengineering, giotechnology, reproductive medicine/science & ethics, cancer biology, science, community & society

School of Computing; www.cs.kent.ac.uk

adv/computer science – artificial intelligence/consultancy/networks, business administrration/information science, computing & business administration, computer intelligence, business information technology, computing security, future computing, networks & security, adv programming for multicore systems, business/IT/information science, software engineering, web computing/applications

School of Engineering and Digital Arts; www.eda.kent.ac.uk;

advanced/electronic/computer systems engineering, computing systems, digital visual effects/arts, electronic & communications engineering, drama & multimedia, information security/biometrics, mobile communication methods, multimedia technology & design, web computing, wireless communication & signal processing

School of Mathematics, Statistics & Actuarial Science; www.kent.ac.uk/lsmsas

applied/actuarial science, bioscience, drug, financial & accounting mathematics, pure/applied maths, statistics, finance, investment, risk, mathematics & applications

Medway School of Pharmacy; www.msp.kent.ac.uk

medicines management, general pharmacy practice, pharmacy, independent supplementary prescribing, drug discovery

School of Physical Sciences; www.kent.ac.uk/physical-sciences

astrophysics, astronomy, forensic chemistry/science, physics, planetary/space science; BA(Hons), BEng, BSc(Hons), DClinPsych, MD, MRes, MPhil, MSc, Msurg, PCert, PDip, PhD

Faculty of Social Sciences; www.kent.ac.uk/socsci

School of Anthropology and Conservation; www.kent.ac.uk/sac

anthropology (social/biological/medical), biodiversity conservation & management, conservation biology, environmental anthropology, ethnicity, ethnobotany, evolution & human behaviour, conservation & int wildlife trade/tourism, social/visual anthropology, wildlife conservation; BA(Hons), BSc(Hons), MA, MSc, PhD

Kent Business School; www.kent.ac.uk/kbs

accounting, business administration, business/management studies, finance, financial services/management, HRM, international business, logistics, management science, marketing management, sustainability management, tourism management, value chain management; BA(Hons), BBA, BSc(Hons), MBA, MEBA, MPhil, MSc

School of Economics; www.kent.ac.uk/economics

agricultural economics, applied environmental economics, econometrics, economics, finance, financial economics, economic development, international finance; BSc(Hons), MPhil, PhD, MSc

Kent Law School; www.kent.ac.uk/law

international/criminal justice, English law, European legal studies/law, numerous joint degrees, international environmental/commercial/economic law, international criminal justice, medical law & ethics, public international law, senior status; BA(Hons), LlB, LlM, MPhil, PhD

Centre for Journalism; www.kent.ac.uk/journalism

journalism, multimedia journalism, journalism & the news industry; BA(Hons)

School of Politics and International Relations; www.kent.ac.uk/politics

comparative federalism, conflict, peace & security, European governance, international conflict analysis/law/human relations, politics, peace & multicultural studies, political theory, politics of international terrorism, security & terrorism; BA(Hons), MA, MPhil, PhD

Dept of Psychology; www.kent.ac.uk/psychology

applied psychology, cognitive psychology/neuropsychology, clinical/ developmental psychology, forensic psychology, group processes & intergroup relations, psychology, social psychology; BSc(Hons), MPhil, MSc, PhD

School of Social Policy, Sociology and Social Research; www.kent.ac.uk/sspssr

autism studies, criminal justice studies, criminology, cultural studies, health & social care, intellectual & development disabilities, international/social policy, sociology, social work/science, migration studies, substance misuse management; BA(Hons), BSc(Hons), Certificate and Diplomas, MA, MPhil, MSc, PhD

Centre for Sports Studies; www.kent.ac.uk/sports-studies
health & fitness, fitness & training, human anatomy & physiology, rehabilitation, sports massage/therapy, sports & exercise/for health/management/psychology/nutrition; BA, BSc, BSc(Hons), MA

KINGSTON UNIVERSITY
www.kingston.ac.uk

Faculty of Art, Design and Architecture; www.kingston.ac.uk/faculties/#design
architecture, advertising & the creative economy, aesthetics & art theory, art & design/history/market/space, art market appraisal, building surveying, design, communication design & the creative economy, computer generated design, curating contemporary design, design for development, design & human wellbeing/product & space, European art practice, experimental film, fashion/retailing, film studies/making, fine art (painting, sculpture, intermedia, print), graphic design, heritage, historic building conservation, history of art, design & film, illustration & animation, interior design, landscape architecture/planning/urbanism, museum & gallery studies, photography, planning & sustainability, product & furniture design, product design for film & TV, professional practice (design), property planning & development, quantity surveying consultancy, real estate management, residential property; BA(Hons), FdA, FDA, FdSc, MA, MSc, PGCert/Dip

Faculty of Arts and Social Sciences; www.fass.kingston.ac.uk
applied/development/business/international business/financial economics, business & economic forecasting, international politics & economics; child centred interprofessional practice, children's special educational needs/inclusive education, early years education & childcare/management & leadership/teaching, primary/secondary teaching (QTS), English language teaching, writing fiction/children's literature/travel, creative writing, criticism, literature & theory, English language & communication, English literature, film studies/making, history (early modern/European/international/British/women's & gender), TV & new broadcasting media, French, translation studies, journalism (fashion/magazine/in open society), media and cultural studies, Spanish, language & society, philosophy, publishing, translation studies; dance, drama, film studies/making, music, music education/performance/creative technology, performance, classical theatre, pop music, playwriting, electroacoustic composition, psychology (applied, clinical, child), law with criminology/HR/international relations/ criminology, cybercrime, Europolitics, environmental politics, international conflict/relations, nationalism, terrorism & political violence, social science; BA(Hons), MA, PgCert/Dip, EdD

Faculty of Law & Business; www.business.kingston.ac.uk

Kingston Business School:
accounting, banking, finance, business, management, business information technology & management, marketing & communications, creative industries, general management, leadership, HRM, services management

Kingston School of Law:
law, criminology, international/corporate & financial/employment/general law, human rights, immigration law, international commercial law, conflict, international relations, law of international trade, legal studies; BA(Hons), BSc(Hons), DBA, FdA, GradDip Law, HND, LlM, MA, MBA, MSC, PhD

Faculty of Science, Engineering & Computing; www.sec.kingston.ac.uk
Aerospace & Aircraft Engineering: aerospace engineering, astronautics & space technology, aircraft engineering/maintenance/repair, aviation studies, renewable energy engineering
Civil Engineering & Construction: civil engineering, construction management, construction management & law, structural design, sustainable construction
Computing & Information Systems: computer science, computer graphics & digital imaging/vision & image analysis, electronic analysis, embedded systems, games programming, health information systems, informatics, information management & knowledge sharing, intelligent transport sytems & services, IT & strategic innovation, network & data

communications, network communications, computing/studies, cyber security & computer forensics, games technology, information sytems, internet business, IT & e-business, medical technologies, mobile computing, network & data security, networking & data communication, software engineering/communication, web development, wireless communication, Geography, Geology and the Environment: applied & environmental geology, environmental/hazards & disaster management/& earth resources management, environmental/management/science/systems, GIS & science, geography/human/physical, sustainable development, sustainability environment & change, sustainable environmental development & management studies

Life Sciences: acupuncture, biochemistry, biology, biomedical science, biotechnology, cancer biology, cell & molecular biology, exercise & nutritional health, exercise for health, forensic biology/science, & investigative analysis, human biology, medical biochemistry, nutrition, pharmacology, sports science/analysis & coaching

Mathematics: actuarial mathematics & statistics, mathematical science, mathematics, statistics

Mechanical & Automotive Engineering: advanced industrial & mechanical systems, advanced product design engineering, automative engineering, commercial vehicle /motorcycle technology, communication systems, computer graphics technology, creative technology, engineering projects & systems management, mechanical engineering, mechatronic systems, media technology, motorsport engineering, professional engineering, TV & video technology

Pharmacy & Chemistry: analytical chemistry, chemistry, forensic analysis, pharmaceutical analysis/science, pharmaceutical & chemical sciences, pharmacy; BSc(Hons), BEng, FdSc, FdEng, HND, MComp, MComp, MPharmSci, MPhil, MSc, PhD, PGCert/Dip, MEng

Faculty of Health & Social Care Sciences; www.healthcare.kingston.ac.uk

advanced practice (health care), brain imaging, breast evaluation, clinical practice, CPD, diagnostic therapy/radiography, exercise for health, health education/healthcare practice & clinical leadership, maternal & child health/social/cultural perspective, mammography, medical imaging, midwifery/registered midwife, nursing/registered nurse, oncology practice, paramedic science, physiotherapy, profession education & training in human services, rehabilitation, social work, specialist/professional child & family studies, specialist/ professional studies in community care; BSc(Hons), DipHE, FdSc, MREs, MPhil, MSc, MA, MSW, PGCert/Dip, PhD,PGDip

LANCASTER UNIVERSITY
www.lancs.ac.uk

Faculty of Arts and Social Sciences; www.lancs.ac.uk/fass/faculty

European Languages and Cultures; www.lancs.ac.uk/fass/eurolang
German, Italian, French, Spanish, modern languages, film studies, European institutions & policy/languages & cultures/legal studies/languages & management studies

Applied Social Science; www.lancs.ac.uk/fass/appsocsci
criminology, social work

Educational Research; www.lancs.ac.uk/fass/edres
educational research

English and Creative Writing; www.lancs.ac.uk/fass/english
English language/literature studies, film studies, creative writing/art, contemporary literature

History; www.lancs.ac.uk/fass/history
history, medieval & Renaissance studies, modern European/ social history

Lancaster Institute for the Contemporary Arts; www.lancs.ac.uk/fass/licr
contemporary arts, fine art, marketing & design, music, innovation & design, theatre studies, film studies, design/management & policy

School of Law; www.lancs.ac.uk/fass/law
law, bioethics, medical law, European legal studies, humanitarian/diplomatic/international law, business & corporate law, international human rights/law, law

& criminology, human rights & the environment, terrorism law, international relations

Linguistics & English Language;
www.ling.lancs.ac.uk
English language/the media, applied/linguistics, creative writing, English literature, English language & literary studies, language & linguistics/literature, teaching English (TESOL/TEFL), discourse studies, sociolinguistics

Politics, Philosophy & Religion;
www.lancs.ac.uk/fass/ppr
politics, international relations/law, medical law, religious studies, philosophy, diplomacy, foreign policy, international law, religion, conflict, development & security, conflict resolution & peace studies, religion & conflict

Sociology; www.lancs.ac.uk/fass/sociology
sociology, environment, culture & society, gender and women's studies, media & cultural studies, social research; BSc(Hons), LlB, LlM, MA, MPhil, MSc, PGDip, PhD

School of Health and Medicine;
www.lancs.ac.uk/shm/faculties

Biomedical & Life Sciences;
www.lancs.ac.uk/shm/bls
biochemistry/with biomedicine or genetics, biomedical/(applied)biological science, medical statistics, cell biology, clinical psychology, learning disabilities, life care, premedical studies, public mental health, applied bioscience & business management, medical biotechnology & leadership

Lancaster Medical School;
www.lancs.ac.uk/shm/med
basic biomedical research, biomedicine, environment & biochemistry, health research, medical education, medical statistics & epidemiology, medicine, premedical studies, toxicology, clinical psychology; BSc(Hons), CertHE, DClinPsych, MBChB, MBiomed, MD, MHospice leadership, MPhil, MRes, MSc, PgDip/Cert, PhD

Lancaster University Management School; www.lums.lancs.ac.uk
accounting, advertising, banking, business studies/analytics & consultancy, e-business & innovation, economics, European management, quantitative/finance, financial management/analysis, HR, information technology, knowledge management, management entrepreneurship/IT/organisation, management & law/organizational change/analytics/organization, marketing, operational research; BA(Hons), BBA, BSc(Hons), LlM, MBA, MPhil, MRes, MSc, PhD

Faculty of Science and Technology;
www.lancs.ac.uk/shm/sci-tech/faculties

Computing & Communication;
www.lancs.ac.uk/sci-tech/departments/computing_and_communication
accountancy, finance & computer science, business information & information systems, computer science, communications/computer/systems engineering/& electronics, computer science & music, language degree science, cyber security, software engineering, IT for creative industries, management & IT, network & internet systems

Engineering; www.engineering.lancs.ac.uk
chemical engineering, engineering, electronic/electrical engineering, mechatronic/mechanical engineering/systems engineering, nuclear engineering, sustainable engineering, computer systems engineering, decommissioning & environmental clean-up, microelectronics, safety engineering, systems-on-chip engineering

Lancaster Environment Centre;
www.lec.lancs.ac.uk
biological/biochemical/biomedical science, cell biology, conservation biology, contaminated land & remediation & conservation, genetics, ecology & conservation, environmental informatics/science/technology/biology/geology environmental change & sustainable development, environmental informatics/science & technology, biochemical toxology, earth science, geography, management & conservation, sustainable water management, volcanology & geological hazard

Mathematics and Statistics;
www.maths.lancs.ac.uk
mathematics, computer science and mathematics, statistics, environmental/mathematics/& philosophy/statistics/psychology/theoretical physics, quantitative methods/finance, mathematics with science/languages/business

Natural Sciences;
www.naturalsci.lancs.ac.uk
combined science, combined technology, natural sciences

Physics; www.lancs.ac.uk/depts/physics
astrophysics, cosmology, biomedical physics, physics, space science, theoretical physics/with mathematics, particle physics

Psychology; www.psych.lancs.ac.uk
development psychology/disorders, language, speech & learning, psychology, psychology of advertising, social psychology, psychological research methods; BEng(Hons), BSc(Hons), MChem, MEng (Hons), MPhil, MPhys (Hons), MRes, MSc, MSci(Hons), PGDip, PhD

Degrees validated by Lancaster University offered at:

BLACKPOOL AND THE FYLDE COLLEGE
www.blackpool.ac.uk

acting, music theatre, graphic design, illustration, fashion & costume for performance, sports coaching/studies & development, events management, catering resource management, hospitality management, health & social care, teaching & learning, education, international resort tourism management, working with young people, professional practice (early years), literacies for life, information technology, creative design, mechanical & production engineering, mechatronics, sustainable energy, electronic & electrical engineering, project management, automotive engineering, management in the workplace, history, English language, media writing, criminology & criminal justice; FD, HNC, HND, BEng, BA(Hons), BSc/(Hons)

EDGE HILL UNIVERSITY
www.edgehill.ac.uk

Faculty of Education;
www.edgehill.ac.uk/education
education with QTS (primary, secondary design & technology/English/ICT/mathematics/modern foreign language/RE/science), post compulsory education & training, children's & young people's learning & development, early years professional practice & leadership, early years education/leadership/practice, teaching, learning & mentoring practice, EYPS, FE/HE management, teaching lifelong sector, PGCE (early years, primary, numerous secondary subjects, post-compulsory education & training), education, management of international HE, simulation & clinical learning, specialist dyslexia training; BA(Hons), BSc(Hons), CertHE, FD, PGCE, MA, MTL, PGCert

Faculty of Health & Social Care;
www.edgehill.ac.uk/health
children's nursing & social work, health & social care, midwifery, nursing studies (adult, learning disabilities, mental health, children's) operating dept practice, paramedic practice, children's health & wellbeing, health & social wellbeing, nutrition & health, complementary therapies, counselling, playwork, support of offenders, working with/support of families & communities, public health, social work, non-medical prescription, return to professional practice; BSc(Hons), Dip/CertHE, FDA, FdSc, MCh, MPhil, MSc, PhD

Faculty of Arts and Science

Business School; www.edgehill.ac.uk/business
accounting, business, management/administration, equality & diversity management, HRM, int business, leisure & tourism, marketing, information systems, sustainable systems, IT for business, public administration, voluntary 3rd sector management, web systems/development, information security & IT management

Dept of English and History; www.edgehill.ac.uk/history
Chinese studies, creative writing, English language/literature, film studies, history, culture, humanities

Law & Criminology; www.edgehill.ac.uk/law
criminology & criminal justice, law, international business & commercial/justice & human rights law, law, law with management

Media; www.edgehill.ac.uk/media
digital SFX/animation, advertising, film & TV production, journalism, media, film & TV or music & sound/enterprise, PR, TV production management

Dept of Natural, Geographical and Applied Sciences; www.edgehill.ac.uk/ngas
biogeography, biology, environmental science, geography, geology, human/physical geography

Performing Arts; www.edgehill.ac.uk/performingart
drama & dance, design for performance, physical theatre, music & sound/enterprise, performance & health, making performance, dance movement & therapy

Dept of Psychology; www.edgehill.ac.uk/psychology
psychology, educational psychology, childhood & youth studies, social work & sociology, social research methods, sport & exercise psychology

Dept of Sport & Physical Activity; www.edgehill.ac.uk/sport
applied sport & exercise science, coach education, physical education & school sport, sport & exercise psychology/science, sports development/studies/therapy, football rehabilitation;
BA(Hons), BSc(Hons), FDA, FDSc, LlB(Hons), MA, MSc, PhD, MBA

UNIVERSITY OF LEEDS
www.leeds.ac.uk

Faculty of Arts; www.leeds.ac.uk/arts

School of English; www.leeds.ac.uk/english
American literature & culture, English language/literature, modern & contemporary/Renaissance literature, post-colonial literary & cultural studies, romantic literature & culture, theatre & global studies, theatre making/studies, Victorian literature

School of History; www.leeds.ac.uk/history
history, international history & politics, medieval history, modern history, race & resistance, social & cultural history

School of Humanities; www.leeds.ac.uk/humanities
classical civilization/studies, classics, Greek, Latin, philosophy, development studies, health care ethics, history and philosophy of science, pastoral studies, mind and knowledge, philosophy of religion/physics, religion/theology and public life/pastoral care, religious studies, science communication, theology

Institute for Colonial and Post-colonial Studies; www.leeds.ac.uk/icps
post-colonial literary & cultural studies, race & resistance, world cinema, modern languages & cultures

School of Modern Languages and Cultures; www.leeds.ac.uk/smlc
Arabic & Middle Eastern studies, Chinese, Japanese, South/East Asian studies, French, German, Italian, linguistics & phonetics, modern languages & cultures, professional language & intercultural studies, Russian, Spanish, Portuguese and Latin American studies, translation & interpreting, world cinema; BA(Hons), MA, MPhil, PGDip, PhD

Faculty of Biological Studies; www.fbs.leeds.ac.uk
biochemistry, biology, bioscience (biotechnology/bioinformatics & computational biology/human disease & therapy/infection & immunology/plant science), ecology & environmental biology, biodiversity & conservation, genetics, human physiology, medical biochemistry/microbiology/sciences, microbiology, neuroscience, pharmacology, virology, molecular biology, sport & exercise sciences, zoology; BSc(Hons), MRes, MSc, PhD

Faculty of Business; www.fbs.leeds.ac.uk

Leeds University Business School; www.leeds.ac.uk/lbs
accounting, advertising & design, banking, business economics, computing & management, corporate

communications & PR, diversity management, economics, actuarial/finance, financial economics/mathematics/risk, HRM, international business/finance/marketing management, management, organizational psychology, textile innovation, manufacturing leadership, marketing, transport studies; BSc(Hons), ExecMBA, MA, MBA, MPhil, MSc, PhD

Faculty of Education, Social Sciences & Law; www.essl.leeds.ac.uk

School of Education; www.education.leeds.ac.uk

childhood studies, clinical education, deaf education, ICT, lifelong learning, mathematics/science education, PGCE biology/chemistry/English/mathematics/modern foreign languages/physics, children with learning difficulties/developmental disorders, special educational needs, teaching, teaching English (TESOL) for young learners/studies/teacher education

School of Law; www.law.leeds.ac.uk

criminal law & rights law, European law/& society, international & comparative criminal justice, law, policing, European & international business law/corporate law/trade law, intellectual property law, European human rights law, senior status

School of Politics and International Studies; www.leeds.ac.uk/polis

economic/political geography, global development (Africa, gender, international political economy), politics (parliamentary, political theory), international relations/development, conflict, development & security, security, terrorism & insurgency

School of Sociology and Social Policy; www.sociology.leeds.ac.uk

disability studies/& global development, crime, gender & culture/studies, gender, sexuality & queer studies, global genders, interdisciplinary social policy & sociology, social & public policy/political thought, international social transformation, politics & society, racism & ethnicity studies, social science/policy, society & international relations, sociology; BA(Hons), LLM, MA, MEd, MPhil, MSc, PGCert, PGCE, PhD

Faculty of Engineering; www.engineering.leeds.ac.uk

School of Civil Engineering; www.engineering.leeds.ac.uk/civil

architectural engineering, civil & environmental engineering/structural engineering/with construction management, international construction management/public health engineering, environmental engineering, engineering project management, water, sanitation & health engineering

School of Computing; www.engineering.leeds.ac.uk/comp

artificial intelligence, adv/computer science/& mathematics, computing & business management, information technology

School of Electronic and Electrical Engineering; www.engineering.leeds.ac.uk/elec

adv electronic devices, digital communication tetworks, electrical engineering, electronic/& communications engineering/& signal processing, mechatronics & robotics, music, multimedia & electronics, electronics/& nanotechnology, broadband wireless & optical comm, embedded systems engineering

Mechanical Engineering; www.engineering.leeds.ac.uk/mech

aeronautical & aerospace engineering, automotive engineering, adv/mechanical engineering, mechatronics & robotics, medical engineering, oilfield corrosion engineering, nuclear engineering, tribology & engineering interfaces, product design

School of Process, Environmental and Materials Engineering; www.engineering.leeds.ac.uk/speme

aviation technology/management, pilot studies, chemical & energy/materials/minerals/nuclear engineering, pharmaceutical science & engineering, chemical engineering, computational fluid dynamics, energy & environment, computational fluid mechanics, energy engineering, fire & explosion, petroleum engineering; BEng, MEng, MSc, MSc(Eng), MPhil, PhD

Faculty of the Environment; www.leeds.ac.uk/foe

School of Earth & Environment; www.see.leeds.ac.uk

engineering geology, environment & business/management, climatic/& atmospheric change, ecological economics, environmental sustainability/

management/science/conservation, exploration geophysics, geochemistry, geological/geophysical sciences, hydrogeology, meterology & climate change, physics of the earth & atmosphere, structural geology & geophysics, sustainability (transport/business environment & corporate responsibility/environmental consultancy/environment & development/ environmental politics & policy/project management). sustainable & environmental science/management

School of Geography; www.geog.leeds.ac.uk

geography, activism & societal change, catchment dynamics & management, geography/with transport planning, geography– geology, GIS, social & cultural geography

Institute for Transport Studies; www.its.leeds.ac.uk

economics with transport studies, geography with transport planning, planning & the environment, transport economics, engine, sustainabilty (transport)

Earth & Biosphere Institute; www.earth.leeds.ac.uk/ebi

global change & the biosphere; BA(Hons), BSc(Hons), MA, MGeol, MGeophys, MRes, MSc, DGCert/Dip, PhD, MEnv,MGeol

Faculty of Mathematics and Physical Science; www.maps.leeds.ac.uk

School of Chemistry; www.chemi.leeds.ac.uk

chemistry, chemical process, colour & imaging science, analytical chemistry, medicinal chemistry, polymer & surface coatings science, chemical biology & drug design

School of Food Science and Nutrition; www.food.leeds.ac.uk

food biotechnology/quality & innovation, nutrition, food studies/science

School of Physics and Astronomy; www.physics.leeds.ac.uk

astrophysics, nanotechnology, physics/with mathematics, medical physics, quantum technologies, theoretical physics

School of Mathematics; www.amsta.ac.uk

actuarial/financial mathematics, mathematics/with finance, statistics/computer science, atmosphere ocean dynamics; BSc(Hons), MChem, MMath, MNatSci, MPhil, MPhys, MSc, PhD

Faculty of Medicine & Health; www.leeds.ac.uk/medhealth

Leeds Dental Institute; www.leeds.ac.uk/dental

hygiene & therapy, dental nursing/surgery/technology/therapy

School of Healthcare; www.healthcare.leeds.ac.uk

adult/child nursing, cardiology, clinical physiology, counselling, diagnostic imaging, audiology, medicines management, mental health, midwifery, nursing, public health, radiography, social work

Leeds School of Medicine; www.leeds.ac.uk/medicine

child health, clinical embryology/psychology, family therapy, health informatics/management, hospital management, medical physics/imaging, medicine, nutrition, obesity & health, patient safety, primary health care, psychiatry, psychoanalytical observation, public health, statistical epidemiology, surgery

Institute of Psychological Sciences; www.psych.leeds.ac.uk

psychology, psychological approach to health, memory & its disorders; BHSc, BSc(Hons), CPD, DClinPsych, GradDip, MA, MBChB, MD, MMedSci, MPH, MPsycObs, MSc, PGDip/Cert, PhD

Faculty of Performance, Visual Arts and Communication; www.leeds.ac.uk/pvac

Institute of Communication Studies; www.ics.leeds.ac.uk

broadcast journalism, cinema & photography, communications studies, international/political communications, journalism, new/media industries

School of Design; www.design.leeds.ac.uk

textile design & performance clothing, advertising & design, art & design, design, technology management, fashion design, graphic and communication design, textile innovation & branding

School of Fine Art, History of Art and Cultural Studies; www.leeds.ac.uk/fine_art

art history with museum studies, cultural studies, fine art, history of art

School of Music; www.ics.leeds.ac.uk/music

composition, app/psychology of music, music, music technology, musicology, performance

School of Performance & Cultural Industries; www.ics.leeds.ac.uk/paci
choreography, culture, creativity & entrepreneurship, dance, managing performance, performance design/culture performance, writing for performance and publication; BA(Hons), GradDip, MFA, BMus, BSc(Hons), MA, MMus, MSc, PhD[a]Degrees validated by University of Leeds offered at:

ASKHAM BRYAN COLLEGE
www.askham-bryan.ac.uk

agriculture, animal management, business & IT, countryside & environment, engineering, plant & construction, equine, floristry, food, forestry & arboriculture, horticulture, land management, sports & leisure, surface & greenkeeping, teacher education; BA(Hons), BSc(Hons), Nat Dips, FD

COLLEGE OF THE RESURRECTION
www.mirfield.org.uk

theology & pastoral studies, theological studies, ministry & theology; BA(Hons), DipHE, MA, MPhil, PGDip, PhD

LEEDS COLLEGE OF ART
www.leeds-art.ac.uk

art & design, creative advertising, digital film, games & animation, fashion/concept & communication, fine art, furniture making, graphic design, interior design, photography, printed textiles & surface pattern design, visual communication; BA(Hons), FD, HNC, National Diploma

LEEDS COLLEGE OF MUSIC
www.lcm.ac.uk

music (classical/pop/production), composition, jazz, musicology, performance, composition; BA (Hons), FD, MA, PGDip

LEEDS TRINITY UNIVERSITY COLLEGE
www.leedstrinity.ac.uk

Faculty of Arts and Social Sciences; www.leedstrinity.ac.uk/departments/fass
English, history, psychology, sport, health, leisure & nutrition, theology & religious studies, Victorian studies; BA(Hons), BSc(Hons), MA, MSc, PGCE

Faculty of Education & Theology
Catholic education, children, education studies, working with children, young people & families, PGCE programmes, primary education, secondary education, supporting learning, teaching assistants, youth & community work, improving professional practice, school leadership, theology/& religious studies, Christian theology, theology & ministry, religion & public life; BA(Hons), FD, MA, PGCert, PGCE

Faculty of Media, Business & Marketing; www.leedstrinity.ac.uk/departments/FMBN
broadcast/magazine/print journalism, business & management, business studies, management, marketing, media, film & culture, public communications, PR, sports journalism; BA(Hons), MA/PGDip, MB

University of Leeds

NORTHERN SCHOOL OF CONTEMPORARY DANCE
www.nscd.ac.uk

contemporary dance, choreography; BPA(Hons), PgDip, MA,FD

YORK ST JOHN UNIVERSITY
www.yorksj.ac.uk

Faculty of Arts
film & TV production, music composition/performance/production, American studies, creative writing, dance, documentary/film production, English literature, film/literature studies, fine arts, history, media, music/composition, product design, theatre; FD, BA(Hons), PgCert/Dip, MA

Faculty of Education & Theology
PGCE, primary/secondary education, religious studies, supporting learning, theology & ministry, Christian theology/studies teacher education, working with children & young people, education studies, children, school leadership, young people & families, youth & community work; MFL, BA(Hons), GradDip, PgDip

Faculty of Health & Life Sciences
counselling, occupational therapy, physiotherapy, professional health & social care studies, community & clinical social care, psychology/of child & adolescent development, CPD & lifelong learning, sport; BA(Hons), MA, PgDip/Cert

York St John Business School
accounting, business management/& HRM, web technologies, language & linguistics, design & creativity, international tourism/ business management/business strategy, HRM, marketing/ management, TESOL, managing finance, global marketing, languages, leadership & management, innovation & change, TESOL, web technologies; BA(Hons), FD, MA, PGDip/Cert, MBA

LEEDS METROPOLITAN UNIVERSITY
www.leedsmet.ac.uk

Faculty of Arts, Environment & Society; www.leedsmet.ac.uk/aet The Leeds School of Architecture, Landscape & Design; www.leedsmet.ac.uk/aet/#art-architecture-design
architecture, contemporary art practice, fine art, urban design, garden art & design, design, interior architecture, landscape architecture & design

School of Built Environment & Engineering; www. www.leedsmet.ac.uk/aet/#built-environment-engineering
building studies, engineering studies, civil engineering, construction/commercial/management, strategic/ project management, facilities management; architectural technology, building/quantity surveying, housing, housing, regeneration & urban management, human geography/& planning, planning law & practice, project management/construction, town & regional planning, heritage planning, construction law & dispute resolution

School of Computing & Creative technology;. www.leedsmet.ac.uk/aet/#computing-creative-technology
advanced engineering development, business information systems, computer forensics, computing, computer security & ethical hacking, information management, systems & networking, green computing, managing software development, mobile & distr computer networks, web applications development, software development/engineering, mobile device applications, information & technology, broadcast media technologies, computer animation technology, photographic journalism, computer animation/& special effects, games design, digital animation & creative visualization, digital video & special effects, mobile device development, multimedia/entertainment, creative technology

School of Film, Music & Performing Arts; www.leedsmet.ac.uk/aet/#film-music-performingarts

music performance/production/technology, audio post-production, moving image, music for interactive games, sound design, multimedia/entertainment, creative technology

Northern Film School

animation, film and moving image production, film & TV production, art events, performance, dance, performance works

School of Cultural Studies & Humanities; www.lmu.ac.uk/as/cs

English, English literature, history, media, communication & culture, cultural planning & policy, English contemporary literature, screen media cultures (Hons), BSc(Hons), DipHE, FdAA, GradCert, MPhil, MRes, MSc, PGDip

Faculty of Business and Law; www.leedsmet.ac.uk/fbl

Leeds Business School; www.leedsmet.ac.uk/fbl/leeds_business_school

accounting, advertising management, business studies, economics for business, events management, tourism & hospitality management, finance, financial services, HRM, international business/communications/business law, leadership, management, marketing, organizational behaviour, PR, purchasing & supply/logistics, strategy & economic analysis

Leeds Law School; www.leedsmet.ac.uk/lbs/law

law, legal practice, commercial/employment/family/property/business law, paralegal practice, UK planning law & practice; BA(Hons), HND, LlB(Hons), LlM, MA, MSc, PGDip/Cert, MBA

Faculty of Health & Social Sciences; www.leedsmet.ac.uk/hss

applied psychology, advanced nutrition, applied/biomedical sciences, criminology, applied/psychology research (education/forensic/health), psychotherapy practice, social work, youth work & community development, psychotherapy, biomedical sciences, clinical language science (speech & language therapy), community specialist practitioner – community/children's/district/practice nursing, dietetics, environmental health, international relations & global development, physiology, pharmacology), mental health studies, health & social care chaplaincy, international political economy/relations, occupational therapy, peace & development, physiotherapy, psychology, youth work & community development, acoustics & noise control, advanced practice, epilepsy practice, Parkinson's disease practice, public health – health promotion, psychological therapies, specialist community public health nursing – health visiting/occupational health nursing/school nursing, stroke practice, sports therapy; BA(Hons), BSc(Hons), CertHE, HNC, MA, MSc, PGDip/Cert, Prof Dip, DipHE, FdAA, GradCert, MPhil, MRes, PGDip

Carnegie Faculty; www.leedsmet.ac.uk/carnegie

English language teaching, business & EFL/marketing/tourism management, language studies, French, German, Spanish, contemporary European studies, childhood & educational studies, QTS with primary early childhood, PE, learning, teaching, leadership, international tourism & hospitality/business management/leadership & management, international/resort/student hospitality management, consumer/retail marketing, international business admin, sports/events management, conference & exhibitions management, culture/sports events, international festival management; BA(Hons), Bsc(Hons), FSc, PGCE, PGCert/Dip, MA, PhD

UNIVERSITY OF LEICESTER
www.le.ac.uk

College of Arts, Humanities and Law;
www2.le.ac.uk/colleges/artshumlaw

School of Archaeology & Ancient History; www.le.ac.uk/ar
ancient history, archaeology, classical Mediterranean, history, historical archaeology, archaeology of the Roman world

School of English; www.le.ac.uk/ee
American studies/history, English studies, English(EU), history of art, visual culture, modern literature & creative writing, Victorian studies

Dept of History of Art and Film; www.le.ac.uk/ha
the country house in art, history & culture, film studies and the visual arts, history of art, humanities, film & film cultures

School of Historical Studies; www.le.ac.uk/hi
contemporary history, English local history, history, history and politics/international relations/ancient history/archaeology/American studies, archaeology, urban history/conservation, European urbanization

School of Law; www.le.ac.uk/law
law, law – international/human rights/commercial/public/employment), law with French law, human rights, legal research

School of Modern Languages; www.le.ac.uk/ml
European studies, French, German, Italian, modern language studies, modern languages with film studies/history of art, Spanish, humanities, translation studies, film & film culture

Museum Studies; www.le.ac.uk /ms
museum studies, digital heritage, interpretation, representation, & heritage studies, learning & visitor studies; BA(Hons), BSc(Hons), LlB, LlM, MSC, MA/GradDip, MPhil, PhD

College of Science and Engineering;
www2.le.ac.uk/colleges/science

Dept of Chemistry; www.le.ac.uk/ch
biochemistry, chemistry, cancer chemistry, biological/physical chemistry, forensic science, green/pharmaceutical chemistry

Dept of Computer Science; www.cs.le.ac.uk
advanced computational methods/distributed systems/software engineering, computer science, computers, computing, web applications & services

Dept of Engineering; www2.le.ac.uk/departments/engineering
advanced control & dynamics, advanced engineering, aerospace engineering, communications & electronic engineering, control & signal processing, electrical engineering, embedded systems & control engineering, general engineering, information & communication engineering, mechanical engineering, software

Dept of Geography; www.le.ac.uk/geography
environmental informatics, geography, geology, GIS, global environmental change, human/physical geography, sustainable management of natural resources, social change & resistance, geospatial intelligence

Dept of Geology; www2.le.ac.uk/departments/geology
applied & environmental geology, crustal processes, geology, borehole/geophysics, palaeobiology

Centre for Interdisciplinary Science; www2.le.ac.uk/departments/interdisciplinary-science
communication science, complex systems, evolution, laboratory science, mathematics for science, nanoscale frontiers, sustainable livelihoods in Africa, virtual worlds

Dept of Mathematics; www2.le.ac.uk/departments/mathematics
actuarial science, computational mathematics, financial mathematics, mathematical modelling, mathematics

Dept of Physics and Astronomy; www2.le.ac.uk/departments/physics
astronomy, physics, radio & space plasma physics, physics with nanotechnology/astrophysics/space science & technology/planetary science; BA(Hons), BSc(Hons), BEng/MEng, MA, MChem, MComp, MGeol, MMath, MPhil, MPhys, MSc, MSci, PGDip, PhD

College of Medicine, Biological Sciences and Psychology; www2.le.ac.uk/colleges/medbiopsych

School of Biological Sciences; www.le.ac.uk/lbs

bioinformatics, biology, clinical science, biological sciences (biochemistry/genetics/microbiology/physiology with pharmacology/zoology), microbiology, medical biochemistry/microbiology/physiology, molecular biology/genetics/toxicology, cell physiology & pharmacology, molecular biology/genetics/toxicology, pharmacology, zoology

School of Medicine, Leicester Medical School; www.le.ac.uk/sm/le

medicine, cancer studies & molecular medicine, cardiovascular sciences, health sciences, infection, immunity & inflammation, medical statistics, medical & social care education, molecular pathology/toxicology, occupational psychology, operating dept practice, pain management, physiotherapy, primary care research, social science applied to health, child & adolescent social work, integrated provision for children & families

School of Psychology; www2.le.ac.uk/departments/psychology

psychology/with sociology/cognitive neuroscience/media, clinical/forensic psychology, applied forensic psychology, forensic legal psychology, occupational psychology, psychology of work; DocClinPsych, BSc, MBChB, MBioSci, MD, MSc, PostgradDip/Cert, PhD

College of the Social Sciences www.le.ac.uk/colleges/socsci

Dept of Criminology; www.le.ac.uk/criminology

applied/clinical/criminology, terrorism, security & policing

Dept of Economics; www2.le.ac.uk/ec

banking & finance, business/financial economics, economics, business analysis & finance, money & banking

School of Education; www.le.ac.uk/education

educational studies, educational learning & teaching, dyslexia, education leadership, mentoring & coaching, TESO/applied linguistics, education, learning & teaching, leadership & management in education, international education, teaching mathematics, PGCE primary/scondary education, TESOL & applied linguistics

The Centre for Labour Market Studies; www2.le.ac.uk/departments/clms

HRM, HRM & training, performance management/industrial relations & workplace learning

Institute of Lifelong Learning; www2.le.ac.uk/departments/lifelong-learning

higher education, humanities & arts, cognitive behaviour therapy, counselling/drugs & alcohol, managing political & community orgs, emergency planning, risk crisis, disaster management

School of Management; www.le.ac.uk/ulsm

accounting, finance, management studies, marketing, finance, organisational studies, economics, politics, business administration

Dept of Media & Communication; www.le.ac.uk/mc

communications & globalization, media/communications & society/PR/advertising, new media & sociology, mass communications, new media governance & democracy

Dept of Politics and International Relations; www.le.ac.uk/politics

diplomatic studies, politics, international relations/& history, economics, politics & sociology/history/management, human rights & global ethics, international security, political research

Dept of Sociology; www.le.ac.uk/sociology

sociology, contemporary civil society, social research; BA(Hons), DocSocSci, EdD, FD, MA, MBA, MPhil, MSc, PGCE, PGDip/Cert, PhD

Degrees validated by the University of Leicester offered at:

NEWMAN UNIVERSITY COLLEGE
www.newman.ac.uk

art & design, counselling, creative arts/writing, drama, early years, education & professional studies, English/literature, history, information technology, management & business, media & communication, theology, psychology & counselling, science, PE & sports studies, teacher training, working with children, young people & families, youth & community work; BA/BSc(Hons), FD,MA, MPhil, PGCE, PhD

UNIVERSITY OF LINCOLN
www.lincoln.ac.uk

Faculty of Agriculture, Equine & Food; www.lincoln.ac.uk/afas
agriculture & environment, bioveterinary science, clinical/animal behaviour & welfare, conservation biology, equine science/sports science, food manufacture, process & business improvement/quality assurance; BSc, FdSc, MPhil, MSc, PhD

Faculty of Art, Architecture & Design; www.lincoln.ac.uk/aad
animation, architecture/sustainable, art, architecture/ & design, conservation of historic objects/studies/ restoration, contemporary cultural practice, creative advertising, construction project management, contemporary lens media, design, design/exhibition & museums, development & regeneration, fashion studies, fine art, graphic design, interior design/architecture, jewellery & objects, product design, planning/& urban design; BA(Hons), BArch, GradDip, MA, March, MPhil, PhD

Faculty of Business & Law; www.lincoln.ac.uk /bl
accountancy, advertising, business administration/management/studies, engineering management, event management, finance, hospitality, HRM, HRD, international business/tourism, management studies, marketing strategy, tourism, law & business/criminology, legal studies, logistics management, marketing, personal executive & corporate coaching, PR, tourism/marketing/management; BA(Hons), BSc(Hons), LlB(Hons), LlM, MA, MBA, MPhil, MRes, MSc, PhD

Faculty of Health, Life & Social Sciences; www.lincoln.ac.uk/hlss
adv professional practice in social work, child studies, clinical/forensic psychology, contemporary culture & communication, criminology/& international relations/politics/forensic investigation, employment-based social work, forensic science, globalisation, health & social care, health, crime & social justice, health science, herbal medicine, human nutrition, human rights, journalism (sport/science & environment/war & international human rights), crime & social justice, international relations, politics & social policy, media & cultural studies, nursing (adult, mental health), psychology with criminology/marketing, social policy/child studies/care/science, sports & exercise science, sports coaching/science; BA(Hons), BSc(Hons), CertHE, DClinPsy, MA, MClinRes, MPhil, PGCert, PhD

Faculty of Media, Humanities and Performance; www.lincoln.ac.uk/mhp
21st-century literature, audio production, adv performance practice, choreography, community radio, creative writing, dance, digital imaging, drama, film & TV, English, games/computing, history, historical studies, medieval studies, arts/investigative/science & environmental/war & international human rights, sports journalism, culture & communications, web technology, media & culture, media production, play writing & script development, politics, photography, PR; BA(Hons), MA, MRes, MPhil, PhD

Faculty of Science; www.lincoln.ac.uk/science
Lincoln School of Engineering
Lincoln School of Computer Technology
School of Life Science
animal behaviour & welfare/science, animal management & welfare, biochemistry, biology, biomedical science, bioveterinary science, clinical animal behaviour, computer information systems/science, computing, ecology & conservation biology, intelligence systems, forensic science, games computing, mechanical engineering, pharmaceutical science, signals intelligence, sustainable power & energy engineering, zoology; BA(Hons), BSc(Hons), BEng(Hons), FdSC, MA, MComp, MPhil, MRes, MSc, PhD, EMM

Centre for Educational Research & Development; www.lincoln.ac.uk/cerd
educational development, HE teaching & learning; EdD, PhD, PGCE

School of Theology & Ministry Studies; www.lincoln.ac.uk/home/theology
theology & Ministry Studies; BA(Hons), Cert/Dip Theology

Degrees validated by the University of Lincoln offered at:

EAST RIDING COLLEGE
www.eastridingcollege.ac.uk

access to higher education, early childhood policy & practice, computing, applied digital media, sport, exercise & health science; BA(Hons), FdA, FdEd, FdSc

HULL COLLEGE
www.hull-college.ac.uk

Faculty of Arts

Hull School of Art & Design; www.hull-college.ac.uk/hull-school-of-art-and-design
3D design crafts, animation, appl creative media, architectural design, contemporary fine art practice, costume design & interpretaion, design, games/graphic design, illustration, interactive multimedia, lens-based photo media journalism, media & communications, TV & film design, visual arts, web design; BA(Hons), FdA, MA

School of Performing Arts & Media
acting, broadcast media, dance, music performance/production/theatre, stage management & technical theatre; BA, FdA

Faculty of Business & Science
automotive technology, business & management, computing, business information technology, computer network management, construction management, counselling practice, crime & community safety, criminology with applied social science, education/& professional development, engineering technology, express logistics, ports & logistics, education, sports studies, travel & tourism management, young children's learning & development; FdA, FdSc, BSc(Hons), BA(Hons), PGCE

NORTH LINDSEY COLLEGE
www.northlindsey.ac.uk

business studies, business & HRM, leadership & management, children's services, early childhood, computing information systems, counselling, education/& training, learning support, electrical/mechanical/electronic engineering, English, history, health & social science, sport performance & exercise development; BA(Hons), Dips, FdA/Sc/Ed/Eng, Grad Cert Ed, Cert Ed

UNIVERSITY OF LIVERPOOL
www.liv.ac.uk

Faculty of Health & Life Sciences; www.liv.ac.uk/health_and_life_sciences

Institute of Learning & Teaching; www.liverpool.ac.uk/learning-and-teaching/

Dentistry; www.liverpool.ac.uk/dentistry/
dental hygiene/therapy/surgery, conscious sedation, orthodontics

Health Sciences; www.liverpool.ac.uk/health-sciences/
diagnostic radiography, health & veterinary studies, medical diagnostic ultrasound, nursing, occupational therapy, orthoptics, physiotherapy, radiotherapy, health sciences

Medicine; www.liverpool.ac.uk/medicine/
medicine, surgery, medical science, public health

Psychology; www.liverpool.ac.uk/psychology/
psychology, addictive behaviour, critical & major incidents, investigative & forensic psychology, research methods

Life Sciences; www.liverpool.ac.uk/life-sciences/
anatomy & human biology, biochemistry, biological sciences, genetics, life sciences/medicine, microbiology, microbial biotechnology, molecular biology, pharmacology, physiology, post genomic science, tropical disease biology, zoology, advanced biological science (numerous subjects)

Veterinary Science; www.liverpool.ac.uk/veterinary-science/
veterinary science, bioveterinary science/reproduction, veterinary practice

Institute of Ageing & Chronic Disease; www.liv.ac.uk/ageing-and-chronic-disease
anatomy & human science, clinical science

Institute of Infection & Global Health; www.liv.ac.uk/infection-and-global-health
clinical science

Institute of Integrative Biology; www.liv.ac.uk/integrative-biology
advance biological sciences

Institute of Psychology, Health & Society; www.liv.ac.uk/psychology-health-and-society
clinical psychology, health service research, medical education, psychology, psychiatry

Institute of Translational Medicine; www.liv.ac.uk/translational-medicine
physiology, pharmacology, anatomy & human biology, biomedical science & translational medicine BSc(Hons), BN, BVSc, BDS, MBChB, FD, PGCert/Dip, MRes, MSc, MPhil, PhD, MD, BDS, MChOrth, MCommH, D/MClinPsychol, MDS, MPH, MRCPsych, MTCH&CP, MTropMed, MTropPaed

Faculty of Humanities & Social Sciences; www.liv.ac.uk/humanities_and_social_sciences/hss

School of the Arts; www.live.ac.uk/arts

Architecture; www.liv.ac.uk/lsa/index.htm
architecture, architectural design, sustainable architectural design, design studies

Communications & Media; www.liv.ac.uk/communication-and-media/index.htm
communications, business studies, media, pop music, English/politics & communications studies, politics & mass media

English Language
applied linguistics, TESOL, English language

English; www.liv.ac.uk/english/index.htm
English, medieval, Renaissance, 17th/18th century, Victorian, romantic literature, 20th century poetry, science fiction, applied linguistics & TESOL, modern & contemporary literature, reading in practice

Music; www.liv.ac.uk/music/index.htm
music, pop music, music industry, musicology, composition, performance

Philosophy; www.liv.ac.uk/philosophy/index.htm
philosophy & maths, politics, art, aesthetics & cultural institutions, philosophy as a way of life, metaphysics, language, mind

School of History, Language & Culture

History; www.liv.ac.uk/history/index.htm
history – social & economic, modern (& politics), Atlantic, cultural, medieval, & Renaissance studies, 18th century world, 20th century history, international slavery studies, archive & record management

Irish Studies; www.liv.ac.uk/irish/index.htm
Irish studies, English history/politics, understanding conflict

Politics; www.liv.ac.uk/politics/index.htm
politics, international politics & policy, politics & international business, international relations & security, politics & Irish studies/modern history/philosophy/communication studies

Archaeology, Classics & Egyptology; www.liv.ac.uk/sace/index.htm
ancient history, archaeology/of ancient civilisations, human evolution, Egyptian archaeology, classics & modern languages, Egyptology, palaeoanthropology, Manx studies, 18th century worlds

Culture, Language & Area studies; www.liv.ac.uk/soclas/index.htm
French, German, Hispanic studies, Italian, linguistics, Latin American studies, Caribbean & American studies, modern European languages, film studies, classical studies, business studies, critical theory, gender studies, colonial/post-colonial slavery, travel writing
BA(Hons), MA, MArch, MPhil, PhD

School of Law & Social Justice; www.liv.ac.uk/law-and-social-justice/index.htm

Liverpool Law School; www.liv.ac.uk/law/index.htm
law, law & business/accountancy, finance/business studies/criminology/philosophy, international human rights /business law, European law, law, medicine & healthcare, technology & intellectual property law

Sociology & Social Policy; www.liv.ac.uk/sociology-social-policy-and-criminology/
sociology, sociology & social policy/criminology, research methods, cities, culture & regeneration

School of Management; www.liv.ac.uk/management
University of Liverpool Management School: accounting, business economics/studies, consumer marketing, e-business strategy & systems, international business, marketing, business finance & management, economics & finance, football industries, operations & supply chain management, programme & project management, entrepreneurship, HRM, management
BA(Hons), MA, MMus, MPhil, MBA, PhD, MRes, PGDip/Cert

Faculty of Science & Engineering; www.liv.ac.uk/science_and_engineering

School of Engineering; www.liv.ac.uk/engineering
adv manufacturing systems & technology, aerospace engineering, maritime/civil & structural engineering, materials science & engineering, mechanical engineering, aerospace & mechanical systems, adv engineering materials/manufacture, energy manufacture, engineering applications of lasers, materials engineering, product design & management, simulation in aerospace engineering

Electrical Engineering & Electronics; www.liv.ac.uk/eee
avionic systems, pilot studies, computer science, electronic engineering, electrical engineering, electronics, engineering, communications engineering, mechatronics & robotic systems, medical electronics & instrumentation, micoelectronic systems & telecomunications, information & intelligent engineering, energy & power systems

Dept of Computer Science; www.csc.liv.ac.uk
adv/computer science, computing, computer information systems, knowledge representation, privacy & security, electronic commerce computing, information systems, internet computing, software development, computation & games theory

School of Environmental Sciences; www.liv.ac.uk/environmental-sciences
civic design, ecology, the environment, environmental science, geography, geology, geophysics, ocean science, marine biology, town & regional planning, environmental management & planning, urban regeneration & management, marine planning & management, globalization & development, environmental & climate change, conservation & resource management

School of Physical Sciences;

Chemistry; www.liv.ac.uk/chemistry/index.htm
chemistry, medicinal chemistry, materials chemistry, pharmacology, adv chemical science (organic with catalysis/chemical synthesis/biomolecular chemistry/nanoscale with interfacial chemistry)

Mathematical Sciences; www.liv.ac.uk/mathematical-sciences/
mathematics, pure/applied mathematics, mathematical sciences, maths with joint subjects, financial

mathematics, mathematical/theoretical physics, statistics & probability
Physics; www.liv.ac.uk/physics/
physics, astronomy, astrophysics, mathematical/theoretical physics, nuclear science, medical applications, new technology, ocean & climate science, radiometrics, radioactive waste, advanced science; BSc(Hons), MChem, BEng, MEng, DEng, MPhil, MMath, MPhys, MESci, MRes, MSc, PhD, MSc(Eng)

Degrees validated at the University of Liverpool offered by:

LIVERPOOL HOPE UNIVERSITY
www.hope.ac.uk

Faculty of Arts & Humanities; www.hope.ac.uk/artsand humanities
drama, dance, performance, English language/literature, fine art, art history & curating, design, music, politics, history, media & communications, theology, philosophy, religious studies, creative practice, theatre studies, philosophy & ethics/religion, Christian chaplaincy/education leadership/theology

Faculty of Education; www.hope.ac.uk/education
education studies, teacher education, graduate education, professional development, PGCE courses, childhood & youth studies (early childhood studies/special education/mentoring & coaching/teaching & learning), CPD

Faculty of Science & Social Science; www.hope.ac.uk/scienceandsocialscience
Business School: business, management, marketing HRM, accounting, finance, marketing
Mathematics & Computer Science: systems engineering, intelligent systems, simulation & modelling, mathematics, networks & security
Geography: environmental science/management, tourism management, geography, international studies
Health Sciences: health, biology, human biology, nutrition, health nutrition & fitness, psychology
Psychology: psychology, sports psychology
Social Work, Care & Justice: social work, criminology, social policy, young persons and children's rights, crime deviance; BA(Hons), BMin, BSc(Hons), BDes, FdA, FdSc, MA, MBA, MMin, MPhil, PGCE, PhD

LIVERPOOL JOHN MOORES UNIVERSITY
www.ljmu.ac.uk

Faculty of Business and Law; *www.ljmu.ac.uk/BLW*

Liverpool Business School; www.ljmu.ac.uk/lbs
accounting, business/studies/communications/management, finance, HRM, management, marketing, personnel & development, international accounting/finance, operations management, banking/business/management/administration

School of Law; www.ljmu.ac.uk/LAW
law, criminal justice, forensic psychology, international business corporate & financial law, legal practice; BA(Hons), BSc(Hons), DBA, HND, LlB, LlM, MA, MBA, MPhil, MRes, MSc, PgDip/Cert

Faculty of Education, Community and Leisure; *www.ljmu.ac.uk/ECL*
CPD, adv educational practice (dyslexia/leadership & management/mentoring & coaching/SEN), education studies & early years, early childhood studies, education & society, PGCE (art & design/design & technology/early years/modern languages/PE/science/secondary/ICT), mathematics & education, education studies & English, applied community studies, special and inclusive education, outdoor education, primary & secondary education, science education, primary early years (primary French (TS)), special needs, sport & inclusive needs, teacher training courses (primary, secondary), work-related learning; BA(Hons), BSc(Hons), EdD, FD, MA, MPhil, MRes, PGCert, PgDip, PhD

Faculty of Media, Arts & Social Science; www.ljmu.ac.uk/MAS

Liverpool School of Art & Design; www.ljmu.ac.uk/LSA

architecture, art & design, fashion, graphic design, illustration, history of art, fine art, interior design, pop music, spatial design, urban design

Liverpool Screen School; www.ljmu.ac.uk/LSS

creative writing, film studies, English, drama, media studies, international/journalism, screen & interactive media, screenwriting, writing

School of Humanities & Social Science; www.ljmu.ac.uk/HSS

critical social science, criminology, psychology, sociology, English, media & cultural studies, modern/history, mass communications, media, culture, communication, literature, policing studies, cultural history, critical & creative arts, social science; BA, BA(Hons), BDes, DipArch, DipHE, MA, MPhil, MRes, PG, PGCE, PhD

Faculty of Science; www.ljmu.ac.uk/faculties/scs

School of Sport & Exercise Science; www.ljmu.ac.uk/sps

sport science, science & football, exercise sciences, app sports psychology/physiology, biomechanics of gait & posture, clinical exercise physiology

School of Pharmacy & Biomolecular Sciences; www.ljmu.ac.uk/PBS

biomedical sciences, biochemistry, biotechnology, forensic science, applied chemical & pharmaceutical science, clinical/pharmacy, virology

School of Natural Sciences & Psychology; www.ljmu.ac.uk/NSP

animal behaviour, applied sports psychology, criminal justice, forensic anthropology, human/forensic/applied psychology, health/occupational psychology, geography, zoology, biology, wildlife conservation, criminal justice; BSc(Hons), MPhil, MPhys, MRes, MSc, PGCE, PhD

Astrophysics Research Institute; www.ljmu.ac.uk/astro

physics, astronomy, astrophysics

Faculty of Technology & the Environment; www.ljmu.ac.uk/faculties/TAE

School of Computing & Mathematical Sciences; www.ljmu.ac.uk/cmp

computer animation & visualization, adv/computer studies/ forensics, computing information systems, IT & multimedia, computer games techn, software engineering, wireless & mobile computing, cyber security, mathematics

School of Engineering & Technology; www.ljmu.ac.uk/ENG

audio & music technology, broadcast & media production, computer aided design, industrial engineering & control engineering, international trade & logistics, manufacturing/ systems engineering, mechanical/electrical/electronic/marine/automotive engineering, product innovation & development, computer technology, microelectronic systems design, telecommunications, maritime business/management operations/port management, marine & offshore engineering, manufacturing transport & logistics, power & control engineering, telecommunications engineering, transport & business

School of the Built Environment; www.ljmu.ac.uk/BLT

architectural technology, applied facilities management, commercial/building surveying, civil engineering, commercial property development practice & commercial management, construction management, quantity surveying, real estate management, environmental planning, building service engineering/project management, water, energy & environment; BA(Hons), BSc(Hons), FdSc, MPhil, MSc, PgCert, PGCE, PgDip, PhD

Faculty of Health & Applied Social Services; www.ljmu.ac.uk/HEA

adv healthcare practice, child nursing, environmental health, health and social care/for families, individuals & communities/practice, health sciences, midwifery, nursing (adult/child/mental health/paramedic practice), neonatal/diabetes care, public health, social work, specialist community practitioner (district nursing/public health nursing, school visisting/health visiting), counselling, psychotherapy, adv paediatric nursing; BA(Hons), BSc, DNurs, DMidw, DPH, DipHE, FD, FdA MPhil, MRes, MSc, PGDip/Cert

UNIVERSITY OF THE ARTS LONDON
www.arts.ac.uk

Camberwell College of Art & Design; www.camberwell.arts.ac.uk

3D design, art & design, book arts, conservation, design & communication, community & art, designer–maker, design practice, digital arts, drawing, graphic design, fine art, visual art, illustration, painting, printmaking, sculpture; BA(Hons), Dip, FdA, MA, MPhil, PGDip, PhD

Central Saint Martins College of Art & Design; www.csm.arts.ac.uk

acting, architecture: spaces and objects, art & design/science, art, exhibition studies/moving image/theory & philosophy, character animation, criticism, curation & communication/art & design, exhibition studies, fashion, fine art, graphic design, jewellery design, performance design & practice, photography, product design, directing, writing, textile design; BA(Hons), FdA, FD, GradDip, MA, MPhil, PGCert/Dip, PhD

Chelsea College of Art & Design; www.chelsea.arts.ac.uk

art theory/practice, art & design, curating, fine art, graphic design communication, graphic design, interior & spatial design, textile design; BA(Hons), FdA, Foundation Dip, GradDip, MA, MPhil, PGCert/Dip, PhD

London College of Communication; www.lcc.arts.ac.uk

3D design, animation, architecture, artefact & spatial design, book arts, curation & criticism, design, digital arts/media, documentary research, events management, film, video & broadcast, games design, graphic design, illustration, interactive media, journalism, marketing, advertising, media & cultural studies, photography, print media & production, printmaking, product design, PR, publishing, screenwriting, sound art, surface design, theatre design, typography; BA(Hons), FdA, ABCDip, MA, MDes, MRes, MSc, PgDip

London College of Fashion; www.fashion.arts.ac.uk

access & fashion journalism/history & culture/illustration/magazines/marketing/photography/retail/textiles, beauty therapy & spa management, broadcasting, buying & merchandising, cosmetic science, costume, curation, digital arts/media, fashion design, textiles, make-up & image styling, pattern cutting, PR, theatre design & performing arts, visual merchandising; BA(Hons), BSc(Hons), diplomas, FD MA, PgDip/Cert

Wimbledon College of Art; www.wimbledon.arts.ac.uk

acting & directing, animation, costume, design, digital arts/media, film video & broadcast, drawing, fine art, interactive media, painting, pattern cutting, printmaking, sculpture, sonic arts, theatre, design & performing arts/technical arts, technical effects, visual language of performance; BA(Hons), FdA, MA

LONDON CONTEMPORARY DANCE SCHOOL
www.theplace.org.uk

advanced dance training, choreography, contemporary dance, dance training & education, improvisation, performance studies; BA, PGDip, MA

LONDON METROPOLITAN UNIVERSITY
www.londonmet.ac.uk

Faculty of Social Sciences & Humanities; www.londonmet.ac.uk/faculties/faculty-of-social-sciences-and-humanities

anthropology, community development & leadership/work, creative writing, English literature, criminology/& law/community policing, psychology/sociology/youth studies, dance, digital media design, early childhood studies, early years teaching, education studies, film & TV studies, health & social care/policy/management, journalism, film & TV, mass communications, media & communications/& journalism, montessori early childhood practice, public health & social care, social media, social sciences/work, sociology/& social policy, youth studies/work, specific learning difficulties (dyslexia), child abuse, comparative European social studies, conference/legal interpreting, creative industries, digital information management/media, PGCE (early years & primary/range of secondary subjects), equality & diversity, filmmaking, health & social policy, health interpreting, housing & inclusion, information management, international ELT & applied language studies, international journalism, interpreting, labour & TU studies, learning & teaching in HE, media studies, mental health & wellbeing, mentoring & coaching in schools, migration & social cohesion, organising for social & community development, practice education in social work, primary ELT, professional writing, public health, public service interpreting, screenwriting, social research/& evaluation, sustainable cities, teaching adult dyslexic learners in H/FE, TESOL & applied linguistics woman & child abuse; BA(Hons), BSc(Hons), MA, MPhil, MRes, MSc, PGCert/Dip, PhDFdA, PGCE,

Faculty of Architecture and Spacial Design; www.londonmet.ac.uk/faculties/faculty-of art-and-design

architectural history, theory & interpretation, architecture/& digital design systems, interior architecture & design, cities, design & urban cultures, energy & sustainability, cities integration of renewable energy in buildings, rapid design & rare resources, spatial planning & urban design; BA(Hons), MA, MSc, PhD, ProfDip

Faculty of Computing; www.londonmet.ac.uk/depts/cctm

Communications Technology
computer networking/systems engineering/science, computing/& business technology, electronic & computer/communications engineering, electronics, telecommunications & network eng, embedded systems, professional information technology, mobile & satellite communication, network management & security

Applied Computing
business computing, business IT/information systems, computer forensics & IT security/science, computing & IT, internet computing & technology, IT security, software engineering

Mathematics
mathematics & computing, financial mathematics, mathematical sciences, mathematics, statistics

Multimedia
computer animation, computer games modelling & design, interactive media & games
BSc(Hons), FdSc, MEng, MRes, MSc, PhD

Faculty of Humanities, Arts, Language and Education; www.londonmet.ac.uk/depts/hale

applied social sciences, humanities, arts & languages, education

Faculty of Law, Governance and International Relations; www.londonmet.ac.uk/depts/hale/lgr

law, law & business management, business/international/European/human rights/ law, international banking & insurance law, trade, transport & maritime law, comparative IP law, European law, human rights law and social justice, international law & politics, governance & international relations/law, international commercial law & business, legal practice, international development, peace & conflict studies, politics, European studies, international relations (globalization/interdisciplinary), international security studies, peace & conflict studies, public service management/administration; BA(Hons), BSc(Hons), FdG, LlB, LlM, MA, PGCE

London Metropolitan University

Faculty of Life Sciences;
www.londonmet.ac.uk/depts/fls

School of Human Science;
www.londonmet.ac.uk/depts/hhs

biochemistry, bioethics, biological sciences, biology, biotechnology, biomedical sciences, blood science, chemistry, food science, forensic & bioanalytical science, pharmaceutical sciences, herbal medicinal science, human biology/nutrition, international/ public health nutrition, public health/sports/dietetics, medical bioscience, medical genetics, obesity & weight management, personal training and fitness consultancy, pharmaceutical science, pharmacology, sports dance therapy, sports psychology & coaching, public health, nutrition, sports therapy

School of Psychology;
www.londonmet.ac.uk/depts/dops

psychology, addiction psychology & treatment, psychology of health, child adolescent & family psychology, business/consumer/criminal/forensic/occupational/organisational psychology, cognitive behaviour therapy; BSc(Hons), DipHE, FdSc, GradDip/Cert, MOst, MOstMed, MSc, Prof Doc

London Metropolitan Business School;
www.londonmet.ac.uk/lmb

accounting & banking/finance/business management, financial markets & derivatives, business/operations management, corporate finance & investment, international financial services/banking & finance/financial studies, international financial strategy

ecomomics, business economics & finance, international business/economics & finance, international bus & marketing, sustainable business, energy & finance, HRM & employment law, international business/business management & business law, human resources & employment management, HRM, organisational change & consultancy, business management/studies/administration, corporate social responsibility, project management, international business management, marketing, law & business management

advertising, marketing communications & PR, digital & experiential marketing, international marketing communications, fashion marketing/buying & retailing/PR, marketing, PR, marketing & business management/journalism; arts & heritage management, aviation management, international events management & PR, international hospitality/tourism management/hotel & restaurant management, international sustainable tourism, international tourism, management & development, international trade & transport, logistics & supply chain management, media business/events/musical culture/business management, music industry & media digital business, purchase & supply chain management, executive & professional courses

DPS, FdSc, GradConv, HND, MA, MBA, MSc, PGDip, ProfDoc

Sir John Cass Dept of Art Media and Design;
www.londonmet.ac.uk/jcmd

applied art, art design, curating the contemporary, design, digital film & animation, drawing, fine art, furniture design, graphic design, interior design, jewellery design, media & commerce, mixed media, music & technology, musical instruments, painting, photography, printmaking, product design, restoration & conservation, sculpture & installation, texvisual culture; BA(Hons), PGCert, FdA, MA, MPhil, MSc, PhD

THE LONDON SCHOOL OF OSTEOPATHY
www.lso.ac.uk

---

osteopathy; MOst

LONDON SOUTH BANK UNIVERSITY
www.lsbu.ac.uk

Faculty of Arts and Human Sciences; www.lsbu.ac.uk/#ahs

Arts, Media; www.lsbu.ac.uk/ahs/departments/artsmedia
digital film & video/media arts/photography, game cultures, music & sonic media; BA(Hons), MA, MPhil, PhD

Culture, Writing & Performance; www.lsbu.ac.uk/ahs/departments/cwp
communications, critical/arts management, creative writing, drama & performance, English, independant film practice, media studies, photographic culture, film studies, cultural & media studies, multimedia journalism, creative media industries, media arts/writing, new media, theatre practice; BA(Hons), MA, PhD, MPhil

Education; www.lsbu.ac.uk/departments/education
early years, education for sustainability, graduate teacher training/PGCE with QTS (primary/secondary maths), learning and teaching, in HE, post-compulsory education, secondary mathematics, sustainability equality & diversity; (BA(Hons), Cert, FdA, MA, MPhil, PhD, PgDip/Cert, EdDoc, PGCHE

Law; www.lsbu.ac.uk/departments/law
common law, crime & litigation, international human rights and development, law, legal studies, criminality; GradDip, LlB(Hons), LLM, CPE

Psychology; www.lsbu.ac.uk/departments/psychology
addiction psychology & counselling, investigative forensic psychology, psychology, criminology, clinical psychology, child development; BSc(Hons), GradDip, MSc, PhD

Social Sciences; www.lsbu.ac.uk/ahs/departments/socialsciences
criminology with law/psychology, development studies, development & urbanisation, international politics, refugee studies, social policy, social research methods, sociology; BA(Hons), BSc(Hons), MSc, PhD, PGDip/Cert

Urban, Environmental & Leisure Studies; www.lsbu.ac.uk/ahs/departments/uels
built environment studies, housing studies, international tourism & hospitality/travel management, planning policy and practice, town planning, urban planning design, sustainable communities, urban and environmental planning/regeneration and community development, urban planning design/regeneration, tourism, leisure & hospitality management; BA(Hons), FdA, HNC, MA, MSc, PGCert/Dip, MPhil, PhD

Faculty of Business; www.bus.lsbu.ac.uk
accounting, business administration/management/project management/studies, international business by e-learning, finance, professional accounting, charity finance/accounting, corporate governanace, international finance/bankin/investment, management in civil society, financial management, business information technology/intelligence, computing, computer systems management, high performance/human centred computing, IT, internet & database systems, multimedia computing, strategic information IT, web design/& mobile computing, business administration, digital marketing, public administration, HRM/D, HR practice, international business, international health services & hospital management, international human resources/HRM/management/marketing, learning & development in practice, management in civil society, marketing & fundraising, marketing/communications management, Chinese business practice, charity finance, public administration, management in civil society/financial management/fundraising & marketing;
MA, D/MBA, PGDip/Cert, MSc, BTEC, HND, DMS, CM, BSc(Hons), BA(Hons), MPA, CM

Faculty of Engineering, Science & Built Environment; www.lsbu.ac.uk/esbe

Dept of Applied Science; www.lsbu.ac.uk/esbe/departments/appsci
applied biology, applied science, bioscience/clinical, chemical & process engineering, biochemistry, culinary art, engineering, environmental biology, food & nutrition, food safety & control, food science, forensic science, human biology, human nutrition, integrated sciences, microbiology, petroleum engineering, sport & exercise science; BA(Hons), BEng(Hons), BSc(Hons), FdSc, MSc/PgCert/PgDip

Dept of Engineering & Design;
www.lsbu.ac.uk/esbe/departments/engdes

computer-aided design/engineering, computer systems & network(s/ing), design & manufacturing management, electrical & electronic engineering, engineering product design, enterprise, mechanical engineering/design, mechatronics/engineering, power distribution, product design/ computing, sports product design, telecommunications & computer networks engineering, embedded & distributed systems, quality engineering management systems for environmental services; BEng(Hons), BSc(Hons), FdEng, HNC, HND, MRes, MSc, PgDip

Dept of the Built Environment;
www.1lsbu.ac.uk/esbe/departments/builtenv

architecture, architectural technology, built environment, commercial management (quantity surveying), construction/management/project management, planning buildings for health, property development & planning management, building surveying, real estate; BA(Hons), FdSc, HNC, PgDip/Cert, MSc

Dept of Urban Engineering;
www1.lsbu.ac.uk/esbe/departments/urbeng

architectural engineering, building services engineering, civil engineering, environmental & architectural acoustics, railway civil engineering, structural engineering, transport engineering & planning, sustainable energy systems; BEng(Hons), BSc(Hons), FdEng, HNC, HND, MSc, PgDip/Cert

Faculty of Health & Social Care;
www.lsbu.ac.uk/faculties/hsc

health & social care (acute hospital care/maternity support/mental health care/primary care/rehabilitation therapy/service user support) nursing (advanced/children's/learning disabilities/mental health/neonatal), midwifery, radiography (diagnostic/therapeutic/reporting), operating dept practice, occupational therapy, social work, primary & social care, adv cardiac catheter pract/neuromuscoloskeletal management, non medical prescribing, breast imaging, ultrasound, child health/nursing, acute & psychiatric intensive care, cognitive behaviour therapy, forensic/mental health, careers guidance, health visiting, leadership & service improvement in healthcare practice, primary care, public health & health practice, schools nursing, workplace health management, continuous professional development, traditional Chinese medicine; FdSc, BSc, BSc(Hons), DipHE(Hons), MSc, PgDip/Cert, PhD, University AdvDip, ProfDoc, MCMAc

UNIVERSITY OF EAST LONDON
www.uel.ac.uk

School of Arts and Digital Industries;
www.uel.ac.uk/ad

advertising, animation, communication studies, community arts projects, creative and professional writing, computer games design/technology, culture studies, digital fashion, English literature, fine art, film & video, graphic design, history, illustration, interactive media, sports/journalism, media studies, moving images, multimedia design technology, music culture/& production, photography, pop music performance, printed textile design, print making, textiles & fashion, theatre studies; BA(Hons), BSc/BA, FdA, GradCert, MA, MPhil, MSc, PGC, PhD, ProfDoc

School of Combined Honours;
www.uel.ac.uk/combined

range of subjects for which combined honours courses are conducted

School of Architecture, Computing and Engineering; www.uel.ac.uk/ace

architecture/computing/design, architecture interpretation & theories/sustainability & design, urban design/environments & energy studies, landscape architecture, bus inf systems, computing networks, computing, computer games/networks/systems engineering/forensics, information technology/security, internet systems engineering, technology management, mobile communications, software engineering, civil engineering surveying, construction practice, electrical & electronic eng, mathematics, product design, environmental adaptability and sustainability, geotechnics & energy management, renewable energy & built environment; BA/BEng(Hons), BA/BSc, BSc(Hons), MPhil, MSc, PhD, ProfDoc

Royal Docks Business School; www.uel.ac.uk/business
accounting, business management (finance/HR/marketing) investment/risk management, economics, finance, hospitality & international tourist management, HRM, international accounting/HRM/marketing/risk business/finance, Islamic finance, financial & risk/investment, project management, retail, brand management, marketing, sports/tourism management; BA(Hons), DBA, HND, LlB, MA, MBA, MPhil, MSc, PGDip, PhD

Cass School of Education & Communities; www.uel.ac.uk/education
child care, children & young people, early years education, enhancement programme, secondary/primary education, English & languages, post-compulsory training, primary/secondary teaching, professional development, social work, special needs, teacher training, teaching assistants, youth & community work; BA(Hons), EdD, FdA, MA, PGCE, PGDip, ProfDoc, UnivCert

School of Health, Sport and Bioscience; www.uel.ac.uk/hsb
biochemistry, biomedical science, biotechnology, cellular & molecular pharmacy, clinical science, conservation, fitness & health, forensic science, health studies, medical/microbiology, paediatrics, toxology, public health, pharmacology, pharmaceutical sci, physiotherapy, podiatry, sports & exercise science/rehabilitation, sports coaching/development/therapy; BA(Hons), BSc(Hons), FdSc, MPhil, MSc, PGCert, PhD, ProfDoc

School of Law & Social Science; www.uel.ac.uk/law
law, criminology/ & criminal justice, human rights, international law & finance/world economy/criminal justice/financial markets, international development/relations, innovation, NGOs & development, Islamic & Middle East law, native American studies, psychosocial studies, social enterprise/science, sociology, refugee studies, transport sustenance & science; BA(Hons), BSc(Hons), LlB, LlM, MSc, PostGDip

School of Psychology; www.uel.ac.uk/psychology
counselling, mentoring, psychology, critical/developmental/forensic/educational/child psychology, psychosocial studies, coaching, careers guidance, spiritual, religious & cultural care; BA(Hons), BSc(Hons), ClinPSyD, FdA, GradDip/Cert, MA, MSc, ProfDoc, UnivCert

UNIVERSITY OF WEST LONDON
www.uwl.ac.uk

Faculty of the Arts; www.uwl.ac.uk/the_university/faculties_and_schools/Faculty_of_the_Arts
London College of Music; www.uwl.ac.uk/music/London_College_of_Music
audio technology, ballet, music theatre, theatre production, music (performance & composition), management & artist development, performance/technology, composing concert music, music industry management, record production, pop music; BA, BMus, BSc, DipHE, FdA, FdMus, MA, MMus, PGCert, PGDip

School of Art Design, & Media; www.uwl.ac.uk/art_design_media/School_of_Art_Design_and_Media
digital animation/media production, fashion & textiles, games development (games art/games design), graphic design, new media art & design, photography, digital imaging, web design, advertising, broadcast journalism, broadcasting, media studies, PR, video production & film studies; BA, FdA, MA, DipHE

Faculty of Health & Human Studies; www.uwl.ac.uk/the_university/faculties_and_schools/Faculty_of_Health_and_Human_Sciences
School of Psychology, Social Care & Human Sciences; www.uwl.ac.uk/school_of_psychology_social_work_and_human_sciences/School_of_Psychology_Social_Work_and_Human_Sciences
substance use & misuse studies, nutrition, nutitional therapeutics, counselling theory, food & consumer health, clinical hypnotherapy, communicable diseases, criminology, enhancing professional practice, forensic sciences, health psychology, health promotion & public health, end of life care, human science, leadership for health & care, psychology, psychology & health/criminology/counselling theory, manipulation of diet in health, nutritional therapeutics/therapy, psychology, strategic workforce planning, social

work/care; BSc, CertHE, DipHE, FdSc, MA, MPhil, MSc, PGCert, PGDip, PhD

School of Nursing, Midwifery & Healthcare; www.uwl.ac.uk/school_of_nursing_midwifery_and_healthcare/School_of_Nursing_Midwifery_and_Healthcare
adv/professional practice, advancing practice/community nursing/midwifery, health & social care/leadership, healthcare, enhancing professional practice, learning disability/adult/child/mental health nursing, midwifery/& women's health, operating dept practice, psychosocial intervention for psychosis, public health, primary care, working with children & young people; BSc, DipHE, MA, MM, MPhil, PGDip, PhD, FdSc

Faculty of Professional Studies

West London Business School; www.uwl.ac.uk/businessschool/Business_School
accounting & finance, business studies/finance/internship/marketing, credit management, English studies, finance & risk management, global capital markets, HRM, marketing, management, managing human resources, information & communication, international business management/marketing hotel management, culinary arts management, corporate communication, management studies (health & social care), project management, PR, purchasing & supply, tourism management; DMS, FdA, GradCert, GradDip, HND, MA, MBA, MPhil, MSc, PGDip, PhD

Ealing Law School; www.uwl.ac.uk/law/Ealing_Law_School
law, criminology, employment law, intellectual property law, investment & arbitration law, international/business & commercial/banking & finance law, finance law, legal practice; GradDip, LLB, LLM, PhD

London School of Hospitality & Tourism; www.uwl.ac.uk/hospitality/London_School_of_Hospitality_and_Tourism
airline & airport management, business travel & tourism, cruise ship management, events management, food & professional cookery, hospitality/operations management, fundraising & special events management, gastronomic food management, international culinary arts/hotel management, tourism, travel & tourism/management; BA, DipHE, FdA, GradCert, HND, MA, MPhil, PGDip, PhD

School of Computing & Technology; www.uwl.ac.uk/computing/School_of_Computing_and_Technology
applied sound engineering, computing/science, information systems/for business, software engineering, computer interaction design/systems management, library/information management, electronic/electrical engineering, information & communications technology, mechanical engineering, mechatronics, microelectronics, network & mobile communications, software engineering. civil & environmental engineering,built environment: construction management/architectural technology; BSc, FdSc, HND, MSc

UNIVERSITY OF LONDON; BIRKBECK
www.bbk.ac.uk

School of Arts; www.bbk.ac.uk/arts
English & humanities, European cultures & languages, history of art & screen media, media & cultural studies, Iberian & Latin American studies, French, Spanish, German, Japanese, Polish, Portugese

School of Business, Economics and Informatics; www.bbk.ac.uk/business
computer science, information systems, economics, mathematics & statistics, management, organizational psychology, business studies; BSc, CertHE, MPhil, PhD MSc, MRes

School of Law; www.bbk.ac.uk/law
law, law (public/company/medical/European/constitutional), criminology & criminal justice, human rights law, international criminal law & social justice; LlB, MPhil, PhD

School of Science; www.bbk.ac.uk
astronomy, biological sciences, pharmacy, biomedicine, chemistry, chemical & molecular biology, biological science; earth and planetary sciences: environmental/geology, earth science, ecology, forensic science, planet science & astronomy; psychological sciences: psychology; BSc, MPhil, PhD,FD

School of Social Sciences, History and Philosophy; www/bbk.ac.uk
applied linguistics & communication,· classics, sociology, social sciences, social research, archaeology, geography, environment & development studies, early modern/European/medieval history, Victorian

studies, politics, philosophy & history, history of ideas, psychosocial studies, social policy & education; BA, BSc, MA, MRes, MPhil, PhD, CertHE

UNIVERSITY OF LONDON; COURTAULD INSTITUTE OF ART
www.courtauld.ac.uk

conservation of easel paintings, curating the art museum, history of art, conservation of wall painting; BA(Hons), GradDip, MA, PGDip, MPhil, PhD

UNIVERSITY OF LONDON; GOLDSMITHS
www.goldsmiths.ac.uk

Dept of Anthropology; www.gold.ac.uk/anthropology
anthropology/media/& cultural policy, applied anthropology & community relations, area studies (Latin America), development & rights, cultural politics, history, sociology, social/visual anthropology, community development, community & youth work, development & rights, health with body in 21st century; BA(Hons), MPhil, PhD, MRes

Dept of Art; www.gold.ac.uk/art
fine art & history of art, art writing, curating; BA(Hons), MFA, MPhil, PhD

Centre for English Language & Academic Writing; www.gold.ac.uk/eap
humanities, social science, media, communication, creative & culture industries, counselling, therapy; GradDip, IntCert

Centre for Cultural Studies; www.gold.ac.uk/cultural-studies
cultural studies/industry, creating social media, interactive media: critical theory & practice, post-colonial culture & global policy; MA, MPhil, PhD

Dept of Computing; www.gold.ac.uk/computing
computing, computer science, computational arts, computer games & entertainment, computer studio art/technology, creative computing, creative & cultural entrepreneurship, digital journalism/society, games programming, information systems, music computing; BMus, BA/BSc(Hons), MFA, MPhil, MSc, PhD

Dept of Design; www.gold.ac.uk/design
creativity & design, design, design education, design & innovation/environment, design – critical practice/education/futures, creative & cultural entrepreneurship, innovation & practice; BA(Hons), BA/BSc(Hons), BEng/MEng, MPhil, MRes, PhD

Dept of Educational Studies; www.gold.ac.uk/educational-studies
artist teachers & contemporary practice, education, culture & society, education:culture, language & society/school-based exploration, writer/teacher, education teacher training (PGCE) – primary/secondary art & design, design & technology, drama, English, geography, mathematics, modern languages, music, biology, chemistry, general science or physics; BA(Hons), DPS, MA, MPhil, PhD

English and Comparative Literature; www.gold.ac.uk/ecl
American literature, applied linguistics, comparative literature, creative/& life writing, drama, English, history, media & modern literature/languages, sociocultural linguistics, comparative literary studies; BA(Hons), MA, MPhil, MRes, PhD

Dept of History; www.gold.ac.uk/history
history, history & anthropology/history of ideas/politics; BA (Hons), MA, MPhil, MRes, PhD

Institute for Creative and Cultural Entrepreneurship; www.gold.ac.uk/ccl
creative cultural entrepreneurship, social entrepreneurship, arts administration & cultural politics; MA, MPhil, PhD

Institute of Management Studies; www.gold.ac.uk/institute-management-studies
leadership & talent management, management of innovation, digital enterprise studies, occupational psychology; MSc

Dept of Media and Communications; www.gold.ac.uk/media-communications

anthropology & media, media & communications/sociology/modern literature, brands communications & culture, creative & cultural entrepreneurship, digital media/journalism, filmmaking, gender & culture, image & communication, electronic graphics, TV/journalism, promotional media, global media & transnational communications, the image & the electronics age, radio screen documentary, screen & film studies, script writing, media & communications, political communication; BA(Hons), MA, MPhil, PhD, MRes

Dept of Music; www.gold.ac.uk/music

arts administration & cultural policy, composition, contemporary music, pop music, creative practice, creative & cultural entrepreneurship, ethnomusicology, historical musicology, music, music computing/performance & related studies, studio composition; BMus(Hons), BMus/BSc(Hons), MA, MMus, MPhil, PGCert, PhD

Dept of Politics; www.gold.ac.uk/politics

art & politics, economics, politics & public policy, history, international studies, politics, sociology, political science; BA(Hons), DPS, MA, MPhil, MRes, PhD

Dept of Professional and Community Education; www.gold.ac.uk/pace

counselling, social work, social & cultural studies, performing arts, dance movement/art psychotherapy, community & youth work, rational-emotive cognitive behaviour therapy; BA(Hons), DipHE, GradDip, PGCert, MSC

Dept of Psychology; www.gold.ac.uk/psychology

cognitive & clinical neuroscience, music, mind & brain, clinical psychology & health service, organizational behaviour, psychology, research methods; FD, BSc(Hons), MPhil, MSc, PhD

Dept of Sociology; www.gold.ac.uk/sociology

critical & creative analysis, digital sociology, gender, media & culture, photography & urban cultures, social research, sociology & anthropology/media/politics, sociology, world cities & urban life; BA(Hons), MA, MPhil, PhD

Dept of Visual Cultures; www.gold.ac.uk/visual-cultures

aural & visual cultures, contemporary art theory/history, fine art, global art, history of art, research architecture; BA(Hons), MA, MPhil, PGDip, PhD

UNIVERSITY OF LONDON; HEYTHROP COLLEGE
www.heythrop.ac.uk

Abrahamic religions, biblical studies, canon law, Christian spirituality/theology, Christianity & inter-religious relations, contemporary ethics, divinity, pastoral/mission/theology, philosophy, religion & ethics/theology, philosophy in education, psychology of religion, study of religions, theology; BA, Certs, FD, GradDip, MA

UNIVERSITY OF LONDON; INSTITUTE IN PARIS
www.ulip.ac.uk

French/Paris studies – history & culture; BA, MA, MPhil, PhD

UNIVERSITY OF LONDON; INSTITUTE OF EDUCATION
www.ioe.ac.uk

teacher training; primary/secondary PGCE, post-compulsory education, adult literacy/numeracy, lifelong learning, leadership, adv educational practice, applied leadership & management, art & design in education, special & inclusive education, teaching English to speakers in other languages (TESOL), bilingual learners, child development, clinical education, comparative education, curriculum, pedagogy, assessment, development education, development & educational psychology, early years education, economics of education, education citizenship history/RE/psychology, education, gender & international development/health promotion/technology, educational assessment/neuroscience/planning/economics, effective learning, English learning/education/globalisation & language policy, geography education, higher & professional education, history of education, inspection & regulation, language & communication, leadership, learning technologies, lifelong learning, literacy learning/difficulties, maths/science education, media, culture & education, museums & galleries in education, music education, philosophy/psychology/sociology of education, policy studies, psychology of education, psychosocial studies, reading recovery & literacy leadership, social justice & education, sociology of education, special & inclusive education, teaching & learning in HE & professional education; BEd, Certs, DedPsy, EdD, GradDip, MA, MBA, MPhil, MRes, MSc, MTg, PGCE, PhD

UNIVERSITY OF LONDON; KING'S COLLEGE LONDON
www.kcl.ac.uk

The School of Arts & Humanities; www.kcl.ac.uk/humanities
Abrahamic religions, adv musical studies, ancient history, biblical studies, Byzantine/modern Greek studies, Christianity & the arts, classics, classical studies/archaeology, comparative literature, conflict resolution & divided society, culture, media & creative cities, digital asset management/culture, early modern Eng lit/history, 18/19th-century studies, English/literature/language, European public policy/studies (French/German/Spanish), film studies, French, German, Turkish/modern Greek, French literature & culture, German & comparative literature, Hispanic studies, medieval/ history, international political economy, learning & cognition, life writing, war studies, Jewish studies, late antique & Byzantine studies, linguistics, medical humanities, medieval history, Middle East & Mediterranean studies, political economy of Middle East, music, philosophy/of medicine/mental disorder/psychology, Portuguese & Brazilian studies, religion in the contemporary world, Spanish & Portuguese, Latin American studies, religion, systematic theology, philosophy & ethics, world history & culture; BA(Hons), MA, MMus, MRes, MSc

School of Biomedical Sciences; www.kcl.ac.uk/biohealth
analytical science/toxicology, anatomy, developmental & human biology, aviation medicine, biomedical science/& scientific English, biomedicine & molecular science, biopharmaceuticals, chemistry with biomedicine, drug discovery/development, forensic science, human & applied physiology, molecular genetics/biophysics, neuroscience, pain science & society, clinical/pharmacology, pharmacy practice, pharmaceutical analysis & quality control/technology, pharmaceutics, physiology, space physiology & health, translational medicine; BSc, DHC, MB, MPharm, MRes, MSc, GradDip, PGDip/Cert, MPhil, PhD, MD

Dental Institute; www.kcl.ac.uk/dentistry
dentistry, adv general dental practice, aesthetic dentistry, conscious sedation, dental public health, developmental & human biology, endodontology, maxillofacial & craniofacial/prosthodontal treatment, regenerative/technology, orthodontics, paediatric dentistry, periodontology, fixed & removable/prosthodontics, sedation & special care dentistry; BDS, MClinDent, MOrth, MScDL, PGDip

Institute of Psychiatry; www.iop.kcl.ac.uk
addiction, advanced psychosocial practice, adv care in dementia, identification of alcohol & drug use in the workplace, child & adolescent mental health, clinical forensic psychiatry/neuroscience, cognitive behavioural therapies/for psychosis, epilepsy, family therapy, forensic mental health, global mental health, health psychology, mental health studies, neuroscience, neuroimaging, mental health/learning disabilities/population research, social work with children & adults, organizational psychiatry & psychology, psychology, social, genetic & developmental psychiatry, war & psychiatry; BSc, DClinPsy, GradCert, MSc, PGDip, MPhil, PhD, MD

School of Law; www.kcl.ac.uk/law
construction law & dispute resolution, criminology & criminal justice, English & French/German/

American/Hong Kong/Australian law, politics, philosophy & law, transnational law, medical ethics & law, EU competition/competition law, European/EU law, global ethics & human values, intellectual property & information law, international business/tax law, medical law, UK/US/EU copyright law; LlB, LLM, MA, MPhil, MSc, PhD

School of Medicine; www.kcl.ac.uk/schools/medicine

medicine, nutrition, chemistry with biomedicine, dietetics, physiology, cardiovascular res, immunology, translational cancer medicine, clinical pharmacology, drug development, clinical/medical imaging, medical engineering/physics, radiopharmaceutics, medical/vascular ultrasound, nuclear medicine, pain, science & society, palliative care, primary health care, public health, adv physiotherapy/paediatrics, clinical dermatology, imaging, rheumatology, translational medicine; MBBS, MPH, MSc, DDip/Cert, MD, MPhil, PhD

Florence Nightingale School of Nursing & Midwifery; www.kcl.ac.uknursing

advanced practice; cancer nursing, cardiac care, child health, critical care, dermatology, diabetes care, infection control, leadership, midwifery, neuroscience care, nurse practitioner, community matron, case manager, palliative care nursing, specialist community health nursing/health visiting/school nursing, women's healthcare, clinical nursing for international students, education for healthcare professionals, health studies; care/education/leadership/midwifery/primary care, gastrointestinal nursing, nursing studies – adult nursing/child nursing/mental health nursing, midwifery studies, public health/women's health, health & social care; BSc(Hons), DipHE, DHC, DPhil, MRes, MSc, PGCert/Dip

School of Natural & Mathematical Sciences; www.kcl.ac.uk/nms

biomedical engineering, chemistry with biomedicine, computer science/with management/mathematics/robotics/intelligent systems, adv computing, adv software engineering, bioinformatics, complex systems modelling, computing & internet systems/security/IT, law & management, mobile & personal communication, mobile internet research, telecommunications/& internet technology, web intelligence
mathematics: mathematics & philosophy/physics/computer science/management & finance, financial mathematics
physics: physics & mathematics/philosophy/medical applications/ theoretical physics, robotics & intelligent systems
electronic engineering/engineering with business management, robotics; BEng, BSc, MSc, MPhil, MSci, GradDip, PhD

School of Social Science and Public Policy; www.kcl.ac.uk/sspp

business management, accounting, accountability & financial management, HRM & organizational analysis, risk analysis
assessment in education, education studies, assessment, child studies, creative arts in the classroom, education – professional studies/management/policy & society/arts & cultural setting/English, ELT/& applied linguistics, ICT education, inclusive education & technology, international child education, ministry & leadership, teaching & learning, FE management, PGCE (various subjects), science/mathematics education
bible & ministry, ethics/mission in modern age, religious/Christian/Jewish education, contemporary ecclesiology/worship, English language & communication, ministry & leadership, theology, politics & faith-based organisations, youth ministry
international politics/studies/conflict studies/management/marketing/peace & security/relations/studies, air power, war studies & history/philosophy, European public policy, science & security, S.Asia & global security, politics of international economics, conflict security & development, intelligence & international security, non-proliferation & international security, geopolitics territory & security
geography, creatice/cities, disasters, adaptation & development, carbon science, society & change, environment & development/politics & globalization, environmental monitoring/modelling/management, geopolitics, global environmental change, acquatic resource management, social science & health
ageing & society, gerontology, health & society/promotion, medicine, science & society, public policy, public services
English language & communication, French, applied linguistics, language – cultural diversity/ethnicity & education, 19th-century studies; BA, MA, MSc, MRes, GradDip, PGDip/Cert, FD, DThMin, DrPS, MPhil, PhD, EdD

UNIVERSITY OF LONDON; LONDON SCHOOL OF ECONOMICS & POLITICAL SCIENCE
www.lse.ac.uk

Departments at LSE:
Accounting, Anthropology, Economics, Finance, Geography & Environment, Government, International History, International Relations, Law, Management, Mathematics, Media and Communications, Philosophy, Logic and Scientific Method, Social Policy, Sociology, Statistics

accounting/organisations & institutions, anthropology/& development, applicable mathematics, applied statistics & actuarial science, China in a comparative perspective, city design & social science, comparative politics (conflict studies/democracy/Latin America/nationalism & ethnicity/politics & markets), criminal justice, policy, culture & society, decision science, diplomacy & international studies, econometrics, economics, economic history, European political economy/public & economic policy/social policy, finance, financial mathematics/studies, gender, geography, global history/media/politics/communication, government, health policy, international relations/history/theory, planning & finance, human geography, international employment rights & HRM, human rights, international development/political economy/history/relations, language studies, law, anthropology & society, management/& regulation of risk/science/& human resources, management information systems & innovation, managerial economics, mathematics, mathematical economics, media & communications, methodology, OR, organizational behaviour, philosophy, political science/economy/sociology/theory, logic & scientific method, poltical economy of Europe, political sociology/theory, population & development, politics & governance in Europe, political sociology, private equity, public & economic policy, public policy/& management/& social policy/administration, risk & stochastics, social anthropology/policy studies/psychology, social policy (Europe & common social policy) social research methods, sociology/contemporary social thought, statistics, urbanization & development; BA(Hons), BSc(Hons), Dips, EMBA, Ll, M, MBA, MPA, MPhil, MRes, MSc, PhD

UNIVERSITY OF LONDON; LONDON SCHOOL OF JEWISH STUDIES
www.lsjs.ac.uk

Jewish education, Jewish studies, applied professional studies; BA(Hons), MA

UNIVERSITY OF LONDON; QUEEN MARY
www.qmul.ac.uk

Humanities & Social Sciences

School of Business & Management;
www.busman.qmul.ac.uk
accounting, business/law/management, finance, global business, management & organisational innovation, marketing, interrnational business & politics/financial management/HRM & employment relations In addition to the above taught degrees there are numerous compulsory modules, a number of which are required to be taken on MSc courses

School of Economics & Finance;
www.econ.qmul.ac.uk
accounting, banking, economics, econometrics, finance, geography, investment, law, management, mathematics, mathematical finance, politics, financial economics, statistics; BSc, MPhil, MSc(Econ), PhD

School of English and Drama;
www.sed.qmul.ac.uk
Dept of Drama
drama, drama & English/French/German/Hispanic studies/Russian/film studies, theatre & performance theory

Dept of English
English/& drama/film studies/history/modern language/French/German/Hispanic studies/Russian, English literature & linguistics, English in Renaissance, writing & society 1700–1820; BA(Hons), MA, MRes, PhD

School of Languages, Linguistics & Film; www.sllf.qmul.ac.uk
French/German/Hispanic studies/Russian/Catalan languages/Portuguese, English language with business management/film studies/linguistics, European studies, Anglo-German cultural relations, languages & literature, comparative literature, film studies with languages/history; BA(Hons), MA, PhD

Dept of Geography; www.geog.qmul.ac.uk
cities & cultures, community organizing, environmental geography/science, business management, geography, global change, environmental science, integrated management of freshwater environment, economy/globalization & development, London studies, physical geography; BA(Hons), BSc(Econ), BSc(Hons), MA, MSc, PhD

Dept of History; www.history.qmul.ac.uk
modern & contemporary/history, history & politics/film studies/English/German language/comparative literature, Islam & the West, European Jewish history, medieval history, Paris studies, modern & contemporary British history, history of political thought & intellectual history; BA(Hons), MA, PhD

School of Law; www.law.qmul.ac.uk law
banking & finance law, commercial & corporate law, comparative & international dispute resolution, competition law, computer & communications law, economic regulation, English and European law, environmental law, human rights law, intellectual property law, international business law, law & development/politics, legal theory & history, management of intellectual property, trade mark law & practice, insurance law, international dspute resolution, medical law, public international law, public law, tax law, media law; Dips, LlB, LlM, MPhil, MSc, PGDip, PhD

Dept of Philosophy; www.philosophy.qmul.ac.uk
philosophy; MPhil, PhD

School of Politics & International Relations; www.politics.qmul.ac.uk
international relations, public policy, politics, politics & economics/law/geography/business management/French/German/Russian/Hispanic studies, global & comparative politics, globalization & development, international business & politics, global & comparative politics, migration/& law
numerous postgraduate modules available; BA(Hons), MA, MPhil, MRes, PhD

School of Medicine & Dentistry; www.smd.qmul.ac.uk

Barts and The London School of Medicine and Dentistry; www.smd-edu.qmul.ac.uk/medicine/
medicine, surgery, dentistry, dental surgery, biomedical engineering, clinical specialisations, community & public health, aesthetic plastic surgery, burn care, cancer therapeutics, clinical dermatology, clinical drug development, clinical microbiology, endocrinology & diabetes, forensic medical sciences, gastroenterology, global public health & policy, healthcare research methods, health systems & global policy, inflammation, international primary health care, mental health/ psychological therapies/transcultural mental health care, molecular pathology & genomics, neuroscience & translational medicine, sport & exercise science, surgical skills & science, trauma science; dental clinical science/public health/technology, endodontic practice, experimental oral practice, oral biology/medicine, orthodontics, paediatric dentistry, periodontology, prosthodontics

Research Institutions;
Barts Cancer Institute
Bizard Institute of Cell and Molecular Science
Institute of Dentistry
Institute of Health Science and Education
William Harvey Research Institute
Wolfson Institute of Preventative Medicine
BDS, BMedSci, FD, BDental Science, MBBS, MClinDent, MD, MRes, MPhil, MSc, NVQ, PGDip, PhD, MPrth, Certs, Dips

Department of Science & Engineering

School of Biological and Chemical Sciences; www.sbcs.qmul.ac.uk
aquatic biology, biochemistry, biology, biomedical sciences, chemistry, freshwater & coastal sciences, genetics, marine ecology & environmental management, medical/genetics, pharmaceutical chemistry, psychology, zoology with aquatic biology; BSc(Hons), FD, MPhil, MSci, PhD

School of Electronic Engineering & Computer Science; www.eecs.qmul.ac.uk

audio systems engineering, computer science/& mathematics/business management, computing/& information systems, digital music processing, electrical engineering, electronic engineering, information/systems/management & communication technologies, multi/media & arts technology, software engineering, telecommunications systems, web technologies, mobile & wireless networks; BEng, BSc(Eng), MEng, MSc, PhD

School of Engineering and Materials Science; www.sems.qmul.ac.uk

aerospace engineering, biomedical engineering, computer-aided engineering, design & innovation, materials & design, materials science & engineering/research, dental materials, biomaterials, mechanical engineering, medical materials/engineering/electronics & physics, polymer science & technology, sustainable energy systems/engineering/materials; BEng, BSc, MEng, MPhil, MRes, PhD

School of Mathematical Sciences; www.maths.qmul.ac.uk

mathematics, pure mathematics, statistics, astrophysics, financial economics, mathematical finance, maths with business management/psychology/computing/physics/accountancy; BSc(Hons), MPhil, MSc, MSci, PGDip/Cert, PhD

School of Physics & Astronomy; www.phy.qmul.ac.uk

astrophysics, astronomy, physics, condensed material physics, theoretical physics & nanoscience, particle physics; BSc(Hons), MSc, MSci, PGDip, PhD

UNIVERSITY OF LONDON; ROYAL HOLLOWAY
www.rhul.ac.uk

Faculty of Arts; www.rhul.ac.uk/departments/arts

Dept for Classics & Philosophy; www.rhul.ac.uk/classicsandphilosophy

ancient history & philosophy, comparative literature & culture & philosophy, late antique & Byzantine studies, combinations of: classics, philosophy, classical studies, drama, Italian, French, Greek, Latin, German; music & philosophy, philosophy, politics & international relations, classical art & archaeology, moderrn philosophy; BA(Hons), MPhil, PhD

Dept of Drama & Theatre; www.rhul.ac.uk/drama

drama & theatre studies, international theatre, English & drama, drama & creative writing/philosophy/French/German/Italian/music/classical studies, theatre; applied drama/directing/physical theatre & performance, playwriting; BA(Hons), MPhil, PhD

Dept of English; www.rhul.ac.uk/english

English, English & philosophy/classics/comparative literature/modern languages/film studies/drama, creative writing, English literature, literature of modernity, medieval studies, poetic practice, Shakespeare, Victorian literature, art, culture

Dept of Media Arts; www.rhul.ac.uk/media-arts

documentary by practice, international broadcasting, production, media arts, film & TV studies, screenwriting/producing for TV & film; BA(Hons), MA, MPhil, PhD

Dept of Modern Languages, Literature & Culture; www.rghul.ac.uk/mllc

French, German, Italian, Spanish, Hispanic studies, modern literature & culture/film studies, critical theory, film, visual & performing arts, linguistics, comparative literature & culture

Dept of Music; www.rhul.ac.uk/Music

advanced musical studies, music, composition, ethnomusicology, musicology, performance, music with performance studies, music history; BA(Hons), BMus, MMus, MPhil, PhD

Faculty of History & Social Sciences; www.rhul.ac.uk/departments/hss

Centre for Criminology & Sociology; www.rhul.ac.uk/criminology & sociology

criminology & sociology/psychology, criminal justice systems, social policy, psychology of morality & behaviour

University of London; Royal Holloway

Dept of Economics; www.rhul.ac.uk/economics
economics, economics of public policy, economics & management/politics/international relations/political studies/modern languages/mathematics/music/political studies, financial & business economics/industrial economics

Dept of European Studies; www.rhul.ac.uk/EuropeanStudies
European studies (French/Spanish/Italian/German), European research

Dept of Social Work www.rhul.ac.uk/socialwork
social work, work with children & families; BA(Hons), MA, MSc

Dept of History; www.rhul.ac.uk/history
history, public history, late antique & Byzantine studies, Hellenic studies, crusader studies, medieval studies, modern history & politics, history/French/German/Spanish/international relations/archeology/philosophy/music

School of Management; www.rhul.ac.uk/management
accounting, economics, entrepreneurship, HR, business/information systems, marketing, international accounting/business/HRM/management, leadership & management in health, Asia Pacific business, European business, sustainability/& management, sport management

Dept of Politics & International Relations; www.rhul.ac.uk/politics-and-IR
politics/with international relations/theory/philosophy, economics, politics & philosophy, European studies/politics/French/German/Italian/Spanish/contemporary political theory, geography, global politics, democracy, politics & governance, new political communication, transnational security studies; BA(Hons), BSc(Hons) MA, MBA, MSc, MPhil, PhD, PGCert, Grad Dip, PGDip

Faculty of Science; www.rhul.ac.uk/departments/science

School of Biological Sciences; www.rhul.ac.uk/biological-sciences
biochemistry, biology, biotechnology, ecology & environment, molecular biology, biomedical sciences, medical biochemistry/neuroscience, psychology, zoology; BA(Hons), BSc(Hons), MSc, PhD

Dept of Computer Science; www.cs.rhul.ac.uk
computer science & (AI)/mathematics/management, business information systems, computing & business, information security; BSc(Hons), MPhil, MSc, PhD

Dept of Earth Sciences; www.gl.rhul.ac.uk
environmental geology/geoscience, geology, geoscience, petroleum geology/geoscience, environmental geology/diagnosis & management, physical geography & geology, petroleum geoscience (basin evolution/tectonics); BSc, MSC, MSci, PhD

Dept of Geography; www.gg.rhul.ac.uk
cultural geography, earthscience, geography, geology, human/physical geography, politics & international relations, practising sustainable development, sustainability & management, quarternary science, creative writing, place, environment, writing, geopolitics & security; BA, BSc, MA, MSc, PhD

Dept of Mathematics; www.ma.rhul.ac.uk
information security, mathematics, mathematics for applications, maths of cryptology & communication, statistics, joint degrees; BSc(Hons), MSc, MSci, PhD

Dept of Physics; www.rhul.ac.uk/physics
physics/with mathematics/philosophy/music, applied physics, astrophysics, low temperature physics, nanotechnology, particle physics, theoretical physics; BSc(Hons), MPhil, MPhys, MSc, PhD

Dept of Psychology; www.rhul.ac.uk/psychology
applied social psychology, cognitive behavioural theory, psychology with biology/mathematics/music; BSc(Hons), DClinPsych, MSc, PhD

UNIVERSITY OF LONDON; ROYAL VETERINARY COLLEGE
www.rvc.ac.uk

bioveterinary sciences, control of infectious diseases in animals, intensive/livestock health & production, veterinary nursing/medicine, wild animal health/biology, veterinary pathology/physiotherapy/education/epidemiology, public health; BSc(Hons),

BVetMed, FdSc, MPhil, PhD, MVMed, MRes, MSc, PGDip/Cert

UNIVERSITY OF LONDON; SCHOOL OF ORIENTAL AND AFRICAN STUDIES
www.soas.ac.uk

Faculty of Languages & Cultures;
www.soas.ac.uk/languagecultures

African language and culture/literature/studies, ancient Near Eastern languages/studies, anthropological research, applied linguistics & language pedagogy, Arabic cultural studies/language teaching/literature, Arabic/& Islamic studies, Asian politics, banking law, Bengali, Chinese (modern and classical), Chinese/literature/studies, comparative literature (Africa/Asia), contemporary Pakistan, cultural studies, gender studies, Burmese (Myanmar), Hausa, Hebrew & Israeli studies, Hindi, Indonesian, international management & SE Asian studies, Iranian studies, Islamic law/studies/societies, Japanese literature/studies, Korean studies, languages & cultures of south Asia, language documentation & description, languages & literatures of south east Asia, linguistics, Near & Middle Eastern studies, Nepali, Pacific studies, Persian, postcolonial studies, Sandskrit, Sinology, south Asian/area studies, Taiwan studies, Thai, Turkish studies, Urdu

Faculty of Law & Social Sciences;
www.soas.ac.uk/lawsocialsciences

international management & SE Asian studies, development economics, economics, international management (China/Japan & Korea/Middle East & North Africa), banking/comparative/environmental/international economic law, law in M East & N SAfrica, S Asian law, globalisation & multinational corporations, international studies & diplomacy, African politics, Asian politics, development economics, development studies/C Asia, economics (reference Asia/S Asia/Asia Pacific region/M East), finance & development, globalisation & development, labour, social movements & development, ME politics, migration mobility & development, political economy of development, political studies, politics of China, research: international development

Faculty of Arts & the Humanities;
www.soas.ac.uk/artshumanities

history of art (Asia, Africa, Europe), history of art &/or archaeology, study of religions, music, social anthropology/of development, anthropological research methods/& Nepali, anthropology of travel, tourism & pilgrimage/food, art & archaeology of E Asia, art & architecture of Islamic M East, contemporary art of Asia & Africa, film & history, history, media in development, medical anthropology, music & development, religions of Asia & Africa, religious arts of Asia, traditions of yoga & meditation, critical media & cultural studies, global cinemas & the transcultural, global media & postnational communication, historical research methods, migration & diaspora studies, ethnomusicology, performance;- BA(Hons), LlB, LlM, MMus, MPhil, MSc, PGDip, PhD

UNIVERSITY OF LONDON; THE SCHOOL OF PHARMACY
www.pharmacy.ac.uk

clinical pharmacy, drug delivery, drug discovery & development/pharmacy management, medicine management, pharmacognosy, pharmacy practice; Certs, MPharm, MSc, PGDip, PhD

UNIVERSITY OF LONDON; UNIVERSITY COLLEGE LONDON (UCL)
www.ucl.ac.uk

UCL School of Life and Medical Science (including UCL Medical School); www.ucl.ac.uk/slms

Faculty of Brain Sciences; www.ucl.ac.uk/brain-sciences

Faculty of Life Sciences; www.ucl.ac.uk/life-sciences

Faculty of Medical Sciences; www.ucl.ac.uk/medical-sciences

Faculty of Population Health Sciences; www.ucl.ac.uk/populationhealth-sciences

cognitive/& decision sciences/behavioural therapy for children & young people/neuroscience, developmental psychology & psychopathology/psychology & clinical practice, human-computer interaction, business psychology, language sciences, linguistics, phonetics, neuroscience, language & communication, psychoanalytic development psychology, social cognition, speech & language sciences/therapy, theoretical psychoanalytic studies, adv audiology, otology, audiological science, audio vestibular medicine, adv neuroimaging, brain & mind sciences, clinical neurology, mental health/psychiatric research, anatomy, biochemistry, biological sciences, biomedical sciences, biotechnology, environmental biology, molecular biology, genetics/of human disease, human genetics/sciences, immunology/& infection, clinical pharmacy, drug delivery/discovery, pharmacology, pharmacy practice, pharmogenetics & stratified medicine, physiology, synthetic biology, surgery, zoology, paediatrics, adv ageing & mental health, adv aesthetic dentistry, cancer, cardiorespiratory physiotherapy, cell & gene therapy, child & adolescent mental health, clinical & applied paediatric neuropsychology, clinical biochemistry/dentistry/neuroscience/experimental medicine/ophthalmology, clinical & public health nutrition, community child health, conservative/implant dentistry, dental public health/sedation & pain management, genetics of human disease, global health & development, haemaglobinopathy, health informatics/psychology/care, history of medicine, immunology, implant dentistry, infection & immunity, international child health, medical mycology, medicine, mental health science, molecular biology/medicine, musculoskeletal science, nanotechnology & regenerative medicine, neuroimaging, oral & maxillofacial surgery/medicine, orthodontics, radiation biology, reproductive science & women's health, sexually transmitted infections and HIV, sports & exercise medicine, surgical science, synthetic biology, theoretical psychoanalytical studies, trauma & orthopaedics, urology, voice pathology, zoology; BSc(Hons), DipCDSc, IbSc, MBBS, MClinDent, MD(Res), MPhil, MRes, MSc, MSci, PGCert/Dip, PhD

The Bartlett, Faculty of the Built Environment

Built Environment; www.barlett.ucl.ac.uk

architecture, advanced architectural studies, advanced spatial analysis & visualisation, adaptive architecture & computation, architectural design/history, energy demand studies, environmental design & engineering, construction economics & management, development administration & planning, environment & sustainable development, facility & environment management, heritage science, international planning, light & lighting, mega infrastucture planning & real estate, planning design & development, project & enterprise management, project design for construction, international real estate planning, sustainable heritage/urbanism, social development practice, spatial planning, strategic management of projects, urban design & management/development planning/economic development/management/regeneration/studies; BSc(Hons), Diplomas, EngD, MA, MArch, MPhil, MSc, PhD, PGDip, MRes

Faculty of Engineering Sciences; www.ucl.ac.uk/engineering

Civil, Environmental & Geomatic Engineering; www.rege.ucl.ac.uk

civil engineering, earthquake engineering with disaster management, environmental engineering/mapping, environmental systems engineering, GIS, hydrographic surveying, remote sensing, transport studies

Biochemical Engineering; www.ucl.ac.uk/biochemeng

biochemical engineering, bioprocessing of new medicines

Chemical Engineering; www.ucl.ac.uk/chemeng
chemical engineering/with biochemical engineering, chemical process engineering

Computer Science; www.cs.ucl.ac.uk/
computer science, computational statistics & machine learning, computer graphics, vision & imaging, financial systems engineering/computation, human-computer interaction with ergonomics, ICT innovation, information security, mathematics of computation, networked computer systems, software systems engineering, web science

Electronic and Electrical Engineering; www.ee.ucl.ac.uk
communications engineering/computer science/nanotechnology, electrical & electronic engineering, internet engineering, nanotechnology, photonics systems, spacecraft technology/& satellite communications, telecommunications/engineering, wireless & optical communications

Management Science and Innovation; www.ucl.ac.uk/msi
business economics, information management for business, innovation management, entrepreneurial finance, decision & risk analysis, business strategy, international business, marketing/communications, strategic HRM, organizational change/behaviour, project management, marketing communications, managing technology entrepreneurship

Mechanical Engineering; www.ucl.ac.uk/mecheng
engineering with business finance, marine engineering, mechanical engineering, naval architecture, power systems engineering, biomaterials & tissue engineering, engineering with innovation & enterprise

Medical Physics & Bioengineering; www.ucl.ac.uk/medphys
human physiology, medical imaging, physics/& medical physics, medical physics, physics & engineering in medicine

countering organised crime & terrorism, crime/& forensic science; BEng, BSc, Certs, MEng, MPhil, MRes, MSc, PgDip, PhD

Faculty of Mathematical and Physical Sciences; www.ucl.ac.uk/maps-faculty

Chemistry; www.ucl.ac.uk/chemistry
chemistry, chemical physics, drug discovery, chemical research, energy & the environment

Earth Sciences; www.es.ucl.ac.uk
earth science, environmental geoscience, geology, geophysical hazards, geophysics, geosciences, natural hazards for insurers, natural sciences

Mathematics; www.ucl.ac.uk/mathematics
mathematics with mathematical physics/economics/modern languages/management studies/physics/statistical science, mathematical modelling, financial mathematics

Physics and Astronomy; www.phys.ucl.ac.uk
astronomy, astrophysics, physics, theoretical physics, high energy physics, planetary science, ultra precision – techniques & applications, managing nanotechnology

Science and Technology Studies; www.ucl.ac.uk/sts
history, philosophy & social studies of science, science, science & society, science, technology, medicine & society

Space and Climate Physics; www.mssl.ucl.ac.uk
astrophysics, climate extremes, space plasma physics, plasma science, solar & stellar physics, space science & engineering, systems engineering management

Statistical Science; www.ucl.ac.uk/stats
economics, finance, mathematics, statistical science, statistics/& management for business, medical statistics; BSc, BSc(Econ), EngD, MRes, MSc, MSci, PhD

Faculty of Arts & Humanities; www.ucl.ac.uk/ah

English Language & Literature: English linguistics, issues in modern culture, Shakespeare in history, old & middle English literature, film studies

European Social & Political Studies, Dutch, French, German, Italian, Russian, Spanish, Scandinavian studies, Spanish & Latin American studies, East European language & culture, Hebrew & Jewish studies, anthropology, economics, geography, planning, political science

Greek & Latin: classics: languages & literature, ancient world studies, reception of classical world

Hebrew & Jewish studies: Jewish history, language & culture, holocaust studies, modern Israeli studies, history (central & E Europe)

Information Studies: library & information studies, electronic communication/& publishing, archive & information studies/records management, digital humanities publishing, programming, information systems/science, web technologies, database systems

Philosophy: philosophy of mind & language, politics & modern philosophy, metaphysics & epistemology, history of philosophy, political philosophy, ethics, Aristotle, early Wittgenstein, epistimology, moral philosophy etc

European Languages, Culture & Society: French, Dutch, German, Spanish & Latin American studies, comparative literature, translation studies, modern languages, language culture & history

Slade School of Art

painting, fine art, sculpture, media, history & theory of art, critical studies; BA(Hons), BFA, MA, MPhil, MRes, PhD, MFA

Faculty of Law; www.ucl.ac.uk/laws

law, law & adv studies/another legal system (Australia, Singapore), French/German/Hispanic law, competition/comparative/corporate law, criminal justice, family & social welfare, dispute resolution, environmental law & policy, family law, human rights/intellectual property law, international banking & finance/commercial law, international law, jurisprudence & legal theory, legal history, litigation & dispute resolution, public law; LlB and Baccalaureus Legum, LlBHons, LlM, MPhil, PhD

Faculty of Historical and Social Sciences; www.ucl.ac.uk/shs

Anthropology; www.ucl.ac.uk/anthropology

anthropology, digital/social & cultural anthropology, culture, materials & design, human evolution & behaviour, human science, medical anthropology, materials & visual culture, palaeoanthropology, palaeolithic archaeology; BA(Hons), BSc(Hons), MA, MPhil, MRes, MSc, PhD

Archaeology; www.ucl.ac.uk/archaeology

archaeology & anthropology, archaeology of eastern Mediterranean/& Middle East, artefact studies, classical archaeology & classical civilization, comparative art & archaeology, conservation for archaeology & museums, culture, materials & design, cultural heritage studies, Egyptian archaeology, environmental archaeology, forensic archaeological science, GIS, managing archaeological sites, museum studies, palaeoanthropology & palaeolithic archaeology, principles of conservation, public archaeology, skeletal & dental bioarchaeology, technology & analysis of archaeological materials; BA(Hons), BSc(Hons), MA, MPhil, MSc, PhD

Economics; www.ucl.ac.uk/economics

applied/economics, statistical methods, microeconomics, macroeconomics, international trade, industrial economics, economics of growth/corporate finance/information, economic development, urban economics, economic policy; BSc(Hons), MSc, PhD

Geography; www.geog.ucl.ac.uk

aquatic science, climate change, environmental mapping/modelling, environment, science & society, ecology, geography/& economics, geography (international), geospatial analysis, global migration, globalization, GIS, natural resources/water management, population/political/physical/human geography, quaternary science, remote sensing, urban studies; BA(Hons), BSc(Hons), MSc, PhD

History; www.ucl.ac.uk/history

history, ancient history, Dutch & the golden age, Egyptology, late antique & Byzantine studies, European history, history of political thought & intellectual history, medieval & Renaissance studies, transnational studies, China, health & humanity; BA(Hons), MA, MPhil, PhD

History of Art; www.ucl.ac.uk/art-history

history of art/with material studies, contemporary art & globalization, politics of the image Germany, inhabiting art: communes colonisation, squatting, technologies of representation in 18th & 19th century France, value of design in the Italian renaissance, the writing of art; BA(Hons), MA, MPhil, PhD

Political Science; www.ucl.ac.uk/spp

political studies, international relations, European social & human rights, security studies, democracy & comparative politics, European public policy, global government & ethics, international public policy, legal & political theory; MA, MPhil, MSc, PhD

School of Slavonic and Eastern European Studies; www.ssees.ucl.ac.uk
central SE/E European studies, economics & business with the EU, political studies, economy, state & society, comparative business economics, Russian studies, politics, security & integration, history, identity, culture and power, politics & East European studies, institutions, politics & economics of the EU, Russian & East European literature & culture; BA(Hons), MA, MPhil, MRes, PhD

UNIVERSITY OF LOUGHBOROUGH
www.lboro.ac.uk

Faculty of Engineering; www.lboro.ac.uk/eng

Aeronautical and Automotive Engineering; www.lboro.ac.uk/departments/tt/
advanced methods/aeronautical engineering, automotive engineering/systems engineering

Chemical Engineering; www.lboro.ac.uk/departments/cg
advanced/chemical engineering, advanced process engineering, chemical engineering/management/IT, science & engineering

Civil and Building Engineering; www.lboro.ac.uk/departments/cv
air transport management, architectural engineering & design management, building services engineering, civil engineering, commercial management & quantity surveying, construction engineering management/project management/construction business management, energy studies, transport & business management, building surveying, low carbon building design, transport, building, infrastructure in emergencies, water & waste engineering/environmental management

Electronic, Electrical & Systems Engineering; www.lboro.ac.uk/departments/el
advanced/systems engineering, computer networks, security & forensics, digital/mobile communication, electronic & electrical engineering, electronics & computer systems engineering/software engineering, networked communications, renewable energy systems technology, signal processing in communication systems, systems engineering

Mechanical and Manufacturing; www.lboro.ac.uk/departments/mm
adv engineering, adv manufacturing engineering & management, engineering design, manufacture, innovative manufacturing engineering, mechanical engineering, mechatronics, product design engineering, sports technology, sustainable engineering

Systems Engineering; www.loboro.ac.uk/programmes/systems
BEng, BSc(Hons), MDes, MRes, MSc, PhD, Cert, Dip

Faculty of Science; www.lboro.ac.uk/sci

Faculty of Chemistry; www.lboro.ac.uk/departments/cm
analytical & pharmaceutical science, analytical chemistry/& environmental science, chemistry/& analytical science/sport science, pharmaceutical science & medicinal chemistry, medicinal chemistry; BSc, MSc, PhD

Dept of Computer Science; www.lboro.ac.uk/departments/co
computer science/& mathematics, AI, IT management for business, computing & management, international computing for the internet, internet computing & network security, IT, networks, visualisation systems & technology; BSc(Hons), MSc, PhD, PGDip/Cert

Dept of Information Sciences; www.lboro.ac.uk/departments/is
information management & computing/web design/business technology, business technology, information & knowledge management, library management, publishing with English, web development & design; BSc(Hons), MPhil, PhD

Dept of Materials; www.lboro.ac.uk/departments/materials
automotive materials, design with engineering materials, materials engineering/science & technology, polymer science & technology, technology; BEng/MEng, BSc(Hons), Diploma in Industrial Studies, MSc, PGDip/Cert, PhD

School of Mathematics; www.lboro.ac.uk/departments/ma
financial mathematics, industrial mathematical modelling, mathematical finance, mathematics,

mathematics & accounting & financial management/sports science/computer science/economics/management/mathematics education/statistics; BSc(Hons), MSc, PhD

Dept of Physics; www.lboro.ac.uk/departments/ph
astrophysics & cosmology, engineering physics, experimental condensed matter physics, materials physics & applications, physics, physics & maths/management/sports science/cosmology/IT/computing, psychophysics, quantum, string & phase transition, science of the internet, surface physics, experimental/theoretical condensed matter physics; BSc(Hons), MSc, PhD

Faculty of Social Sciences and Humanities; www.lboro.ac.uk/ssh

School of the Arts; www.loboro.ac.uk/departments/sota
3D design/new practice, fine art, graphic communication, illustration, textile innovation & design, 2D/3D visualisation, art & design, arts & the public sphere, studio ceramics, arts research by practice; BA(Hons), MA, MSc, MPhil, PhD

School of Business & Economics; www.loboro.ac.uk/departments/sbe
Business: accounting & financial management, banking, business analysis & management, finance & management, international business/strategy, management sciences/& strategy/information systems, marketing, management, HRM, organizational behaviour
Economics: economics, business economics & finance/accounting, international economics, banking & finance/financial markets, money
Executive Education: management & leadership, automotive management, occupational health & safety management, security management; BSc, MA, MSc, MRes, MPhil, PhD, Cert, Dip, MBA

Loughborough Design School; www.loboro/departments/ds
design/ergonomics, ergonomics (human factors in design), product/industrial design & technology, design for innovation & sustainability, international design, product design in business, user-centred/virtual product design, road & vehicle safety; BA, MA, MSc, MDes, PGCE with QTS

Dept of English & Drama; www.lboro.ac.uk/departments/ea
creative writing, drama, English, history, North American studies, performance & multi-media, sports science; BA(Hons), MA, PhD

Dept of Politics, International Relations & European Studies; www.lboro.ac.uk/departments/eu
history & geography/English, international relations, politics, res methods (European & international); BSc(Hons), MPhil, MSc, PhD

Dept of Geography; www.lboro.ac.uk/departments/gy
environmental monitoring for management, geography, geography & management/economic, sports management & science, global transformations, globalization & society/sport, human geography research, international financial & political relations, space & sport; BSc, MPhil, MSc, PhD

School of Sport, Exercise and Health Sciences; www.lboro.ac.uk/departments/ssehs
human biology, physical activity & public health, physical education & QTS, psychology, PE & QTS, sociology of sport, sport biomechanics, sport coaching, sports science & management, sport and exercise nutrition/psychology/science, exercise science/physiology, sport management/science; BSc(Hons), MPhil, MSc, PhD

Dept of Social Sciences; www.lboro.ac.uk/departments/ss
communications and media studies, criminology & social policy, digital media & culture, global media & cultural industries, media & cultural analysis, social psychology, sociology; BSc(Hons), MPhil, MSc, PhD

Teacher Education Unit; www.lboro.ac.uk/departments/teu
design & technology, PE, science, physics with mathematics, initial teacher training; MSc, PGCE

UNIVERSITY OF MANCHESTER
www.manchester.ac.uk

Faculty of Engineering and Physical Sciences; www.eps.manchester.ac.uk

School of Chemical Engineering and Analytical Science; www.ceas.manchester.ac.uk

biotechnology, adv chemical engineering, chemical engineering with chemistry/environmental technology/management/design, adv chemical process design for energy, environmental & sustainable technologies, refinery design & operation, petroleum engineering; BEng, MEng, MSc, PhD

School of Chemistry; www.chemistry.manchester.ac.uk

chemistry, forensic & analytical/medicinal chemistry/industrial experience, polymer & materials science & engineering; BSc(Hons), EngD, MChem, MEnt, MPhil, MSc, PhD

School of Computer Science; www.cs.manchester.ac.uk

adv web technologies, AI, computer science/security, computer science with/business & management/mathematics, computer systems engineering, computing for business applications, data & knowledge management, digital biology, engineering, internet computing, multicore computing, semantic technology, software engineering BSc(Hons), MEng, MEnt, MPhil, MSc, PhD

School of Earth, Atmospheric & Environmental Sciences; www.seas.manchester.ac.uk

earth sciences, environmental sciences/policy & management, geochemistry, geography, geology, planetary science, environmental & resource geology, petroleum engineering, geoscience/engineering, pollution & environmental control; BSc(Hons), MEarthSci, MEng, MSc, PhD

School of Electrical and Electronic Engineering; www.eee.manchester.ac.uk

communication engineering, advanced control & systems engineering, digital image & signal processing, electrical /& electronic engineering/industrial experience, electrical energy conversion systems, electrical power systems engineering, mechatronic engineering, renewable & clean technology; BEng(Hons), Dip, BSc(Hons), EngD, MEng(Hons), MPhil, MSc, PhD

School of Materials; www.materials.manchester.ac.uk

advanced/engineering materials/composites, biomaterials/science & tissue engineering, composite materials, corrosion control engineering, design management for fashion retailing, fashion & textile retailing, international fashion retailing, materials & surface design, materials science & engineering, textile science & technology, marketing & management of fashion textiles, material & surface design, polymer material science & engineering, textile design & design management/technology BSc, MEng, MPhil, PhD

School of Mathematics; www.maths.manchester.ac.uk

actuarial science, applied maths, biostatistics, computational science, financial mathematics, mathematical finance, mathematics, statistics, pure mathematics & logic, mathematics jt degrees; BSc, MMath, MPhil, MSc, PhD

School of Mechanical, Aerospace and Civil Engineering; www.mace.manchester.ac.uk

adv manufacturing technology & systems management, aerospace engineering, civil engineering/enterprise, maintenance engineering & asset management, management of projects, mechanical engineering/design, nuclear engineering, structural engineering, thermal power & fluid engineering, renewable energy & clean technology; BEng, EngD, MEng, MEnt, MPhil, MSc, PhD

School of Physics & Astronomy; www.physics.manchester.ac.uk

physics, physics & astrophysics/mathematics/astrophysics/theoretical physics/philosophy, nuclear science & technology, radio imaging & sensing; BSc, EngD, MMath & Phys, MPhys, MSc, PhD

Faculty of Humanities; www.humanities.manchester.ac.uk

School of Arts, Histories and Cultures; www.arts.manchester.ac.uk

American studies/history/culture, ancient history, applied theatre, art gallery & museum studies, archaeology/& anthroplogy, art history, arts management/policy & practice, biblical studies, classical studies, classics, comparative religion & social anthropology, composition, contemporary literature & culture, creative writing, cultural history, drama/& screen studies, early modern history, economic & social history, English & American studies, electro-acoustic music composition, English literature, French, gender, sexuality & culture, global history, Greek, history & culture 1200-1700, history of art, humanitarianism & conflict response, international disaster management, Jewish studies, Latin/& English literature/linguistics/Spanish/French, linguistics, medieval studies, modern British/European history, modern history & economics/politics, music, musicology, performance, screen & visual cultures, politics, post-1900 literatures, post-colonial literatures & cultures, religion & political life/theology, screen studies, social anthropology, south Asian studies, Spanish, study of religion & theology, theatre studies/ & performance, theological studies in philosophy & ethics, Victorian times, war, culture & history, world history; BA(Hons), MA, MMus, PhD

School of Education;
www.education.manchester.ac.uk
applied community & youth work studies, counselling, digital technology, communication & education, education (international/research), educational leadership & improvement, educational technology & TESOL, language, literacy & communication, critical learning, disability studies, management & leisure, PGCE primary/secondary (business education, design technology, English, mathematics, modern languages, science), teaching & learning; BA(Hons), DCons, DEd, EdD, MA, MEd, MPhil, MSc, PGCE, PGCert/Dip, PhD, UGCert/Dip

School of Environment and Development;
www.sed.manchester.ac.uk
architecture/& urbanism, city & regional development, environmental impact assessment & management, global urban development & planning, planning, urban regeneration & development, environmental monitoring, modelling & reconstruction/governance, GIS, competition, regulation & development, development economics & policy/finance/studies, globalisation studies, HR development/management (international development), HRM & development, ICTs for development, industry, trade & development, politics & governance, development management, economics & management of rural development, environment & development, poverty conflict & reconstruction, public policy & management, social policy & spatial development, management & implementaion of development projects, information systems, change & development, organisational change/poverty & development, town & country planning, urban development; BSc, MA, MPlan, MSc, MTCP, PGDip, PhD

School of Languages, Linguistics and Cultures; www.llc.manchester.ac.uk
Caribbean studies, English language, European languages and cultures/studies, French/Italian/German/Spanish/Japanese/Chinese/Portuguese/Persian/Russian/Arabic/Hebrew studies, Latin American cultural studies, Caribbean studies, English, English literature & modern languages, modern languages & business & management/history of art, linguistics & English literature/Middle East language/sociology/screen studies, Middle Eastern languages/studies, modern Middle Eastern history, intercultural communication: languages & culture, modern languages, screen studies, Spanish, conference interpretation, translation & interpreting studies; BA(Hons), MA, MML, MPhil, PhD

School of Law; www.law.manchester.ac.uk
law, bioethics and medical jurisprudence, corporate governance, crime/law & society, criminology/& socio-legal studies, health care ethics, intellectual property law, international business & commercial law, international financial law/trade transactions, law & economics/development, politics; BA, LlB, LlM, MA, MPhil, MRes, PGDip, PhD

Manchester Business School;
www.mbs.manchester.ac.uk
accounting/& finance/management & information systems, information technology for business, international business finance & economics, international management/with American business studies, management accounting & finance/human resources/innovation/sustainability estates, analytics: OR & risk analysis, business administration, Chinese business & management, corporate communications & reputation management, finance & business economics, enterprise, finance, global business analysis, international business & management/commercial & contract management, healthcare management, HRM & industrial relations, information systems (business IT, e-business technology, organization & management), innovation management & entrepreneurship, international business & management, management,

managerial psychology, marketing, operations, supply chain management, organizational psychology, quantitative finance (financial engineering, risk management, healthcare governance); BA, BSc, MBA, MBus, MDA, MEnt, MPA, MRes, MSc, PhD, DBA, PGCert

School of Social Sciences;
www.socialsciences.manchester.ac.uk
accounting, anthropology, archaeology, business studies, criminology, democracry & elections, development studies/economics, econometrics, economics, employment/sociology/political economy, ethics & political philosophy, European politics and policy, finance, financial economics, governance & public policy, human rights, international relations, political economy/science/theory, philosophy, politics, political economy of development/space & evolution, social anthropology, social change/history, statistics, sociological research, sociology, visual anthropology; BAEcon, BSc, MA, MRes, MSc, PGDip, PhD

Centre for Educational Leadership;
www.cel.manchester.ac.uk
educational leadership, process consultancy; MEd, PGCert

Faculty of Life Sciences;
www.lf.manchester.ac.uk
anatomical sciences, biochemistry, bioinformatics & systems biology, biological sciences, biology, biomechanics, biomedical and forensic studies in Egyptology, biomedical sciences, biotechnology/& enterprise, cell biology, cancer research & molecular biomedicine, cognitive neuroscience and psychology, developmental biology, genetics, history of science, technology and medicine, immunology and immunogenetics, integrative biology, life sciences, medical biochemistry, microbiology, molecular biology/parasitology & vector biology, neuroscience, optometry, pharmacology, physiology, plant sciences, zoology; BSc, MNeuroSci, MRes, MSc, PhD

Faculty of Medical & Human Sciences;
www.mhs.manchester.ac.uk

School of Dentistry;
www.dentistry.manchester.ac.uk
dental implantology, dental public health, dentistry, endodontics, fixed & removable prosthodondics, prosthodontics, oral & maxillofacial surgery, oral health sciences, orthodontics, periodontology, restorative & aesthetic dentistry; BDS, BSc, MDen, MDPH, MSc, MSc(Clin), PGDip/Cert, PhD

School of Medicine;
www.medicine.manchester.ac.uk
applied mental health, clinical biochemistry/rheumatology, digital biology, cardiovascular health, maternal & foetal health, genetic medicine/counselling, healthcare ethics & law, investigative ophthalmology & vision science, medical education/imaging/microbiology/sciences/virology, occupational hygiene/medicine, primary care, psychiatry, public health, pharmaceutical cancer, interdisciplinary molecular medicine, oncology, pharmaceutical cancer, forensic mental health; ChB, MB, MD/ChM, MPH, MPhil, MRes, MSc, PGCert, PGDip, PhD

School of Nursing and Midwifery & Social Work; www.nursing.manchester.ac.uk
advanced nursing/midwifery studies, adv audiology studies, health & social care, midwifery, adult/child/mental health nursing, psychosocial interventions for psychosis, dementia care, primary health care, social work; BMidwif, BNurs, MA, MClinRes, MPhil, MRes, MSc, PGCert, PGD, PGDip, PhD

School of Pharmacy & Pharmaceutical Sciences; www.pharmacy.manchester.ac.uk
clinical & health services pharmacy, community pharmaceutical public health service, pharmaceutical industrial advanced training, pharmacy, modelling & simulation in pharmacokinetics/dynamics; MPharm, MPhil, MSc, PGCert/Dip, PhD

School of Psychological Sciences;
www.psych-ci.manchester.ac.uk
audiology, clinical & health psychology, cognitive brain imaging, cognitive neuroscience & psychology, deaf education, psychology, speech & language therapy, adv audiology studies; BSc, MPhil, MRes, MSc, PGDip, PhD, ClinPsyD

MANCHESTER METROPOLITAN UNIVERSITY
www.mmu.ac.uk

Manchester School of Art; www.artdes.mmu.ac.uk

acting, architecture/& urbanism, contemporary art history, fashion, film & video/curating, interactive art/design, creative practice, design & art direction, fashion, film & media studies, filmmaking, fine art, illustration, animation, graphic design, interior/3D design, landscape architecture/design, media arts, movement practice for theatre, photography, product design, textiles in practice, visual culture; BA(Hons), BArch, BL and Arch, MA, MEnterprise, MPhil, PGDip/Cert, PhD

Faculty of Health, Psychology & Social Care; www.hpsc.mmu.ac.uk

Health Professions; Nursing; Social Work & Social Change

acupuncture, adult nursing, cardiorespiratory physiotherapy, clinical communication, community health, contemp health practice, counselling, CPD, criminology, critical psychology, disability studies, health & social care, psychoanalytical studies, physiotherapy, social work/adv practice/ leadership, social care, musculoskeletal/neurological physiotherapy, public health/school nursing, emergency management/medicine, forensic psychology, health visiting; BA(Hons), BSc(Hons), BA/BSc, MA, FdA, DipHE, PGCert/Dip, PhD, MPhil

Faculty of Humanities, Law & Social Science; www2.hlss.mmu.ac.uk

applied criminology, applied/linguistics, sociology, digital media, communications, contemp European/film & culture, critical theory, film, the Gothic, multimedia journalism, English studies/contemporary literature & film/critical theory, American literature, creative writing, French, German, Spanish, Italian, medieval/modern/political/social/local & American history, European urban culture/philosophy, library & information management, information management/& communications, politics, public services, global change, sociology, web development; TESOL, TEFL; BA(Hons), BSc(Hons), PGDip/Cert, MA, MPhil, PhD, LlB, LlM, MSc

Faculty of Science & Engineering; www.sci-eng.ac.uk

School of Healthcare Science; www.shs.mmu.ac.uk

biological psychology, biomedical science, clinical physiology, dental technology, healthcare science, human biology, human movement science in health & disease, physical activity & health, physiology; BSc(Hons), MSc, PGCert/Dip

School of Computing, Mathematics & Digital Technology; www.scmdt.mmu.ac.uk

adv/computing, computing forensics & security, computer games technology, computer science, games design & development, media technology, multimedia & web computing, software engineering, digital media computing, mobile application dev, web & mobile applications development, mathematics; FDSc, BSc(Hons), MSc PGDip/Cert, PhD

School of Engineering; www.soe.mmu.ac.uk

automotive engineering, mechanical engineering, automation & control, computer-aided/communications/computer engineering, electrical/electronic engineering, design engineering, engineering & technology/management, electronic systems design, computer & network technology, industrial communications, mechanical/product/design & technology, computer networks, manufacture with management, sports technology; BSc(Hons), BEng(Hons), MSc, PGDip/Cert, MPhil, PhD

School of Science & the Environment; www.ssty.mmu.ac.uk

Biology & Conservation Ecology

animal behaviour, biology, conservation biology, ecology & conservation, environmental management & business/sustainable development, wildlife biology, ornithology, applied/GIS, GI technology, microbiology & molecular biology, tropical ecology, countryside/env management, sustainable aviation, zoo studies/conservation biology; BSc(Hons), MSc, PGDip/Cert, MPhil, PhD

Chemistry & Environmental Science

applied chemistry, chemistry, chemical & pharmaceutical science, environmental science, forensic/

medicinal & biochemical/pharmaceutical chemistry; MChem, BSc(Hons)

Geography & Environmental Management
geography, environmental management & sustainability, human/physical geography, GIS & management/environment; BSc(Hons), PGCert/Dip, MSc, MPHil, PhD

Manchester Metropolitan University Business School;
www.business.mmu.ac.uk

accounting, finance, financial planning & wealth management, PR, business/administration, economics, management/finance, IT, HRM, marketing, business economics, financial studies/services, planning & management, international business management/marketing/creative advertising/HRM, retail marketing, sports marketing/management, business IT/internet/retailing, regulated financial planning, leadership in health & social care, digital/business management/marketing & communications, logistics & supply chain management, project management, strategic financial management, sustainable business; BA(Hons), BSc(Hons), MA, MSc, MBA, DBA, PhD, FD

Institute of Education;
www.ioe.mmu.ac.uk

childhood studies, early childhood/years studies, education studies, initial teacher training (CPD: supporting teaching & education; education) primary education, primary early years education, (QTS), professional studies (early years education/careers education and guidance/education/special educational needs), school administration/business management, secondary education, specific learning difficulties, teaching, youth & community work; BA(Hons), BA/BSc, Certs, EdD, FD, MA, MPhil, MSc, PGDip/Cert, PhD

Hollings Faculty;
www.hollings.mmu.ac.uk

Department of Clothing Design & Technology
fashion materials & technology, clothing product design, fashion buying & merchandising, fashion design/sportswear, int fashion marketing/practice, fashion design & technology, strategic fashion buying

Department of Food & Tourism Management
food and nutrition, food technology, human nutrition, hospitality/business management, events/tourism management, trading standards, environmental health, food management/safety/innovation, international food management/events management/tourism management/hospitality management, hospitality with culinary arts, hospitality events/business management/nutrition & health, hospitality/business management; BA(Hons), BSc(Hons), FdA, FdSc, HND, MA, MPhil, PhD, BTech, HND

MMU Cheshire;
www.cheshire.mmu.ac.uk

Dept of Business & Management Studies; www.cheshire.mmu.ac.uk/bms
business, business management (financial management/HRM/ legal studies/marketing), HRM, marketing/management, strategic leadership & change, sport management; BA/BSc, BA(Hons), FD, HNC, HND, MBA, MSc, MPhil, PhD

Dept of Contemporary Arts; www.cheshire.mmu.ac.uk/dcu
contemporary arts, contemporary theatre & performance, creative music production, creative writing, dance, drama, music, popular music; BA(Hons), MA, MPhil, PhD

Dept of Exercise & Sports Science; www.cheshire.mmu.ac.uk/exspsci
coaching and sport development, coaching studies, exercise & sport/biological medicine/coaching studies/physiology/sport development/sport injuries, PE & sports pedagogy, sport/ development/science, sport & exercise science, psychology of sport and exercise; BA, BSc, FD, MA, MSc

MIDDLESEX UNIVERSITY
www.mdx.ac.uk

School of Arts and Education; www.mdx.ac.uk/schools/arts

Art & Design; www.mdx.ac.uk/aboutus/Schools/art-and-design/index.aspx

animation, 3D animation & games, creative technology, digital product, fashion/styling/promotion/textiles, fine art, graphics des, illustration in design, engineering & manufacturing management, interior architecture, jewellery & accessories, photography, product design, film, TV, animation, professional practice; BA(Hons), FdA, MA, MSc

Dance, Music & the Theatre Arts

dance technology pedagogy, education (drama), dance performance/studies, music & arts management, jazz, pop music, technical theatre design/performance/solo performance, theatre arts (design & technical theatre/performance/theatre direction); BA(Hons), BMus, MA, MMus

English Literature & Language; www.mdx.ac.uk/courses/undergraduate/english/index.aspx

English/English literature

Film, Television & Media Arts

digital arts, film TV production/technical arts, animation, creative techniques, teleanimation; BA(Hons)

Media, Culture & Communication; www.mdx.ac.uk/research/areas/media/index.aspx

advertising, PR and media, communication, creative & media writing, journalism, magazine publishing, media & communication studies/management, design for interactive media, digital media, moving image; BA(Hons), MA

Language & Translation Studies; www.mdx.ac.uk/courses/undergraduate/language_translation_studies/index.aspx

international business & Arabic/Mandarin/Russian/Spanish, TEFL, public service/interpreting, translation; BA(Hons), MA

Teaching & Education

early years, early childhood studies, early years education studies, primary education, inclusive education, leadership management & change, learning & teaching, professional studies; PGCE primary, secondary qualifications in range of subjects, supported learning, lifelong learning, TESOL/with applied linguistics; BA(Hons), FdA, MA, PGCE, PGCert

Middlesex University Business School; www.mdx.ac.uk/schools/bs

Accounting & Finance; www.mdx.ac.uk/research/areas/finance-and-accounting/index.aspx

accounting, business accounting, banking, corporate accountability, finance, financial management/services, investment, statistics; BA(Hons), BSc(Hons), MSc

Business & Management; www.mdx.ac.uk/courses/undergraduate/business_and_management/index.aspx

business administration/management, international business/& Arabic/Mandarin/Russian/Spanish, international business management, business enterprise & entrepreneurship, business & marketing, human rights, management for personal assistants/ studies, professional practice;BA(Hons), BSc(Hons), MSc, MBA, DProf, DBA

Economics & Statistics

banking, business economics, economics, finance, international finance, financial economics/services, business & management; BSc(Hons), MA, MBA, MSc, DBA, ProDoc

Human Resource Management; www.mdx.ac.uk/research/areas/HR/index.aspx

international HRM, HR management/development, personal & professional development, public works HR practice; AdvDip, BA(Hons), FdA, PGCert, PGDip

Marketing & Enterprise; www.mdx.ac.uk/research/areas/law/index.aspx

international business/marketing, business & marketing, digital marketing/media, marketing, marketing communications/management, e-marketing & social media, visual analytics; BA(Hons), BSc(Hons), MA, MSc

Law

law, business/employment law, human rights & business, international business law, minorities, rights & the law; BA(Hons), GradDip, LlBHons, LlM, MA, PGDip

The School of Engineering and Information Sciences; www.mdx.ac.uk/schools/eis

Computing & Information Technology; www.mdx.ac.uk/courses/undergraduate/computing_it/index.aspx

business information/systems/management/technology, computer & network security, computer networks/science/communication, computing, graphics, games creative technology, electronic security & digital forensics, engineering & computing, forensic computing, information technology & business information/networking, multimedia computing, interaction applications development, internet application development, multimedia computing, network eng/ management & security; BSc, MSc

Product Design and Engineering; www.mdx.ac.uk/courses/undergraduate/product_design_engineering/index.aspx

design engineering/digital systems/electronics, embedded systems, engineering & computing, manufacturing management, mechatronics, mobile/ telecommunication engineering, product design, project management, telecommunications engineering; BA(Hons), BSc(Hons), MSc

School of Health & Social Sciences; www.mdx.ac.uk/schools/hssc

Biomedical and Biological Sciences; www.mdx.ac.uk/courses/undergraduate/Biomedical_and_Biological_Sciences/index.aspx

biomedical science, bioscience, medical microbiology, clinical biochemistry, cellular pathology, haematology & transfusion science, healthcare science, medical microbiology, molecular pathology; BSc(Hons), MSc

Complementary Health Sciences; www.mdx.ac.uk/research/areas/complementary-health/index.aspx

ayurvedic medicine, acupuncture, Chinese herbal med, complementary medicine, traditional Chinese medicine; AdvDip, BSc(Hons), MSc, MCM

Criminology & Sociology; www.mdx.ac.uk/research/areas/criminology/index.aspx

criminal justice, criminology, community safety, comparative drug & alcohol studies, psychology, sociology, forensic psychology, policing, public protection, serious crime investigation, sociology with psychology, youth justice; BA(Hons), BSc(Hons), MA, MSc

Environment & Public Health; www.mdx.ac.uk/courses/undergraduate/public_health/index.aspx

environmental health, public health, health promotion, occupational safety & health, food control, environmental pollution control/health, sustainable development/environmental management; BSc(Hons), MA, MSc

Nursing, Midwifery & Health; www.mdx.ac.uk/research/areas/Health/index.aspx

child, adolescent, nursing (child, adult, family/mental health/specialist practice), child/adolescent mental health, health promotion, dual diagnosis, promoting mental health in young people, leadership & management of care services, mental health studies, midwifery, public & community health services; AdvDip, BSc, BSc(Hons), Dip, MSc, PGCert, FdA

Social Science, Politics & Development; www.mdx.ac.uk/courses/undergraduate/social_science_politics_development/index.aspx

criminology, global government (public policy, housing), international politics, international relations/development, psychology, global, liberal arts, social science, sociology; BA, BSc, CertHE, FdA, FdSc, MA

Social Work; www.mdx.ac.uk/research/areas/social-work/index.aspx

social work (adolescents, children, families); BA(Hons), MA

Psychology; www.mdx.ac.uk/research/areas/psychology/index.aspx

applied/criminal health/psychology, criminology, counselling, forensic psychology, health psychology, psychology; BA(Hons), BSc(Hons), GradDip; MSc

Sport & Exercise Science; www.mdx.ac.uk/facilities/sport/index.aspx

coaching and sports development, sport and exercise science/rehabilitation, sport & community, sport massage therapy & rehabilitation, sport rehabilitation & injury prevention, strength & conditioning, teaching & coaching sport, sport performance, performance analysis; BSc(Hons), FdSc, MSc

UNIVERSITY OF NEWCASTLE UPON TYNE
www.ncl.ac.uk

Faculty of Humanities and Social Sciences; www.ncl.ac.uk/hass

School of Architectural Planning and Landscape; www.ncl.ac.uk/apl
architecture, architecture & practice/management/planning design/theory & criticism, digital architecture, future landscape, geography, architectural planning/landscape, planning & environmental research, planning in developing countries/studies/practice, planning for sustainable & climate change, spatial planning, sustainable building & environment, town planning, urban design; BA, BArch, Cert, Dip, MA, MPhil, MSc, PGCert, PhD

School of Arts and Cultures/music; www.ncl.ac.uk/sacs
Music; www.ncl.ac.uk/sacs/music/
folk & traditional music, music, music & education, popular & contemporary music, composition, performance, theoretical & cultural musicologies, ethnomusicology, early modern & medieval music; BA, BMus, Diploma, MA, MLitt, MMus, MPhil, PhD
Fine Art; www.ncl.ac.uk/sacs/fineart/
fine art, history of art; BA(Hons), MFA, MPhil, PhD
Digital Media; www.ncl.ac.uk/sacs/digitalmedia/
digital media/theoretical foundations/techniques, understanding user experience; Dip, MA, MRes
Museum, Gallery and Heritage Studies; www.ncl.ac.uk/sacs/icchs/
art museum & gallery education/gallery studies, art as enterprise, heritage education & interpretation/management, museum studies; MA, MPhil, MPrac, PGCert, PGDip, PhD
Media & Cultural Studies; www.ncl.ac.uk/sacs/macs/
media & journalism/PR/cultural studies, international multimedia journalism, mass media, media communications & cultural studies; BA(Hons), MA, PhD

Business School; www.ncl.ac.uk/nubs
accounting, advanced business management, arts, business & creativity, banking, business accounting, business management, e-business (information systems/emarketing), economics, finance, e-marketing, financial & business economics, financial regulation, HRM, international business management/economics & finance/financial analysis/HR/marketing, Islamic finance, law, management, marketing, operations management & logistics/supply chain management, strategic planning & investment, quantitative finance & marketing; BA, BSc, DBA, MA, MBA, MSc, PhD

School of Education, Communication and Language Sciences; www.ncl.ac.uk/ecls
applied linguistics & TESOL, cross-cultural communication & applied linguistics/education/international management/marketing/international relations/media studies, education leadership & management, information communication & educational technology, international development & education, pedagogy & education, practitioner enquiry (leadership & management), evidence-based practice in common disorders, PGCE primary/secondary (numerous subjects), educational psychology, education, speech & language science, languge pathology, international development/multimedia; BA(Hons), BSc(Hons), DedPsych, EdD, MA, MEd, MSc, PGCE, PhD

School of English Literature, Language, Linguistics; www.ncl.ac.uk/elll
English language/literature, English lit: 1500-1900, linguistics, creative writing, film theory, language acquisition, modern & contemporary studies; BA(Hons), MA, MLitt, MPhil, PGCert, PhD

Geography, Politics and Sociology; www.ncl.ac.uk/gps
applied policy research, geography (human, physical), geography & planning, local & regional development, European Union studies, international political economy, international politics (global justice & ethics/critical geopolitics/globalization, politics/& economics/sociology/history, poverty, development), sociology, social research, world politics & popular culture; BA(Hons), BSc(Hons), MA, MSc, PhD

Global Urban Research Unit; www.ncl.ac.uk/guru
cities and international development, power, place & materiality, planning & environmental dynamics, cities, security & vulnerability; MPhil, PhD

Institute of Health and Society;
www.ncl.ac.uk/ihs/
public health & health services res, social sciences; MSc, PGDip/Cert

School of History, Classics & Archaeology Studies; www.ncl.ac.uk/historical
ancient history, archaeology, British history, Byzantine & Roman archaeology, classical studies, classics, early medieval & Byzantine archaeology, east Asian history, late/European history, Greek & Roman/Byzantine archaeology, history, politics, history of medicine, history of the Americas, Latin American studies, Roman frontier studies, archaeology, rulership, power & court societies in the ancient world; BA(Hons), MA, MLitt, MPhil, PhD

Centre for History of Medicine; www.ncl.ac.uk/historical
history of medicine, medical history; BA(Hons), MLitt, MPhil, PhD

Centre for Knowledge, Innovation, Technology and Enterprise;
innovation, creativity & enterprise, e-business & information science, arts, business & creativity; DBA, MSc, PhD

Newcastle Law School; www.ncl.ac.uk/nuls
environmental regulation & sustainable development, criminology, international legal studies, international business law, law (complete range of legal areas taught at undergrad level); LlB, LlM, MPhil, PhD

Centre for Learning and Teaching;
www.ncl.ac.uk/cflat
PGCE primary & secondary education, educational leadership and management, education & communication, graduate skills enhancement, information, communication and entertainment technology, inclusive education, international development & education, practitioner enquiry, pedagogy & learning, educational psychology; EdD, MA, MEd, PGCE

Newcastle Centre for the Literary arts/
www.ncl.ac.uk/ncla
creative writing; MA, PhD

School of Modern Languages;
www.ncl.ac.uk/sml
Chinese, French, German, Japanese, Spanish, Portuguese & Latin American studies, Catalan, Dutch, Quecha, linguistics/for European languages, linguistics & language acquisition, modern languages & business studies/linguistics, Spanish Portuguese & Latin American studies, film theory & practice, Spanish, translating and interpreting – Chinese strand; BA(Hons), MA, MLitt, PhD

Newcastle Institute for the Arts, Social Sciences and Humanities
Policy, Ethics and Life Sciences Research Centre; www.ncl.ac.uk/peals
ageing, biosecurity, bioinformation & security studies, clinical ethics, disability, fertility, genetics, human stem cell research, public participation; PhD

Centre for Research in Linguistics and Language Science; www.ncl.ac.uk/linguistics
applied linguistics & TESOL, cross-cultural communication, education (TESOL), English language & literature, human communication sciences, linguistics, language acquisition/pathology, linguistics, speech & language science; MA, MEd, MSc, PhD

Centre for Urban and Regional Development Studies; www.ncl.ac.uk/curds
local/and regional development; MA

Faculty of Medical Sciences;
www.ncl.ac.uk/aboutpeoplestudies
academic/biosciences

Biomedical and Biomolecular Sciences & Medicine; www.ncl.ac.uk/biomed
biochemistry, biomedical genetics/science, medical microbiology, biotechnology, medical science, pharmacology, psychological science, clinical education/psychology, sociology
medicine, surgery, infection prevention & control, public health & health services, medical & molecular bioscience, minimal access surgery, oncology & palliative care, therapeutics, social services & health psychology, clinical/& health psychology, cognitive behavioural therapy, neuroscience, psychological therapies; BSc(Hons), DClinPsychol, MB, MClinEd, MClinRes, MD, MRes, MSc, MSci, PGCert/Dip, PhD, MClinRes, MBBS

Dentistry; www.ncl.ac.uk/dental
clinical dental implants, conscious sedation in dentistry, dental surgery, endodontics, orthodontics, restorative dentistry; BDS, DDS, MSc, PGDip, PhD

Faculty of Science, Agriculture & Engineering; www.ncl.ac.uk/aboutpeoplestudies/academic/sage

School of Agriculture, Food and Rural Development; www.ncl.ac.uk/afrd
adv food marketing, & management agri-business management, agricultural & environmental science, agriculture, agronomy, animal production/science/behaviour & welfare, biodiversity, conservation & ecosystems, countryside management, organic farming & food production systems, environmental resource assessment/science, food & human nutrition, food & rural development, medicinal plants & functional foods, rural social science/studies, wildlife conservation & management; BSc(Hons), MPhil, MSc, PhD

School of Biology; www.ncl.ac.uk/biology
biology, cellular & molecular biology, conservation & ecotourism, ecological & environmental biology, ecological consultancy, industrial & commercial biotechnology, zoology; BSc(Hons), MSc, MRes, PhD

School of Chemical Engineering and Advanced Materials; www.ncl.ac.uk/ceam
applied process control, chemical engineering, chemical & processing engineering, clean technology, industrial quality technology, materials and process engineering, materials, design & engineering, process automation/ control, sustainable chemical engineering; BEng(Hons), MEng(Hons), MSc, PGDip

School of Chemistry; www.ncl.ac.uk/chemistry
chemistry, drug chemistry, medicinal chemistry, chemical nanoscience; BSc(Hons), MChem, MPhil, MSc, PhD

Civil Engineering and Geosciences; www.ncl.ac.uk/ceg
civil engineering, environmental engineering/consultancy, geochemistry, geotechnical engineering, petroleum geochemistry/geoscience, engineering geology, environmental & petroleum geochemistry, geotechnical engineering, intelligent transport systems & intelligent mobility, transport engineering & operations, transport & business operations/environment, transport planning & policy, structural engineering, surveying & mapping science, physical geography, applied hydrology, flood risk management, hydroinformatics & water management, hydrology & climate change, water environment; BEng, BSc(Hons), MEng, MPhil, MSc, PhD

Computing Science; www.cs.ncl.ac.uk/
computer game engineering, computer security and resilience, bioinformatics, biocomputing, computational systems biology, adv/computing science, distributed systems/games and virtual environments/software engineering, e-business & information systems, neuroinformatics, software engineering, synthetic biology, internet technologies & enterprise computing; network systems & internet technology; BSc(Hons), MPhil, MSc, MComp, PhD

Electrical, Electronic and Computer Engineering; www.ncl.ac.uk/eece
adv sensor technology, automation and control, communications & signal processing, electrical & electronics engineering/computer engineering, electrical power, electronic communications, computer engineering, microelectronics, power distribution, wireless embedded systems; BEng, EngD, MEng, MPhil, PhD

Newcastle Institute for Research on Sustainability; www.ncl.ac.uk/
research projects; MPhil, MRes, PhD

Digital Institute; www.ncl.ac.uk/iri
research projects; PhD

Newcastle Centre for Railway Research; www.ncl.ac.uk/newrail
rail freight & logistics

School of Marine Science and Technology; www.ncl.ac.uk/marine
aquaculture enterprise & technology, engineering & science in marine environments, international marine environmental consultancy, marine & offshore power systems/technology, marine biology, marine engineering/structures & integrity/transport & management/technology, marine zoology, marine electrical power technology, naval architecture, oceanography, offshore & environmental technology, offshore engineering, pipeline engineering, renewable energy enterprise & management, small craft technology/design, subsea engineering & management, tropical coastal management; BEng, BSc(Hons), MEng, MRes MSc

Mathematics and Statistics; www.ncl.ac.uk/math
applied/financial mathematics/with management, mathematics, mathematical sciences, pure

mathematics, statistics; BSc(Hons), MMath, MMath-Stat, MPhil, PhD

School of Mechanical & Systems Engineering; www.ncl.ac.uk/mech
bioengineering, biomedical engineering, manufacturing engineering, mechanical engineering/design, mechatronics, mechanical engineering/with microsystems, low carbon transport engineering, BEng, MEng, MSc

Centre for Rural Economy; www.ncl.ac.uk/cre
food & rural development; MPhil, MSc, PhD, MRes

Sir Joseph Swan Institute for Energy Research; www.ncl.ac.uk/energy
biosciences, renewable energy, novel geoenergy, energy conversion, storage & distribution, social impact; MRes, MSc, PhD

Centre for Software Reliability; www.csr.ncl.ac.uk

UNIVERSITY OF NORTHAMPTON
www.northampton.ac.uk

School of Science & Technology; www.northampton.ac.uk/science-technology

Division of Computing; www2.northampton.ac.uk/computing
computing/internet technology & security/computer networks engineering/security/software engineering/mobile computing, computer systems engineering/graphics & visualization; BA/BSc, BSc(Hons), HND, MSc, PhD

Division of Engineering; www2.northampton.ac.uk/engineering
electrical and electronic engineering, engineering, lift (& escalator) technology/engineering, mechanical/production engineering, non-destructive testing;BSc(Hons), BTEC, FdSc, HNC, HND, MSc, ProfCert

Geographical & Environmental Science; www2.northampton.ac.uk/geographical-and-environmental sciences
applied conservation biology, biology, biological conservation, environmental management/science, geography, physical geography; BA/B/Sc, BSc(Hons), FdSc, HND, MBA, MSc, UnivCerts

Institute for Creative Leather Technologies; www2.northampton.ac.uk/leather technology
leather technology (international environmental management/marketing), environment, leather science (marketing or business); BSc(Hons), BTEC NC, Cert/Dip, MSc, PhD/MPhil

The School of The Arts; www.northampton.ac.uk/info/20300/school-of-the-arts

Division of Design; www2.northampton.ac.uk/arts/home/Design
architectural technology, creative advertising, graphic communication, illustration, interactive digital media, interior design, product design, design (textiles/footwear/graphic communication/photographic communication/product & spatial innovation); BA(Hons), BSc(Hons), MA, HND

Division of Fine Art; www2.northampton.ac.uk/arts/home/Fine Art
art and design, drawing, fine art, painting, photographic practice; BA(Hons), FDA, MA

Division of Media, English and Culture; www2.northampton.ac.uk/arts/home/Media English Culture
creative writing, English, film & TV studies, journalism, media production, digital film making, screen studies, modern English studies; BA(Hons), MA, HND

Division of Performance Studies; www2.northampton.ac.uk/arts/home/performance
acting, dance, drama, music production/practice, popular music, theatre, performing arts; BA(Hons), HND, MA, PhD

Division of Fashion;
www2.northampton.ac.uk/arts/home/
Division of Fashion
fashion, footware & accessories, printed textile fashion, surface design & printed textiles; BA(Hons), MA

School of Education;
www.northampton.ac.uk/departments/
education
early years education/professional studies/sector-endorsed/studies, education (primary), early years (primary/early years/secondary/PGCE), education studies, graduate teacher programme (GTP), initial teacher training, learning & teaching, level childhood & youth, special education needs & inclusion, post-compulsory education & training; BA(Hons), GTP, PGCE, BSc(Hons), CertHE, FD, PhD

School of Health;
www.northampton.ac.uk/departments/
health
autonomous healthcare practice, adult/children's/dental nursing, health studies, applied cancer studies, children's, young people, families & care, sociology & community development, health & social care (acute & community/children's workforce/dementia support), mental health, human bioscience, leadership in health & social care, maternal & neonatal health, mental health & learning disabilities, midwifery, non-medical prescribing, occupational therapy, palliative & supportive care, paramedic science, podiatry, social care, social work, specialist community pharmacy, sport development, work-based learning; BSc(Hons), MPhil, PGCert, PhD

Northampton Business School;
www.northampton.ac.uk/departments/
business
accounting, advertising, applied management, banking & financial planning, business, business computing systems/entrepreneurship/studies, construction management, corporate governance, economics, enterprise development, events management, financial services management, healthcare management, HRM, information science, international accounting/banking & finance/business/business communications/development/logistics & trade financing, IT service management, leadership & management, leisure & lifestyle management, management, marketing management, sports marketing/enterprise, tourism & hospitality management, travel & tourism management, web design; BA(Hons), BA/BscHons, CMS, DBA, DMS, FdA, HND, MA, MBA, MSc, PGDip (marketing), MBL, ProfDip

School of Social Sciences;
www.northampton.ac.uk/info/20040/
school-of-social-sciences

History; www.northampton.ac.uk/info/200178/history
history, social & cultural history; BA(Hons), MA, PhD

Law; www.northampton.ac.uk/info/200180/law
international business law/criminal law & security, law, appl criminal justice, offender management, police & criminal justice; LlB, LlM, BSc, PhD, FdA

Psychology; www.northampton.ac.uk/info/200176/subject-areas/853/psychology
child & adolescent health, development & educational/sport & exercise psychology, counselling, psychology, transpersonal psychology & consciousness; BA/BSc, BSc(Hons), PhD

Sociology; www.northampton.ac.uk/info/200176/subject-areas/171/sociology
international relations, sociology; BA(Hons), MA police & criminal justice service, probation & policing, urban affairs; BSc, FdA

Politics; www.northampton.ac.uk/info/200176/subject-areas/169/politics
media studies, philosophy, politics, media, philosophy, politics, international relations, politics, international relations; BA/BSc(Hons)

Criminology; www.northampton.ac.uk/info/200176/subject-areas/160/criminology
criminology; BA, MA

Human Geography; www.northampton.ac.uk/info/200176/subject-areas/164/human-geography
geography(human/physical); BSc(Hons)

Probation & Policing; www.northampton.ac.uk/info/200176/subject-areas/170/probation-and-policing
police & criminal justice studies, offender management; FdA

Urban Affairs; www.northampton.ac.uk/info/200176/subject-areas/167/urban-affairs
sustainable communities; FdA

UNIVERSITY OF NORTHUMBRIA AT NEWCASTLE
www.northumbria.ac.uk

Newcastle Business School;
www.newcastlebusinessschool.ac.uk
accounting, advertising management, business administration/communication/development, business creation/management/studies, business with economics/finance/HRM/international management/logistics & supply chain management/marketing/entrepreneurship/financial management/arts management, corporate management, economics, finance, global financial management, global/logistics & supply chain management, hospitality & tourism management, HRM, investment management, legal management, international business management with French/Spanish, international business administration/hospitality & tourism management/HRM/management/banking & finance/business, investment management, leadership & corporate management/performance coaching/development, trade finance, marketing management/studies, multidisciplinary design innovation, music management, public administration, tourism & hospitality management, strategic marketing, travel & tourism management; BA, DBA, MA, MBA, MSc, PhD

School of Life Sciences;
www.northumbria.ac.uk/sd/academic/lifesciences

Biology, Food & Nutrition Science;
www.northumbria.ac.uk/sd/academic/lifesciences/ad/bfns/bfnug;
www.northumbria.ac.uk/sd/academic/lifesciences/ad/bfns/bfnpg
applied biology, applied sciences, biology with forensic biology, biotechnology, food science & nutrition, human nutrition, nutrition science, microbiology; BSc(Hons), MSc, PhD

Chemical & Forensic Science;
www.northumbria.ac.uk/sd/academic/lifesciences/ad/cfs/cfsug;
www.northumbria.ac.uk/sd/academic/lifesciences/ad/cfs/cfspg
analytical/applied chemistry, applied sciences, biomedical sciences, chemistry/forensic science, drug design with pharmacology, science (chemistry); BSc, BSc(Hons), MChem, MRes, MSc

Biomedical Sciences;
www.northumbria.ac.uk/sd/academic/lifesciences/ad/biomed/bmsug;
www.northumbria.ac.uk/sd/academic/lifesciences/ad/biomed/bmspg
applied science, biomedical science, chemistry, human biology, medical science; BSc(Hons), Dip, PostDoc

Psychology; www.northumbria.ac.uk/sd/academic/lifesciences/ad/psych/courses;
www.northumbria.ac.uk/sd/academic/lifesciences/ad/psych/psychpg
psychology with criminology/sport science, health psychology, occupational psychology, organisational psychology, psychology of health & wellbeing, psychology of sport & exercise behaviour; BSc(Hons), MSc, ProfDoc

Sport & Exercise Science;
www.northumbria.ac.uk/sd/academic/lifesciences/ad/ses/sesugcses;
www.northumbria.ac.uk/sd/academic/lifesciences/ad/ses/sespg
applied science with coaching/exercise science, psychology & sport science, sport exercise nutrition, clinical exercise psychology, psychology of sport & exercise behaviour; BSc(Hons), MSc

Sport Development;
www.northumbria.ac.uk/sd/academic/lifesciences/ad/sdmc/ugcses;
www.northumbria.ac.uk/sd/academic/lifesciences/ad/sdmc/pgcses
sport, sport coaching, sport development/management, athlete lifestyle, international sport management; BA(Hons), BSc(Hons), MSc, ProfDoc

School of Arts & Social Sciences; www.northumbria.ac.uk/sd/academic/sass

Dept of Arts; www.northumbria.ac.uk/sd/academic/sass/about/arts/?view=Standard
music management & promotion, conservation of fine art, cultural management, dance, drama & scriptwriting, performance, events & conference management, film & TV studies, fine art, museum & heritage management, contemporary photographic practice, preventive conservation; MA, MSc, MERes, BA(Hons), FD

Dept of Humanities; www.northumbria.ac.uk/sd/academic/sass/about/humanities/?view=Standard
creative writing, English literature/& place, gender studies, history, (America,/British/European/early modern), linguistics, English language/literature; BA(Hons), MA, PGCert, MRes, PhD

Dept of Media; www.northumbria.ac.uk/sd/academic/sass/about/media/?view=Standard
mass communication/management/& business, media, media cultures/production, journalism/& English literature, advertising; BA(Hons), MA

Dept of Social Sciences; www.northumbria.ac.uk/sd/academic/sass/about/socscience/?view=Standard
criminology & sociology/psychology, history & English literature/politics, international development, public administration/services, social sciences, politics, sociology, regeneration, media culture & society, psychology, Eng lit & history; BA(Hons), BSc(Hons), MA, MSc, MRes, MPA, PhD, PGCert/Dip

School of Built & Natural Environment; www.northumbria.ac.uk/sd/academic/sobe

architectural technology/engineering/environment/studies, architecture, building design management/project management/services engineering, building surveying, built environment, commercial/quantity surveying, construction management, project management/for construction, geography/& crime science, disaster management & development, environmental health/management, international/real estate management, geography, housing policy/with professional practice, interior architecture, housing policy & management, international/real estate management, occupational safety & health, planning & development/quantity surveying, project management, surveying (minerals), sustainable development in the built environment; BA(Hons), BSc(Hons), FdSc, MA, MSc, PGDip/Cert, PhD, ProfDip

School of Computing, Engineering & Information Science: northumbria.ac.uk/sd/academic/ceis

Business Information Systems;
business information management/systems/technology, IT management for business; BSc(Hons), FdSc, MSc

Computing
applied computing, computer animation & digital SFX/forensics/games design & production/network technology/science/studies, computing and IT, ethical hacking for computer security, games programming, IT management, web design & development/computing; BSc(Hons), MSc

Engineering
computer & network technology, electrical & electronic engineering, electrical power engineering, electronic design engineering, ethical hacking for computer security, IT management, mobile communication engineering, mechanical design/engineering, microelectronic & communications engineering, pipeline integrity management, product design technology, professional engineering, renewable sustainable energy technologies; BEng(Hons), BSc(Hons), MSc

Information and Communications Management
communication & PR, computing and IT, business information systems management, information & library/web/communications management, librarianship, records management; BSc(Hons), MA, MScPGDip

Mathematics & Statistics
mathematics/with business management; BSc(Hons)

Physics
physics, astrophysics; BSc(Hons)

School of Design; www.northumbria.ac.uk/sd/academic/scd

3D design, design, design for industry/management/entrepreneurship/professional practice, fashion, fashion communication/management/marketing, graphic design, interactive media design, interior design, motion graphics & animation, multidisciplinary design innovation, transportation design; BA(Hons), DocDesPract, BSc(Hons), MA, MSc, PhD

School of Health, Community & Education Studies; www.northumbria.ac.uk/sd/academic/shes

Health: emergency care practice, midwifery studies, nursing studies/registered nurse/child/mental health/adult/learning disabilities, leadership & management in integrated children/services, occupational therapy, operating dept practice, physiotherapy; AdvDipHE, BSc, MSc, PGDip

Education: academic practice, autism, early primary education, early years education, PGCE early years & primary/secondary, education studies/leadership, professional practice, graduate teacher training, post-compulsory education & training; literacy/HE/curriculum development/teaching & learning, adult learners with learning difficulties/disablement, teaching assistants, lifelong learning /English literacy/(CPD)/mathematics/numeracy/maths; BA(Hons), MSc, MA, MTL, Cert/DipHE, PGDipCert

Social Work: social work/with children, young people & their families/in mental health services; BSc(Hons), PGDip/Cert, ProfDoc

Northumbria Law School: northumbria.ac.uk/sd/academic/law

law, business/child/commercial property/commercial/employment law, information rights law and practice, international commercial/trade law, law with business/international business/environment/property management, legal practice, medical law, mental health law, policy & practice, solicitors; GradCert, LlM, LlB, LPC, PGCert, MLaw, MSc, MBA

School of Life Sciences; www.northumbria.ac.uk/sd/academic/lifesciences

Biology, Food Science & Nutritional Sciences: applied biology/sciences, biology, forensic biology, biotechnology, food science & nutrition, human nutrition, microbiology, nutrition science; BSc(Hons), MSc

Biomedical Sciences: applied science, biomedical science, chemistry, human biosciences, medical sciences, practical anatomy; BSc(Hons), MSc, ProfDoc, PGCert/Dip

Psychology: sport & exercise behaviour, criminology, sport science, business/health/occupational/organisational psychology, psychology of health & welbeing/sport & exercise behaviour; BSc(Hons), MSc, MRes

Sport & Exercise Science: applied sport science & coaching, sport & exercise science, psychology of sport science, sport & exercise behaviour/psychology, sport exercise & nutrition, clinical exercise physiology, psychology of sport & exercise behaviour

Sport Development: sport coaching, development/management/marketing, athletic lifestyle, international sport management; BSc(Hons), MSc, ProfDoc

---

UNIVERSITY OF NOTTINGHAM
www.nottingham.ac.uk

Faculty of Arts; www.nottingham.ac.uk/arts

School of American and Canadian Studies; www.nottingham.ac.uk/american

American studies with English studies/history/film & TV studies/politics, American studies (& history/culture/Canadian literature/Canadian studies/European studies), English; BA(Hons), MA, MRes, PhD

Dept of Archaeology; www.nottingham.ac.uk/archaeology/index.aspx

archaeological materials, archaeology, ancient history/geography, classical civilization, bioarchaeology, medieval archaeology, Mediterranean archaeology, Roman archaeology, Viking studies, natural science; BA(Hons), BSc(Hons), MA, MPhil

Art History; www.nottingham.ac.uk/art-history
art history & classical civilisation/English studies/archaeology/history, Renaissance to the present day, modern art, criticism & display, art, photography & film; BA(Hons), MA

Dept of Classics; www.nottingham.ac.uk/classics
classical civilisation, ancient history/drama, classical literature, classics, Greek (ancient), Latin, ancient drama & its reception, visual culture of classical antiquity, history, warrior societies; BA(Hons), MPhil/PhD

Dept of Culture, Film & Media; www.nottingham.ac.uk/cfm
cultural studies, culture & entrepreneurship, international media & communications studies, critical theory & politics, contemporary Middle East studies, film & TV studies, global Hollywood; BA(Hons), MA, MPhil

Centre for English Language Education; www.cele.nottingham.ac.uk
arts & social sciences, business & English, teaching English for academic purposes; BA(Hons), FCert, PGCert

School of English Studies; www.nottingham.ac.uk/english
applied linguistics, communication & entrepreneurship, creative & professional practice in arts & education, English studies/language teaching/language/literature, creative writing, literary linguistics, the 20th century & contemporary literature, Viking studies, world Englishes; BA(Hons), MA, MPhil, MSc, PGDip, PhD

Dept of French & Francophone Studies; www.nottingham.ac.uk/french
French, classical civilization, critical theory & cultural studies, modern European studies, modern language & critical theory, medieval studies, francophone & post-colonial studies, French culture & society, early modern French studies, 20th/21st-century French thought, numerous jt degrees; BA(Hons), MA, MPhil, PhD

Dept of German Studies; www.nottingham.ac.uk/german
German, classical civilization, E European civilization, modern & contemporary German studies, law & German law, modern language studies, modern languages & critical theory, comparative literature, literature in English translation; BA(Hons), MA, MPhil, PhD

School of History; www.nottingham.ac.uk/history
history, ancient history, archaeology, British history, gender history, contemporary Chinese studies, art history, politics, medieval/ modern history, Viking studies, warrior societies; BA(Hons), MA, MPhil, PhD

School of Humanities; www.nottingham.ac.uk/humanities
archaeology, art history, classics, music, philosophy, theology & religious studies, Viking studies; BA(Hons), BSc(Hons), MA, MSci, MSc

School of Modern Languages & Cultures; www.nottingham.ac.uk/modern-languages
culture film & media, comparative literature, French & francophone studies, German studies, Russian & Slavonic studies, Spanish Portuguese & Latin American & Canadian studies, translation & interpreting; BA(Hons), MA, MPhil, PhD

Music; www.nottingham.ac.uk/music
music, early music, music on stage & screen, music theory & analysis, musicology, history & culture; BA(Hons), MPhil, PhD

Dept of Philosophy; www.nottingham.ac.uk/philosophy
philosophy, theology, philosophy & literature, systematic & philosophical theology, metaphysics, mind & knowledge, ethics, philosophy of language, aesthetics; BA(Hons), MA, MPhil, PhD

Russian & Slavonic Studies; www.nottingham.ac.uk/slavonic
Russian studies, international media communications, Serbian & Croatian studies, Russian and East European civilisations, Slavonic studies; BA(Hons), MA, MPhil

Spanish, Portuguese and Latin American Studies; www.nottingham.ac.uk/splas
Hispanic studies, Portuguese/Spanish (beginners), Hispanic & Latin American studies, Portuguese & Lusophone studies, modern language studies; BA(Hons), MA, MPhil, PhD

Department of Theology and Religious Studies; www.nottingham.ac.uk/theology

biblical interpretation & theory, church history, philosophical theology, philosophy, philosophy & literary masters/theology, systemic & philosophical theory, religious studies, theology; BA(Hons), MA, MPhil/PhD

Faculty of Science; www.nottingham.ac.uk/science

School of Biology; www.nottingham.ac.uk/biology

biology, biochemistry & genetics, zoology, human/genetics, biological photography & imaging; BSc(Hons), MSc, MRes, MSci, Phd

School of Biosciences; www.nottingham.ac.uk/biosciences

Agricultural and Environmental Sciences; www.nottingham.ac.uk/biosciences/divisions/agrenv/index.aspx

agriculture, integrative systems biology, adv genomic & proteonomic science, environmental science

Plant and Crop Sciences; www.nottingham.ac.uk/biosciences/divisions/plantcrop/index.aspx

agriculture & biotechnology, applied biology, crop improvement/science, technology & entrepreneurship, environmental biology & genetics, genomic & proeonomic science, integrative systems biology, plant genetic manipulation, plant science

Animal Sciences; www.nottingham.ac.uk/biosciences/divisions/animal/index.aspx

animal science, preveterinary science

Food Sciences; www.nottingham.ac.uk/biosciences/divisions/food/index.aspx

applied biomolecular technology, biopharmacy, food & biotechnical industries, brewing science & food production management, food microbiology/science, industrial biochemistry, microbiology, nutrition & food science, sustainable energy/bioenergy

Nutritional Sciences; www.nottingham.ac.uk/biosciences/divisions/nutritional/index.aspx

advanced dietetic practice, dietetics, food science, nutrition, nutritional biochemistry; BSc(Hons), Cert, Grad Dip, MRes, MSc, MNutrition, MPhil, PhD

School of Chemistry; www.nottingham.ac.uk/chemistry

biochemistry, biological chemistry, chemistry, nanoscience chemistry/& entrepreneurship, molecular physics, medicinal chemistry; BSc(Hons), MChem, MPhil, MSc, MSci, PhD

School of Computer Science; www.nottingham.ac.uk/computerscience

artificial intelligence, adv/computer science, computer science & entrepreneurship/IT/mathematics/economics, computing & information systems, digital economy, human-computer interaction, management/of information technology, scientific computation, software engineering, BSc(Hons), MPhil, MSc

School of Mathematical Sciences; www.maths.nottingham.ac.uk/

financial mathematics, gravity, particles & fields, mathematics, numerical techniques for finance, pure mathematics, statistics, scientific computation/with industrial mathematics/mathematical medicine & biology, statistics with biomedical applications/applied probability; BSc(Hons), MSc, PhD

School of Pharmacy; www.nottingham.ac.uk/pharmacy

medicinal & biological chemistry, pharmacy, nanoscience, stem cell technology; MPharm, MRes, MSc, MSci, PhD

School of Physics & Astronomy; www.nottingham.ac.uk/physics

astronomy, mathematical physics, medical physics, nanoscience, physics, physics & philosophy, theoretical astrophysics/physics, chemistry & molecular physics; BSc(Hons), MSc, MSci, PhD, MRes, MPhil

School of Psychology; www.nottingham.ac.uk/psychology

cognitive neuroscience, brain imaging, neuroimaging, psychology/philosophy; BSc(Hons), MSc, PhD, DAppPsych, DEdPsych

Faculty of Engineering; www.nottingham.ac.uk/engineering

Dept of Architecture & Built Environment; www.nottingham.ac.uk/abe

architectural environment engineering, architecture, design, energy conversion & management, environmental design, renewable energy & architecture, sustainable built environment/energy & entrepreneurship, sustainable tall buildings/building technology, technology, theory & design, urban design; BA(Hons), BArch (Hons), BEng (Hons), Dip Arch, MEng, MPhil, PhD

Dept of Chemical and Environmental Engineering; www.nottingham.ac.uk/scheme
chemical engineering, environmental engineering, environmental & resource engineering; BEng(Hons), MEng(Hons), MPhil, MRes, MSc, PhD

Dept of Electrical & Electronic Engineering; www.nottingham.ac.uk/eee
biophotonics, electrical & electronic engineering, electrical technology for sustainable & renewable energy systems, electromagnetics design, electronic communications & computer engineering, electronic & ultrasonic instrumentation, photonic & optical engineering techniques, power electronics & drive, machines & drive, sustainable transmission & electric power; BEng, MEng, MPhil, MRes, MSc, PGDip, PhD

Dept of Civil Engineering; www.nottingham.ac.uk/civil
civil engineering/mechanics, civil engineering: engineering surveying/environmental fluid mechanics/management, engineering surveying & GIS/geodosy, environmental management & earth observation, GNNS technology, pavement engineering, structural engineering, transportation, positioning & navigation technology, risk & reliability methods; BEng(Hons), MEng(Hons), MPhil, MSc, PhD

Dept of Mechanical, Materials and Manufacturing Engineering; www.nottingham.ac.uk/schoolm3
advanced materials/manufacture, aerospace technology, applied ergonomics, materials failure and analysis, human factors, manufacturing engineering & management, mechanical engineering; BEng, MEng, MSc, PGCert, PhD

Faculty of Medicine & Health Science; www.nottingham.ac.uk/mhs/index.aspx

School of Biology; www.nottingham.ac.uk/biology
biochemical genetics, biological photography & imaging, biology, human genetics; BSc, MSc, MSci, PhD

School of Biomedical Sciences; www.nottingham.ac.uk/biomedsci
biochemistry, biological chemistry, biology, biotechnology, genetics, pharmacy, pharmacology, physiology, medicine, neuroscience, integrated physiology in health & disease, sport & exercise science; BSc(Hons), MPhil, MRes, MSc, PhD, BMBS, BMedSci

School for Clinical Sciences; www.nottingham.ac.uk/scs
assisted reproduction/stem cell technology, sports & exercise medicine, translational neuroimaging; DM, MSc, PhD

School of Community Health Sciences; www.nottingham.ac.uk/chs
applied epidemiology, applied/work & organization/rehabilitation/work & occupational/management/occupational health/criminological/health psychology, medicine, mental health studies, occupational health & safety leadership, psychology & health, workplace health & wellbeing, medical education, public health, psychological research methods; MBBS, BMedSci, MMedSci, MPH, MSc, PGDip/Cert, PhD

School of Graduate Entry Medicine & Health; www.nottingham.ac.uk/gem
health care science; BSc, MRes, MPhil, PHD, DM

School of Molecular Medical Sciences; www.nottingham.ac.uk/mol
clinical microbiology, molecular medicine, microbiology/& immunology, immunology & allergy, cancer immunology, molecular genetics & diagnostics, clinical genetics, oncology, MSc, PhD

School of Nursing, Midwifery & Physiotherapy; www.nottingham.ac.uk/nursing
nursing science/studies, healthcare studies/practice, adult/critical care, advanced clinical practice/skills, advanced nursing, clinical leadership for innovative practice, cognitive behaviour therapy, nursing(adult/child/mental health), health and social care/practice teacher, health communication, health care sciences, midwifery, physiotherapy-manual therapy/neurohabilitation, psychological therapies; BMid(Hons), BSc(Hons), DHSci, MA, MNursSci, MPhil, MSc, PGDip/Cert, PhD

School of Veterinary Medicine & Science; www.nottingham.ac.uk/vet
laboratory animal medicine, veterinary medicine & surgery/science; BVMBVS, BVMedSci, MPhil, MRes, PhD, DVM, DVS

Institute of Work, Health & Organisations; www.nottingham.ac.uk/who
clinical psychology, work/management/occupational/forensic/criminological/rehabilitation/health/clinical psychology

Politics
psychology & health; MSc, DForPsych, DClinPsych

Faculty of Social Sciences, Law & Education; www.nottingham.ac.uk/social-sciences/index.aspx

School of Contemporary Chinese Studies; www.nottingham.ac.uk/chinese
Chinese/English translation & interpreting, accounting & finance for contemporary Chinese, corporate finance/banking & financial markets/management in contemporary China, global issues & contemporary Chinese studies; BA, MSc, MSci, PhD

Economics; www.nottingham.ac.uk/economics
applied economics, behavioural economics, economic development & policy analysis, economics, economics with modern languages/philosophy/mathematics/politics, international/development/financial economics, econometrics, philosophy; BA(Hons), BSc(Hons), MPhil, PGDip, PhD

School of Education; www.nottingham.ac.uk/education
counselling/children & young people, teacher training (PGCE) – secondary (English, geography, history, humanistic counselling, mathematics, modern languages, science), PGCE (primary), mentoring & coaching, educational leadership & management, special needs, international HE, trauma studies, TESOL, learning technology & education, special needs, TESOL, creative & professional writing, fine art, humanities, teaching Chinese; BA(Hons), MA, MPhil, MRes, PGCE, PGCert/Dip, PhD, SCITT, EdD

School of Geography; www.nottingham.ac.uk/geography
geography, environmental management/history, GIS, human geography/with Chinese, physical geography, landscape & culture, contaminated land management, economy, space, society, geospatial intelligence; BA(Hons), PhD

School of Law; www.nottingham.ac.uk/law
law, French/German/Spanish/Euro/Chinese, Canadian/New Zealand/South East Asian/Australian/American law, environmental law, human rights law, international commercial law/criminal justice and armed conflict, criminal law, international commercial law, international law/and development, law & environmental science, maritime law, public international law, senior status; BA(Hons), LlB, LlM, MA, MSc, PhD

Nottingham University Business School; www.nottingham.ac.uk/business
corporate social responsibility/strategy and governance, entrepreneurship, finance accounting & management, finance & investment, industrial economics, innovation & policy/with insurance, industrial engineering & operations management, international business, logistics & supply chain management, management studies, management with Asian studies/Chinese studies/French/German/Spanish, manufacturing systems, marketing, operations management, risk management, supply chain & operations management, sustainable environment/communications/entrepreneurship; BA(Hons), ExecMBA, MA, MBA, MSc

Politics & International Relations; www.nottingham.ac.uk/politics
diplomacy, international relations & global issues, international security & terrorism, politics & economics/contemporary history/American studies/German/French, social and global justice, war & contemporary conflict; BA(Hons), MA, MPhil, MRes, PhD

School of Sociology and Social Policy; www.nottingham.ac.uk/sociology
global citizenship, identities & human rights, health communication, cultural sociology, public administration/policy, social & cultural studies, international/social policy, social work, sociology, trauma studies; BA(Hons), MA, MPA, MPhil, MSWS, PhD, PGCert

NOTTINGHAM TRENT UNIVERSITY
www.ntu.ac.uk

School of Animal, Rural and Environmental Sciences; www.ntu.ac.uk/ares
animal biology/studies, biodiversity conservation, environmental design & management/conservation science, equestrian practice & sports science, equine health & welfare/sports science, geography, endangered species recovery & conservation, wildlife

conservation, zoo biology; BSc(Hons), MSc/MRes/ PGCert/PGDip, FdSc

School of Architecture, Design and Built Environment; www.ntu.ac.uk/adbe

adv project design engineering, architecture, architectural technology & design, interior architecture & design, international real estate investment & finance, civil engineering, furniture & product design, building/quantity surveying, planning & development, real estate, construction management, planning, urban design & sustainable development, project management, innovation & management, structural engineering, smart design; BSc(Hons), MA, MSc, MArch, PGDip/Cert, PhD

School of Art & Design; www.ntu.ac.uk/art

branding & identity design, costume design & marketing, curation by registered provision, contemporary craft practice, creative pattern design decorative arts, design for film & TV/events/publication, illustration, fashion accessory design/design/knitwear design and knitted textiles/management/design/communication & promotion/marketing and branding/marketing communications, film practice, fine art, graphic design, international fashion business, interaction design, motion graphic design, media creativity, multimedia, photography, puppetry and digital animation, textile design and innovation, theatre design; BA(Hons), GradDip, MA, MPhil, PhD

School of Arts & Humanities; www.ntu.ac.uk/hum

English, broadcasting/magazine/newspaper journalism, broadcasting, creative writing, global studies, European studies, history, games & play, Holocaust & genocide studies, museum & heritage management, environmental change, English language, international development, linguistics, media, philosophy, French, Spanish, Latin American studies, TESOL; BA(Hons), MA, PGDip/Cert, MPhil, PhD

Nottingham Business School; www.ntu.ac.uk/nbs

management, management & entrepreneurship/business/HRM/international business, investment studies/mental health, marketing (advertising & communication/retail), economics & finance, international/strategic accounting & finance/business, HRM; BA(Hons), DBA, MBA, MSc

School of Education; www.ntu.ac.uk/edu

business & education development, education, education studies, secondary design & technology education, early years & educational development/ & psychology & education, psychology/& special & inclusive education, educational support, HE, ICT & education, physical science education, primary education, psychology & education/educational development, sport & leisure, teaching adult literacy, numerous PGCE secondary courses, TESOL, teacher training; BA(Hons), MA, PGCE, PGCert, ProfCert, ProfDoc

Nottingham Law School; www.ntu.ac.uk/nls

corporate/commercial law, international criminal justice, health law, human rights, insolvency law, corporate law, international trade law, sports law, professional practice/business/criminology/psychology; GDL, GradDip, LlB, LlM, LPC, PhD

School of Science & Technology; www.ntu.ac.uk/sat

analytical chemistry, adv materials engineering, applied biosciences, biological sciences, bioinformatics, biomedical science, biotechnology, chemistry, forensics, coaching & sport science, computer science (games systems/networks, forensics and security), computer systems (engineering/networks/forensics & security/games technology), computing & technology, digital media, electronic systems, engineering management, engineering & cybernetics & communications/electronics/internet & security/enterprise computing), forensic science/biology, environmental management, exercise nutrition & health, financial mathematics, forensic science, games technology/& play, geonomic & proteonomic science, healthcare science, information & communication technology, information systems, materials science, mathematics, medical & materials imaging, molecular cell biology, multimedia games engineering, neuroscience, nutrition and health, pharmaceutical and medicinal chemistry, pharmacology, pharmacological analysis, physics and mathematics/astrophysics/nuclear technology, software engineering, sport sciences/& management/exercise science, sport & exercise science; BSc, FdSc, MChem, MRes, MSc, MSci, PhD

School of Social Sciences; www.ntu.ac.uk/soc

applied child psychology, careers/guidance, child care practice, criminology, children's services, counselling & psychotherapy, forensic mental health/ health & wellbeing psychology, health & social care, health & safety risk management, international relations, psychology with criminology/sociology/

sports science, politics, public health, safety & environment, social work, sociology, youth studies/ justice/work; BA(Hons), MA, MRes, MSc, Pfdip/Cert, PGDip/Cert, PhD, ProfDoc

Degrees validated by Nottingham Trent University offered at:

SOUTHAMPTON SOLENT UNIVERSITY
www.solent.ac.uk

Art & Design; www.solent.ac.uk/courses/course-areas/art-design.aspx
Art & Design
advertising/& PR, promotional media, PR & communication, creative advertising, PR
Animation
animation, computer-generated imagery, special effects
Fashion
fashion, fashion graphics, fashion management with marketing, fashion photography/writing/styling, fashion with photography/PR, fashion merchandising management,
Graphic Design
graphic design
Interactive Design
computer & video games
Interior Design
interior design/decoration
Media & Fashion Styling
fashion styling/make-up for media, make-up & hair design
Media Production, Media Technology, Media Writing, Media Studies
media culture & production, special effects, media production, media, communication & culture, pop music production, audio technology, live & studio sound, media technology, music studio technology, English & advertising/film/magazine, journalism/media/PR/screenwriting/writing/media writing, screenwriting, creative writing, industry & practice, writing fashion & culture, media
Photography
photography
Visual Arts
fine art, illustration, visual arts

Business & Law; www.solent.ac.uk/courses/course-areas/business-law.aspx
Accountancy
accountancy/& finance
Business & Business IT
business, business & finance/management/marketing, business management, international business management, business(customer service/management, organisational improvement), MBA, business studies, business information technology
Event Management
events management
Sport
sport & development
Human Resources/Personnel
HRM, personnel & development
International Business
international politics
Law
legal practical course, law & practice, LlB/LlM courses
Management
leadership & management development, management, management & finance/international business
Marketing
digital marketing/& media, marketing/with advertising management, marketing management
Sport
sport & development

Computing; www.solent.ac.uk/courses/course-areas/computing.aspx
Business IT
business information systems/technology, information & computer technology, information technology for business, software engineering/management, computer network management, web design, computer systems & networks, network security management, internet technology, computer games development, computing

Engineering & Construction; www.solent.ac.uk/courses/course-areas/engineering-construction.aspx
Architecture
architectural technology
Civil Engineering
Construction
construction management
Electrical/Electronic Engineering
electronic engineering

Engineering(General)
engineering with business

Mechanical Engineering
mechanical design, manufacturing & mechanical engineering

Surveying
quantity surveying

Entertainment Technology; www.solent.ac.uk/courses/course-areas/entertainment-technology.aspx

Acoustics

Media Technology
audio technology, live & studio sound, media technology, music studio/technology

Music & Music Technology
sound technology, sound for film, TV & games

Outside Broadcasting
outside broadcasting (production operations)

Maritime; www.solent.ac.uk/courses/course-areas/maritime.aspx

Geography
geography with environmental studies/marine studies

Maritime Industry
marine engineering & management, marine operations management/engineering/operations, maritime business, ship and port management, international maritime studies – ship & shipping management/shipping and logistics, shipping operations

Yacht and Boat Design
yacht and powercraft design, yacht production and surveying watersports technology

Media; www.solent.ac.uk/courses/course-areas/media.aspx

Advertising/Communications
advertising/& PR, promotional media, PR/ & communication

Film and TV Studies
film/& TV/studies, film, sports broadcasting

Graphic Design
graphic design

International Business
politics and international relations

Journalism
journalism, magazine journalism & feature writing, multimedia/photo/sport journalism, writing fashion & culture

Journalism and Media Writing
publishing, multimedia journalism

Media Production
media culture/& production media, communication and culture, popular music production, special effects

Media Studies
media, popular music

Media Writing
English, English & advertising film, magazine journalism, English & media/PR/screenwriting, media writing, creative writing, writing fashion and culture, multimedia communications

Music and Music Technology
digital music, music promotion, pop music and record production, popular music journalism/performance, music festival industries

Performing Arts
comedy – writing and performance, performance,

Television Production
TV & video production/post-production/studio production television

Visual Arts
illustration

Social Sciences; www.solent.ac.uk/courses/course-areas/social-sciences.aspx

Business
communications in crisis management

Criminology
criminal investigation with psychology criminology/& psychology/ criminal justice

Housing
managing change in the workplace

Psychology
psychology (counselling/criminal behaviour/education/health psychology)

Social Work
adult social care, social work/with adults

Sport and Tourism; www.solent.ac.uk/courses/course-areas/sport-tourism.aspx

Health and Fitness
management/fitness & personal training, health, exercise & physical activity

Leisure Management
introduction to special event logistics/staging

Marketing
promoting & marketing sports activities, outdoor & watersports, adventure & extreme sports management outdoor learning & watersports management

Sport
football studies/& business, sport coaching & development, sports studies, applied sport science, sport

coaching, young people & physical activity, sport & development
Tourism
cruise industry management, international/tourism management
Teaching & Learning
teaching & learning in HE, blended learning

Degrees, Diploma, certificates conferred
BA(Hons), MA, MPhil, PhD, Cert, CIM, FdA, GradDip, LLM, MA, MBA, MProf, PGDip, BEng(Hons), BSc(Hons), FdSc, HNC, HND, MPhil, MSc, PhD

THE OPEN UNIVERSITY
www.open.ac.uk

Arts and Humanities Studies; www3.open.ac.uk/study/undergraduate/arts-and-humanities/index.htm
art history, classical studies, creative writing, English language & literature, history, humanities, literature, music, politics, philosophy, economics, psychological studies, religious studies; BA(Hons), MA, PGDip

Business and Management; www3.open.ac.uk/study/undergraduate/business_and_management/index.htm
accounting, business management/administration/studies, computing & IT, public services, finance, financial services/strategy, leadership and management, retail management, clinical leadership, HRM, international finance; BA/BSc, Diplomas, DipHE, FD, MA, MSc, PGDip

Childhood and Youth; www3.open.ac.uk/study/undergraduate/childhood-and-youth/index.htm
childhood practice, childhood & youth studies, early years, primary teaching & learning, youth work, working with young people, youth justice studies; BA(Hons), Diplomas, DipHE, Certificates

Computing and ICT; www3.open.ac.uk/study/undergraduate/computing-and-ICT/index.htm
advanced networking, computing/for commerce and industry, computing & IT/practice, information systems, management of software, software development, strategic management of IT systems; BSc(Hons), Certs, Diplomas, DipHE, FD, MSc, PGDip

Education; www3.open.ac.uk/study/undergraduate/education/index.htm
childhood practice, childhood & youth studies, early years, education, educational technology, mathematics & its learning, online & distance education, primary teaching & learning, QTS, secondary education in physics, working together for children, working with young people, youth work; BA/BSc, Certs, DipHE, FD, MA, PGCE

Engineering, Technology & Design; www3.open.ac.uk/study/undergraduate/engineering_and-technology-and-design/index.htm
adv networking, computing and IT/practice, design & innovation, ECT practice, engineering, information & communications technology, information systems, materials fabrication & engineering, systems thinking in practice, technology management; BEng, FD, MBA, MEng, MSc, PGDip,DipHE

Environment, Development and International Studies; www3.open.ac.uk/study/undergraduate/environment-development-and-international-studies/index.htm
conflict/environment & development, development management, environmental science/studies, environmental policy/decision making/management, international studies, human rights & development; BSc(Hons), MSc, PGDip/Cert

Health and Social Care; www3.open.ac.uk/study/undergraduate/health-and-social-care/index.htm
adult nursing, advancing professional practice/healthcare practice, childhood & youth studies, health studies/science, health & social care, managing care, mental health nursing, nursing practice, promoting public health, social working with young people, youth justice, youth work; BA(Hons), BA/BSc, CertHE, DipHE, FD

Languages; www3.open.ac.uk/study/ undergraduate/languagesstudies/ index.htm
French, German, applied linguistics, language studies, Spanish, English language & literature, humanities, education; BA(Hons), Dip/CertHE

Law; www3.open.ac.uk/ undergraduate/law/index.htm
law, agreements, ownership & trusts, legal system, criminal justice, business/studies, human rights & corporate responsibility, company law, employment law, English law; Certs, Dips, LlB(Hons), PGDip

Mathematics and Statistics; www3.open.ac.uk/study/undergraduate/ mathematics_ and_ statistics/index.htm
computing IT, economics & mathematical sciences, statistics, mathematics, mathematics education, mathematics & its learning; BA/BSc, BSc(Hons), MMath, MSc, UGCert

Psychology & Counselling; www3.open.ac.uk/study/undergraduate/ psychology-and-counselling/index.htm
counselling, psychology, combined social studies, behaviour & psychological studies, forensic psychology & criminology, psychological studies & criminology; BA/BSc, MSc, PGDip, UGDip

Science; www3.open.ac.uk/study/ undergraduate/science/index.htm
astronomy, biology, chemistry, geography, planetary science/studies, earth science, environmental studies/science, health sciences, medical physics, medicinal chemistry, natural sciences, paramedic sciences, physics, professional science, science & society, secondary education in physics; BSc(Hons), DipHE, FD, MSc

Social Sciences; www3.open.ac.uk/study/ undergraduate/social_sciences/index.htm
counselling, economics, environmental studies, criminology/& social policy, philosophy, social sciences; BA(Hons), BA/BSc, FD, MA, PGDip

UNIVERSITY OF OXFORD
www.ox.ac.uk

Division of Humanities; www.ox.ac.uk/ divisions/humanities

Rothermere American Institute; www.rai.ox.ac.uk/
American studies/history/politics; MSt

Faculty of Classics; www.classics.ox.ac.uk
ancient & modern history, classical archaeology & ancient history, classical philology & linguistics, Greek and Latin literature, philosophy; BA(Hons), MPhil, MSt

Ruskin School of Drawing and Fine Art; www.ruskin-sc.ox.ac.uk
art history & theory, contemporary art, drawing, fine art, theoretical & practice-led research, history of art & visual culture; BFA, MLitt, DPhil

Faculty of English; www.english.ox.ac.uk
English language and literature (650–1550; 1550–1700; 1600–1830; 1800–1914; 1900–present day), literature in English, English & American studies, history & English, medieval studies, history & English, Shakespeare; BA(Hons), DPhil, MLitt, MPhil, MSt

History of Art Department; www.hoa.ox.ac.uk
history of art, authenticity & replication in art and visual culture, media & modernity: Gothic; artistic originality & transmission of style & mass culture, 1880–2000, theories of vision; BA(Hons), DPhil, MLitt, MSt

Faculty of History; www.history.ox.ac.uk
ancient & modern history, economic & social history, international global & imperial history, Gothic, history of science, medicine, technology, media & modernity: art & mass culture, late antique & Byzantine studies, medieval history/studies, modern British & European history, US history, women, art & culture in early modern Europe; BA(Hons), DPhil, MPhil, MSc, MSt, MLetters

Faculty of Linguistics, Philology and Phonetics; www.ling-phil.ox.ac.uk
comparative philology & comparative linguistics, historical philology, history & structure of language, linguistics theory, philology & phonetics, modern languages & linguistics; BA, MPhil, PhD

Faculty of Medieval & Modern Languages; www.mod-langs.ox.uk

Celtic, comparative literature or medieval literature, cultural studies, Czech, Catalan, Galician, French, German, linguistics, literature, modern Greek, Italian, medieval literature, language history, medieval & modern languages, European enlightenment/cultural studies, film, Polish, Portuguese, Russian, Russian, Spanish, Slavonic languages, Yiddish; BA(Hons), DPhil, MPhil, MSt

Faculty of Music; www.music.ox.ac.uk

aesthetics & criticism, chamber music, choral studies/conducting performance, composition & analysis, dance music, ethnomusicology, historical musicology, jazz, musical history/theory, orchestration, performance & interpretation, theory & analysis, source studies Western music theory; BMus, DPhil, MA(Hons), MPhil, MSt, MLitt

Faculty of Oriental Studies; www.orinst.ox.ac.uk

Arabic, Persian, Turkish, Sanskrit, Buddhist studies, Chinese studies, classic & oriental studies, eastern Christianity, Egyptology & ancient Near East, European & Middle East languages, Asia & Near Asian studies, Hebrew & Jewish studies, Islamic world, Japanese studies, Korean studies, theology; BA(Hons), DPhil, MPhil, MSt

Faculty of Philosophy; www.philosophy.ox.ac.uk;

philosophy & modern language/theology/physics/mathematics, aesthetics, Aquinas, Aristotle, ethics, formal logic, history of philosophy Descartes to Kant, knowledge & reality, logic & language, medieval philosophy, philosophy of mind/ physics/religion/language & linguistics, Plato, post-Kantian philosophy, PPP Russell, Wittgenstein; BA(Hons), BPhil, MPhil, PhD

Faculty of Theology; www.theology.ox.ac.uk

theology/& pastoral studies/religious studies, oriental studies, pastoral studies, the Old Testament/New Testament studies, biblical interpretation, scholastic/modern/reformation theology, ecclesiastical history, Christian ethics/doctrine, philosophy & theology, philosophical theology, eastern Christian studies, Judaism & Christianity in Graeco-Roman world, applied theology, study of religion; BA(Hons), BTh, MTh, MSt, MLitt, MPhil, DPhil, PGDip/Cert

Division of Mathematical, Physical and Life Sciences; www.ox.ac.uk/divisions/mpls

Dept of Chemistry; www.chemistry.ox.ac.uk

inorganic chemistry, mathematical techniques, medical chemistry, molecular biochemistry/& chemical biology, organic reactions/synthesis, organometallic chemistry, physical & theoretical chemistry, quantum mechanics, reaction mechanisms, solid state chemistry, spectroscopy, theoretical chemistry, thermodynamics; DPhil, MChem, MSc

Dept of Computer Science; www.cs.ox.ac.uk

computer science, mathematics, modelling & scientific computing, mathematics & foundations of computer science/philosophy, software engineering, software & systems security; BA(Hons), MSc, DPhil

Dept of Engineering Science; www.eng.ox.ac.uk

biomedical engineering, chemical engineering, computer engineering, process engineering, civil & offshore engineering, electrical engineering, electronic & information engineering, structures, materials & dynamics, engineering science, engineering, economics & management, information/control & vision engineering, materials engineering, mechanical/civil/structural engineering; DPhil, MEng, MSc

Life Science Interface; Doctoral Training Centre; www.lsi.ox.ac.uk

biological physics, computational biology, medical imaging & signals, bioinformatics, evolution & genetics; DPhil

Division of Materials; www.materials.ox.ac.uk

materials science, materials structures & mechanical properties of metals, electrical/mechanical properties, nanoelectronics, non-metallic materials; composites, polymers, packaging/superconducting/semiconducting materials, etc; DPhil, MEng, MSc, MS, MEm

Mathematical Institute; www.maths.ox.ac.uk

algebra, analysis, applied maths, mathematics & foundations of computer science, mathematics & scientific computing, mathematical finance, statistics, geometry, pure maths; BA(Hons), DPhil, MCF, MFoCS, MS, MSc, MMath

University of Oxford

Dept of Physics; www.physics.ox.ac.uk
physics, atmospheric oceanic & planetary physics, astrophysics, condensed matter physics, particle physics, physics, atomic & laser/theoretical physics; BA(Hons), DPhil, MPhys, MPhysPhil

Dept of Plant Science; www.lps.plants.ox.ac.uk/plants
biochemistry & systems biology, cell biology/physiology, comparative developmental genetics, ecology, evolution & systematics, plant science; BA(Hons), DPhil, MRes, MSc

Dept of Statistics; www.stats.ox.ac.uk
applied statistics, mathematics & statistics; BA(Hons), DPhil, MMath, MSc, PGDip

Dept of Zoology; www.zoo.ox.ac.uk
animal behaviour/welfare, ageing biology, biological science, disease, ecology, evolution, food science, molecular biology & bioinformatics, indigenous biology, ornithology, integrative bioscience, wildlife conservation; BA(Hons), DPhil, MRes, MSc

Division of Medical Science; www.oc.ac.uk/divisions/medical_science

Medical Sciences; www.medschool.oc.ac.uk
pre-clinical/post-clinical medicine, neuroscience, global health, immunology, athletic performance, psychological research, pharmacology, diagnostic imaging, neuroradiology, musculoskeletal sciences, clinical embryology, medicinal chemistry for cancer, health care, therapeutics; MB, BCh, MSc, DPhil, PhD

Dept of Biochemistry; www.bioch.ox.ac.uk
biochemistry (molecular & cellular), biomedicine, chromosome & developmental biology, genetics & molecular biology, immunity & translational medicine, infection, integrated systems, medical sciences, molecular biochemistry & chemical biology, neuroscience, structural biology; DPhil, MBiochem, MSc, PhD

Dept of Cardiovascular Medicine; www.cardiov.ox.ac.uk
cardiovascular science; DPhil

Nuffield Dept of Clinical Laboratory Sciences; www.ndcls.ox.ac.uk
clinical laboratory sciences; DPhil, MSc

Dept of Clinical Neurology; www.clneuro.ox.ac.uk
clinical immunology, cardiovascular disease, structural biology, genetics, developmental biology, cancer, endocrinology, metabolic medicine, neurodegeneration, neurology, neurogenetic immunology/pathology, epidemiology, integrated immunology, global health science, multiple sclerosis; DPhil, MSc

Nuffield Dept of Clinical Medicine; www.ndm.ac.uk
cancer biology, clinical immunology, gerentology, immunity & infectious diseases, musculo-skeletal med, physiology, cellular & molecular biology, clinical trials & epidemiology, endricinology & metabolic medicine, genetics & genomics, physiology, cellular & molecular biology, professional science & structural biology, tropical & global med; PhD, MSc

Dept of Pharmacology; www.pharm.ox.ac.uk
clinical pharmacology, experimental therapeutics, practical drug therapy, medical chemistry for cancer; MSc, DPhil

Dept of Experimental Psychology; www.psy.ox.ac.uk
clinical/ experimental psychology, psychology, philosophy & linguistics, neuroscience, psychological research; BA(Hons), DPhil, MSc

Dept of Oncology; www.oncology.ox.ac.uk
oncology, radiation biology, experimental therapeutics, clinical pharmacy, medical oncology, radiation oncology & biology; DPhil, MRes, MSc

Wellcome Trust Centre for Human Genetics; www.well.ox.ac.uk
biology, immunity, cardiovascular disease, neuroscience, structural biology; PhD

Wetherall Institute of Molecular Medicine; www.imw.ox.ac.uk
clinical genetics, computational biology, stem cell biology, HIV immunity, global health, paediatrics, human immunology, molecular immunology/oncology/parasitology/haematology; DPhil

Nuffield Dept of Obstetrics & Gynaecology; www.obs-gyn.ox.ac.uk
clinical embryology, human reproduction, obstetrics, gynaecology, antenatal care, sexual & reproductive health; MSc, DPhil

Nuffield Laboratory of Ophthalmology; www.eye.ox.ac.uk
retinal genetics, artificial vision, bodyclocks, ocular biology, vision & disease, gene therapy, genetic/ocular biology, photoreceptors, ophthalmology, neuroscience, sleep; DPhil, MSc

Nuffield Centre of Clinical Neuroscience; www.cineuro.oc.ac.uk;
cerobrovascular disease, functional neurosurgery, muliple sclerosis, neurodegeneration/genetics/muscular/immunology pathology

Nuffield Department of Orthopaedics, Rheumatology and Musculoskeletal Sciences; www.ndorms.ox.ac.uk
orthopaedics, rheumatology, musculoskeletal sciences; MSc, DPhil

Dept of Paediatrics; www.paediatrics.ox.ac.uk
paediatric infection & immunity/gastroenterological & nutrition/neurology/vaccine/endocrine & diabetes, childhood care; PhD, MSc

Dept of Physiology, Anatomy, and Genetics; www.dpag.ox.ac.uk
ion channels, transporters & signalling, metabolism & endrinoconology, functional genomics, neuroscience, development and reproduction; MPhil, MSc, DPhil

Dept of Psychiatry; www.psychiatry.ox.ac.uk
child & adolescent psychiatry, eating disorders, evidence-based mental health, experimental psychopathology and cognitive therapy, forensic psychiatry, molecular neuropathology, neurobiology of ageing, neuroimaging, psychopharmacology, social psychiatry, suicide research; DPhil, MRCPsych

Division of Primary Care Health Science; www.dphpc.ox.ac.uk
cancer, monitoring & diagnosis, tobacco addiction, health therapeutics, infectious disease, health services & policy, global health science, health economics/services; DPhil, MSc

Nuffield Dept of Surgical Science; www.surgery.ox.ac.uk
endovascular neurosurgery, diagnostic imaging, integrated immunology, surgical science & practice; DPhil, MCh, MSc

Division of Social Sciences; www.socsci.ox.ac.uk

School of Anthropology and Museum Ethnography, www.anthro.ox.ac.uk
human science, humanities, social anthropology, medical anthropology, cognitive & evolutionary anthropology, visual, material, & museum anthropology, migration studies, refugee & forced migration studies, material anthropology & museum ethnography; BA, BSc, DPhil, MPhil

PittRivers Museum; www.prm.ox.ac.uk
material anthropology, museum ethnography; DPhil, MPhil, MSc

School of Archaeology; www.arch.ox.ac.uk
archaeology & anthropology, classical archaeology & ancient history, archaeological science; BA(Hons), DPhil, MLitt, MSc, MSt

SAID Business School; www.sbs.ox.ac.uk
accounting, engineering/materials/economics & management, major project management, finance, financial strategy/economics, general management, global business, law management science, marketing, innovation/change/organizational behaviour/leadership, general management, public policy, Dip

Dept of Economics; www.economics.ox.ac.uk
economics/development, engineering/materials/economics & management, history & economics, financial economics, micro economics, macroeconomics, philosophy, politics & economics; BA(Hons), DPhil, MEng, MSc

Dept of Education; www.education.ox.ac.uk
applied linguistics, child development and education, comparative & international education, e-learning, educational research methodology, HE, learning and teaching/technology, PGCE (numerous secondary subjects), teaching English in university setting; DPhil, MSc, PGCE, PGDip

School of Geography & the Environment; www.geog.ox.ac.uk
biodiversity, ecosystems & conservation, climate systems & policy, landscape dynamics, biogeography, conservation & management, dryland environment, earth systems processes/dynamics, earth science, environmental change & management, geographical techniques/controversies, geographical technology, geography & finance, nature, society &

environmental policy, transport, water science, policy & management; BA(Hons), DPhil, MSc

School of Interdisciplinary Area Studies; www.area-studies.ox.ac.uk
African studies, modern Japanese/Chinese studies, Russian & east European studies, public policy, Latin American studies; MSc, MPhil, DPhil

Dept of International Development; www.qeh.ox.ac.uk
development studies, economics for development, refugee & forced migration studies, global governance, diplomacy; Cert/Dip, DPhil, MPhil, MSc

Oxford Internet Institute; www.oil.ox.ac.uk
social science of the internet; DPhil, MSc

Faculty of Law; www.law.ox.ac.uk
common/comparative/company/competition/corporate/labour law, constitutional & administration/criminal law, philosophy of/criminology, environmental law, EU/family/human rights law, intellectual property law, judicial process, law & finance, law of obligation, legal history, media law, property & trusts, Roman law, socio-legal studies; BA(Hons), BCL, Dip, DPhil, MJur, MLitt, MPhil, MSc, MSt, PGDip

Oxford Martin School; www.oxfordmartin.ox.ac.uk
research in health & medicine, energy & environment, technology & society, ethics & governance

Oxford-Man Institute of Quantitative Finance; www.oxford-man.ox.ac.uk
research in quantitative finance, alternative investment etc

Dept of Politics & International Relations; www.politics.ox.ac.uk
comparative government, history and politics, international relations, philosophy, political theory, politics and economics, politics (comparative government/European politics and society/political theory), PPE; BA(Hons), DPhil, MLitt, MPhil, MSc

Dept of Social Policy & Intervention; www.spi.ox.ac.uk
comparative social policy, educational policy, evidence-based social intervention, family policy, ageing, poverty, inequality, health & social policy, housing & homelessness, social policy & the environment, labour markets/policy; BA, MPhil, MSc

Dept of Sociology; www.sociology.ox.ac.uk
political sociology, quantitative methods in politics and sociology, sociological theory, introduction to/sociology, sociology of industrial societies; BA(Hons), DPhil, MPhil, MSc

OXFORD BROOKES UNIVERSITY
www.brookes.ac.uk

Faculty of Business; www.brookes.ac.uk/about/faculties/business

Business School; www.business.brookes.ac.uk
accounting & finance, business & management/marketing management, economics, finance & international business/politics & international relations, international business/management, business management, applied accounting, international management/& international relations, international transport & logistics, HRM, business, management & communications, business & enterprise, e-business, international business/economics/trade & logistics, BA(Hons), BSc(Hons), Certs, DCM, DBA, Dips, MA, MBA, MRes, MSc, PhD, FdA

Oxford International Centre for Publishing; www.publishing.brookes.ac.uk
publishing, publishing media; BA(Hons), European Master's in Publishing; MA

Oxford School of Hospitality; www.hospitality.brookes.ac.uk
international hospitality management/& tourism management, international tourism & hotel marketing, food, wine & culture; BSc(Hons), MSc

Faculty of Human & Life Sciences; www.hls.brookes.ac.uk

Dept of Biological & Medical Sciences; www.bms.brookes.ac.uk
animal behaviour & wellbeing/biology & conservation, biological sciences, biology, biomedical science, biotechnology/with business, conservation ecology,

environmental management/science, human biology, biosciences, medical science, equine science/& management/thoroughbred management; BA(Hons)/BSc(Hons), MSc, PGDip, PhD, BMedSci

Dept of Clinical Health Care;
www.chc.brookes.ac.uk
adult/children's nursing, cancer studies, children's nursing, emergency care, health and social care, nursing studies, leadership in clinical practice, non-medical prescribing, palliative care, paramedic emergency practice; BScHons, FdSC, MA, MSc

Dept of Psychology;
www.psychology.brookes.ac.uk
psychology, cognitive neuroscience, developmental psychology; BSc(Hons), BA(Hons), MPhil, PhD, MSc, PGDip/Cert

Dept of Social Work & Public Health;
www.swph.brookes.ac.uk
management in/health & social care/studies, health promotion, social work, children, young people & family wellbeing, community childrens' nursing, district nursing, higher professional education, infection prevention & control, public health, specialist public health nursing; BSc(Hons), BA(Hons), PGDip/Cert, Cert HE, MA, MSc

Dept of Sport & Health Science;
www.shs.brookes.ac.uk
nutrition, occupational health, osteopathy, physiology, sport & exercise science, sports coaching & PE, sports science, applied human nutrition, applied sports & exercise nutrition, contemporary occupational therapy, rehabilitation; BSc(Hons), MSc, PGDip/Cert, MOst, MSc, PhD

Faculty of Humanities & Social Sciences; www.brookes.ac.uk/about faculties/hss

School of Education;
www.education.brookes.ac.uk
early/childhood studies, advanced early years specialisation, early years, e-pedagogy, gifted & talented education, artist teacher studies, educational studies, education & lifelong learning, English language & communications, education (leadership & management/TESOL), mentoring new teachers, working with literacy difficulties, PGCE primary/secondary/post-compulsory education, learning & teaching, primary teacher education, support for learning; BA(Hons), BA/BSc(Hons), CertEd, FdA, MA, MPhil, PGCE, PGDip, PhD

Dept of English & Modern Languages;
www.english-language.brookes.ac.uk
English, creative writing, drama, European business, culture & language, French, Spanish, Japanese studies; BA(Hons), MA

Dept of History, Philosophy & Religion
www.history.brookes.ac.uk
history, history of medicine, history of art, philosophy, religion & theology, communication, media & art, ministry; BA(Hons), MA, FdA

School of Law; www.law.brookes.ac.uk
law, international/economic/human rights/trade & commerce law, public international law, legal practice; BA/BSc, LlB, PGDip, GradDip, LlM

Dept of Social Sciences; www.social-sciences.brookes.ac.uk
anthropology, geography, international relations /& politics, primate conservation, international studies (international relations/global political economy/environment/security), international management & international relations/law, sociology, policing; BA/BSc, MA, MSc, GradDip, FdA

Faculty of Technology, Design & Environment; www.brookes.ac.uk/tde

School of Architecture; http://architecture.brookes.ac.uk
architecture, interior architecture, applied design in architecture; BA(Hons), MArch, MArchD, PhD

School of Arts; www.arts.brookes.ac.uk
fine art, composition & sonic art, contemporary art, & music, social sculpture; music, composition & sonic art, fine art: drawing for fine art practice, archaeological illustration, contemporary arts/& music, social sculpture, music & popular culture, music on stage and on screen, contemporary practice in composition, music in 19th-century culture, film studies; BA(Hons), BA/BSc, MA, MPhil, PhD

Dept of Planning; http://planning.brookes.ac.uk
environmental assessment & planning, spatial planning, historic conservation, city & regional planning, planning & property development, tourism environment & development, urban design/planning development & transitional regions; BA(Hons), MPlan, MSc, PhD, MPhil, PGCip/Cert

Dept of Real Estate & Construction; http://rec.brookes.ac.uk

construction, quantity surveying & commercial management, international/real estate, spatial planning, construction project management; BSc(Hons), MSc, PhD

Dept of Computing & Communication Technologies; http://cct.brookes.ac.uk

computer science, mobile computing, media technology, computer vision, computer games & animation, ebusiness, network computing, software engineering, multimedia production, sound technology & digital music, broadband networks, mobile & high-speed telecommunications, wireless communication science, digital media production; BSc(Hons), MSc, PhD

Dept of Mechanical Engineering & Mathematical Science; http://mems.brookes.ac.uk

mathematics, mathematical science, statistics, mechanical engineering, motorsport engineering, automotive engineering, computer aided mechanical engineering, adv engineering design, racing engine design, medical statistics; BSc(Hons), BA(Hons), BEng, MEng, MSc, MRes, MPhil, PhD

UNIVERSITY OF PLYMOUTH
www.plymouth.ac.uk

Faculty of Arts; www.plymouth.ac.uk/arts

School of Architecture, Design, Environment; www.plymouth.ac.uk/pages/view.asp?page=27259

architecture, architectural technology & the environment, architectural conservation, 3D design, design/service practice/spatial practice, sustainable futures, design thinking, building surveying & the environment, sustainable construction/cost management/project management, construction management & the environment; BA(Hons), MA, MRes, MArch, MSc

School of Art & Media; www.plymouth.ac.uk/schools/artmedia

creativity & enterprise, creative practice, digital art & technology, media & animation, graphic communication with typography, film & video, fine art, media arts, contemporary art/film practice, photography/& the book, publishing, TV arts; BA(Hons), MA, MArch, BA(Hons), GradDip, MA, MRes, PhD, MSc, BSc

School of Humanities & Performing Arts; www.plymouth.ac.uk/schools/hpa

art history, computer music, dance, literature, English & creative writing/history/French/Spanish/culture, fine art & art history, history with international relations/politics, music, performance practice, theatre & performance, the speaking dance; BA(Hons), MA, PGDip/Cert, MRes, PhD

Faculty of Health, Education & Society; www.plymouth.ac.uk/faculties/health

School of Social Science & Social Work; www.plymouth.ac.uk/schools/sssw

health & social care studies, mental health, social work, sociology, cognitive behavioural therapy, social & market/education research, social research & evaluation, sociology; BA(Hons), BSc(Hons), MA, MSc, PGDip

School of Nursing & Midwifery; www.plymouth.ac.uk/schools/nm

midwifery, adult/child health/mental health nursing, adv practice in education for health professionals, healthcare/service improvement, genetic healthcare; BSc(Hons), MSc, PGDip

School of Health Professions; www.plymouth.ac.uk/schools/hp

dietetics, mental health, neurological rehabilitation, adv/occupational therapy, adv professional practice (dietetic/neurological rehabilitation/occupational therapy/paediatric dietetics/physiotherapy), operating dept practice, optometry, paramedic practitioner (community emergency/studies), physiotherapy, podiatry, women's health, work & wellbeing; BSc(Hons), DipHE, MSc, PGCert, PGDip

School of Education; www.plymouth.ac.uk/schools/education

primary – art & design, digital literacy, early childhood studies, English, humanities, mathematics, music, PE, science, special education: early childhood studies (IMP) education, learning for sustainability, teaching & learning; PGCE; primary/early years, secondary (large range of secondary subjects), special educational needs coordination; BEd, Cert Ed, MA, MSc, Masters in Teaching & Learning, PGCE, Dip, PGCert, ProfDoc

Plymouth Business School; www.plymouth.ac.uk/faculties/pbs

Plymouth Law School; www.plymouth.ac.uk/schools/law

criminology & criminal justice studies, law, law with business studies/politics/psychology/sociology, legal practice; BA(Hons), BSc(Hons), LlB, LlM, MSc, PGDip

School of Management; www.plymouth.ac.uk/schools/man

accounting, business admin/economics/management/ studies, finance, business & management, marketing, economics/with international relations/law/politics, financial economics, HRM, international business/ economics/finance/logistics/management/trade & operations management/supply chain management/ shipping, maritime business & logistics, supply chain management, port management, public administration/management/services; BA(Hons), BSc(Hons), MA, MBA, DBA, MSc, PGCert/Dip, DMS, DPA

School of Tourism & Hospitality; www.plymouth.ac.uk/schools/th

business & tourism, cruise management, event management, international/hospitality management, hospitality tourism & events management, international tourism & marketing, tourism & hospitality management; BSc(Hons), BA(Hons), MSc, PGDip

Faculty of Science & Technology; www.plymouth.ac.uk/faculties/scitech

School of Biomedical & Biological Sciences; www.plymouth.ac.uk/schools/bio

animal behaviour/welfare, appl bioscience (aquaculture/plant sciences), biomedical/biological science/ diversity, healthcare science/nurition, exercise & health, human bioscience, environmental biology, life science, physiological sciences, sustainable aquaculture systems, zoo conservation; BSc(Hons), PGDip, MSc

School of Computing & Mathematics; www.plymouth.ac.uk/schools/compmath

applied statistics, computing, computer science/systems & networks, civil engineering, computer networks/engineering, computer & information security, computer systems & networks, games development, electrical & electronic engineering, mathematics/with statistics/education/finance, multimedia computing, network systems engineering, robotics, signal processing, web applications dev; BSc, MSc, MRes

School of Geography, Earth, & Environmental Science; www.plymouth.ac.uk/schools/sogees

analytical chemistry, applied/geology, environmental science/consultancy, extended science, holistic science, geography/& international relations/ocean science, physical geography, geosciences, planning, sustainable environmental management; BA(Hons), BSc(Hons), MGeol, MSc, MRes, MSc, PGCert

School of Marine Science & Engineering; www.plymouth.ac.uk/schools/mse

applied marine science, civil /coastal engineering, marine & composites technology, marine biology & coastal ecology/oceanography, marine studies (merchant shipping/navigation/ocean yachting), marine technology, mechanical design & manufacture, mechanical engineering technology & composites, ocean exploration/science, coastal engineering, hydrography, marine sport science/technology, marine renewable energy, navigation & marine science, ocean exploration science; BSc(Hons), MEng, MRes, MSc, BEng, FdSc, PGDip

School of Psychology; www.plymouth.ac.uk/schools/psychology

psychological studies, psychology/with law, human biology/sociology, criminology & criminal justice studies, psychology research methods; BSc(Hons), MSc, PGDip

Plymouth University Peninsular School of Medicine and Dentistry; www.pcmd.ac.uk

medicine, surgery, dentistry, clinical science/education, infection prevention & control, remote treatment, environmental & human health, diabetes, cardiovascular risk & ageing, neuroscience, health services, professional studies, public health, simulation & palliative studies/primary care/restorative dentistry/leadership/trauma,; MBBS, BDS, MD, MS, MPhil, PhD

Degrees validated by the University of Plymouth offered at:

SOUTH DEVON COLLEGE
www.southdevon.ac.uk

animal science, biosciences, business, computing, creative digital media, teaching in the lifelong learning sector, law, early years care & education, education, electrical & electronics engineering, engineering technology, exercise science & fitness, events & conference management, healthcare practice, illustrative arts, modern music production, outdoor education, performance practice & events management, 3D design, sustainable construction & building, tourism & hospitality management, uniformed public services, yacht operations; BSc(Hons), FD, HNC, HND, PGCE

TRURO & PENWITH COLLEGE
www.trurocollege.ac.uk

action photography, applied media, archaeology, bioscience, children & young people's workforce, commercial fashion/music, community & cultural studies, computer techniques, contemporary world jazz, community studies, complementary body therapies, counselling, dance, digital visualization, early childhood education, education/and training, education in lifelong learning sector, English studies, environmental & public health/nutrition, exercise, health & fitness, hairdressing & salon management, history & heritage, information, advice & guidance, interior design, law, libraries, museums & archives, management & business resources, media advertising, post-compulsory education & training, music performance, outdoor education, photography & digital imaging, public services, salon & spa management, silversmithing & jewellery, sound engineering, sports coaching & therapy/rehabilitation, web technology; BA(Hons), BSc, FdA, FdSc, HNC, HND, PCET, PGCE, UnivCert/Dip

UNIVERSITY OF PORTSMOUTH
www.port.ac.uk

Portsmouth Business School;
www.port.ac.uk/departments/faculties/portsmouthbusinessschool

Department of Accounting and Finance; www.port.ac.uk/departments/academic/accountingandfinance
accountancy, business, business English/communication, finance, & business/management, finance with business communication, financial decision analysis/management, forensic accounting, international finance & trade; BA(Hons), BSc(Hons), MSc

Department of Economics; www.port.ac.uk/departments/academic/economics
applied economics, business law, banking, economics & law, economics for business, business economics/finance & business/marketing, international/economics, business & enterprise, finance; BA(Hons), BScEcon(Hons), MA, MSc, PGDip

Department of Human Resource and Marketing Management; www.port.ac.uk/departments/academic/hrmm
business administration/studies/communication, coaching & development, digital marketing, hospitality management/with tourism, HRD, international/HRM, HRM with psychology, marketing/with digital business communications/psychology, sales management, training management & consultancy; BA(Hons), MA, MPhil, PGCert/Dip, PhD

School of Law; www.port.ac.uk/departments/academic/law
law with European studies/international relations/business/bus communications/criminology, corporate governance & law, international business law; BA(Hons), LlB, LlM

Department of Strategy and Business Systems; www.port.ac.uk/academic/sbs

business development/information technology, business management, European business, innovation management & entrepreneurship, international business studies, leadership & management, leadership in health & wellbeing, leadership, business & management, management, project management & leadership, risk management, strategic quality management; BA(Hons), FdA, HND, MBA, MSc, PGDip/Cert

Faculty of Creative and Cultural Industries; www.port.ac.uk/departments/faculties/facultyofcreativeartsandindustries

Portsmouth School of Architecture; www.port.ac.uk/departments/academic/architecture/

architecture, interior design, professional practice, sustainable architecture, urban design, historic building conservation; BA(Hons), MA, MArch, MSc

School of Art, Design and Media; www.port.ac.uk/departments/academic/adm

design for digital media, art, contemporary fine art fashion & textile design with enterprise, fine art, graphic design, illustration, photography; BA(Hons), MA

School of Creative Arts, Film and Media; www.port.ac.uk/departments/academic/scafm

creative & media writing, drama, English, entertainment technology, film & TV studies, media studies; BA(Hons), MA

School of Creative Technologies; www.port.ac.uk/departments/academic/ct

animation, computational sound, computer animation/games enterprise/technology, computing & digital sound, creative professional practice, digital media, entertainment technology, TV & film production/broadcasting, video & games technology; BA(Hons), BSc(Hons), FdSc, MSc

Faculty of Humanities and Social Science; www.port.ac.uk/departments/faculties/facultyofhumanities

Institute of Criminal Justice Studies; www.port.ac.uk/departments/academic/icjs

counter fraud & counter corruption studies, crime & criminology/community safety/criminal justice/criminal psychology/crime culture, forensic studies/psychology/accounting/IT, criminality, investigation & evidence, law/sociology & criminology, sociology & criminality, police studies, policing, policy & leadership, risk & security management; BSc(Hons), FdA, LlB, MScDCrim Studs

School of Education and Continuing Studies; www.port.ac.uk/departments/academic/iecs

childhood & youth studies/with psychology, early childhood studies/with psychology, early years care & education, education administration, education & training studies/management, PGCE in numerous subject courses/post-compulsory education, learning support, learning & teaching/in HE; BA(Hons), CertEd, FdA, MA, MSc, PGCE, PGCert, EYPS

School of Languages & Area Studies; www.port.ac.uk/departments/academic/slas

American studies & history, applied languages, combined modern languages, communication & English studies, English language, European studies, French studies, German studies, international trade & business, international development studies/& languages, international relations/trade & business communication, international trade, logistics & business communications, languages & European studies/law, linguistics & business English, logistics & business communications, Spanish & Latin American studies, technical communication, TESOL & language/English lit; BA(Hons), MA

School of Social, Historical and Literary Studies; www.port.ac.uk/departments/academic/sshls

English & history/media studies/languages & literature, English literature, European law & policy/studies, government, history/& politics, history of war, culture & society, international relations & history/politics/European studies, journalism/with English literature/media studies, media studies, politics, psychology, sociology/& criminology,

187

literature, culture & identity, public administration; BA(Hons), BSc(Hons), FdA, MPA, MSc

Faculty of Science; www.port.ac.uk/departments/faculties/faculty of science

School of Biological Sciences; www.port.ac.uk/departments/academic/biology

applied aquatic biology, biology, biochemistry, marine biology; BSc(Hons), MSc, MPhil, PhD, MRes

School of Earth and Environmental Sciences; www.port.ac.uk/departments/academic/isees

applied physics, engineering geology & geotechnics, environmental science, geological hazards, geology, marine environmental science, palaeobiology; BSc(Hons), MEng(Hons), MSc

Department of Geography; www.port.ac.uk/departments/academic/geography

environmental geography, coastal & marine resources management, geography, GIS, human geography, physical geography, science; BA(Hons), BSc(Hons), MSc

The Dental Academy; www.port.ac.uk/departments/academic/dentalacademy

dental hygiene/therapy nursing, science & dental therapy; BSc (Hons), CertHE, FdSc

School of Health Sciences and Social Work; www.port.ac.uk/departments/academic/shssw

applied clinical healthcare, child care social work, human physiology, language & communication science, operating dept practice, paramedic science, social work radiography (diagnostic/therapy), langauge & communication science; DipHE, FdSc, GradDip, BSc(Hons), MSc

Pharmacy & Biomedical sciences; www.port.ac.uk/departments/academic/pharmacy/

applied/biomedical science, pharmacy/practice, medicines management, pharmacology, biomedicine; FdSc, BSc(Hons), MSc

Psychology; www.port.ac.uk/departments/academic/psychology/

psychology, forensic/psychology, applied psychology of intellectual disabilities, child forensic studies, science; BSc(Hons), MSc, PGCert, MPhil, PhD

Sport & Exercise Science; www.port.ac.uk/departments/academic/sportscience/

sport & exercise science, sports development/business management/performance, clinical exercise science, science; BSc(Hons), MSc

Faculty of Technology www.port.ac.uk/departments/faculties/facultyoftechnology

Civil Engineering & Surveying; www.port.ac.uk/departments/academic/sces

civil engineering, construction engineering management, property development, environmental/geotechnical/ structural engineering, construction project management, quantity surveying; BSc(Hons), BEng(Hons), MEng, MSc

Computing; www.port.ac.uk/departments/academic/comp

business information systems, computer science, computing & information systems/digital image/information security, forensic computing, information technology, information systems/technology, software engineering, web technologies, forensic/IT; BSc(Hons), MSc

Mathematics; www.port.ac.uk/departments/academic/maths

mathematics, mathematics for finance & management/with statistics, logistics & transportation/supply chain management, supportability management; BSc(Hons) MSc,PgCert/Dip, MPhil, PhD

Engineering; www.port.ac.uk/departments/academic/eng

communication systems/engineering, computer-aided product design, computer engineering, computer networks, electronic engineering, electronic systems engineering, engineering & technology, mechanical & manufacturing engineering, mechanical engineering, petroleum engineering, product design & modern materials/innovation, adv manufacturing technology, technology management, adv manufacturing technology, communication network planning & management, computer network administration & management, digital systems engineering, electronic engineering, mechanical engineering, technology management; BSc(Hons), BEng(Hons), MEng, MSc

**Learning at Work; www.port.ac.uk/
departments/academic/learning atwork**
occupational health & safety management; PGCert, MSc

QUEEN MARGARET UNIVERSITY COLLEGE
www.qmuc.ac.uk

School of Arts, Social Sciences and Management; www.qmuc.ac.uk/assam
business management, events/festival management, film & media/media/PR/marketing, international hospitality management, hospitality and tourism management, marketing, international management & leadership, public service governance, retail business, theatre & film studies, acting for stage & screen, costume design & construction, drama and performance, film, media, PR, marketing, cultural management, psychology, sociology; BA/BA(Hons), BA(Hons), BSc(Hons), MA, MBA, PhD

The School of Health Sciences; www.qmuc.ac.uk/hs
applied pharmacology, audiology/hearing aid, dance movement therapy, human biology, dietetics, mammography, music therapy, nursing, nutrition, occupational & arts therapies, palliative/primary care, public health practice, psychology & sociology, physiotherapy, podiatry, radiography (therapy/diagnostic), speech & language therapy, person centred/social care workers, care; BSc(Hons), BA(Hons), MA, MSc, HECert,

Institute for International Health and Development; www.qmuc.ac.uk/iild
health systems, human resources for health, international health, sexual & reproductive health, social justice, development & health; PgDipCert, MSc, PhD

UNIVERSITY OF READING
www.reading.ac.uk

Faculty of Arts & Humanities; www.reading.ac.uk/fah

School of Arts & Communication Design; www.reading.ac.uk/sacd
Art: art, fine art, history of art, art & philosophy/film & theatre/psychology, history of art & ancient history/classics/English/architecture
Film, Theatre and Television: film & theatre & TV/English literature/art/film/German/Italian/history of art, theatre/film studies, theatre & history of art/German/Italian, English literature
Typography & Graphic Communication: graphic communication & English/history/history of art, book/information typeface design, typography & graphic communication; BA(Hons), MA, MA(Res), MFA, MPhil, PhD

School of Humanities; www.reading.ac.uk/humanities
Classics: ancient history, & history/history of art, the city of Rome, classical & medieval studies, classical studies & English/English literature/history of art, the classical tradition, classics
History of Art: history of art & architecture/art/English/history/ancient history/ classics
History: history, modern history, history & economics/English/European literature & culture/international relations/modern European languages/medieval studies
Philosophy: philosophy & ethics value/politics/modern European language; BA(Hons), MA, MPhil, PhD

School of Literature & Languages; www.reading.ac.uk/literature-and-languages

Dept of Modern Languages & European Studies; www.reading.ac.uk/modern-languages-and-european-studies/mles-home.aspx

French studies, French studies & English literature, French & history of art/economics/German/international relations/Italian/management studies/politics/history/philosophy/English language/international management & business administration; German studies, German studies & history of art/economics/French/international relations/Italian/management studies/politics/philosophy/English literature/film & theatre/international management & business administration/history; Italian studies, Italian studies & history of art/classical studies/economics/French/international relations/German/management studies/politics/English literature/history/philosophy; European Studies, European cultures & histories, English & European Literature & culture, Franco-British history, modern Italian history; BA(Hons), MA, MA(Res), PhD

Dept of English Language & Literature; www.reading.ac.uk/english-literature/ell-home.aspx

English language/& literature, applied linguistics, English, English language teaching, English literature & classical studies/French studies/history of art & architecture /German studies/Italian studies/history/international relations, English literature & culture/film & theatre/philosophy/politics & international relations, American literature; BA(Hons), MA, MA(Res), PhD

Dept of English Literature;

English/& politics and international relations/philosophy/film & theatre, English literature & classical studies, English & European literature & culture/French studies/German studies/history/history of art & architecture/Italian studies/international relations, modern & contemporary writing, children's literature, early modern literature & drama, 19th century literature; BA(Hons), MA, MA(Res)

Faculty of Social Sciences; www.reading.ac.uk/internal/fss

Institute of Education; www.reading.ac.uk/education

children's development & learning, early years, education (art/English/music specialism), theatre art, education & deaf studies, PGCE (secondary, primary, graduate teacher programme, subject knowledge enhancement), instrument teaching, education for sustainable global future; BA(Hons), FdA, PGCE, PhD, EdD

School of Law; www.reading.ac.uk/law

law, law & economics, advanced legal studies, European Union law & citizenship/governance, legal studies in Europe, international law & world order/commercial law/corporate finance/financial regulation/banking law, law & society, oil & gas; DPhil, LlB, LLM, MARes, MRes, MScPhD

School of Politics & International Relations; www.reading.ac.uk/spirs

international relations & politics/economics/English literature/history/philosophy/modern European language, politics & economics/English literature/history/philosophy/modern European language, public policy, international relations (diplomacy/international law & order/international security/strategy), war, peace & international relations, military history & strategy; BA(Hons), MA, MPhil, MRes, PhD

The School of Economics; www.reading.ac.uk/economics

banking and finance/business & management in emerging economies, business economics, econometrics, economic development in emerging markets, economics of climate change, economics of international business & finance, international business & economic development, public policy, international banking & financial services; BA(Hons), BSc(Hons), MSc, PhD

Henley Business School; www.henley.ac.uk

accounting, finance, informatics, management, real estate & planning; MBA, DBA, Masters, PhD

Faculty of Life Sciences; www.reading.ac.uk/internal/lifesci

School of Agriculture, Policy & Development; www.reading.ac.uk/apd

agriculture, agricultural business management/development economics, applied development studies, animal science, climate change & development, communications for innovation, consumer behaviour & marketing, development finance/policy, environment & development, environmental & countryside management, food marketing/& business security, research agricultural & food economics, social development & sustainable livelihoods; BA(Hons), BSc(Hons), MPhil, PhD

School of Biological Sciences; www.reading.ac.uk/biologicalsciences

applied ecology & conservation, biochemistry, biological sciences, biomedical sciences, food security & development, horticulture, microbiology, plant diversity, policy practice & processing, species identification & survey skills, wildlife management & conservation, zoology; BSc(Hons), MPhil, MSc, PhD

School of Chemistry, Food & Pharmacy; www.reading.ac.uk/fcfp

chemistry, food science/technology, forensic analysis, medical chemistry, nutrition & food science, pharmacy, quality assurance; BSc(Hons), MPharm, MSc, PhD

School of Psychology & Clinical Language Science; www.reading.ac.uk/pcls

psychology, childhood and ageing, psychology & maths/biology/philosophy/art, psychology – mental & psychological health, clinical aspects, speech & language therapy, cognitive neuroscience, development & psychopathology; BSc(Hons), MSc, PhD

Faculty of Science; www.reading.ac.uk/internal/facsci

School of Systems Engineering; www.reading.ac.uk/sse

artificial intelligence, computer science and informatics, cybernetics, digital signal processing & communications, electronic engineering, IT, robotics, software engineering, systems engineering; BEng, BSc(Hons), FdSc, MEng, MPhil, MRes, MSc, PhD

School of Construction Management and Engineering; www.reading.ac.uk/CME

building/quantity surveying, construction management, built environment/project management, intelligent buildings, renewable energy, technology & sustainability; BSc(Hons), MPhil, MSc, PGDip, PhD

School of Mathematical & Physical Sciences; www.smps.reading.ac.uk/

applied/meteorology, atmosphere, oceans & climate, computational mathematics, mathematics, mathematics and economics/meteorology/psychology, statistics/applied statistics, mathematics of scientific and industrial computation, meteorology, biometrics; BSc(Hons), MMath, MPhil, MSc, PhD

School of Human & Environmental Science; www.reading.ac.uk/shes

archaeology/with ancient history/classical studies/history/Italian/environmental science, medieval archaeology, geoarchaeology, geography/physical/human, economics, environmental management/science, soils & environmental pollution; BSc(Hons), MSc, MA, MPhil, PhD

ROBERT GORDON UNIVERSITY
www.rgu.ac.uk

Faculty of Health and Social Care

School of Applied Social Studies; www.rgu.ac.uk/social

applied social sciences, corporate responsibility & energy, mental health, social care/work, sociology; BA(Hons), GradCert, MSW, MSc, PGDip, PhD

School of Health Sciences; www.rgu.ac.uk/health

applied medical science, bioscience, biomedicine, biochemistry, forensic & analytical science, clinical practice, diagnostic radiography, occupational therapy, pharmacy, physiotherapy, radiography, applied sport & exercise science, sports nutrition & dietetics, laboratory, biochemical & sport sciences, analytical instrumental science; BSc(Hons), CertHE, MPhil, MSc, PhD, MN, BN, MPhysiotherapy

School of Nursing & Midwifery; www.rgu.ac.uk/nursing

acute/adult/children's/mental health/community nursing occupational health, adv clinical practice, children & young people, community health, midwifery; BN, DipHE, MPhil, MSc, PhD, MN, MRes, MNurs

School of Pharmacy & Life Sciences; www.rgu.ac.uk/pharmacy-life

applied/biomedical science, adv pharmacy practice, bioscience, nutrition, dietetics, pharmacy, prescribing science, clinical pharmacy, forensic & analytical science, instrumental analytical science; MPharm, MSc, PGDip, PhD, DocProfPract

Robert Gordon University

Aberdeen Business School;
www.rgu.ac.uk/abs

Accounting & Finance: accounting, finance, strategic accounting, financial management, oil & gas accounting

Management: int/business/management, HRM, marketing, management studies, project management, energy management, health, safety & risk management, international business management, oil & gas management, public administration, purchasing & supply chain management, quality management

Communication & Media: PR, journalism, media studies, publishing

Information management: information management, information & library studies

Events & Fashion Management: events/fashion management

Hospitality & Tourism: international hospitality/tourism management, management & marketing, corporate communication & public affairs, international marketing management

Law: law, law & management, online law, construction law & arbitration, employment law, international commercial/tax, oil & gas law, legal practice; BA/BA(Hons), DBA, DInfSc, LlB, LlM, MBA, MPA, MPhil, MSc, PGDip/Cert, PhD

Faculty of Design & Technology

School of Computing; www.rgu.ac.uk/computing

business information systems technology, computer science, computing for graphics & animation/internet & multimedia, information systems technology, computing: information engineering with network management, network management with design, applications of software design, forensic graphics & animation, internet, multimedia, digital media; design, production & development, software technology with network technology, information engineering, software technology, computer network management & engineering, communications & computer network engineering, engineering, multimedia development; BSc(Hons), MSc, PGCert/Dip

School of Engineering; www.rgu.ac.uk/eng

electrical/electronic/mechanical/offshore engineering, oil & gas /drilling & well/ petroleum production engineering, computer network management & engineering, communications & computer network engineering; BSc, BSc(Hons), MPhil, MSc, PhD

Gray's School of Art, Design & Craft; www.rgu.ac.uk/grays

art & design, commercial photography/design, contemporary art practice, design for digital media, fashion & textile design, fine art, painting, 3D design; BA/BA(Hons), BDes/BDes(Hons), MDes, MRes, PGDip/MAa

The Scott Sunderland School of Architecture and Built Environment; www.rgu.ac.uk/sss

advanced/architecture studies, architecture, architectural technology, construction project management, quantity/surveying; GradDip, MArch, MSc, PhD, BSc(Hons)

ROEHAMPTON UNIVERSITY
www.roehampton.ac.uk

Dept of Dance; www.roehampton.ac.uk/dance

ballet studies, dance anthropology/choreography/studies, SE Asia dance studies, community dancing, global dancing/politics/identities & institutions, teaching dance; BA, MA, PGDip/Cert, MRes

Dept of Drama, Theatre & Performance; www/roehampton.ac.uk/drama_theatre_and_performance

drama, theatre & performance studies, performance & creative research; BA(Hons), MPhil, MRes, PhD

Dept of English & Creative Writing; www.roehampton.ac.uk/english_and_creative_writing

creative/professional writing, modern literature & culture, English literature, children's literature; BA, MA, MPhil, PhD

Dept of Humanities; www.roehampton.ac.uk/humanities

classical civilization, classics, history, philosophy, Christian ministry, theology & religious studies, religion & gender, ministerial theology; BA, MTh, PGDip, MPhil, PhD

Department of Education;
www.roehampton.ac.uk/education

applied music (education), art, craft and design education, education leadership & management, early childhood studies, English education, PGCE (primary education/secondary education), social research methods, special education needs & inclusion, sports coaching, supporting learning & teaching; BA(Hons), BA/BSc, EdD, FdA, Froebel Cert and Grad Cert, MA, MPhil, PGCE Primary/Secondary, PhD

Dept of Life Sciences;
www.roehampton.ac.uklif-sciences

Anthropology: anthropology, biological anthropology

Biosciences & Health Sciences: biological/biomedical sciences, biomechanics, health studies/sciences, nutrition & health, ecology, clinical neuroscience/nutrition, health & community, obesity-risk & prevention, primate biology, behaviour & conservation, stress & health

Sport & Exercise Sciences: sport psychology, sport & exercise physiology/science; BA, BSc, MSC, MPhil, PGDip, PhD

Dept of Media, Culture & Language;
www.roehampton.ac.uk/media-culture-and-language

English language & linguistics, EFL, journalism, film/ & TV, language testing & assessment, media & culture studies, modern languages, photography, Spanish, French, TESOL, translation and interpreting, audiovisual translation, documentary practice, media, culture & identity; BSc, BA, MA, MRes, MPhil, PGDip, PhD

Dept of Psychology;
www.roehampton.ac.uk/psychology

applied music psychology, art psychotherapy, counselling, counselling psychology, forensic psychology, integrative counselling, psychotherapy, play/music/drama/dance movement therapy, attachment studies, applied psychological research; BSc, PsychD, MA, MPhil, PhD

Dept of Social Sciences;
www.roehampton.ac.uk/social-sciences

childhood & society, criminology, human rights & society/international relations, sociology; BA/BSc, BSc, MA, PGDip/Cert, PhD

Roehampton Business School;
www.roehampton/business

business management & accounting/economics/entrepreneurship/retail marketing/HRM, international business/management, marketing, international management with finance/HRM/information systems/marketing, HRM, web & creative technologies, finance, international supply chain & logistics management; MBA, PGDip/Cert, BA/BSc, BSc(Hons), MSc, MPhil, PhD

THE ROYAL ACADEMY OF DANCE
www.rad.org.uk

ballet education, dance education, professional dancer's teaching diploma; BA, PGCert

ROYAL ACADEMY OF DRAMATIC ART
www.rada.org

acting, technical theatre & stage management, theatre lab/directing, text & performance; BA, MA, PGDip, FD

ROYAL AGRICULTURAL COLLEGE
www.rac.ac.uk

agriculture (livestock production, crop production, farm mechanisation, farm business, countryside management, agricultural science & sustainable soil management), agricultural management, business management, countryside management, equine business & management, equine science, food production & supply management, environmental conservation & heritage management, global/international food industry, international rural development, international agri-food business, national and international real estate, property agency & management, rural estate management, rural land management, wine business management; FdSc, BSc(Hons), BSc(Hons) Top-up, GradDip, MSc, MA, MBA

ROYAL BALLET SCHOOL
www.royalballetschool.co.uk

classical ballet training, performing dancing/arts, professional dance; BTEC, NatDip

ROYAL COLLEGE OF ART
www.rca.ac.uk

School of Architecture; www.rca.ac.uk/Default.aspx?ContentID=160131
architecture, interior design

School of Communication; www.rca.ac.uk/Default.aspx?ContentID=160132
animation, information experience design, visual communication

School of Design; www.rca.ac.uk/Default.aspx?ContentID=501976
design interactions/products, innovation design engineering, service design, vehicle design

School of Fine Art; www.rca.ac.uk/Default.aspx?ContentID=160134
painting, photography, printmaking, sculpture

School of Humanities; www.rca.ac.uk/Default.aspx?ContentID=160135
critical writing in art & design, curating contemporary art, critical and historical studies, history of design

School of Material; www.rca.ac.uk/Default.aspx?ContentID=160133
ceramics & glass, fashion menswear/womenswear, goldsmithing, metalwork & jewellery, silversmithing, textiles; MA, MPhil, PGCert, PhD

ROYAL COLLEGE OF MUSIC
www.rcm.ac.uk

advanced vocal performance, composition, composition for screen, conducting, opera, performance, historical/orchestral performance, physics & musical performance, vocal studies; DipRCM, BMus, BSc, PGDip, MMus, DMus, GradDip, MPerf, MSc, ArtDip

THE ROYAL COLLEGE OF ORGANISTS
www.rco.org.uk

teaching, choral directing; CertRCO, ARCO, FRCO, LTRCO, DipCHD

ROYAL CONSERVATOIRE OF SCOTLAND
www.rsmad.ac.uk

School of Music
keyboard, education, vocal studies, opera, strings, woodwind, brass, timpani & percussion, Scottish music, composition, academic studies, conducting, jazz; BA(Hons), BMus(Hons), MA, MMus, MOpera, MPhil, PGDip, PhD

School of Drama
acting, classical & contemporary text, contemporary performance practice, digital film & TV, technical & production arts, musical theatre, directing

School of Dance
modern ballet; BA(Hons), BMus(Hons), MA, MMus, MOpera, MPhil, PGDip, PhD

ROYAL NORTHERN COLLEGE OF MUSIC
www.rncm.ac.uk

Schools: composition, keyboard studies, strings, vocal studies, wind, brass & percussion, musicology, music psychology, popular music practice/performance; BA(Hons), MusB, MMus, MPhil, PhD, BA(Hons)

UNIVERSITY OF ST ANDREWS
www.st-andrews.ac.uk

Faculty of Arts

School of Art History; www-ah.st-andrews.ac.uk
art history (with numerous joint degrees), history of photography, archaeology, modern languages (French & German) & ancient history, museum & gallery studies: GradCert, GradDip, MA, MLitt, MPhil, PhD

School of Classics; www.st-andrews.ac.uk/classics
ancient history & archaeology, classics, classical studies, Greek, Latin; MA, MLitt, MPhil, PGDip, PhD

School of Economics & Finance; www.st-andrews.ac.uk/economics
analytical finance, finance, applied economics/quantitative finance, economics, international strategy & economics, money, banking & finance, microeconomics, macroeconomics, sustainable development; BSc, MA, MSc, MPhil, PhD

School of English; www.st-andrews.ac.uk/english
creative writing, English, medieval English, Romantic/Victorian studies, Shakespeare & Renaissance literature, women, writing & gender; GradDip, MA, MLitt, MPhil, PhD

School of History; www.st-andrews.ac.uk/history
Arabic, book history, central & Eastern European studies, environmental history, history, Iranian studies, medieval history, Middle East studies/history, early/modern history, reformation studies, Scottish historical studies/history; GradDip, MA, DLitt, MPhil, PhD

School of International Relations; www.st-andrews.ac.uk/intrel

international relations (numerous jt hons degrees), international security studies, international political theory, Middle East & Central Asian security studies, peace & conflict, sustainable development, terrorism studies; MA, MLitt, MPhil, MRes, PhD

School of Management; www.st-andrews.ac.uk/management

corporate social responsibility/finance, finance & accounting/management, entrepreneurship/& small business development, global business management, HRM, information technology, dynamic strategic management, international business/marketing/banking, management, managing in the creative industries, marketing, organizational studies, sustainable development; BSc, DipRes, MA, MLitt, MSc, MRes, PhD

School of Modern Languages; www.st-andrews.ac.uk/modlang

Arabic, comparative literature, cultural identity studies, French/German/Italian studies, language/& linguistics, modern Hispanic literature & film, Russian, Central & Eastern European studies, Spanish, Spanish & Latin American studies, medieval studies; DLang, MA, MLitt, MPhil, PGDip, PhD

School of Philosophical, Anthropological & Film Studies; www.st-andrews.ac.uk/philosophy

Philosophy: analytical/classical philosophy, logic & philosophy of science, philosophy of Scottish enlightenment, Kant, metaphysics, political philosophy, advanced logic, philosophy of perception, contemporary metaphysics

Social Anthropology: social anthropology & Pacific studies, Americindian studies, anthropology, art & perception

Film Studies: film studies, film culture, theory of entertainment film theory & history, world cinema

Music: opera, advanced performance, Scottish/bagpipe/electronic music; BSc, MA, MLitt, MPhil, MRes, PhD

Faculty of Divinity

School of Divinity; www.st-andrews.ac.uk/divinity

bible & the contemporary world, biblical studies, divinity, New Testament, Old Testament, theological studies/interpretation of scripture, biblical language & literature, scripture & theology, systematic & historical theology; BD, MA, MLitt, MPhil, MTheol, PGDip, PhD

Faculty of Medicine

Bute Medical School; www.medicine.st-andrews.ac.uk

health psychology, medicine, surgery, community health, molecular medicine; BSc, MD, MPhil, MSc, PhD, MRes

Faculty of Science

School of Biology; www.biology.st-andrews.ac.uk

behavioural biology, biochemistry, biology, biology & geology/psychology, cell biology/ecology & conservation, environmental biology/& geography, marine biology, molecular biology, neuroscience, psychology with biology, zoology, marine mammal science, ecosystem-based management of marine systems, environmental, behavioural & neural sciences, sustainable aquaculture; BSc, MPhil, MRes, PhD, PG Dip/MSc

School of Chemistry; www.ch.st-andrews.ac.uk

biomolecular/chemical sciences, biological chemistry, inorganic/physical/organic chemistry, materials science, medicinal chemistry; BSc, MChem, MSci, PGDip, PhD,PG Dip/MSc

School of Computer Science; www.cs.st-andrews.ac.uk

advanced/computer science, AI, component technology, dependable software systems, internet programming, internet computer science, information technology, computer management & IT, networks & distributed systems, software engineering; BSc, MPhil, MSc, PhD, MSci(Hons)

School of Geography & Geosciences; www.st-andrews.ac.uk/gg

environmental geoscience/history, evolutionary biology, geography, geoscience, geology, general sciences, earth sciences, managing environmental change, sustainable development; BSc, MA, MLitt, MPhil, MRes, MSc, PGCert, PGDip, PhD, MGeol

School of Mathematics & Statistics; www.maths.mcs.st-andrews.ac.uk

applied mathematics/statistics & data mining, mathematics, pure mathematics, statistics; BSc, GradDip, MA, MLitt, MMath, MPhil, MSc, PhD

School of Physics & Astronomy; www.st-andrews.ac.uk/physics
astrophysics, physics, theoretical physics, photonics & optoelectronic devices; BSc, EngDoc, MPhys, MSc, PhD, MSci

School of Psychology; www.psy.st-andrews.ac.uk
behavioural & neural sciences, evolutionary & comparative psychology, learning disabilities, neuroscience, perception, psychology, health psychology; BSc, MA, MPhil, MRes, MSc, PhD

UNIVERSITY OF SALFORD
www.salford.ac.uk

College of Arts & Social Sciences; www.famss.salford.ac.uk

School of Art & Design; www.salford.ac.uk/art-design
advertising design, animation, art & design, arts & museum management, communication design, computer & video games, contemporary fine art, creative games/technology, design for digital media/management/the creative industries, design futures, fashion, graphic design, heritage studies, interior design, journalism & design studies, museum & heritage exhibition design, photography, product design, visual arts; BA(Hons), BSc(Hons), HND, MA, PGDip, PhD

School of Humanities, Languages & Social Sciences; www.salford.ac.uk/humanities
contemporary history & politics, contemporary military & international history, criminology/& sociology, drama, creative writing, English, English language/& linguistics/English literature, international relations & politics, law with criminology, modern language studies (Arabic/French/Spanish/French and EFL/Italian), politics, psychology & criminology, sociology, intelligence & security services, translation & interpreting (combinations of Arabic/EFL/Chinese/French/German/Italian), international relations & globalisation, literary culture & production, terrorism & security, TESOL & applied linguistics, translating for foreign management & business; BA(Hons), MA, PGDip/Cert

School of Media, Music & Performance; www.smmp.salford.ac.uk
animation, film studies, TV & radio, computer & video games, TV documentary, fiction, film production, wildlife documentary, film screenwriting, post production for TV & film, TV & radio scriptwriting, journalism, media technology, professional broadcast techniques, social meda, music, performance, digital performance, film screenwriting; BA(Hons), BSc(Hons), MA, PGDip/Cert

Salford Business School; www.salford.ac.uk/business-school
business & management studies/with law, business information technology, business management, business studies with financial management/HRM/international business management/marketing/ quantitative business management, business with economics, events management, finance & accounting, hospitality/& tourism, management, leisure/& tourism management, financial services management, HRM/& development, information systems management, international banking & finance/business/corporate finance/events management/management, Islamic banking and finance, marketing, procurement, logistics & supply chain management, project management, The Salford MBA; BA(Hons), BSc(Hons), CertHE, DipHE, FD, GradCert, HNC, HND, MA, MBA, MPhil, ProfDip, ProfPGDip, PhD

Salford School of Law; www.salford.ac.uk/law
construction law & practice, environmental/health case law, international law & regulation, law/& criminality/finance/Spanish; LlB, LlM, MA, MSc, PGCert/Dip

College of Health & Social Care; www.fhsc.salford.ac.uk

School of Health Science; www.salford.ac.uk/health-science
sports science (strength & conditioning), diagnostic radiography, exercise, physical activity & health, occupational therapy, physiotherapy, podiatry, prosthetics & orthotics, psychology & counselling/criminology, psychology, sport rehabilitation, adv medical imaging (radiology), adv medical imaging (ultrasound), adv occupational therapy, advancing physiotherapy, applied psychology (therapies), dental

implantology, lower limb health, disease & rehabilitation, upper limb orthopaedics, media psychology, nuclear medicine imaging, psycho-oncology, public health, sports injury rehabilitation, strength & conditioning, surgical practice, trauma orthopaedics; BSc(Hons), MSc, PgDip/PgCert

School of Nursing, Midwifery & Social work; www.salford.ac.uk/nmsw

midwifery, nursing/RN children & young people's/adult/mental health, professional counselling studies, integrated practice in learning disability nursing/& social work, social policy, adv practice (health & social care/neonatal), cognitive behavioural psychotherapy/therapy,child & adolescent mental health, counselling & psychotherapy, international hospital & health care management, leadership & management for health care practice, nursing, (education, research, practice, international), midwifery, health & social care, health care, counselling, adult care, child care, therapeutic interventions, enhancing professional health care practice; BSc(Hons), MA, ProfDoc, MSc, PgDip/PgCert

College of Science & Technology; www.fsee.salford.ac.uk

School of the Built Environment; www.sobe.salford.ac.uk

accessibility & building design, architectural design & technology, BIM & integrated design, building surveying, construction & property, construction law & practice/management, digital architectural design, facilities management, project management in construction, property management & investment, quantity surveying (mechanical & electrical), real estate development/management, sustainable building design, urban design; BSc(Hons), DBEnv, DConst-Mangt, DRealEst, MSc, PGDip/Cert, PhD, ProfDoc

School of Computing, Science & Engineering; www.cse.salford.ac.uk

acoustics, advanced control systems, adv computer science, aeronautical engineering, aerospace design & manufacture/engineering, aircraft engineering, animation, audiotechnology/production, aviation technology, civil/& architectural engineering, computer networks/science, creative games, data telecommunications & networks, databases and web-based systems, digital broadcast technology, gas engineering & management, industrial & commercial combustion engineering, information security management, internet computing, interactive media, manufacturing systems & management, materials physics, mathematics, mechanical engineering, multimedia & internet technology, petroleum & gas engineering, pure & applied/physics, pilot studies, professional sound & video technology, robotics & automation, software engineering, space technology, sound & video technology, structural engineering, transport engineering & planning, vacuum engineering & applications; BEng, BSc(Hons), HND, MEng, MEnt(Tech), MPhys, MSc, PGDip, PG(Tech)

School of Environmental & Life Sciences; www.els.salford.ac.uk

applied microbiology, applied bioscience, biology, human biology & infectious disease, wildlife & practical conservation, wildlife conservation with zoo biology, zoology

Biomedicine: biochemistry, biomedical science, pharmaceutical science

Environment: environmental studies/health/management, geography

Bioscience: analytical bioscience & drug design, biotechnology, molecular parasitology & vector biology

Geography: GIS

Environmental Studies: environmental assessment & management, environmental/& public health, occupational safety & health, safety, health & environment

Housing & Regeneration: housing, regeneration & sustainability

Wildlife: wildlife documentary production

BSc(Hons), BA(Hons), MSc, MA, FD

Degrees validated by University of Salford offered at:

RIVERSIDE COLLEGE, HALTON
www.riversidecollege.ac.uk

business & management, childcare, counselling, health and social care, sport, teacher education and teaching assistants; Dip, FD, FdSc, PGDip

UNIVERSITY OF SHEFFIELD
www.sheffield.ac.uk

Faculty of Arts & Humanities;
www.sheffield.ac.uk/faculty/arts-and-humanities

Dept of Archaeology; www.sheffield.ac.uk/archaeology
archaeology, archaeology, religion, theology & the bible, archaeological materials, archaeology & history/Slavonic studies/Hispanic studies/French/German, Aegean/classical & ancient world, environmental archaeology & palaeoeconomy, European historical archaeology/prehistory, experimental archaeology, geoarchaeology, human osteology and funerary archaeology, landscape archaeology, material culture studies, palaeoanthropology, cultural heritage management, medieval archaeology, environmental archaeology & palaeoeconomy, osteoarchaeology, cultural heritage management; BA(Hons), BSc(Hons), MA, MPhil, MSc, PhD, MSt

Dept of Biblical Studies; www.sheffield.ac.uk/biblicalstudies
archaeology/the bible & ancient cultures, biblical sites, religion, theology & the Bible/& linguistics, religion, conflict & theology, biblical literature and English, French/German/philosophy & religion, theology and music, theological studies, social scientific biblical studies; BA(Hons), MA, PGDip/Cert

Dept of French; www.sheffield.ac.uk/french
French studies, French & archaeology/business management/economics/English/German/ Hispanic studies/history/journalism/linguistics/music/philosophy/politics/ religion/Russian, modern languages; BA(Hons), MA, MPhil, PhD

School of English Literature, Language and Linguistics; www.sheffield.ac.uk/english
18th/19th-century studies, applied linguistics with TESOL, creative writing, culture of the British Isles, English language studies, English literature, English language & linguistics, language acquisition, theatre & performance studies; BA(Hons), MA, MPhil, PhD

Dept of Germanic Studies; www.sheffield.ac.uk/german
German studies, German & archaeology/business management/economics/English/French/Hispanic studies/history/journalism/linguistics/music/ philosophy/politics/ religion/Russian, modern languages, 19th century studies, historical research, applied linguistics; BA(Hons), MPhil, PhD

Dept of Hispanic Studies; www.sheffield.ac.uk/hispanic
Hispanic studies & archaeology/business management/economics/English/French/Hispanic studies/history/journalism/linguistics/music/philosophy/politics/ religion/Russian, applied Hispanic studies, Catalan studies, Portuguese studies, Latin American studies, BA(Hons), MA, MPhil, PhD

Dept of History; www.sheffield.ac.uk/history
18th/19th-century studies, American history, early/modern history, historical research, history, international/medieval/ history; BA(Hons), MA, MPhil, PhD

School of Languages & Cultures; www.sheffield.ac.uk/slc
Catalan, Czech, Dutch, French, German, Hispanic studies, European gender studies, intercultural communication, modern languages, multilingual information management, Polish, Russian, Russian and Slavonic studies, screen translation, translation studies; BA(Hons), MA, MPhil, PhD

Department of Music; www.sheffield.ac.uk/music
ethnomusicology, music, music management/performance, music psychology in education, psychology of music/for musicians sonic arts, world music, numerous jt degrees; BA(Hons), BMus(Hons), DPhil, MA, MMus, PhD

Dept of Philosophy; www.sheffield.ac.uk/philosophy
philosophy, metaphysics, epistemology, logic, philosophy of language & the mind, ethics, politics & value, political theory, cognitive studies, numerous joint degrees; BA(Hons), MA, MPhil, PhD

Russian & Slavonic Studies; www.sheffield.ac.uk/russian
Russian studies, Polish studies, Czech, translation studies, screen translation, intercultural communication, multilingual information management, numerous jt degree courses; BA(Hons), MA, MPhil, PhD

Faculty of Engineering;
www.sheffield.ac.uk/faculties/
engineering

Dept of Aerospace Engineering; www.sheffield.ac.uk/aerospace

aerospace materials/engineering, aerospace engineering with private pilot instruction, aerostructures & aerodynamics, avionics, control systems; BEng, MEng, MPhil, MSc, PhD, PGDip

Dept of Automatic Control & Systems Engineering; www.sheffield.ac.uk/acse

control systems, gas turbine control, computer systems engineering, electronic/mechanical systems engineering, mechatronics, systems & control engineering; BEng, MEng, MPhil, MSc, PhD

Dept of Bioengineering; www.sheffield.ac.uk/bioengineering

bioengineering, biomedical engineering, biomaterials science with tissue engineering, biological systems bioprocessing, medical devices & systems; BEng, MEng

Dept of Chemical & Biological Engineering; www.sheffield.ac.uk/cbe

biological and bioprocessing engineering, chemical engineering, chemical & process engineering, environmental & energy engineering, fuel technology, process safety & loss prevention; BEng, MEng, MPhil, MSc, MSc(Eng), PhD

Dept of Civil & Structural Engineering; www.sheffield.ac.uk/civil

architectural engineering design, civil/structural engineering, civil structures, contaminant hydrogeology, earthquake & civil engineering dynamics, environmental management of urban land & water, groundwater & water engineering, steel construction, structural/& concrete engineering, urban water engineering & management; BEng, MEng, MPhil, MSc, PGDip/Cert, PhD

Dept of Computer Science; www.sheffield.ac.uk/dcs

advanced computer science, advanced software engineering, computer science with speech & language processing, enterprise computing, software engineering, AI, data communications, information systems, information technology management for business, software systems & internet technology; BEng, BSc, MComp, MEng, MPhil, MSc, MSc(Eng), PhD

Dept of Electronic & Electrical Engineering; www.sheffield.ac.uk/eee

avionic systems, computer vision engineering, data communications, digital electronics, semiconductor photonics & electronics, electrical/communications/electronic engineering, microelectronics; BEng, MEng, MPhil, MSc, PhD

Dept of Materials Science & Engineering; www.sheffield.ac.uk/materials

aerospace materials, adv metallurgy, materials science & engineering, biomaterials/& regenerative medicine, metallurgy, ceramic science & engineering, polymers & polymer composites, adv solid state chemistry, industrial management, nuclear environmental science/technology, nanomaterials for nanoengineering, bionanotechnology; BEng, EngD, MEng, MPhil, MSc, MRes, PhD

Dept of Mechanical Engineering; www.sheffield.ac.uk/mecheng

advanced mechanical engineering, advanced manufacturing technology, aerodynamics & aerostructures, automotive engineering, mechanical engineering with Spanish/French/Italian/German/industrial management, nuclear technology; BEng, MEng, MPhil, MSc, MSc(Res), PhD

Faculty of Medicine, Dentistry & Health;
www.sheffield.ac.uk/faculties/
medicine-dentistry-health

The Medical School; www.sheffield.ac.uk/medicine

cancer, human metabolism/nutrition, infection & immunity, medicine, medical education, molecular/& genetic medicine, musculoskeletal science, nephrology, neuroscience, orthoptics, surgery, vision & strabismus, pharmacokinetics/dynamics; BMedSci, MBChB, MD, PhD, PGCert/Dip

Dept of Cardiovascular Science; www.sheffield.ac.uk/cardiovascularscience

cell biology, coronary artery disease, haemostasis, medical physics, molecular medicine – cardiovascular pathway, non-mammalian models, pulmonary vascular, platelets, inflammatory signals, translational neuroscience, vascular biology; MPhil, PhD, DM

School of Clinical Dentistry; www.sheffield.ac.uk/dentalschool
adult dental care, dental hygiene and therapy, dental implantology, dental materials science, dental public health, dental surgery, dentistry, oral pathology, oral health, orthodontics, paediatric dentistry, periodontics, restorative dentistry, social science & oral health; BDS, ClinDent, Diploma, MSc, MClinD, MDPH, MMedSci, MPhil, PhD

Health & Related Research; www.sheffield.ac.uk/scherr
adv emergency care, clinical research, health services, public health (management & leadership, international development), economics/health economics & decision modelling, European public health, health informatics, international health, technical assessment, psychotherapy studies, social science & health, statistics appl to medicine; MSc, PGDip/Cert, MPH, MEuro PubHealth

Dept of Human Communication Sciences; www.sheffield.ac.uk/hcs
cleft palate studies, clinical/human communication sciences, language & communication impairment in children, speech/difficulties; AdvCert, BMedSci(Hons), BSc(Hons), MMedSci, MPhil, MSc, PGCert/Dip, PhD

Dept of Human Metabolism; www.sheffield.ac.uk/humanmetabolism
molecular medicine, translational neuroscience; BMedSci, MSc, MRCPsych

Dept of Infection & Immunity; www.sheffield.ac.uk/infectionandimmunity
molecular medicine, translational neuroscience; BMedSci, MSc, MRCPsych

Dept of Neuroscience; www.sheffield.ac.uk/neuroscience
clinical neurology of translational neuroscience, neuroscience; BMedSci, MSc, MRCPsych

Dept of Oncology; www.sheffield.ac.uk/oncology
clinical oncology, cancer studies, supportive care, surgical oncology, urology, inflammation & tumour targeting, MSc, MSD, PhD

School of Nursing & Midwifery; www.sheffield.ac.uk/snm
acute care, cancer care, advanced nursing studies, advancing practice, enhancing neonatal practice, health & social care studies/human sciences, high dependency & critical care, infection control, long term conditions, maternity care, midwifery nursing studies, occupational health nursing, palliative care, public health, primary/critical/cancer/neonatal intensive care; BMedSci, MMedSci, MMid, MPhil, PGCert, PhD

The Faculty of Science; www.sheffield.ac.uk/faculties/science

Dept of Animal & Plant Science; www.sheffield.ac.uk/aps
animal behaviour, biology, conservation & biodiversity, ecology, plant sciences, evolution & behaviour, plant-environment interaction/science, ecology & conservation biology/environment, plant & microbiol biology, molecular science, plant science, plant-environment interchange, population & community ecology, zoology; MBiolSci, PhD, MPhil, MEnv Sci

Dept of Biomedical Science; www.sheffield.ac.uk/bms
biomedical science/with biomaterials & tissue engineering, molecular & cellular basis of human disease, developmental & cell biology, physiology & pharmacology, medical science stem cell & regenerative medicine; BSc(Hons), MSc, PhD

Dept of Chemistry; www.sheffield.ac.uk/chemistry
chemistry, polymers for advanced technologies, science communication, biological chemistry, chemical physics; BSc, MChem, MPhil, MPhys, PhD

Dept of Molecular Biology & Biotechnology; www.sheffield.ac.uk/mbb
biochemistry, biology, genetics, medical genetics/microbiology, microbiology, molecular/cell biology, biology, mechanistic biology, microbrewing; BSc(Hons), MBiolSci, PhD

Dept of Physics & Astronomy; www.sheffield.ac.uk/physics
astronomy, astrophysics, medical physics, nanoscale science and technology, nanoelectronics & nanomechanics, physics, theoretical physics; BS(Hons), MPhys, MSc, PhD

Dept of Psychology; www.sheffield.ac.uk/psychology
cognitive studies/neuroscience, cognitive & computational neuroscience, human neuroimaging, science communication, psychology, psychological research; BA(Hons), BSc(Hons), DClinPsych, MA, MPhil, MSc, PhD

School of Mathematics & Statistics; www.math.dept.sheac.uk/maths
mathematics, financial maths, statistics/with medical applications; BSc, MSc, PhD, MMath, MComp

Faculty of Social Science; www.sheffield.ac.uk/faculty/social-science

School of Architecture; www.sheffield.ac.uk/architecture
architectural design, architecture/& landscape, computer-aided environmental design, conservation & regeneration, designing learning environments, structural engineering, sustainable architectural studies, urban design; BA(Hons), MArch, MPhil, MSc, PhD, MEng

School of East Asian Studies; www.sheffield.ac.uk/seas
Chinese studies, East Asian studies, Japanese studies, Korean studies, teaching Chinese as foreign language; BA(Hons), MA, PhD

Dept of Economics; www.sheffield.ac.uk/economics
development economics & policy, accounting, business finance, economics, economics & mathematics/politics/philosophy/ finance/management, financial economics, health economics, international finance and economics, money, banking & finance; Adv Cert, BA(Hons), BSc(Hons), MSc, PhD

Sheffield School of Law; www.sheffield.ac.uk/law
biotechnological law and ethics, commercial law, law (European & international), law with French/German/Spanish/criminology, social policy & criminology, European health law & policy, criminology, international commercial law & practice, global policy & law, European law, politics & governance, legal practice; LlB, LlM, MAPhil, PhD, GradDip

Sheffield Management School; www.sheffield.ac.uk/management
accounting & financial management/& economics/informatics/mathematics, HRM, information systems management, business management & economics/informatics/sociology/social policy/various foreign language studies/mathematics, entrepreneurship, international business management/management & marketing, leadership, management, logistics & supply chain management, management (creative & cultural industries/international business), marketing management practice, occupational/work psychology; MSc, MPhil, PhD, Sheffield MBA, ExecMBA

Dept of Politics; www.sheffield.ac.uk/politics
politics, European law/& global affair/governance & politics, contemporary global security, international politics/relations/history/political economy/security studies, sociology, global politics and law security/justice, globalisation & development, governance & public policy, politics/ & history/sociology/economics/philosophy, French/German /Russian, international studies, philosophy, political theory; BA, MA, MPhil, PhD

Dept of Sociological Studies; www.sheffield.ac.uk/socstudies
business management & social policy/sociology, criminology, global & international/social policy, social policy/work, sociology & English language/history/politics/criminology, professional practice; BA(Hons), MA, MPhil, PhD

Dept of Town & Regional Planning; www.sheffield.ac.uk/trp
architecture/ & town & regional planning, commercial property, geography, international development & planning, landscape architecture, planning /& development, planning research, town & regional planning, urban studies/design & planning, TR; BA(Hons), MA, MPlan, PhD

The School of Education; www.sheffield.ac.uk/education
education, culture & children, globalising education, policy & practice, PGCE (English, geography, history, mathematics, modern languages & science), initial teacher education, psychology & education, working with communities: identities, regeneration and change, educational research; EdD, MA, MEd, MPhil, PhD, PCHE

Dept of Geography; www.sheffield.ac.uk/geography
arid land studies, environmental science/change & international development, geography & planning, human geography, international development, polar & alpine change, social & cultural geography, environmental analysis of terrestrial systems, physical geography, social & spatial inequalities; BA(Hons), BSc(Hons), MEnvSci, PhD

School of Information; www.sheffield.ac.uk/is

accounting & financial management, informatics & business management, electronic & digital library management, health informatics, information literacy, information management/in business, information systems/management, librarianship, multilingual information management; MA, MChem, MSc, MSc(Res), PhD/MPhil

Dept of Journalism Studies; www.sheffield.ac.uk/journalism

global/magazine/web journalism journalism studies, international political communication, broadcast/print/web/science journalism; BA, MPhil, PhD

Dept of Landscape; www.sheffield.ac.uk/landscape

landscape architecture/with ecology/planning, landscape management, architecture & landscape, landscape studies, landscape research; BA(Hons), BSc(Hons), MA, PGDip, PhD, MLA

SHEFFIELD HALLAM UNIVERSITY
www.shu.ac.uk

Faculty of Arts, Computing, Engineering & Science; www.shu.ac.uk/art/faculties.aces

Art & Design; www.shu.ac.uk/prospectus/subject/art-design/

animation & special effects, creative art practice, design & technology education, fashion design, graphic design, industrial practice/design, interior design, product design/jewellery & fashion, product design finance, networking & journalism; BA(Hons), MA, MArt, MDes

Media, PR & Journalism; www.shu.ac.uk/prospectus/subject/media-pr-journalism/

corporate/communication, international broadcast journalism, PR, film & media production, media, professional communication, journalism, technical communication, cultural policy & management; BA(Hons), MA, MPhil, PhD, PGCert/Dip

Computing; www.shu.ac.uk/prospectus/subject/computing/

animation for special effects/computer games, applied computing, business information systems, computing, computer & network engineering/information security, computer science, computer security with forensics, database professionals, digital media production, electronics/management & IT, forensic & security technologies, games & interactive technology, games/software design, IT professional (databases), information systems/security/with SAP, internet media with animation, internet & management, mobile computing applications, multimedia technology, networking technology & management/design, software engineering, web & cloud computing, web systems design; BEng, BSc(Hons), FDSc, GradDip, HND, MComp, MSc

Engineering; www.shu.ac.uk/prospectus/subject/engineering/

aeronautical/aerospace/electronic engineering, advanced design/aeronautical materials engineering/engineering metals, automotive & control engineering, automotive design/manufacturing engineering, computer-aided engineering, design technology, advanced engineering & management, computer & network engineering, design technology, electrical & electronic engineering, electronics & information technology, energy engineering, forensic engineering, industrial management, integral engineering, logistics & supply chain management, materials engineering, mechanical engineering, mobile computing applications, engineering materials & product design, software development/engineering, sports technology, telecommunication engineering; BSc(Hons), BEng FdSc, MBA, MSc, PhD

Mathematics; www.shu.ac.uk/mathematics

specialist teaching, education & QTS, mathematics & education, mathematics; BSc(Hons), MSc, PhD

Media Arts; www.shu.ac.uk/prospectus/subject/media-arts/

animation/& special effects, computer games, digital media production, games design/software development, international documentary production, fine art, journalism, interactive/media, photography, PR & media; BA(Hons), MA, MComp, MArt

Faculty of Development & Society;
www.shu.ac.uk/faculties/ds

Built Environment; www.shu.ac.uk/prospectus/subject/construction-building-surveying/

architectural technology, architecture, construction & community management, environmental design, building surveying/studies, built environment, construction/management & real estate, planning & property development, project management, quantity surveying, real estate; BSc(Hons), HNC, HND, MPhil, MSc, PGDip/Cert, PhD

Criminology & Community Justice; www.shu.ac.uk/prospectus/subject/law/

criminology & psychology/sociology/politics, forensic criminology, international criminal justice; BEng, BSc(Hons), FdSc, MA/PgDip/PgCert, MSc

Education; www.shu.ac.uk/prospectus/subject/education-studies/

Asperger's syndrome, autism spectrum, children & playwork, early/childhood studies, early years/education with QTS, design & technology, education, education & disability studies/learning support, English & educational studies, languages & TESOL, learning & teaching in HE, mentoring & coaching in educational leadership/early years mathematics with education, technologically enhanced learning, analysis & change, teaching & learning in the primary sector/with QTS/early years, special knowledge enhancement (various subjects), education studies, learning & skills, education & training, primary ed with QTS, design & technology/science with education & QTS, PGCE (early years education, learning & skills, primary, secondary – broad range of taught subjects – secondary citizenship), post education education & training, youth work; BA(Hons), CertE, EdD, FdA, MA, MPhil, MSc, PGCert/Dip, PhD

Environment; www.shu.ac.uk/prospectus/subject/environment/

environmental management business/international resource & climate management, wildlife & landscape conservation/science, sustainable communities & environment, environmental conservation/science/studies, public rights of way & countryside access; BA(Hons), BSc(Hons), MPlan, MSc/PGDip/PGCert

English; www.shu.ac.uk/prospectus/subject/english/

creative writing, history, English/language/literature, Shakespeare & Renaissance literature, writing; BA(Hons), MA, PgDip, MPhil, PhD

History; www.shu.ac.uk/prospectus/subject/history/

history, English & history, criminology, politics, local & global, history, imperialism & culture; BA(Hons), MA, PGDip, MPhil, PhD

Stage & Screen; www.shu.ac.uk/prospectus/subject/stage-screen/

animation & visual effects, film studies, film and media/production, international documentary production, performance & professional practice/for stage & screen, screenwriting, performing arts/music, drama; BA(Hons), FdA, MA, MA/PGDip/PGCert

Geography; www.shu.ac.uk/prospectus/subject/geography/

geography/with planning, GIS, human geography; BA(Hons), BSc(Hons), MSc, PGDip/Cert

Forensics; www.shu.ac.uk/forensics

analytical chemistry, biochemical laboratory sciences, biomedical sciences, analytical criminology/engineering/psychology, intelligence & forensics management, forensic & security technologies, forensic science, pharmaceutical analysis, pharmacology & biotechnology; BSc(Hons), FdSc, MSc

Law; www.shu.ac.uk/prospectus/subject/law/

antisocial behavioural law & strategy, business law, criminality & community, international commercial law, forensic accounting/criminology/psychology/science, law, law and criminology, maîtrise en droit Frañcais; LlB, LLM, MSc, PGCert/Dip

Planning, Regeneration & Housing; www.shu.ac.uk/planning/

geography & planning, GIS, housing for environmental health, housing policy and practice/professions, int real estate, sustainable communities/and environments, transport/planning and management, urban and regional/environmental planning, urban regeneration; BA(Hons), BSc(Hons), MPlanning and Transport, MSc/PGDip, DipHE

Psychology; www.shu.ac.uk/psychology

psychology, applied cognitive neuroscience, cognitive analytic therapy, criminal psychology, developmental/forensic/organizational, health psychology,

psychology & science, sexual & relationship psychotherapy; BSc(Hons), MRes/PGDip/PGCert, MSc

Sociology & Politics; www.shu.ac.uk/prospectus/subject/sociology-politics/
applied social science, business, cultural studies, criminology, sociology, education, health & society, history, international relations, politics, psychology, public health, social sciences, social work, planning and policy, youth & community work, working with children, young people & families; BA(Hons), GradDip, MA, MPhil/PhD, MRes/PgDip/PgCert

Faculty of Health & Wellbeing; www.shu.ac.uk/faculties/hwb

Sport and Active Lifestyles; www.shu.ac.uk/prospectus/subject/sport-active-lifestyles/
PE & youth sport, sport performance/coaching, sport, culture & community/society, sport development with coaching, sport science for performance, sport journalism/technology/engineering, physical activity, health & exercise science, sport & exercise science, international/sport business management, physical ed & youth sport, sport & community development/exercise psychology, BA(Hons), BSc(Hons), MA, MSc, PgDip/Cert, PRofDoc

Biosciences; www.shu.ac.uk/bio/
analytical chemistry, biochemistry, biology, biomedical laboratory science, biosciences, biotechnology, chemistry, forensic science, forensic biosciences, human biology, molecular & cell biology, pharmaceutical analysis, pharmacology and biotechnology; BSc(Hons), MSc/PGDip/PGCert, ProfDocBiomedSci

Diagnostic Radiography; www.shu.ac.uk/prospectus/subject/diagnostic-radiography/
advanced diagnostic imaging practice, applying radiography, breast imaging & diagnosis, diagnostic radiography, medical imaging, medical ultrasound, radiological studies, health & social care leadership; DocProf Studies (Health and Social Care), BA(Hons), BSc(Hons), MSc/PGDip/PGCert

Management and Leadership; www.shu.ac.uk/faculties/hwb/cpod/
health & social care, leadership/management/services management; BA(Hons), DipHE, MSc, PhD

Nursing & Midwifery
clinical education, health and social care leadership, learning disabilities & generic social work, maternal health care, midwifery, adult, child or mental health nursing, supportive and palliative care, primary care nursing/district nursing, health visiting and school nursing, primary care radiological studies, social work; AdvDip, AdvProfDev, BA(Hons), BSc(Hons), DocProfStud, FD,MSc/PGDip/PGCert

Medical & Dental; www.shu.ac.uk/faculties/hwb/medical/
cardiovascular medicine, clinical education; MSc, PGCert/Dip

Occupational Therapy; www.shu.ac.uk/occupational
applying/occupational therapy, paediatric practice, vocational rehabilitation, health and social care leadership; BSc(Hons), DocProf, MSc/PGDip/PGCert

Operating Department Practice; www.shu.ac.uk/odp/
operating dept practice; BA(Hons), BSc(Hons), DipHE, DocProfStud, MSc/PGDip/Cert

Paramedic Studies; www.shu.ac.uk/paramedic/
paramedic practice, health and social care leadership, BSc(Hons), DipHEMSc,PGDip/Cert

Physiotherapy; www.shu.ac.uk/physio/
advancing/applying physiotherapy, physiotherapy (practice based), sport injury, professional practice (paediatrics), radiological studies, health and social care leadership; BA(Hons), BSc(Hons), MSc, PGCert, PGDip

Radiotherapy and Oncology; www.shu.ac.uk/radiotherapy/
radiotherapy planning, radiotherapy & oncology practice, supportive and palliative care, health and social care leadership; BA(Hons), BSc(Hons), DipHE, MSc/PGDip/PGCert

Social Work; www.shu.ac.uk/socialwork/
applied nursing & generic social work (learning disability), social work, specialist mental health practice/practitioner, working with children, young people & families, youth & community work studies, youth work, health and social care leadership; BA(Hons), GradDip, MScPgDip, MSW, PGCert, Doc SocWork

Sheffield Business School; www.shu.ac.uk/sbs/

Accounting, Banking & Finance; www.shu.ac.uk/prospectus/subject/accounting-banking-finance/
accounting & finance, audit management & consultancy, banking, business accounting/economics/financial management, forensic accounting, risk management, international finance/banking/economics/stockbroking; BA(Hons), MA, MSc, PGDip/Cert

Business & Management; www.shu.ac.uk/prospectus/subject/business-management/
business and management, business admin/economics/studies, enterprise management, finance, financial management, ICT, international business studies, global marketing/business/strategic marketing, HRM/HR development, leadership, industrial management, international business & management/HRM/marketing/business studies, marketing, tourism; BSc(Hons), DBA, FD, GradDip, HNC, HND, MBA, MPhil, MSc, PGCert, PGDip, PhD

Facilities Management; www.shu.ac.uk/prospectus/course/875/
food management, events management, tourism, hospitality & facilities management; BA(Hons), BSc(Hons), Cert, FD, MA, MPhil, MSc, PGCert, PGDip, PhD

Languages; www.shu.ac.uk/prospectus/subject/languages/
business & English, English language teaching, educational studies & TESOL, int business studies & languages, teaching English for academic purposes; GradDip/Cert, MPhil, PGCert, PhD

Tourism, Hospitality & Events Management; www.shu.ac.uk/prospectus/subject/tourism-hospitality-events/
events/& leisure management, events management with arts & entertainment, international events and conference management, international hospitality/& tourism management, hospitality business management with conference & events; BSc(Hons), FdSc, HND, MA, MPhil, MSc, PGCert, PGDip, PhD

UNIVERSITY OF SOUTHAMPTON
www.soton.ac.uk

Faculty of Business and Law; www.southampton.ac.uk/faculties/faculty_business_law.html

School of Law; www.soton.ac.uk/law
commercial & corporate law, European & comparative property law, European law/legal studies, IT & commerce/telecommunications, international law/business law/legal studies, maritime law; LlB, LlM, MPhil, PhD

Management Business School; www.southampton.ac.uk/management
accounting, business & administration, business analytics & management studies, corporate risk & security management, digital marketing, entrepreneurship, finance, HRM/strategies, international banking, financial studies/markets/marketing, knowledge & information systems management, marketing analytics, management, risk management; BSc(Hons), MSc, PhD, MBA, DBA

Winchester School of Art; www.wsa.soton.ac.uk
advertising design, design/fashion management, graphic/communications design, illustration, luxury brand management, photography, motion graphics, luxury illustration & digital animation, fine art, fashion & fibre, fashion promotion & marketing, new media, painting, printmaking, sculpture, textile design; BA(Hons), MA, MPhil, PhD

Faculty of Engineering & the Environment; www.southampton.ac.uk/faculties/faculty_engineering_environment.html

Acoustical Engineering
acoustical engineering, acoustics & music, engineering; BEng, MEng, BSc(Hons)

Aerospace Engineering
aeronautics & astronautics, aeronautics & astronautics/advanced materials/aerodynamics/airvehicle systems design/engineering management/European studies/spacecraft engineering/structural design,

engineering, space systems engineering; BHEng, MEng

Audiology
environmental science, healthcare science(audiology); BSc, BSc(Hons)

Civil & Environmental Engineering
civil engineering /& architecture, environmental engineering; BEng, MEng

Environmental Sciences
environmental sciences; BSc, BSc(Hons), MEnvSci(Hons)

Mechanical Engineering
mechanical engineering, mechanical engineering / advanced materials/aerospace/automotive/bioengineering engineering management/mechatronics/naval engineering/sustainable energy systems; BEng, MEng

Ship Science
engineering, ship science, ship science/advanced materials/engineering management/naval architecture/naval engineering/yacht & small craft; BEng, MEng

Taught Master(MSc) Degrees
advanced tribology, aerodynamics & computation, applied digital signal processing, audiology, biodiversity & conservation bioengineering, civil engineering, coastal & marine engineering & management, computational engineering design, energy & sustainability (energy resources & climate change/energy, environment & buildings), engineering acoustics, engineering & the environment, engineering in the coastal environment, engineering materials, environmental monitoring & assessment, environmental pollution control, integrated environmental studies, marine technology (classification & survey/conversion & repair/defence/general /marine engineering/naval architecture/offshore engineering/small craft design/advanced materials/marine engineering/maritime computational fluid dynamics/naval architecture/ship science/yacht & small craft, mechatronics, race car aerodynamics, sound & vibration studies, space systems engineering, structural dynamics, sustainable energy technologies, transportation planning & engineering, unmanned vehicle systems design/air-vehicle/marine water resources management; Research Degrees; MPhil, PhD, EngD

Faculty of Health Sciences; www.soton.ac.uk/about/faculties/faculty_health_sciences

advanced diplomates, clinical practice/specialist practice community nursing healthcare science (cardiovascular & respiratory & sleep science), nursing (adult, children, mental health), midwifery, occupational therapy, physiotherapy, podiatry, health & social care, public health practice, mental health practitioner, health & rehabilitation, advanced clinical practice (CAMHS/critical care/long-term conditions/midwifery/neonatal/specialist community practice/
standard/urgent care, clinical leadership in cancer, palliative & end of life care, clinical research, health science (health & rehabilitation), leadership & management health & social care, mental health studies, physiotherapy, public health practice; BSc(Hons), MSc, PGDip, MPhil, PhD, MRes, DocClinPract

Faculty of Humanities; www.soton.ac.uk/about/faculties/faculty_humanities

Archaeology; www.southampton.ac.uk/archaeology/
archaeology & history/geography, archaeological computing (spatial technologies/virtual pasts), Rome & provinces, ceramic & Lithic/maritime/social archaeology, osteoarchaeology, maritime conservation, archaeological survey & landscape, palaeolithic

English; www.southampton.ac.uk/english/
English, English & jt degrees, English literary studies, language & linguistics, 18th-century studies, 20th/21st century literature, medieval & Renaissance studies, creative writing

Film; www.southampton.ac.uk/film/
film studies/ film & cultural management, film (jt degrees)

History; www.southampton.ac.uk/history/
history, modern history, jt hons incl archaeology, English, foreign language, philosophy, Jewish history & culture studies, 18th century studies, medieval & Renaissance studies

Modern Languages; www.southampton.ac.uk/ml/
modern languages-contemporary Europe/English language studies/French/German/linguistics studies/Spanish, Portuguese, Latin American studies

Music; www.southampton.ac.uk/music/
performance, composition, music therapy, musicology, 18th century studies, medieval & Renaissance studies

Philosophy; www.southampton.ac.uk/philosophy/
philosophy: jt hons degrees incl sociology, politics, mathematics, foreign language, aesthetics
BA(Hons), MA, MRes, MPhil, PhD, CetHE, MMus

Faculty of Medicine; www.southampton.ac.uk/faculties/faculty_medicine.html

Medicine; www.southampton.ac.uk/medicine
allergy, biomedical sciences/cell biology & immunology of cancer, immunology & infection, stem cell science, medicine, public health/nutrition; BM, MSc, BMedSci, PGDip/Cert, PhD, DM

Faculty of Natural and Environmental Sciences; www.soton.ac.uk/about/faculties/faculty_natural_environmental-sciences

Biological Sciences; www.soton.ac.uk/biosc
biochemistry, biology, biomedical sciences, biological sciences & chemistry, cellular & molecular sciences, molecular biosciences, neurosciences, pharmacology, zoology, ecology & the environment; BSc(Hons), Cert/DipHE, MPhil, PhD

Chemistry; www.soton.ac.uk/chemistry
chemistry/with biological sciences/ocean & earth sciences/mathematics/medical science, electrochemistry, computational systems chemistry, molecular diagnostics & therapeutics, magnetic resonance, molecular assembly, function & structure; BSc(Hons), B/MNatSci, MPhil, PhD

National Oceanography Centre, Southampton www.noc.soton.ac.uk

School of Ocean and Earth Science; www.soton.ac.uk/soes
geology, geophysical science, ocean chemistry/science, oceanography, earth & climate science, engineering in the coastal environment, physical geography, marine science/biology/policy & law, marine resource management, engineering in the coastal environment, marine environment & resources, vertebrate palaeontology; BSc(Hons), MSci, BNatSci, MRes, MPhil, PhD

Faculty of Physical and Applied Sciences; www.soton.ac.uk/about/faculties/faculty_physical-applied_sciences

Electronics and Computer Science; www.ecs.soton.ac.uk
bionanotechnology, computer science, AI, distributed networks, engineering & sustainability with electrical power engineering, microelectronic systems design/mechanical systems, nanoelectronics & nanotechnology, software engineering, systems-on-a-chip, systems & signal processing, web science/technology, image & multimedia systems, mobile & secure systems, software/electrical/electronic/electromechanical engineering, optical communication, power systems, wireless communications; BEng, MEng, MSc, MComp, PhD

Optoelectronics Research Centre; www.orc.soton.ac.uk
photonics, photonic technologies; MSc, PhD

Physics & Astronomy; www.phy.soton.ac.uk
astronomy, adv quantum mechanics, coherent light/matter, theoretical particle physics, physics with astronomy/nanotechnology/space science/photonics/mathematics; BSc(Hons), European Masters, PhD

Faculty of Social and Human Sciences; www.soton.ac.uk/about/faculties/facultysocial_human-sciences

School of Education; www.southampton.ac.uk/education
educational studies, education & training (primary), educational studies with psychology, education (management & leadership/practice & innovation/specific learning difficulties (dyslexia)/mathematics & science), post-compulsory education & training, PGCE (primary, numerous secondary subjects), PCET; BSc(Hons), BA(Hons), MSc, MA(Ed), CertEd, MPhil, PhD, EdD

Geography & Environment; www.soton.ac.uk/geography
geography, geology, physical geography, oceanography, applied GIS & remote sensing, city & regional development, geo-information science & earth sciences; BSc(Hons), BA(Hons), MA, MSc, MPhil, PhD

School of Mathematics; www.soton.ac.uk/maths
actuarial science, mathematical studies, mathematics with actuarial science/astronomy/biology/computer

science/economics/finance/management science/music/OR/physics/statistics, OR/& finance, mathematics, OR & statistics, applications in medicine; BSc(Hons), MMath, MSc, PGDip, PhD

School of Psychology; www.southampton.ac.uk/psychology
psychology/& educational studies, clinical psychology, management arts & science, companion animal behaviour counselling, health psychology, human animal behaviour; BSc(Hons), MSc, MPhil, PhD

School of Social Sciences; www.southampton.ac.uk/socsci
applied social sciences (anthropology/criminology/psychological studies/accounting), economics/& finance, actuarial science, finance, management sciences, politics, international relations, sociology, modern history & politics, philosophy & politics/international relations/modern European languages, international political economy, philosophy & sociology, social policy, gerontology, international comparative studies, econometrics, citizenship & democracy, global politics, governance & policy, demographics, official/social statistics, social work, social policy/research; BSc(Hons), BA(Hons), MEcon, MSc, MPhil, PGDip, PhD

Southampton Statistical Sciences Research Institute; www.southampton.ac.uk/s3ri
PhD

STAFFORDSHIRE UNIVERSITY
www.staffs.ac.uk

Staffordshire University Business School; www.staffs.ac.uk/business
Accounting & Finance: accounting & business/finance, business administration with finance
Business, Management & Enterprise: business management, business management & enterprise, business start-up, international business management, business administration (finance/HRM/international), economics for business analysis, economics of international trade & European integration, international business/marketing, management practice/studies, management
Education: education, post-compulsory education, teaching assistants, teaching in the lifelong learning sector, business education/business & economics (PGCE), education (learning & assessment/negotiated), leading enterprise learning, mentoring & coaching, leading community learning, educational leadership, teaching in the lifelong learning sector
Economics: economics for business analysis, economics of international trade & European integration, business & economics education
Human Resource Management: HRM, strategic HRM, personnel practice. professional development
Marketing; marketing management, international marketing
Tourism & Events: tourism management, events management
Professional Courses; BA, BSc, HNC, HND, MA, MBA, MPhil, MSc, PGCert/Dip, PhD, PGCE

Faculty of Arts, Media & Design; www.staffs.ac.uk/faculties/art_and_design
Art & Design; art, design, fashion accessories/design crafts, advertising & brand management, animation, cartoon & comic arts, fine art, photography, graphic design, illustration, photojournalism, product design, stop motion animation & puppet-making, surface pattern design, textile surfaces, transport design, visual effects & concept design
Film, Journalism and Broadcast Media: advertising & commercial film production, broadcast/celebrity/journalism, experimental film production, film, TV & radio studies, media (film) production, music broadcasting, music journalism & broadcasting, radio production, screenwriting with film studies, scriptwriting, sports journalism/PR & journalism
Humanities, Community & Society: creative writing, crime, deviance & society/security, drama, performance & theatre arts, English & creative writing, English literature, ethics, philosophy & society, modern/& international history, philosophy, sociology, theatre studies & technical stage production arts, media & design, broadcast journalism, ceramic design, community & participatory arts, community practice, continental philosophy, creative futures, design management, film production, practice & theory/& visual cultures global society & media, communication, international history/policy & diplomacy/relations, regeneration, social & cultural theory, sociology, sports broadcast journalism, transnational

Staffordshire University

organised crime, youth & community work philosophy; BA, FdA, MA, MFA, MPhil, MSc, PhD

Faculty of Computing, Engineering & Technology; www.staffs.ac.uk/faculties/comp_eng_tech

3D games modelling, advanced programming, aeronautical technology, applied multimedia systems/internet communication/ network management/computing, automotive electronics/engineering/technology, automotive & autosport engineering, bioinformatics, business computing/information technology, computer science/systems/solutions for business, computer game design/development/programming/networks & seurity, cyber security, database telecommunication/administration & management, design & technology, digital feature film production, digital forensics, 3D games technology, electrical/electronic/electronic & broadcast engineering, film production technology, geoinformatics, information/communication technology, forensic computing, games technology, mathematics & applied statistics, mechanical engineering, mechatronics, medical engineering/devices, mobile computer systems & e-learning, multimedia computing, network computing, web development/multimedia, software engineering, motorsport technology, music technology, network computing/engineering/systems management, product design engineering/technology, telecommunications engineering; BA, BEng, BSc, FdSc, HND, MEng, MSc, MPhil, MRes, PGCE, PGCert, PGDip, PhD

Faculty of Health; www.staffs.ac.uk/faculties/health

advice work/& law, advanced clinical practice, ageing, mental health & dementia, clinical practice/biomechanics (& diabetes/orthotic therapy/pain management), clinical podiatric biomechanics, community nursing in the home/mental health nursing, health management & policy/social care, hypnosis & stress, major incident medical management, medical education, midwifery practice, negotiated learning – health & social care, musculoskeletal diagnosis, nursing practice: teacher-enabling learning in nursing practice, adult/children's/district/mental health nursing, specialist/clinical practice, public health – health visiting/specialist practice, operating dept practice, osteopathy, paramedic science, peri-operative care, professional practice, specialist community public health nursing/health visiting & school nursing, social care/work, applied sport & exercise psychology/science, PE & youth sports coaching, physical activity/public health, sport & exercise science, sport development & coaching, footware in diagnosis & therapy; BSc, MA, MPhil, MSc, PGCE, PGCert, PGDip, PhD

Faculty of Sciences; www.staffs.ac.uk/faculties/sciences

animal biology & conservation, biology, biomedical science, clinical psychology, cognitive behavioural therapy, counselling, child development, crime scene development, criminology, early childhood studies, environment & sustainability, sustainability & environmental management, fire investigation, forensic biology/investigation/psychology/science, geography/& mountain leadership, governance & sustainable development, habitat conservation & management, health psychology, health care science, human biology, molecular biology, policing & criminal investigation, psychology/& child development, psychotherapeutical investigation, sport & exercise psychology/science, urban biology; BA, BSc, DClinPsy, DHealthPsy, FdSc, MA, MSc, MPhil, PGCert, PGDip, PhD

Law School; www.staffs.ac.u/faculties/law

business law, criminology, environmental/family/employment/international trade & commerce law, human rights law, law, legal practice, international/sports law, healthcare & ethics; LLB, LLM, MPhil, PhD

UNIVERSITY OF STIRLING
www.external.stir.ac.uk

School of Applied Social Science; www.dass.stir.ac.uk

applied social research, sociology & social policy, criminology, housing studies, applied studies (child welfare & protection/management & leadership in social services/management of social welfare organisations), adult services, suport & protection, child welfare & protection, management for team leadership, social work studies, drug & alcohol studies, dementia studies, child welfare & protection, criminology, crime & justice, social policy, sociology; BA, GradCert, MSc, PGCert, PGDip, PhD

School of Arts & Humanities; www.stir.ac.uk/schools/arts-and-humanities

Dept of English Studies; www.english.stir.ac.uk
English studies, creative writing, English language & literature, the Gothic imagination, modern Scottish writing, post-colonial studies, international publishing management, publishing studies, Renaissance studies; BA, MLitt, MPhil, MRes, MSc, PhD

Dept of Film, Media & Journalism; www.fmj.stir.ac.uk
film & media studies, journalism studies, digital media, publishing & law, media & culture/management, public communications management, strategic PR; BA, MLitt, MPhil, MSc, PGDip, PhD

History & Politics; www.historyandpolitics.stir.ac.uk
History, Politics: large range of taught modules at undergraduate and postgraduate levels; BA(Hons), MSc, MRes, MA, DPhil, PhD

School of Languages, Culture and Regions; www.slcr.stir.ac.uk
hermeneutics, humanities, French/Spanish & Latin American studies, translation studies, TESOL, film studies, global cinema & culture; BA, MLitt, MRes, PhD

Dept of Philosophy; www.philosophy.stir.ac.uk
philosophy, philosophy of logic & language, legal, moral & social philosophy, epistemology & philosophy of mind, history of early analytical philosophy; BA, MLitt, MPhil, PhD

Stirling Law School; www.law.stir.ac.uk
law, international commercial law, financial law & finance, environmental policy & governance, digital publishing, media & the law, corporate social responsibility, business/commercial law, law; BA, LLB, LLM, MSc, MLitt, PhD

School of Education; www.ioe.stir.ac.uk
education (primary/secondary), tertiary education (TQFE/TQAE), English language teaching, EFL, educational leadership, applied linguistics, computer-assisted language learning, international policing, professional learning & leadership, enquiry, teaching qualifications in adult education/FE, TESOL with translational studies/applied linguistics, tertiary education; BA, BSc, EdD, MEd, MPhil, MRes, MSc, PGCert/Dip, PhD, UnivCert

School of Natural Sciences; www.stir/schools/natural-sciences

Institute of Aquaculture; www.aqua.stir.ac.uk
aquaculture & the environment/development, aquacultural business management/biotechnology/veterinary studies, marine biology, sustainable aquaculture; BSc, MPhil, MSc, PGCert, PGDip, PhD

School of Biological & Environmental Sciences; www.sbes.stir.ac.uk
animal/cell/conservation biology, biology & professional education/psychology, conservation biology & management, ecology, energy & the environment, environmental geography/history/management/professional education/science/outdoor education, sports & exercise science; BSc, MPhil, MRes, MSc, PGCert, PGDip, PhD

Dept of Computing Science & Mathematics; www.cs.stir.ac.uk
advanced/computing, computing for financial markets, IT, mathematics/& its applications, information technology; BSc, MSc, PhD, MBA

Dept of Psychology; www.psychology.stir.ac.uk
psychology, psychological research methods, autism/child development/evolution & behaviour/measuring perception/psychology of faces, primary care, psychology applied to health; BA, BSc, MSc, PGDip, PhD

School of Nursing & Midwifery & Health; www.nm.stir.ac.uk
advanced/professional practice/care practice, health & wellbeing in older person, non-medical prescribing, health profession & paramedical practice, studies/research, midwifery, nursing (adult, mental health), supporting self-care; BM, BN, BSc, DAHP, DM, DN, MPhil, MRes, MSc, PGDip, PhD, DipHE

School of Sport; www.sports.stir.ac.uk
health & exercise sciences, performance coaching, psychology of sport, sport & exercise science, sport coaching/management/nutrition; BA, BSc, MPhil, MSc, PGDip, PhD

University of Stirling

Stirling Management School;
www.stir.ac.uk/management/

Accounting & Finance Division
accountancy, finance, international accounting & finance, investment analysis, computing for financial markets

Business & Marketing Division
business & management, business studies, HRM, international business, marketing, management science & socioeconomic development, retail marketing, public service management

Division of Economics
money, banking & finance, economics, environmental economics; BA, BSc, MBA, MSc, PhD, BAcc, MPhil, PGDip, MBA, MRes

Institute for People-centred Healthcare Management;
PhD

Institute for Retail Studies
retail studies; PhD

Institute for Social Marketing
PhD

Institute for Socio-management
PhD

STOCKPORT COLLEGE
www.stockport.ac.uk

access to HE, art & design, media, building/services/construction, business & IT technology/management, child development & wellbeing, early childhood studies, photography, enterprise computing, illustration, graphic art & design, health & social care, engineering, forensic science, graphic communication, photography, social work/counselling; BA, FdA, FDSc

UNIVERSITY OF STRATHCLYDE
www.strath.ac.uk

Strathclyde Business School;
www.strath.ac.uk/business

Undergraduate Courses:
accounting, business enterprise, business technology, economics, finance, hospitality & tourism studies, HRM, management/science, marketing, business law

Postgraduate Courses:
applied economics, management of business information technology systems, business analysis & consulting, business & management, finance, global enterprise management, HRM, hospitality & tourism leadership, international accounting & finance/banking/hospitality & management tourism management/management/marketing, investment & finance, marketing, equality in pay, operational research; BA, MSc, MBA, DBA, MPhil, PhD, MRes, PGCert/Dip, MBM

Faculty of Engineering;
www.strath.ac.uk/engineering

Dept of Architecture; www.strath.ac.uk/architecture
architecture, adv architectural design/studies, sustainable engineering, urban design; MArch, MRes, MSc, PGCert, PGDip

Bioengineering Unit; www.strath.ac.uk/bioeng
bioengineering, medical devices, biomedical engineering, medical technology; EngD, MPhil, MRes, MSc, PGCert, PGDip, PhD

Dept of Chemical & Process Engineering; www.strath.ac.uk/chemeng
adv chemical & processing engineering, chemical engineering, chemical processing, chemical/process & technology management; BEng, MEng, MSc, PGCert, PGDip

Dept of Civil & Environmental Engineering; www.strath.ac.uk/civeng
architectural/civil/environmental engineering, environmental engineering/health, hydrogeology, sustainability & environmental studies; BEng, BSc, MEng, MPhil, MRes, MSc, PhD

Dept of Design, Manufacture & Engineering Management; www.strath.ac.uk/dmen
adv engineering technology & systems, computer-aided engineering design, digital creativity, engineering design, environmental entrepreneurship, global innovation management, integrated product development, management of competitive manufacturing, mechatronics & automation, operations management in engineering, product design engineering/design & innovation, production engineering & management, sports engineering, supply chain & ops management, management; BEng, BSc, MEng, MSc, PGCert, PGDip

Dept of Electronic & Electrical Engineering; www.strath.ac.uk/eee
communications/technology & policy, computer & electronic systems, control & digital processing systems, digital multimedia & communication systems, electrical energy systems, electrical & electronic engineering with/business studies/international studies, mechanical/ electrical power/electronic engineering, electronic & digital systems; BEng, MEng, MSc, PGCert, PGDip

Dept of Mechanical & Aerospace Engineering; www.strath.ac.uk/mecheng
adv mechanical engineering, aero-mechanical/enviro-mechanical/mechanical engineering, mechanical engineering with aeronautics/financial management, materials engineering, power plant engineering/technologies, sustainable renewable energy systems & the environment; BEng, MEng, MPhil, PGCert, PGDip, PhD

Dept of Naval Architectural & Marine Engineering; www.strath.ac.uk/na-me
marine engineering/technology, naval architecture, with marine engineering/ocean engineering/small craft engineering, subsea engineering, offshore renewable energy/floating systems, technical ship management; BEng, MEng, MPhil, MSc, PGCert, PGDip, PhD

National Centre for Prosthetics & Orthotics; www.strath.ac.uk/prosthetics
prosthetics & orthotics, rehabilitation studies; BSc, MPhil, MSc, PGCert, PGDip, PhD

Faculty of Humanities & Social Sciences; www.strath.ac.uk/humanities

School of Applied Social Sciences; www.strath.ac.uk/humanities/school of appliedsocialsciences
community education, adv professional studies, human/ geography, social work/management, residential child/community care, mental health officer social work, sociology, social research, refugee & migration studies, investigatory journalism, media & communication; BA(Hons), Cert, MPhil, PhD, MSc, MRes, MLitt

School of Education; www.strath.ac.uk/humanities/schoolofeducation
autism, childhood practice, early childhood studies, education & social services, maths recovery, applied educational research, educational support, management & leadership in education, philosophy with children, school leadership & management, PGCE (primary, secondary), supporting bilingual learners; BA, BSc, EdD, BEd, MSc, PGCE, PGCert, MEd, MPhil, PGDE, PGDip, PhD

School of Government & Public Policy; www.strath.ac.uk/humanities/schoolofgovernmentandpublicpolicy
European/international public policy, political research, politics, public policy; BA, MSc, PhD

School of Humanities; www.strath.ac.uk/humanities/schoolofhumanities
creative writing, English, history, French, Spanish, Italian, politics, journalism, psychology, sociology, law, hospitality & tourism, HRM, applied social science, education, government, psychological sciences & health, music; MA, MLitt, MPhil, MRes, PGDip/Cert, PhD

School of Law; www.strath.ac.uk/humanities/lawschool
law, advocacy, construction law, criminal justice & penal change, human rights law, international economic law, international law & sustainable development, internet law & policy, mediation & conflict resolution, Scots law; BA, LLB, LLM, PGCert, PGDip, MSc

School of Psychological Science & Health; www.strath.ac.uk/humanities/schoolofpsychologicalsciencehealth
psychology, sport & physical activity, speech & language pathology, educational psychology,

counselling; BA, BSc, MRes, DEdPsy, PGCert/Dip, MCounselling

Faculty of Science; www.strath.ac.uk/science

Dept of Pure & Applied Chemistry; www.chem.strath.ac.uk
chemistry, applied chemistry & chemical engineering, forensic & analytical chemistry, chemistry with drug discovery, chemistry with teaching, forensic science; BSc, MChem, MSc, PGDip, PhD

Dept of Computer & Information Sciences; www.strath.ac.uk/cis
business information systems, computer & electronic systems, adv/computer science/with law, information & library studies, information management, software engineering; BEng, BSc, MEng, MPhil, MRes, MSc, PGCert, PGDip

Dept of Mathematics & Statistics; www.mathstat.strath.ac.uk
mathematics, mathematics & science/business/humanities & social sciences/statistics, research topics; BSc, MSc, PhD

Dept of Physics; www.strath.ac.uk/physics
physics, nanoscience, optical technologies, high power frequency science & engineering, photonics & device fabrication, quantum information & coherence, physics with teaching; BSc, MPhys, MSc, PhD

Strathclyde Institute of Pharmacy & Biomedical Sciences; www.strath.ac.uk/sipbs
biomedical sciences, biochemistry, quality & good manufacturing practice, analysis of medicines, clinical pharmacy, pharmacy; BSc, MPharm, MPhil, MSc, PGCert, PGDip, PhD

UNIVERSITY CAMPUS SUFFOLK
www.ucs.ac.uk

School of Arts & Humanities; www.ucs.ac.uk/SchoolsAndNetwork/SchoolOfArtsAndHumanities
arts practice, design context & practice, computer games design, dance, English, history, film, fine art, graphic/design/illustration, interior architecture & design, photography, journalism; BA, FdA, MA, PGCert, PGDip

School of Science, Technology & Health; www.ucs.ac.uk/SchoolsAndNetwork/UCSSchools/SchoolofScience,TechnologyandHealth
Division of Health
advanced healthcare practice (advanced nurse practitioner; allied health professionals), health & wellbeing, diagnostic radiography, radiotherapy & oncology, health sciences (diagnostic imaging), health administration, operating department practice, health sciences (mammography), acute healthcare practice

Division of Science and Technology
bioscience, nutrition & human health, sport & exercise science, regenerative medicine, science of healthy ageing; FdSc, FdSc, MA, PGCert, PGDip,-Cert/DipHE, BSc(Hons), MSc

School of Nursing & Midwifery; www.ucs.ac.uk/study/SchoolsAndCentres/SchoolOfArtsAndHumanities/events/events
adult/children's/mental health nursing, health care practice, midwifery, care practice, continuing care, clinical practice, nursing practice, education for health & social care professionals, leadership & service innovation; BSc(Hons), FdA, MA

School of Applied Social Science; www.ucs.ac.uk/SchoolsAndNetwork/UCSSchools/SchoolofAppliedSocialSciences
Children, Young People and Education
children, young people & policy, children's care, learning & development, criminology/& youth studies, early childhood studies, early learning, psychology & criminology/sociology/youth studies, sociology & youth studies, SCITT, early years professional status, childhood & youth studies, learning & teaching

Social Policy and Social Work
social care practice, social work, mental health; BA(Hons), BSc(Hons), FdAPG Cert, PG Dip, MA

School of Business, Leadership & Enterprise; www.ucs.ac.uk/ SchoolsAndNetwork/ UCSSchools/ SchoolofBusiness, LeadershipandEnterprise/Courses
business administration/management & HRM/marketing, event management, HR strategy, HRM, hospitality management, leadership & management, leisure/tourism management, network & communication technologies; BA, FdA, FdSc, MHRStrat, MBA, PGDip

UNIVERSITY OF SUNDERLAND
www.sunderland.ac.uk

Faculty of Applied Sciences; www.sunderland.ac.uk/faculties/apsc

Dept of Computing, Engineering & Technology; www.sunderland.ac.uk/faculties/apsc/ourfaculty/ourdeparts/cet
applied computing engineering, automotive/electronic & electrical/manufacturing/engineering, business computing, computer systems engineering, computing, engineering management, health information management, information communications technology, IT management, low carbon vehicle technology, mechanical engineering, network systems/computing, project management, renewable energy eng, telecommunications engineering; BA, BEng, BSc, FdSc, MSc

Dept of Pharmacy, Health & Well-being; www.sunderland.ac.uk/faculties/apsc/ourfaculty/ourdepartments/phw
advanced clinical practice, biomedical sciences, biopharmaceutical science, clinical skills, community & public health, clinical pharmacy, cognitive behavioural therapy, drug & alcohol studies, drug discovery & devlopment, health & social care, healthcare science, medicine management, proteomics & metabolomics, public health, nursing, pharmacological science, medicines management, pharmacy, recovery in psychosis & complex mental health; BA, BSc, FdA, MPharm, MSc, PGCE, Univ Dip, PGDip, Adv Dip

Dept of Psychology; www.sunderland.ac.uk/faculties/apsc/ourfaculty/ourdepartments/psychology
counselling, psychology; BA, FdA, MA, MSc

Dept of Sport & Exercise Sciences; www.sunderland.ac.uk/faculties/apsc/ourdepartments/sport/
sport & exercise development/sciences, sport studies, sports coaching/journalism; BA, BSc, FdA MSc

Faculty of Arts, Design & Media; www.sunderland.ac.uk/faculties/adm

Dept of Arts & Design; www.sunderland.ac.uk/faculties/adm/ourfaculty/ourdepartments/departmentofartsdesign
dance, drama, music, design, fine art, glass & ceramics, photography; BA, BSc, FdA, MA

Dept of Media; www.sunderland.ac.uk/faculties/adm/ourfaculty/ourdepartments/departmentofmedia
media & cultural studies, film, media, & cultural studies, journalism & PR, TV, video & news media; BA, BSc, FdA, MA

Faculty of Business & Law; www.sunderland.ac.uk/faculties/bl

Sunderland Business School; www.sunderland.ac.uk/faculties/bl/departments/business/
accounting, applied management, banking & finance, financial management, applied investment/professional practice, business & management/enterprise management/HRM/marketing, hospitality management, HRM, innovation & enterprise, events/travel management, international management, business admin, sports management

Dept of Law; www.sunderland.ac.uk/faculties/bl/departments/law/
law, criminology, business law, legal practice, criminal law & procedure, human rights

University of Sunderland

Dept of Tourism, Hospitality & Events; www.sunderland.ac.uk/faculties/bl/departments/tourism/
international hospitality & tourism management, tourism management, events management, travel & tourism; BA,(Hons), BA/BSc, CertHE, FdA, GradDip, LLB, LLM, MA, MBS, MSc, PGDip, MBA

Faculty of Education & Society

Dept of Education; www.sunderland.ac.uk/faculties/es/ourfaculty/ourdepartments/departmentofeducation
secondary education (chemistry education, design & technology, English education, GTP, information technology with QTS, mathematics education, advanced pedagogy, post compulsory education & training, professional learning & teaching, training & work-based learning, advanced professional practice (primary/secondary/business/geography/design & technology), teaching & learning with ICT, TESOL, international education, children's literature, PGCE secondary (various subjects)/primary (5–11)/teaching of French, special needs & inclusive education, teaching & learning with ICT), TESOL; BA, BSc, MA, PGCE, FD, Dip, MSc

Dept of Culture; www.sunderland.ac.uk/faculties/es/ourfaculty/ourdepartments/departmentofculture
English & creative writing, English education/language & literature, TESOL, history, politics, religious studies, French, German, Spanish, EFL, world literatures; BA, BSc, MA, PGCE

Dept of Social Sciences; www.sunderland.ac.uk/faculties/es/ourfaculty/ourdepartments/departmentofsocialsciences
career guidance, childhood studies, community & youth studies, criminology, early years professional status, education & care/curriculum studies, health & social care, interprofessional practice education, social work, sociology, understanding community development, working with young people; BA, FdA, MA, BA(Hons), BEng(Hons), BSc(Hons), EdEng, FdSc, LLM, MBA, MSc, PGCE, PGCert

Degrees validated by University of Sunderland offered at:

CITY OF SUNDERLAND COLLEGE
www.citysun.ac.uk

accountancy & management, applied arts, art and design, business & management, counselling, early years, education & care, health & social care, network security technology, dance, drama, biomedical science, exercise health & fitness, health & safety management, leadership & management, sports coaching, travel & tourism; FdA

UNIVERSITY OF SURREY
www.surrey.ac.uk

Faculty of Arts & Human Sciences; www2.surrey.ac.uk/fahs/

School of Arts; www.surrey.ac.uk/school of arts
acting, dance, cultures, film studies, creative writing, theatre studies, music, creative music technology, music & sound recording, professional acting, musical theatre, practice of voice & singing, professional, with creative writing; MPhil, PGDip, PhD

School of English & Languages; www.surrey.ac.uk/englishandlanguages
French/German/Spanish & translation, French/German/Spanish/ for international communication, business management & French/German/Spanish, English literature/with creative writing, audiovisual translation, business translation & interpreting, monolingual subtitling & audio description, public service interpreting, translation/studies/with intercultural communication, business interpreting in Chinese & English, communications & international

marketing, intercultural communication with international business, English literature, creative writing

School of Politics; www.surrey.ac.uk/politics
politics, international politics/with English for international communication, international politics with French/German/Spanish, politics & sociology/economics, politics with policy studies, international intervention, European & international politics, European politics, business & law

School of Psychology; www.surrey.ac.uk/psychology
psychology, environmental/forensic/health/social, occupational & organisational psychology, research methods, supervision & consultation: psychotherapeutic organisational approaches, psychological intervention, clinical psychology, psychotherapeutic & counselling psychology

School of Sociology; www.surrey.ac.uk/sociology
sociology, criminology, criminal justice & social research, sociology, culture & media, media studies BA(Hons), BSc(Hons), MA, MSc, PsychD, PGDip

Dept of Economics; www.econ.surrey.ac.uk
finance, economics, energy economics & policy, business/international economics, finance & development; BSc, MSc, PhD

Dept of English; www.english.surrey.ac.uk
communication & international marketing, English literature, creative writing, intercultural communication with international business; BA, MA, MPhil, PGDip, PhD

Dept of Languages & Translation Studies; www.surrey.ac.uk/languages
audiovisual translation, French/German/Spanish, business translation, international communication, interpreting, monolingual subtitles & audio description, public service translation; BA, BSc, MA, MSc, PGDip

Dept of Music & Sound Recording; www.surrey.ac.uk/music
creative music technology, music, music & sound recording, musicology; BMus, BSc, MMus, MPhil, MRes, PGDip, PhD

Dept of Political, International & Policy Studies; www2.surrey.ac.uk/politics
European politics/business & law, international politics & languages, international intervention; BA, LLB, MA, MPhil, PhD

Dept of Psychology; www.psy.surrey.ac.uk
applied psychology & sociology, clinical/environmental/forensic/health/occupational & organizational/social psychology, psychology, subversion & consultation, psychological intervention; BSc, MSc, PhD, PsychD

Dept of Sociology; www.soc.surrey.ac.uk
criminology, criminal justice & social research, media studies, social research methods, sociology; BSc, MSc, PhD

Faculty of Engineering & Physical Sciences; www.surrey.ac.uk/feps

Dept of Computing; www2.surrey.ac.uk/computing
computer science/& engineering, computing & information technology, information systems, internet computing, security technologies & applications; BSc, MSc, PhD

Dept of Electronic Engineering; www.ee.surrey.ac.uk
advanced systems, communications networks & software, satellite communications engineering, electronics engineering/with computer systems, medical imaging, microwave engineering & wireless subsystems, mobile & satellite communication, mobile communication systems, multimedia technology & systems, nanotechnology & nanoelectronic devices, signal processing & machine intelligence, space systems communications, space technology & planetary exploration; BEng, MEng, MPhil, MSc, PhD

Dept of Mathematics; www.maths.surrey.ac.uk
financial mathematics, statistics, mathematics/with jt degrees, research including nonlinear mathematics; BSc, MMath, MSc, PhD

Dept of Physics; www.surrey.ac.uk/physics
medical physics, physics, nuclear astrophysics, satellite technology, radiation & environmental protection; BSc, MSc, MPhys

Division of Civil, Chemical & Environmental Engineering; www.surrey.ac.uk/cce
chemical engineering, bio-systems engineering, civil engineering, information & process/business systems

engineering, process & environmental systems engineering, renewable energy, petroleum refining, process systems engineering, bridge engineering, structural engineering, water & environmental engineering, corporate environmental management, environmental strategy & engineering, process systems engineering, sustainable development, transport planning & practice, water regulation & management; BEng, MEng, MSc, PGCert, PGDip

Division of Mechanical, Medical & Aerospace Engineering; www.surrey.ac.uk/mma

advanced materials, aerospace/mechanical engineering, biomedical/medical engineering; BEng, MEng, MSc, PGCert, PGDip

Faculty of Health & Medical Sciences; www2.surrey.ac.uk/fhms

Division of Biochemistry & Physiology; www2.surrey.ac.uk/biochem

applied/genetic toxicology, biochemistry, clinical biochemistry/pharmacology, biomedical science, microbiology, neuroscience, toxicology, veterinary bioscience, adv gynaecological endosystems; BSc, MSc

Division of Chemistry; www.surrey.ac.uk/chemistry

chemistry/with forensic investigation, medicinal chemistry, drug

School of Health & Social Care; www.surrey.ac.uk/healthandsocialcare

advanced/clinical practice, health & social care, learning & teaching for professional practice, midwifery studies, nursing studies: adult/child/mental health nursing, operating department practice, paramedic practice, public health practice; BSc, DipHE, MSc, PGCert/Dip, PhD,DClinPract

Division of Microbial & Cellular Sciences; www.surrey.ac.uk/microbial

applied toxicology, biomedical science, clinical/biochemistry, food science, medical/microbiology, veterinary biosciences; BSc, MSc

Division of Nutritional & Metabolic Sciences; www.surrey.ac.uk/nutrition

nutrition, food science, dietetics, nutritional medicine; BSc, MSc, PGCert, PGDip

Faculty of Business, Economics & Law; www.surrey.ac.uk/fbel

Surrey Business School; www.surrey.ac.uk/sbs

accounting & finance, banking & finance, business/& retail management, corporate environment management, entrepreneurship, finance, HRM, international business/financial/marketing/retail management, event/tourism management, operations & logistics management, international retail management, marketing management; BSc, DBA, MBA, MSc, PhD

School of Law; www.surrey.ac.uk/law

health/European/international/international commercial law, law & international studies/criminology; LLB, LLM, MA, PhD

School of Hospitality & Tourism Management; www.surrey.ac.uk/shtm

food management, international hospitality/& tourism management, international event/hotel management, tourism development/management/marketing, sustainable tourism; BSc(Hons), MSc, PhD, MBA

School of Economics; www.surrey.ac.uk/economics

economics, economics & finance, business economics, energy economics & policy, international economic finance & development; BSc(Hons), MSc, PhD

Dept of Health Care Management & Policy; www.surrey.ac.uk/hcmp

health care management; MSc, PhD

Degrees validated by the University of Surrey offered at:

FARNBOROUGH COLLEGE OF TECHNOLOGY
www.farn-ct.ac.uk

accounting, aeronautical engineering, business management, childcare, complementary therapy, computing with gaming/networking, education, early childhood/years/learning support, electrical/electronic engineering, graphic design animation & interactive media, holistic therapies, hospitality management, media/music production, multimedia, photography, psychology & marketing/criminology, public service (uniformed), salon & spa management, software engineering, sports science/performance & personal training, theatre, dance & film; BA, BSc, FdA, FdSc

NESCOT (NORTH EAST SURREY COLLEGE OF TECHNOLOGY)
www.nescot.ac.uk

acoustics, environment & noise control, biomedical science, business management, psychodynamic counselling, health & social care, computing, early years, music technology, orthopaedic medicine, osteopathy, photography, photo-imaging, perfusion sci, sports therapy, teacher training, teaching & learning in lifelong learning sector, travel & tourism management; BA(Hons), BSc(Hons), DipHE, FdA, FdSc, HNC, HND, MSc, PGDip, Masters

ST MARY'S COLLEGE
www.smuc.ac.uk

applied linguistics & ELT, applied physics, applied sport nutrition/physiology, sport & exercise physiology, bioethics & medical law, business law, Catholic school leadership, charity management, clinical hypnosis, creative & professional writing, drama, applied theatre, & theatre arts, coaching science, drama & physical theatre, education in context, integrated children's services, education, leading innovation & change/pedagogy & professional values & practice/RE, education & social science, English, geography, Gothic culture, subculture, counterculture, health, exercise & PE, health chaplaincy, history, international business practice, international tourism management, Irish studies, law, managing for sustainability, media arts, mentoring, sports/nutrition, physical activity for public health, pastoral theology/ministry, philosophy, physical theatre, physical & sport exercise, PGCE (primary, secondary), psychology & counselling, screen media, sociology, sport science/coaching, science/journalism/rehabilitation, sport & tourism management, strength & conditioning, teaching & learning in the lifelong learning sector, theatre directing, theology & religious studies, youth ministry; BA, BSc, FdA, LlB, LLM, MA, MPhil, MSc, PGCE, PGCert, PGDip, PhD

UNIVERSITY OF SUSSEX
www.sussex.ac.uk

Brighton & Sussex Medical School; www.bsms.sussex.ac.uk
clinical education, commissioning & leadership, epidemiology, evidence-based practice, global health, health & social care, diabetes, leadership & management in health care, medical education, medicine, nephrology, psychiatry, psychopharmacology, public health, surgery, trauma & orthopaedics; MA, MD, MPhil, PGCert, PGDip, PhD

School of Business, Management & Economics; www.sussex.ac.uk/aboutus/schoolsdepartments/bmec

Dept of Business & Management; www.sussex.ac.uk/Units/spru/bams
accounting & finance, banking & finance, business & management studies, business admin/finance, international banking & finance/business, international accounting & corporate governance, HRM, international management/marketing, management & entrepreneurship/finance, managing innovation & projects, marketing & management; BA, BSc, MSc, PGDip, LlB, MPhil, DPhil

Dept of Economics; www.sussex.ac.uk/economics

economics, economics & international development/international relations/management studies/politics, development economics, finance & business, mathematics with economics, PPE, international economics, international finance; BA, BSc, GradDip, MSc, MPhil, DPhil

Dept of Science & Technology Policy Research (SPRU); www.sussex.ac.uk/spru

science & technology policy, energy policy for sustainability, innovation & sustainability for international development, technology & innovation management; DPhil, MPhil, MSc

School of Education & Social Work; www.sussex.ac.uk/aboutus/schoolsdepartments/esw

Dept of Education; www.sussex.ac.uk/education

education, education studies, working with children & young people, initial teacher education; PGCE 11–18/7–14 maths/modern foreign languages/secondary(numerous subjects)/international; BA, MA, PGCE, PGCert/ Dip, EdD, MPhil, DPhil, MSc

Dept of Social Work & Social Care; www.sussex.ac.uk/socialwork

children's & youth studies, leadership, management & supervision of children's services, effective practice in children's services, practice education, social work, social research methods; BA, DPhil, MA, MPhil, MSc, PGCert

School of Engineering & Informatics www.sussex.ac.uk/ei

Engineering: advanced mechanical engineering, aerospace technology, automotive/mechanical engineering, electrical/electronic/computer engineering, digital communications & embedded systems, product design, satellite communications & space systems, sustainable engineering technology

Informatics: computer science, adv/computing & AI, computing for business & management/digital media, evolutionary & adaptive systems, games & multimedia environments, human-computer interaction, IT with business & management, intelligent systems, music informatics; BA, BSc, BEng, MEng, DPhil, MA, MComp, MPhil, MSc, PGCert

School of English; www.sussex.ac.uk/aboutus/schoolsdepartments/english

English language/literature/studies, American studies, drama & English/studies, early modern literature & culture, English (jt degrees) English literature & culture 1700–1900, literature, film & visual culture, literature, culture & thought, modern & contemporary culture, sexual dissidence & culture, creative & critical writing, critical theory, literature & philosophy, applied/linguistics; BA, DPhil, MA, MPhil

School of Global Studies; www.sussex.ac.uk/aboutus/schoolsdepartments/global

Dept of Anthropology; www.sussex.ac.uk/anthropology

anthropology & cultural studies/history/modern languages, anthropology & international development/geography/international relations, anthropology of development/social transformation, media practice for international development; BA, DPhil, MA, MSc

Dept of Geography; www.sussex.ac.uk/geography

geography & international relations/development/anthropology/modern languages, applied geomorphology, climate change/environment & policy/development, migration studies; BA, BSc, DPhil, MA, MPhil, MSc

International Development; www.sussex.ac.uk/development

international development, anthropology & international development/of social transformation, environmental development & policy, gender & development, globalization, ethnicity and culture, social development, human rights; BA, MA, MPhil, DPhil

Dept of International Relations; www.sussex.ac.uk/ir

conflict, security & development, geopolitics & grand strategy, global political economy, international relations & anthropology/ contemporary European studies/law/modern languages/law/politics/sociology/economics/geography/development, international security; BA, DPhil, MA

School of History, Art History & Philosophy; www.sussex.ac.uk/aboutus/schoolsdepartments/hahp

Dept of American Studies; www.sussex.ac.uk/americanstudies
American studies, American studies with history/English/film studies/politics/law/psychology; BA, MA, MPhil, DPhil, LlB

Dept of Art History; www.sussex.ac.uk/arthistory
art history & museum curating/philosophy/cultural studies/film studies/French/Italian/Spanish/English; BA, MA, MPhil, DPhil

Dept of History; www.sussex.ac.uk/history
contemporary history, history/& American studies/English/philosophy/sociology/anthropology/film studies, intellectual history, modern European history; BA, MPhil, DPhil, MA

Dept of Philosophy; www.sussex.ac.uk/philosophy
philosophy, philosophy & cognitive science, philosophy & English/French Spanish/Italian/Music, PPE, social & political thought; BA, MA, MPhil, DPhil

School of Law, Politics & Sociology; www.sussex.ac.uk/aboutus/schoolsdepartments/lps

Dept of Politics; www.sussex.ac.uk/politics
contemporary European studies, European politics, politics & international relations/languages/history/law/sociology/philosophy, PPE; BA, DPhil, MPhil

Sussex Law School; www.sussex.ac.uk/law
law, international criminal law/trade law/commercial law, law & business/American studies/international relations, development, law & criminology; DPhil, GradDip, LLB, LLM, MPhil, MSc

Dept of Sociology; www.sussex.ac.uk/sociology
sociology with cultural studies/politics/psychology/media studies/international relations/philosophy/politics/media, international development, gender studies, social sciences; BA, DPhil, MA, MPhil, MSc

School of Mathematical & Physical Sciences; www.sussex.ac.uk/aboutus/schoolsdepartments/mps

Dept of Mathematics; www.sussex.ac.uk/maths
mathematics, corporate & financial risk management, financial mathematics, mathematics with computer science/economics/physics, scientific computation; BSc, DPhil, MMath, MPhil, MSc, PGDip

Dept of Physics & Astronomy; www.sussex.ac.uk/physics
astronomy, astrophysics, cosmology, physics, astrophysics, theoretical/particle physics, frontiers of quantum technology; BSc, DPhil, MPhil, MPhys

School of Life Sciences; www.sussex.ac.uk/aboutus/schoolsdepartments/lifesci

Biochemistry & Molecular Biology; www.sussex.ac.uk/lifesci/biochemistry/
biochemistry, biomedical science, genetic manipulation & molecular cell biology

Evolution, Behaviour & Environment; www.sussex.ac.uk/lifesci/ebe/
biology, ecology & environment, developmental cell biology, environmental science

Genome Danger & Stability; www.sussex.ac.uk/gdsc/
various research topics

Neuroscience; www.sussex.ac.uk/lifesci/neuroscience/
neuroscience, medical neurosciences, neuroscience with cognition science/psychology, cellular & molecular neuroscience; BSc, DPhil, MPhil, MChem, MSc

School of Media, Film & Music; www.sussex.ac.uk/aboutus/schoolsdepartments/mfm

Dept of Media & Film; www.sussex.ac.uk/mediaandfilm/
computing for digital media, English & media studies, media & conservation, media studies & Italian/Spanish/cultural studies/sociology, film studies & American studies/art history/drama studies/English/history/French/Spanish/Italian, creative media practice, media/cultural studies, digital documentary/media, film studies, gender & media/cultural studies, media practice/studies, global film culture, journalism, media practice for international development

University of Sussex

Dept of Music; www.sussex.ac.uk/music/
music, music informatics, philosophy & music, music & sonic media
BA, BSc, DPhil, MA, MPhil, PhD, PGDip

School of Psychology; www.sussex.ac.uk/aboutus/ schoolsdepartments/psychology
psychology, psychology with American studies/cognitive science/neuroscience/sociolology, applied social psychology, experimental psychology, clinical psychology & mental health, health psychology, cognitive/ neuroscience, psychological methods/therapy; BSc, MRes, MSc, PGDip

SWANSEA UNIVERSITY
www.swansea.ac.uk

College of Arts & Humanities; www.swansea.ac.uk/artsandhumanities
classics, creative writing, English language studies, English literature/language studies, finance, French, German, Italian, Spanish, language & communication, Latin, media practice & PR, English literature/language & TEFL, translation & language/interpreting/with language technology/Chinese-English,-Welsh, American studies, ancient Egyptian culture/history, ancient & medieval history, classical/civilization, classics, European history, French/German/Italian/Spanish/Welsh with business/computer/legal studies, politics & intercultural studies, Greek, international communication/relations, early modern history, medieval studies, philosophy, politics & economics (PPE), PPL, political communications/theory, social history & social policy, TEFL, war & society, Welsh, Welsh writing in English; BA, MA, MPhil, MSc, MScEcon, PhD

College of Business & Economics & the Law; www.swansea.ac.uk/business
accounting & finance, business economics/with computing/finance, business management/with accountancy/finance/information systems/marketing/economics, economics/with politics/social policy/geography/marketing, financial economics/with accountancy, international business economics, management (finance/international management/marketing); BA, BSc, MBA, MPhil, MSc, MScEcon, PhD

College of Engineering; www.swansea.ac.uk/engineering
aerospace engineering/chemical engineering, biochemical engineering/bioprocess engineering, computational engineering/modelling/mechanics/& finite elements, civil engineering, communication systems, computational mechanics, electronic & electrical engineering, electronic systems design engineering, environmental engineering/management, information materials engineering/science, mechanical engineering, medical engineering, medical radiation physics, product design engineering, simulation-driven product design, sports science, steel technology, telecommunications engineering, nanomedicine/technology/electronics eng/science, structural materials for gas turbines; BEng, EngD, MEng, MPhil, MRes, MSc

College of Human & Health Sciences; www.swansea.ac.uk/Human & HealthSciences
audiology, advanced clinical practice/(infection control), applied social studies, health & chronic condition management, clinical physiology with cardiology/respiratory physiology, childhood studies, clinical technology (medical physics), cognitive neuroscience, ageing studies, enhanced professional practice, health & social care, health care law & ethics/science/management/informatics, public health/promotion/partnerships in care, infection prevention & control, medical sciences & humanities, midwifery, nursing (adult/child/mental health), specialist community public health nursing, paramedic science, osteopathy, ageing studies, early childhood, developmental & therapeutic play, abnormal & clinical/psychology, social policy/work/studies/history, developmental & therapeutic play; BA, BSc, BMid, BN, DipHE, HND, LLB, MA, MPhil, MSc, MScEcon, PGCert/Dip,PhD

School of Law; www.swansea.ac.uk/law
international/commercial/maritime/trade law, law, law & criminology, legal practice/& advanced

drafting, numerous jt degrees; GradDip, LLB, LLM, MA, MPhil, PGDip, PhD

College of Medicine; www.swansea.ac.uk/medicine

medical genetics, medical biochemistry, trauma surgery, biochemistry general medicine, liquid chromatography & mass spectrometry, health service research, basic biomedical & physiological science, bioinformatics, cell biology of cancer & reproduction, diabetes, immunity & allergy, medical physics & clinical engineering, microbiology & infection, neuroscience & molecular psychiatry, nanomedicine & medical devices; BSc, MBBCh, MD, MPhil, MSc, PhD

College of Science; www.swansea.ac.uk/science

Dept of Biosciences; www.swansea.ac.uk/biosci

biology, biological science & genetics, maritime biology, zoology, environmental biology, conservation & resource management, aquatic ecology & conservation, sustainable aquaculture & fisheries

Dept of Computer Science; www.swansea.ac.uk/compsci

computer science, computing/& communications, computer science & pure mathematics/physics/geoinformatics, adv computer science, software technology, human-computer interaction, visual computing, safety & secure systems

Dept of Geography; www.swansea.ac.uk/geography

geography, human geography, physical earth geography, geography & geoinformatics/European studies, environmental dynamics & climate change, geographical information & climate change, global migration

Dept of Physics; www.swansea.ac.uk/physics

physics, theoretical physics, physics & nanotechnology, particle physics & cosmology, modelling, uncertainty & data

Dept of Mathematics; www.swansea.ac.uk/maths

mathematics, pure/applied mathematics, mathematics for finance, mathematics & physics/geoinformatics/computing for finance, modelling, uncertainty & data; BSc, MEng, MMath, MPhil, MPhys, MRes, MSc, PhD

UNIVERSITY OF TEESSIDE
www.tees.ac.uk

School of Arts & Media; www.tees.ac.uk/schools/sam

broadcast media production, creative writing, dance, design, digital arts, English studies/& cultural history, fine art, future design/in creative media, graphical design, history, interior architecture/design, media & journalism/& news practice, local & regional/social & cultural history, multimedia PA/journalism/PR, music technology, performance & events production, performing arts, performing for live & recorded material, product design, professional dance practice, TV & film production; BA(Hons), BSc(Hons), FdA, MA, MPhil, MSc, PhD

School of Computing; www.tees.ac.uk/schools/scm

applied/computing, adv computer science, animation & games, computer & digital forensics, computer animation/& visual effects, computer character animation, computer games animation/art/design/programming, computer science, computing/networking/mathematics, creative animation production, creative digital media, information & communication technologies, instrumentation & control engineering, graphics/art/visual effects, network systems, web & multimedia design, digital/character animation, creating digital media, computing networking, ICT, software development, networks & communication, network systems, graphic design (multimedia & web publishing), music technology, web multimedia design/design/development; BA, BSc, DProf, FdSc, HNC, HND, MA, MPhil, MProf, MSc, PGDip, PhD

School of Health & Social Care; www.tees.ac.uk/schools/soh

adv clinical practice, neurological rehabilitation musculoskeletal studies, behavioural analysis, cardiac care, clinical psychology, dental hygiene/therapy/nurse practice, diagnostic radiography, evidence-based medicine (various surgical/anaesthesia/adv cardiac care/nurse practice/surgical care practice), forensic radiography, leadership in/managing/health & social care, long-term health conditions, midwifery, nursing studies (adult, child, learning disabilities, mental health, surgery), nusing in home/district nursing, manipulative therapy, medical ultrasound, neurological rehabilitation, occupational therapy, operating dept practice, orthopaedics, physiotherapy, practice innovation (acute care), primary care, profession health/nursing services, public health, specialist community public health nursing (health visiting/occupational therapy/schools nursing), surgical care, social work; BA, BSc, DipHE, FdSc, HND, MA, MPhil, MSc, PGCert/Dip

Science & Engineering; www.tees.ac.uk/schools/sse

adv manufacturing systems, aeronautical/aerospace engineering, automotive engineering, chemistry, biological sciences, biotechnology, chemical/civil engineering, computer & digital forensics, control & electronics, crime & investigation, crime scene science, disaster management, electrical & electronic engineering, electronics & communications, energy & environmental engineering, engineering/management, environmental science/health, fire scene investigation, food, nutrition & health science, forensic biology/science, instrumentation & control engineering, mechanical engineering, petroleum technology, project management, renewable energy engineering; BEng, BSc, FdEng, HNC, HND, MPhil, MRes, MSc, PGDip, PhD

School of Social Sciences & Law; www.tees.ac.uk/schools/ss

business/criminal law, international/medical law, counselling & psychology, childhood & youth studies, clinical psychology, criminal investigation/law, criminology with sociology/law/psychology/youth studies/investigation, contemporary drug use, early childhood studies, education studies, legal/& forensic psychology, global development, health psychology, human rights, international/criminal law, investigative skills, law, outdoor education, police studies, policing & investigation, professional policing, promoting inclusive practice in education, social research methods, social sciences, sociology, sport & exercise (exercise science/sport science/coaching), sports therapy, fitness instruction & sports massage, adv sports therapy & rehabilitation science, strength & conditioning psychology/development/therapy & rehabilitation), teaching in lifelong learning, youth & community studies/criminology/psychology; BA, BSc, DProf, FdA, FdSc, FdSocSc, GradCert, HNC,CertEd, HND, LLB, LLM, MA, MPhil, MProf, MSc, PhD

Teesside Business School; www.tees.ac.uk/schools/tubs/

accounting & finance, advertising, business administration/finance/management, business with law, economic crime management, financial investigation & financial crime, fraud management, hospitality management, HRM, international/management, marketing, project management, tourism & aviation, travel & tourism/management, leadership & management; BA, BSc, DBA, FdA, FdSc, HND, MA, MBA, MSc, PGDip

---

TRINITY COLLEGE LONDON
www.trinitycollege.co.uk

---

dance, drama & speech, music, performing arts, English language, teaching English; PGDip, SfL, TESOL

UNIVERSITY OF ULSTER
www.ulster.ac.uk

Faculty of Art, Design & the Built Environment; www.adbe.ulster.ac.uk

School of Architecture & Design; www.adbe.ulster.ac.uk/schools/archi_design
3D design (interior, product & furniture design), architectural studies/technology & management, architecture, interior design; BA, BDes, BSc, CertHE, MArch, MLA, MSc

School of Art & Design; www.adbe.ulster.ac.uk/schools/art_design
art & design, art in public, design for visual communication, fine & applied arts, fine art, photography, textile material product, textiles & fashion design; BA, BDes, BSc, MA, MDes, MFA, PGDip

School of the Built Environment; www.adbe.ulster.ac.uk/schools/built_environment
building engineering & materials, building services & energy engineering, civil engineering, construction engineering/business project management, energy & building services engineering, environmental health, fire safety engineering, housing management/studies, hydrogen safety engineering, infrastructure engineering, property investment & development/planning, quantity surveying & commercial management, renewable engineering & energy management, transportation; BEng, BSc, MEng, MPhil, MSc, PGCert, PGDip, PhD

Faculty of Arts; www.arts.ulster.ac.uk
documentary practice, film & TV management & policy, interactive media arts, journalism, languages & translation, media studies, photo-imaging
The following can be taken single subject or in a large number of joint degrees: drama, music, English, history, Irish, film studies, French, German, Spanish, Irish, Chinese; BA, MA, MPhil, PGDip, PhD, MRes, BMus, MMus, MDes, CertHE

Faculty of Computing & Engineering; www.compeng.ulster.ac.uk

School of Computing & Information Engineering; www.compeng.ulster.ac.uk/cie
computing, computing artificial intelligence/digital games development/internet systems, telecommunications & internet systems,computing with accountancy/business, education/geography/physics; BSc, MSc, PGDip, PhD

School of Computing & Intelligent systems; www.scis.ulster.ac.uk
creative computing (games/design), information & communications technologies, computer science (intelligent systems/mobile computing/software systems development), computer games development, multimedia computer games/computing & design, computing with accounting/HRM/management studies/marketing, computing & creative technologies/intelligent systems/financial services; BEng, BSc, MSc, PGDip, PhD

School of Computing & Mathematics; www.infj.ulst.ac.uk/cm/
computing & information systems, computer security, computing science/& mathematics, computing/web technologies/healthcare informatics/communication/artificial intelligence, creative computing, information & communication technologies, interactive multimedia design,computing science (artificial intelligence/healthcare/technologies/network technologies), software engineering; BSc, MSc, PGCert, PGDip, PhD

School of Engineering; www.seng.ulster.ac.uk/eme
biomedical engineering, clean technology, electronic engineering, communications & software, engineering management, mechanical engineering, mechatronics engineering, sports technology, technology/design, adv composites & polymers, medical electronics, nanotechnology; BSc, BEng, MEng, MSc, PGDip, PhD

University of Ulster

Faculty of Life & Health Sciences;
www.science.ulster.ac.uk

School of Biomedical Sciences; www.biomed.science.ulster.ac.uk
applied biosciences, biology, biomedical science, biotechnology, cataract & refractory studies, clinical visual sciences, dietetics, food regulatory affairs, food & forensic studies, human nutrition, optometry, pathology, pharmaceutical sciences, pharmacy/management, stem cell biology, systems biology, veterinary public health; BSc, DMedSc, GradCert, MPharm, MSc, PGCert, PGDip

School of Environmental Sciences; www.science.ulster.ac.uk/envsci
coastal zone management, coastal & marine tourism, environmental management/science/studies/toxicology & pollution monitoring, GIS, geography, marine science/spatial planning; AB, BSc, DEnvSci, MPhil, MRes, MSc, PGCert, PGDip, PhD

School of Health Sciences; www.science.ulster.ac.uk/health
advanced practice, clinical physiology research/cardiology/respiratory, health science, occupational therapy, physiotherapy, podiatry, radiography (diagnostic/therapeutic), speech & language therapy; BSc, MClinRes, MSc

School of Nursing; www.science.ulster.ac.uk/nursing
community & public health nursing, dementia studies, health promotion & population health, health & social care/wellbeing, independent & supplementary prescribing, learning disabilities, midwifery, nursing practice/adult/public health, palliative care, primary care & general practice, specialist midwifery/nursing practice; BSc, CertHE, MSc, PGCert, PGDip, MPhil, PhD

School of Psychology; www.science.ulster.ac.uk/psychology
applied behaviour analysis, applied psychology (mental health), careers guidance, health psychology, psychology; BSc, MSc, PGDip

Ulster Sports Academy; www.ulster.ac.uk/science
physical activity & population health, sport & exercise sciences, applied sport & exercise psychology, sports management/coaching/studies/technology/development, sports & exercise nutrition; BSc, FdSc, MPhil, MSc, DPhil, PGDip, PhD

Faculty of Social Sciences;
www.socsci.ulster.ac.uk

School of Communication; www.socsci.ulster.ac.uk/comms
advertising & marketing, PR, counselling/& therapeutic communication, communication with advertising/counselling/PR, political lobbying & public affairs, language & linguistics with advertising/communications/counselling/PR, linguistics/in advertising; BSc, MPhil, MSc, PGCert, PGDip, PhD

School of Economics; www.socsci.ulster.ac.uk/ecompolitics
applied/ business economics, economics, economics with accountancy/marketing/politics; BSc, MSc, PGDip

School of Education; www.socsci.ulster.ac.uk/education
PGCE (post-primary, primary, in numerous school subjects, FE), Certificate in Teaching, contemporarysociety, educational leadership & management, education with numerous jt degree subjects, ICT, inclusive & special education, international development, teaching & learning, library & information management; TESOL, MEd, PGCE, PGCert, PGDip, BA(hons), BSc(Hons)

School of Law; www.socsci.ulster.ac.uk/law
law, law & criminology/politics, human rights law & transitional justice, clinical legal education; LLB, LLM

School of Criminology, Politics & Social Policy; www.socsci.ulster.ac.uk/policy
criminology/ & criminal justice, health & social care policy, politics, public administration, social policy, international studies, procurement executive development, politics with criminology/economics sociology/law/international studies; BSc, MPA, PGCert, PGDip

School of Sociology & Applied Social Studies; www.socsci.ulster.ac.uk/sociology
community development/youth work, restorative practices, profession development/in social work, sociology/with international politics/social work/criminology/HRM/law/politics; BSc, MSc, PGCert, PGDip

Graduate School of Professional Legal Education; www.socsci.ulster.ac.uk/gsple
legal practice; PGDip

Ulster Business School;
www.business.ulster.ac.uk
accounting & law/advertising/HRM/finance/marketing, accounting, advanced accounting, advertising & HRM, accounting computing, drama, psychology, agri-food business development, applied management, business, business development & innovation, business improvement, business information systems business, management, business studies, business with accounting/business/drama/education/environmental science/French/geography/German/HRM/international development/Irish/marketing/media studies/psychology/retail studies/Spanish, consumer studies, creative advertising technologies, culinary arts management, cultural management, event management, executive leadership, finance & investment analysis, financial services, HRM, innovation management in the public service, international business/by e-learning, international hospitality management/tourism development, travel & tourism management/studies with languages, leisure & events management, management & corporate governance/& leadership development, management practice, marketing, social enterprise, sport management; BSc, CertHE, HND, MBA, MBS, MSc, PGDip

UNIVERSITY OF WALES: GLYNDWR UNIVERSITY
www.newi.ac.uk

Institute for Arts, Science & Technology;
www.glyndwr.ac.uk/en/
UniversityInstitutes/
ArtsScienceandTechnology

Creative Industries, Media & Performance;
www.glyndwr.ac.uk/en/
UniversityInstitutes/
ArtsScienceandTechnology/
CreativeIndustries/

Applied Art: design, applied arts, garden design, art/design practice.
Communications Technology: music technology, studio recording & performance technology
Design, Communication & Digital Art: design communication/creative media, digital media design & production
Creative Computing: computer game development, creative media computing
Journalism & Media: broadcasting, journalism, media communications, screen studies, English, journalism; BA(Hons), BSc(Hons), FdSA, FdSc, CertHE, MA, MPhil, PhD

Electrical and Electronic Engineering;
www.glyndwr.ac.uk/en/
Undergraduatecourses/
ElectricalandElectronicEngineering/

advanced electronic techniques, digital & RF communication systems, electrical & electronic engineering/systems, sound & broadcast engineering, automation systems, instrumentation & control, renewable energy & sustainability/distributed generation; BEng(Hons), FdEng, HNC/D, MSc, PhD, MPhil, MRes

Computing; www.glyndwr.ac.uk/en/
UniversityInstitutes/
ArtsScienceandTechnology/Computing/

applied/computing, computer studies, computer game development, computer network management & security, creative audio/computing/media technology, information technology support, library & information practice, computer networking/science, high performance computing; BSc(Hons), FdEng, MSc, MRes, PhD

Aeronautical & Mechanical Engineering;
www.glyndwr.ac.uk/en/
Undergraduatecourses/
AeronauticalandMechanicalEngineering/

Aeronautical Engineering: aeronautical & electronic engineering (avionics)/mechanical engineering, aeronautical engineering (manufacture/logistics), aircraft maintenance/electronics & control
Mechanical Engineering: mechanical technology, manufacturing engineering, composites. performance car technology; BEng(Hons), FdEng, HNC/D, MPhil, PhD, MSc, MRes

Materials & Analytical Science;
www.glyndwr.ac.uk/en/
UniversityInstitutes/
ArtsScienceandTechnology/
ScienceandTechnology/
MaterialsandAnalyticalSciences/

forensic science, environmental science; BSc(Hons), FdSc

Natural & Built Environment

Built environment: architectural design technology, building studies (construction/maintenance management), estate agency/management, housing studies, sustainable development, housing & sustainable communities, supported housing, regeneration & sustainability, environmental science, occupational health, safety, & environmental management

Animal Studies & Equestrian Psychology: animal studies, equestrian psychology, Welsh; BSc(Hons), FdSc

Management & Business

business accounting/management/marketing/administration, business & events marketing, accounting & finance, interrnational business, IT management, marketing, logistics & operations management, HRM, marketing management; BA(Hons), FdA, HNC, PhD, MPhil, MA, MBA, MSc, ProfDoc

Humanities; www.glyndwr.ac.uk/en/ UniversityInstitutes/ ArtsScienceandTechnology/Humanities/

English: creative writing/history, history, history & Welsh language studies, local history, library & information practice/management, information management

Languages: history & Welsh language studies, professional Welsh, Welsh translation, languages & language education, Adv English for speakers of other languages

Screen Studies: broadcasting, journalism/media communication & screen studies; BA(Hons), FdA, FdSc, PhD, MA;

Welsh; www.glyndwr.ac.uk/en/ UniversityInstitutes/ ArtsScienceandTechnology/Welsh/

professional Welsh; BA(Hons)FdA

Institute for Health, Medical Science & Society; www.glyndwr.ac.uk/en/ UniversityInstitutes/ HealthMedicalScienceandSociety

Art & Design; www.glyndwr.ac.uk/en/ UniversityInstitutes/ ArtsScienceandTechnology/ArtandDesign/

design: animation & games art/film & photography/graphic design & multimedia/illustration/graphic novels & children's publishing, fine art, applied arts; BA(Hons)

Education & Childhood Studies; www.glyndwr.ac.uk/en/ Undergraduatecourses/ EducationChildhoodStudies/

education/families & childhood studies, early childhood care & education, learning & development of babies & young children; BA(Hons), FdA

Education; www.glyndwr.ac.uk/en/ UniversityInstitutes/ HealthMedicalSciencesandSociety/ Education/

post-compulsory/professional education & training, learning & teaching support, dyslexia, e-learning, theory & practice, professional development in education, teaching of psychology, professional development (education); BA(Hons), FdA, PGCert, GradCert, ProDoc, MPhil, PhD, MA, MSc

Health & Medical Sciences; www.glyndwr.ac.uk/en/ UniversityInstitutes/ HealthMedicalSciencesandSociety/

Complementary Medicine: acupuncture, complementary therapies for healthcare, occupational Health & Safety; occupational health, safety, occupational & environmental risk management, public health

Nursing & Health Care studies (pre reg): advanced clinical practice, nursing (adult/mental health)

Health & care studies (post reg): community practice, community specialist practice (community children's/district/general practice nursing), health studies, healthcare/& social care leadership & management, specialist community professions, palliative care, professional education, public health nursing (health visiting/occupational health/school nursing), clinical/community practice, counselling/with children & young people, occupational therapy

Psychology: psychology of religion, teaching of psychology; BSc(Hons), FdSc, BN(Hons), Dip/CertHE, MSc, MPhil, PhD, MA, ProfDoc

Science & Environment

polymer science & technology; MRes, MPhil, PhD

Society & Community

Counselling: counselling studies, person-centred & experiential counselling & psychotherapy

Criminal Justice: criminology & criminal justice

Social Care: social work, therapeutic childcare, counselling & psychotherapy, counselling studies/with children & young people

Social Science: public & social policy. Youth & Community, youth & community work/studies;

Cer/DiptHE, BA(Hons), FdA, MPhil, PhD, MA, ProfDoc

Social Sciences
social science; MRes, MPhil, PhD

Sport & Exercise Sciences;
www.glyndwr.ac.uk/en/
UniversityInstitutes/
HealthMedicalSciencesandSociety/
SportandExerciseSciences/
sport & exercise sciences, sports coaching; BSc(Hons), MRes, MPhil, PhD

UNIVERSITY OF WALES: NEWPORT
www.newport.ac.uk

Faculty of Arts & Business

Newport Business School;
www.newport.ac.uk/Newport-Business-School
accounting & economics/finance/financial management/law/business, business studies, business & marketing/management/law/HRM, HRM, law, management, marketing, business leadership/enterprise development/psychology/studies, digital strategy/marketing, evaluation studies, leadership & management, managing customer service excellence, project management, public sector management, sports management, strategic decision making, strategic marketing, telecommunications with management; BA, BSc, BEng, FdSc, HNC, HND, MBA, MSc

School of Design, Engineering, Fashion & Technology; www.newport.ac.uk/Design-Engineering-fashion-and-technology
Design: advertising design, art design & media, computer games design, creative writing, creative & therapeutic arts, fashion design, photography for fashion & advertising, smart clothes & wearable technology
Computing: forensic computing, information security systems, computing, cyber crime forensics, ICT & education
Engineering: building studies, systems engineering, electrical engineering, electronic & communications engineering, engineering, fire safety engineering, mechanical & manufacturing engineering, telecommunications with management

School of Film, Photography & Digital Media; www.newport.ac.uk/Film-Photography-and-Digital-Media
Film & Screen Media: animation, creative audiovisual media, documentary, film & TV, film & video, scriptwriting/screen media & film

School of Performing Arts;
applied drama, creative music/practice, performance (theatre & film), scriptwriting for screen media & film
Photography; documentary photography, photographic art, photography for fashion & advertising, contemporary photographic practice; BA(Hons), BSc(Hons), BEng, MA, MSc, MFA, FD, MFA

Faculty of Education & Social Sciences

School of Education; www.newport.ac.uk/
http:/www.newport.ac.uk/study/subjectareas/education
adult literacy/numeracy, applied drama, autism, child & adolescent mental health, childhood studies, SEN development coordination disorders, ESOL, early years, education & ICT, education leadership & management (PCET/health education), inclusive education, education studies, secondary teaching, mobility & orientation, post-compulsory education & training, GCE/adult numeracy/literacy, primary studies with QTS, RE, rehabilitation (visual impairment), returning & supply teachers, secondary teaching design & technology (QTS)/mathematics/science, secondary design & technology, SEN specific learning difficulties/hearing impairment, visual impairment, teaching English as an additional language, special educational needs, TESOL, TAEL; BA, BSc, FdA, MA, PGCE, PGCert, PGDip, CertHE, Univ Cert

School of Humanities & Lifelong Learning; www.newport.ac.uk/Humanities-and-Lifelong-Learning/
Education: see School of Education
English: creative writing, English
History: history, regional history
Religious Studies: religious studies, Buddhist studies, religious education, professional development

Sustainable Development/Global Citizenship: energy management, professional development, education for sustainable development & citizenship; BA(Hons), MA, PGDip/Cert

School of Sport, Health & Applied Social Sciences; www.newport.ac.uk/Sport-Health-and-Applied-Social-Sciences

Health: community health & wellbeing, counselling studies, nutrition, psychological & counselling studies, rehabilitation (visual impairment), art psychotherapy, autism, child & adolescent mental health, childhood studies, consultative supervision, counselling/ children & young people, developmental disorders, leadership & management (healthcare & education), mobility & orientation in education, music therapy, SEN dyspraxia, hearing/visual impairmant, specifics, learning difficulties, special educationProfessional Development: managing customer service excellence, business psychology, community health studies, cognitive behavioural therapy, counselling/studies, criminology & criminal justice, social work, social studies, sports coaching, sports studies/management, working with young people, youth justiceSport: sports coaching/studies; BSc(Hons), BA(Hons), MA, MSc, PGCert/Dip, CertHE, FD

UNIVERSITY OF WALES: SWANSEA METROPOLITAN UNIVERSITY
www.smu.ac.uk

Faculty of Applied Design & Engineering; www.smu.ac.uk/index.php/potential-students/faculty-of-applied-design-and-engineering

School of Applied Computing; www.smu.ac.uk/index.php/potential-students/faculty-of-applied-design-and-engineering/school-of-applied-computing

business information technology, computer games development, computer networks/systems & electronics, computing & information systems, e-commerce, electronic engineering, software engineering, web development; BEng, BSc, HND, MSc

School of Automotive Engineering; www.smu.ac.uk/index.php/potential-students/faculty-of-applied-design-and-engineering/school of automotive engineering

automotive engineering, motorcycle engineering, motorsport engineering & design/technology; BEng, BSc, HND

School of Built & Natural Environment; www.smu.ac.uk/index.php/potential-students/faculty-of-applied-design-and-engineering/school-of-natural-environment

building studies, civil engineering & environmental management, facilities management, project & construction management, quantity surveying; BSc, HNC, HND, MSc

School of Digital Media; www.smu.ac.uk/index.php/potential-students/faculty-of-applied-design-and-engineering/school-of digital-media

3D/computer animation, creative computer games design, interactive digital media, multimedia, music technology; BA, BSc, HND, MA, MSc

School of Industrial Design; www.smu.ac.uk/index.php/potential-students/faculty-of-applied-design-and-engineering/school-of-industrial-design

automotive design, industrial design, product design/& innovation, transportation design; BA, BSc, MA, MSc

School of Logistics & Manufacturing Engineering; www.smu.ac.uk/index.php/potential-students/faculty-of-applied-design-and-engineering/school-of-logistics-a-manufacturing

logistics, lean & agile manufacturing, mechanical & manufacturing engineering, food logistics, motorsport management, non-destructive testing & evaluation; BSc, BEng, HND, MA, MSc

Welsh School of Architectural Glass; www.smu.ac.uk/index.php/faculty-of-applied-design-a-engineering/welsh-school-of-architectural-glass

architectural glass, stained glass; BA, MA

Faculty of Art & Design;
www.smu.ac.uk/index.php/potential-students/faculty-of-art-and-design

School of Contextual Studies & Visual Communication; www.smu.ac.uk/index.php/potential-students/faculty-of-art-and-design/csvc

graphic/design for advertising, general illustration; BA, HND

School of Fine Arts; www.smu.ac.uk/index.php/potential-students/faculty-of-art-and-design/school-of-fine-arts

fine art: combined media/painting & drawing/3D & sculpture, photography & video: photography in the arts, photojournalism, documentary video, video arts, surface pattern (textiles); surface pattern design (contemporary arts practice/textiles for fashion/for interiors), digital film & TV production, visual communication, graphic design, advertising & brand design, general illustration; BA, FdA, MA

Faculty of Humanities; www.smu.ac.uk/faculty-of-humanities

Swansea School of Education; www.smu.ac.uk/index.php/faculty-of-humanities/swansea-school-of-education

educational studies, drama & educational support, post-compulsory education & training, professional development (education & training/teaching & learning), learning support, introduction to teaching, maths education, PGCE primary/secondary (in numerous subjects), secondary education, primary education (Welsh medium); BA, MA, FD, MRes, MA, GradDip

School of Performance & Literature; www.smu.ac.uk/index.php/faculty-of-humanities/school-of-performance-a-literatuture

performing arts, drama & counselling/educational studies/psychology, technical theatre; BA, HNC, HND, MPhil, PhD

School of Psychology & Counselling; www.smu.ac.uk/index.php/faculty-of-humanities/school-of-psychology-and-counselling

counselling & educational studies/psychology/drama, psychology & education studies/counselling/drama, counselling practice; BA, MPhil, PhD, Dip, PGDip, MA

Faculty of Business & Management;
www.smu.ac.uk/faculty-of-businss-and-management

Swansea Business School; www.smu.ac.uk/index.php/faculty-of-humanities/swansea-business-schools

accounting, business & finance, business, HRM, HR development, financial services/management, marketing management, international business international tourism, events management, leisure management, tourism management, international travel & tourism management, sports management; BA, FdA, GradDip, HND, MA, MA(Ed), MRes, PGCE, MBA, MSc

School of Public Service Leadership; www.smu.ac.uk/index.php/faculty-of-humanities/school-of-public-service-leadership

health & social care, public services; BA, MPhil, PhD

UNIVERSITY OF WALES: TRINITY SAINT DAVID
www.trinitysaintdavid.ac.uk

Faculty of Humanities;
www.trinitysaintdavid.ac.uk/en/facultyofhumanities/

School of Archaeology, History & Anthropology; www.trinitysaintdavid.ac.uk/en/archaeologyhistoryandanthropology/

anthropology, archaeology, history, medieval studies, modern historical studies, landscape management & environmental archaeology, ancient history & archaeology, cultural astronomy & astrology, local history; BA, MA, PhD

School of Cultural Studies; www.trinitysaintdavid.ac.uk/en/schoolofculturalstudies/

Chinese studies, creative writing, creative & script writing, English & creative writing/TEFL, medieval &

early modern literature, modern literature, applied/philosophy, European philosophy

School of Classics; www.trinitysaintdavid.ac.uk/en/schoolofclassics/
ancient history/civilizations, ancient history & archaeology, classical studies, ancient & medieval history, classics, Greek, Latin; BA, MA, MPhil, PhD

Dept of Theology & Religious Studies & Islamic Studies; www.trinitysaintdavid.ac.uk/en/schooloftheologyreligiousstudiesandislamicstudies/
biblical interpretation, Celtic Christianity, Christian theology, church history, Islamic studies, philosophy, religious history/studies, study of religions, jt hons in numerous subjects, theology; BA, DMin, DPT, LTh, MA, MMin, MTh

Faculty of Arts & Social Studies; www.trinitysaintdavid.ac.uk/en/facultyofartsandsocialstudies/

School of Business; www.trinitysaintdavid.ac.uk/en/schoolofbusiness/
business information technology/management, internet/computing, management & information technology, prof practice, tourism/management, social/entrepreneurship, HRM, information security/management, leadership, marketing, professional practice, professional arts management, heritage tourism management, technology enhanced learning; BA, MBA, MA, MSc, MPhil, PhD, GradCert, GradDip

School of Creative Arts; www.trinitysaintdavid.ac.uk/en/creativearts/
applied art, art & design, 3D designer maker-craft product, ceramics & jewellery, digital illustration, fashion: apparel design & construction, fine art, graphic communication, photography, textiles, art, design, craft, film & visual culture, new media production, fine art: contemporary practice, painting, drawing & printmaking, sculpture, photography; BA(Hons), MPhil, PhD

School of Sport, Health & Outdoor Education; www.trinitysaintdavid.ac.uk/en/schoolofsporthealthandoutdooreducation/
health, nutrition & lifestyle, PE with SQTS, health & exercise/sport studies, outdoor education; BA, BSc, MA

School of Performing Arts; www.trinitysaintdavid.ac.uk/en/schooloftheatreandperformance/
acting, theatre design & production, drama & education – context & practices, theatre & society; BA, MA

Faculty of Education & Training; www.trinitysaintdavid.ac.uk/en/facultyofeducationandtraining

School of Early Childhood; www.trinitysaintdavid.ac.uk/en/schoolofearlychildhood/
early years education, early childhood, nursery management, Welsh & bilingual practice in early years, foundation phase; MA, BA, CertHE, PGDip

School of Initial Training & Education; www.trinitysaintdavid.ac.uk/en/schoolofinitialteachereducationandtraining/
primary education with QTS, professional development, education; MA, BA, GradDip

School of Welsh & Bilingual Studies; www.trinitysaintdavid.ac.uk/en/schoolofwelshandbilingualstudies/
Celtic studies, bilingualism & multilingualism; BA, MA, MPhil, PhD

Welsh International Academy of Voice; www.trinitysaintdavid.ac.uk/en/schoolofwelshandbilingualstudies/
advanced vocal studies; MA

UNIVERSITY OF WARWICK
www.warwick.ac.uk

Faculty of Arts; www2.warwick.ac.uk/fac/arts

Dept of Classics & Ancient History; www2.warwick.ac.uk/fac/arts/classics
ancient history & classical archaeology, ancient visual & material culture, visual & material culture in ancient Rome, classical civilization/with philosophy, classics, English & Latin literature, Italian & classics, Italian literature; BA, MA, MPhil, PhD

Dept of English & Comparative Literary Studies; www2.warwick.ac.uk/fac/arts/english
English literature, creative writing, English & theatre studies, pan-romanticisms, philosophy, film & literature, world literatures, writing, English & French/German/Latin/Italian; BA, MA, MPhil, PhD

Dept of Film & TV Studies; www2.warwick.ac.uk/fac/arts/film
film & literature/TV studies, research in film & TV, history & film; BA, MA, MPhil, PhD

Dept of French Studies; www2.warwick.ac.uk/fac/arts/french
English & French, French studies with history of art/German/Italian studies/film studies/ stage & theatre German/history/international studies/Italian/politics/film/sociology, film, French culture & thought, French & francophone studies; BA, MA, MPhil, PGDip, PhD

Dept of German Studies; www2.warwick.ac.uk/fac/arts/german
German cultural studies, German studies, German with business studies/French/international studies/Italian/Spanish/history, pan-romanticism, translation, writing & cultural differences; BA, MA, MPhil, PGDip, PhD

Dept of History; www2.warwick.ac.uk/fac/arts/history
history, 18th-century studies, comparative American history, global history, history & politics/sociology/Italian/French/German, history, history of race in America, literature & culture of the Americas, historical studies, modern European, modern history, Renaissance & early modern, medieval world, histography, history of medicine, religious & social history, 1500–1700; BA, MA, MPhil, PhD

Dept of History of Art; www2.warwick.ac.uk/fac/arts/arthistory
art history with Italian, history of art/& French, Venice, British art; BA, MA, MPhil, PGDip, PhD

Dept of Italian; www2.warwick.ac.uk/fac/arts/italian
comparative Italian/& European studies, Italian & French/German/Classics/theatre studies/international studies/history of art/European literature, translation, writing & cultural differences; BA, MA, MPhil, PGDip, PhD

School of Comparative American Studies; www2.warwick.ac.uk/fac/arts/cas
comparative American studies, literature, film & politics of the USA, literature & culture of the Americas, history of race in the Americas; BA, MA, PhD

School of Theatre, Performance & Cultural Policy Studies; www2.warwick.ac.uk/fac/arts/Theatre_s
theatre consultancy, international cultural policy & management, creative & media enterprise, global media & communication, theatre & performance studies; BA, MA, MPhil, PhD

Faculty of Medicine; www2.warwick.ac.uk/fac/med

Warwick Medical School
adv clinical practice, child health, chronic kidney disease, clinical systems improvement, diabetes, emergency care, health sciences, health services management, medical education/leadership, medicine & surgery, mental health, occupational health, oral surgery, orthodontic surgery, orthopaedics, palliative care, philosophy & ethics of mental health, pre-hospital critical care, public health/& epidemiology, sexual & reproductive health care, systems leadership & management, dentistry, implant dentistry, ortho/endodontics, restorative dentistry; MBChB, MD, MMedSci, MPhil, MSc, PhD

Faculty of Science; www2.warwick.ac.uk/fac/sci

Dept of Life Sciences; www2.warwick.ac.uk/fac/sci/lifesci

biochemistry, biomedical science, biological sciences, biotechnology, bioprocessing & business management, cell biology, food science, environmental resources, food security, medical microbiology, molecular genetics, sustainable crop production virology; BSc, MD, MPhil, MSc, PhD

Dept of Chemistry; www2.warwick.ac.uk/fac/sci/chemistry

analytical science, chemical biology, chemistry, molecular/physical chemistry, chemical physics, materials chemistry, synthetics, polymer chemistry, chemistry with scientific writing; BSc, MChem, MSc, PhD

Dept of Computer Science; www2.warwick.ac.uk/fac/sci/dcs

computer & management sciences, cognitive systems, computer science/& applications, computing systems, discrete mathematics; BSc, MEng, MPhil, MSc, PhD

School of Engineering; www2.warwick.ac.uk/fac/sci/eng

automotive engineering, biomedical engineering, civil engineering, computer & information engineering, electronic engineering/systems, electronic systems with communications/sensor technology, engineering systems, energy & power electronic systems, engineering/& business, engineering business management, manufacturing & mechanical engineering/systems, mechanical systems, systems engineering, tunnelling & underground space; BEng, BSc, EngD, MPhil, MSc, PhD

Dept of Mathematics/Warwick Mathematics Institute; www2.warwick.ac.uk/fac/sci/maths

financial/interdisciplinary mathematics, mathematics, mathematics & business studies/economics/philosophy; BSc, MMath, MSc, PhD

Dept of Physics; www2.warwick.ac.uk/fac/sci/physics

mathematics & physics, physics/& business studies, Master project options; BSc, MPhys, MSc, PhD, MMathPhys

Dept of Psychology; www2.warwick.ac.uk/fac/sci/psych

philosophy with psychology, behavioural & economic science, clinical applications of psychology, psychology; BSc, MPhil, MSc, PhD

Dept of Statistics; www2.warwick.ac.uk/fac/sci/statistics

statistics & mathematics/economics, operational research, financial mathematics; MMathStat, MPhil, MSc, PgDip, PhD

Faculty of Social Studies; www2.warwick.ac.uk/fac/soc

Centre for Applied Linguistics; www2.warwick.ac.uk/fac/soc/al

English language teaching/for young learners/specific purposes/ICT & multimedia/testing & assessment methods, intercultural communication/for business & the professions, English, translation & cultural studies, teaching English as a second language; BEd, BA(Hons), EdD, MA, MPhil, PGCert, PGDip, PhD

Dept of Economics; www2.warwick.ac.uk/fac/soc/economics

economics, economics & industrial organisation/politics & international studies, mathematics, operational research, statistics & economics, economic development & growth, international financial economics, economics, behavioural & economic science, PPE; BA, BSc, BSc/Ec, MEcMSc, PGDip, PhD

Dept of Philosophy; www2.warwick.ac.uk/fac/soc/philosophy

continental philosophy, philosophy, philosophy & literature/maths/psychology, philosophy of mind, philosophy, politics & economics; BA, BSc, MA, MPhil, PGDip, PhD

Dept of Politics & International Studies; www2.warwick.ac.uk/fac/soc/pais

politics & international studies/French/ German/ sociology/history/economics/international studies, globalization & development, international politics & East Asia/Europe, international relations/security/political economy, politics, public policy; BA, MA, MPhil, PhD

Dept of Sociology; www2.warwick.ac.uk/fac/soc/sociology

gender & international development, science, media & public policy, social & political thought, sociology/

& law/politics/French, social policy; BA, MA, MPhil, PGDip, PhD

School of Health & Social Studies; www2.warwick.ac.uk/fac/soc/shss
applied social research, health studies, health & social studies, nursing, health care, ethnic relations, social work; MA, MPhil, PGDip, PhD

Warwick Business School; www2.wbs.warwick.ac.uk/fac/soc/
accounting & finance, business (behavioural science/finance & accounting/marketing/analytics & consulting), finance & IT/economics/behavioural science, financial mathematics, industrial relations & managing human resources, information systems, management & innovation & management, information & technology, international business/employment relations/management, management & organizational analysis, management science & operational research, marketing & strategy, public leadership & management; BA, BSc, MA, MBA, MPA, MPhil, MSc, PGDip, PhD

Warwick Institute of Education; www2.warwick.ac.uk/fac/soc/wie
accreditation of prior learning, adv teaching of Shakespeare, childhood, children in society, education & society, drama & theatre education, educational assessment/leadership & innovation studies/research methods, mathematics education, TSA school direct, PGCE: primary/secondary/qualified teacher programme; BA, EdD, FdA, MA, MPhil, MSc, PGCE, PhD

Warwick School of Law; www2.warwick.ac.uk/fac/soc/law
advanced legal studies, European law, international corporate governance & financial regulation, international economic/ development law & human rights, law & business/sociology; BA, LLB, LLM, MPhil, PhD, PGCert, PGDip

UNIVERSITY OF WEST OF SCOTLAND
www.uws.ac.uk

Faculty of Business & Creative Industries; www.uws.ac.uk/subhomepb.aspx?pageid=2147483907&terms=creative

Business School; www.uws.ac.uk/schools/business-school
accounting, business, business administration, international financial management/marketing/HRM/marketing management, event management/& tourism, hospitality management, HRM, marketing, economics/financial management/marketing, law, logistics & supply chain management; BA, BSc, MSc, MBA

School of Creative and Cultural Industries; www.uws.ac.uk/schools/school-of-creative-and-cultural-industries
broadcast journalism/production, commercial music/sound production, contemporary art practice/screen acting, creative media practice, digital art, filmmaking & screen writing, journalism, musical theatre, music, innovation & entrepreneurship, songwriting & performance, sports journalism, research methods for business, cultural & social research; BA, BA(Hons), BAcc, ExecMBA, MA, MSc, PGDip, PhD

School of Science; www.uws.ac.uk/schools-of-science
adv/applied biomedical science and psychology/zoology/forensic investigation, biomedical science, chemistry, forensic science, general science, occupational safety & health, physics, sport & exercise science, sports coaching/development, biotechnology, drug design & discovery, environmental & clean technology, project management, quality management, waste management with environmental management; BSc/BSc(Hons), CertHE,GradDip/Cert, MSc, PhD

School of Engineering; www.uws.ac.uk/schools/school-of-engineering
civil/chemical/mechanical/aircraft/motorsport design engineering, computer-aided design, product design & development, engineering management, product design & development, mechatronics, sensor design; BEng(Hons), PGDip/Cert, MSc

School of Health, Nursing & Midwifery; www.uws.ac.uk/schools/school-of health-nursing-and-midwifery
adv clinical practice, acute & critical care, cancer care, health studies, non-medical prescribing, midwifery, adult/mental health/public health nursing, maternal

& child health, health care, occupational health, integrated public services, non-medical prescribing, cancer & palliative care, veterinary nursing, vulnerability; BSc(Hons), MSc, PGCert/Dip, DipHE

School of Social Sciences; www.uws.ac.uk/schools/school-of-social-sciences
alcohol & drug studies, careers guidance & development, criminal justice, politics, psychology, race equality, social policy, social sciences, social studies, social work, sociology; BA, BA(Hons), MSc, Grad Cert, PGDip/Cert, Cert HE

School of Computing; www.uws.ac.uk/schools/school-of-computing
advanced computer systems development, business technology, computer animation BA(Hons), BSc, BSc(Hons), MSc, PGDip/Cert, CertHE

School of Education; www.uws.ac.uk/schools/school-of-education
artist teacher, chartered teacher, childhood practice/studies, community learning & participation, leadership for learning, leadership & learning in HE, inclusive education, primary/secondary education; BA, BEd MEd, PGCert/Dip

THE UNIVERSITY OF WESTMINSTER
www.wmin.ac.uk

School of Architecture & the Built Environment; www.westminster.ac.uk/schools/architecture
architectural technology, architecture, property & planning, architecture & interiors/digital media, cultural identity & globalisation, interior/design architecture, building engineering/surveying, business & property, construction project/property/management, domestic interior design, facilities & property management, international planning & sustainable development, logistics & supply chain management, planning, housing & urban development, property with business/urban development, property finance, property & planning/construction, quantity surveying/& commercial management, real estate development, tourism & planning, air/transport planning & management, events management/business, tourism management, travel & tourism, conference & events management, urban & regional planning/design; BA, BSc, MA, MPhil, MSc, PGCert, PGDip, PhD, MArch

School of Electronics & Computer Science; www.westminster.ac.uk/schools/computing
business & information systems, business intelligence & analytics, computer games development/science, computer software/systems engineering, computer network security, computer forensics, database systems, microelectronic systems design, mobile wireless & broadband communications, multimedia computing & animation, networks & communications, multimedia communications, electronic engineering, embedded systems, multimedia, IT security, media technology, mobile & web computing, software engineering; BEng, BSc, MEng, MPhil, MSc, PhD

School of Law; www.westminster.ac.uk/schools/law
law/with French, commercial/corporate finance law, dispute prevention & resolution, entertainment law, EU law, European legal studies, international & commercial dispute resolution, international commercial/banking /law, legal practice; GradDip, LLB, LLM, LPC

School of Life Sciences; www.westminster.ac.uk/schools/science
applied/microbiology & biotechnology, biochemistry, biochemical engineering, biological sciences (cancer biology/forensic biology/nutrition/molecular biosystems) biomedical sciences, biotechnology, cellular pathology, Chinese medicine/acupuncture, clinical chemistry, complementary therapies, drug discovery & development, environmental biotechnology, forensic biology, nutritional therapy, international/public health nutrition, herbal medicine, haematology, human nutrition (nutrition & exercise science)/microbiology, medical biotechnology/microbiology/molecular biology, genetics, nutrition/& medical science, nutrition & exercise science, physiology & pharmacology; BSc, FdSc, MA, MPhil, MSc, PGCert, PhD

School of Media, Arts & Design; www.westminster.ac.uk/schools/media

animation, audio production, ceramics, clinical photography, commercial music performance, communication, contemporary media practice, design for communication, diversity, fashion/buying, management/design/merchandise management, film & TV directing/production/theory, global media, graphic communication design, illustration & visual communication, international media, journalism (international/broadcasting/online/print), media development/management, mixed media, fine art, film & TV, music business management, photographic arts/studies, digital imaging, photojournalism, PR, radio production, TV production, theory, culture & industry; BA, BMus, BSc, FdA, GradDip, MA, PGDip

School of Social Sciences, Humanities & Languages; www.westminster.ac.uk/schools/humanities

creative writing/writing the city, cultural studies, English literature & creative writing/French/German/Spanish/linguistics, cultural & critical studies, English language & Arabic/Chinese/creative writing/French/Gernan/Spanish/linguistics, various jt degree combinations of (English language, English literature and Arabic/Chinese/French/Spanish/ creative writing/sociology), history & politics/sociology, international liaison & culture, international relations & Arabic/Chinese/French/German/Spanish/politics/democratic politics/security/development studies, TESOL, visual culture, bilingual translation, conference interpreting, museums, galleries & contemporary culture, specialist & technical translation, translation studies (Chinese/Arabic/French German), interpreting, visual culture, politics, contemporary political theory, applied cognitive neuroscience/rehabilitation, business/health psychology, applied market & social research, sociology & criminology, criminal justice, sociology; BA, MA, MPhil, PhD

Westminster Business School; www.westminster.ac.uk/schools/business

business/international, business management (accounting/economics/entrepreneurship, finance & financial services, HRM, business management (international business law/marketing/operations & supply chain management, international business (communication/Arabic/Chinese/French/German/Spanish), international marketing, marketing communications/management, business & management research, HRM, international business & management/development/management/HRM, management, marketing communications, marketing management, Master of Business Administration, project management, purchasing & supply chain management; BA, MA, MBA, MPhil, MSc, PGCert, PhD

THE UNIVERSITY OF WINCHESTER
www.winchester.ac.uk

Faculty of Arts; www.winchester.ac.uk/aboutus/universitystructure/

American studies/literature, creative/critical writing, dance practice & production, cultural & arts management, English/literature in context, digital media design/development, film & cinema techniques, film studies/production, journalism, media production/studies, cultural studies, choreography & dance, global radio production, performing arts (contemporary performance), drama, media & production/studies, popular/devised performance, street arts, theatre & media as development, theatre production (stage & arts management), vocal & choral studies, writing for children; BA ,FdA, MA, PGCert/Dip, PhD

Faculty of Humanities and Social Sciences; www.winchester.ac.uk/aboutus/universitystructure/hss

Dept of Archaeology; www.winchester.ac.uk/academicdepartments/archaeology/Pages/Archaeology.aspx

archaeology, archaeological practice, ancient, classical & medieval studies, cultural heritage & resource management, regional & local history & archaeology

Dept of Theology and Religious Studies; www.winchester.ac.uk/ academicdepartments/theology/Pages/ TheologyandReligiousStudies.aspx

religious studies, theology & religious studies, death, religion & culture, orthodox studies, religion, ethics & society

Dept of History; www.winchester.ac.uk/ academicdepartments/history/Pages/ history.aspx

history, regional and local history &/or archaeology, historical studies, history & the medieval world/ modern world, global history & politics, ancient, classical & medieval studies

Dept of Psychology; www.winchester.ac.uk/ academicdepartments/psychology/Pages/ Welcome.aspx

psychological science/disorders, child development, cognition, psychology, psychological research methods; BA, BSc, MA, MPhil, MRes, MSc, PGCert, PGDip, PhD

Faculty of Education, Health & Social Care; www.winchester.ac.uk/aboutus/ universitystructure/ Educationhealthsocialcare

childhood studies, educational studies, modern liberal arts, early childhood/years, social work & community studies, community education, interprofessional studies (children, health, social work, & community), modern liberal arts, primary practice, youth & community studies, teacher education; PGCE secondary/(RE)/primary ed with QTS, health & social care practice/wellbeing, GP education, humanistic counselling, medical education, nursing studies, social care studies, social work; BA, FdA, MA(Ed), MPhil, PGCE, PhD, Dip

Faculty of Business Law & Sport; www.winchester.ac.uk/research/ attheuniversity/ faculty%20of%20business%20law%20 and%20sport/pages/ facultyofbusinesslawandsport.aspx

Winchester Business School; www.winchester.ac.uk/ academicdepartments/ Winchester%20Business%20School/Pages/ WinchesterBusinessSchool.aspx

accounting & finance, business management, enterprise & innovation, economics, logistics, retail, business administration/management, event management, HRM, management, managing contemporary issues with environment & development, marketing, sustainable business; BA, FdA, MBA, MSc, PGCert, PGDip, FD

Dept of Law; www.winchester.ac.uk/ academicdepartments/Law/Pages/ LawDepartment.aspx

law, public/European/criminal/contract & restitution/ equity law; BA/LLB, LLB

Dept of Sports Studies; www.winchester.ac.uk/ academicdepartments/SportsStudies/ Pages/Sportsstudies.aspx

sports coaching & development/management/ science/studies, sport & society, applied sport & exercise science; BA, BSc, FdA

UNIVERSITY OF WOLVERHAMPTON
www.wlv.ac.uk

School of Applied Sciences; www.wlv.ac.uk/default.aspx?page=6878

adv technical management, biomedical science (cellular biology/clinical biochemistry/medical microbiology/physiological science/biomedical science), informatics, biotechnology, cognitive behaviour therapy, counselling psychology, environmental health/ management/technology, forensic science & criminology/human identification, genetics, healthcare, human physiology/biology, medical sciences/ biotechnology, molecular biology, occupational psychology, pharmaceutical science (drug discovery & design/pharmaceutical analysis/manufacture), pharmacology, occupational/psychology, psychology (counselling/criminal behaviour), PGCE; secondary education: biology; BA, BSc, DBMS, FdSc, GradDip, HND, MPharm, MSc, PGDip

School of Art & Design; www.wlv.ac.uk/default.aspx?page=6963

animation, applied arts, art & design, computer games design, commercial video production, design & applied arts, digital & visual communication, fashion & textiles, fine art, graphic communication, illustration, interior design, photography, product design, video & film production; BA, FdA, HND, MA

School of Education; www.wlv.ac.uk/default.aspx?page=6965

adult numeracy/literacy, childhood & family studies, conductive education, CPD, early years services/learning, primary ed, education studies, learning assistants, TESOL, post-compulsory education, PGCE (numerous secondary subjects)/early/primary education/adult education/numeracy/literacy, ESOL, learning assistants, preparing to teach, special needs & inclusion studies, subject specialists in English (ESOL/literacy/mathematics/numeracy), social policy, sociology, special needs & inclusive study, support of children in primary years; BA, EdD, FdA, MA, PGCert, PGDip, PhD

School of Technology; www.wlv.ac.uk/default.aspx?page=24367

advanced technology management, architectural studies/design technology, interior architecture & property development, armed forces & combat engineering, automotive systems engineering, building services engineering, building surveying/studies, civil engineering, computer science/games development/software development/security, computer systems engineering, computer networks/security, software development, games design, commercial management & quantity surveying, computer-aided design & construction, construction, construction law/management/project management, design technology, electronics & communications engineering, engineering design management, business information systems, information technology/management, interior mathematics, mechanical engineering, mechatronics, polymer engineering, rapid production design & development, sustainable design & manufacture; BDes, BEng, BSc, FdSc, HNC, MEng, MSc, PGCert

School of Health & Wellbeing; www.wlv.ac.uk/default.aspx?page=6067

adult/children's/mental health nursing, emergency practitioner, health & social care practice/& wellbeing, health studies, midwifery, specialist community nursing (district/general practice/health/school), nursing studies (acute/cancer/cardiac/older person/critical diabetes/emergency/lymphoedema/mental health/neonatal intensive/ophthalmic/orthopaedic/palliative/renal/stroke), specialist social work (adults/children, young people & families), non-medical prescribing, primary, public health nursing (visiting/school nursing), social care & criminology & social justice/deaf studies/social policy/sociology, specialist community public health nursing (health visiting, therapeutic practice, district nursing, social work, health & social care practice (acute/cardiac/critical/emergency/lymphoedema care) (mental health/psychological health/neonatal intensive/offender rtreatment/palliative & end of life/renal/stroke); BA, BSc, DipHE, FdA, GradDip, MA, MPH, MSc, PGCert, PGDip

School of Law, Social Sciences & Communications

armed forces & combat engineering/medicine, accountancy/business & law, broadcasting & journalism, conflict studies, consumer protection, contemporary media, corporate & financial law, creative & professional writing, criminology & criminal justice, deaf studies, drama, English/language, film studies, history, HRM, inclusion & deaf studies, international corporate & financial law (oil & gas), interpreting, law, langauage & information processing, linguistics, media & communication/cultural studies, philosophy, policing, politics, popular culture, public sector, religious studies, social policy, sociology, TESOL, transmedia screenwriting, voluntary & public sectors: policy & practice, uniformed public services, war studies, world & sign language; BA, FdA, LLB, LLM, MA

School of Sport, Performing Arts & Leisure; www.wlv.ac.uk/default.aspx?page=6970

creative music production, dance/& drama/science, drama & performance/creative professional writing/English/film studies, event & venue management, international hospitality management, music/theatre/& popular music/technology, physical activity, exercise & health, physical education; BA, BSc, FdA, FdSc, MA, MSc

University of Wolverhampton Business School; www.wlv.ac.uk/default.aspx?page=6971

accounting & finance, business administration, international/business management, business & finance/HRM/marketing management, coaching & mentoring, employability & enterprise, HRM, HRD &

organisational change, innovation & entrepreneurship, management studies, marketing & enterprise management/HRM, marketing management healthcare leadership, leadership, HRD/M; BA, FdA, HND, MA, MBA, PGDip/Cert, MSC

UNIVERSITY COLLEGE WORCESTER
www.worc.ac.uk

Institute of Education; www.worc.ac.uk/departments/661.html
early childhood, education (early years), education studies, education & Christianity, Christian discipleship, integrated working with children & families, educational management & leadership, improving practice in education, integrated children's service, church school leadership, learning support, teaching & learning in HE, English/PGCE (primary, secondary, graduate teacher), primary intial teacher, professional practice, mentoring & coaching for leadership, mentoring in early childhood, religious education, retraining to teach, special & inclusive education, teaching primary languages; BA, CertHE, FdA, MA, MSc, PGCE, PGCert, PGDip

Institute of Health & Safety; www.worc.ac.uk/departments/659.html
advancing practice, applied health sciences, applied social policy: health & society/law & the family/older adults, birth & beyond practitioner, business/occupational psychology, counselling/psychology, CPD, developmental psychology, health & social care, health sciences, psychology, child & adolescent mental health, dance & movement therapy, drama therapy, dynamics of domestic violence, health sciences, learning disabilities, midwifery, nursing studies, nutritional therapy, paramedical science, psychodrama/therapy, psycho therapies/intervention, applied/psychology, social welfare social work & community studies, sports therapy, substance misuse, systemic youth work, young people services, youth & community services; BSc, DipHE, FdA, FdSc, GradDip, MA, MSc, PGCert, PGDip

Institute of Humanities & Creative Arts; www.worc.ac.uk/departments/663.html
animation, art & design, creative & professional writing, creative digital media, dance, drama & performance, English language/literary studies/literature, film making/studies, fine art practice, graphic design & multimedia, illustration, history, journalism, media & cultural studies, performance (costume & make-up), screenwriting, sociology, urban & electronic music; BA, HND, MA, MSc

Science & the Environment; www.worc.ac.uk/departments/652.html
animal biology, arboriculture, archaeology & heritage studies/landscape studies, airborne infectious agents & allergies, biochemical biology, archaeological landscapes, garden design, conservation ecology, ecology, environmental management/science, human/physical/geography, medical communication, organic & sustainable/horticulture, plant science, sustainable developmental advocacy; BSc, FdSc, HNC, HND, MSc, PGCert, PGDip

Institute of Sport & Exercise Science; www.worc.ac.uk/departments/652.html
applied sport science, outdoor adventure leadership & management/education, PE, sport & exercise psychology/science, sports coaching/management/performance & coaching/therapy/business management; BSc, HND, MSc

Worcester Business School; www.worc.ac.uk/departments/655.html
accountancy, accounting, advertising, business administration, business IT/management, computer game design & development, economics, entrepreneurship, executive leadership & management (health & social care), finance, financial management, hospitality, retail, tourism & travel, HRM, innovation, international business/management, IT for education, leadership, management/studies, management & human resources, marketing/advertising & PR/management, web design/development; BA, BSc, DMS, GradCert, MBA, MSc

UNIVERSITY OF YORK
www.york.ac.uk

Dept of Archaeology; www.york.ac.uk/depts/arch
archaeology, archaeology of buildings, archaeological information systems, bioarchaeology, coastal & marine/digital/field/landscape/medieval archaeology, conservation studies, cultural heritage management, early prehistory, heritage studies, historical archaeology, mesolithic studies, zooarchaeology; BA, BSc, MA, MPhil, MSc, PhD

Dept of Biology; www.york.ac.uk/depts/biol
biology, biochemistry, bioscience technology, biotechnology & microbiology, computational biology, ecology & environmental management, post-genomic biology, genetics, molecular cell biology; BSc, MPhil, MRes, MSc, PhD

Dept of Chemistry; www.york.ac.uk/depts/chemistry
chemistry, chemistry with biological & medicinal chemistry/management & industry/resources & the environment, chemoinformatics, computational biology, green chemistry & sustainable industrial technology; BSc, MChem, MPhil, MSc, PhD

Dept of Computer Science; www.cs.york.ac.uk/depts
computer science/with AI/embedded systems/software engineering/philosophy/mathematics, cyber security, natural computation, human-centred interactive technologies, information technology, large-scale complex IT systems, safety critical systems, safety critical systems, engineering, social media & interactive technology; BEng, BSc, MEng, MMath, MPhil, MSc, PGCert, PGDip

Dept of Economics & Related Studies; www.york.ac.uk/depts/econ
economics, econometrics & finance, economics & economic history/sociology/philosophy/politics, environmental economics & management, development economics & emerging markets, financial engineering, project analysis, finance & investment, health/public/economics, economic & social policy analysis; BA, BSc, MSc, PGCert, PGDip, PhD

Dept of Education; www.york.ac.uk/depts/educ
applied linguistics for language teaching, English in education, psychology in education, educational studies, language & literature in education, teaching English (young learners/TESOL), PGCE (English, history, maths, foreign languages, sciences), global & international citizenship, science education & learning, sociology & education; BA, MA, MPhil, PhD

Dept of Electronics; www.york.ac.uk/depts/elec
avionics, communications engineering, computer engineering, digital systems engineering & signal processing, digital media systems, electronic engineering, engineering management, internet & wireless technology, music technology/systems, electrical engineering with nanotechnology/business management, computer engineering; BEng, MEng, MSc, MPhil, PhD

Dept of English & Related Literature; www.york.ac.uk/depts/engl
English, English & history/history of art/linguistics/philosophy/politics, culture & thought after 1945, cultures of empire, resistance & postcoloniality, eighteenth century studies, English literary studies, film & literature, medieval literatures, modern & contemporary literature & culture, nineteenth-century literature & culture in Renaissance literature, 1500–1700, romantic & sentimental literature; BA, MA, MPhil, PhD

Dept of Environment; www.york.ac.uk/depts/eeem
environmental economics & management, environmental geography/science, ecology & environmental management, environment, economics, & ecology, corporate social responsibility & environmental management, marine environmental development; BSc, MPhil, MSc, PGDip, PhD

Dept of Health Sciences; www.york.ac.uk/depts/healthsciences
haematopathology, health sciences, public health/international, midwifery practice, nursing studies (adult/child/learning disability/mental health); BA, BSc, DipHE, MPhil, MSc, PGCert, PGDip, PhD

Dept of History; www.york.ac.uk/depts/hist
history, history with politics/history of art/philosophy/economics/French/English, medieval history, railway studies & transport history, early/modern history, public history; BA, GradCert, MA, MPhil, PhD

Dept of History of Art; www.york.ac.uk/depts/histart
history of art, stained glass conservation & heritage management; BA, MA, MPhil, PhD

Hull York Medical School; www.hyms.ac.uk
undergraduate qualifying medical courses, human evolution, medical education; MBBS, MSc, PGCert, MD, PhD, MPhil

Dept of Language & Linguistic Science; www.york.ac.uk/depts/lang
linguistics, phonetics & phonology, psycholinguistics, sociolinguistics, combinations of French/German/Spanish/English, linguistics & French/German/Spanish, philosophy & French/German, syntax & semantics, phonological development in childhood, forensic speech science; BA, MA, MPhil, MSc, PhD

York Law School; www.york.ac.uk/depts/law
law, law & society/practice, international corporate & commercial law, international human rights & practice; LLB, LLM, MPhil, PhD

Dept of Mathematics; www.york.ac.uk/depts/maths
mathematics, mathematics with computer science/economics/physics/statistics/finance/linguistics/philosophy, financial engineering, statistics & computational finance, financial mathematics, mathematical finance; BA, BSc, MMath, MPhil, MRes, MSc, PGCert, PGDip, PhD

Dept of Music; www.york.ac.uk/depts/music
music, community music, music technology, composition, performance; BA, MA, MPhil, PhD

Dept of Philosophy; www.york.ac.uk/depts/phil
philosophy, history of philosophy, practical ethics, PPE, philosophy, theology & ethics; BA, BSc, GradDip, MA, MPhil, PGCert, PGDip, PhD

Dept of Physics; www.york.ac.uk/depts/physics
physics, physics with astrophysics, theoretical physics, fusion energy; BA, BSc, MMath, MPhil, MPhys, MSc, PhD

Dept of Politics; www.york.ac.uk/depts/poli
politics with international relations/English/history/economics/philosophy/contemporary history & international politics, political research, conflict, governance & development, international political economy/relations, political philosophy, public administration & public policy, PPE, postwar recovery; BA, MA, PGDip, PhD

Dept of Psychology; www.york.ac.uk/depts/psych
cognitive neuroscience, applied forensic psychology, development disorders of learning & cognition, psychology; BSc, MPhil, MRes, MSc, PhD

Dept of Social Policy & Social Work; www.york.ac.uk/depts/spsw
applied social science (children & young people/crime & criminal justice), international development, public administration, public policy & management, social policy, social work, sociology & political science, comparative & international social policy; BA, MA, MPhil, MRes, PGCert, PhD, MPA

Dept of Sociology; www.york.ac.uk/depts/soci
sociology /with criminology/economics/education/philosophy/politics/social psychology, social research, social media & management/interactive technology; BA, MA, MPhil, MSc, PhD

School of Social & Political Sciences; www.york.ac.uk/sps
social & political sciences, comparative cultural class analysis, environmental politics, science & technology, social media & communications, urban social science & criminology, women's studies; BA(Hons), MA, MRres, PhD

Dept of Theatre, Film & Television; www.york.ac.uk/depts/tft
cinema, TV & society, post-production with visual effects/sound design, theatre, film & TV production, theatre writing, directing & performance; BA, MA, MPhil, MSc, PhD

Hull York Medical School;
www.hyma.york.ac.uk
medicine, medical education; BMBS, MD, MPhil, MSc, PGCert, PhD

School of Politics, Economics & Philosophy;
www.york.ac.uk/depts/pep
economics, philosophy, politics, development, political economy, public affairs; BA, MA, MRes, PGCert, PhD

York Management School;
www.york.ac.uk/depts/management
accounting, business finance & management, management, international business & strategic management, financial management, corporate social responsibility & environmental management, HRM; BA, BSc, MA, MPhil, MRes, MSc, PhD

YORKSHIRE COAST COLLEGE
www.yorkshirecoastcollege.ac.uk

Higher education; http:/www.yorkshirecoastcollege.ac.uk/highereducation/index.php
historical & performance costume for stage & screen, fine art, teacher education; BA, FdA, GradCert

Part 5

Qualifications Awarded by Professional and Trade Associations

THE FUNCTIONS OF PROFESSIONAL ASSOCIATIONS

Qualifications

Some associations qualify individuals to act in a certain professional capacity. They also try to safeguard high standards of professional conduct. Few associations have complete control over the profession with which they are concerned. Some professions are regulated by the law, and their associations act as the central registration authority. Entry to others is directly controlled by associations that alone award the requisite qualifications. If a profession is required to be registered by the law and is controlled by the representative council, a practitioner found guilty by his or her council of misconduct may be suspended from practice or completely debarred by the removal of his or her name from the register of qualified practitioners. In other professions the consequence of misdemeanour may not be so serious, because the profession does not exercise the same degree of control.

The professions registered by statute, and therefore subject to restrictions on entry and loss of either privileges or the right to practise on erasure, are listed in Table 5.1. Certain other professions are closed.

Table 5.1 Professions registered by statute

Profession	Statutory committee controlling professional conduct
Architects	Architects Registration Board
Dentists	General Dental Council
Doctors	General Medical Council
Professions supplementary to medicine: arts therapists, biomedical scientists, chiropodists/podiatrists, clinical scientists, dieticians, hearing aid dispensers, occupational therapists, operating department practitioners, orthoptists, paramedics, physiotherapists, practitioner psychologists, prosthetists/orthotists, radiographers, speech and language therapists and social workers	Health and Care Professions Council (HCPC)
Nurses and midwives	Nursing and Midwifery Council
Opticians	General Optical Council
Patent agents	Chartered Institute of Patent Attorneys
Teachers	The Teaching Agency

Study

Some associations give their members an opportunity to keep abreast of a particular discipline or to undertake further study in it. Such associations are especially numerous in medicine, science and applied science. Many qualifying associations also provide an information and study service for their members. Some of the more famous learned societies confer added status upon distinguished practitioners by electing them to membership or honorary membership.

Protection of Members' Interests

Some associations exist mainly to look after the interests of individual practitioners and the group. A small number are directly concerned with negotiations over salary and working conditions.

MEMBERSHIP OF PROFESSIONAL ASSOCIATIONS

Qualifying associations

The principal function of qualifying associations is to examine and qualify people who wish to become practitioners in the field with which they are concerned. As already indicated, some regulate professional conduct and many offer opportunities for further study. Membership is divided into grades, usually classified as corporate and non-corporate. Non-corporate members are those not yet admitted to full membership, mainly students; they are divided from corporate membership by barriers of age and levels of responsibility and experience. The principal requirement for admission to membership is the knowledge and ability to pass the association's exams; candidates may be exempted from the association's exams if they have acceptable alternative qualifications.

Non-corporate or affiliated members

Non-corporate members are those who are as yet unqualified or only partly qualified. They are accorded limited rights and privileges, but may not vote at meetings of the corporate body. Most associations have a student membership grade. Students are those who are preparing for the exams that qualify them for admission to corporate membership. Some associations have licentiate and graduate membership grades, which are senior to the student grade. Graduates are those who have passed the qualifying exams but lack other requirements, such as age and experience, for admission to corporate membership.

Corporate or full members

Corporate members are the fully qualified constituent members of incorporated associations. They are accorded full rights and privileges and may vote at meetings of the corporate body. Corporate membership is often divided into two grades: a senior grade of members or fellows and a general grade of associate members or associates.

Honorary members

Some associations have a special class of honorary members or fellows for distinguished members or individuals who have made an outstanding contribution to the profession in question.

Examinations and requirements

Professionals normally become corporate members by exam or exemption, with or without additional requirements. Many final professional exams are of degree standard, and a number of professional qualifications are accepted by employers as evidence of competence at operational level. Ongoing professional development is encouraged by most associations to ensure members' skills and knowledge are up to date and relevant.

The transition from the general grade of membership to the senior can be automatic in some associations (for instance, on reaching a prescribed age), but in others the higher grade is reached only after the submission of evidence of research or progress in the profession.

Qualifying exams are usually conducted in two or more stages. The first stage leads to an Intermediate or Part I qualification, the second leads to a Final or Part II or Part III qualification, which is about the standard of a degree.

Gaining professional qualifications

Prospective students can study by any of the following means:

- correspondence courses (distance learning and/or online support);

- personal attendance at the schools maintained by some associations (eg the Architectural Association School of Architecture);
- further and higher education institutions.

ACCOUNTANCY
Membership of Professional Institutions and Associations

ASSOCIATION OF ACCOUNTING TECHNICIANS

140 Aldersgate Street
London EC1A 4HY
Tel: 0845 863 0802
Fax: 020 7397 3009
E-mail: aat@aat.org.uk
Website: www.aat.org.uk

AAT is the UK's leading qualification and membership body for accounting professionals. We have over 125,000 members including students, people working in accountancy and self-employed business owners, in more than 90 countries worldwide. Established in 1980 to ensure consistent training and regulation for accounting staff, our qualifications provide a progression route to CIMA, CIPFA, ICAS, ICAEW and ACCA.

MEMBERSHIP
Student member
Affiliate member
Full member (MAAT)
Fellow member (FMAAT)

QUALIFICATION/EXAMINATIONS
AAT Accounting Qualification
AAT Access Level 1 in accounting
AAT Level 2 Award in Bookkeeping

DESIGNATORY LETTERS
MAAT and FMAAT

ASSOCIATION OF CHARITY INDEPENDENT EXAMINERS

The Gatehouse
White Cross
South Road
Lancaster
Lancashire LA1 4XQ
Tel: 01524 34892
Fax: 01524 34892
E-mail: info@acie.org.uk
Website: www.acie.org.uk

ACIE provides support, training, conferences, resources and qualifications for independent examiners of charity accounts throughout the UK (*subscriptions apply*). Further information at the website; www.acie.org.uk
  Registered charity in E&W 1139609 & SC039066. Registered company limited by guarantee 7461134; registered in England at 4-6 Grimshaw St, Burnley BB11 2AZ.

MEMBERSHIP
Affiliate
Full Member (with category of Associate or Fellow)

Accountancy

QUALIFICATION/EXAMINATIONS
Associate (limited re: size and type of charity by 1 of 5 authorisation bands – see website for details): ACIE
Fellow (all UK charities eligible for IE): FCIE

DESIGNATORY LETTERS
ACIE, FCIE

CHARTERED INSTITUTE OF INTERNAL AUDITORS

13 Abbeville Mews
88 Clapham Park Road
London SW4 7BX
Tel: 020 7498 0101
Fax: 020 7978 2492
E-mail: info@iia.org.uk
Website: www.iia.org.uk

The Chartered Institute of Internal Auditors (IIA) is the only professional body in the UK and Ireland focused exclusively on internal auditing and we are passionate about supporting, promoting and training the professionals who work in it. Every year we help internal auditors at every stage of their career with training, qualifications and technical resources.

MEMBERSHIP
Student Member
Affiliate Member
Voting Member (PIIA, CMIIA)
Head of Internal Audit Service Member
Fellow (FIIA, CFIIA)

QUALIFICATION/EXAMINATIONS
IIA Certificate in Internal Audit and Business Risk (IA Cert)
IIA Diploma in Internal Audit Practice (PIIA)
IIA Advanced Diploma in Internal Auditing and Management (CMIIA)
IT Auditing Certificate

DESIGNATORY LETTERS
IA Cert, PIIA, CMIIA, FIIA, CFIIA

CIMA – THE CHARTERED INSTITUTE OF MANAGEMENT ACCOUNTANTS

26 Chapter Street
London SW1P 4NP
Tel: 020 8849 2251
Fax: 020 8849 2450
E-mail: cima.contact@cimaglobal.com
Website: www.cimaglobal.com

CIMA is the employers' choice when recruiting financially qualified business leaders.

The Chartered Institute of Management Accountants, founded in 1919, is the world's leading and largest professional body of Management Accountants, with 183,000 members and students operating at the heart of business in 168 countries. CIMA works closely with employers and sponsors leading-edge research, constantly updating its qualification, professional experience requirements and continuing professional development to ensure it remains the most relevant international accountancy qualification for business.

MEMBERSHIP
Member
Associate (ACMA)
Fellow (FCMA)

QUALIFICATION/EXAMINATIONS
Certificate in Business Accounting
Chartered Management Accounting Qualification
Certificate in Islamic Finance
Diploma in Islamic Finance

DESIGNATORY LETTERS
ACMA, FCMA

ICAEW (THE INSTITUTE OF CHARTERED ACCOUNTANTS IN ENGLAND AND WALES)

Metropolitan House
321 Avebury Boulevard
Milton Keynes MK9 2FZ
Tel: 01908 248 250
Fax: 01908 248 260
E-mail: careers@icaew.com
Website: icaew.com/careers

ICAEW is a world leader of the accountancy profession, with more than 136,000 members in over 160 countries. Our members work at the highest levels of business, across all industry sectors around the world. Our professional qualification, the ACA, delivers essential knowledge, skills and technical expertise in accountancy and business.

MEMBERSHIP
ACA (Associate of the Institute of Chartered Accountants in England and Wales) FCA (Fellow Chartered Accountant)

QUALIFICATION/EXAMINATIONS
The ACA qualification consists of 15 examined modules in the Professional and Advanced Stages, 450 days of technical work experience, structured training in ethics and initial professional development. It takes between three and five years to complete depending on your entry route to starting your training and students undertake the ACA with an ICAEW authorized training employer. Find out more information at icaew.com/careers
The Certificate in Finance, Accounting and Business (CFAB) consists of the knowledge modules of the ACA qualification. There are no entry requirements in order to start CFAB and it can be studied via distance learning or self-study. Students do not need to be in an ICAEW training agreement in order to study CFAB. Find out more information at icaew.com/cfab

DESIGNATORY LETTERS
ACA, FCA

ICAS (INSTITUTE OF CHARTERED ACCOUNTANTS OF SCOTLAND)

CA House
21 Haymarket Yards
Edinburgh EH12 5BH
Tel: 0131 347 0186
E-mail: caeducation@icas.org.uk
Website: icas.org.uk

ICAS is a professional body for around 19,000 world class business professionals who work in the UK and in more than 100 countries around the world. Our members have all achieved the internationally recognised and respected CA qualification. We are an educator, examiner, regulator, and thought leader. ICAS is the first professional body for accountants and was created by Royal Charter in 1854.

MEMBERSHIP
To qualify as a CA, trainees must enter and complete a training contract with an ICAS authorised employer for a prescribed period, normally three years. They must achieve relevant work experience requirements and key competencies, study for and pass three stages of examinations and complete a course and assignment in Business Ethics. For further information please see the ICAS website.

QUALIFICATION/EXAMINATIONS
The CA qualification syllabus contains ten subjects leading to three stages of exams.
Test of Competence (TC) contains five subjects: Financial Accounting, Principles of Auditing and Reporting, Finance, Business Management, Business Law.

Accountancy

Test of Professional Skills (TPS): Taxation, Advanced Finance, Financial Reporting, Assurance and Business Systems.

Test of Professional Expertise (TPE) contains a multidisciplinary case study designed to apply theoretical knowledge and practical skills to a real-life situation.

In addition to including ethics within the three levels, Business Ethics forms a standalone subject and assessment.

DESIGNATORY LETTERS
CA

INSTITUTE OF FINANCIAL ACCOUNTANTS

Burford House
44 London Road
Sevenoaks
Kent TN13 1AS
Tel: 01732 458080
Fax: 01732 455848
E-mail: mail@ifa.org.uk
Website: www.ifa.org.uk

The IFA was established in 1916 and is the oldest body of non-Chartered Accountants in the world. We represent members and students in more than 80 countries, providing qualifications for those wishing to work in financial management and accountancy, and CPD for qualified Financial Accountants, particularly in SMEs.

MEMBERSHIP
Affiliate
Financial Accounting Executive
Associate (AFA)
Fellow (FFA)

QUALIFICATION/EXAMINATIONS
Financial Accounting Diploma
Professional Financial Accountant

DESIGNATORY LETTERS
AFA, FFA

INTERNATIONAL ASSOCIATION OF BOOK-KEEPERS

Suite 30
40 Churchill Square
Kings Hill
West Malling
Kent ME19 4YU
Tel: 01732 897750
Fax: 01732 897751
E-mail: mail@iab.org.uk
Website: www.iab.org.uk

The IAB specializes in providing high-quality, accredited and regulated financial and business qualifications. We continue to be the leading international membership body for professional book-keepers. Established in 1973, we now have many thousands of students and members worldwide.

MEMBERSHIP
Associate (AIAB)
Member (MIAB)
Fellow (FIAB)

QUALIFICATION/EXAMINATIONS
Award in Bookkeeping (Level 1)
Award in Manual Bookkeeping (Level 1)
Award in Computerized Bookkeeping (Level 1)

Certificate in Bookkeeping (Level 2)
Award in Manual Bookkeeping (Level 2)
Award in Computerized Bookkeeping (Level 2)
Certificate in Applied Bookkeeping (Level 2)
Certificate in Bookkeeping (Level 3)
Certificate in Manual Bookkeeping (Level 3)
Award in Computerized Bookkeeping (Level 3)
Certificate in Applied Bookkeeping (Level 3)
Diploma in Accounting to International Standards (Level 4)
Award in Payroll (Level 1)
Certificate in Payroll (Level 2)
Award in Practical Payroll (Level 2)
Award in Computerized Payroll (Level 2)
Award in Applied Payroll (Level 2)
Certificate in Payroll (Level 3)
Award in Computerized Payroll (Level 3)

DESIGNATORY LETTERS
AIAB, MIAB, FIAB

THE ASSOCIATION OF CHARTERED CERTIFIED ACCOUNTANTS

London WC2A 3EE
Tel: 020 7059 5000
Fax: 020 7059 5050
E-mail: info@accaglobal.com
Website: www.accaglobal.com

ACCA is the largest and fastest-growing international accountancy body, with over 424,000 students and 147,000 members in 170 countries. The ACCA Qualification is an established route to professional status, and we offer continued support to our members throughout their careers.

MEMBERSHIP
Associate (ACCA)
Fellow (FCCA)

QUALIFICATION/EXAMINATIONS
Foundations in Accountancy
Certified Accounting Technician (CAT) qualification
The ACCA Qualification
BSc in Applied Accounting (awarded by Oxford Brookes University)
MBA (awarded by Oxford Brookes University; accredited by the Association of MBAs)

DESIGNATORY LETTERS
ACCA, FCCA

THE ASSOCIATION OF CORPORATE TREASURERS

51 Moorgate
London EC2R 6BH
Tel: 020 7847 2540
Fax: 020 7374 8744
E-mail: enquiries@treasurers.co.uk
Website: www.treasurers.org

The ACT is the international body for professionals working in treasury, risk and corporate finance. We are the leading examining body for international treasury, providing the widest scope of benchmark qualifications and continuing development through training, conferences and publications – including *The Treasurer* magazine.

MEMBERSHIP
Student Member
Faculty Member
Associate Member (AMCT)
Member (MCT)
Fellow (FCT)
Corporate Member
International Affiliate

QUALIFICATION/EXAMINATIONS
Advanced Diploma in Treasury, Risk and Corporate Finance (MCT)
Diploma in Treasury (AMCT)
Certificate in Financial Fundamentals for Business

(CertFin)
Certificate in International Treasury Management (CertITM)
Certificate in Corporate Finance and Funding (CertCFF)
Certificate in Financial Maths and Modelling (CertFMM)

Certificate in International Cash Management (CertICM)
Certificate in Risk Management (CertRM)

DESIGNATORY LETTERS
AMCT, MCT, FCT

THE ASSOCIATION OF INTERNATIONAL ACCOUNTANTS

Staithes 3
The Watermark
Metro Riverside
Newcastle upon Tyne
Tyne & Wear NE11 9SN
Tel: 0191 493 0277
Fax: 0191 493 0278
E-mail: aia@aiaworldwide.com
Website: www.aiaworldwide.com

AIA was founded in 1928 as a global accountancy body and has recognition as a Recognised Qualifying Body for statutory auditors, supervisory status for its members in the Money Laundering Regulations 2007 and an Awarding Body in the UK. AIA is a Prescribed Body in the ROI and is recognised in over 30 countries worldwide.

MEMBERSHIP
Student Member
Graduate Member
Affiliate Member (AMIA)
Academic Member
Associate (AAIA)
Fellow (FAIA)
Honorary Member
Retired Member

QUALIFICATION/EXAMINATIONS
Professional Accountancy Qualification
Statutory Audit Qualification
Audit Diploma
Corporate Finance Diploma
IFRS Diploma
Management Accounting & Costing Diploma

DESIGNATORY LETTERS
AMIA, AAIA, FAIA

THE CHARTERED INSTITUTE OF PUBLIC FINANCE AND ACCOUNTANCY

3 Robert Street
London WC2N 6RL
Tel: 020 7543 5656
Fax: 020 7543 5700
E-mail: students@cipfa.org.uk
Website: www.cipfa.org.uk

The CIPFA is the professional body for people in public finance. Our 14,000 members work throughout the public services and as the only UK professional accountancy body to specialize in public services, CIPFA's qualifications are the foundation for a career in public finance.

MEMBERSHIP
Student Member
Affiliate
Associate
Full Member

QUALIFICATION/EXAMINATIONS
CIPFA Professional Qualification
Certificate in Charity Finance and Accountancy
Certificate in International Treasury Management – Public Finance

THE INSTITUTE OF CERTIFIED BOOKKEEPERS

Victoria House
64 Paul Street
London EC2A 4NG
Tel: 0845 060 2345
Fax: 01635 298960
E-mail: info@bookkeepers.org.uk
Website: www.bookkeepers.org.uk

The ICB is the largest bookkeeping institute in the world. Our aims are to promote bookkeeping as a profession, to improve training in the principles of bookkeeping, and to establish qualifications and the award of grades of membership that recognize academic attainment, work experience and professional competence, and thereby enable qualified bookkeepers to gain recognition as an integral part of the financial world.

MEMBERSHIP
Registered Student
Affiliate
Associate Member (AICB)
Member (MICB)
Fellow (FICB)

QUALIFICATION/EXAMINATIONS
Level 1: Certificate in Basic Bookkeeping
Level 2: (Intermediate): Certificate in Computerized Bookkeeping
Level 2: (Intermediate): Certificate in Manual Bookkeeping
Level 3: (Advanced): Diploma in Computerized Bookkeeping
Level 3: (Advanced): Diploma in Manual Bookkeeping
Level 3: (Advanced): Diploma in Payroll Management
Level 3: (Advanced): Diploma in Self-Assessment Tax Returns
Level 4: (Advanced) Diploma in Financial Management (Drafting Financial Statements, Management Accounting, Personal Taxation and Business Taxation)

DESIGNATORY LETTERS
AICB, MICB, FICB

ACOUSTICS
Membership of Professional Institutions and Associations

INSTITUTE OF ACOUSTICS

St Peter's House
45–49 Victoria Street
St Albans
Hertfordshire AL1 3WZ
Tel: 01727 848195
Fax: 01727 850553
E-mail: ioa@ioa.org.uk
Website: www.ioa.org.uk

The IOA is the UK's professional body for those working in acoustics, noise and vibration, and has more than 3,000 members in research, educational, environmental, government and industrial organizations. It offers professionally recognized courses and is licensed by the Engineering Research Council to offer registration at Chartered and Incorporated Engineer levels.

MEMBERSHIP
Student
Affiliate
Technician Member (TechIOA)
Associate Member (AMIOA)
Member (MIOA)
Fellow (FIOA)
Honorary Fellow (HonFIOA)
Incorporated Engineer (IEng)
Chartered Engineer (CEng)
Sponsor

QUALIFICATION/EXAMINATIONS
Certificate of Competence in Environmental Noise Measurement
Certificate of Competence in Workplace Noise Risk Assessment
Certificate Course in the Management of Occupational Exposure to Hand–Arm Vibration
Certificate Course in Building Acoustics Measurements
Diploma in Acoustics and Noise Control

DESIGNATORY LETTERS
TechIOA, AMIOA, MIOA, FIOA, HonFIOA, IEng, CEng

ADVERTISING AND PUBLIC RELATIONS
Membership of Professional Institutions and Associations

CHARTERED INSTITUTE OF PUBLIC RELATIONS

52–53 Russell Square
London WC1B 4HP
Tel: 020 7631 6900
Fax: 020 7631 6944
E-mail: info@cipr.co.uk
Website: www.cipr.co.uk

The CIPR, founded in 1948, is the professional body for PR practitioners and has more than 9,000 members, to whom it offers information, advice, support and training. Our aim is to raise standards within the profession through the promotion of best practice and our members abide by our strict code of professional conduct.

MEMBERSHIP
Student
Affiliate
Associate (ACIPR)
Member (MCIPR)
Fellow (FCIPR)
Honorary Fellow (Hon FCIPR)

QUALIFICATION/EXAMINATIONS
Foundation Award in Public Relations
Advanced Certificate
Diploma

DESIGNATORY LETTERS
ACIPR, MCIPR, FCIPR

INSTITUTE OF PRACTITIONERS IN ADVERTISING

44 Belgrave Square
London SW1X 8QS
Tel: 020 7235 7020
Fax: 020 7245 9904
E-mail: training@ipa.co.uk
Website: www.ipa.co.uk

The IPA is the UK's leading professional body for advertising, media and marketing communications agencies. We promote the services of our member agencies, which have access to a range of services and benefits, including a Legal Department, Information Centre and training courses provided by our Professional Development Department.

MEMBERSHIP
Personal Member (MIPA)
Fellow/Honorary Fellow (FIPA)
Member Agency

QUALIFICATION/EXAMINATIONS
Foundation Certificate
Advanced Certificate
LegRes Certificate
Excellence Diploma

DESIGNATORY LETTERS
MIPA, FIPA

INSTITUTE OF PROMOTIONAL MARKETING

70 Margaret Street
London W1W 8SS
Tel: 020 7291 7733
E-mail: enquiries@theipm.co.uk
Website: www.theipm.org.uk

The Institute of Promotional Marketing represents promoters, agencies and service partners engaged in promotional marketing in the UK by protecting, promoting and progressing effective sales promotion across all media channels through its education, legal advice, awards, and other products and services.

MEMBERSHIP
Personal Member (MISP)
Corporate Member

QUALIFICATION/EXAMINATIONS
Certificate in Experiential Marketing
Diploma in Motivation
Certificate in Promotional Marketing
Diploma in Promotional Marketing

DESIGNATORY LETTERS
MISP

LONDON SCHOOL OF PUBLIC RELATIONS

118A Kensington Church Street
London W8 4BH
Tel: 020 7221 3399
Fax: 020 7243 1730
E-mail: info@lspr-education.com
Website: www.lspr-education.com

The LSPR provides up-to-date training for those wishing to enter public relations as a career or for those already in PR or an information/communications job who require up-to-date practical training awarded with a professional development qualification. Our Diploma, *An Integrated Approach to Public Relations*, is awarded to delegates upon successful completion of a 10-day full-time intensive course or an 8-week part-time evening course (twice weekly – 6.30pm – 8.30pm).

LSPR also runs training programmes in Leadership, CSR, Reputation Management, Stakeholder Analysis, Crisis and Issues Management, Branding, Corporate Identity, Media Relations and Feature and Press Release Writing.

LSPR training programmes are approved and recognised by the Institute of Training and Occupational Learning (ITOL). LSPR operates globally with franchises, in association with international PR bodies and agencies.

MEMBERSHIP
Institute of Training and Occupational Learning

QUALIFICATION/EXAMINATIONS
Diploma

AGRICULTURE AND HORTICULTURE
Membership of Professional Institutions and Associations

INSTITUTE OF HORTICULTURE

Capel Manor College
Bullsmoor Lane
Enfield
Middlesex EN1 4RQ
Tel: 01992 707025
E-mail: ioh@horticulture.org.uk
Website: www.horticulture.org.uk

The IoH represents all those professionally engaged in horticulture in the UK and the Republic of Ireland. Our main aim is to promote the profession and its importance in food and ornamental plant production, improving the environment, providing employment and as the leisure pursuit of gardening. We are also developing CPD and mentoring schemes for our members and liaise with government and other bodies on matters of interest or concern.

MEMBERSHIP
Student Member, Affiliate, Associate (AI Hort), Member (MI Hort), Fellow (FI Hort), Group Membership

DESIGNATORY LETTERS
AI Hort, MI Hort, FI Hort

ROYAL HORTICULTURAL SOCIETY

RHS Qualifications
RHS Garden Wisley
Woking
Surrey GU23 6QB
Tel: 0845 260 9000
E-mail: qualifications@rhs.org.uk
Website: www.rhs.org.uk

RHS Qualifications is a recognized awarding body offering a range of qualifications in horticultural knowledge and skills. Part-time courses leading to RHS qualifications are offered by approved centres throughout the UK and Ireland, and by distance-learning providers. The RHS School of Horticulture provides courses in practical horticultural skills.

QUALIFICATION/EXAMINATIONS
RHS Level 1 Award in Practical Horticulture
RHS Level 2 Certificate in the Principles of Plant Growth, Propagation and Development
RHS Level 2 Certificate in the Principles of Garden Planning, Establishment and Maintenance
RHS Level 2 Certificate in the Principles of Horticulture
RHS Level 2 Certificate in Practical Horticulture
RHS Level 2 Diploma in the Principles and Practices of Horticulture
RHS Level 3 Certificate in the Principles of Plant Growth, Health and Applied Propagation
RHS Level 3 Certificate in the Principles of Garden Planning, Construction and Planting
RHS Level 3 Certificate in Practical Horticulture
RHS Level 3 Diploma in the Principles and Practices of Horticulture
Master of Horticulture (RHS)
Wisley Diploma in Practical Horticulture
Certificate in Practical Horticulture
Specialist Option Certificates in:
Ornamental Horticulture
Fruit Cultivation
Rock and Alpine Gardening
Orchid Culture and Glasshouse Technique
Estate Management with Arboriculture
Plant Centre Management Skills

THE ROYAL BOTANIC GARDEN EDINBURGH

20A Inverleith Row
Edinburgh EH3 5LR
Tel: 01312 482825
Fax: 01312 482901
E-mail: education@rbge.org.uk
Website: www.rbge.org.uk

The RBGE was founded in the 17th century as a physic garden, growing medicinal plants. Now it extends over four gardens boasting a rich living collection of plants, and is a world-renowned centre for plant science and education.

QUALIFICATION/EXAMINATIONS
Certificate in Practical Field Botany
Certificate in Practical Horticulture
Diploma in Botanical Illustration
Diploma in Garden Design
Diploma in Herbology
HND/BSc in Horticulture with Plantsmanship
MSc in The Biodiversity and Taxonomy of Plants

AMBULANCE SERVICE
Membership of Professional Institutions and Associations

AMBULANCE SERVICE INSTITUTE

Suite 183
Maddison House
226 High Street
Croydon CR9 1DF
E-mail: enquiries@asi-international.com
Website: www.asi-international.com

The ASI is a non-union, non-political, independent institute whose membership is dedicated to raising the standards and quality of ambulance provision and thereby improving the professionalism and quality of care available to patients. Membership is open to non-NHS personnel as well as to employees of NHS Ambulance Services.

MEMBERSHIP
Student
Member (MASI)
Licentiate (LASI)
Associate (AASI)
Graduate (GASI)
Fellow (FASI)

QUALIFICATION/EXAMINATIONS
The Institute offers professional examinations and qualifications in the areas of Pre-Hospital Care, Control and Communications, and Management, for those who desire a career in the ambulance service.

DESIGNATORY LETTERS
MASI, LASI, AASI, GASI, FASI

ARBITRATION
Membership of Professional Institutions and Associations

THE CHARTERED INSTITUTE OF ARBITRATORS

12 Bloomsbury Square
London WC1A 2LP
Tel: 020 7421 7444
Fax: 020 7404 4023
E-mail: info@ciarb.org
Website: www.ciarb.org

The CIArb is a not-for-profit, UK-registered charity with 12,000 members worldwide that exists to promote and facilitate the settlement of private disputes by arbitration and alternative dispute resolution. We provide training for arbitrators, mediators and adjudicators and act as an international centre for practitioners, policy-makers, academics and those in business concerned with the cost-effective and early settlement of disputes.

MEMBERSHIP
Associate (ACIArb)
Member (MCIArb)
Fellow (FCIArb)

QUALIFICATION/EXAMINATIONS
Introductory Certificate
Advanced Certificate
Diploma

DESIGNATORY LETTERS
ACIArb, MCIArb, FCIArb

ARCHAEOLOGY
Membership of Professional Institutions and Associations

THE INSTITUTE FOR ARCHAEOLOGISTS

SHES
University of Reading
Whiteknights
PO Box 227
Reading RG6 6AB
Tel: 0118 378 6446
Fax: 0118 378 6448
E-mail: admin@archaeologists.net
Website: www.archaeologists.net

The IfA is a professional organization for all archaeologists and others involved in protecting and understanding the historic environment, with more than 2,700 members. We advance the practice of archaeology and allied disciplines by promoting professional standards and ethics for conserving, managing, understanding and enjoying our heritage.

MEMBERSHIP
Student
Affiliate
Practitioner (PIfA)
Associate (AIfA)
Member (MIfA)
Registered Organization

ARCHITECTURE
Membership of Professional Institutions and Associations

ARCHITECTS REGISTRATION BOARD

8 Weymouth Street
London W1W 5BU
Tel: 020 7580 5861
Fax: 020 7436 5269
E-mail: info@arb.org.uk
Website: www.arb.org.uk

The ARB is the regulatory body for architects in the UK. Only individuals registered with the Board can use the title 'architect'. Applicants must have passed the recognized exams at a school of architecture in the UK (or have an equivalent non-UK professional qualification) and have at least 2 years' practical experience working under the supervision of an architect.

Architecture

CHARTERED INSTITUTE OF ARCHITECTURAL TECHNOLOGISTS (CIAT)

397 City Road
London EC1V 1NH
Tel: 020 7278 2206
Fax: 020 7837 3194
E-mail: info@ciat.org.uk
Website: www.ciat.org.uk

CIAT represents professionals working and studying in the field of Architectural Technology. We are internationally recognised as the qualifying body for Chartered Architectural Technologists (MCIAT) and Architectural Technicians (TCIAT).

MEMBERSHIP
Student member
Profile candidate
Associate (ACIAT)
Architectural Technician (TCIAT)
Chartered Architectural Technologist (MCIAT)
Honorary Member (HonMCIAT)

DESIGNATORY LETTERS
ACIAT, TCIAT, MCIAT

ROYAL INSTITUTE OF BRITISH ARCHITECTS

60 Portland Place
London W1B 1AD
Tel: 020 7580 5533
Fax: 020 7255 1541
E-mail: info@inst.riba.org
Website: www.architecture.com

The Royal Institute of British Architects is the UK body for architecture and the architectural profession. We provide support for our 40,500 members worldwide in the form of training, technical services, publications and events, and set standards for the education of architects, both in the UK and overseas. We also work with government to improve the design quality of public buildings, new homes and new communities.

MEMBERSHIP
Student Member
Affiliate Member
Associate Member
Chartered Member
Chartered Practice

ART AND DESIGN
Membership of Professional Institutions and Associations

BRITISH ASSOCIATION OF ART THERAPISTS

Claremont
24–27 White Lion Street
London N1 9PD
Tel: 020 7686 4216
E-mail: info@baat.org
Website: www.baat.org

The BAAT is the professional organization for art therapists in the UK and has its own Code of Ethics of Professional Practice. We maintain a comprehensive directory of qualified art therapists and work to promote art therapy in the UK through 20 regional groups. We also have a European section and an international section.

MEMBERSHIP
Trainee Member
Associate Member
Full Member
Honorary Member
Fellow
Corporate Member

QUALIFICATION/EXAMINATIONS
The BAAT organizes a programme of CPD courses for Art Therapists. For details see the website.

BRITISH ASSOCIATION OF PAINTINGS CONSERVATOR-RESTORERS

PO Box 258
Norwich NR13 4WY
Tel: 01603 516237
Fax: 01603 510985
E-mail: office@bapcr.org.uk
Website: www.bapcr.org.uk

The BAPCR (founded in 1943 as the Association of British Picture Restorers) is the professional association for conservator-restorers of paintings and has more than 400 members worldwide. Our aims are to advance the profession by providing means for CPD to our members and thereby a service to the public.

MEMBERSHIP
Associate (Student)
Associate
Fellow

D&AD (BRITISH DESIGN & ART DIRECTION)

9 Graphite Square
Vauxhall Walk
London SE11 5EE
Tel: 020 7840 1111
Fax: 020 7840 0840
E-mail: info@dandad.co.uk
Website: www.dandad.org

Founded in 1962, D&AD is a professional association and educational charity with a membership of more than 2,000, working on behalf of the design and advertising communities. Our mission is to set creative standards, educate and inspire the next creative generation, and promote the importance of good design and advertising to business as a whole.

MEMBERSHIP
Student
New Creative
Elected Associate
Associate
Member

SOCIETY OF DESIGNER CRAFTSMEN (SDC)

24 Rivington Street
London EC2A 3DU
Tel: 07531 798983
E-mail: info@societyofdesignercraftsmen.org.uk
Website: www.societyofdesignercraftsmen.org.uk

The Society, which was founded in 1887 as the Arts and Crafts Exhibition Society, is the largest and oldest multi-craft society in the UK. Our aim is to emphasize designer-making where innovation, originality and quality are important; we provide promotional services and exhibiting opportunities to members.

MEMBERSHIP
Associate
Licentiate (LSDC)
Member (MSDC)
Fellow (FSDC)

DESIGNATORY LETTERS
LSDC, MSDC, FSDC

THE CHARTERED SOCIETY OF DESIGNERS

1 Cedar Court
Royal Oak Yard
Bermondsey Street
London SE1 3GA
Tel: 020 7357 8088
Fax: 020 7407 9878
E-mail: info@csd.org.uk
Website: www.csd.org.uk

The CSD, which was founded in 1930, is the professional body for designers and has more than 3,000 members. We promote sound principles of design in all areas in which design considerations apply, further design practice and encourage the study of design techniques for the benefit of the community.

MEMBERSHIP
Student Member

Graduate Member
Member (MCSD)
Fellow (FCSD)

DESIGNATORY LETTERS
MCSD, FCSD

THE INDEX OF PROFESSIONAL MASTER DESIGNERS

Kensington House
33 Imperial Square
Cheltenham Spa
Gloucestershire GL50 1QZ
Tel: 08701 161823
Fax: 08702 626146
E-mail: masterdesigners@kensington-house.com

The Index was formed to provide a register of designers practising in all areas of design. Our objectives are to enable designers to achieve recognition and attain qualifications and also to accredit schools and training organizations offering suitable courses.

MEMBERSHIP
Student
Professional Designer (IPMD (DIP))
Master Designer (IPMD (MAS))

QUALIFICATION/EXAMINATIONS
Certificate of Excellence – Interior Design Students

DESIGNATORY LETTERS
IPMD (DIP), IPMD (MAS)

ASTRONOMY AND SPACE SCIENCE
Membership of Professional Institutions and Associations

THE BRITISH INTERPLANETARY SOCIETY

27/29 South Lambeth Road
London SW8 1SZ
Tel: 020 7735 3160
Fax: 020 7587 5118
E-mail: mail@bis-spaceflight.com
Website: www.bis-spacef.com

The BIS was formed in 1933 and has been at the forefront of actively promoting new ideas on space exploration at technical, educational and popular levels for over 70 years. We serve the interests of those professionally involved with space, promote fundamental space research, technology and applications, encourage technical and scientific space studies, and undertake educational activities on space topics.

MEMBERSHIP
Member
Fellow (FBIS)

DESIGNATORY LETTERS
FBIS

AVIATION
Membership of Professional Institutions and Associations

THE GUILD OF AIR PILOTS AND AIR NAVIGATORS

Cobham House
9 Warwick Court
London WC1R 5DJ
Tel: 020 7404 4032
Fax: 020 7404 4035
E-mail: gapan@gapan.org
Website: www.gapan.org

The Guild, an active Livery Company of the City of London, represents pilot and navigator interests within all areas of aviation. Most of our members are, or have been, professional licence holders, or hold a private licence. Our aims include promoting the highest standards of air safety, liaising with all authorities connected with licensing, training and legislation, providing advice and facilitating exchange of information.

MEMBERSHIP
Associate
Freeman
Upper Freeman

QUALIFICATION/EXAMINATIONS
Master Air Pilot Certificate
Master Air Navigator Certificate

THE GUILD OF AIR TRAFFIC CONTROL OFFICERS

4 St Mary's Road
Bingham
Nottingham
Nottinghamshire NG13 8DW
Tel: 01949 876405
Fax: 01949 876405
E-mail: caf@gatco.org
Website: www.gatco.org

Founded in 1954, GATCO is an independent professional organization that exists to promote honourable practice and the highest standards in all aspects of aviation. It is dedicated to the safety of all who seek their livelihood or pleasure in the air.

MEMBERSHIP
Student Member
Associate Non-Operational Member
Associate Operational Member
Full Member
Corporate Member

QUALIFICATION/EXAMINATIONS
Qualifying criteria apply to all memberships categories. Further information should be sought from GATCO Ltd, Central Administrative Facility (CAF).

BANKING

Membership of Professional Institutions and Associations

IFS SCHOOL OF FINANCE

8th Floor
Peninsular House
36 Monument Street
London EC3R 8LJ
Tel: 01227 818609
Fax: 01227 784331/786030
E-mail: customerservices@ifslearning.ac.uk
Website: www.ifslearning.ac.uk

The ifs School of Finance is a world-class provider of financial learning, and has more than 50,000 students in over 90 countries. Having built a reputation for excellence in learning, all the qualifications it provides combine innovation and quality, and draw from over 130 years of educational experience.

MEMBERSHIP
Member
Affiliate
Associate
Fellow
Chartered Associate
Adviser Membership (for financial and mortgage advisers)

QUALIFICATION/EXAMINATIONS
The ifs offers a wide range of qualifications for those employed or aspiring to a career in the financial services industry, and for consumers. For details see www.ifslearning.ac.uk.

THE CHARTERED INSTITUTE OF BANKERS IN SCOTLAND

Drumsheugh House
38B Drumsheugh Gardens
Edinburgh EH3 7SW
Tel: 0131 473 7777
Fax: 0131 473 7788
E-mail: info@charteredbanker.com
Website: www.charteredbanker.com

The Chartered Institute of Bankers in Scotland provides world-class professional qualifications for both the UK and international markets. Our vision for the financial services industry is one of professionalism. We are the only organisation in the world entitled to award the designation 'Chartered Banker' to its members.

MEMBERSHIP
Student
Affiliate
Associate (ACIBS)
Member (MCIBS)
Fellow (FCIBS)

QUALIFICATION/EXAMINATIONS
Certificate
Diploma
Advanced Diploma
Chartered Banker

DESIGNATORY LETTERS
ACIBS, MCIBS, FCIBS

BEAUTY THERAPY AND BEAUTY CULTURE
Membership of Professional Institutions and Associations

ASSOCIATION OF THERAPY LECTURERS

18 Shakespeare Business Centre
Hathaway Close
Eastleigh
Hampshire SO50 4SR
Tel: 0844 875 2022
Fax: 023 8062 4399
E-mail: info@fht.org.uk
Website: www.fht.org.uk

(Part of the Federation of Holistic Therapists)

The ATL began in 1963 as the Society of Beauty Teachers, when Beauty Therapy teaching was still in its infancy. In the 1990s it amalgamated with the National Beauty Teachers and Lecturers Association (NBTLA) and today it represents Lecturers in a wide range of therapies.

MEMBERSHIP
Member

QUALIFICATION/EXAMINATIONS
Please see www.fht.org.uk for details.

BRITISH ASSOCIATION OF BEAUTY THERAPY AND COSMETOLOGY LTD

BABTAC Limited
Ambrose House, Meteor Court
Barnett Way
Barnwood
Gloucester GL4 3GG
Tel: 0845 065 9000
Fax: 0845 065 9001
E-mail: enquiries@babtac.com
Website: www.babtac.com

BABTAC was formed in 1977 and is a non-profit-making organization for beauticians and therapists in the UK. Members work to a rigorous code of ethics and good practice, both in terms of the treatments and therapies they offer and the way they conduct their relationships with their clients. CIBTAC, an international, educational awarding body that works closely with BABTAC, offers over 30 internationally recognized diplomas in beauty and complementary therapies to accredited colleges and students in the UK and abroad.

MEMBERSHIP
Student Member
Associate Member
Nail Technician
Full Member
Overseas Member
Salon Plan Member

QUALIFICATION/EXAMINATIONS
BABTAC offers a programme of short courses. For details see the BABTAC website. For CIBTAC diplomas see www.cibtac.com/courses_home.htm.

BRITISH INSTITUTE AND ASSOCIATION OF ELECTROLYSIS LTD

40 Parkfield Road
Ickenham
Middlesex UB10 BLW
Tel: 08445 441373
E-mail: sec@electrolysis.co.uk
Website: www.electrolysis.co.uk

The BIAE is a non-profit-making organization that demands a high standard of skill and ethical conduct from its members, who are spread throughout the UK and overseas. Candidate Electrolysists must complete the rigorous assessments, both theoretical and practical, of the BIAE Examining Board before being accepted onto the Register.

MEMBERSHIP
Member

QUALIFICATION/EXAMINATIONS
Certificate in Remedial Electrolysis (CRE)

FEDERATION OF HOLISTIC THERAPISTS

18 Shakespeare Business Centre
Hathaway Close
Eastleigh
Hampshire SO50 4SR
Tel: 0844 875 2022
Fax: 023 8062 4396
E-mail: info@fht.org.uk
Website: www.fht.org.uk

The FHT is the leading and largest professional beauty, sports and complementary therapist association in the UK, which has been representing the interests of holistic therapists since 1962. The FHT leads the industry by offering its members a Code of Ethics, public liability insurance, access to regulation, a robust CPD programme with auditing, class-leading journal, local therapist network, and comprehensive business and public affairs updates.

MEMBERSHIP
Student
Affiliate
Associate
Member
Fellow
International

QUALIFICATION/EXAMINATIONS
Please see the FHT's website.

DESIGNATORY LETTERS
MFHT, FFHT, AFHT, AfFHT

ITEC

2nd Floor, Chiswick Gate
598–608 Chiswick High Road
London W4 5RT
Tel: 020 8994 4141
Fax: 020 8994 7880
E-mail: info@itecworld.co.uk
Website: www.itecworld.co.uk

ITEC is an international examination board offering a variety of qualifications in the beauty therapy, complementary therapy and sports therapy sectors worldwide. We also offer teacher training courses in: Skincare; Make-up; Manicure and Pedicure; Waxing; Holistic Massage; Aromatherapy; Reflexology; Body Treatments; and other areas as required.

QUALIFICATION/EXAMINATIONS
Please see the ITEC website.

BIOLOGICAL SCIENCES
Membership of Professional Institutions and Associations

INSTITUTE OF BIOMEDICAL SCIENCE

12 Coldbath Square
London EC1R 5HL
Tel: 020 7713 0214
Fax: 020 7837 9658
E-mail: mail@ibms.org
Website: www.ibms.org

The IBMS is the professional body for biomedical scientists in the UK. We aim to promote and develop the role of biomedical science within healthcare to deliver the best possible service for patient care and safety.

MEMBERSHIP
Associate
Licentiate (LIBMS)
Member (MIBMS)
Fellow (FIBMS)
Company member

QUALIFICATION/EXAMINATIONS
Certificate of Competence (also required for registration with the Health and Care Professions Council (HCPC))
Specialist Diploma in:
Cellular Pathology, Clinical Biochemistry, Clinical Immunology, Cytopathology, Haematology & Transfusion Science, Histocompatibility & Immunogenetics (developed in conjunction with BSHI), Medical Microbiology, Transfusion Science, Virology.
Diploma of Specialist Practice
Higher Specialist Diploma in:
Cellular Pathology, Clinical Chemistry, Cytopathology, Haematology, Immunology, Histocompatibility & Immunogenetics (developed in conjunction with BSHI), Medical Microbiology, Transfusion Science, Virology.
Diploma of Higher Specialist Practice
Complementary qualifications/examinations related to areas of scientific expertise (available to Members and/or Fellows)
Certificates and Diplomas of Expert Practice
Advanced Specialist Diplomas

DESIGNATORY LETTERS
LIBMS, MIBMS, FIBMS

SOCIETY OF BIOLOGY

9 Red Lion Court
London EC4A 3EF
Tel: 020 7936 5900
Fax: 020 7936 5901
E-mail: info@societyofbiology.org
Website: www.societyofbiology.org

The Society of Biology aims to be a single unified voice for biology: advising government and influencing policy; advancing education and professional development; supporting members; and engaging and encouraging public interest in the life sciences.

MEMBERSHIP
Associate Member (AMSB)
Member (MSB)
Fellow (FSB)
Chartered Biologist (CBiol)

DESIGNATORY LETTERS
AMSB, MSB, FSB, CBiol

BREWING
Membership of Professional Institutions and Associations

INSTITUTE OF BREWING & DISTILLING

33 Clarges Street
Mayfair
London W1J 7EE
Tel: 020 7499 8144
Fax: 020 7499 1156
E-mail: enquiries@ibd.org.uk
Website: www.ibd.org.uk

The IBD is a members' organization dedicated to the education and training needs of brewers and distillers and those in related industries. We do this by offering a range of internationally recognized qualifications and the training to support them, through either direct instruction or distance learning.

MEMBERSHIP
Member
Honorary Member
Senior Member
Fellow (FIBD)
Honorary Fellow
Corporate Member

QUALIFICATION/EXAMINATIONS
Certificate in the Fundamentals of Brewing and Packaging of Beer (FBPB) (City & Guilds Level 2)
Certificate in the Fundamentals of Distilling (FD) (City & Guilds Level 2)
General Certificate in Brewing (GCB) (City & Guilds Level 3)
General Certificate in Distilling (GCD) (City & Guilds Level 3)
General Certificate in Packaging (GCP) (City & Guilds Level 3)
Diploma in Packaging (Dipl.Pack) (City & Guilds Level 4)
Diploma in Brewing (Dipl.Brew) (City & Guilds Level 4)
Diploma in Distilling (Dipl.Distil) (City & Guilds Level 4)
Master Brewer (MBrew)

DESIGNATORY LETTERS
Dipl.Brew, Dipl.Distil, Dipl.Pack, MBrew, FIBD, Hon FIBD

BUILDING
Membership of Professional Institutions and Associations

INSTITUTE OF ASPHALT TECHNOLOGY

Paper Mews Place
280 High Street
Dorking
Surrey RH4 1QT
Tel: 01306 742792
Fax: 01306 888902
E-mail: secretary@instofasphalt.org
Website: www.instofasphalt.org

The IAT is the UK's professional body for persons working in asphalt technology and those interested in aspects of the manufacture, placing, technology and uses of materials containing asphalt or bitumen. A fully audited CPD system for members has been available since 1994 and is now also offered in computerized format for ease of data entry and auditing, via members' own PCs.

MEMBERSHIP
Student
Technician (Tech IAT)
Affiliate (AIAT)
Member (MIAT)
Fellow (FIAT)

DESIGNATORY LETTERS
Tech IAT, AIAT, MIAT, FIAT

THE CHARTERED INSTITUTE OF BUILDING

Englemere
Kings Ride
Ascot
Berkshire SL5 7TB
Tel: 01344 630700
Fax: 01344 630777
E-mail: educationadmin@ciob.org.uk
Website: www.ciob.org

The CIOB is the international voice of the construction industry. CIOB members are largely Construction Managers engaged in managing the development, conservation and improvement of the built environment, with a common commitment to achieving and maintaining the highest possible standards.

MEMBERSHIP
Student Member
Associate (ACIOB)
Incorporate (ICIOB)
Member (MCIOB)
Fellow (FCIOB)
Chartered Environmentalist (CENV)

QUALIFICATION/EXAMINATIONS
The CIOB has routes to membership to suit a range of professionals from those with degrees or vocational qualifications to those with experience but no formal qualifications. All our members have a strong commitment to improve and develop themselves in a challenging and exciting career.

Chartered Member status is recognized internationally as the mark of a skilled professional in the construction industry. CIOB members are from a wide range of professions in the construction industry.

To find out more about our membership qualifications and joining the CIOB just visit our website www.ciob.org

The CIOB Awarding Body offers a suite of qualifications to enable site operatives to progress into management roles.
Level 3 Diploma in Site Supervisory Studies
Level 4 Certificate in Site Management
Level 4 Diploma in Site Management
The CIOB qualifications develop the skills and confidence to manage and coordinate all types of construction projects. The site management qualifications are nationally recognized and allow the learner to progress to higher education and National Vocational Qualifications (NVQs).
For more information on the Site Management Qualifications visit the website at www.ciob.org.uk/education/courseinfo/sitemanagement

DESIGNATORY LETTERS
ACIOB, ICIOB, MCIOB, FCIOB, CENV

THE INSTITUTE OF CARPENTERS

32 High Street
Wendover
Buckinghamshire HP22 6EA
Tel: 0844 879 7696
Fax: 01296 620981
E-mail: info@instituteofcarpenters.com
Website: www.instituteofcarpenters.com

The IOC was founded in 1890 to oversee training for carpenters and joiners and maintain high professional standards at a time when many feared that traditional skills were being lost. Today, while remaining committed to our original aims, we embrace many other wood craftsmen, such as shopfitters, furniture and cabinetmakers, boat builders (woodworking skills), structural post & beam carpenters (heavy structural timber framers), wheelwrights, wood carvers and wood turners, and offer professional status to those holding recognized qualifications.

MEMBERSHIP
Student
Mature Student
Affiliate
Licentiate (LIOC)
Member (MIOC)
Fellow (FIOC)
College Member
Corporate Member
Corporate Associate

QUALIFICATION/EXAMINATIONS
Certificate of Competence in Joinery & Shopfitting Setting-Out
Foundation Certificate in Carpentry and Joinery
Intermediate Examination
Advanced Craft Examination
Fellowship Examination

DESIGNATORY LETTERS
LIOC, MIOC, FIOC

THE INSTITUTE OF CLERKS OF WORKS AND CONSTRUCTION INSPECTORATE OF GREAT BRITAIN INC

28 Commerce Road
Lynch Wood
Peterborough PE2 6LR
Tel: 01733 405160
Fax: 01733 405161
E-mail: info@icwgb.co.uk
Website: www.icwgb.org

The ICWCI is the professional body that supports quality construction through inspection. As a membership organization, we provide a support network of meeting centres, technical advice, publications and events to help keep our members up to date with the ever-changing construction industry.

MEMBERSHIP
Student
Licentiate (LICWCI)
Member (MICWCI)
Fellow (FICWCI)

DESIGNATORY LETTERS
LICWCI, MICWCI, FICWCI

BUSINESS STUDIES
Membership of Professional Institutions and Associations

ASSOCIATION OF BUSINESS RECOVERY PROFESSIONALS (R3)

8th Floor
120 Aldersgate Street
London EC1A 4JQ
Tel: 020 7566 4200
Fax: 020 7566 4224
E-mail: association@r3.org.uk
Website: www.r3.org.uk

The Association of Business Recovery Professionals (known by its brand name 'R3') is the leading professional association for insolvency, business recovery and turnaround specialists in the UK. A not-for-profit organization, it promotes best practice for professionals working with financially troubled individuals and businesses, and provides a forum for debate on key issues facing the profession.

MEMBERSHIP
Student Member
Networking Member
Associate Member (AABRP)
Full Member (MABRP)
Fellow (FABRP)

QUALIFICATION/EXAMINATIONS
R3 provides comprehensive Continuing Professional Education in the field of Insolvency and Restructuring. For details of courses see R3's website.

DESIGNATORY LETTERS
AABRP, MABRP, FABRP

INSTITUTE OF ASSESSORS AND INTERNAL VERIFIERS

PO Box 148
Wirral CH62 7WB
Tel: 01925 485 786
E-mail: office@iavltd.co.uk

The IAV is the professional organization representing assessors and internal verifiers in the UK in vocational training and assessment.

MEMBERSHIP
Affiliate Member
Associate Member
Licentiate Member

Business Studies

THE ACADEMY OF EXECUTIVES & ADMINISTRATORS

Head Office
Warwick Corner
42 Warwick Road
Kenilworth
Warwickshire CV8 1HE
Tel: 01926 259342
E-mail: info@academyofexecutivesandadministrators.org.uk
Website: www.academyofexecutivesandadministrators.org.uk

The Academy of Executives & Administrators was founded in 2002 to give professional status and recognition to the knowledge and skills of executives and administrators. We encourage excellence and flexibility in the changing environment of executive and administrative roles, and support lifelong learning to help members fulfil their career ambitions.

MEMBERSHIP
Student Member (StudAEA)
Associate Member (AMAEA)
Member (MAEA)
Fellow (FAEA)
Companion (CAEA)

QUALIFICATION/EXAMINATIONS
Certified Business Economist
Certified Financial Analyst
Certified Accounting Assistant
Certified Corporate Accountant
Certified Trainer

THE ACADEMY OF MULTI-SKILLS

Head Office
219 Bow Road
London
Middlesex E3 2SJ
Tel: (0)709 201 2910
E-mail: The MSAcademy@yahoo.co.uk
Website: www.academyofmultiskills.org.uk

The Academy of Multi-Skills was founded in 1995 to give professional recognition to multi-skilled personnel, skilled trades, crafts and professions. The Academy encourages a positive and energetic attitude to the challenges of careers that require diversity, creativity and intellect, and recognizes the valuable contribution that these skills provide to society.

MEMBERSHIP
Technician (TAMS)
Associate (AAMS)
Fellow (FAMS)
Doctoral Fellow (DFAMS)

QUALIFICATION/EXAMINATIONS
Members may choose to enhance their qualifications via our diploma, HND, post-graduate and doctoral diploma courses.
We have arrangements with other prestigious organisations which our members may choose to join to obtain further qualifications.
Discounts are available to our members from organisations ranging from books to overseas conferences.

DESIGNATORY LETTERS
TAMS, AAMS, FAMS, DFAMS

THE FACULTY OF SECRETARIES AND ADMINISTRATORS (1930) WITH THE ASSOCIATION OF CORPORATE SECRETARIES

Brightstowe
Catteshall Lane
Godalming
Surrey GU7 1LL
Tel: 01483 427323

The Faculty and Association is a professional body for company and corporate secretaries whose prime qualified designation is that of Certified Public or Corporate Secretary.

MEMBERSHIP
Membership Fellows (FFCS)
Associates (AFCS)
Member (MACS)
Ordinary Member
Student Member

QUALIFICATION/EXAMINATIONS
Part 1 The Generic Business Assessment to ONC/D Level
Part 2 Professional Papers in Company Secretarial Practice, Company Law and Management, Secretarial and Administrative Practice, Commercial Law
Part 3 Professional Meetings Law and Procedure, Company Taxation, Accountancy and Finance, Company Law

DESIGNATORY LETTERS
FFCS, AFCS, MACS

THE INSTITUTE OF CHARTERED SECRETARIES AND ADMINISTRATORS

16 Park Crescent
London W1B 1AH
Tel: 020 7580 4741
Fax: 020 7323 1132
E-mail: studentsupport@icsaglobal.com
Website: www.icsaglobal.com

The Institute of Chartered Secretaries and Administrators is the international qualifying and membership body for the Chartered Secretary profession. With a global community of 37,000 members we provide Chartered Membership, training and a professional qualifying scheme to set you on the path to a diverse, challenging and rewarding career.

MEMBERSHIP
Affiliate
Graduate (GradICSA)
Associate (ACIS)
Fellow (FCIS)

QUALIFICATION/EXAMINATIONS
Chartered Secretaries Qualifying Scheme (CSQS)
Certificate in Offshore Finance and Administration
Diploma in Offshore Finance and Administration
Certificate in Company Secretarial Practice and Share Registration Practice
Certificate in Irish Company Secretarial Practice and Share Registration Practice
Certificate in Employee Share Plans
Postgraduate Certificate in Charity Management
ICSA Certificate in Further Education Governance

DESIGNATORY LETTERS
GradICSA, ACIS, FCIS

CATERING AND INSTITUTIONAL MANAGEMENT
Membership of Professional Institutions and Associations

BII

Wessex House
80 Park Street
Camberley
Surrey GU15 3PT
Tel: 01276 684449
E-mail: info@bii.org
Website: www.bii.org

Founded in 1981, BII is the professional body for the licensed retail sector with a remit to raise standards throughout the industry. BIIAB, the wholly owned awarding body of BII, does this through offering qualifications specifically tailored to, and designed in conjunction with, the industry.

MEMBERSHIP
There is a wide range of membership grades available, from those who have just started their careers in licensed retailing to those who have been in the industry for many years. The grade of membership awarded depends on both experience and qualifications and is determined by a points system. Member of the Hotel Catering and Management Association, HCIMA.

QUALIFICATION/EXAMINATIONS
Qualifications for licensing
National Certificate for Personal Licence Holders (Level 2)
Scottish Certificate for Personal Licence Holders
Scottish Certificate for Licensed Premises Staff
National Certificate for Door Supervisors (Level 2)
National Certificate for Door Supervisors (Scotland)
National Certificate for Door Supervisors (Northern Ireland) (Level 2)
Certificate in Physical Interventions (in conjunction with Maybo)
National Certificate for CCTV Operators (Public Space Surveillance) (Level 2)
National Certificate for Security Guards (Level 2)
National Certificate for Security Guards (Scotland)
National Certificate for Licensees (Drugs Awareness) (Level 2)
Scottish Licensee's Certificate in Drug Awareness
National Certificate for Designated Premises Supervisors (Level 2)

Qualifications for new licensed retail managers
National Certificate in Licensed Retailing (Level 2)
Award in Beer and Cellar Quality

Qualifications for staff development
Award in Responsible Alcohol Retailing (Level 1)
Award in Conflict Management
Award in Essentials of Catering (Level 1)
Award in Cooking Theory and Practice (Level 2)
Certificate in Kitchen Management (Level 3)
Award in Customer and Drinks Service (Licensed Hospitality) (Level 1)
Scottish Award in Customer and Drinks Service (Licensed Hospitality)

Qualifications for management development
Profitable Business Portfolio (professional development programme)
Advanced Certificate in Licensed Hospitality (Level 3)
Diploma in Licensed Hospitality (Level 3)

Qualifications for personal and social responsibility
Certificate in Alcohol Awareness (Level 1)
Scottish Certificate in Alcohol Awareness
Award for Music Promoters (Level 2)

CONFEDERATION OF TOURISM AND HOSPITALITY

37 Duke Street
London W1U 1LN
Tel: 020 7258 9850
Fax: 020 7258 9869
E-mail: info@cthawards.com
Website: www.cthawards.com

The Confederation of Tourism and Hospitality (CTH) was established in 1982 to provide recognised standards of management and vocational training appropriate to the needs of the hotel and travel industries, via its syllabuses, examinations and awards. We work with approved centres worldwide and are acknowledged by leading hotel and travel industry organisations such as Virgin Atlantic, Gordon Ramsey Holdings and Radisson Edwardian.

MEMBERSHIP
Student Member
Associate Member (AMCTH)
Member (MCTH)
Fellow (FCTH)

QUALIFICATION/EXAMINATIONS
Level 3 Diploma in Hospitality and Tourism Management
Level 4 Diploma in Hotel Management
Level 4 Diploma in Tourism Management
Level 5 Advanced Diploma in Hotel Management
Level 5 Advanced Diploma in Tourism Management
Level 6 Pro-Graduate Diploma in Hospitality and Tourism Management
Level 7 Postgraduate Diploma in Hospitality and Tourism Management

DESIGNATORY LETTERS
AMCTH, MCTH, FCTH

GUILD OF INTERNATIONAL PROFESSIONAL TOASTMASTERS

Life President: Ivor Spencer
12 Little Bornes
Alleyn Park
London SE21 8SE
Tel: 020 8670 5585
Fax: 020 8670 0055
Website: www.guildoftoastmasters.co.uk

The Guild of Professional Toastmasters was established over 30 years ago to improve standards in the profession and support its members. A 5-day course is offered to prospective members, who may apply for membership upon successful completion of the course. Applications are considered by the Fellows of the Guild.

MEMBERSHIP
Fellow (FGIntPT)

DESIGNATORY LETTERS
FGIntPT

CHEMISTRY
Membership of Professional Institutions and Associations

INSTITUTE OF HOSPITALITY

Trinity Court
34 West Street
Sutton
Surrey SM1 1SH
Tel: 020 8661 4900
Fax: 020 8661 4901
E-mail: awardingbody@instituteofhospitality.org
Website: www.instituteofhospitality.org

The Institute of Hospitality is the professional body for managers and aspiring managers in the hospitality, leisure and tourism industries. We are an accredited awarding body in the UK and have more than 10,000 members worldwide, whose professional and career development we promote to ensure the highest standards.

MEMBERSHIP
Student Member
Affiliate
Associate (AIH)
Member (MIH)
Fellow (FIH)

DESIGNATORY LETTERS
AIH, MIH, FIH

SOCIETY OF COSMETIC SCIENTISTS

Suite 6
Langham House East
Mill Street
Luton
Bedfordshire LU1 2NA
Tel: 01582 726661
Fax: 01582 405217
E-mail: ifscc.scs@btinternet.com
Website: www.scs.org.uk

The main object of the Society, which was formed in 1948, is to advance the science of cosmetics. We endeavour to do this by attracting highly qualified scientists with both academic and industrial experience in cosmetics or a related science to our membership of around 900 members, and by means of our publications, educational programmes and scientific meetings.

MEMBERSHIP
Student
Affiliate
Associate Member
Member – B Grade
Member – A Grade
Honorary Member

QUALIFICATION/EXAMINATIONS
Diploma in Cosmetic Science (validated by De Montfort University)

THE OIL AND COLOUR CHEMISTS' ASSOCIATION

1st Floor
3 Eden Court
Eden Way
Leighton Buzzard
Bedfordshire LU7 4FY
Tel: 01525 372530
Fax: 01525 372600
E-mail: membership@occa.org.uk
Website: www.occa.org.uk

OCCA, founded in 1918, is a learned society comprising individual qualified persons employed in, or associated with, the worldwide surface coatings industries. Most of our members work in a technical capacity, but there are senior personnel from throughout the surface coating industries. The word 'oil' in our title refers to vegetable oils, which once formed a major part of surface coatings' formulations.

MEMBERSHIP
Student Member
Ordinary Member
Honorary Member
Licentiate (LTSC)
Associate (ATSC)
Fellow (FTSC)

DESIGNATORY LETTERS
LTSC, ATSC, FTSC

THE ROYAL SOCIETY OF CHEMISTRY

Thomas Graham House
Science Park
Milton Road
Cambridge CB4 0WF
Tel: 01223 420066
Fax: 01223 423623
E-mail: membership@rsc.org
Website: www.rsc.org

The RSC is the UK professional body for chemical scientists and an international learned society for advancing the chemical sciences. With over 46,000 members worldwide and an internationally acclaimed publishing business, our activities span education and training, conferences, science policy and the promotion of the chemical sciences to the public.

MEMBERSHIP
Affiliate
Associate Member (AMRSC)
Member (MRSC)
Fellow (FRSC)

QUALIFICATION/EXAMINATIONS
NVQ Analytical Chemistry (Level 5)
Qualified Person (QP) for the Pharmaceutical Industry
Mastership in Chemical Analysis (MChemA)
Chartered Chemist (CChem)
Chartered Scientist (CSci)

DESIGNATORY LETTERS
AMRSC, MRSC, FRSC, CChem

CHIROPODY
Membership of Professional Institutions and Associations

BRITISH CHIROPODY AND PODIATRY ASSOCIATION

The New Hall
149 Bath Road
Maidenhead
Berkshire SL6 4LA
Tel: 01628 632440
Fax: 01628 674483
E-mail: membership@bcha-uk.org
Website: www.bcha-uk.org

The BChA, formed in 1959, is the largest professional organization in the UK representing the interests of independent private chiropodists / podiatrists. Since 2005 we have added foothealth practitioners to include our 7,000 members, most of whom work mainly in private practice. Those who are registered with the Health Professions Council may work in the NHS or in education.

MEMBERSHIP
Member (MSSCh & MBChA) – Podiatrists
Fellow (FSSCh) – Podiatrist
Associate members are foothealth practitioners trained by The SMAE Institute.

QUALIFICATION/EXAMINATIONS
Diploma in Podiatric Medicine (DipPodMed)
Foothealth practitioners carry the qualification – MAFHP

DESIGNATORY LETTERS
MSSCh, MBChA, FSSCh and MAFHP

THE INSTITUTE OF CHIROPODISTS AND PODIATRISTS

27 Wright Street
Southport
Merseyside PR9 0TL
Tel: 01704 546141
Fax: 01704 500477
E-mail: secretary@iocp.org.uk
Website: www.inst-chiropodist.org.uk

The IOCP represents all levels of the profession and our CPD is open to both members and non-members, as by elevating professional standards we aim to improve public safety. We have branches throughout the UK and the Republic of Ireland, and members overseas, and hold lectures, seminars and workshops to enable members to keep up to date.

MEMBERSHIP
Full Member
Fellow

THE SOCIETY OF CHIROPODISTS AND PODIATRISTS

1 Fellmongers Path
Tower Bridge Road
London SE1 3LY
Tel: 020 7234 8620
Fax: 0845 450 3721
E-mail: enq@scpod.org
Website: www.feetforlife.org

The SCP is the professional body and trade union for registered podiatrists. Membership is restricted to those qualified for registration and the Society represents around 10,000 NHS podiatrists, private practitioners and students. We monitor standards of undergraduate education and provide opportunities for CPD for our members.

MEMBERSHIP
Member (MChS)
Fellow (FChS)

DESIGNATORY LETTERS
MChS, FChS

CHIROPRACTIC
Membership of Professional Institutions and Associations

MCTIMONEY CHIROPRACTIC ASSOCIATION

Crowmarsh Gifford
Wallingford
Oxfordshire OX10 8DJ
Tel: 01491 829211
Fax: 01491 829494
E-mail: admin@mctimoney-chiropractic.org
Website: www.mctimoneychiropractic.org

The McTimoney Chiropractic Association is the professional association for McTimoney chiropractors, who in the UK are registered with the General Chiropractic Council.

MEMBERSHIP
Provisional Member
Full Member
Fellow

DESIGNATORY LETTERS
MMCA

SCOTTISH CHIROPRACTIC ASSOCIATION

1 Chisholm Avenue
Bishopton
Renfrewshire PA7 5JH
Tel: 0141 404 0260
Fax: 0141 404 0260
E-mail: admin@sca-chiropractic.org
Website: www.sca-chiropractic.org

The SCA was formed in 1979 and now has more than 60 members practising in Scotland and over 120 associated members elsewhere in the UK and abroad. Our aims are to enhance the chiropractic profession in the UK, maintain high standards of professional practice, and provide advice and support to our members.

MEMBERSHIP
Member

UNITED CHIROPRACTIC ASSOCIATION

1st Floor
45 North Hill
Plymouth
Devon PL4 8EZ
Tel: 01752 658785
Fax: 01752 658786
E-mail: admin@united-chiropractic.org
Website: www.united-chiropractic.org

The UCA is a UK-based organization for qualified, professional, principal-based chiropractors, associates and students. Full membership is open to qualified, GCC-registered chiropractors from any recognized school of chiropractic.

MEMBERSHIP
Student
Associate
Affiliate
1st Year Graduate
2nd Year Graduate
Full Member
Overseas Member

THE CHURCHES
Membership of Professional Institutions and Associations

BAPTIST UNION OF SCOTLAND

48 Speirs Wharf
Glasgow G4 9TH
Tel: 0141 423 6169
Fax: 0141 424 1422
E-mail: admin@scottishbaptist.org.uk
Website: www.scottishbaptist.org.uk

The Baptist Union of Scotland was formed in 1869, when 51 churches with a total congregation of about 3,500 united. Today, with 165 churches and about 11,450 members, the Union strives for simplicity in organizational structure and promotes increasing contact between the local churches and the National Team, who function under the overall direction of the General Director.

QUALIFICATION/EXAMINATIONS
BD or BA in Theology;
Graduate Diploma in Applied Theology through Work Based Learning
Graduate Diploma in Pastoral Studies
(awarded by the Scottish Baptist College, Paisley, and validated by the University of Paisley)

BRISTOL BAPTIST COLLEGE

The Promenade
Clifton Down
Clifton
Bristol BS8 3NJ
Tel: 0117 946 7050
Fax: 0117 946 7787
E-mail: admin@bristol-baptist.ac.uk
Website: www.bristol-baptist.ac.uk

The central aim of the College is to train men and women for ministry in the Church and in the world. We do this by enabling critical reflection upon the Bible and Christian theological tradition and on the contexts from which we come and within which we are placed.

QUALIFICATION/EXAMINATIONS
Certificate in Theological Studies
Diploma in Theological Studies
BA in Theological Studies
MA in Biblical Studies
MA in Mission Studies
(all validated by the University of Bristol)

METHODIST CHURCH IN IRELAND

Board of Examiners
Secretary: Rev Peter D Murray, BA, BD
28 Windermere Drive
Bangor
Co Down BT20 4QF

MEMBERSHIP

Candidates for training must normally have the standard of general education for university entrance. They must be accredited Local Preachers of the Methodist Church, and are examined by written papers in Biblical Studies and Theology and by oral aptitude and personality tests. After admission to training, candidates normally spend 3 years at Edgehill Theological College, Belfast, studying for a diploma or degree of Queen's University, Belfast, in New Testament Greek, Hebrew, the English Bible, Theology, Church History, Pastoral Psychology, or Homiletics. This is followed by 3 years as a probationer Minister working under a superintendent Minister. During probation the candidate continues study within a tutorial system and is examined by continuous assessment.

THE CHURCH OF ENGLAND

Ministry Division of The Archbishops' Council
Church House
Great Smith Street
London SW1P 3AZ
Tel: 020 7898 1404
Fax: 020 7898 1421
E-mail: david.way@churchofengland.org (ordination training)
susan.hart@churchofengland.org (Reader training)
Website: http:/ www.churchofengland.org/clergy-office-holders/ministry.aspx
www.archbishopofcanterbury.org/1027

The Church of England's Ministry Division oversees training for ordination and issues certificates for successful completion for Reader ministry. Enquiries about entry into training should be directed to the candidate's own diocese. In addition, The Archbishop's Examination in Theology offers means of study at three postgraduate levels.

QUALIFICATION/EXAMINATIONS
Archbishop's Examination:
PG Diploma of Student of Theology
Master of Philosophy
Doctor of Philosophy

THE CHURCH OF SCOTLAND

Church of Scotland Offices
121 George Street
Edinburgh EH2 4YN
Tel: 0131 225 5722
Fax: 0131 220 3113
Website: www.churchofscotland.org.uk

The Ministries Council runs an enquiry process to help those who sense a call to any of the ministries within the Church of Scotland to consider it in a supportive environment. Attendance at one of our enquirers' conferences, which are held twice each year, is the first stage of the enquiry process. For more information see; www.churchofscotland.org.uk/serve/ministries_in_the_church/training_for_ministries

THE METHODIST CHURCH

Formation in Ministry Office (Initial Development of Ministries)
25 Marylebone Road
London NW1 5JR
Tel: 020 7486 5502

Candidates for Diaconal or Presbyteral Ministry in the Methodist Church must have been members of the Methodist Church at least 2 years and are expected to offer at least 10 years of ministerial service. The first stage of preparation is Foundation Training, which requires 1 year (FT) or 2 years (PT) to complete, during which a person may apply to become a candidate for ordained ministry. The process of selection takes 6 months. To enter into training for Presbyteral Ministry, a candidate must be a trained Local Preacher, which involves taking the Methodist Local Preachers' Training Course, Faith & Worship. Deacons become members of the Methodist Diaconal and are not required to be preachers. Accepted candidates for either order receive 1 or 2 years of further theological training, which in most cases leads to a degree or diploma in Theology or Ministry. Upon completion of training, a candidate serves as a Methodist Minister for 2 years on probation before ordination. For Presbyters, the appointment may be to an itinerant appointment (stipendiary) or to a local appointment (usually non-stipendiary) or as licensed to minister in secular employment. Deacons are always itinerant.

THE MORAVIAN CHURCH IN GREAT BRITAIN AND IRELAND

Moravian Church House
5–7 Muswell Hill
London N10 3TJ
Tel: 020 8883 3409
Fax: 020 8365 3371
E-mail: moravianchurchhouse@btinternet.com
Website: www.moravian.org.uk

Candidates for Moravian Church Service must be members of the Moravian Church and would normally have completed the Lay Training Course and have the support of their local church committee. They should make an initial application to the Provincial Board of the Moravian Church. Their qualifications are examined by the Church Service Advisory Board, which reports on them to the Provincial Board, with whom the final decision rests. Normally the standard of education required for the work of the Ministry is a university Divinity degree or Certificate together with a thorough acquaintance with the history, principles and methods of the Moravian Church. Candidates receive guidance for the Ministry during a period of supervised service under the direction of experienced Ministers. A class of non-stipendiary Ministers has been established for those who wish to serve on a non-maintained basis. Training varies according to candidates' needs. In all cases applications should be made to the address given above.

THE PRESBYTERIAN CHURCH IN IRELAND

The Director of Ministerial Studies
Union Theological College
108 Botanic Avenue
Belfast BT7 1JT
Tel: 02890 205088
Fax: 02890 205099

Qualifications required: Under 30 – a non-theological degree; over 30 but under 40 (as reckoned on 1 October following application) – either a non-theological degree or 2 years, non-graduating Arts or 4 modules of PT BD study or 6 modules of PT study in Humanities acceptable to the Board of Studies; over 40 – not normally accepted, except in exceptional circumstances, where candidate is already possessed of good educational background and/or professional experience.

THE PRESBYTERIAN CHURCH OF WALES

Tabernacle Chapel
81 Merthyr Road
Whitchurch
Cardiff CF14 1DD
Tel: 02920 627465
Fax: 02920 616188
E-mail: swyddfa.office@ebcpcw.org.uk
Website: www.ebcpw.org.uk

The Presbyterian Church of Wales (PCW) is a Protestant non-conformist denomination. Ordination is dependent on successful application through the local church and Presbytery to the Candidates and Training Department.

MEMBERSHIP
Ministers are ordained to the full-time, part-time or non-stipendary ministry.

QUALIFICATION/EXAMINATIONS
Pastoral Studies course

THE ROMAN CATHOLIC CHURCH

Candidates for the priesthood in the RC Church attend a residential seminary course of at least 6 years. Among subjects studied are Philosophy, Psychology, Dogmatic and Moral Theology, Scripture, Church History, Canon Law, Liturgy, Catechetics, Communications and Pastoral Theology. Each college/seminary has its own arrangements for the university education of its students. Those who do not attend university take a final internal exam.

THE SALVATION ARMY

UK Headquarters
101 Newington Causeway
London SE1 6BN
Tel: 020 7367 4500
E-mail: thq@salvationarmy.org.uk
Website: www.salvationarmy.org.uk

Salvation Army officers engaged in FT service are ordained ministers of religion, and are commissioned following a 2-year period of residential training at the William Booth College, Denmark Hill, London SE5 8BQ. This course – an HE Diploma in Salvation Army Officer Training – may now be undertaken by distance learning, or a mixture of residential and distance learning. Officers may be appointed to corps (church) work, to social services centres (for which additional professional qualifications are required) or to administrative posts.

THE SCOTTISH EPISCOPAL CHURCH

Theological Institute of the Scottish Episcopal Church
Forbes House
21 Grosvenor Crescent
Edinburgh EH12 5EE
Tel: 0131 225 6357
Fax: 0131 346 7247
E-mail: tisec@scotland.anglican.org
Website: www.scotland.anglican.org

Candidates are trained for lay and ordained, stipendiary and non-stipendiary ministries in the Scottish Episcopal Church, Methodist Church and the United Reformed Church.

The curriculum is delivered centrally through residential sessions and regionally through diocesan groups. The Diploma in Theology for Ministry course run by the Institute is validated by York St John's University. Some students undertake further studies through universities, leading to degree qualifications.

THE SCOTTISH UNITED REFORMED AND CONGREGATIONAL COLLEGE

113 West Regent Street
Glasgow G2 2RU
Tel: 0141 248 5382
E-mail: Scottishcollege@urcscotland.org.uk
Website: www.scotland.urc.org.uk

The College is recognized as a resource centre for learning by the General Assembly of the United Reformed Church and is one of the institutions charged with responsibility for initial ministerial education.

QUALIFICATION/EXAMINATIONS

The College awards only its own certificate, which is part of the process of accreditation of ordinands as ministers of the United Reformed Church. Students, however, are normally concurrently matriculated for a degree, normally in Theology or Religious Studies, at a university.

THE UNITARIAN AND FREE CHRISTIAN CHURCHES

Essex Hall
London WC2R 3HY
Tel: 020 7240 2384
Fax: 020 7240 3089
E-mail: info@unitarian.org.uk
Website: www.unitarian.org.uk

Candidates accepted for training for the ministry in the Unitarian and Free Christian Churches take courses of training either at Manchester Academy & Harris College, Oxford (2 to 4 years' study for an Oxford degree in Theology/or Theology & Philosophy or an Oxford Certificate in Theology/Religious Studies), or at the Unitarian College (Luther King House, Brighton Grove, Rusholme, Manchester; an individually designed contextual theology course of the Partnership for Theological Education which may lead to a degree or other academic qualification validated by Chester or Manchester University). Alternative arrangements can be made for candidates wishing to study through the Welsh language. Placement work and Unitarian studies are also integral to ministerial preparation. Training normally takes 2 or more years.

THE UNITED REFORMED CHURCH

Church House
86 Tavistock Place
London WC1H 9RT
Tel: 020 7916 2020
Fax: 020 7916 2021
E-mail: training@urc.org.uk
Website: www.urc.org.uk

Stipendiary Ministry: URC Ministers are usually trained in the Church's theological colleges. All training is ecumenical. Candidates must been a member of the URC for at least 2 years and go through a candidating process in the other Councils of the Church to decide whether they should be sponsored for training. Most then take a 3- or 4-year degree in Theology or a diploma of the university to which their college is attached. In certain cases it is possible to train PT on an ecumenical course. The minimum requirement on training completion is a Theology diploma and 800 hours placement in a church.

Non-Stipendiary: A training programme of PT study usually over 4 years is open to committed members of the URC. Candidates must be recommended by their local church and go through the process indicated above. A Director of Training guides the student. Most students study PT on a recognized ecumenical course, with an additional programme to study Reformed History Ethics and Worship, but some train FT in a college. A Leaving Certificate for a call to the ordained ministry is granted. Training is arranged by the Board of Studies of the Training Committee.

Church-related Community Workers: They help lead and strengthen the local church's mission through community development in an area where specialist help is required to meet unusual needs. Candidates must be members of the URC and show capabilities for leadership. They are required to obtain at least a Diploma in Theology and a Diploma in Community Work before being commissioned.

Lay Preacher's Certificate: Training for Learning & Serving is the qualifying course for this. The course takes 3 years. Work is done in local groups and there are five residential weekend courses each year. Candidates are also expected to undertake some practical work in churches.

THE WESLEYAN REFORM UNION

Wesleyan Reform Church House
123 Queen Street
Sheffield S1 2DU
Tel: 0114 272 1938
E-mail: admin@thewru.co.uk
Website: www.thewru.com

The Wesleyan Reform Union has no training college of its own and encourages candidates for its Ministry to enter a Bible College for 2 or 3 years. All candidates are, however, under the personal supervision of a Union Tutor, who directs a Biblical Studies & Training Department offering fairly extensive courses. Candidates attend Headquarters once a year for an oral exam in Theology conducted by the Tutor in the presence of the Union Examination Committee; they also take written exams.

UNITED FREE CHURCH OF SCOTLAND

11 Newton Place
Glasgow G3 7PR
Tel: 01413 323435
Fax: 01413 331973
E-mail: office@ufcos.org.uk
Website: www.ufcos.org.uk

The United Free Church of Scotland is a small presbyterian denomination which came into being in 1929. Those seeking to become candidates for the ministry should normally have been members of the denomination for at least a year. They will require to undertake a degree course in theology.

THE CHURCH IN WALES

St Michael's College
Llandaff
Cardiff CF5 2YJ
Tel: 029 205 63379
Fax: 029 208 38008
Website: www.stmichaels.ac.uk

The Church in Wales expects candidates for ordination to satisfy the requirements of recognized theological courses. University graduates usually spend at least 2 years at a theological college, and if they are non-theological graduates, they are encouraged to study for a university degree or diploma in Theology. Non-graduate candidates must have at least 5 passes at GCSE and normally study for a university diploma in Theology or a degree in Theology if they have obtained the necessary grades at A level. These requirements may be modified in the case of older candidates.

CINEMA, FILM AND TELEVISION
Membership of Professional Institutions and Associations

BRITISH KINEMATOGRAPH SOUND AND TELEVISION SOCIETY (BKSTS)

Pinewood Studios
Pinewood Road
Iver Heath
Buckinghamshire SL0 0NH
Tel: 01753 656656
E-mail: info@bksts.com
Website: www.bksts.com

The BKSTS was founded in 1931 to serve the growing film industry and today arranges meetings, presentations, seminars, international exhibitions and conferences, as well as organizing an extensive programme of training courses, lectures, workshops and special events. We ensure that our members remain up to date with the latest techniques through master classes and our print and electronic publications.

MEMBERSHIP
Student Member
Intermediate Member
Associate Member
Full Member (MBKS)
Retired Member
Fellow (FBKS)

DESIGNATORY LETTERS
MBKS, FBKS

THE LONDON FILM SCHOOL

24 Shelton Street
Covent Garden
London WC2H 9UB
Tel: 020 7836 9642
Fax: 020 7497 3718
E-mail: info@lfs.org.uk
Website: www.lfs.org.uk

The LFS is one of the foremost independent film schools in Europe and is recognized by Skillset as a Centre of Excellence. It is a registered charity and a non-profit-making company, limited by guarantee. Since 1956 we have trained thousands of directors, cinematographers, editors and other film professionals from around the world.

QUALIFICATION/EXAMINATIONS
MA in Filmmaking (validated by London Metropolitan University)
MA in Screenwriting (validated by London Metropolitan University)

THE NATIONAL FILM AND TELEVISION SCHOOL

Beaconsfield Studios
Station Road
Beaconsfield
Buckinghamshire HP9 1LG
Tel: 01494 671234
Fax: 01494 674042
E-mail: info@nfts.co.uk
Website: www.nfts.co.uk

A Skillset Screen & Media Academy, the UK's leading film and television school offers full-time MA and Diploma courses in all the key film and television disciplines, from Animation to VFX. Purpose-built studios include two film stages, a large television studio, and post-production facilities rivalling those of many professional companies.

QUALIFICATION/EXAMINATIONS
Diploma (in 1 of 3 disciplines)
MA in Film and Television (specializing in 1 of 13 disciplines)

CLEANING, LAUNDRY AND DRY CLEANING
Membership of Professional Institutions and Associations

BRITISH INSTITUTE OF CLEANING SCIENCE

9 Premier Court
Boarden Close
Moulton Park
Northampton NN3 6LF
Tel: 01604 678710
Fax: 01604 645988
E-mail: info@bics.org.uk
Website: www.bics.org.uk

The BICSc is the largest independent professional and educational body within the cleaning industry. Our aim is to raise the status and standards of the cleaning industry through training and education. We offer our 5,000 members a range of assessment schemes and training courses, together with a telephone and e-mail helpline.

MEMBERSHIP
Practitioner
Associate
Member
Corporate Member

QUALIFICATION/EXAMINATIONS
Cleaning Professional Skills Suite
Qualifications and Credit Framework

THE GUILD OF CLEANERS AND LAUNDERERS

5 Portland Place
London W1B 1PW
Tel: 0845 600 1838
E-mail: enquiries@gcl.org.uk
Website: www.gcl.org.uk

The Guild, formed in 1949, is a technical and professional society whose aim is to further knowledge and skill in all branches of the industry. We keep our members up to date through lectures, seminars and written reports, exchange information of mutual benefit with other organizations in the industry, and voice our opinion in relevant forums.

MEMBERSHIP
Young Guilder
Member
Associate (AGCL)
Advanced Member (AdGCL)
Licentiate (LGCL)
Fellow (FGCL)

DESIGNATORY LETTERS
AGCL, AdGCL, LGCL, FGCL

COLOUR TECHNOLOGY
Membership of Professional Institutions and Associations

PAINTING AND DECORATING ASSOCIATION

32 Coton Road
Nuneaton
Warwickshire CV11 5TW
Tel: 024 7635 3776
Fax: 024 7635 4513
E-mail: info@paintingdecoratingassociation.co.uk
Website: www.paintingdecoratingassociation.co.uk

The PDA is a registered trade and employers' organization, catering exclusively for the needs of professional painting and decorating trade employers. The Association conducts no examinations, but all membership applications are scrutinized at branch level to ensure that only bona fide firms that agree to abide by our code of conduct are admitted.

MEMBERSHIP
Full Member
Associate

THE SOCIETY OF DYERS AND COLOURISTS

Perkin House
82 Grattan Road
Bradford BD1 2JB
Tel: 01274 761792
Fax: 01274 392888
E-mail: members@sdc.org.uk
Website: www.sdc.org.uk

An educational charity, professional body and chartered society, serving globally all aspects of the coloration industries including the textile supply chain through the knowledgeable and enthusiastic involvement of its professional members and industry partners.

Recognized as the authority for colour science and technology, delivering high-quality international qualifications and training programmes.

MEMBERSHIP
Professional Voting Member (FSDC, ASDC, LSDC, CCol)
Ordinary Voting Member
Individual Member
Individual Student Member
Educational Institute Member
Corporate (Company) Member

QUALIFICATION/EXAMINATIONS
Diploma of Fellowship (FSDC)
Diploma of Associateship (ASDC)
Diploma of Licentiateship (LSDC)
Chartered Colourist (CCol)

DESIGNATORY LETTERS
FSDC, ASDC, LSDC, CCol.

COMMUNICATIONS AND MEDIA
Membership of Professional Institutions and Associations

THE PICTURE RESEARCH ASSOCIATION

Box 105 Hampstead House
176 Finchley Road
London NW3 6BP
Tel: 07771 982308
Website: www.picture-research.org.uk

The PRA, founded in 1977, is a professional organization for picture researchers, picture editors and anyone specifically involved in the research, management and supply of visual material to the media industry. Our aims are to provide information and give support to our members, and to promote their interests and specific skills to potential employers.

MEMBERSHIP
Introductory Member
Associate Member
Full Member

COMPUTING AND INFORMATION TECHNOLOGY
Membership of Professional Institutions and Associations

ASSOCIATION OF COMPUTER PROFESSIONALS

ACP
Chilverbridge House
Arlington
East Sussex BN26 6SB
Tel: 01323 871874
Fax: 01323 871875
E-mail: admin@acpexamboard.com
Website: www.acpexamboard.com

The ACP is an independent professional examining body, founded in 1984 to set and maintain standards of education that reflect the constantly changing requirements of the computer industry, both in the UK and overseas. We do so through the provision of course syllabuses and examinations to our carefully vetted training centres around the world.

MEMBERSHIP
Student
Practitioner
Graduate (GradACP)
Licentiate (LACP)
Associate (AACP)
Member (MACP)
Fellow (FACP)

QUALIFICATION/EXAMINATIONS
Please see the ACP's website for details of certificates and diplomas.

DESIGNATORY LETTERS
GradACP, LACP, AACP, MACP, FACP

BRITISH COMPUTER SOCIETY

1st Floor, Block D
North Star House
North Star Avenue
Swindon
Wiltshire SN2 1FA
Tel: 01793 417417
Fax: 01793 417444
E-mail: customerservices@hq.bcs.org.uk
Website: www.bcs.org.uk

The BCS is the professional membership and accreditation body for IT and has more than 70,000 members, including practitioners, businesses, academics and students, in the UK and internationally. Our aim is to promote the academic study and professional practice of computing and to show the public that IT is about far more than simply using a PC.

MEMBERSHIP
Student
Affiliate
Associate Member (AMBCS)
Professional Fellow (FBCS)
Honorary Fellow
Distinguished Fellow
Incorporated Engineer (IEng)
Chartered Engineer (CEng)
Chartered IT Professional (MBCS CITP)
Chartered Fellow (FBCS CITP)
Chartered Scientist (CSci)
Education Affiliate (institutional member)

QUALIFICATION/EXAMINATIONS
Certificate in IT
Certificate in IT for Insurance Professionals (developed jointly with The Chartered Insurance Institute)
Diploma in IT
Professional GradDip in IT

See the BCS website for details of other qualifications.

INSTITUTE FOR THE MANAGEMENT OF INFORMATION SYSTEMS

Suite A, (Part) 2nd Floor
3 White Oak Square
London Road
Swanley
Kent BR8 7AG
Tel: 0845 850 0006
Fax: 0845 850 0007
E-mail: central@imis.org.uk
Website: www.imis.org.uk

IMIS is one of the leading professional associations in the IT sector. A registered charity, it plays a prominent role in fostering greater understanding of IS management, in working to enhance the status of those engaged in the profession, and in promoting higher standards through better education and training worldwide.

MEMBERSHIP
Student Member
Practitioner Member
Licentiate Member (LIMIS)
Associate Member (AIMIS)
Full Member (MIMIS)
Fellow (FIMIS)

QUALIFICATION/EXAMINATIONS
Foundation
Diploma
Higher Diploma

DESIGNATORY LETTERS
LIMIS, AIMIS, MIMIS, FIMIS

INSTITUTION OF ANALYSTS AND PROGRAMMERS

Charles House
36 Culmington Road
London W13 9NH
Tel: 020 8567 2118
Fax: 020 8567 4379
E-mail: dg@iap.org.uk
Website: www.iap.org.uk

The IAP is a professional organization for people who work in the development, installation and testing of business systems and computer software. Our aim is to promote high standards of competence and conduct among our members, to encourage them to develop their skills and progress their career, and to facilitate the advancement and spreading of knowledge within the profession.

MEMBERSHIP
Licentiate
Graduate (GradIAP)
Associate Member (AIAP)
Member (MIAP)
Fellow (FIAP)

DESIGNATORY LETTERS
GradIAP, AIAP, MIAP, FIAP

COUNSELLING

Membership of Professional Institutions and Associations

COUNSELLING LTD

Registered Office
5 Pear Tree Walk
Wakefield
West Yorkshire WF2 0HW
E-mail: E-mail via the website
Website: www.counselling.ltd.uk

Counselling, a registered charity founded in 1998, is a membership organization for counsellors and psychotherapists in the UK that has established a network of about 2,700 affiliated CCC-registered counsellors, many of whom are able to provide occasional free or discounted face-to-face counselling with clients on low incomes.

MEMBERSHIP
Affiliate

COUNSELLORS AND PSYCHOTHERAPISTS IN PRIMARY CARE

Queensway House
Queensway
Bognor Regis
West Sussex PO21 1QT
Tel: 01243 870701
Fax: 01243 870702
E-mail: cpc@cpc-online.co.uk
Website: www.cpc-online.co.uk

CPC is a professional membership association for individual practitioners, whose names are entered in a Register of Members. The aims of the Association are to represent counsellors and psychotherapists working in an NHS setting and to lead the way in establishing national standards and guidelines for further development of professional and effective counselling throughout the NHS.

MEMBERSHIP
Student
Subscriber
Intermediate Member
Registered Member
Supervisor
Organizational Member

QUALIFICATION/EXAMINATIONS
PGDip in Supervision for the Primary Care Setting

CSCT COUNSELLING TRAINING

13 Coleshill Street
Sutton Coldfield
West Midlands B72 1SD
Tel: 0121 321 1396/0870 1
Fax: 0121 355 5581
E-mail: info@counsellingtraining.com
Website: www.counsellingtraining.com

CSCT has been producing counselling training courses for over 25 years, during which time we have trained over 50,000 students. Our courses are offered PT via a network of colleges and private providers throughout the UK. Our training materials are written to the specifications of the appropriate awarding body and we provide 24-hour e-mail and telephone support from Client Services and the Academic Team.

QUALIFICATION/EXAMINATIONS
Please see the CSCT's website.

CREDIT MANAGEMENT
Membership of Professional Institutions and Associations

INSTITUTE OF CREDIT MANAGEMENT

The Water Mill
Station Road
South Luffenham
Oakham
Leicestershire LE15 8NB
Tel: 01780 722900
Fax: 01780 721333
E-mail: info@icm.org.uk
Website: www.icm.org.uk

The ICM is the largest professional credit management organization in Europe and the only one accredited by Ofqual as an awarding body. We represent the credit profession across trade, consumer and export credit, as well as in related activities such as collections, credit reporting, credit insurance and insolvency, promote excellence in credit management and raise awareness of its vital role in business and the community.

MEMBERSHIP
Affiliate
Associate Member (AICM)
Graduate Member (MICM(Grad))
Member (MICM)
Fellow (FICM)

QUALIFICATION/EXAMINATIONS
Diploma in Credit Management (Level 2)
Diploma in Credit Management (Level 3)
Diploma in Credit Management (Level 5)

DESIGNATORY LETTERS
AICM, MICM (Grad), MICM, FICM

DANCING
Membership of Professional Institutions and Associations

BRITISH BALLET ORGANIZATION

Woolborough House
39 Lonsdale Road
Barnes
London SW13 9JP
Tel: 020 8748 1241
Fax: 020 8748 1301
E-mail: info@bbo.org.uk
Website: www.bbo.org.uk

The BBO, founded in 1930, is an awarding body offering teacher training and examinations in classical ballet, tap, modern dance and jazz. We have schools throughout the UK and in several other countries.

MEMBERSHIP
Student Member
Senior Student Member
Affiliated Member
Student Teacher Member
Teacher Member

QUALIFICATION/EXAMINATIONS
Please see the BBO website for details.

IMPERIAL SOCIETY OF TEACHERS OF DANCING

Imperial House
22/26 Paul Street
London EC2A 4QE
Tel: +44 (0)20 7377 1577
Fax: +44 (0)20 7247 8309
E-mail: education@istd.org
Website: www.istd.org

The ISTD is a registered educational charity and examinations board. We aim to promote knowledge of dance, to maintain and improve teaching standards, and to qualify (by examination) teachers of dancing. Our dance techniques cover more than 12 different genres and are taught by more than 7,500 members by our members worldwide.

MEMBERSHIP
A range of 9 categories from Student to Life Membership.

QUALIFICATION/EXAMINATIONS
Please see our website www.istd.org or www.dance-teachers.org.

DESIGNATORY LETTERS
ISTD

INTERNATIONAL DANCE TEACHERS' ASSOCIATION LIMITED

International House
76 Bennett Road
Brighton BN2 5JL
Tel: 01273 685652
Fax: 01273 674388
E-mail: info@idta.co.uk
Website: www.idta.co.uk

The IDTA is one of the world's largest dance examination boards, with more than 7,000 members in 55 countries. Our aims are to promote knowledge and foster the art of dance in all its forms, to maintain and improve dancing standards, and to offer a comprehensive range of professional qualifications in all dance genres.

MEMBERSHIP
Associate (AIDTA)
Licentiate (LIDTA)
Fellow (FIDTA)

DESIGNATORY LETTERS
AIDTA, LIDTA, FIDTA

THE BENESH INSTITUTE

36 Battersea Square
London SW11 3RA
Tel: 020 7326 8031
Fax: 020 7924 3129
E-mail: beneshinstitute@rad.org.uk
Website: www.benesh.org

The Benesh Institute is the international centre for Benesh Movement Notation (BMN) founded in 1962 to promote, develop and offer education in BMN. We also function as an examining body and professional centre, and are responsible for coordinating technical developments. Since 1997 The Benesh Institute has been incorporated within the Royal Academy of Dance.

MEMBERSHIP
Fellow (FI Chor)

QUALIFICATION/EXAMINATIONS
Certificate in Benesh Movement Notation (CBMN) (validated by the Royal Academy of Dance)
Diploma for Professional Benesh Movement Notators (DPBMN) (validated by the Royal Academy of Dance)
Associate of the Institute of Choreology (AI Chor)

DESIGNATORY LETTERS
FI Chor

DENTISTRY
Membership of Professional Institutions and Associations

GENERAL DENTAL COUNCIL

37 Wimpole Street
London W1G 8DQ
Tel: 0845 222 4141
Fax: 020 7224 3294
E-mail: information@gdc-uk.org
Website: www.gdc-uk.org

The GDC regulates dental professionals in the UK. All dentists, clinical dental technicians, dental hygienists, dental nurses, dental technicians, dental therapists and orthodontic therapists must be registered with the GDC in order to work in the UK.

THE BRITISH DENTAL ASSOCIATION

64 Wimpole Street
London W1G 8YS
Tel: 020 7935 0875
Fax: 020 7487 5232
E-mail: enquiries@bda.org
Website: www.bda.org

The BDA, which was founded in 1880, is the professional association and trade union for dentists in the UK. Our aims are to advance the science, arts and ethics of dentistry, improve in UK's oral health, and promote the interests of our members. Membership, which is voluntary, stands at around 23,000, mostly in general practice.

MEMBERSHIP
Student Member
(Recently) Qualified Member
Ordinary Member
Retired Member
Overseas Member

BRITISH SOCIETY OF DENTAL HYGIENE AND THERAPY

3 Kestrel Court
Waterwells Business Park
Gloucester GL2 2AT
Tel: 01452 886365
Fax: 01452 886468
E-mail: enquiries@bsdht.org.uk
Website: www.bsdht.org.uk

The BSDHT is the only nationally recognized body that represents dental hygienists, dental hygienist-therapists and students of dental hygiene. We have a membership of more than 3,500 in the UK and beyond, and look after their interests through liaising with the Department of Health, General Dental Council, British Dental Association and other organizations.

MEMBERSHIP
Member

BRITISH ASSOCIATION OF DENTAL NURSES

PO Box 4, Room 200
Hillhouse International Business Centre
Thornton-Cleveleys
Lancashire FY5 4QD
Tel: 01253 338360
Fax: 01253 773266
E-mail: admin@badn.org.uk
Website: www.badn.org.uk

The BADN represents dental nurses, whether qualified or unqualified, working in general practice, hospital, the community, the armed forces, industry, practice management or reception, and has representation on the National Examining Board, the Dental Nurses Standards and Training Advisory Board and its Registration Committee, the Joint Consultative Committee, and other bodies.

MEMBERSHIP
Associate Member
Full Member

CLINICAL DENTAL TECHNICIANS ASSOCIATION

Room 3b, Ground Floor
Tower House Business Centre
Fishergate
York YO10 4UA
Tel: 01904 625130
Fax: 01904 658361
Website: www.cdta.org.uk

The CDTA provides political and educational representation for its members, who are registered with the General Dental Council and trained in designing, creating, constructing, repairing and rebasing removable appliances to ensure optimal fit, maximum comfort and general wellbeing of patients. We are committed to team dentistry and ensure that our members work to the highest professional standards.

MEMBERSHIP
Member

DENTAL TECHNOLOGISTS ASSOCIATION

3 Kestral Court
Waterwells Drive
Waterwells Business Park
Gloucester GL2 2AT
Tel: 0870 243 0753
E-mail: sueadams@dta-uk.org
Website: www.dta-uk.org/

The DTA is an organization that supports the development of the dental technology profession by encouraging and promoting education, including CPD, and for the exchange of views between dental technicians. We advise, develop and support dental technicians and maintain links with the government, other dental organizations, service providers and the public.

MEMBERSHIP
Member

DIETETICS

Membership of Professional Institutions and Associations

THE BRITISH DIETETIC ASSOCIATION

5th Floor
Charles House
148–49 Great Charles Street Queensway
Birmingham B3 3HT
Tel: 0121 200 8080
Fax: 0121 200 8081
E-mail: info@bda.uk.com
Website: www.bda.uk.com

The BDA, established in 1936, is the UK's leading professional association and trade union for dietitians. Our aims are to advance the science and practice of dietetics and associated subjects, to promote education and training in the science and practice of dietetics and associated subjects, and to regulate relations between our 6,700+ members and their employers.

MEMBERSHIP
Full Member
Associate Member
Affiliate Member
Alliance Member
Student Member

DISTRIBUTION

Membership of Professional Institutions and Associations

THE CHARTERED INSTITUTE OF LOGISTICS AND TRANSPORT (UK)

Earlstrees Court
Earlstrees Road
Corby
Northamptonshire NN17 4AX
Tel: 01536 740104
Fax: 01536 740101
E-mail: membership@ciltuk.org.uk
Website: www.ciltuk.org.uk

The Chartered Institute of Logistics and Transport in the UK – CILT(UK) – is the independent professional body for transport, logistics, supply chain management and has more than 18,000 members in the industry. Our aim is to facilitate the development of personal and professional excellence.

MEMBERSHIP
Learner Affiliate
Student Affiliate
Affiliate
Member (MILT)
Chartered Member (CMILT)
Chartered Fellow (FCILT)
Corporate Member

QUALIFICATION/EXAMINATIONS
Regulated Qualifications (cover eight professional sectors in Supply Chain, Transport Planning, Rail, Active Travel and Travel Planning, Bus & Coach, Ports Maritime and Waterways, Freight Forwarding and Aviation)
Award (Level 1)
Award (Level 2)
Award (Level 3)
Certificate (Level 2)

Certificate (Level 3)
Diploma (Level 2)
Professional Diploma (Level 5)
Advanced Diploma (Level 6)

Accredited Qualifications
Humanitarian Logistics (3 programmes)
Supply Chain Practitioner Award (Foundation, Professional and Master programmes)

Partnerships
Certified European Logistician (Junior, Senior, Master programmes)
MSc in International Transport and Logistics or International Logistics and Supply Chain Management

DESIGNATORY LETTERS
MILT, CMILT, FCILT

DIVING
Membership of Professional Institutions and Associations

DIVING CERTIFICATES

Health & Safety Executive, Diving Operations Strategy Team
Wren House, Hedgerows Business Park
Colchester Road, Springfield
Chelmsford
Essex CM2 5PF
Tel: 01245 706256
Fax: 01245 706222
E-mail: cathy.uprichard@hse.gsi.gov.uk
Website: www.hse.gov.uk/diving

The Health and Safety Executive (HSE) issues diver competence certificates to divers who have been assessed as competent by an HSE-recognized diver-training organization (a list of which can be obtained from the HSE) for the following competencies: SCUBA, Surface Supplied, Surface Supplied (top-up) and Closed Bell.

DRAMATIC AND PERFORMING ARTS
Membership of Professional Institutions and Associations

EQUITY

Guild House
Upper St Martins Lane
London WC2H 9EG
Tel: 020 7379 6000
Fax: 020 7379 7001
E-mail: info@equity.org.uk
Website: www.equity.org.uk

Equity is the UK trade union representing professional performers and other creative workers from across the entertainment, creative and cultural industries. The main function of Equity is to negotiate minimum terms and conditions of employment for its members and to represent its members' interests to the government and other bodies.

MEMBERSHIP
Youth Member
Student Member
Graduate Member
Full Member

NATIONAL COUNCIL FOR DRAMA TRAINING

249 Tooley Street
London SE1 2JX
Tel: 020 7407 3686
Fax: 020 7387 3860
E-mail: info@ncdt.co.uk
Website: www.ncdt.co.uk

The NCDT is a partnership of employers in the theatre, broadcast and media industries, employee representatives and training providers. We accredit vocational courses, act as a champion for the sector and work to optimize support for professional drama training and education in acting, stage management and technical theatre, embracing change and development.

THE BRITISH (THEATRICAL) ARTS

12 Deveron Way
Rise Park
Romford
Essex RM1 4UL
Tel: 01708 756263
Website: www.britisharts.org

The British Arts is a non-profit-making organization dedicated to maintaining and where necessary raising the standard of the teaching of Performing Arts subjects. We work to encourage a strong technical foundation combined with an understanding of professional theatrical presentation and conduct exams in Dramatic Art, Classical & Stage Ballet, Mime, Tap, Musical Theatre and Modern Dance.

MEMBERSHIP
Student Member
Companion
Associate (Teaching and Non-teaching)
Member (Teaching and Non-teaching)
Advanced Teacher Member
Fellow

QUALIFICATION/EXAMINATIONS
Please see the British Arts website.

DRIVING INSTRUCTORS
Membership of Professional Institutions and Associations

REGISTER OF APPROVED DRIVING INSTRUCTORS

The Axis Building
112 Upper Parliament Street
Nottingham NG1 6LP
Tel: 0300 200 1122
E-mail: ADIReg@dsa.gsi.gov.uk

The Register of Approved Driving Instructors (ADI) and the licensing scheme for trainee instructors (PDI) are administered under the provisions of the Road Traffic Act 1988 by the Department for Transport (DfT). It is an offence for anyone to give professional instruction (that is instruction paid for by or in respect of the pupil) in driving a motor car unless: (a) his or her name is on the Register of Approved Driving Instructors; or (b) he or she holds a 'trainee's licence to give instruction' issued by the Registrar.

Embalming

QUALIFICATION/EXAMINATIONS
Please see the Business Link website (www.businesslink.gov.uk) for details of the qualifying examinations.

EMBALMING
Membership of Professional Institutions and Associations

INTERNATIONAL EXAMINATIONS BOARD OF EMBALMERS

39 Poplar Grove
Kennington
Oxford OX1 5QN
Tel: 01865 735788
Fax: 01865 730941

The Board examines candidates who wish to become qualified members of the British Institute of Embalmers (qv), which is not itself an examining body but can provide information packs (also available from the above address) that contain lists of approved schools and accredited tutors.

THE BRITISH INSTITUTE OF EMBALMERS

Anubis House
21c Station Road
Knowle
Solihull
West Midlands B93 0HL
Tel: 01564 778991
Fax: 01564 770812
E-mail: enquiries@bioe.co.uk
Website: www.bioe.co.uk

The BIE, founded in 1927, is an organization for professional embalmers. Its objectives include supporting and protecting the status, character and interests of embalmers, promoting the efficient tuition of persons seeking to become embalmers, and encouraging the study and practice of improved methods of embalming.

MEMBERSHIP
Member (MBIE)
Fellow (FBIE)

DESIGNATORY LETTERS
MBIE, FBIE

EMPLOYMENT AND CAREERS SERVICES
Membership of Professional Institutions and Associations

RECRUITMENT AND EMPLOYMENT CONFEDERATION

4th Floor
Albion House
Chertsey Road
Woking
Surrey GU21 6BT
Tel: 020 7009 2100
Fax: 01483 714979
E-mail: info@rec.uk.com
Website: www.rec.uk.com

The REC is the representative body for the UK's £27 billion private recruitment and staffing industry, with a membership of more than 8,000 Corporate Members comprising agencies and businesses from all sectors, and 6,000 members of the Institute of Recruitment Professionals (IRP) made up of recruitment consultants and other industry professionals.

MEMBERSHIP
Affiliate (AIRP)
Member (MIRP)
Fellow (FIRP)

QUALIFICATION/EXAMINATIONS
Certificate in Recruitment Practice (CertRP)
Diploma in Recruitment Practice (DipRP)
BA in Recruitment Practice (run jointly with Middlesex University Business School)
MA in Recruitment Practice (run jointly with Middlesex University Business School)

DESIGNATORY LETTERS
AIRP, MIRP, FIRP

THE INSTITUTE OF CAREER GUIDANCE

Ground Floor
Copthall House
1 New Road
Stourbridge
West Midlands DY8 1PH
Tel: 01384 376464
Fax: 01384 440830
E-mail: hq@icg-uk.org
Website: www.icg-uk.org

The ICG is the largest UK-wide professional association for career guidance practitioners. Our aim is to promote access to high-quality career guidance and development services, delivered by professionally qualified staff working within an appropriate ethical framework, and to underpin this our members adhere to a strict code of ethics.

MEMBERSHIP
Student Member
Full Member
Fellow
Honorary Fellow
School Member
Organizational Member

QUALIFICATION/EXAMINATIONS
Qualification in Career Guidance (QCG)
Qualification in Career Coaching (QCC)
Certificate in Professional Practice (CPP)
Certificate in Career Guidance Theory (CCGT)

ENGINEERING, AERONAUTICAL
Membership of Professional Institutions and Associations

ROYAL AERONAUTICAL SOCIETY

4 Hamilton Place
Hyde Park Corner
London W1J 7BQ
Tel: 020 7670 4300
Fax: 020 7670 4309
E-mail: raes@aerosociety.com
Website: www.aerosociety.com

The RAeS, founded in 1866 to further the science of aeronautics, is a multidisciplinary professional institution dedicated to the global aerospace community. We work on our members' behalf to promote the highest professional standards in all aerospace disciplines, to provide specialist information and act as a central forum for the exchange of ideas, and to play a leading role in influencing opinion on aviation matters.

MEMBERSHIP
Student Affiliate
Affiliate
Associate (ARAeS)
Associate Member (AMRAeS)
Member (MRAeS)
Companion (CRAeS)
Fellow (FRAeS)
Engineering Technician (EngTech)
Incorporated Engineer (IEng)
Chartered Engineer (CEng)

ENGINEERING, AGRICULTURAL
Membership of Professional Institutions and Associations

BRITISH AGRICULTURAL AND GARDEN MACHINERY ASSOCIATION

Middleton House
2 Main Road
Middleton Cheney
Oxfordshire OX17 2TN
Tel: 01295 713344
Fax: 01295 711665
E-mail: info@bagma.com
Website: www.bagma.com

BAGMA is the trade association representing agricultural and garden machinery dealers in the UK. We have some 850 dealer members and 75 affiliated suppliers and allied industry companies. We offer a range of training and assessment courses through our online learning package and at approved Training and Assessment Centres.

QUALIFICATION/EXAMINATIONS
Please see the BAGMA website.

THE INSTITUTION OF AGRICULTURAL ENGINEERS

The Bullock Building
University Way
Cranfield
Bedford
Bedfordshire MK43 0GH
Tel: 01234 750876
Fax: 01234 751319
E-mail: secretary@iagre.org
Website: www.iagre.org

The IAgrE is the professional body for engineers, scientists, technologists and managers in agricultural and allied land-based industries, including forestry, food engineering and technology, amenity, renewable energy, horticulture and the environment. The IAgrE also administers the Landbased Engineering Technician Accreditation schemes (LTA) for the industry.

MEMBERSHIP
Student
Associate (AIAgrE)
Associate Member (AMIAgrE)
Member (MIAgrE)
Fellow (FIAgrE)
Honorary Fellow

QUALIFICATION/EXAMINATIONS
Chartered Engineer (CEng), Chartered Environmentalist (CEnv), Incorporated Engineer (IEng), Engineering Technician (EngTech)

DESIGNATORY LETTERS
AIAgrE, AMIAgrE, MIAgrE, FIAgrE

ENGINEERING, AUTOMOBILE
Membership of Professional Institutions and Associations

INSTITUTE OF AUTOMOTIVE ENGINEER ASSESSORS

Brooke House
24 Dam Street
Lichfield
Staffordshire WS13 6AA
Tel: 01543 266906
Fax: 01543 257848
E-mail: secretary@iaea-online.co.uk
Website: www.iaea-online.org

The IAEA, a Professional Affiliate of the Engineering Council, was founded in 1932 and now represents more than 1,500 automotive engineer assessors responsible for activities such as vehicle damage assessment, accident reconstruction, investigation of mechanical failures, electrical failures and vehicle fires, providing expert witness testimony, repair assessment, car fleet surveys, and conciliation and arbitration.

MEMBERSHIP
Student
Graduate
Associate
Licensed Estimator
Incorporated Member (IMInstAEA)
Member (MInstAEA)
Fellow (FInstAEA)

QUALIFICATION/EXAMINATIONS
Basic Principles of Maths & Physics Application to Accident Reconstruction
Motor Vehicle Legislation as related to Insurance Principles

Engineering, Automobile

Principles and Practice of Vehicle Damage Assessment
Motor Insurance

DESIGNATORY LETTERS
IMInstAEA, MInstAEA, FInstAEA

SOCIETY OF AUTOMOTIVE ENGINEERS

PO Box 13312
Birmingham B28 1BG
E-mail: info@sae-uk.org
Website: www.sae-uk.org

SAE-UK is the only professional society dedicated solely to the vehicle and component manufacturing industries and has more than 2,000 members. Our aims are to improve the standards of design, use of materials, methods of manufacturing and safety, to encourage the development and continuous updating of automotive technology, and to improve the status of our members.

MEMBERSHIP
Personal Member
Corporate Member

THE INSTITUTE OF THE MOTOR INDUSTRY

Fanshaws
Brickendon
Hertford SG13 8PQ
Tel: 01992 511521
Fax: 01992 511548
E-mail: imi@motor.org.uk
Website: www.motor.org.uk and www.automotivetechnician.org.uk

The IMI is the professional association for individuals working in the motor industry and exists to help individuals and employers improve professional standards and performance by qualifying, recognizing and developing people. We are the Sector Skills Council for the automotive retail industry, a Licensed Member of the Engineering Council and the governing body for Automotive Technician Accreditation (ATA) – the UK's first national voluntary assessment system for vehicle technicians.

MEMBERSHIP
Affiliate (AffIMI)
Licentiate (LIMI)
Associate (AMIMI)
Member (MIMI)
Fellow (FIMI)
For technicians only, there are two special IMI awards recognizing technical qualifications and experience:
AAE (Advanced Automotive Engineer)
CAE (Certificated Automotive Engineer)

DESIGNATORY LETTERS
AffIMI, LIMI, AMIMI, MIMI, FIMI, AAE, CAE

ENGINEERING, BUILDING SERVICES
Membership of Professional Institutions and Associations

THE CHARTERED INSTITUTION OF BUILDING SERVICES ENGINEERS

222 Balham High Road
London SW12 9BS
Tel: 020 8675 5211
Fax: 020 8675 5449
Website: www.cibse.org

CIBSE is the professional body for people involved in the design, construction, operation and maintenance of the engineering elements of a building other than its structure and enables it to operate efficiently by saving energy and contributing to a low carbon built environment. This includes heating, ventilation, air conditioning, electrical services, lighting etc.

MEMBERSHIP
Student Affiliate
Affiliate
Graduate
Companion
Licentiate (LCIBSE)
Associate (ACIBSE)
Member (MCIBSE)
Fellow (FCIBSE)

QUALIFICATION/EXAMINATIONS
Please see the CIBSE website.

DESIGNATORY LETTERS
LCIBSE, ACIBSE, MCIBSE, FCIBSE

ENGINEERING, CHEMICAL
Membership of Professional Institutions and Associations

THE INSTITUTION OF CHEMICAL ENGINEERS

Davis Building
Railway Terrace
Rugby
Warwickshire CV21 3HQ
Tel: 01788 578214
Fax: 01788 560833
E-mail: onlineassistance@icheme.org
Website: www.icheme.org

The IChemE, founded in 1922, is an international professional membership organization for chemical, biochemical and process engineers, and we have some 30,000 members in more than 113 countries. We promote competence and a commitment to sustainable development, advance the discipline for the benefit of society, and support the professional development of our members.

MEMBERSHIP
Student
Affiliate
Associate Member (AMIChemE)
Member (MIChemE)
Fellow (FIChemE)
Chartered Chemical Engineer (CEng MIChemE)
Chartered Engineer (CEng)
Chartered Scientist (CSci)
Chartered Environmentalist (CEnv)

DESIGNATORY LETTERS
AMIChemE, MIChemE, FIChemE, CEng MIChemE, CEng, CSci, CEnv

ENGINEERING, CIVIL
Membership of Professional Institutions and Associations

INSTITUTION OF CIVIL ENGINEERS

1 Great George Street
Westminster
London SW1P 3AA
Tel: 020 7222 7722
Fax: 020 7233 0515
E-mail: membership@ice.org.uk
Website: www.ice.org.uk

The ICE is a UK-based international organization with 80,000 members that strives to promote and progress civil engineering around the world. Our purpose is to qualify professionals engaged in civil engineering, exchange knowledge and best practice, and support our members, and in the UK we liaise with government and publish reports on civil engineering issues.

MEMBERSHIP
Student
Graduate
Affiliate
Technician Member
Associate Member (AMICE)
Member (MICE)
Companion
Fellow (FICE)

ENGINEERING, ELECTRICAL, ELECTRONIC AND MANUFACTURING
Membership of Professional Institutions and Associations

INSTITUTION OF LIGHTING PROFESSIONALS

Regent House
Regent Place
Rugby
Warwickshire CV21 2PN
Tel: 01788 576492
Fax: 01788 540145
E-mail: info@theilp.org.uk
Website: www.theilp.org.uk

The ILP is a professional lighting association with about 2,200 members, including lighting designers, consultants and engineers. We are dedicated to excellence in lighting and to raising awareness about the important contribution of lighting in road safety, crime prevention and the environment. We support members by providing technical advice and encourage their CPD through our bimonthly journal and by holding a wide range of conferences, regional meetings, seminars and courses.

MEMBERSHIP
Student
Affiliate
Associate Member (AMILP)
Member (MILP)
Fellow (FILP)
Silver Group Member
Gold Group Member
Engineering Technician (EngTech)
Incorporated Engineer (IEng)
Chartered Engineer (CEng)

QUALIFICATION/EXAMINATIONS	DESIGNATORY LETTERS
Exterior Lighting Diploma	AMILP, MILP, FILP, EngTech, IEng, CEng

THE INSTITUTION OF ENGINEERING AND TECHNOLOGY

Michael Faraday House
Stevenage
Hertfordshire SG1 2AY
Tel: 01438 313311
Fax: 01438 765526
E-mail: postmaster@theiet.org
Website: www.theiet.org

The IET is a world leading professional organisation sharing and advancing knowledge to promote science, engineering and technology across the world. It is the professional home for life for engineers and technicians, and a trusted source of essential engineering intelligence. The IET has more than 150,000 members in 127 countries.

Member (MIET)
Fellow (FIET)
Honorary Fellow
ICT Technician (ICTTech)
Engineering Technician (EngTech)
Incorporated Engineer (IEng)
Chartered Engineer (CEng)

MEMBERSHIP
Student
Associate

DESIGNATORY LETTERS
FIET, ICTech, EngTech, IEng, CEng, MIET

ENGINEERING, ENERGY
Membership of Professional Institutions and Associations

ENERGY INSTITUTE

61 New Cavendish Street
London W1G 7AR
Tel: 020 7467 7100
Fax: 020 7255 1472
E-mail: info@energyinst.org.uk
Website: www.energyinst.org.uk

The EI is the leading professional body for the energy industries, with almost 15,000 members internationally. A Chartered professional body, promoting good practice and professionalism throughout the sector, we offer a wide range of professional qualifications, including Chartered, Incorporated and Engineering Technician status for engineers, as well as Chartered Scientist, Chartered Energy Manager and Chartered Environmentalist.

Member (MEI)
Fellow (FEI)
Engineering Technician (EngTech)
Incorporated Engineer (IEng)
Chartered Engineer (CEng)
Chartered Scientist (CSci)
Chartered Environmentalist (CEnv)
Chartered Energy Manager (exclusive EI title)
Chartered Energy Engineer (exclusive EI title)
Chartered Petroleum Engineer (exclusive EI title)

MEMBERSHIP
Student Member
Affiliate
Graduate Member (Grad EI)

DESIGNATORY LETTERS
GradEI, MEI, FEI, EngTech, IEng, CEng

ENGINEERING, ENVIRONMENTAL
Membership of Professional Institutions and Associations

INSTITUTE OF ENVIRONMENTAL MANAGEMENT AND ASSESSMENT

St Nicholas House
Lincoln LN1 3DP
Tel: 01522 540069
Fax: 01522 540090
E-mail: info@iema.net
Website: www.iema.net

The IEMA is a not-for-profit membership organization that provides recognition and support to environmental professionals and promotes sustainable development through improved environmental practice and performance. We have about 15,000 individual and corporate members in 87 countries, in the public, private and non-governmental sectors.

MEMBERSHIP
Student Member
Affiliate Member
Graduate Member
Associate (AIEMA)
Full Member (MIEMA)
Fellow (FIEMA)
Chartered Environmentalist (CEnv)
Corporate Member

QUALIFICATION/EXAMINATIONS
Foundation Certificate in Environmental Management
Associate Certificate in Environmental Management
Diploma

DESIGNATORY LETTERS
AIEMA, MIEMA, FIEMA, CEnv

THE CHARTERED INSTITUTION OF WATER AND ENVIRONMENTAL MANAGEMENT

15 John Street
London WC1N 2EB
Tel: 020 7831 3110
Fax: 020 7405 4967
E-mail: admin@ciwem.org
Website: www.ciwem.org

Founded in 1895, CIWEM is an independent professional body and registered charity with 12,000 members that advances the science and practice of water and environmental management for a clean, green and sustainable world by promoting environmental excellence and professional development and training, supplying independent advice and evidence-based opinion, and providing a forum for debate through conferences, technical meetings and its publications.

MEMBERSHIP
Student
Associate ACIWEM
Graduate
Member MCIWEM C.WEM
Fellow FCIWEM C.WEM
Environmental Partner
Chartered Engineer (CEng)
Chartered Environmentalist (CEnv)
Chartered Scientist (CSci)

QUALIFICATION/EXAMINATIONS
Online training courses in partnership with Staffordshire University, accredited university courses at 12 leading institutions, CPD modules and Rural Environmental Management Programme

DESIGNATORY LETTERS
CEng, CEnv, CSi, C.WEM

THE SOCIETY OF ENVIRONMENTAL ENGINEERS

The Manor House
High Street
Buntingford
Hertfordshire SG9 9AB
Tel: 01763 271209
Fax: 01763 273255
E-mail: office@environmental.org.uk
Website: www.environmental.org.uk

The SEE, founded in 1959, is a professional society that promotes awareness of the discipline of environmental engineering (the measurement, modelling, control and simulation of all types of environment). We provide members with information, training and representation within this field and encourage communication and good practice in quality, reliability, and cost-effective product development and manufacture.

MEMBERSHIP
Student
Member
Corporate Member
Engineering Technician (EngTech)
Incorporated Engineer (IEng)
Chartered Engineer (CEng)

DESIGNATORY LETTERS
EngTech, IEng, CEng

ENGINEERING, FIRE
Membership of Professional Institutions and Associations

ASSOCIATION OF PRINCIPAL FIRE OFFICERS

10/11 Pebble Close
Amington
Tamworth
Staffordshire B77 4RD
Tel: 01827 302300
Fax: 01827 302399
E-mail: enquiries@apfo.org.uk
Website: www.apfo.org.uk

The APFO is the staff association of the most senior Fire Officers in the UK. Our objectives are: to represent and promote the interests of members in conditions of service and legal and employment matters; to negotiate and promote the settlement of disputes involving members; to provide assistance to members and their dependants in exceptional circumstances; and to provide support to members in matters concerning employment or a work-related injury.

MEMBERSHIP
Associate Member
Lifetime Past Member

CHIEF FIRE OFFICERS' ASSOCIATION

9–11 Pebble Close
Amington
Tamworth
Staffordshire B77 4RD
Tel: 01827 302300
Fax: 01827 302399
Website: www.cfoa.org.uk

The CFOA is a professional membership association of the most senior fire officers in the UK. We provide independent advice to the government, local authorities and others. Our aim is to reduce loss of life, personal injury and damage to property by improving the quality of fire fighting, rescue, fire protection and fire prevention in the UK.

MEMBERSHIP
Member

THE INSTITUTION OF FIRE ENGINEERS

London Road
Moreton-in-March
Gloucestershire GL56 0RH
Tel: 01608 812580
Fax: 01608 812581
E-mail: info@ife.org.uk
Website: www.ife.org.uk

The IFE, founded in 1918, is a non-profit-making professional body for fire professionals and has more than 12,000 members worldwide. Our aim is to encourage and improve the science and practice of fire extinction, fire prevention and fire engineering, to enhance technical networks, and to give advice and support to our members for the benefit of the community at large.

MEMBERSHIP
Student
Affiliate Member
Technician (TIFireE)
Graduate (GIFireE)
Associate (AIFireE)
Member (MIFireE)
Fellow (FIFireE)
Engineering Technician (EngTech)
Incorporated Engineer (IEng)
Chartered Engineer (CEng) Affiliate Organization

QUALIFICATION/EXAMINATIONS
Level 2 Certificate Level 3 Certificate
Level 3 Diploma Level 4 Certificate

DESIGNATORY LETTERS
TIFireE, GIFireE, AIFireE, MIFireE, FIFireE, EngTech, IEng, CEng

ENGINEERING, GAS
Membership of Professional Institutions and Associations

THE INSTITUTION OF GAS ENGINEERS AND MANAGERS

IGEM House
High Street
Kegworth
Derbyshire DE74 2DA
Tel: 0844 375 4436
Fax: 01509 678198
Website: www.igem.org.uk

IGEM is licensed by EC(UK) and serves a wide range of professionals in the UK and international gas industry through membership and technical standards, having a diverse membership ranging from university students to qualified professionals. Anyone working or interested in the gas industry can form positive connections to enhance their career through IGEM.

MEMBERSHIP
Student Member
Associate (AIGEM)
Associate Member (AMIGEM)
Graduate Member (GradIGEM)
Member Manager (MIGEM)
Technician Member (Eng Tech (MIGEM))
Incorporated Member (I Eng (MIGEM))
Chartered Member (C Eng (MIGEM))
Fellow (C Eng (FIGEM))
Industrial Affiliate (company membership)

DESIGNATORY LETTERS
MIGEM, Eng Tech (MIGEM), I Eng (MIGEM), C ENG (MIGEM), C Eng (FIGEM)

ENGINEERING, GENERAL
Membership of Professional Institutions and Associations

ASSOCIATION OF COST ENGINEERS

Lea House
Sandbach
Cheshire CW11 1XL
Tel: 01270 764798
Fax: 01270 766180
E-mail: enquiries@acoste.org.uk
Website: www.acoste.org.uk

The ACostE represents the professional interests of those with responsibility for the prediction, planning and control of resources for engineering, manufacturing and construction. As a Professional Affiliate of The Engineering Council, we can propose suitably qualified members for the award of the titles of Chartered Engineer (CEng) and Incorporated Engineer (IEng).

MEMBERSHIP
Student
Associate (AA Cost E)
Companion (Companion A Cost E)
Graduate (Grad A Cost E)
Member (MA Cost E)
Fellow (FA Cost E)
Honorary Fellow (Hon FA Cost E)
Certified Cost Engineer (CCE)
Engineering Technician (EngTech)
Incorporated Engineer (IEng)
Chartered Engineer (CEng)

DESIGNATORY LETTERS
AA Cost E, Companion A Cost E, Grad A Cost E, MA Cost E, FA Cost E, CCE, EngTech, IEng, CEng

Engineering, General

INSTITUTE OF MEASUREMENT AND CONTROL

87 Gower Street
London WC1E 6AF
Tel: 020 7387 4949
Fax: 020 7388 8431
E-mail: membership@instmc.org.uk
Website: www.instmc.org.uk

The IMC is a multidisciplinary body that brings together thinkers and practitioners from the many disciplines that have a common interest in measurement and control. Our object is to promote for the public benefit, by all available means, the general advancement of the science and practice of measurement and control technology and its application.

MEMBERSHIP
Student Member
Affiliate Member
Associate Member
Member (MemInstMC)
Fellow (FInstMC)
Honorary Fellow (HonFInstMC)

SEMTA – THE SECTOR SKILLS COUNCIL FOR SCIENCE, ENGINEERING AND MANUFACTURING TECHNOLOGIES

14 Upton Road
Watford
Hertfordshire WD18 0JT
Tel: 01923 238441
Fax: 01923 256086
E-mail: customerservices@semta.org.uk
Website: www.semta.org.uk

Semta is part of the Skills for Business network of 25 employer-led Sector Skills Councils in the UK and works with employers in the aerospace, automotive, electrical, electronics, marine, mechanical, metals and science & bioscience sectors to ascertain their current and future skills needs and provide short- and long-term solutions to meet those needs.

THE ENGINEERING COUNCIL

2nd Floor
246 High Holborn
London WC1V 7EX
Tel: 020 3206 0500
Fax: 020 3206 0501
Website: www.engc.org.uk

The Engineering Council holds the national registers of Chartered Engineers (CEng), Incorporated Engineers (IEng), Engineering Technicians (EngTech) and Information and Communications Technology Technicians (ICTTech). We set and maintain internationally recognized standards of competence and ethics, ensuring that employers, government and society can have confidence in registrants' skills and commitment.

DESIGNATORY LETTERS
ICTTech, EngTech, IEng, CEng

THE INSTITUTION OF BRITISH ENGINEERS

Clifford Hill Court
Clifford Chambers
Stratford upon Avon
Warwickshire CV37 8AA
Tel: 01789 298739
Fax: 01789 294442
E-mail: info@britishengineers.com
Website: www.britishengineers.com

MEMBERSHIP
Vice President
Fellow (FIBE)
Member (MIBE)
Associate Member (AMIBE)
Graduate Member (GradIBE)
Qualified Sales Engineer (SEng)
Bi-Lingual Engineer (BLEng)
Diploma in Business Engineering (DBE)
Certificate of Competence in Engineering

DESIGNATORY LETTERS
FIBE, MIBE, AMIBE, GradIBE, SEng, BLEng, DBE

WOMEN'S ENGINEERING SOCIETY

Michael Faraday House
Six Hills Way
Stevenage
Herts SG1 2AY
Tel: 01438 765506
E-mail: info@wes.org.uk
Website: www.wes.org.uk

The WES, founded in 1919, is a professional, not-for-profit network of women engineers, scientists and technologists, who offer inspiration, support and professional development. Working in partnership, we campaign to encourage women to participate and achieve as engineers, scientists and as leaders.

MEMBERSHIP
Student Member
Associate Member (MWES)
Group Member
Corporate Member

DESIGNATORY LETTERS
WES

ENGINEERING, MARINE
Membership of Professional Institutions and Associations

THE INSTITUTE OF MARINE ENGINEERING, SCIENCE AND TECHNOLOGY

80 Coleman Street
London EC2R 5BJ
Tel: +44 (0)20 7382 2600
Fax: +44 (0)20 7382 2670
E-mail: membership@imarest.org
Website: www.imarest.org

The IMarEST, established in 1889, is the leading international membership body and learned society for marine professionals and has more than 15,000 members worldwide. We have a strong international presence, with a network of 50 international branches, affiliations with major marine societies around the world, representation on the key marine technical committees and non-governmental status at the International Maritime Organization.

MEMBERSHIP
Membership Categories
IMarEST membership is open to everyone with an interest in the marine world across scientific, engineering and technological disciplines and applications.

Categories of membership are available to those who are seeking professional recognition, those who are currently studying or just starting out in their careers, or those who simply have a general interest in the IMarEST and its activities. There are no academic requirements for Non-corporate Membership of the IMarEST. However, professionals seeking Corporate Membership will require certain academic qualifications according to the type of membership being sought.

Corporate Membership Categories
Fellow (FIMarEST)
Fellows are those who qualify for the category of Member and have demonstrated to the satisfaction of Council a level of knowledge and understanding, competence and commitment involving superior responsibility for the conceptual design, management or the execution of important work in a marine related profession, and have given a commitment to abide by the Institute's Code of Professional Conduct.
Member (MIMarEST)
Members are those who qualify for the category of Associate Member and have demonstrated to the satisfaction of Council that they have achieved a position of professional standing having normally been professionally engaged in the marine sector for a period of 5 years that includes significant responsibility and have given a commitment to abide by the Institute's Code of Professional Conduct.
Associate Member (AMIMarEST)
Associate Members are those demonstrating to the satisfaction of Council that they have achieved a position as a technician, or are professionally engaged in Initial Professional Development or occupy an occupational role in the marine sector, and have given a commitment to abide by the Institute's Code of Professional Conduct.
Non-corporate Membership Categories
Affiliate
Affiliates may either be those with an interest in, or who may contribute to, the activities of the Institute; or persons who, in the opinion of Council, can contribute to, or wish to have access to, the technical services of the Institute, being resident in a recognized overseas territory and also members of a professional society with which the Institute has a reciprocal arrangement.
Student (SIMarEST)
Student members are those enrolled on a programme of further or higher education accredited or recognized by the IMarEST.
Professional Registration
In addition to membership, the IMarEST is licensed to provide a range of registers covering the fields of engineering, science and technology. In addition, the IMarEST's Royal Charter empowers the Institute to offer registers designed to meet the specific needs of the marine profession. Corporate members can become registered (chartered) as follows:
Engineers
Chartered Engineer (CEng)
Chartered Marine Engineer (CMarEng)

Incorporated Engineer (IEng)
Incorporated Marine Engineer (IMarEng)
Engineering Technician (EngTech)
Marine Engineering Technician (MarEngTech)
Scientists
Chartered Scientist (CSci)
Chartered Marine Scientist (CMarSci)
Registered Marine Scientist (RMarSci)

Marine Technician (MarTech)
Technologists
Chartered Marine Technologist (CMarTech)
Registered Marine Technologist (RMarTech)
Marine Technician (MarTech)

DESIGNATORY LETTERS
SIMarEST, AMIMarEST, MIMarEST, FIMarEST

ENGINEERING, MECHANICAL
Membership of Professional Institutions and Associations

INSTITUTION OF MECHANICAL ENGINEERS

1 Birdcage Walk
Westminster
London SW1H 9JJ
Tel: 020 7304 6999
E-mail: membership@imeche.org
Website: www.imeche.org

The IMechE is a professional engineering body with about 80,000 members. Our aims are to promote sustainable energy and engineering sustainable supply, economic growth while mitigating and adapting to climate change and the depletion of natural resources, and safe, efficient transport systems to ensure less congestion and emissions, and to inspire, prepare and support tomorrow's engineers so we can respond to society's changes.

MEMBERSHIP
Affiliate
Associate Member (AMIMechE)
Member (MIMechE)
Fellow (FIMechE)
Engineering Technician (EngTech)
Incorporated Engineer (IEng)
Chartered Engineer (CEng)

DESIGNATORY LETTERS
AMIMechE, MIMechE, FIMechE, EngTech, IEng, CEng

ENGINEERING, MINING
Membership of Professional Institutions and Associations

INSTITUTE OF EXPLOSIVES ENGINEERS

Wellington Hall 289
Cranfield University
Defence Academy of the UK
Shrivenham, Swindon
Wiltshire SN6 8LA
Tel: 01793 785322
Fax: 01793 785772
E-mail: iexpe@cranfield.ac.uk
Website: www.iexpe.org

The Insitute of Explosives Engineers promotes the occupational competency, education and professional standing of those who work with explosives and provides consultative facilities for organizations and government departments within the explosives field.

MEMBERSHIP
Student
Associate (AIExpE)
Member (MIExpE)
Fellow (FIExpE)
Company

DESIGNATORY LETTERS
AIExpE, MIExpE, FIExpE

THE INSTITUTE OF MATERIALS, MINERALS AND MINING (IOM^3)

1 Carlton House Terrace
London SW1Y 5DB
Tel: 020 7451 7300
Fax: 020 7839 1702
Website: www.iom3.org

IOM^3 is a major UK engineering institution whose activities encompass the whole materials cycle, from exploration and extraction, through characterization, processing, forming, finishing and application, to product recycling and land reuse. We promote and develop all aspects of materials science and engineering, geology, mining and associated technologies, mineral and petroleum engineering and extraction metallurgy, as a leading authority in the worldwide materials and mining community.

MEMBERSHIP
Student
Graduate
Affiliate
Member (MIMMM)
Fellow (FIMMM)

DESIGNATORY LETTERS
MIMMM, FIMMM

THE INSTITUTE OF QUARRYING

7 Regent Street
Nottingham NG1 5BS
Tel: 0115 945 3880
Fax: 0115 948 4035
E-mail: mail@quarrying.org
Website: www.quarrying.org

The Institute of Quarrying, which dates from 1917, is the international professional body for quarrying, construction materials and related extractive and processing industries, and has 6,000 members in some 50 countries. Our aim is to improve all aspects of operational performance through education and training at supervisory and management level.

MEMBERSHIP
Student
Associate
Member (MIQ)
Fellow (FIQ)

QUALIFICATION/EXAMINATIONS
Professional Examination

DESIGNATORY LETTERS
MIQ, FIQ

ENGINEERING, NUCLEAR
Membership of Professional Institutions and Associations

THE NUCLEAR INSTITUTE

Allan House
1 Penerley Road
London SE6 2LQ
Tel: 020 8695 8220
Fax: 020 8695 8229
E-mail: admin@nuclearinst.com
Website: www.nuclearinst.com

The NI (a Nominated Body of the Engineering Council) is a registered charity established to support the nuclear sector. We organize lectures, seminars and events at a regional and national level, and can award EngTech, IEng and CEng to suitably qualified individuals.

MEMBERSHIP
Student Member
Learned Member
Graduate Member
Technician Member (TNucI)
Associate Member (AMNucI)
Member (MNucI)
Fellow (FNucI)
Honorary Fellow

DESIGNATORY LETTERS
TNucI, AMNucI, MNucI, FNucI

ENGINEERING, PRODUCTION

Membership of Professional Institutions and Associations

THE INSTITUTE OF OPERATIONS MANAGEMENT

CILT(UK)
Earlstrees Court
Earlstrees Road
Corby
Northamptonshire NN17 4AX
Tel: 01536 740105
E-mail: info@iomnet.org.uk
Website: www.iomnet.org.uk

The Institute of Operations Management (IOM) is the UK professional body for operations management in manufacturing, service industries and the public sector. Our aim is to equip operations professionals with the skills and resources they need to maximize individual potential and organizational process.

MEMBERSHIP
Learner Affiliate
Student Affiliate
Associate
Member (MIOM)
Fellow (FIOM)
Corporate Membership
APICS Membership

QUALIFICATION/EXAMINATIONS
Regulated Qualifications
Certificate in Operations Management COM (Level 3)
Diploma in Operations Management DOM (Level 5)

Accredited Qualifications
Advanced Diploma in Operations Management

Partnerships
APICS Certified in Production and Inventory Management (CPIM)
APICS Certified Supply Chain Professional (CSCP)

DESIGNATORY LETTERS
MIOM, FIOM

ENGINEERING, REFRACTORIES

Membership of Professional Institutions and Associations

INSTITUTE OF REFRACTORIES ENGINEERING

25 Woodland Way
Long Newton
Stockton-on-Tees
Co Durham TS21 1DJ
Tel: 01642 583840
Fax: 01642 589397
E-mail: secretary@ireng.org
Website: www.ireng.org

The IRE is a non-profit-making organization dedicated to fostering the science, technology and skills of refractories engineering and to serving the needs of refractories engineers worldwide. Our members have a background in R&D, design, engineering, manufacturing and installation contracting in the iron & steel, cement, non-ferrous, glass, chemical/petrochemical incineration, power generation, ceramics/bricks and similar industries.

MEMBERSHIP
Student

Associate Member (AMI Ref Eng)
Member (MI Ref Eng)
Fellow (FI Ref Eng)

DESIGNATORY LETTERS
AMI Ref Eng, MI Ref Eng, FI Ref Eng

ENGINEERING, REFRIGERATION
Membership of Professional Institutions and Associations

THE INSTITUTE OF REFRIGERATION

Kelvin House
76 Mill Lane
Carshalton
Surrey SM5 2JR
Tel: 020 8647 7033
Fax: 020 8773 0165
E-mail: ior@ior.org.uk
Website: www.ior.org.uk

The IOR is the professional body for the refrigeration and air conditioning industries. We promote the technical advancement and perfection of refrigeration, and the minimization of its effects on the environment, encourage the extension of refrigeration, air conditioning and heat pump services for the benefit of the community, and provide advice, CPD and support to our members.

MEMBERSHIP
Student
Technician Affiliate
Associate Member (AMInstR)
Member (MInstR)
Fellow (FInstR)
Engineering Technician (EngTech)
Incorporated Engineer (IEng)
Chartered Engineer (CEng)

QUALIFICATION/EXAMINATIONS
REAL Zero CPD, REAL Skills Europe CPD

DESIGNATORY LETTERS
AMInstR, TMInstR, MInstR, FInstR

ENGINEERING, ROAD, RAIL AND TRANSPORT
Membership of Professional Institutions and Associations

INSTITUTE OF HIGHWAY ENGINEERS

De Morgan House
58 Russell Square
London WC1B 4HS
Tel: 020 7436 7487
Fax: 020 7436 7488
E-mail: secretary@theihe.org
Website: www.theihe.org

The IHE is the professional body for highway and traffic professionals. We are run by engineers for engineers and technicians, and work to keep the standards of the profession high, to safeguard the interests of our members, and to ensure that their contribution is recognised.

MEMBERSHIP
Student Member
Graduate Member
Associate Member (AMIHE)
Member (MIHE)
Fellow (FIHE)
Engineering Technician (EngTech)
Incorporated Engineer (IEng)
Chartered Engineer (CEng)

QUALIFICATION/EXAMINATIONS
Prof Cert in Traffic Sign Design
Prof Cert in Traffic Signal Control
Prof Cert in Transport Development Management

DESIGNATORY LETTERS
AMIHE, MIHE, FIHE, EngTech, IEng, CEng

INSTITUTION OF RAILWAY SIGNAL ENGINEERS

4th Floor
1 Birdcage Walk
Westminster
London SW1H 9JJ
Tel: 020 7808 1180
Fax: 020 7808 1196
E-mail: hq@irse.org
Website: www.irse.org

The Institution of Railway Signal Engineers, known more usually as the IRSE, is an international organization, active throughout the world. It is the professional institution for all those engaged or interested in railway signalling and telecommunications and allied disciplines. Membership is open to anyone engaged or interested in the management, planning, design, installation, telecommunications or associated equipment.

MEMBERSHIP
Student
Associate
Accredited Technician
Associate Member
Member
Fellow
Companion

QUALIFICATION/EXAMINATIONS
Professional Examination

DESIGNATORY LETTERS
AMIRSE, MIRSE, FIRSE, CompIRSE

SOCIETY OF OPERATIONS ENGINEERS

22 Greencoat Place
London SW1P 1PR
Tel: 020 7630 1111
Fax: 020 7630 6677
E-mail: soe@soe.org.uk
Website: www.soe.org.uk

SOE is a professional membership organisation representing more than 16,000 individuals and companies in the engineering industry. It was formed in 2000 by the merger of the Institute of Road Transport Engineers (IRTE) and the Institution of Plant Engineers (IPlantE). The Society's third Professional Sector, the Bureau of Engineer Surveyors (BES), joined in 2004.

MEMBERSHIP
Associate Member (AMSOE)
Member (MSOE)
Fellow (FSOE)
Honorary Fellow (HonFSOE)
Companion (CompanionSOE)
Engineering Technician (EngTech)
Incorporated Engineer (IEng)
Chartered Engineer (CEng)

THE CHARTERED INSTITUTION OF HIGHWAYS AND TRANSPORTATION

119 Britannia Walk
London N1 7JE
Tel: 020 7336 1555
Fax: 020 7336 1556
E-mail: info@ciht.org.uk
Website: www.ciht.org.uk

The CIHT is a learned society and membership organization concerned with the planning, design, construction, maintenance and operation of land-based transport systems and infrastructure. CIHT provides professional development and networking opportunities to members, with routes to qualifications, cutting-edge technical conferences and exciting social events.

MEMBERSHIP
Student
Associate Member (AMCIHT)
Member (MCIHT)
Fellow (FCIHT)
Incorporated Engineer (IEng)
Chartered Engineer (CEng)

QUALIFICATION/EXAMINATIONS
Transport Planning Professional (TPP) status (awarded jointly with the Transport Planning Society (TPS))

DESIGNATORY LETTERS
AMCIHT, MCIHT, FCIHT, IEng, CEng

ENGINEERING, SHEET METAL
Membership of Professional Institutions and Associations

INSTITUTE OF SHEET METAL ENGINEERING

102 Richmond Drive
Perton
Wolverhampton
West Midlands WV6 7UQ
Tel: 07891499146
E-mail: ismesec@googlemail.com
Website: www.isme.org.uk

The ISME is a learned body with individual membership open to those employed in the sheet metal and associated industries and corporate membership open to relevant companies. Our aims are to promote the science of working and using sheet metal by providing opportunities for the exchange of ideas and information, and to encourage the professional development of our members.

MEMBERSHIP
Student Member
Member (MISME)
Fellow (FISME)
Corporate Member

DESIGNATORY LETTERS
MISME, FISME

ENGINEERING, STRUCTURAL
Membership of Professional Institutions and Associations

THE INSTITUTION OF STRUCTURAL ENGINEERS

11 Upper Belgrave Street
London SW1X 8BH
Tel: 020 7235 4535
Fax: 020 7235 4294
E-mail: membership@istructe.org
Website: www.istructe.org

The Institution of Structural Engineers, founded in 1908, is the world's largest membership organization dedicated to the art and science of structural engineering. Our aims include: maintaining professional standards for structural engineering; ensuring continued technical excellence; advancing safety, creativity and innovation; and promoting a sustainable approach to both the structural engineering profession and the built environment.

MEMBERSHIP
Student
Affiliate
Graduate
Technician (TIStructE)
Associate Member (AMIStructE)
Associate (AIStructE)
Chartered Member (MIStructE)
Fellow (FIStructE)

DESIGNATORY LETTERS
TIStructE, AMIStructE, AIStructE, MIStructE, FIStructE

ENGINEERING, WATER
Membership of Professional Institutions and Associations

INSTITUTE OF WATER

4 Carlton Court
Team Valley
Gateshead
Tyne and Wear NE11 0AZ
Tel: 0191 422 0088
Fax: 0191 422 0087
E-mail: info@instituteofwater.org.uk
Website: www.instituteofwater.org.uk

The IW is the only institute concerned with the UK water industry. Our aim is to promote high standards of integrity, conduct and ethics, and to provide our members with an opportunity for CPD and growth through sharing knowledge, experience and networking opportunities.

MEMBERSHIP
Student Member
Associate Member
Full Member
Fellow
Honorary Member
Engineering Technician (EngTech)
Incorporated Engineer (IEng)
Chartered Engineer (CEng)
Chartered Environmentalist (CEnv)
Company Member

DESIGNATORY LETTERS
EngTech, IEng, CEng, CEnv

ENGINEERING DESIGN
Membership of Professional Institutions and Associations

THE INSTITUTION OF ENGINEERING DESIGNERS

Courtleigh
Westbury Leigh
Westbury
Wiltshire BA13 3TA
Tel: 01373 822801
Fax: 01373 858085
E-mail: ied@ied.org.uk
Website: www.ied.org.uk

Established in 1945, the IED represents 4,000 members worldwide working in engineering design, product design and CAD. Benefits include a bimonthly journal, access to an extensive library, legal advice helpline, local branch activities, and guidance and support to registration with the EC(UK) for suitably qualified members.

MEMBERSHIP
IED membership has two divisions: Engineering Design, and Product Design and Technology.

Each division has a range of membership grades: Student Member (StudIED), Graduate/Diplomate Member (GradIED/DipIED), Competent Draughting Associate (CDAIED), Associate (AIED), Member (MIED), Fellow (FIED).

QUALIFICATION/EXAMINATIONS
Registration with EC(UK) for suitably qualified members

DESIGNATORY LETTERS
AIED, MIED, FIED

ENVIRONMENTAL SCIENCES
Membership of Professional Institutions and Associations

INSTITUTE OF ECOLOGY AND ENVIRONMENTAL MANAGEMENT

43 Southgate Street
Winchester
Hampshire SO23 9EH
Tel: 01962 868626
Fax: 01962 868625
E-mail: enquiries@ieem.net
Website: www.ieem.net

Founded in 1991 to advance the science, technology and practice of ecology, environmental management and sustainable development to further conservation and the enhancement of biodiversity through education, training, study and research. IEEM now has more than 4,400 members drawn from local authorities, government agencies, industry, environmental consultancy, teaching/research and NGOs.

MEMBERSHIP
Student Member
Affiliate Member
Graduate Member (Grad IEEM)
Associate Member (AIEEM)
Full Member (MIEEM)
Fellow (FIEEM)

DESIGNATORY LETTERS
Grad IEEM, AIEEM, MIEEM, FIEEM

EXPORT
Membership of Professional Institutions and Associations

THE INSTITUTE OF EXPORT

Export House
Minerva Business Park
Lynch Wood
Peterborough PE2 6FT
Tel: 01733 404400
E-mail: info@export.org.uk
Website: www.export.org.uk

Established since 1935 offering training and professional qualifications to those working within international trade. We are the only professional institute in the UK offering qualifications ranging from the new 14–19 Diploma up to a level 5 Diploma as well as standard and bespoke training courses for individuals and companies.

MEMBERSHIP
Affiliate
Student
Associate
Member MIEx (Grad)
Member MIEx
Fellow
Business
Corporate

QUALIFICATION/EXAMINATIONS
Diploma in International Trade (DIT)
Certified International Trade Advisor (CIT)
Advanced Certificate in International Trade (ACIT)

FISHERIES MANAGEMENT
Membership of Professional Institutions and Associations

INSTITUTE OF FISHERIES MANAGEMENT

18 Lomond Road
Spring Bank West
Hull
East Yorkshire HU5 5BN
Tel: 0845 388 7012
E-mail: info@ifm.org.uk
Website: www.ifm.org.uk

The Institute of Fisheries Management is an international organization of persons sharing a common interest in the modern and sustainable management of recreational and commercial fisheries. It is a non-profit-making body and is a constituent body of the Society for the Environment.

MEMBERSHIP
Subscriber
Student Member
Associate Member (AMIFM)
Registered Member (MIFM)
Fellow (FIFM)
Honorary Fellow (Hon FIFM)
Corporate Member

QUALIFICATION/EXAMINATIONS
Certificate
Diploma (accredited by The Open University)

DESIGNATORY LETTERS
AMIFM, MIFM, FIFM, Hon FIFM

FLORISTRY
Membership of Professional Institutions and Associations

SOCIETY OF FLORISTRY LTD

Tel: 07896 639520
E-mail: info@societyoffloristry.org
Website: www.societyoffloristry.org

The SOF, founded in 1951, is an awarding body that promotes the highest standards in professional floristry. We are responsible for preparing and setting the highest floristry qualifications and for designing programmes for the training of SOF judges and examiners. We provide help, advice and information to our more than 1,000 members, who include business owners, florists, training providers, and students.

MEMBERSHIP
Member
Corporate Member

QUALIFICATION/EXAMINATIONS
Level 4 Higher Diploma in Floristry (ICSF)
Level 5 Master Diploma in Professional Floristry (NDSF)

FOOD SCIENCE AND NUTRITION
Membership of Professional Institutions and Associations

INSTITUTE OF FOOD SCIENCE AND TECHNOLOGY

5 Cambridge Court
210 Shepherd's Bush Road
London W6 7NJ
Tel: 020 7603 6316
Fax: 020 7602 9936
E-mail: info@ifst.org
Website: www.ifst.org

IFST is the leading independent qualifying body for food professionals in Europe and the only professional body in the UK concerned with all aspects of food science and technology. As a registered charity we are independent of government, industry, lobby or special interest groups.

MEMBERSHIP
Associate
Member (MIFST)
Fellow (FIFST)
Chartered Scientist (CSci)

DESIGNATORY LETTERS
MIFST, FIFST, CSci

FORESTRY AND ARBORICULTURE
Membership of Professional Institutions and Associations

INSTITUTE OF CHARTERED FORESTERS

59 George Street
Edinburgh EH2 2JG
Tel: 0131 240 1425
Fax: 0131 240 1424
E-mail: icf@charteredforesters.org
Website: www.charteredforesters.org

The ICF is the Royal Chartered body for foresters and arboriculturists in the UK. We have over 1,000 members, to whom we offer advice, guidance and support. We also strive to foster a greater public understanding and awareness of the profession, as the environment and its management become more relevant to everyone.

MEMBERSHIP
Student Member
Supporter
Associate Member
Professional Member (MICFor)
Fellow (FICFor)

QUALIFICATION/EXAMINATIONS
Professional Membership Entry (PME) exam

DESIGNATORY LETTERS
MICFor, FICFor

THE ARBORICULTURAL ASSOCIATION

Ullenwood Court
Ullenwood
Cheltenham
Gloucestershire GL53 9QS
Tel: 01242 522152
Fax: 01242 577766
E-mail: admin@trees.org.uk
Website: www.trees.org.uk

The Arboricultural Association, founded in 1964, is the leading body in the UK for the amenity tree care professional in either civic or commercial employment at craft, technical, supervisory, managerial or consultancy level. There are currently over 2,000 members of The Arboricultural Association in a variety of membership classes.

MEMBERSHIP
Individual Membership
Student Member
Ordinary Member
Associate Member
Technician Member
Professional Member
Fellow
Corporate Membership
Corporate Member

QUALIFICATION/EXAMINATIONS
Arboricultural Association Approved Contractor
Arboricultural Association Registered Consultant

DESIGNATORY LETTERS
TechArborA; MArborA; FArborA

THE ROYAL FORESTRY SOCIETY

102 High Street
Tring
Hertfordshire HP23 4AF
Tel: 01442 822028
Fax: 01442 890395
E-mail: rfshq@rfs.org.uk
Website: www.rfs.org.uk

The RFS was founded in 1882 and now has over 3,600 members. We are dedicated to promoting the wise management of trees and woodlands, and to increasing people's understanding of forestry. We publish a popular magazine, the *Quarterly Journal of Forestry*, arrange outdoor meetings, organize woodland study tours in the UK and overseas, run exams in arboriculture and manage model woodlands.

MEMBERSHIP
Member

FOUNDRY TECHNOLOGY AND PATTERN MAKING
Membership of Professional Institutions and Associations

THE INSTITUTE OF CAST METALS ENGINEERS

National Metalforming Centre
47 Birmingham Road
West Bromwich
West Midlands B70 6PY
Tel: 01216 016979
Fax: 01216 016981
E-mail: info@icme.org.uk
Website: www.icme.org.uk

The ICME is the professional body for those in the castings and associated industry. It was formed in 1904, granted its first Royal Charter in 1921, a Third Supplemental Charter in 1994 and changed its name in 2001. The granting of the Third Supplemental Charter aligned its membership requirements with those of the EC(UK).

MEMBERSHIP
Student
Member (MICME)
Professional Member (Prof MICME)
Fellow (FICME)
Engineering Technician (EngTech)
Incorporated Engineer (IEng)
Chartered Engineer (CEng)
European Engineer (EurIng)

DESIGNATORY LETTERS
MICME, Prof MICME, FICME, EngTech, IEng, CEng, EurIng

FREIGHT FORWARDING
Membership of Professional Institutions and Associations

BRITISH INTERNATIONAL FREIGHT ASSOCIATION (BIFA)

Redfern House
Browells Lane
Feltham
Middlesex TW13 7EP
Tel: 020 8844 2266
Fax: 020 8890 5546
E-mail: bifa@bifa.org
Website: www.bifa.org

BIFA is the principal trade association providing representation, training and support to British companies engaged in the international movement of freight to and from the UK by air, rail, road and sea. It is a not-for-profit organisation. Members are encouraged to contribute to the running of the Association.

MEMBERSHIP
Associate Member
Trade Member

FUNDRAISING
Membership of Professional Institutions and Associations

INSTITUTE OF FUNDRAISING

Park Place
12 Lawn Lane
London SW8 1UD
Tel: 020 7840 1000
Fax: 020 7840 1001
E-mail: info@institute-of-fundraising.org.uk
Website: www.institute-of-fundraising.org.uk

The Institute of Fundraising is the professional body for fundraisers in the UK, representing over 5000 individual fundraisers and 340 organisations. We offer professional support, act as a voice for fundraisers and promote best practice. We offer professional qualifications and training, and the annual IoF National Convention is the largest fundraising conference of its type in Europe.

MEMBERSHIP
Associate
Full Member (MInstF)
Fully Certificated Member MInstF(Cert)
Diploma Qualified Member MInstF(Dip)
Organisational Member

QUALIFICATION/EXAMINATIONS
Introductory Certificate in Fundraising
Certificate in Fundraising
Diploma in Fundraising
Advanced Diploma in Fundraising (in development)
Certificate in Direct Marketing

DESIGNATORY LETTERS
MInstF, MInstF(Cert), MInstF(Dip), FInstF, FInstF(Cert), FInstF(Dip)

FUNERAL DIRECTING, BURIAL AND CREMATION ADMINISTRATION

Membership of Professional Institutions and Associations

NATIONAL ASSOCIATION OF FUNERAL DIRECTORS

618 Warwick Road
Solihull
West Midlands B91 1AA
Tel: 0845 230 1343
Fax: 0121 711 1351
E-mail: info@nafd.org.uk
Website: www.nafd.org.uk

The NAFD, founded in 1905, is an independent trade association whose members include more than 3,200 funeral homes throughout the UK, suppliers to the profession, and overseas funeral directing businesses. We provide support to our members and offer informed opinion to government.

MEMBERSHIP
Funeral Director (Category A) Member
Supplier (Category B) Member
Overseas Member

QUALIFICATION/EXAMINATIONS
Advanced Certificate in Funeral Services
National Certificate in Funeral Arranging and Administration (NCFAA)
National Diploma in Funeral Directing (NDipFD)
Advanced Diploma in Funeral Arranging and Administration

NATIONAL ASSOCIATION OF MEMORIAL MASONS

1 Castle Mews
Rugby
Warwickshire CV21 2AL
Tel: 01788 542264
Fax: 01788 542276
E-mail: enquiries@namm.org.uk
Website: www.namm.org.uk

The NAMM was formed in 1907 to promote excellence and craftsmanship within the memorial masonry trade. Our services to members include training, business advice, technical advice, promotion, a legal helpline, a conciliation and arbitration service, trade exhibitions and a conference. We protect members' interests through representation to the British Standards Institution (BSI) and the Burial & Cemeteries Advisory Group (BCAG).

MEMBERSHIP
Individual Associate Member
Affiliate Retail Member
Full Retail and Wholesale Members
Company Associate Member
Corporate Associate Member

THE INSTITUTE OF BURIAL AND CREMATION ADMINISTRATION

Kelham Hall
Newark
Nottinghamshire NG23 5QX
Tel: 01636 708311
Fax: 01636 706311

MEMBERSHIP
Student
Registered Licentiate (LInstBCA)
Associate Member (AInstBCA)
Member (MInstBCA)
Fellow (FInstBCA)

QUALIFICATION/EXAMINATIONS
Diploma
Final Diploma

DESIGNATORY LETTERS
LInstBCA, AInstBCA, MInstBCA, FInstBCA

FURNISHING AND FURNITURE
Membership of Professional Institutions and Associations

FLOORING INDUSTRY TRAINING ASSOCIATION

4c St Marys Place
The Lace Market
Nottingham NG1 1PH
Tel: 0115 9506836
E-mail: info@fita.co.uk
Website: www.fita.co.uk

FITA was set up and is fully supported by the CFA and the NICF to provide training for the floor-covering industry. We have a fully equipped training centre at Loughborough, where the majority of our courses are run. We also offer tailor-made courses to suit individual specifications and requirements.

QUALIFICATION/EXAMINATIONS
FITA Training Courses
The Flooring Industry Flooring Association was set up by, and is fully supported by the CFA and NICF to provide training.
FITA has a fully equipped training centre at Loughborough in Leicestershire where the majority of our standard courses are run. FITA also offers tailor-made courses to suit your specifications and requirements, quotations on request.
FITA instructors have all passed assessments and knowledge exams and are supported on courses by technicians with specialist knowledge from the trade.

FITA also enjoys the support of a considerable number of suppliers who freely donate materials, accessories and tools.

Fully trained staff are an asset to any company. The outlay for training courses far outweighs the initial cost.

Please be sure to book early to reserve your place on a course. Go to our Course Dates page for details of our latest courses and the training centres where they are being held.
Training courses considered suitable for Domestic Installers
Carpet Fitting – Basic
Carpet Fitting – Intermediate
Domestic Sheet Vinyl Fitting
Profitable Measuring and Quoting
Subfloor Preparation – Domestic
Training courses considered suitable for Commercial Installers
Commercial Vinyl Fitting – Advanced
Commercial Vinyl Fitting – Basic

Commercial Vinyl Fitting – Intermediate
Cost Effective Estimating and Planning
Subfloor Preparation – Commercial
Training courses considered suitable for Domestic & Commercial Installers
Carpet Fitting – Advanced
Laminate and Wood Fitting – Basic
Moisture – Preventing floor failures
Resilient / Luxury Vinyl Tile Fitting – Advanced
Resilient / Luxury Vinyl Tile Fitting – Basic
Wood Fitting – Advanced
Wood Fitting – Intermediate
Wood Sanding and Finishing
Assessments designed for FITA QA Accreditation
QA Card Adhered Carpet Assessment
QA Card Carpet Tile Assessment
QA Card Floating Timber Assessment
QA Card Resilient Sheet Assessment
QA Card Subfloor Preparation Assessment
QA Card Vinyl Tile Assessment

NATIONAL INSTITUTE OF CARPET AND FLOORLAYERS

4c St Marys Place
The Lace Market
Nottingham NG1 1PH
Tel: 0115 9583077
Fax: 0115 9412238
E-mail: info@nicfltd.org.uk
Website: www.nicfltd.org.uk

The NICF furthers the interests of its members by promoting excellence in the field of carpet and floorlaying and providing a range of benefits, products and services.

MEMBERSHIP
Master Fitter Member
Fitter Member
Trainee Fitter Member
Retailer Member
Associate Member
Patron Member

QUALIFICATION/EXAMINATIONS
Fitter qualification assessment
Master Fitter qualification assessment

GEMMOLOGY AND JEWELLERY
Membership of Professional Institutions and Associations

THE GEMMOLOGICAL ASSOCIATION OF GREAT BRITAIN

27 Greville Street
London EC1N 8TN
Tel: 020 7404 3334
Fax: 020 7404 8843
E-mail: education@gem-a.com
Website: www.gem-a.com

The Gemmological Association of Great Britain (Gem-A), a UK-registered charity, is the world's longest established provider of gem and jewellery education, our first diploma having been awarded in 1913. We are committed to promoting the study of gemmology and to providing CPD to our members – an international community of gem professionals and enthusiasts.

MEMBERSHIP
Member
Fellow (FGA)
Diamond Member (DGA)
Corporate Member

QUALIFICATION/EXAMINATIONS
Foundation Certificate in Gemmology

Diploma in Gemmology
Gem Diamond Diploma

DESIGNATORY LETTERS
FGA, DGA

THE NATIONAL ASSOCIATION OF GOLDSMITHS

78A Luke Street
London EC2A 4XG
Tel: 020 7613 4445
Fax: 020 7613 4450
E-mail: nag@jewellers-online.org
Website: www.jewellers-online.org

The NAG, established in 1894, serves and supports the jewellery industry of Great Britain and Ireland. We promote high professional standards among our members, who must adhere to a code of professional practice. In return, we offer them advice, support and CPD in the form of distance learning courses, seminars and tutorials.

MEMBERSHIP
Alumni Member
Allied Member
Affiliate Member
Ordinary Member

QUALIFICATION/EXAMINATIONS
Professional Jewellers' Diploma
Professional Jewellers' Gemstone Diploma
Professional Jewellers' Management Diploma
Professional Jewellers' Valuation Diploma

GENEALOGY
Membership of Professional Institutions and Associations

SOCIETY OF GENEALOGISTS

14 Charterhouse Buildings
Goswell Road
London EC1M 7BA
Tel: 020 7251 8799
Fax: 020 7250 1800
E-mail: info@sog.org.uk
Website: www.sog.org.uk

The Society (founded 1911) is the National Family History Centre. A registered educational charity, it was founded to encourage and foster the study, science and knowledge of genealogy. This it does chiefly through its library, publications and extensive education programme of courses and events. It currently does not hold exams.

MEMBERSHIP
Member
Fellow (FSG)
Honorary Fellow (FSG Hon)

DESIGNATORY LETTERS
FSG, FSG Hon

THE HERALDRY SOCIETY

PO Box 772
Guildford GU3 3ZX
Tel: 01438 237373
E-mail: memsec@theheraldrysociety.com
Website: www.theheraldrysociety.com

The Heraldry Society is a registered charity that aims to encourage interest in heraldry through publications, lectures, visits and related activities. Members receive *The Heraldry Gazette*, which contains heraldic news and comments, and Society information quarterly. We maintain contact with heraldic societies in many parts of the UK and abroad.

MEMBERSHIP
Associate Member
Ordinary Member
Fellow (FHS)
Honorary Fellow (Hon FHS)
Institutional Member

QUALIFICATION/EXAMINATIONS
Elementary Certificate
Intermediate Certificate
Advanced Certificate
Diploma (DipHS)

DESIGNATORY LETTERS
FHS, Hon FHS

THE INSTITUTE OF HERALDIC AND GENEALOGICAL STUDIES

79–82 Northgate
Canterbury
Kent CT1 1BA
Tel: 01227 768664
Fax: 01227 765617
E-mail: registrar@ihgs.ac.uk
Website: www.ihgs.ac.uk

The IHGS, founded in 1961, is an independent educational charitable trust that offers a wide range of courses on family history, heraldry and related historical subjects, and has an extensive library, archive and research facilities. We also publish a monthly e-mail newsletter and a quarterly journal, *Family History*.

MEMBERSHIP
Associate Member
Graduate Member
Licentiate (LHG)
Fellow (FHG)

QUALIFICATION/EXAMINATIONS
Correspondence Course in Genealogy
Higher Certificate in Genealogy
Diploma in Genealogy

DESIGNATORY LETTERS
LHG, FHG

GEOGRAPHY
Membership of Professional Institutions and Associations

ROYAL GEOGRAPHICAL SOCIETY (WITH THE INSTITUTE OF BRITISH GEOGRAPHERS)

1 Kensington Gore
London SW7 2AR
Tel: 020 7591 3000
Fax: 020 7591 3001
E-mail: info@rgs.org
Website: www.rgs.org

The RGS-IBG is the learned society and professional body for geography. We aim to foster an understanding and informed enjoyment of our world: developing, supporting and promoting geographical research, expeditions and fieldwork, education, public engagement, and providing geography input to policy.

MEMBERSHIP
Young Geographer
Member
Postgraduate Fellow
Fellow
Chartered Geographer (CGeog)
Corporate Member

DESIGNATORY LETTERS
FRGS, CGeog

GEOLOGY
Membership of Professional Institutions and Associations

THE GEOLOGICAL SOCIETY

Burlington House
Piccadilly
London W1J 0BG
Tel: 020 7434 9944
Fax: 020 7439 8975
E-mail: enquiries@geolsoc.org.uk
Website: www.geolsoc.org.uk

The Geological Society, founded in 1807, is the UK's national organization for professional Earth scientists. The normal grade of membership is Fellow. Students may become Candidate Fellows. Members of the public not eligible for any other status may join as Friends.

MEMBERSHIP
Friend
Candidate Fellow
Fellow
Chartered Geologist

DESIGNATORY LETTERS
FGS, CGeol

GLASS TECHNOLOGY
Membership of Professional Institutions and Associations

BRITISH SOCIETY OF SCIENTIFIC GLASSBLOWERS

Unit W1, MK2 Business Centre
Barton Road
Bletchley
Milton Keynes
Buckinghamshire MK2 3HU
Tel: 01908 821191
Fax: 01908 821195
E-mail: bssg@biochemglass.co.uk
Website: www.bssg.co.uk

The Society was founded in 1960 for the benefit of those engaged in Scientific Glassblowing and its associated professions, and to uphold and further the status of Scientific Glassblowers. We welcome written submissions to our quarterly journal, which is circulated to members.

MEMBERSHIP
Associate
Student Member
Fellow
Full Member
Master
Honorary Member
Retired Member
Overseas Member

SOCIETY OF GLASS TECHNOLOGY

9 Churchill Way
Chapeltown
Sheffield
South Yorkshire S35 2PY
Tel: 0114 2634455
Fax: 0871 8754085
E-mail: info@sgt.org
Website: www.sgt.org

The objects of the Society of Glass Technology are to encourage and advance the study of the history, art, science, design, manufacture, after treatment, distribution and end use of glass of any and every kind.

MEMBERSHIP
Personal Member
Fellow (FSGT)
Fellow Emeritus
Honorary Fellow (HonFSGT)
Corporate Member

QUALIFICATION/EXAMINATIONS
Peer review by the Board of Fellows

DESIGNATORY LETTERS
FSGT, HonFSGT

HAIRDRESSING

Membership of Professional Institutions and Associations

HABIA

Oxford House
Sixth Avenue
Sky Business Park, Robin Hood Airport
Doncaster
South Yorkshire DN9 3GG
Tel: 0845 2 306080
Fax: 01302 774949
E-mail: info@habia.org
Website: www.habia.org

Habia is the government-appointed standards-setting body for hair, beauty, nails, spa therapy, barbering and African-type hair, and creates the standards that form the basis of all qualifications, including NVQs, SVQs, apprenticeships, diplomas and foundation degrees, as well as industry codes of practice.

MEMBERSHIP
Habia offers a membership programme for training providers (Habia Members) and a wider, free membership for industry professionals and educators.

THE GUILD OF HAIRDRESSERS

Archway House
Barnsley S71 1AQ
Tel: 01226 786555
Fax: 01226 786555

The Guild of Hairdressers dates back to 1340, when it was part of the Guild of Barbers and Surgeons. Then in the late 16th century, when the surgeons split off, it became the Guild of Hairdressers, Wigmakers and Perfumers. Today it still exists for the benefit of its members, who adhere to a code of ethics and to whom it provides help and advice.

HEALTH AND HEALTH SERVICES
Membership of Professional Institutions and Associations

BRITISH OCCUPATIONAL HYGIENE SOCIETY – FACULTY OF OCCUPATIONAL HYGIENE

5/6 Melbourne Business Court
Millennium Way
Pride Park
Derby DE24 8LZ
Tel: 01332 298101
Fax: 01332 298099
E-mail: admin@bohs.org
Website: www.bohs.org

BOHS is a professional membership organisation and learned society, promoting public and professional awareness, good practice and high standards of occupational hygiene, to help reduce work-related ill-health. The Faculty is our professional arm and examining board, and administers examinations and awards qualifications in occupational hygiene and allied subjects.

MEMBERSHIP
Individual
Student
Affiliate (corporate)
Retired
Associate (AFOH)
Licentiate (LFOH)
Member (MFOH)
Specialist Member (MFOH(S))
Fellow (FFOH)

QUALIFICATION/EXAMINATIONS
A range of UK and international qualifications in occupational hygiene and related subjects, which include stand-alone modules covering general principles and practical applications at the technician level, through to BOHS's own professional level Certificate and Diploma qualifications.

The Occupational Hygiene Modules are aimed at those who want to gain a qualification in a particular topic of occupational hygiene to demonstrate technical expertise in that area or, grouped together, to gain exemption from the Faculty's professional level Certificate Core examination.

The International Occupational Hygiene Modules are based on the Occupational Hygiene Modules, without specific reference to UK or other legislation.

The Proficiency Modules cover both theory and practical training in a specific subject, and are aimed at those needing to demonstrate a level of proficiency to carry out the area of work covered by the Module.

Our professional qualifications are as follows: The Certificate of Competence in an individual subject is for candidates wanting to establish their competence in a specific field, and follows on from successful completion of one of the Occupational Hygiene Modules. This is an oral examination, supported by submission of a written report. The Certificate of Operational Competence in Occupational Hygiene is the qualification required to join the Faculty of Occupational Hygiene as a Licentiate, and demonstrates knowledge and competence in the broad principles and practice of occupational hygiene. This is a two-part written and oral examination. The Diploma of Professional Competence in Occupational Hygiene is the highest professional occupational hygiene qualification. Candidates must already hold the Certificate of Operational Competence, and be able to demonstrate 5 years' experience in the field of occupational hygiene. Award of the Diploma qualifies the holder to become a Member of the Faculty, and demonstrates knowledge of, and competence in, assessment of health hazards and the extent of risk in various workplace circumstances, and an ability to advise on suitable control procedures. This is also a two-part, written and oral, examination.

For further information see www.bohs.org/education/examinations/

DESIGNATORY LETTERS
AFOH, LFOH, MFOH, FFOH, MFOH(S)

CHARTERED INSTITUTE OF ENVIRONMENTAL HEALTH

Chadwick Court
15 Hatfields
London SE1 8DJ
Tel: 020 7827 5800
Fax: 020 7827 5832
E-mail: customerservices@cieh.org
Website: www.cieh.org

The CIEH is a professional, awarding and campaigning body at the forefront of environmental and public health and safety.

MEMBERSHIP
Student member
Associate
Accredited Associate
Graduate Member
Fellow

QUALIFICATION/EXAMINATIONS
The CIEH offers a range of Ofqual-regulated qualifications at four levels in health and safety, food safety, environmental protection and train the trainer.

ERGONOMICS SOCIETY

Elms Court
Elms Grove
Loughborough
Leicestershire LE11 1RG
Tel: 01509 234904
Fax: 01509 235666
E-mail: ergsoc@ergonomics.org.uk
Website: www.ergonomics.org.uk

The Ergonomics Society, founded in 1949, is a UK-based professional society for ergonomists worldwide. We encourage and maintain high standards of professional practice through education, accreditation and development, promote the interests of our members across government, academia, business and industry, and raise awareness of ergonomics in general.

MEMBERSHIP
Student Member
Associate Member
Graduate Member
Registered Member (MErgS)
Fellow (FErgS)

INSTITUTE OF HEALTH PROMOTION AND EDUCATION

c/o Helen Draper
School of Dentistry, University of Manchester
Coupland 3, Oxford Road
Manchester M13 9PL
Tel: 01612 756610
E-mail: honsec@ihpe.org.uk
Website: www.ihpe.org.uk

The IHPE was established 50 years ago to bring together professionals with a common interest in health education and promotion to share their experience, ideas and information. Our members come from a diverse range of backgrounds, including nursing, midwifery, health visiting, medicine, dentistry, public health, stress management, psychology and teaching.

MEMBERSHIP
Student Member
Associate Member (AIHPE)
Full Member (MIHPE)
Fellow (FIHPE)
Corporate Member

DESIGNATORY LETTERS
MIHPE, AIHPE, FIHPE

INSTITUTE OF HEALTH RECORDS AND INFORMATION MANAGEMENT

Marshall House
Heanor Gate Road
Heanor
Derbyshire DE75 7RG
Tel: 01773 713927
Fax: 01773 713927
E-mail: ihrim@zen.co.uk
Website: www.ihrim.co.uk

IHRIM was founded in 1948, primarily as an educational body, to provide qualifications as well as career and professional assistance to members. We encourage professionalism and high standards among our members who work in the fields of health records, information management, clinical coding and information governance.

MEMBERSHIP
Student
Affiliate
Licentiate
Certificated Member (CHRIM)
Accredited Clinical Coder (ACC)
Associate (AHRIM)
Fellow (FHRIM)
Corporate Affiliate

QUALIFICATION/EXAMINATIONS
Certificate of Technical Competence
Foundation exam
Certificate exam
Diploma exam
National Clinical Coding Qualification

DESIGNATORY LETTERS
CHRIM, ACC, AHRIM, FHRIM

INSTITUTE OF HEALTHCARE ENGINEERING AND ESTATE MANAGEMENT

2 Abingdon House
Cumberland Business Centre
Northumberland Road
Portsmouth PO5 1DS
Tel: 023 92 823186
Fax: 023 92 815927
E-mail: office@iheem.org.uk
Website: www.iheem.org.uk

IHEEM is the learned society and professional body for those working in the Healthcare Estates sector. Our members are architects, builders, engineers, estate managers, surveyors, medical engineers and other related professionals. We provide benefits to members to keep them up to date with developing technology and changing regulations.

MEMBERSHIP
Graduate (GIHEEM)
Associate Member (AMIHEEM)
Member (MIHEEM)
Fellow (FIHEEM)

DESIGNATORY LETTERS
GIHEEM, AMIHEEM, MIHEEM, FIHEEM

INSTITUTE OF HEALTHCARE MANAGEMENT

18–21 Morely Street
London SE1 7QZ
Tel: 020 7620 1030
Fax: 020 7620 1040
E-mail: enquiries@ihm.org.uk
Website: www.ihm.org.uk

The IHM is the professional organization for managers throughout healthcare, including the NHS, independent providers, healthcare consultants and the armed forces. Our focus is on improving patient/user care by publishing standards of management practice, promoting the IHM Code (which covers behavioural and ethical aspects of management practice) and establishing a CPD framework for our members.

MEMBERSHIP
Associate Member
Full Member (MIHM)
Fellow (FIHM)
Companion (CIHM)

QUALIFICATION/EXAMINATIONS
Certificate in Health Management Studies (CertHMS)
Certificate in Health Services Management (CertHSM)
Certificate in Managing Health Services (CertMHS)
Certificate in Managing Health & Social Care (CertMHSC)
Diploma in Health Services Management (DipHSM)

DESIGNATORY LETTERS
MIHM, FIHM, CIHM

THE ROYAL SOCIETY FOR PUBLIC HEALTH

John Snow House
59 Mansell Street
London E1 8AN
Tel: 020 7265 7300
Fax: 020 7265 7301
E-mail: info@rsph.org.uk
Website: www.rsph.org.uk

The RSPH was formed in October 2008 by the merger of the Royal Society for the Promotion of Health (RSPH/RSH) and the Royal Institute of Public Health (RIPH). We offer a wide range of vocationally related qualifications in the fields of food safety and nutrition, hygiene, health and safety, pest control, health promotion and the built environment.

MEMBERSHIP
Associate (ARSPH)
Licentiate (LRSPH)
Member (MRSPH)
Fellow (FRSPH)

QUALIFICATION/EXAMINATIONS
Please see the RSPH's website.

DESIGNATORY LETTERS
ARSPH, LRSPH, MRSPH, FRSPH

HORSES AND HORSE RIDING
Membership of Professional Institutions and Associations

THE BRITISH HORSE SOCIETY

Contact: Equestrian Qualifications GB Limited
c/o The British Horse Society
Abbey Park
Kenilworth
Warwickshire CV8 2XZ
Tel: 02476 840500
Fax: 02476 840501
E-mail: exams@bhs.org.uk
Website: www.bhs.org.uk

The British Horse Society offers vocational and work-based examinations for grooms, stable managers, riding instructors and coaches. Founded in 1947, the BHS exams system is world renowned as credible and rigorous, producing competent, practical people who follow safe practices. We also offer competency certificates for the recreational rider.

MEMBERSHIP
Individual Member
Trade Member
Corporate Member

QUALIFICATION/EXAMINATIONS
Equestrian Qualifications GB Limited awards examinations and qualifications for grooms, stable managers, riding instructors and coaches on behalf of The British Horse Society and British Equestrian Federation. Please see the EQL website, www.equestrian-qualifications.org.uk, for details.

HOUSING
Membership of Professional Institutions and Associations

THE CHARTERED INSTITUTE OF HOUSING

Octavia House
Westwood Way
Coventry CV4 8JP
Tel: 024 7685 1700
Fax: 024 7669 5110
E-mail: customer.services@cih.org
Website: www.cih.org

The CIH is the professional body for people involved in housing and communities. We are a registered charity and not-for-profit organization. We have a diverse and growing membership of over 22,000 people – both in the public and private sectors – living and working in over 20 countries on five continents across the world.

MEMBERSHIP

From January 2012 two new grades of membership have been introduced and replaced the previous six grades of membership.
CIH Member (formerly Student, Affiliate, Practitioner, Associate)
CIH Chartered Member (formerly Corporate and Fellow).
Visit www.cih.org to find out more about CIH membership.

QUALIFICATION/EXAMINATIONS
Certificate Courses

The CIH offers a range of certificated courses at Levels 2, 3 and 4 delivered at various centres across the UK. They are also available by distance learning. We also offer a suite of certificated courses in repairs and maintenance, also at Levels 2, 3 and 4, developed in partnership with the Chartered Institute of Building (CIOB).
Professional Qualifications
The CIH Professional Qualification can be achieved at either undergraduate or postgraduate level, FT or PT.
Please see the CIH's website for details.

DESIGNATORY LETTERS
CIH Members: CIH Member or CIHM, CIH Chartered Members: CIH Chartered Member or CIHCM (existing Fellows can continue to use FCIH and Honorary Members can use (Hon).

INDEXING
Membership of Professional Institutions and Associations

SOCIETY OF INDEXERS

Woodbourn Business Centre
10 Jessell Street
Sheffield S9 3HY
Tel: 01142 449561
E-mail: admin@indexers.org.uk
Website: www.indexers.org.uk

The Society of Indexers is the professional body for indexing in the UK and Ireland, and exists to promote indexing, the quality of indexes and the profession of indexing. We offer information to publishers and other organizations on commissioning indexes and our online directory 'Indexers

Available' provides an up-to-date guide to indexers currently working in a wide range of fields.

MEMBERSHIP
Student Member
Member
Professional Member (MSocInd)
Advanced Professional Member (MSocInd(Adv))
Fellow (FSocInd)
Corporate Member

QUALIFICATION/EXAMINATIONS
Training in Indexing course
Advanced Test
Fellowship index submission

DESIGNATORY LETTERS
MSocInd, MSocInd(Adv), FSocInd

INDUSTRIAL SAFETY
Membership of Professional Institutions and Associations

BRITISH SAFETY COUNCIL

70 Chancellors Road
London W6 9RS
Tel: 020 8741 1231
Fax: 020 8741 4555
E-mail: mail@britsafe.org
Website: www.britsafe.org

The BSC is one of the world's leading health and safety organizations. Our mission is to keep people healthy and safe at work. Our range of charitable initiatives, such as free health and safety qualifications for school children, is supported by a broad mix of commercial activities centred on membership, training, auditing and qualifications.

MEMBERSHIP
UK Member
International Member

QUALIFICATION/EXAMINATIONS
Certificate in Process Safety
Certificate in COSHH Risk Assessment (Level 2)
Certificate in DSE Risk Assessment (Level 2)
Certificate in Fire Risk Assessment (Level 2)
Certificate in Manual Handling Risk Assessment (Level 2)
Certificate in Risk Assessment (Level 2)
Certificate in Supervising Staff Safely (Level 2)
Certificate in Occupational Health and Safety (Level 3)
Diploma in Occupational Health and Safety (Level 6)
Diploma in Environmental Management (DipEM)
International Certificate in Occupational Health and Safety
International Diploma in Environmental Management
International Diploma in Occupational Health and Safety

Industrial Safety

HEALTH & SAFETY EXECUTIVE APPROVED MINING QUALIFICATIONS

Mining Qualifications, The Health & Safety Executive
2nd Floor, Foundry House
3 Millsands, Riverside Exchange
Sheffield
South Yorkshire S3 8NH
Tel: 0114 291 2394
Fax: 0114 291 2399
E-mail: sarah.johnson@hse.gsi.gov.uk
Website: www.hse.gov.uk/mining

The HSE issues First and Second Class Certificates of Qualification as required under the Management and Administration of Safety and Health at Mines Regulations (MASHAM) 1993 for the appointment of a manager and undermanager respectively, in mines of coal, shale and fireclay in the UK. It also issues certificates to Mining Mechanical and Mining Electrical Engineers, Mechanics and Electricians Class I and Class II, Mines Surveyor, and Mines Deputy. For details see; www.hse.gov.uk/mining

INTERNATIONAL INSTITUTE OF RISK AND SAFETY MANAGEMENT

Suite 7a
77 Fulham Palace Road
London W6 8JA
Tel: 020 8741 9100
Fax: 020 8741 1349
E-mail: info@iirsm.org
Website: www.iirsm.org

The IIRSM is a professional body for health & safety practitioners and specialists in associated professions. Our aim is to advance professional standards in accident prevention and occupational health throughout the world. We have more than 8,100 members, in the UK and over 70 other countries, to whom we provide support and offer advice via a technical helpline.

MEMBERSHIP
Student
Affiliate
Associate (AIIRSM)
Member (MIIRSM)
Specialist Member (SIIRSM)
Fellow (FIIRSM)

DESIGNATORY LETTERS
AIIRSM, MIIRSM, SIIRSM, FIIRSM

NEBOSH (THE NATIONAL EXAMINATION BOARD IN OCCUPATIONAL SAFETY AND HEALTH)

Dominus Way
Meridian Business Park
Leicester LE19 1QW
Tel: (+44) 116 263 4700
Fax: (+44) 116 282 4000
E-mail: info@nebosh.org.uk
Website: www.nebosh.org.uk

NEBOSH offers globally recognized qualifications designed to meet the health, safety, environmental and risk management needs of all places of work. Courses leading to NEBOSH qualifications attract over 35,000 candidates annually in over 100 countries around the world. NEBOSH also offers qualifications in Oil and Gas, and Health and Well-being.

MEMBERSHIP

NEBOSH's National General Certificate, National Certificate in Fire Safety and Risk Management, National Certificate in Construction Health and Safety, and the International General Certificate are all accepted as meeting the academic requirements to apply for Technician Membership (Tech IOSH) of the Institution of Occupational Safety and Health (IOSH), and Associate Membership (AIIRSM) of the International Institute of Risk and Safety Management (IIRSM).

NEBOSH's National Diploma and International Diploma are accepted as meeting the requirements to apply for Graduate Membership (Grad IOSH) of the Institution of Occupational Safety and Health (IOSH). Diplomates may also apply to become full Members (MIIRSM) of the International Institute of Risk and Safety Management (IIRSM). The National Diploma provides a sound basis for progression to MSc level: a number of UK universities offer MSc programmes that accept the National Diploma as a full or partial entry requirement.

The NEBOSH Environmental Diploma fulfils the academic requirements for Specialist Membership of the International Institute of Risk and Safety Management (IIRSM).

QUALIFICATION/EXAMINATIONS

NEBOSH Award in Health and Safety at Work
NEBOSH Health, Safety and Environment in the Process Industries Qualification
NEBOSH National Certificate in Construction Health and Safety
NEBOSH National Certificate in Environmental Management
NEBOSH National Certificate in Fire Safety and Risk Management
NEBOSH National General Certificate in Occupational Health and Safety
NEBOSH International General Certificate in Occupational Health and Safety
NEBOSH International Technical Certificate in Oil and Gas Operational Safety
NEBOSH National Certificate in the Management of Health and Well-being at Work
NEBOSH International Certificate in Construction Health and Safety
NEBOSH International Certificate in Fire Safety and Risk Management
NEBOSH National Diploma in Environmental Management
NEBOSH National Diploma in Occupational Health and Safety
NEBOSH International Diploma in Occupational Health and Safety

THE INSTITUTION OF OCCUPATIONAL SAFETY AND HEALTH

The Grange
Highfield Drive
Wigston
Leicestershire LE18 1NN
Tel: 0116 257 3100
Fax: 0116 257 3101
E-mail: membership@iosh.co.uk
Website: www.iosh.co.uk

IOSH is the world's largest organization for health and safety professionals, with more than 36,000 members worldwide, including 13,000 Chartered Safety and Health Practitioners. The Institution was founded in 1945 and is an independent, not-for-profit organization that sets professional standards, supports and develops members, and provides authoritative advice and guidance on health and safety issues.

MEMBERSHIP
Affiliate Member
Technician Member (Tech IOSH)
Graduate Member (Grad IOSH)
Chartered Member (CMIOSH)
Chartered Fellow (CFIOSH)

DESIGNATORY LETTERS
Tech IOSH, Grad IOSH, CMIOSH, CFIOSH

INSURANCE AND ACTUARIAL WORK
Membership of Professional Institutions and Associations

ASSOCIATION OF AVERAGE ADJUSTERS

Secretariat: The Baltic Exchange
St Mary Axe
London EC3A 8BH
Tel: 020 7623 5501
Fax: 020 7369 1623
E-mail: aaa@balticexchange.com
Website: www.average-adjusters.com

The AAA was founded in 1869 to promote correct principles in the adjustment of marine insurance claims and general average, uniformity of practice among average adjusters and the maintenance of good professional conduct. It ensures the independence and impartiality of its members by imposing a strict code of conduct and has close links with other international associations and insurance markets.

MEMBERSHIP
Subscriber
Associate
Fellow

QUALIFICATION/EXAMINATIONS
The Association's examination consists of 6 modules. Passes in Modules 1 & 2 are required for Associateship, passes in Modules 3–6 for Fellowship. For details see the Association's website.

THE CHARTERED INSTITUTE OF LOSS ADJUSTERS

51–55 Gresham Street
London EC2V 7HQ
Tel: 020 7216 7580
Fax: 020 7216 7581
E-mail: info@cila.co.uk
Website: www.cila.co.uk

The CILA, which was founded in 1941, is the professional body representing the claims specialists who investigate, negotiate and agree the conclusion of insurance and other claims on behalf of insurers and policyholders. We safeguard the interests of our members and maintain the high standards of the profession by requiring them to abide by our code of professional conduct.

MEMBERSHIP
Student Member
Ordinary Member
Certificate Member (Cert CILA)
Associate (ACILA)
Fellow (FCILA)
Honorary Member

QUALIFICATION/EXAMINATIONS
CILA examination

DESIGNATORY LETTERS
Cert CILA, ACILA, FCILA

THE CHARTERED INSURANCE INSTITUTE

42–48 High Road
South Woodford
London E18 2JP
Tel: 020 8989 8464
Fax: 020 8530 3052
E-mail: customer.serv@cii.co.uk
Website: www.cii.co.uk

The CII is the premier professional body for those working in the insurance and financial services industry. We are dedicated to promoting higher standards of competence and integrity through the provision of relevant qualifications for employees at all levels across all sectors of the industry.

MEMBERSHIP
Ordinary Member
Qualified Member
Associate Member (ACII)
Fellow (FCII)

QUALIFICATION/EXAMINATIONS
Award in Financial Planning
Award in Insurance
Certificate in Equity Release
Certificate in Financial Administration
Certificate in Financial Planning
Certificate in Insurance
Certificate in Life and Pensions
Certificate in Mortgage Advice
Diploma in Financial Planning
Diploma in Insurance
Advanced Diploma in Financial Planning
Advanced Diploma in Insurance
MSc in Insurance and Risk Planning (in association with Cass Business School)

DESIGNATORY LETTERS
ACII, FCII

THE FACULTY AND INSTITUTE OF ACTUARIES

Faculty of Actuaries
Maclaurin House
18 Dublin Street
Edinburgh EH1 3PP
Tel: 0131 240 1313
E-mail: faculty@actuaries.org.uk
Website: www.actuaries.org.uk

Institute of Actuaries
Staple Inn Hall
High Holborn
London WC1V 7QJ
Tel: 020 7632 2111
E-mail: institute@actuaries.org.uk

Napier House
4 Worcester Street
Oxford OX1 2AW
Tel: 01865 268211
E-mail: institute@actuaries.org.uk

Actuaries are experts in assessing the financial impact of tomorrow's uncertain events. They enable financial decisions to be made with more confidence by analysing the past, modelling the future, assessing the risks involved, and communicating what the results mean in financial terms.

MEMBERSHIP
Student Member
Affiliate Member
Associate (AFA or AIA)
Fellow (FFA or FIA)
Honorary Fellow

QUALIFICATION/EXAMINATIONS
Certificate in Financial Mathematics

DESIGNATORY LETTERS
AFA, AIA, FFA, FIA

JOURNALISM
Membership of Professional Institutions and Associations

NATIONAL COUNCIL FOR THE TRAINING OF JOURNALISTS

NCTJ Training Ltd
The New Granary
Newport
Saffron Walden
Essex CB11 3PL
Tel: 01799 544014
Fax: 01799 544015
E-mail: info@nctj.com
Website: www.nctj.com

The NCTJ provides a range of journalism training products and services in the UK, including: accredited courses; qualifications and examinations; awards; careers information; distance learning; short courses and CPD; information and research;

publications and events. We play an influential role in all areas of journalism education and training.

QUALIFICATION/EXAMINATIONS
Diploma in Journalism
Diploma in Press Photography and Photojournalism
National Certificate Examination (NCE) for Press photographers and photo-journalists
National Certificate Examination (NCE) for Reporters
National Certificate Examination (NCE) for Sub-editors
National Certificate Examination (NCE) for Sports Reporters

THE CHARTERED INSTITUTE OF JOURNALISTS

2 Dock Offices
Surrey Quays Road
London SE16 2XU
Tel: 020 7252 1187
Fax: 020 7232 2302
E-mail: memberservices@cioj.co.uk
Website: www.cioj.co.uk

The CIoJ, which dates back to 1884, is a professional body and trade union for journalists. We expect our members to uphold high standards in the way they work and to adhere to a strict code of conduct, and in return we champion journalistic freedom, protect their interests in the workplace and campaign for better working conditions.

MEMBERSHIP
Student Member
Affiliate Member
Trainee Member
Full Member
International Member

DESIGNATORY LETTERS
MCIJ – Member, FCIJ – Fellow

LAND AND PROPERTY
Membership of Professional Institutions and Associations

RICS (ROYAL INSTITUTION OF CHARTERED SURVEYORS)

Parliament Square
London SW1P 3AD
Tel: 0870 333 1600
Fax: 020 7334 3811
E-mail: contactrics@rics.org
Website: www.rics.org/careers

RICS, an independent, not-for-profit organization, has around 100,000 qualified members and more than 50,000 students and trainees in some 140 countries, and provides the world's leading professional qualification in land, property, construction and associated environmental issues. We accredit over 600 courses at leading universities worldwide and provide impartial, authoritative advice on key issues for business, society and governments.

MEMBERSHIP
Student
Associate (AssocRICS)
Member (MRICS)
Fellow (FRICS)

DESIGNATORY LETTERS
AssocRICS, MRICS, FRICS

THE COLLEGE OF ESTATE MANAGEMENT

Whiteknights
Reading
Berkshire RG6 6AW
Tel: 0118 921 4696
Fax: 01189 921 4620
E-mail: courses@cem.ac.uk
Website: www.cem.ac.uk

The College of Estate Management is the leading provider of supported distance learning for real estate and construction professionals. We have been playing a key role in the property world for over 90 years. At any one time we have over 4,000 students based all over the world.

QUALIFICATION/EXAMINATIONS
Diploma in Construction Practice
BCSC Diploma in Shopping Centre Management
Diploma in Surveying Practice
BSc(Hons) Building Services Quantity Surveying
BSc(Hons) Building Surveying
BSc(Hons) Construction Management
BSc(Hons) Estate Management
BSc(Hons) Property Management
BSc(Hons) Quantity Surveying
Postgraduate Diploma/MSc Conservation of the Historic Environment
Postgraduate Diploma/MSc Surveying
MBA Real Estate and Construction Management
MSc Real Estate
Postgraduate Diploma in Adjudication
Postgraduate Diploma in Arbitration
RICS Postgraduate Diploma in Project Management
Postgraduate Diploma/MSc Facilities Management
Postgraduate Diploma/MSc Property Investment
RICS Professional Membership Graduate Route – Adaptation 1

THE INSTITUTE OF REVENUES, RATING AND VALUATION

Northumberland House
5th Floor
303–306 High Holborn
London WC1V 7JZ
Tel: 020 7831 3505
Fax: 020 7831 2048
E-mail: education@irrv.org.uk
Website: www.irrv.org.uk

The Institute offers professional and technical qualifications for all those whose professional work is concerned with local authority revenues and benefits, valuation for rating, property taxation and the appeals procedure. Our qualifications are widely recognized throughout the profession.

MEMBERSHIP
Student Member
Affiliate Member
Graduate Member
Technician Member (Tech IRRV)
Corporate Member (IRRV)
Diploma Member (Dip IRRV)
Honours Member (IRRV Hons)
Honorary Member
Fellow (FIRRV)

QUALIFICATION/EXAMINATIONS
Level 3 Certificate
Level 3 Local Taxation & Benefits (QCF) / SVQ
Professional Diploma in Local Taxation and Benefits Honours

DESIGNATORY LETTERS
Tech IRRV, IRRV, IRRV (Dip), IRRV (Hons), FIRRV

THE NATIONAL FEDERATION OF PROPERTY PROFESSIONALS

Arbon House
6 Tournament Court
Edgehill Drive
Warwick CV34 6LG
Tel: 01926 417794
Fax: 01926 417789
E-mail: quals@nfopp.co.uk
Website: www.nfopp.co.uk

The NFOPP Awarding Body is committed to raising standards within agency through the provision of accredited, nationally recognized qualifications. We are recognized by the Qualifications and Examinations Regulator (Ofqual) and have to follow strict guidelines and maintain quality standards in the provision of all our qualifications.

MEMBERSHIP

For membership details of the following organizations please refer to the relevant website:
APIP; www.apip.co.uk
ARLA; www.arla.co.uk
ICBA; www.icba.uk.com
NAEA; www.naea.co.uk
NAVA; www.nava.org.uk

QUALIFICATION/EXAMINATIONS

Technical Award in Commercial Property Agency (Level 3)
Technical Award in Real Property Auctioneering (Level 3)
Technical Award in Residential Letting and Property Management (Level 3)
Technical Award in Sale of Residential Property (Level 3)
Diploma in Commercial Property Agency (DipCPA) (Level 5)
Diploma in Commercial Property Agency (DipREA) (Level 5)
Diploma in Residential Letting and Management (DipRLM) (Level 5)

THE PROPERTY CONSULTANTS SOCIETY

Basement Office
Surrey Court
1 Surrey Street
Arundel
West Sussex BN18 9DT
Tel: 01903 883787
E-mail: info@propertyconsultantssociety.org
Website: www.propertyconsultantssociety.org

The Property Consultants Society is a non-profit-making organization that offers advice to qualified surveyors, architects, valuers, auctioneers, land and estate agents, master builders, construction engineers, accountants and members of the legal profession to help them to undertake their property consultancy in a competent, legitimate and publicly acceptable way.

MEMBERSHIP

Student (SPCS)
Licentiate (LPCS)
Associate (APCS)
Fellow (FPCS)
Honorary Member

DESIGNATORY LETTERS

SPCS, LPCS, APCS, FPCS

LANDSCAPE ARCHITECTURE
Membership of Professional Institutions and Associations

LANDSCAPE INSTITUTE

Charles Darwin House
12 Roger Street
London WC1N 2JU
Tel: 020 7685 2640
E-mail: membership@landscapeinstitute.org
Website: www.landscapeinstitute.org

The LI is an educational charity and chartered body responsible for protecting, conserving and enhancing the natural and built environment for the benefit of the public. We champion well-designed and well-managed urban and rural landscape. Our 6,000 members include chartered landscape architects, academics and scientists working for local authorities, government agencies and in private practice, and students.

MEMBERSHIP
Student Member
Affiliate Member
Licentiate Member
Chartered Member (CMLI)
Fellow (FLI)
Academic
Academic Fellow

QUALIFICATION/EXAMINATIONS
Pathway to Chartership oral examination conferring chartered professional status (CMLI).

DESIGNATORY LETTERS
CMLI, FLI

LANGUAGES, LINGUISTICS AND TRANSLATION
Membership of Professional Institutions and Associations

INSTITUTE OF TRANSLATION & INTERPRETING

Fortuna House
South Fifth Street
Milton Keynes MK9 2PQ
Tel: 01908 325250
Fax: 01908 325259
E-mail: info@iti.org.uk
Website: www.iti.org.uk

The Institute of Translation & Interpreting is one of the primary sources of information on these services to government, industry, the media and the general public. We promote the highest standards, providing guidance to those entering the profession and advice to those who offer language services and to their customers.

MEMBERSHIP
Student Associate
Associate
Academic
Qualified Member (MITI)
Corporate Member

QUALIFICATION/EXAMINATIONS
Applicants for qualified membership must take an exam (translators) or attend an interview (interpreters).

THE CHARTERED INSTITUTE OF LINGUISTS

Saxon House
48 Southwark Street
London SE1 1UN
Tel: 020 7940 3100
Fax: 020 7940 3101
E-mail: info@iol.org.uk
Website: www.iol.org.uk

The Chartered Institute of Linguistics, founded in 1910, is a respected language assessment and accredited awarding body, with about 6,500 members. Our aims include promoting the learning and use of modern languages, improving the status of all professional linguistics, and ensuring the maintenance of high professional standards through adherence to our code of conduct.

MEMBERSHIP
Registered Student
Associate Member (ACIL)
Member (MCIL)
Fellow (FCIL)
Chartered Linguist (CL)

QUALIFICATION/EXAMINATIONS
Certificate in Bilingual Skills (CBS)
Diploma in Public Service Interpreting (DPSI)
International Diploma in Bilingual Translation (IDBT)
Diploma in Translation (DipTrans)

DESIGNATORY LETTERS
ACIL, MCIL, FCIL, CL

THE GREEK INSTITUTE

34 Bush Hill Road
London N21 2DS
Tel: 020 8360 7968
Fax: 020 8360 7968
E-mail: info@greekinstitute.co.uk
Website: www.greekinstitute.co.uk

The Greek Institute, which was founded in 1969, is a non-profit-making cultural organization that promotes Modern Greek studies and culture through lectures, publications, literary competitions, Greek cultural evenings and the award of Certificates and a Diploma which are recognized by many UK universities as equivalent to GCSE and GCE A level Modern Greek.

MEMBERSHIP
Member
Associate (AGI)
Fellow (FGI)

QUALIFICATION/EXAMINATIONS
Certificate in Greek Conversation – Basic Stage: Levels 1 and 2
Certificate in Greek Conversation – Intermediate Stage: Levels 3 and 4
Certificate in Greek Conversation – Higher Stage: Levels 5 and 6
Preliminary Certificate
Intermediate Certificate
Advanced Certificate
Diploma in Greek Translation (DipGrTrans)

DESIGNATORY LETTERS
AGI, FGI

LAW

ENGLAND AND WALES

MAGISTRATES

Following the Constitutional Reform Act 2005, which came into force in April 2006, the Lord Chief Justice has become head of the Judiciary. He is responsible for the welfare, training and deployment of magistrates, for approving the names of the candidates recommended for appointment and for disciplinary action, short of removal. The Lord Chancellor also has responsibility for the protection of judicial independence and for working to ensure that the magistracy reflects the diversity of society as a whole.

There are six key qualities that a magistrate must possess: good character, understanding and communication, social awareness, maturity and sound temperament, sound judgement, commitment and reliability.

Before sitting in court, magistrates must undertake some basic training, which includes structured observations in court. This covers practice and procedure in court, structured decision making, sentencing, etc. New magistrates are assigned a mentor for their first two years. Consolidation training takes place about 18 months to two years after appointment, followed by appraisals. Magistrates only sit in adult courts when first appointed. Having got that experience they may apply to sit in youth courts and family courts and have to undertake more training before they can sit.

JUDGES

All judicial office holders are Her Majesty's Judges and as such all appointments are made by the Queen or her Ministers. Since 2006 all candidates for judicial appointment in England and Wales have been selected by the independent Judicial Appointments Commission (JAC), which passes its recommendations to the Lord Chancellor for approval. Once the JAC's selections have been received, the actual appointments are made in slightly different ways depending on the type of post. The Lord Chancellor himself appoints Deputy District Judges and most members of tribunals. He also appoints the 30,000 unpaid magistrates (who are selected by local Advisory Committees, not by the JAC). The Queen appoints High Court and Circuit Judges, Masters, Registrars and District Judges, District Judges (Magistrates' Courts) and Recorders on the advice of the Lord Chancellor. The most senior appointments – the Lord Chief Justice and other Heads of Division, and the Lords Justices who are the judges of the Court of Appeal – are approved by the Lord Chancellor and then passed to the Queen via the Prime Minister. Scotland and Northern Ireland have their own separate court systems, with their own arrangements for appointing members of the judiciary. The Supreme Court has jurisdiction over the whole of the UK, so its Justices are not selected by the JAC, which is an England and Wales body. Rather, a special committee is set up, which is made up of the three judicial appointments bodies from around the UK (England and Wales, Scotland and Northern Ireland), who recommend a name to Ministers. The Queen appoints the Justices on the basis of advice from the Prime Minister.

Appointments to salaried or fee-paid judicial posts are made from among judges or practising lawyers. In general the requirement for appointment is that the candidate must have been a practising barrister or solicitor for at least 10 years (for appointment to the Circuit Bench or above) or for five years (appointments to the District Bench and to most tribunal posts). Certain posts are also open to legal executives, patent agents and trademark agents of the required seniority. Candidates for appointment as Justices of the Supreme Court must be existing holders of high judicial office or must have been practising barristers or solicitors of the senior courts for at least 15 years.

OFFICERS OF THE COURT

Officers of the Court include judicial and administrative staff; the former include Masters and Registrars, the latter secretaries and clerks to the judges and the staff who administer the court service. Details are given in The English Legal System, 13th edition, 2012–13 (Routledge). Qualifications for the judicial offices vary somewhat, but most appointments are limited to established barristers and solicitors.

THE LEGAL PROFESSION

The legal profession consists of two branches. Each performs distinct duties, although there is a degree of overlap in some aspects of their work.

Solicitors undertake all ordinary legal business for their clients (with whom they are in direct contact). They may also appear on behalf of a client in the magistrates' and county courts and tribunals, and with specialist training are able to represent them in the higher courts (Crown Court, High Court and Court of Appeal).

Barristers (known collectively as the 'Bar' and collectively and individually as 'Counsel') advise on legal problems submitted by solicitors and conduct cases in court when instructed by a solicitor; only barristers or qualified solicitor advocates may represent clients in the higher courts.

LEGAL EXECUTIVES

Both graduates and non-graduates can work in a legal office with the option of qualifying as a solicitor through further vocational training.

CORONERS

Coroners must be barristers, solicitors or legally qualified medical practitioners of not less than five years' standing. They are appointed by local authorities. There are approximately 110 coroners' jurisdictions in England and Wales. Coroners are independent judicial officers. When not engaged in coronal duties, coroners (apart from 'whole-time' coroners) continue in their legal or medical practices. Further information from the Coroners' Society of England and Wales, website; www.coronersociety.org.uk

BARRISTERS

Qualification as a barrister at the Bar of England and Wales

There are three stages that must be completed in order to qualify as a barrister. The academic stage consists of an undergraduate degree in law or an undergraduate degree in any other subject with a minimum of a 2:2. For those with an undergraduate degree in a subject other than law a one-year conversion course (CPE/GDL) must be completed. Before commencing the vocational stage candidates must join one of the four Inns and then undertake the Bar Professional Training Course (BPTC), which is either one year full time or two years part time. The main skills taught on the Bar Professional Training Course are: case work skills, legal research, general written skills, opinion-writing (that is, giving written advice), interpersonal skills, conference skills (interviewing clients), resolution of disputes out of court (ReDOC) and advocacy (court or tribunal appearances). The main areas of knowledge taught on the Bar Professional Training Course are: civil litigation and remedies, criminal litigation and sentencing, evidence, professional ethics, and two optional subjects selected from a choice of at least six.

From 2012 three examinations will be set by the BSB. These are Civil Litigation, Criminal Litigation and Ethics. It is planned that applicants will take an Aptitude Test to ensure that those undertaking the BPTC have the required skills to succeed. Introduction of the Aptitude Test (BCAT) (subject to approval) is planned for Autumn 2012 (for those starting the course in September 2013). The test will be available for applicants when the BPTC online application system opens in October 2012.

Once the BPCT has been successfully completed candidates are 'Called to the Bar' by their Inn. The Pupillage Stage consists of one year spent in an authorized pupillage training organization. Pupillage is divided into two parts: the non-practising six months (also known as the first six) and the practising six months (also known as the second six).

To find out more about all three stages of qualification as a barrister visit www.barcouncil.org.uk.

SOLICITORS

Qualification as a solicitor in England and Wales

To practise as a solicitor in England and Wales a person must have been admitted as a solicitor, his or her name having been entered on the Roll of Solicitors, and must hold a practising certificate issued by The Solicitors Regulation Authority (SRA) (Ipsley Court, Berrington Close, Redditch, Worcestershire B98 0TD, Tel: 0870 606 2555). The SRA is the independent regulatory body of the Law Society of England and Wales. People will be admitted as solicitors only if they have passed the appropriate academic and vocational course and have completed a training contract and Professional Skills course, or have transferred from another jurisdiction or the Bar. The SRA controls the training of solicitors. Most solicitors become members of the Law Society, but membership is not compulsory. Intending solicitors other than Fellows of the Institute of Legal Executives and Justices' Clerk's Assistants, and qualified lawyers from other jurisdictions, are required to serve a period of training with a practising solicitor after they have completed the legal practice course.

All new entrants to the profession are required to complete a Criminal Records Bureau standard disclosure prior to admission. Candidates wishing to start training must enrol as a student with the SRA and satisfy it that they have successfully completed the academic stage of training and have no issues that may call their character and suitability into question.

THE COMMON PROFESSIONAL EXAM (CPE)/POSTGRADUATE DIPLOMA IN LAW

The seven taught modules are the foundation subjects prescribed by the Joint Academic Stage Board on behalf of the Law Society and General Council of the Bar: Criminal Law, Obligations A (Contract), Obligations B (Tort), Property Law A (Land Law), Property Law B (Equity and Trusts), UK Public Law, and European Public and Private Law. For an up-to-date list of course providers for the CPE, see the SRA website; www.sra.org.uk/students/courses/trainingprovidersearch.

THE LEGAL PRACTICE COURSE

Stage 1 covers core practice areas: Litigation, Property Law and Practice (PLP), Business Law and Practice (BLP); Course Skills: Research, Writing, Drafting, Interviewing and Advising, and Advocacy – these skills form an integral part of the compulsory and elective subjects; Solicitors Accounts and Professional Conduct and Regulation; Taxation, and Wills and Administration of Estates. Stage 2 covers three vocational electives: from a range of corporate client or private client topics (the range of elective available can differ from institution to institution). An up-to-date list of course providers for the LPC is available from the SRA website; www.sra.org.uk/students/courses/trainingprovidersearch.page

TRAINING CONTRACT

The training contract to be served by all intending solicitors, other than Fellows of the Institute of Legal Executives and Justices' Clerk's Assistants, is two years full time or a maximum of four years part time. The training contract can also be a part-time-study training contract that normally lasts between three and four years. During this period the trainee works and is studying the last two years of a part-time qualifying law degree, the part-time Common Professional Examination course and/or the part-time Legal Practice course.

The law graduate who holds a qualifying law degree must complete the Legal Practice course at a recognized institution, and then serve under the training contract for two years. The non-law graduate must first pass the Common Professional Exam (CPE) or the Postgraduate Diploma in Law, having attended either a one-year full-time or two-year part-time preparatory course. He or she may then serve under the training contract for two years after completion of a Legal Practice course. A Professional Skills course must be attended and successfully completed during the training contract.

Fellows of the Institute of Legal Executives may obtain partial or full exemptions from the CPE and Justices' Clerk's Assistants partial exemptions by virtue of similar subjects passed in their Fellowship exams or the Diploma in Magisterial Law. After passing or being exempted from the CPE, the Fellow/Justices' Clerk's Assistant may be exempt from serving under a training contract following successful completion of an LPC. A Professional Skills course must be taken prior to application for admission.

THE PROFESSIONAL SKILLS COURSE

The aim of the Professional Skills course is to build on the foundations laid in the LPC so as to develop a trainee's professional skills. Providers of the course, trainees and their employers are encouraged to regard the course as the first stage of a trainee's lifetime professional development.

Built upon the LPC, the course provides training in three subject areas: financial and business skills; advocacy and communication skills; client care and professional standards. Elective topics will also be chosen, which fall within one or more of these three core areas. All trainees have to complete all sections of the course satisfactorily before being admitted. The course consists of face-to-face instruction on the core subjects, for a minimum of 18 hours each for Financial and Business Skills and Advocacy and Communication Skills, and a minimum of 12 hours for Client Care and Professional Standards. The elective topics require a minimum total of 24 hours, of which a minimum of 12 hours must be face to face. The instruction must be completed during the training contract. The PSC is offered by accredited external course providers.

QUALIFIED LAWYERS FROM OTHER JURISDICTIONS

UK lawyers together with lawyers from certain foreign jurisdictions and EU lawyers can apply for admission under the Qualified Lawyers Transfer Scheme Regulations 2010. They need to obtain a QLTS Certificate of Eligibility.

Under the European Communities Directive No 2005/36/EC, lawyers from EU jurisdictions may apply for admission if they can prove they have met the requirements of the Directive and implementing legislation. Any lawyer applying for admission under the Directive may be required to pass one or more QLTS Assessments. All international applicants must satisfy the requirements and pass all of the

QLTS Assessments. The Assessments are in three parts. Part 1 is a multiple-choice test; Part 2 is a practical examination that will test interviewing and advocacy skills in the context of three areas of practice – business, civil and criminal litigation, and property and probate; Part 3 is a technical legal skills test that will test the skills of legal research, drafting and writing. The Solicitors Regulation Authority has appointed Kaplan QLTS as the sole assessment organization for the first three years of the operation of the assessments (www.kaplanqlts.com).

EEA, Northern Irish and Scottish lawyers, and barristers qualified in England and Wales will be individually assessed against the Day One Outcomes. All transferees are required to prove their character and suitability to be a solicitor by taking the SRA Suitability Test. With effect from 15 July 2011 the LSB has approved changes to the QLTS Regulations that will enable the SRA to grant an exemption from the Part 1 (MCT) assessment to applicants who have passed the LPC.

Prospective candidates wanting more information on QLTS can consult the website www.sra.org.uk/solicitors/qlts/key-features.page for guidance, or contact the SRA on 0870 606 2555.

SCOTLAND

The Court of Session, High Court of Justiciary, Sheriff Courts and Justice of the Peace Courts are administered by the Scottish Court service, an Executive Agency of the Scottish Government. For further information on Scottish Courts go to www.scotcourts.gov.uk.

The Legal Profession
The profession consists of solicitors and advocates.

Qualification as a Solicitor in Scotland
Solicitors in Scotland have their names inserted in a Roll of Solicitors and are granted annual Certificates entitling them to practise by The Law Society of Scotland (26 Drumsheugh Gardens, Edinburgh EH3 7YR; Tel: 0131 226 7411; Fax: 0131 225 2934; e-mail: lawscot@lawscot.org.uk; website; www.lawscot.org.uk). A Certificate is granted to candidates who have passed approved exams, completed a term of practical training and been admitted as solicitors. (The Law Society will be happy to provide copies of its Careers Information leaflet on request.)

THE QUALIFYING EXAMINATIONS
Prior to September 2011, the standard route to qualification was the LLB, followed by the Diploma in Legal Practice and a two year traineeship. In the academic session 2011/12, the LLB was replaced by a new Foundation Programme, which is offered at the same level as the LLB but with some changes to the programme itself, including changes to the professional subjects.

The Diploma in Legal Practice has become Professional Education and Training Stage 1 (PEAT 1) which is also known as the Diploma in Professional Legal Practice. This vocational stage is the stage of legal education where knowledge, skills, attitudes and values are learnt in a simulated environment. The traineeship has become Professional Education and Training Stage 2 (PEAT 2). Trainees undertaking PEAT 2 work towards reaching the standard of the qualifying solicitor.

A major change is the introduction of outcomes that apply across both PEAT 1 and PEAT 2, in 'professionalism, professional ethics and standards', 'professional communication' and 'business, commercial, financial and practice awareness'. The two stages have never been linked in this way before and the link will provide real clarity across the two.

Trainee CPD has replaced the Professional Competence Course. All trainees starting after 1 September 2011 are required to undertake Trainee Continuing Professional Development.

The CPD requirements for all solicitors have also changed. The new framework retains the existing requirement of a minimum of 20 hours each year. To support solicitors in their CPD activities, from 2011 the Society introduced basic templates, which can be completed online, to assist with identifying training needs, recording CPD undertaken and evaluating the outcome of the training. In addition, a wider range of activities are acceptable as CPD, including activities such as structured and formalized one-to-one training, coaching and online training.

An alternate route to qualifying as a solicitor in Scotland is by a combination of the Law Society's own examinations and three years' pre-Diploma training. To be eligible to sit the Law Society's examinations, non-law graduates must find full-time employment as a pre-Diploma trainee with a qualified solicitor practising in Scotland. A pre-Diploma training contract lasts for three years and during that time training must be given in the three prescribed areas of conveyancing, litigation, and either trusts and executries or the legal work of a public authority. To be eligible to enter into a pre-Diploma training contract, non-law graduates must fulfil certain educational requirements as outlined in Appendix 1 of the leaflet 'Pre-Diploma training' on the Law Society of Scotland website (www.lawscot.org.uk/media/196398/103_pre-diploma training.pdf). During the period of the training contract, a pre-Diploma trainee will study for the Law Society's examinations, having four years from commencement of the first examination in which to complete the core subjects: Public Law and the Legal System, Conveyancing, Scots Private Law, Evidence, Scots Criminal Law, Taxation, and Scots Commercial Law (I). European Community Law must be passed prior to admission as a solicitor, but can be obtained during post-Diploma training. The two routes to qualification (degree and Law Society exams) merge at this point as all intending solicitors are required to complete the Diploma in Legal Practice. Upon successful completion of the Diploma the graduate will enter into a two-year post-Diploma training contract with a qualified solicitor practising in Scotland.

Qualification as an Advocate in Scotland

Barristers in Scotland are called Advocates. Scottish Advocates are not only members of the Faculty of Advocates but also members of the College of Justice and officers of the Court. The procedure for the admission of 'Intrants' is subject in part to the control of the Court and in part to the control of the Faculty; the Court is responsible for most of the formal procedures and the Faculty for the exams and periods of professional training. To become an Intrant, applicants must produce evidence that they hold one of the following standard of degree: a degree with Honours, Second Class (Division 2) or above, in Scottish Law at a Scottish university, or a degree in Scottish Law at a Scottish university together with a degree with Honours, Second Class (Division 2) or above, in another subject at a UK university or an ordinary degree with distinction in Scottish Law at a Scottish university. A Diploma in Legal Practice from a Scottish University is also required, although in exceptional cases this requirement may be waived.

Once this evidence is provided and the relevant references obtained, a notice is posted outside Parliament House for a period of 21 days declaring the candidate's intention to present a Petition. At the end of this period the Petition is presented to the Court. After the Petition has been remitted by the Court to the Faculty and signed off by the Clerk of Faculty and Dean of Faculty the candidate is considered to have matriculated as an Intrant.

An Intrant must also comply with the professional training required by the Faculty, which consists of a period of 21 months' training in a solicitors' office (in some cases 12 months). Subject-for-subject exemptions are granted to Intrants who have passed exams at this standard in the course of a curriculum for a law degree at a Scottish university. Every Intrant must pass or be exempted from exams in nine compulsory subjects and two optional subjects. The compulsory subjects include Roman Law of Property and Obligations, Jurisprudence, Constitutional and Administrative Law, Scottish Criminal Law, Scottish Private Law, Commercial Law and Business Institutions, Evidence, International Private Law and European Law and Institutions. In addition, and prior to the commencement of pupillage (also known as 'devilling') every Intrant must sit the Faculty's entrant examination in Evidence, Practice and Procedure. If successfully passed, the Intrant can then commence his or her pupillage.

During the first five or six weeks of pupillage pupils undertake the Foundation course. After about three months of work with their 'devil master', the pupils will participate in the February Skills course, comprising a series of performance workshops involving the use of documents in evidence, the conduct of a procedure roll discussion, workshops on judicial review, section 275 applications and working with expert evidence. Shortly before admission, the pupils attend the May Preparation for Practice course, covering workshops on vulnerable witnesses, longer motions, reclaiming motions, negotiation and mediation, as well as carrying out civil and criminal appeals before a serving judge.

Intrants who have passed all the necessary exams and undergone the necessary professional training as well as successfully completing their pupillage may apply to be admitted to membership of the Faculty and are admitted at a public meeting of the Faculty. Once admitted, Intrants are introduced to the Court by the Dean of Faculty, make a Declaration of Allegiance to the Sovereign in open Court and are then admitted by the Court to the public office of Advocate. For further information on becoming an advocate contact Dean's Secretariat, Faculty of Advocates, Parliament House, Edinburgh EH1 1RF; Tel: 0131 260 5795; e-mail: admissions@advocates.org.uk; website; www.advocates.org.uk.

NORTHERN IRELAND

As in England and Wales, the superior courts are the Court of Appeal, the High Court and the Crown Court. The latter is an exclusively criminal court. The Court of Appeal hears appeals in civil cases from the High Court and in criminal cases from the Crown Court, and cases stated on a point of law from, inter alia, the County Court and the Magistrates' Courts. Appeals lie from the Court of Appeal to the House of Lords.

Inferior Courts: As in England and Wales, the county courts are principally civil courts, but in Northern Ireland they also hear appeals from conviction in the Magistrates' Courts for summary offences.

Magistrates' Courts: These deal principally with minor criminal offences (summary offences) and are presided over by Resident Magistrates (stipendiaries). Resident Magistrates are appointed by the Crown on the advice of the Lord Chancellor.

Coroners: Coroners in Northern Ireland must be barristers or solicitors who have practised for not less than five years. They are appointed by the Lord Chancellor.

The legal profession

The legal profession in Northern Ireland consists of barristers and solicitors belonging to professional bodies organized on similar lines to those in England and Wales.

Qualification as a barrister in Northern Ireland

To qualify to practise as a barrister in Northern Ireland a candidate must be admitted to the degree of Barrister-at-Law by the Honourable Society of the Inn of Court of Northern Ireland (enquiries to Under Treasurer, Bar Council Office, The Bar Library, 91 Chichester Street, Belfast BT1 3JQ; Tel: Belfast 028 9024 1523; e-mail: chief.executive@barlibrary.com; website; www.barlibrary.com). A candidate must have a recognized law degree of 2.1 honours standard or higher, or equivalent (the list of recognized law degrees can be found at www.qub.ac.uk/schools/InstituteofProfessionalLegalStudies/FileStore/).

To be called to the Bar of Northern Ireland the candidate needs to have obtained his or her Certificate of Professional Legal Studies or otherwise be qualified, to have completed and signed a Memorial and Undertaking, and to have submitted two certificates of good character.

Qualification as a solicitor in Northern Ireland

The solicitors' professional body in Northern Ireland is the Law Society of Northern Ireland (Law Society House, 96 Victoria Street, Belfast BT1 3GN; Tel: 028 9023 1614; website; www.lawsoc-ni.org). It has overall responsibility for education and admission to the profession.

Admission to training is generally dependent upon possession of a recognized law degree from a university. Details of the recognized law degrees are available on the website of the Institute of Professional Legal Studies (www.qub.ac.uk/schools/InstituteofProfessionalLegalStudies/Admissions/RecognisedLawDegrees/). Details are also available on the Graduate School website (see 'Information Booklet for Applicants'; www.socsci.ulster.ac.uk/gsple/info_booklet.pdf). Law graduates must attend a two-year vocational apprenticeship course at the Institute of Professional Legal Studies, The Queen's University of Belfast, or the Graduate School of Professional Legal Education at the University of Ulster's Magee Campus. On completion of the two-year apprenticeship newly qualified solicitors receive restricted practising certificates, which means that although they are fully qualified they cannot practise on their own account or in partnership for at least two more years.

Non-law graduates must satisfy the Society that they possess an acceptable degree in a discipline other than law and have attained a satisfactory level of knowledge of the following subjects: Constitutional Law, Law of Tort, Law of Contract, Criminal Law, Equity, European Law, Land Law, Law of Evidence; that they have been offered a place in the Institute; and that they have obtained a Master (a solicitor with whom the applicant proposes to serve his or her apprenticeship). It is also possible to be accepted as a student of the Law Society if the applicant is 29 years or older and can demonstrate the required experience, knowledge or relevant qualifications (see the Law Society of Northern Ireland website; www.lawsoc-ni.org/joining-the-legal-profession/).

Membership of Professional Institutions and Associations

COUNCIL FOR LICENSED CONVEYANCERS

16 Glebe Road
Chelmsford
Essex CM1 1QG
Tel: 01245 349599
Fax: 01245 341300
E-mail: clc@clc-uk.org
Website: www.clc-uk.org

The CLC was established under the provisions of the Administration of Justice Act 1985 as the Regulatory Body for Licensed Conveyancers. Our purpose is to set entry standards and regulate the profession of Licensed Conveyancers effectively. CLC regulates Probate services provided by its licensed practitioners. CLC is an authorised regulator for ABS.

MEMBERSHIP
Student
Licensed Conveyancer
Probate Practitioner
ABS

QUALIFICATION/EXAMINATIONS
Foundation
Finals
Practical Training

THE LAW SOCIETY OF SCOTLAND

26 Drumsheugh Gardens
Edinburgh EH3 7YR
Tel: 0131 226 7411
Fax: 0131 225 2934
E-mail: lawscot@lawscot.org.uk
Website: www.lawscot.org.uk

The Law Society of Scotland is the membership organization of Scottish solicitors. We promote the interests of the profession and of the public in relation to the profession. Our services include providing initial career advice, overseeing legal education in Scotland, handling admissions to the profession, monitoring trainees, providing post-qualifying legal education, and administering courses and examinations for the Society of Law Accountants in Scotland.

MEMBERSHIP
All practising solicitors in Scotland must be members of the Society and must hold a current Practising Certificate which is issued by the Society.

QUALIFICATION/EXAMINATIONS
Please see the Law Society of Scotland's website.

INSTITUTE OF LEGAL EXECUTIVES

Kempston Manor
Kempston
Bedford MK42 7AB
Tel: 01234 841000
E-mail: info@ilex.org.uk
Website: www.ilex.org.uk

ILEX, founded in 1892, is a professional body representing around 22,000 practising and trainee legal executives (qualified lawyers who specialize in a particular area of law). Our objectives are to provide for the education, training and development of our Fellows, to advance and protect their interests, and to promote cooperation among everyone engaged in legal work.

MEMBERSHIP
Student Member
Affiliate Member
Associate Member (AInstLEX)
Graduate Member (GInstLEX)
Fellow (FInstLEX)

QUALIFICATION/EXAMINATIONS
Level 3 Certificate in Law and Practice
Level 3 Professional Diploma in Law and Practice
Level 6 Certificate in Law
Level 6 Professional Higher Diploma in Law and Practice
Graduate Fast Track Diploma (Level 6)

DESIGNATORY LETTERS
AInstLEX, GInstLEX, FInstLEX

THE ACADEMY OF EXPERTS

3 Gray's Inn Square
Gray's Inn
London WC1R 5AH
Tel: 020 7430 0333
Fax: 020 7430 0666
E-mail: admin@academy-experts.org
Website: www.academy-experts.org

The Academy of Experts is a multidisciplinary body established in 1987 to establish and promote high objective standards for those acting as expert witnesses. We act as an accrediting and professional body, offering training, technical guidance and representation. In addition we promote cost-efficient dispute resolution, maintaining a register of qualified dispute resolvers.

MEMBERSHIP
Non-Practising Subscriber
Associate Member
Associate Member (AMAE)
Full Member (MAE)
Fellow (FAE)
Practising Corporate Member
Dispute Resolver Member

QUALIFICATION/EXAMINATIONS
There are examinations for upgrade.

DESIGNATORY LETTERS
AMAE, MAE, FAE, QDR

THE INSTITUTE OF LEGAL CASHIERS AND ADMINISTRATORS (ILCA)

2nd Floor
Marlowe House
109 Station Road
Sidcup
Kent DA15 7ET
Tel: 020 8302 2867
Fax: 020 8302 7481
E-mail: info@ilca.org.uk
Website: www.ilca.org.uk

The ILCA, which was founded in 1978, is a non-profit-making professional body dedicated to the education and support of specialist financial and administrative personnel working within the legal community. We encourage the development of our members' skills through educational courses, training workshops, seminars, conferences and our bimonthly magazine, *Legal Abacus*.

MEMBERSHIP
Ordinary Member
Diploma Member (ILCA (Dip))
Associate Member (AILCA)
Fellow Member (FILCA)
Affiliated Professional Member

QUALIFICATION/EXAMINATIONS
Diploma
Associateship examination

DESIGNATORY LETTERS
ILCA (Dip), AILCA, FILCA

LEISURE AND RECREATION MANAGEMENT
Membership of Professional Institutions and Associations

INSTITUTE FOR SPORT, PARKS AND LEISURE

Abbey Business Centre
1650 Arlington Business Park
Theale
Reading RG7 4SA
Tel: 0844 418 0077
Fax: 0118 929 8001
E-mail: infocentre@ispal.org.uk
Website: www.ispal.org.uk

ISPAL is the membership body for sport, parks and leisure industry professionals. We promote high standards and provide CPD as well as a wide range of training courses to our members in-house and at venues across the UK. We also work hard to influence government policy on behalf of our members.

MEMBERSHIP
Student
Studying Member
Full Member
Retiree
Local Authority Member
Corporate Member

INSTITUTE OF GROUNDSMANSHIP

28 Stratford Office Village
Walker Avenue
Wolverton Mill East
Milton Keynes MK12 5TW
Tel: 01908 312511
Fax: 01908 311140
E-mail: iog@iog.org
Website: www.iog.org

The Institute of Groundsmanship is the only membership organization supporting the whole of the grounds care industry. Serving the industry for 75 years, we provide a range of quality products, services and events including education, training and membership services, exhibitions, local information days, an annual conference and awards programme.

MEMBERSHIP
Junior Member
Student Member
Amateur Associate
Professional Associate
Full Individual Member
Affiliate Member
Corporate Member

QUALIFICATION/EXAMINATIONS
For details see; www.iog.org/training-training-courses.asp

INSTITUTE OF SPORT AND RECREATION MANAGEMENT (ISRM)

Sir John Beckwith Centre for Sport
Loughborough University
Loughborough
Leicestershire LE11 3TU
Tel: 01509 226474
Fax: 01509 226475
E-mail: info@isrm.co.uk
Website: www.isrm.co.uk

ISRM is the only national professional body for those involved exclusively in providing, managing, operating and developing sport and recreation services in the UK. Our aim is to ensure that the benefits of sport and physical activity are delivered effectively through the professional, safe and efficient management and development of facilities and services.

MEMBERSHIP
Associate Member
Member
Diploma Member
Companion (CInstSRM)
Fellow (FInstSRM/FInstSRM(Hons))
Corporate Affiliate
Further & Higher Education Corporate Affiliate
Commercial Affiliate

QUALIFICATION/EXAMINATIONS
National Pool Plant Operators Foundation Certificate
National Spa Pool Foundation Certificate
National Spa Pool Operators Certificate
National Pool Carers Certificate (Level 2)
Operations Certificate (Level 2)
Events Management Certificate (Level 3)
Fitness Management Certificate (Level 3)
Food and Beverage Management Certificate (Level 3)
Health & Safety Management Certificate (Level 3)
National Pool Plant Operators Certificate (Level 3)
Supervisory Management Certificate (Level 3)
National Pool Lifeguard Qualification (NPLQ)
Pool Technical Management Diploma

DESIGNATORY LETTERS
CInstSRM, FInstSRM, FInstSRM(Hons)

LIBRARIANSHIP AND INFORMATION WORK
Membership of Professional Institutions and Associations

CHARTERED INSTITUTE OF LIBRARY AND INFORMATION PROFESSIONALS

7 Ridgmount Street
London WC1E 7AE
Tel: 020 7255 0500
Fax: 020 7255 0501
E-mail: quals@cilip.org.uk
Website: www.cilip.org.uk

CILIP is the professional body representing those working within libraries and the information profession in the UK.

MEMBERSHIP
Certified Affiliate (ACLIP)
Chartered Member (MCLIP)
Chartered Fellow (FCLIP)
Revalidated Chartered Member or Fellow
Student Membership

QUALIFICATION/EXAMINATIONS
Application for membership qualifications is through the submission of a portfolio of evidence meeting published criteria. Please contact the Institute for further information.

DESIGNATORY LETTERS
ACLIP, MCLIP, FCLIP

MANAGEMENT
Membership of Professional Institutions and Associations

ASSOCIATION FOR PROJECT MANAGEMENT

Ibis House
Regent Park
Summerleys Road
Princes Risborough
Buckinghamshire HP27 9LE
Tel: 0845 458 1944
Fax: 0845 458 8807
E-mail: info@apm.org.uk
Website: www.apm.org.uk

The association is a registered charity with over 19,500 individual and 500 corporate members making it the largest professional body of its kind in Europe. APM's mission statement is 'to develop and promote the professional disciplines of project and programme management for the public benefit'.

MEMBERSHIP
Student Member
Associate Member
Full Member (MAPM)
Fellow (FAPM)
Corporate Member
Honorary member/ Fellow (HonFAPM)

QUALIFICATION/EXAMINATIONS
Introductory Certificate in Project Management (IC)
APMP
APMP for PRINCE2 Practitioners
Practitioner Qualification (PQ)
Risk level 1
Risk level 2
Pan sector standard:
Registered Project Professional (RPP)

Higher Apprenticeship:
Higher Apprenticeship in Project Management

DESIGNATORY LETTERS
MAPM, FAPM, HonFAPM, RPP

ASSOCIATION OF CERTIFIED COMMERCIAL DIPLOMATS (ACCD)

Commercial Diplomats Regulation Authority
ACCD Global Headquarters
Central Administration Office
PO Box 50561, Canary Wharf,
London E16 3WY
Tel: +44(0)8445 864249
Fax: +44(0)8445 864252
E-mail: enquiries@commercialdiplomats.eu or enquiries@chartereddiplomats.org.uk
Website: www.commercialdiplomats.org.uk

Association of Certified Commercial Diplomats is the first independent regulation authority, and global professional awarding body for commercial diplomats. The umbrella of ACCD covers ambassadors, representatives of government, trade commissioners, advisors and negotiators, arbitrators, negotiators of IIAs, policy-makers & government officials involved in trade, commercial and or investment issues, commercial counsellors, IIA experts, academia, private sector & NGO representatives, officials in government ministries, parastatals, corporations, academic, public and private institutions worldwide. Its principal objectives are to provide accreditation and regulation, and to advance the interests of its members as qualified, certified and competent commercial diplomats. As the global voice, ACCD has overall responsibility, including the setting of policy and guidelines, as well as the qualification and accreditation procedures for the commercial diplomatic profession. ACCD is non-partisan, not-for-profit, independent of government, and uniquely the professional regulatory body for commercial diplomats, and institutions of higher learning providing advanced postgraduate, doctoral, and postdoctoral programmes on commercial diplomacy.

MEMBERSHIP
AFFILIATED PROFESSIONAL MEMBERSHIP:
Affiliated Professional Associate
Affiliated Professional Fellow
FULL MEMBERSHIP:
Associate
Member
Fellow

QUALIFICATION/EXAMINATIONS
ACCD REGULATED QUALIFICATIONS/EXAMINATIONS/ACCREDITATIONS:
Qualified Policy Advocate (QA)
Qualified Certified Diplomat (QCD)
Chartered Diplomat (C. Dipl)

DESIGNATORY LETTERS
ACDipl, MCD, DCD, FCDipl, QA, QPA, QCD, C. Dipl

AUA

AUA National Office
University of Manchester
Oxford Road
Manchester M13 9PL
Tel: 0161 275 2063
Fax: 0161 275 2036
E-mail: aua@aua.ac.uk
Website: www.aua.ac.uk

As a member-led organization with over 4,000 members, AUA promotes best practice in higher education management and exists to advance and promote professional recognition and development of those who work in higher and further education by encouraging and fostering sound methods of leadership, management and administration, through a range of professional development initiatives.

AUA members are individually and collectively committed to:
- the continuous development of their own and others' professional knowledge, skills and practices
- actively championing equality of educational and professional opportunity
- the advancement of higher education through the robust application of professional knowledge, skills and practices
- the highest standards of fair, ethical and transparent professional behaviours

AUA is at the forefront of professional development in higher education and has developed a sector-wide framework to support the development of professional services colleagues. Through continuing professional development, individuals, teams and institutions can foster skills and behaviours associated with the profession. AUA also holds the largest professional development annual conference in the UK higher education calendar.

MEMBERSHIP
Member (MAUA)
Associate Member (AUA (A))
International Associate Member (AUA (A))
Fellow (FAUA)

QUALIFICATION/EXAMINATIONS
Postgraduate Certificate in Professional Practice (PG Cert)
This programme is validated by The Open University and credits from the course can be used on a number of MA courses.

BRITISH INSTITUTE OF FACILITIES MANAGEMENT

Number One Building
The Causeway
Bishop's Stortford
Hertfordshire CM23 2ER
Tel: 0845 058 1356
Fax: 01279 712669
E-mail: info@bifm.org.uk
Website: www.bifm.org.uk

The BIFM is the 'natural home' of facilities management (FM) in the UK. Founded in 1993, the Institute provides information, education, training and networking services for nearly 13,000 members – both individual professionals and organizations. The BIFM's mission is to advance the profession – to consolidate FM as a vital management discipline.

MEMBERSHIP
Affiliate
Associate (ABIFM)
Member (MBIFM)
Certified Member (CBIFM)
Fellow (FBIFM)
Corporate Member

Management

QUALIFICATION/EXAMINATIONS
BIFM Level 4 Award in Facilities Mangement
BIFM Level 4 Certificate in Facilities Management
BIFM Level 4 Diploma in Facilities Management
BIFM Level 5 Award in Facilities Management
BIFM Level 5 Certificate in Facilities Management
BIFM Level 5 Diploma in Facilities Management
BIFM Level 6 Award in Facilities Management
BIFM Level 6 Certificate in Facilities Management
BIFM Level 6 Diploma in Facilities Management

DESIGNATORY LETTERS
ABIFM, MBIFM, CBIFM, FBIFM

BUSINESS MANAGEMENT ASSOCIATION

1 High Oak House
Collett Road
Ware
Hertfordshire SG12 7LY
Tel: 01920 898156
Fax: 01920 823261
E-mail: enquiries@businessmanagement.org.uk
Website: www.businessmanagement.org.uk

The Business Management Association is a professional body for business owners and managers. We promote the aims and interests of the small business sector internationally, provide information and advice to our members, encourage networking between members, and seek to provide members with advanced knowledge, skill and qualifications in several aspects of management.

MEMBERSHIP
Affiliate (AffBMA)
Associate (ABMA)
Member (MBMA)
Fellow (FBMA)
Companion (CBMA)
Certified Manager (CertMgr)
Certified Master of Management (CMMgt)
Certified Master of Business Administration (CMBA)
Certified Doctor of Business Administration (CDBA)
Member Certified Business Management Accountant (MCBMA)
Fellow Certified Business Management Accountant (FCBMA)

QUALIFICATION/EXAMINATIONS
Entrepreneurs Award (EA)
Diploma In Business Management (DipBMA)

DESIGNATORY LETTERS
AffBMA, ABMA, MBMA, FBMA, CBMA, CertMgr, CMMgt, CMBA, CDBA, MCBMA, FCBMA

DIPLOMATIC ACADEMY OF EUROPE AND THE ATLANTIC

A Global Force for Regional Prosperity
ACCD Global Headquarters
PO Box 50561, Canary Wharf
Greater London E16 3WY
Tel: 08445 857027
Fax: 08445 857077
E-mail: enquiries@eatcd.org
Website: www.eatcd.org

Diplomatic Academy of Europe is an authoritative knowledge-based professional diplomatic institution whose activities include advanced research and development, provision of postgraduate and post-qualification education, and contribution to responsible commercial diplomatic practice. A key independent extraterritorial diplomatic organization established for the advancement and development of greater knowledge and skills in commercial diplomacy. The Academy offers complete portfolio of specialized mandatory post-graduate programme on commercial diplomatic practice.

MEMBERSHIP
Fellow of the Diplomatic Academy (FDAe)

QUALIFICATION/EXAMINATIONS
EXAMINATIONS:

Master of Commercial Diplomacy
Doctor of Commercial Diplomacy
Fellowship of the Diplomatic Academy
Qualified Certified Diplomat (QCD)
PostQualification Fellowship

DESIGNATORY LETTERS
MCD, DCD, FDAe

FACULTY OF PROFESSIONAL BUSINESS AND TECHNICAL MANAGEMENT

Head Office
Warwick Corner
42 Warwick Road
Kenilworth
Warwickshire CV8 1HE
Tel: 01926 259342
E-mail: info@pbtm.org.uk
Website: www.pbtm.org.uk

PBTM was founded in 1983 to forge the link between business and technology. We give professional recognition to the knowledge and skills of managers in business and technology, supporting lifelong learning to help members fulfil their career ambitions and develop their potential.

MEMBERSHIP
Student Member (SFPBTM)
Associate Member (AMFPBTM)
Member (MFPBTM)
Fellow (FFPBTM)
Companion (CFPBTM)

INSTITUTE OF ADMINISTRATIVE MANAGEMENT

6 Graphite Square
Vauxhall Walk
London SE11 5EE
Tel: 020 7091 9620
Fax: 020 7091 7340
E-mail: info@instam.org
Website: www.instam.org

The IAM is the leading professional body and UK government-recognized awarding body for those involved in the administration and management of business. We offer a range of qualifications, from an introduction to the subject up to a full BA Hons degree.

MEMBERSHIP
Student Member
Associate (AInstAM)
Member (MInstAM)
Fellow (FInstAM)

QUALIFICATION/EXAMINATIONS
Introductory Award in Administrative Management (Level 2)
Certificate in Administrative Management (Level 3)
Diploma in Administrative Management (Level 4)
Advanced Diploma in Administrative Management (Level 5)
BA Hons degree in Business Management, from The Open University, Sheffield Hallam University or The University of Teeside

Management

DESIGNATORY LETTERS
AInstAM, MInstAM, FInstAM

INSTITUTE OF BUSINESS CONSULTING

4th Floor
2 Savoy Court
Strand
London WC2R 0EZ
Tel: 020 7497 0580
Fax: 020 7497 0463
E-mail: ibc@ibconsulting.org.uk
Website: www.ibconsulting.org.uk

The Institute of Business Consulting was formed in 2007 by the merger of the Institute of Business Advisers and the Institute of Management Consultancy, and we are the professional body for business consultants and advisers. Our aim is to raise the standards of professional practice in support of better business performance.

MEMBERSHIP
Student
Affiliate
Associate (AIBC)
Member (MIBC)
Fellow (FIBC)
Certified Business Advisor (CBA)
Certified Management Consultant (CMC)
Practice Member (corporate membership)

QUALIFICATION/EXAMINATIONS
Certificate in Business Support
Certificate in Management Consulting Essentials
Diploma in Business Support
Diploma in Management Consultancy (in conjunction with the Chartered Management Institute)

DESIGNATORY LETTERS
AIBC, MIBC, FIBC

INSTITUTE OF DIRECTORS

116 Pall Mall
London SW1Y 5ED
Tel: 020 7766 2601
Fax: 020 7766 2606
E-mail: professionaldev@iod.com
Website: www.iod.com/development

The IoD represents professional leaders, with individual members ranging from entrepreneurs of start-up companies to CEOs of multinational organizations. The Institute's principal objectives are to advance the interests of its members as company directors, and to provide them with business facilities and a variety of services.

MEMBERSHIP
Associate Member
Member (MIoD)
Fellow (FIoD)
Chartered Director (C Dir)

QUALIFICATION/EXAMINATIONS
Certificate in Company Direction (CertIoD)
Diploma in Company Direction (DipIoD)
Chartered Director (C Dir)

DESIGNATORY LETTERS
MIoD, FIoD, C Dir

INSTITUTE OF LEADERSHIP & MANAGEMENT

Stowe House
Netherstowe
Lichfield
Staffordshire WS13 6TJ
Tel: 01543 266867
Fax: 01543 266893
E-mail: customer@i-l-m.com
Website: www.i-l-m.com

The ILM supports, develops and informs leaders and managers at every stage of their career. With our broad range of industry-leading qualifications, membership services and learning resources, the ILM provides flexible development solutions that can be blended to meet the specific needs of employers and learners.

MEMBERSHIP
Studying Member
Professional Member

QUALIFICATION/EXAMINATIONS
Management
Award in Effective Team Skills (Level 2)
Award and Certificate in Team Leading (Level 2)
Award, Certificate and Diploma in First Line Management (Level 3)
Award, Certificate and Diploma in Management (Level 4)
Award, Certificate and Diploma in Management (Level 5)
Award in Management (Level 6)
Award, Certificate and Diploma in Executive Management (Level 7)
Leadership
Award and Certificate in Leadership (Level 3)
Award in Leadership (Level 4)
Award and Certificate in Leadership (Level 5)
Award, Certificate and Diploma in Strategic Leadership (Level 7)
Leadership and management
Award, Certificate and Diploma in Leadership and Management (Level 3)
Award, Certificate and Diploma in Leadership and Management (Level 5)
Award, Certificate and Diploma in Strategic Leadership and Executive Management (Level 7)
Coaching and mentoring
Award and Certificate in Workplace Coaching for Team Leaders and First Line Managers (Level 3)
Certificate in Workplace Coaching and Mentoring (Level 3)
Certificate in Coaching and Mentoring in Management (Level 5)
Diploma for Professional Management Coaches and Mentors (Level 5)
Certificate in Executive Coaching and Leadership Mentoring (Level 7)
Diploma for Professional Executive Coaches and Leadership Mentors (Level 7)
Specialist management qualifications
Environmental Management
Facilities Management
Managing Equality and Diversity
Managing Volunteers
Sales Management
Site Waste Management

INSTITUTE OF MANAGEMENT SERVICES

Brooke House
Lichfield
Staffordshire WS13 6AA
Tel: 01543 266909
Fax: 01543 257848
E-mail: admin@ims-stowe.fsnet.co.uk
Website: www.ims-productivity.com

The IMS is the primary body in the UK concerned with the promotion, practice and development of methods and techniques for the improvement of productivity and quality. We act as the qualifying body for the management services profession in the UK, focusing developments in practice and knowledge and acting as a forum for information exchange.

MEMBERSHIP
Affiliate
Associate (AMS)
Member (MMS)
Fellow (FMS)

QUALIFICATION/EXAMINATIONS
Management Services Certificate
Management Services Diploma

DESIGNATORY LETTERS
AMS, MMS, FMS

INSTITUTE OF VALUE MANAGEMENT

Westminster
London SW1H 9JJ
Tel: 08709 020905
E-mail: secretary@irm.org.uk
Website: www.ivm.org.uk

The Institute aims to establish Value Management as a process for achieving value in every sector of the economy and to provide support in the innovative use of value management techniques.

MEMBERSHIP
Corporate Membership: Open to any company or organization practising or promoting value techniques. Each corporate member may nominate up to 10 members of their organization as representatives to the Institute. A member nominated by a corporate body can hold executive office and has full voting rights.
Ordinary Membership: Open to any professional person who has an interest in and can demonstrate an involvement in practising value techniques.
Student Membership: Open to students who have an interest in value management and who are registered FT students possessing a valid student card.
Fellow: Awarded to a member as a special honour for outstanding contribution to the field of value management.

QUALIFICATION/EXAMINATIONS
Certificate and Training: The Institute has worked closely with the Commission of the European Communities to establish a European Training System and Certification Procedure.
Roll of Practitioners: The Institute maintains an authorized list of value practitioners who are members of the Institute.
It launched its European Training and Certification System in 1998. This European Commission funded initiative offers, through the IVM's Certification Board, certification in the following categories: Certificated Value Analyst (CVA); Professional in Value Management (PVM); Certificated Value Manager (CVM); Trainer in Value Management (TVM). The Certification Board also approves basic and advanced courses in value management that have been designed by trainers in value management. The Institute provides a list of trainers.

INTERNATIONAL PROFESSIONAL MANAGERS ASSOCIATION

5 Starnes Court
Union Street
Maidstone
Kent ME14 1EB
Tel: 01622 672867
Fax: 01622 755149
E-mail: admin@ipma.co.uk
Website: www.ipma.co.uk

The IPMA is an international examining, licensing and regulatory professional body, which, through its qualifying examinations, enables practising managers to participate in and be part of the process of improving managerial performance and effectiveness in all areas of business, industry and public administration.

MEMBERSHIP
Student member
Graduate Member (GRD PMA)
Licentiate Member (LMPMA)
Certified Associate (AMPMA)
Certified Member (MPMA)
Certified Fellow (FPMA)
Honorary Member (MPMA)
Honorary Fellow (FPMA)

QUALIFICATION/EXAMINATIONS
Certified International Professional Manager (CIPM) examinations

DESIGNATORY LETTERS
GRD PMA, LMPMA, AMPMA, MPMA, FPMA, CIPM

THE ASSOCIATION OF BUSINESS EXECUTIVES

5th Floor, CI Tower
St Georges Square
New Malden
Surrey KT3 4TE
Tel: 020 8329 2930
Fax: 020 8329 2945
E-mail: info@abeuk.com
Website: www.abeuk.com

ABE is a professional membership body and examination board. We develop business and management qualifications at Levels 4, 5, 6 & 7 on the QCF framework. ABE's range of OFQUAL accredited qualifications provide progression routes to degree and Master's programmes worldwide.

MEMBERSHIP
Student Member
Associate Member (AMABE)
Member (MABE)
Fellow (FABE)

QUALIFICATION/EXAMINATIONS
Diploma Levels 4, 5 and 6 in:
Business Management
Management of Information Systems (Pathway)
Financial Management (Pathway)
Human Resource Management
Marketing Management
Travel, Tourism and Hospitality Management
and Postgraduate Diploma (Level 7) in Business Management

DESIGNATORY LETTERS
AMABE, MABE, FABE

THE CAMBRIDGE ACADEMY OF MANAGEMENT

Wellington House
Cambridge CB1 1BH
E-mail: info@cambridge-uk.org
Website: www.businessmanagement.org.uk

The Cambridge Academy of Management (CAM) is a professional, autonomous, not-for-profit institution established to foster the concept of UK management education made available to all internationally. CAM is built on the foundation of promoting state-of-the-art knowledge and expertise in all facets of management education, training and development for the global educational arena.

MEMBERSHIP
Associate Category (ACAM)
Member Category (MCAM)
Fellowship Category (FCAM)

QUALIFICATION/EXAMINATIONS
All programmes offered by Cambridge Academy of Management are accredited by Quality Assurance Commission UK. Programmes offered:
CAM International Foundation Diploma
CAM International Certificate in Restaurant & Catering Management
CAM International Diploma in Business Management
CAM International Diploma in Business (Restaurant & Catering Management)
CAM International Diploma in Business (Tourism Management)
CAM International Advanced Diploma in Business Management
CAM International Advanced Diploma in Business (Restaurant & Catering Management)
CAM International Advanced Diploma in Business (Tourism Management)
CAM International Postgraduate Diploma in Hospitality Management
CAM International Postgraduate Diploma in Business
CAM International Postgraduate Diploma in Business with Specialization in: Marketing, Finance, Human Resource

THE CHARTERED MANAGEMENT INSTITUTE

Membership Department
Management House
Cottingham Road
Corby
Northants NN17 1TT
Tel: 01536 207307
Fax: 01536 400388
E-mail: membership@managers.org.uk
Website: www.managers.org.uk

The CMI is the only chartered professional body dedicated to managers and leaders, and to the organizations they work in. As founders of the National Occupational Standards for Management and Leadership excellence, we set the standards that others follow. As a membership organization we give our members the tools they need to make a genuine impact on business in the UK.

MEMBERSHIP
Associate (ACMI)
Member (MCMI)
Fellow (FCMI)
Chartered Manager (CMgr)

DESIGNATORY LETTERS
ACMI, MCMI, FCMI, CMgr

THE INSTITUTE OF COMMERCIAL MANAGEMENT

ICM House
Castleman Way
Ringwood
Hampshire BH24 3BA
Tel: 01202 490555
Fax: 01202 490666
E-mail: info@icm.ac.uk
Website: www.icm.ac.uk

The Institute is the leading professional body for Commercial and Business Development Managers. It is fully accredited by Ofqual, the Regulator of UK Qualifications. ICM provides Examining and assessment services for those undertaking business and management studies and offers in excess of 200 programmes. ICM is authorized to offer awards from HNDs to doctorates and works with public and private sector education and training providers in more than 100 countries.

MEMBERSHIP
Student Membership

QUALIFICATION/EXAMINATIONS
ICM Awards cover the following areas: Accounting & Finance; Business Studies; Commercial Management; Hospitality Management; Human Resource Development; Journalism; Legal Studies; Management Studies; Maritime Management; Marketing Management; Sales Management; Travel & Tourism.

THE INSTITUTE OF MANAGEMENT SPECIALISTS

Head Office
Warwick Corner
42 Warwick Road
Kenilworth
Warwickshire CV8 1HE
Tel: 01926 259342
E-mail: info@instituteofmanagementspecialists.org.uk
Website: www.instituteofmanagementspecialists.org.uk

The Institute of Management Specialists was founded in 1971 to give professional recognition to the knowledge and skills of managers and specialists. The Institute encourages management excellence and specialist expertise, and supports lifelong learning to help members fulfil their career ambitions.

MEMBERSHIP
Student Member (StudIMS)

Associate Member (AMIMS)
Member (MIMS)
Fellow (FIMS)
Companion (CompIMS)

QUALIFICATION/EXAMINATIONS
Diploma in Management

THE SOCIETY OF BUSINESS PRACTITIONERS

PO Box 11
Sandbach
Cheshire CW11 3GE
Tel: 01270 526339
Fax: 01270 526339
E-mail: info@mamsasbp.org.uk
Website: www.mamsasbp.org.uk

The SBP is an international organization formed by experienced educationalists and executives to fulfil a need to set standards in business practice to be achieved by examinations/assessments. Both inexperienced and mature students should be able to follow careers in further education and/or be proficient in employment and receive the benefits of membership.

MEMBERSHIP
Student (StuSBP)
Member (MSBP)
Certified Professional Manager (CPMSBP)
Professional Memberships *(Senior Professional Qualifications)*
Associateship (ASBP)
Licentiateship (LSBP)
Graduateship (GSBP)
Fellowship (FSBP)
These are certified competency-based Membership Awards open to persons occupied in business practice who are considered suitable by the Membership Committee.
CPD programmes are also offered for the Asia region.

QUALIFICATION/EXAMINATIONS
Diploma in Business Administration
Advanced Diploma in Business Administration
PGDip in Business Administration
PGDip in International Marketing
Diploma in Computer Studies
Advanced Diploma in Computer Studies
GradDip in IT & E-Commerce
GradDip in Entrepreneurship
Advanced Diploma in Accounting
Diploma & Advanced Diploma in Marketing Management (Joint Award with the Managing & Marketing Sales Association)

DESIGNATORY LETTERS
StuSBP, MSBP, CPMSBP, ASBP, LSBP, GSBP, FSBP

MANUFACTURING
Membership of Professional Institutions and Associations

THE INSTITUTE OF MANUFACTURING

Head Office
Warwick Corner
42 Warwick Road
Kenilworth
Warwickshire CV8 1HE
Tel: 01926 259342
E-mail: info@instituteofmanufacturing.org.uk
Website: www.instituteofmanufacturing.org.uk

The Institute of Manufacturing was founded in 1978 to give professional recognition to the knowledge and skills of people in all aspects of manufacturing. The Institute supports lifelong learning to help members fulfil their career ambitions and develop their potential.

MEMBERSHIP
Student Member (StudIManf)

Associate Member (AMIManf)
Member (MIManf)
Fellow (FIManf)
Companion (CompIManf)

MARKETING AND SALES
Membership of Professional Institutions and Associations

LONDON CENTRE OF MARKETING

Buckingham House East
Stanmore
London HA7 4EB
Tel: 020 8385 7766
Fax: 020 8385 7755
E-mail: info@lcmuk.com
Website: www.lcmuk.com

The London Centre of Marketing is an accredited, non-political, non-profit-making institution based in London, which exists with the sole aim of providing internationally recognized professional qualifications in marketing and marketing management.

QUALIFICATION/EXAMINATIONS
Diploma, Higher Diploma, Professional Diploma, Graduate Diploma and Postgraduate Dipolma in:

Business Management & Marketing
Human Resource Development & Marketing
Sales & Marketing Management
Travel & Tourism Marketing
Public Relations & Marketing
Entrepreneurship & Marketing

MANAGING AND MARKETING SALES ASSOCIATION EXAMINATION BOARD

PO Box 11
Sandbach
Cheshire CW11 3GE
Tel: 01270 526339
Fax: 01270 526339
E-mail: info@mamsasbp.org.uk
Website: www.mamsasbp.org.uk

MAMSA is an international organization offering qualifications in Sales, Marketing and Management and its senior specialist Stategic Marketing Diploma. The importance of 'Customer Service' is emphasized throughout all the programmes.

MEMBERSHIP
Graduate (GradMAMSA)
Graduate Affliliate (GradAfMAMSA)
Professional (MMAMSA)
Fellow (FMAMSA)

QUALIFICATION/EXAMINATIONS
Standard Diploma in Salesmanship

Certificate in Sales Marketing
Higher Diploma in Marketing
Advanced Diploma in Sales Management
Certificate in Marketing Strategy
Diploma in Marketing Strategy & Management (Hypothesis/Thesis)
Diploma in Sales and Marketing Practices (Joint Award with the Society of Business Practitioners)
A CPD programme is also offered.

DESIGNATORY LETTERS
GradMAMSA, GradAfMAMSA, MMAMSA, FMAMSA

MRS (THE MARKET RESEARCH SOCIETY)

The Old Trading House
15 Northburgh Street
London EC1V 0JR
Tel: 020 7490 4911
Fax: 020 7490 0608
E-mail: profdevelopment@mrs.org.uk
Website: www.mrs.org.uk

With members in more than 60 countries, MRS is the world's largest association serving those with professional equity in the provision or use of market, social and opinion research. We offer various qualifications and membership grades, and are an awarding body for vocationally related qualifications in market and social research.

MEMBERSHIP
Student Member
Affiliate Member
Associate Member (AMRS)
Full Member (MMRS)
Fellow (FMRS)
Honorary Member (Hon. MMRS)
Honorary Fellow (Hon. FMRS)

QUALIFICATION/EXAMINATIONS
MRS Certificate in Market and Social Reseach
MRS Certificate in Interviewing Skills for Market and Social Research
MRS Advanced Certificate in Market and Social Research Practice
MRS Diploma in Market and Social Research Practice

DESIGNATORY LETTERS
AMRS, MMRS, FMRS, Hon. MMRS, Hon. FMRS

THE CHARTERED INSTITUTE OF MARKETING

Moor Hall
Maidenhead
Berkshire SL6 9QH
Tel: 01628 427120
Fax: 01628 427158
E-mail: qualifications@cim.co.uk
Website: www.cim.co.uk/learningzone

The Chartered Institute of Marketing is the leading international professional marketing body, with 47,000 members worldwide. We aim to improve the skills of marketing practitioners, enabling them to deliver exceptional results for their organization. Qualifications from Introductory to Chartered postgraduate level are offered to anyone wanting to develop their career in marketing.

MEMBERSHIP
Affiliate (Studying/Professional)
Associate (ACIM)
Member (MCIM)
Fellow (FCIM)
Chartered Marketer

QUALIFICATION/EXAMINATIONS
Introductory Certificate in Marketing
Professional Certificate in Marketing
Professional Diploma in Marketing
Chartered Postgraduate Diploma in Marketing
Diploma in Marketing Communications
Diploma in Managing Digital Media
Diploma in Digital Marketing
Diploma in Hospitality and Tourism Marketing

DESIGNATORY LETTERS
ACIM, MCIM, FCIM

THE INSTITUTE OF DIRECT MARKETING

1 Park Road
Teddington
Middlesex TW11 0AR
Tel: 020 8977 5705
Fax: 020 8943 2535
E-mail: enquiries@theidm.com
Website: www.theidm.com

The IDM is Europe's leading professional development body for direct, data and digital marketing. Founded in 1987, we are an educational trust and registered charity. We advocate lifelong learning and maintain an up-to-date education portfolio designed to meet the needs of marketing practitioners throughout their career.

MEMBERSHIP
Affiliate Member
Associate Member
Member
Fellow
Corporate Member

QUALIFICATION/EXAMINATIONS
Certificate in B2B Marketing (Cert BusM)
Certificate in Digital Marketing (Cert DigM)
Certificate in Direct and Interactive Marketing (Cert IDM)
Diploma in B2B Marketing (Dip BusM)
Diploma in Digital Marketing (Dip DigM)
Diploma in Direct and Interactive Marketing (Dip IDM)
Diploma in Integrated Marketing Communications (Dip IMC)

THE INSTITUTE OF SALES AND MARKETING MANAGEMENT

Harrier Court
Woodside Road
Lower Woodside
Bedfordshire LU1 4DQ
Tel: 01582 843260
Fax: 01582 849142
E-mail: education@ismm.co.uk
Website: www.ismm.co.uk

The ISMM offers professional qualifications in sales and marketing. The qualifications are accredited by the Qualification and Curriculum Authority, the body set up by the government to regulate qualifications. The programmes are available through ISMM-accredited centres.

MEMBERSHIP
Student
Associate (AInstSMM)
Member
Fellow

QUALIFICATION/EXAMINATIONS
Award in Basic Sales Skills (Level 1)
Award and Certificate in Sales and Marketing (Level 2)
Award, Certificate and Diploma in Advanced Sales and Marketing (Level 3)
Award, Certificate and Diploma in Operational Sales and Marketing (Level 4)
Award, Certificate and Diploma in Account Management/Sales Management (Level 5)
Diploma in Sales and Account Management (Level 5)
Executive Award, Executive Certificate and Executive Diploma in Strategic Sales and Account Management (Level 6)

DESIGNATORY LETTERS
AInstSMM, MInstSMM, FInstSMM

THE SOCIETY OF SALES & MARKETING

40 Archdale Road
East Dulwich
London SE22 9HJ
Tel: 0845 643 6832
Fax: 0845 643 6834
E-mail: info@ssm.org.uk
Website: www.ssm.org.uk

The Society is the only professional examining body that awards Certificates and Diplomas in all the four areas of selling, namely selling and sales management, marketing, retail management, and international trade and services. The Society celebrated its Silver Jubilee in style in 2005 at Imperial College London.

MEMBERSHIP
Graduate (GSSM)
Associate (ASSM)
Fellow (FSSM)

QUALIFICATION/EXAMINATIONS
Candidates for the Certificate, Advanced Certificate or Diploma choose any one of the following: (A) Selling & Sales Management, (B) Marketing, (C) Retail Management and (D) International Trade & Services.

(A) Selling & Sales Management subjects:
Certificate: (1) Business Communication, (2) Book-keeping & Accounts, (3) Selling & Sales Management, (4) Fundamentals of Marketing
Advanced Certificate: (5) Marketing Research Management, (6) Consumer Behaviour, (7) Principles of Selling, (8) Consumer Law
Diploma: (9) Management Information Systems, (10) Consumerism, Ethics & Social Responsibility, (11) Marketing Planning & Control, (12) Marketing Communication

(B) Marketing subjects:
Certificate: (1) Business Communication, (2) Book-keeping & Accounts, (3) Selling & Sales Management, (4) Fundamentals of Marketing
Advanced Certificate: (5) Marketing Research Management, (6) Consumer Behaviour, (7) Principles of Selling, (8) Consumer Law
Diploma: (9) Management Information Systems, (10) Consumerism, Ethics & Social Responsibility, (11) Marketing Planning & Control, (12) Marketing Communication

(C) Retail Management subjects:
Certificate: (1) Business Communication, (2) Book-keeping & Accounts, (3) Selling & Sales Management, (4) Retail Management
Advanced Certificate: (5) Marketing Research Management, (6) Consumer Behaviour, (7) Principles of Selling, (8) Consumer Law
Diploma: (9) Management Information Systems, (10) Consumerism, Ethics & Social Responsibility, (11) Fundamentals of Marketing, (12) Marketing Communication

(D) International Trade & Services:
Certificate: (1) Business Communication, (2) Book-keeping & Accounts, (3) International Trade & Services, (4) Fundamentals of Marketing
Advanced Certificate: (5) Marketing Research Management, (6) Import & Export Management, (7) Finance for Export, (8) Consumer Law
Diploma: (9) Management Information Systems, (10) Consumerism, Ethics & Social Responsibility, (11) Marketing Planning & Control, (12) Marketing Communication

DESIGNATORY LETTERS
GSSM, ASSM, FSSM

MARTIAL ARTS
Membership of Professional Institutions and Associations

INSTITUTE OF MARTIAL ARTS AND SCIENCES

1 Henrietta Street
Bolton
Lancashire BL3 4HL
Tel: 01942 212378
Fax: 01942 211650
E-mail: admin@institute-of-martialarts-and-sciences.com
Website: www.institute-of-martialarts-and-sciences.com

The IMAS was formed by a group of high-ranking martial arts instructors, educators, researchers and academics to encourage education and research in martial arts, promote professionalism among martial arts instructors, afford martial artists the opportunity of obtaining recognized and accredited qualifications, and to act as a platform to encourage academic debate.

MEMBERSHIP
Associate (AIMAS)
Member (MIMAS)
Fellow (FIMAS)

QUALIFICATION/EXAMINATIONS
Bachelors, Masters and Doctoral in Martial Arts and Sciences

DESIGNATORY LETTERS
Grad.IMAS, MSc, PhD

MASSAGE AND ALLIED THERAPIES
Membership of Professional Institutions and Associations

BRITISH MEDICAL ACUPUNCTURE SOCIETY

BMAS House
3 Winnington Court
Winnington Street
Northwich
Cheshire CW8 1AQ
Tel: 01606 786782
Fax: 01606 786783
E-mail: admin@medical-acupuncture.co.uk
Website: www.medical-acupuncture.co.uk

The BMAS was formed in 1980 as an association of medical practitioners interested in acupuncture and we now have a membership of more than 2,500 registered doctors and allied health professionals who practise acupuncture alongside more conventional techniques. We believe that acupuncture has an important role to play in healthcare and promote its use as a therapy following orthodox medical diagnosis by suitably trained practitioners. We run training programmes in the UK for doctors, dentists and other healthcare professionals.

MEMBERSHIP
Member
Accredited Member
Dental/Veterinary Member
Retired Member
Honorary Member
Overseas Member

QUALIFICATION/EXAMINATIONS
Certificate of Basic Competence (CoBC)
Diploma of Medical Acupuncture (DipMedAc)
University of Hertfordshire MSc in Western Medical Acupuncture

LCSP REGISTER OF REMEDIAL MASSEURS AND MANIPULATIVE THERAPISTS

38A High Street
Lowestoft
Suffolk NR32 1HY
Tel: 01502 563344
Fax: 01502 582220
E-mail: lcsp@btconnect.com
Website: www.lcsp.uk.com

The Register accepts practitioners who currently work in Massage, Remedial Massage or Manipulative Therapy. Applicants must have completed a course of education at an establishment whose training meets or exceeds the National Occupational Standards. The Register offers heavily discounted comprehensive medical malpractice insurance, business support, regular communications and CPD opportunities.

MEMBERSHIP
Student Member
Associate Member (LCSP (Assoc))
Full Member (LCSP (Phys))
Affiliate
Fellow (FLCSP)
Honorary Member

DESIGNATORY LETTERS
LCSP (Assoc), LCSP (Phys), FLCSP

NORTHERN INSTITUTE OF MASSAGE LTD

14–16 St Mary's Place
Bury
Greater Manchester BL9 0DZ
Tel: 0161 797 1800
E-mail: information@nim.co.uk
Website: www.nim.co.uk

The NIM was founded in 1924 and offers professional training in Remedial Massage, Advanced Remedial Massage, and Manipulative Therapy. We also offer a number of CPD seminars and short courses to supplement our main training programme. Research is carried out mostly by therapists on patients from their own clinics or by students completing university courses.

QUALIFICATION/EXAMINATIONS
Diploma in Remedial Massage
Advanced Remedial Massage Diploma
Manipulative Therapy Diploma

SOCIETY OF HOMEOPATHS

11 Brookfield Duncan Close
Moulton Park
Northampton NN3 6WL
Tel: 01604 817890
Fax: 01604 648848
E-mail: info@homeopathy-soh.org
Website: www.homeopathy-soh.org

The Society of Homeopaths was established in 1978 and is now the largest organization registering professional homeopaths in Europe. Our vision is 'homeopathy for all' and we aim to achieve this both by supporting our members and by raising the profile of homeopathy in general.

MEMBERSHIP
Subscriber
Student Member
Student Clinical Member
Registered Member (RSHom)

DESIGNATORY LETTERS
RSHom

MATHEMATICS
Membership of Professional Institutions and Associations

EDINBURGH MATHEMATICAL SOCIETY

School of Mathematics, Edinburgh University
James Clerk Maxwell Building
Mayfield Road
Edinburgh EH9 3JZ
Tel: 01316 505040
Fax: 01316 506553
E-mail: edmathsoc@maths.ed.ac.uk
Website: www.maths.ed.ac.uk

The EMS, founded in 1883, is the principal mathematical society for the academic community in Scotland as well as mathematicians in industry and commerce. We organize meetings, publish a journal and support mathematical activities through various funds.

MEMBERSHIP
Ordinary Member
Reciprocal Member
Honorary Member

THE INSTITUTE OF MATHEMATICS AND ITS APPLICATIONS

Catherine Richards House
16 Nelson Street
Southend-on-Sea
Essex SS1 1EF
Tel: 01702 354020
Fax: 01702 354111
E-mail: post@ima.org.uk
Website: www.ima.org.uk

The IMA, founded in 1964, is the UK's learned society for mathematics and its applications. We promote mathematical research, education and careers, and the use of mathematics in business, industry and commerce. In 1990 the Institute was incorporated by Royal Charter and subsequently granted the right to award the status of Chartered Mathematician, Chartered Scientist and Chartered Mathematics Teacher.

MEMBERSHIP
Student
Affiliate
Associate Member (AMIMA)
Member (MIMA)
Fellow (FIMA)
Chartered Mathematician (CMath)
Chartered Mathematics Teacher (CMathTeach)
Chartered Scientist (CSci)

DESIGNATORY LETTERS
AMIMA, MIMA, FIMA, CMath, CMathTeach, CSci

THE MATHEMATICAL ASSOCIATION

259 London Road
Leicester LE2 3BE
Tel: 01162 210013
Fax: 01162 122835
E-mail: office@m-a.org.uk
Website: www.m-a.org.uk

The MA dates from 1871 and supports and improves the teaching and learning of mathematics and its applications, and provides opportunities for communication and collaboration between teachers and students of mathematics. We publish a number of books, journals and magazines, hold an annual conference and regional meetings, and organize CPD events for our members. We also confer with government re the curriculum and assessment.

MEMBERSHIP
Student Member
Personal Member
Institutional Member

MEDICAL HERBALISM
Membership of Professional Institutions and Associations

THE NATIONAL INSTITUTE OF MEDICAL HERBALISTS

Clover House
James Court
South Street
Exeter
Devon EX1 1EE
Tel: 01392 426022
Fax: 01392 498963
E-mail: info@nimh.org.uk
Website: www.nimh.org.uk

The NIMH is the UK's leading professional organization of qualified medical herbal practitioners. We maintain high standards of practice and patient care, and work to promote the benefits of western herbal medicine. We provide codes of conduct, ethics and practice, and represent the profession, patients and the public through participation in external processes.

MEMBERSHIP
Member (MNIMH) Membership is open to graduates holding a BSc(Hons) degree in Herbal Medicine from: the Scottish School of Herbal Medicine, Edinburgh Napier University, University of Central Lancashire, Leeds Metropolitan University, Middlesex University, University of East London, University of Lincoln or University of Westminster. There is also a student affiliate membership scheme for those who are undergraduates of any of the above schools.

Fellow (FNIMH)

QUALIFICATION/EXAMINATIONS
The NIMH has historically managed its own accreditation process, with universities currently offering a BSc(Hons) degree in Herbal Medicine at Middlesex University, University of Lincoln, University of Westminster and University of East London. The programme at the University of East London is delivered by blended learning.

From 2011 accreditation of the above courses transferred to The European Herbal and Traditional Medicine Practitioners Association (EHTPA), as an umbrella body of Professional Herbal Medicine Associations, although graduates will continue to be eligible to apply for NIMH membership.

DESIGNATORY LETTERS
MNIMH, FNIMH

MEDICAL SECRETARIES
Membership of Professional Institutions and Associations

ASSOCIATION OF MEDICAL SECRETARIES, PRACTICE MANAGERS, ADMINISTRATORS AND RECEPTIONISTS

Tavistock House North
Tavistock Square
London WC1H 9LN
Tel: 020 7387 6005
Fax: 020 7388 2648
E-mail: info@amspar.co.uk
Website: www.amspar.com

AMSPAR is a professional membership and educational organization. We work with City & Guilds to provide non-clinical qualifications for health administration within the UK qualification frameworks. We aim to promote quality and coherence in the delivery of qualifications, and encourage and support standards of excellence in the pursuit of continuous professional development and lifelong learning.

MEMBERSHIP
Associate Member (AAMS)
Member (MAMS)
Fellow (FAMS)

QUALIFICATION/EXAMINATIONS
The Level 5 Diploma in Primary Care & Health Management
The Level 5 Certificate in Primary Care & Health Management
The Level 3 Diploma for Medical Secretaries
The Level 3 Certificate in Medical Administration
The Level 3 Certificate in Medical Terminology
Diploma in Medical Administration
The Level 2 Certificate in Medical Administration
The Level 2 Award in Medical Terminology

DESIGNATORY LETTERS
AAMS, MAMS, FAMS

MEDICINE

A student who wishes to qualify as a doctor in the UK must first obtain a primary qualification. Medical students in the UK typically study for five years to receive their medical degrees (or four years for a graduate entry programme). After graduation, a trainee doctor will enter the two-year Foundation Programme. The trainee is provisionally registered with a licence to practise with the General Medical Council (GMC) while completing the first year and full registration is awarded upon completion of year one.

The GMC is charged with the responsibility under the Medical Act 1983 of keeping a register of all duly qualified medical practitioners. General Medical Council, Regent's Place, 350 Euston Road, London NW1 3JN; Tel: 0161 923 6602; e-mail: gmc@gmc-uk.org; website; www.gmc-uk.org. For information on how to apply to join the register, see www.gmc-uk.org/doctors/registration_applications/join_the_register.asp.

PRIMARY QUALIFICATIONS

A qualifying examination for the purposes of Part II of the Medical Act is an examination held for the granting of one or more primary medical qualifications (PMQs) by any one of the bodies or combinations of bodies in the United Kingdom that are included in a list maintained by the GMC and published on the GMC's website (www.gmc-uk.org/education/undergraduate/awarding_bodies.asp).
Subject to the provisions of the Act any person whose fitness to practise is not impaired and who a) holds one or more primary United Kingdom qualifications and has satisfactorily completed an acceptable

programme for provisionally registered doctors; or b) being a national of any relevant European State, holds one or more primary European qualifications, is entitled to be registered as a fully registered medical practitioner.

LICENSING AND REVALIDATION

A qualifying examination for the purposes of Part II of the Medical Act is an examination held for the granting of one or more primary medical qualifications (PMQs) by any one of the bodies or combinations of bodies in the United Kingdom that are included in a list maintained by the GMC and published on the GMC's website (www.gmc-uk.org/education/undergraduate/awarding_bodies.asp).

Subject to the provisions of the Act any person whose fitness to practise is not impaired and who a) holds one or more primary United Kingdom qualifications and has satisfactorily completed an acceptable programme for provisionally registered doctors; or b) being a national of any relevant European State, holds one or more primary European qualifications, is entitled to be registered as a fully registered medical practitioner.

Revalidation is a new way of regulating licensed doctors that will give extra confidence to patients that their doctors are up to date and fit to practise. Licensed doctors will have to revalidate, usually every five years, by having regular appraisals based on the GMC's core guidance for doctors, *Good Medical Practice*. It is planned that revalidation will be introduced across the UK in early December 2012 and the majority of licensed doctors will be revalidated for the first time by the end of March 2016.

Membership of Professional Institutions and Associations

COLLEGE OF OPERATING DEPARTMENT PRACTITIONERS

197–199 City Road
London EC1V 1JN
Tel: 0870 746 0984
Fax: 0870 746 0985
E-mail: office@codp.org
Website: www.codp.org

The CODP is the professional body for Operating Department Practitioners. It is a membership, not-for-profit organization that sets standards of education for the pre-registration aspect of the profession and promotes the enhancement of knowledge and skills, in the context of the multidisciplinary team, through regional, national and international networks.

MEMBERSHIP
Student Member
Association Member
Full College Member

ROYAL COLLEGE OF GENERAL PRACTITIONERS

1 Bow Churchyard
London EC4M 9DQ
E-mail: info@rcgp.org.uk
Website: www.rcgp.org.uk

The aims of the College are to encourage, foster and maintain the highest possible standards in general medical practice. Full entry to the College is by exam undertaken whilst in training for General Practice, or assessment as a qualified GP.

MEMBERSHIP
Associate in Training
Associate
Member (MRCGP)
Fellow (FRCGP)

Undergraduate medical students and Foundation programme students may register with the College's Student Forum, which exposes the students to life in general practice.

QUALIFICATION/EXAMINATIONS
Assessment for Membership of the RCGP (MRGGP)

DESIGNATORY LETTERS
MRCGP, FRCGP

ROYAL COLLEGE OF OBSTETRICIANS AND GYNAECOLOGISTS

27 Sussex Place
London NW1 4RG
Tel: 020 7772 6200
Fax: 020 7723 0575
E-mail: library@rcog.org.uk
Website: www.rcog.org.uk

The RCOG encourages the study and advancement of the science and practice of obstetrics and gynaecology. We do this through postgraduate medical education and training development, and the publication of clinical guidelines and reports on aspects of the specialty and service provision. The RCOG International Office works with other international organizations to help lower maternal morbidity and mortality in under-resourced countries.

MEMBERSHIP
Junior Affiliate
Affiliate
Associate
Diplomate
Trainee – pre-membership
Member without Examination (MRCOG)
Member (MRCOG)
Fellow (FRCOG)
Fellow *honoris causa*
Fellow *ad eumdem* (FRCOG)
Honorary Fellow (FRCOG)

QUALIFICATION/EXAMINATIONS
MRCOG
DRCOG

DESIGNATORY LETTERS
MRCOG, FRCOG

ROYAL SOCIETY OF MEDICINE

1 Wimpole Street
London W1G 0AE
Tel: 020 7290 2900
Fax: 020 7290 2989
E-mail: membership@rsm.ac.uk
Website: www.rsm.ac.uk

The RSM, founded in 1805, is a medical charity that promotes the exchange of information and ideas in medical science. We provide a broad range of educational activities and opportunities for doctors, dentists, veterinary surgeons, students of these disciplines and allied healthcare professionals, organize conferences, and publish books and journals through our publishing division, RSM Press.

MEMBERSHIP
Student
Associate
Fellow

THE FEDERATION OF ROYAL COLLEGES OF PHYSICIANS OF THE UNITED KINGDOM

MRCP(UK)
11 St Andrews Place
Regent's Park
London NW1 4LE
Tel: +44 (0)20 3075 1649
Fax: +44 (0)20 7935 4143
E-mail: part1@mrcpuk.org
Website: www.mrcpuk.org

The Federation is a partnership between the Royal College of Physicians of Edinburgh, the Royal College of Physicians and Surgeons of Glasgow and the Royal College of Physicians of London. Working together, the colleges develop and deliver membership and specialty examinations that are recognized around the world as quality benchmarks.

MEMBERSHIP

Membership of the Royal Colleges of Physicians (MRCP(UK)): Once candidates have successfully completed their final Part of the examination they must then submit and complete the Form of Faith and a testimonial for election to membership. The testimonial must be completed by a Fellow or Member of the Royal Colleges of Physicians of the United Kingdom. The latter should have worked with the candidate within the previous 3 years and must be a holder of MRCP(UK) for at least 8 years.

QUALIFICATION/EXAMINATIONS

The Federation is responsible for a portfolio of examinations: MRCP(UK) Diploma (Membership of the Royal Colleges of Physicians of the United Kingdom): Candidates for the MRCP(UK) Diploma may enter through the Royal College of Physicians of Edinburgh, the Royal College of Physicians and Surgeons of Glasgow, the Royal College of Physicians of London, or through the online application system. There are three components to the MRCP(UK) Diploma. The part 1 examination has a two-paper format. Each paper is 3 hours in duration and contains 100 multiple choice questions in one from five (best of five) format, where a candidate chooses the best answer from five possible answers. The part 2 written examination has a three-paper format. All papers in the MRCP(UK) part 2 written examination are 3 hours in duration and contain up to 100 multiple choice questions. The questions will usually have a clinical scenario, may include the results of investigations and may be illustrated. The Part 2 clinical examination (PACES) consists of five clinical stations, each assessed by two independent examiners. Candidates will start at any one of the five stations, and then move round the carousel of stations at 20-minute intervals until they have completed the cycle. There is a 5-minute period between each station. Candidates may apply to sit the MRCP(UK) part 1 examination provided they graduated at least 12 months in advance of the examinations date (and have had at least 12 months' experience in medical employment). Candidates who have passed the part 1 examination can proceed to complete the remaining components. The MRCP(UK) Examination provides valid, reliable evidence of attainment in knowledge, clinical skills and behaviour, and is a mandatory component of assessment for Core Medical Training (CMT). The Specialty Certificate Examinations (SCEs): The Federation of Royal Colleges of Physicians of the UK, in association with the Specialist Societies, has developed a programme to deliver Specialty Certificate Examinations within the new specialist training structure. The aim of these national assessments is to ensure that trainees have sufficient knowledge of their specialty to practise safely and competently as consultants. The Specialty Certificate Examination is delivered in computer-based format (referred to as CBT) at a Pearson VUE test centre. Each paper is based on the MRCP(UK) written paper format and contains 100 multiple choice questions in 'best of five' format. A Specialty Certificate Examination is now a compulsory component of assessment for Certificate of Completion of Training (CCT) for all UK trainees whose specialist training began in or after August 2007 and is in one of the following specialties: Dermatology; Endocrinology and Diabetes; Gastroenterology, Geriatric Medicine; Infectious Diseases; Medical Oncology; Nephrology; Neurology; Palliative Medicine; Respiratory Medicine and Rheumatology.

THE INSTITUTE OF CLINICAL RESEARCH

Institute House
Boston Drive
Bourne End
Buckinghamshire SL8 5YS
Tel: 0845 521 0056/01628
Fax: 01628 530641
E-mail: info@icr-global.org
Website: www.icr-global.org

The ICR was founded in 1978 and is now the largest professional clinical research body in Europe and India. Our aim is to promote knowledge and understanding by engaging with the healthcare community and the general public, to support and facilitate communication between our members, and to provide opportunities for learning and development to enhance professional competence.

MEMBERSHIP
Affiliate
Registered Member (RICR)
Professional Member (MICR)
Fellow (FICR)
Honorary Fellow (Hon FICR)

QUALIFICATION/EXAMINATIONS
Please see the ICR's website.

DESIGNATORY LETTERS
RICR, MICR, FICR, HonFICR

THE ROYAL COLLEGE OF ANAESTHETISTS

Churchill House
35 Red Lion Square
London WC1R 4SG
Tel: 020 7092 1500
Fax: 020 7092 1730
E-mail: info@rcoa.ac.uk
Website: www.rcoa.ac.uk

The RCA, which dates from 1948, is the professional body responsible for the specialty of anaesthesia throughout the UK. Our principal responsibility is to ensure the quality of patient care through the maintenance of standards in anaesthesia, pain management and intensive care. We set and run examinations, and provide CPD for all practising anaesthetists.

MEMBERSHIP
Trainee
Affiliate
Associate Member
Member (MRCA)
Associate Fellow
Fellow *ad eundem* (FRCA)
Fellow (FRCA)
Honorary Fellow (FRCA)

QUALIFICATION/EXAMINATIONS
FRCA Examinations

DESIGNATORY LETTERS
MRCA, FRCA

THE ROYAL COLLEGE OF PATHOLOGISTS

2 Carlton House Terrace
London SW1Y 5AF
Tel: 020 7451 6700
Fax: 020 7451 6701
E-mail: info@rcpath.org
Website: www.rcpath.org

The College aims to advance the science and practice of pathology, to provide public education, to promote research in pathology and to disseminate the results.

MEMBERSHIP
Affiliate Member
Associate
Diplomate Member (DipRCPath)
Fellow (FRCPath)

QUALIFICATION/EXAMINATIONS
Training programmes are approved for all pathology specialities and sub-specialities. The exact examination arrangements vary for each speciality but they will all involve a Part 1 and a Part 2 which include, inter alia, written, practical and oral components. In addition the College offers a Diploma in Cytopathology, a Diploma in Dermatopathology and a Diploma in Forensic Pathology. Further details may be obtained from the Examinations Department or the College's website.

DESIGNATORY LETTERS
DipRCPath, FRCPath

THE ROYAL COLLEGE OF PHYSICIANS AND SURGEONS OF GLASGOW

232–242 St Vincent Street
Glasgow G2 5RJ
Tel: 0141 2216072
Fax: 0141 2211804
E-mail: exams@rcpsg.ac.uk
Website: www.rcpsg.ac.uk

The Royal College of Physicians and Surgeons of Glasgow (RCPSG) welcomes professionals from a diverse range of disciplines. At present, our collegiate body includes Physicians, Surgeons, professionals in Dentistry, Travel Medicine, Podiatric Medicine and other professionals allied to medicine. The College aims to provide career support to our membership through education, training, professional development, examinations and assessment, whilst acting as a charity and leading voice on health issues in order to set the highest standards of health care.

MEMBERSHIP
Member   MRCPS(Glasg)/MFDS   RCPS(Glasg)/MRCS(Glasg)/MRCS(ENT)(Glasg)/MFTM RCPS(Glasg)/MFPM RCPS(Glasg)
Fellow   (FRCP(Glasg)/FRCS(Glasg)/FDS RCPS(Glasg))/FFTM   RCPS(Glasg)/FFPM RCPS(Glasg)
Associate Member
Affiliate Member
Associate in Training
Introductory Member

QUALIFICATION/EXAMINATIONS
Diploma in Child Health (DCH)
Diploma in Dermatology (Dip Derm)
Diploma in Geriatric Medicine (DGM)
Diploma in Otolaryngology – Head and Neck Surgey (DOHNS)
Diploma in Travel Medicine (DipTravMed)
Diploma of Membership of the Royal College of Physicians of the United Kingdom (MRCP(UK)) (see MRCP(UK) website)
Diploma of Membership of the Royal College of Surgeons (MRCS(Glasg))
Diploma of Membership of the Royal College of Surgeons (MRCS(ENT)(Glasg))
Diploma of Membership of the Faculty of Dental Surgery (MFDS RCPS(Glasg))

Diploma of Membership of the Faculty of Travel Medicine (MFTM RCPS(Glasg))
Diploma of Membership of the Faculty of Podiatric Medicine (MFPM RCPS(Glasg))
Diploma of Fellowship of the Royal College of Physicians and Surgeons of Glasgow in Ophthalmology (FRCS(Glasg))

Diploma of Fellowship of the Royal College of Physicians and Surgeons of Glasgow (FDS (dental specialty)RCPS(Glasg))
Diploma of Fellowship of the Royal College of Physicians and Surgeons of Glasgow (FRCSGlasg(-surgical specialty))

Diploma of Fellowship of the Faculty of Travel Medicine (FFTM RCPS(Glasg))
Diploma of Fellowship of the Faculty of Podiatric Medicine (FFPM RCPS(Glasg))

DESIGNATORY LETTERS
MFDS RCPS(Glasg), MFTM RCPS(Glasg), MRCP(UK), MRCS(Glasg), MRCS(ENT)(Glasg), MRCPS(Glasg), MFPM RCPS(Glasg), FRCP(Glasg)/FRCSGlasg/FDS RCPS(Glasg)/FRCS(Urol)(Glasg), FFTM RCPS(Glasg)/FFPM RCPS(Glasg)

THE ROYAL COLLEGE OF PHYSICIANS OF EDINBURGH

9 Queen Street
Edinburgh EH2 1JQ
Tel: 01312 257324
Fax: 01312 266124
E-mail: l.tedford@rcpe.ac.uk
Website: www.rcpe.ac.uk

The RCPE promotes the highest standards in internal medicine internationally. Along with our sister Colleges in Glasgow and London we oversee the Member of the Royal College of Physicians (MRCP(UK)) examination enabling doctors to enter higher specialist training, leading eventually to a Certificate of Completion of Specialist Training (CCST).

MEMBERSHIP
e-Associate
Associate
Collegiate Member (MRCPE)
Fellow (FRCPE)

QUALIFICATION/EXAMINATIONS
MRCP(UK)
Specialty Certificate Examinations

DESIGNATORY LETTERS
MRCPE, FRCPE

THE ROYAL COLLEGE OF PHYSICIANS OF LONDON

11 St Andrews Place
Regent's Park
London NW1 4LE
Tel: +44 (0)20 7935 1174
Fax: +44 (0)20 7935 4143
E-mail: DGM@rcplondon.ac.uk; DTMH@rcplondon.ac.uk
Website: www.rcplondon.ac.uk

The Royal College of Physicians of London offers a Diploma in Geriatric Medicine (DGM) Examination and a Diploma in Tropical Medicine and Hygiene, run in conjunction with the London School of Tropical Medicine and Hygiene.

MEMBERSHIP
The Royal College of Physicians of London runs the MRCP(UK) Examination which is the MRCP(UK) membership examination. As the examination is run in conjunction with two other Royal Colleges of

Physicians, this examination and the membership qualification MRCP(UK) are listed in this directory under *The Federation of Royal Colleges of Physicians*

QUALIFICATION/EXAMINATIONS

Diploma in Geriatric Medicine The Diploma in Geriatric Medicine is designed to give recognition of competence in the provision of care of older people to General Practitioner vocational trainees, staff physicians and others working in non-consultant career posts in Departments of Geriatric Medicine, and other doctors with interests in or responsibilities for the care of older people.

The Diploma in Geriatric Medicine is available to all registered doctors. It is not primarily directed towards career geriatricians, but is generally to family doctors, psycho-geriatricians and indeed any doctor involved in the care of older people.

The Diploma in Geriatric Medicine is in two parts, the first of which is a written examination of multiple choice (best of 5) questions, lasting 2 hours and 30 minutes normally held twice a year at the Royal College of Physicians of London.

The second part is a Clinical Examination also held twice a year at various clinical centres in England and Wales. The clinical examination is a four-station standardized examination similar to an Objective Standard Clinical Examination (OSCE).

Diploma in Tropical Medicine and Hygiene The Diploma in Tropical Medicine and Hygiene is intended to test the knowledge required of physicians who wish to practise medicine effectively in developing countries.

Candidates for the Diploma in Tropical Medicine & Hygiene must hold a primary medical qualification recognized by the Royal College of Physicians of London.

The Royal College of Physicians of London will accept applications from candidates who are in the process of completing, or have completed within the last 5 years, the Tropical Medicine courses in London, Liverpool, Sheffield and Glasgow, which are recognized as appropriate training centres for the examination. The examination is held once a year over 2 days (unless required for a viva) and is conducted in the following sections: A **Practical Section** lasting 2 hours and 30 minutes consists of a mixture of microscopy specimens, including 20 'spot' questions that are set up on a microscope for identification. Other specimens require the candidate to use the microscopes themself. They are mainly parasitological and may include faecal, blood and haematological preparations together with some entomological specimens. A **Written Section** (3 hours and 20 minutes in total) consists of three papers. The **Clinical Paper** (1 hour) contains 18 compulsory questions. The first 16 are based on clinical pictures – usually of patients with abnormal physical signs; but occasionally laboratory slides, X-rays, or epidemiological data may be shown. There will be two or three questions on each, asking (for example) identification, diagnosis, further investigation, treatment etc. Each of these 16 questions is worth a maximum of 5 marks. The last 2 questions (17 and 18) are brief clinical cases, with 2 or 3 questions (again concentrating on diagnosis or differential diagnosis, investigation and treatment). The **Multiple Choice Question Paper** (1 hour and 20 minutes) consists of 40 multiple choice questions designed to test the knowledge of tropical medicine and hygiene over a wide area. The **Preventative Medicine Paper** (1 hour including 5 minutes reading time) consists of 10 questions of which the candidate must choose 5. Each question may have several parts, covering all aspects of preventative medicine and international community health in a tropical context. There is also an **Oral ('Viva') Examination** for borderline candidates. The examination is conducted by two examiners. The first part of the examination (10 minutes) is a discussion of an illustrated clinical case history, which candidates are allowed to study for 10 minutes before the examination. The second part of the examination (10 minutes) consists of more general questions.

THE ROYAL COLLEGE OF PSYCHIATRISTS

17 Belgrave Square
London SW1X 8PG
Tel: 020 7235 2351
Fax: 020 7245 1231
E-mail: latkinson@rcpsych.ac.uk
Website: www.rcpsych.ac.uk

The RCPsych is the professional and educational body for psychiatrists in the UK and Ireland. We are committed to improving the understanding of psychiatry and mental health, and are at the forefront in setting and achieving the highest standards through education, training and research. We actively promote psychiatry as a career, and provide guidance and support to our members and associates.

MEMBERSHIP
Pre-Membership Psychiatric Trainee
New Associate
Corresponding Associate
Affiliate
Specialist Associate
Member (MRCPsych)
Fellow (FRCPsych)
Honorary Fellow
International Associate

QUALIFICATION/EXAMINATIONS
MRCPsych qualifying exams
FRCPsych qualifying exams

DESIGNATORY LETTERS
MRCPsych, FRCPsych

THE ROYAL COLLEGE OF RADIOLOGISTS

38 Portland Place
London W1B 1JQ
Tel: 020 7636 4432
Fax: 020 7323 3100
E-mail: enquiries@rcr.ac.uk
Website: www.rcr.ac.uk

The RCR is a professional body representing over 8,900 medical and dental practitioners worldwide that aims to advance the science and practice of clinical radiology and clinical oncology. We promote the highest standards of professional competence, undertake regular audits of training and practice, conduct examinations for Certificates and Diplomas, encourage CPD among our members, and provide information for the public.

MEMBERSHIP
Junior Member
Associate
Member
Fellow (FRCR)
Honorary Member/Fellow (Hon MRCR/Hon FRCR)

QUALIFICATION/EXAMINATIONS
First FRCR Examination
Final FRCR Examination
Diploma in Dental and Maxillofacial Radiology (DDMFR)

DESIGNATORY LETTERS
FRCR, Hon MRCR, Hon FRCR

THE ROYAL COLLEGE OF SURGEONS OF EDINBURGH

Nicolson Street
Edinburgh EH8 9DW
Tel: 0131 527 1600
Fax: 0131 557 6406
E-mail: information@rcsed.ac.uk
Website: www.rcsed.ac.uk

The Royal College of Surgeons of Edinburgh, which dates from 1505, is dedicated to the maintenance and promotion of the highest standards of surgical practice, through education, training and rigorous examination, and its liaison with external medical bodies. Today, with more than 20,000 Fellows and Members, we pride ourselves also on our innovation and adaptability.

MEMBERSHIP
Affiliate
Surgical Associate Member
Member (MRCSEd)
Fellow (FRCSEd)

QUALIFICATION/EXAMINATIONS
Please see the Royal College of Surgeons of Edinburgh website.

DESIGNATORY LETTERS
MRCSEd, FRCSEd

THE ROYAL COLLEGE OF SURGEONS OF ENGLAND

35–43 Lincoln's Inn Fields
London WC2A 3PE
Tel: 020 7405 3474
Fax: 020 7831 9438
E-mail: exams@rcseng.ac.uk
Website: www.rcseng.ac.uk

The Royal College of Surgeons of England is committed to enabling surgeons to achieve and maintain the highest standards of surgical practice and patient care. We examine trainees, supervise the training of and provide support and advice for surgeons, promote and support surgical research in the UK, and liaise with the DoH, health authorities, Trusts and hospitals in the UK and other medical and academic organizations worldwide.

MEMBERSHIP
Intercollegiate Member

QUALIFICATION/EXAMINATIONS
Please see the Royal College of Surgeons of England website.

THE SOCIETY OF APOTHECARIES OF LONDON

Black Friars Lane
London EC4V 6EJ
Tel: 020 7236 1180
Fax: 020 7329 3177
E-mail: registrar@apothecaries.org
Website: www.apothecaries.org

The Society of Apothecaries of London was incorporated by Royal Charter in 1617 and allowed to prepare and sell drugs for medicinal purposes, laying the foundations of the British pharmaceutical industry. Later, apothecaries were permitted to prescribe and dispense medicines, becoming the forerunners of today's GPs. Now the Society is primarily an examining body.

QUALIFICATION/EXAMINATIONS
PGDip in the Forensic and Clinical Aspects of Sexual Assault (DFCASA)
PGDip in Forensic Medical Sciences (DFMS)
PGDip in Genitourinary Medicine (Dip GU Med)
PGDip in the History of Medicine (DHMSA)
PGDip in HIV Medicine (Dip HIV Med)
PGDip in the Medical Care of Catastrophes (DMCC)
PGDip in Medical Jurisprudence (Pathology) (DMJ[Path])
PGDip in the Philosophy of Medicine (DPMSA)

METALLURGY
Membership of Professional Institutions and Associations

INSTITUTE OF CORROSION

7B High Street Mews
High Street
Vimy Road
Leighton Buzzard
Bedfordshire LU7 1EA
Tel: 01525 851771
Fax: 01525 376690
E-mail: admin@icorr.org
Website: www.icorr.org

The Institute of Corrosion has since 1959 been serving the corrosion science, technology and engineering community in the fight against corrosion, which costs the UK around 4 per cent of GNP per annum. We promote the establishment and promotion of sound corrosion management practice, the advancement of cost-effective corrosion control measures, and a sustained effort to raise corrosion awareness at all stages of design, fabrication and operation.

MEMBERSHIP
Student Member
Ordinary Member
Technical Member (TICorr)
Professional Member (MICorr)
Engineering Technician (EngTech)
Incorporated Engineer (IEng)
Chartered Engineer (CEng)
Chartered Scientist (CSci)

QUALIFICATION/EXAMINATIONS
Please see the Institute of Corrosion website.

DESIGNATORY LETTERS
TICorr, MICorr, EngTech, IEng, CEng

Metallurgy

THE INSTITUTE OF METAL FINISHING

Exeter House
48 Holloway Head
Birmingham B1 1NQ
Tel: 01216 227387
Fax: 01216 666316
E-mail: exeterhouse@instituteofmetalfinishing.org
Website: www.uk-finishing.org.uk

The IMF, founded in 1925, provides a focus for surface engineering and finishing activities worldwide through the fulfilment of technical, educational and professional needs at all levels for individuals and companies involved in the coatings industry. We promote R&D within the industry and CPD for our members, cooperate with other institutes, and liaise with legislative bodies to influence decision-making.

MEMBERSHIP
Student
Affiliate
Associate (AssocIMF)
Technician (TechIMF)
Licentiate (LIMF)
Member (MIMF)
Fellow (FIMF)
Engineering Technician (EngTech)
Sustaining Member (company)

QUALIFICATION/EXAMINATIONS
Foundation Certificate
Technician Certificate
Advanced Technician Certificate

DESIGNATORY LETTERS
AssocIMF, TechIMF, LIMF, MIMF, FIMF, EngTech

METEOROLOGY AND CLIMATOLOGY
Membership of Professional Institutions and Associations

MET OFFICE COLLEGE

Met Office
Fitzroy Road
Exeter
Devon EX1 3PB
Tel: 01392 885680
Fax: 01392 885681
E-mail: met-training@metoffice.gov.uk
Website: www.metoffice.gov.uk

The Meteorological Office College is part of the Met Office and is located in Exeter, Devon. We provide meteorological training for our own staff and to meteorological services worldwide, as places become available on a fee-paying basis.

QUALIFICATION/EXAMINATIONS
NVQ in Meteorological Observing (Level 3)
NVQ in Meteorological Weather Forecasting (Level 4)
Forecaster Foundation Training Programme
Professional Development Programme
Specialist Forecaster Programme

ROYAL METEOROLOGICAL SOCIETY

104 Oxford Road
Reading RG1 7LL
Tel: 0118 956 8500
Fax: 0118 956 8571
E-mail: info@rmets.org
Website: www.rmets.org

The RMetS is the learned and professional society for anyone whose profession or interests are connected with weather and climate. It administers the NVQs of the profession and is the accreditation body for the status of Chartered Meteorologist. Its principal aim is the advancement of the understanding of weather and climate for the benefit of everyone.

Associate Fellow
Fellow (FRMetS)
Honorary Member
Chartered Meteorologist (CMet)
Chartered Environmentalist (CEnv)
School Member
Corporate Member

MEMBERSHIP
Student

DESIGNATORY LETTERS
FRMetS, CMet, CEnv

MICROSCOPY
Membership of Professional Institutions and Associations

THE ROYAL MICROSCOPICAL SOCIETY

Oxford OX4 1AJ
Tel: 01865 254760
Fax: 01865 791237
E-mail: info@rms.org.uk
Website: www.rms.org.uk

The RMS, which dates from 1839, is an international scientific society dedicated to advancing the science of microscopy and the interests of its 1,400 members, who range from individuals interested in microscopy to scientists and company members representing manufacturers and suppliers of microscopes, other equipment and services.

MEMBERSHIP
Ordinary Member
Fellow (FRMS)
Corporate Member

DESIGNATORY LETTERS
FRMS

MUSEUM AND RELATED WORK
Membership of Professional Institutions and Associations

MUSEUMS ASSOCIATION

24 Calvin Street
London E1 6NW
Tel: 020 7426 6955
Fax: 020 7426 6962
E-mail: cpd@museumsassociation.org
Website: www.museumsassociation.org

The MA is the oldest museums association in the world, set up in 1889 to guard the interests of museums and galleries. Today, we have 5,200 individual members, 600 institutional members and 250 corporate members. Our aim is to enhance the value of museums to society by sharing knowledge, developing skills, inspiring innovation and providing leadership.

MEMBERSHIP
Student
Volunteer
Professional Member
Associate (AMA)
Commercial Member
Institutional Member

DESIGNATORY LETTERS
AMA

MUSIC
Membership of Professional Institutions and Associations

ABRSM (ASSOCIATED BOARD OF THE ROYAL SCHOOLS OF MUSIC)

24 Portland Place
London W1B 1LU
Tel: 020 7636 5400
Fax: 020 7637 0234
E-mail: abrsm@abrsm.org
Website: www.abrsm.org

ABRSM's mission is to motivate musical achievement. We aim to support the development of learners and teachers in music education worldwide and to celebrate their achievements. We do this through authoritative and internationally recognized assessments, publications and professional development support for teachers, and through charitable donations.

MEMBERSHIP
Licentiate (LRSM)
Fellow (FRSM)

QUALIFICATION/EXAMINATIONS
Certificate of Teaching (CT ABRSM)
Diploma in Instrumental/Vocal Teaching (DipABRSM)
Diploma in Music Direction (DipABRSM)
Diploma in Music Performance (DipABRSM)

Please see the ABRSM website for details of other examinations and awards.

DESIGNATORY LETTERS
CT ABRSM, DipABRSM, LRSM, FRSM

MUSICAL INSTRUMENT TECHNOLOGY
Membership of Professional Institutions and Associations

INCORPORATED SOCIETY OF MUSICIANS

10 Stratford Place
London WIC 1AA
Tel: 020 7629 4413
Fax: 020 7408 1538
E-mail: membership@ism.org
Website: www.ism.org

The ISM, a non-profit-making organization founded in 1882, is the UK's professional body for musicians. We promote the art of music and the interests of musicians through campaigns, support and practical advice. Members also receive our monthly in-house magazine, *Music Journal*, which includes news and information on CPD.

MEMBERSHIP
Student Member
Associate Member
Full Member
Corporate Member

INCORPORATED SOCIETY OF ORGAN BUILDERS

Smithy Steads
Cragg Vale
Hebden Bridge
West Yorkshire HX7 5SQ
Fax: 0870 139 3645
E-mail: admin1@isob.co.uk
Website: www.isob.co.uk/

The ISOB was founded in 1947 to advance the science and practice of organ building, to provide a central organization for organ builders, and to provide for the better definition and protection of the profession by a system of examinations and the issue of certificates and distinctions. We hold regular meetings and conferences around the UK and overseas.

MEMBERSHIP
Student Member
Ordinary Member (MISOB)
Associate Member (AISOB)
Fellow (FISOB)
Councillor (CISOB)

DESIGNATORY LETTERS
MISOB, AISOB, FISOB, CISOB

PIANOFORTE TUNERS' ASSOCIATION

PO Box 1312
Lightwater
Woking
Surrey GU18 5UB
Tel: 0845 602 8796
E-mail: secretary@pianotuner.org.uk
Website: www.pianotuner.org.uk

The PTA is a professional body committed to improving standards, and applicants for membership must pass a theoretical and practical examination to prove their ability as a qualified piano tuner or technician. We publish a regular newsletter and hold an Annual Convention and General Meeting in different towns around Britain, to which members and aspiring non-members are invited.

MEMBERSHIP
Student
Patron
Associate
Technician Member
Member

NAVAL ARCHITECTURE
Membership of Professional Institutions and Associations

THE ROYAL INSTITUTION OF NAVAL ARCHITECTS

10 Upper Belgrave Street
London SW1X 8BQ
Tel: 020 7235 4622
Fax: 020 7259 5912
E-mail: membership@rina.org.uk
Website: www.rina.org.uk

The RINA is an internationally renowned professional institution whose members are involved at all levels in the design, construction, maintenance and operation of marine vessels and structures. Our members are widely represented in industry, universities and colleges, and maritime organizations in over 90 countries.

MEMBERSHIP
Student Member
Associate (AssocRINA)
Associate Member (AMRINA)
Member (MRINA)
Fellow (FRINA)

DESIGNATORY LETTERS
AssocRINA, AMRINA, MRINA. FRINA

NAVIGATION, SEAMANSHIP AND MARINE QUALIFICATIONS
Membership of Professional Institutions and Associations

THE NAUTICAL INSTITUTE

202 Lambeth Road
London SE1 7LQ
Tel: 020 7928 1351
Fax: 020 7401 2817
E-mail: sec@nautinst.org
Website: www.nautinst.org

The Nautical Institute is the international professional body for qualified seafarers and others with an interest in nautical matters. We provide a wide range of services to enhance the professional standing and knowledge of members who are drawn from all sectors of the maritime world. The Institute has over 40 branches worldwide and more than 6500 members in over 100 countries. It provides the strongest possible professional focus, dedicated to improving standards of those in control of seagoing craft while maintaining the Institute as an international centre of nautical excellence.

MEMBERSHIP
Honorary Fellow
Fellow
Associate Fellow (AFNI)
Member (MNI)
Associate Member (AMNI)

QUALIFICATION/EXAMINATIONS
Harbour Master's Certificate
Pilotage Certificate
Command Diploma

DESIGNATORY LETTERS
FNI, AFNI, MNI, AMNI

THE ROYAL INSTITUTE OF NAVIGATION

1 Kensington Gore
London SW7 2AT
Tel: 020 7591 3130
Fax: 020 7591 3131
E-mail: info@rin.org.uk
Website: www.rin.org.uk

The RIN is a learned society with charitable status. Our aims are: to unite those with a professional or personal interest in any aspect of navigation in one unique body; to further the development of navigation in every sphere; and to increase public awareness of both the art and science of navigation, how it has shaped the past, how it impacts our world today, and how it will affect the future.

MEMBERSHIP
Junior Associate Member

Student
Associate
Member (MRIN)
Associate Fellow (AFRIN)
Fellow (FRIN)
Affiliate Club
Affiliate College or University
Corporate Member

DESIGNATORY LETTERS
MRIN, AFRIN, FRIN

NON-DESTRUCTIVE TESTING
Membership of Professional Institutions and Associations

THE BRITISH INSTITUTE OF NON-DESTRUCTIVE TESTING

Newton Building
St George's Avenue
Northampton NN2 6JB
Tel: 01604 89 3811
Fax: 01604 89 3861
E-mail: info@bindt.org
Website: www.bindt.org

The BINDT was formed in 1976 from the merger of the Society of Non-Destructive Examination (SONDE) and the Society of Industrial Radiology and Allied Methods of Non-Destructive Testing, later renamed the NDT Society of Great Britain (NDTS), both formed in 1954. Our aim is to promote and advance the science and practice of non-destructive testing, condition monitoring, diagnostic engineering and all other materials and quality testing disciplines.

MEMBERSHIP
Student Member
Affiliate
Practitioner Member (PInstNDT)
Graduate Member (GInstNDT)
Member (MInstNDT)
Fellow (FInstNDT)
Engineering Technician (EngTech)
Incorporated Engineer (IEng)
Chartered Engineer (CEng)
Licensed Engineering Practitioner
Associate Member (corporate)

DESIGNATORY LETTERS
PInstNDT, GInstNDT, MInstNDT, FInstNDT, EngTech, IEng, CEng

NURSERY NURSING
Membership of Professional Institutions and Associations

COUNCIL FOR AWARDS IN CHILDREN'S CARE AND EDUCATION

Apex House
81 Camp Road
St Albans
Hertfordshire AL1 5GB
Tel: 0845 347 2123
Fax: 01727 818618
E-mail: info@cache.org.uk
Website: www.cache.org.uk

CACHE is an Awarding Body that designs courses and qualifications in the care and education of children and young people. Our courses, which are widely available, range from entry level to advanced qualifications for sector professionals. We regularly lobby the government and other agencies to raise the quality and professionalism of child care.

QUALIFICATION/EXAMINATIONS
Please see the CACHE website.

NURSING AND MIDWIFERY
Membership of Professional Institutions and Associations

THE NURSING & MIDWIFERY COUNCIL

23 Portland Place
London W1B 1PZ
Tel: 020 7333 9333
E-mail: advice@nmc-uk.org
Website: www.nmc-uk.org

We are the nursing and midwifery regulator for England, Wales, Scotland, Northern Ireland and the Islands. We exist to safeguard the health and well-being of the public.

OCCUPATIONAL THERAPY
Membership of Professional Institutions and Associations

BRITISH ASSOCIATION OF OCCUPATIONAL THERAPISTS

106–114 Borough High Street
Southwark
London SE1 1LB
Tel: 020 7357 6480
Fax: 020 7450 2299
E-mail: membership@cot.co.uk
Website: www.cot.org.uk

The British Association and College of Occupational Therapists is the professional body for occupational therapy in the UK. The College has 29,000 members and represents the profession nationally and internationally.

MEMBERSHIP
Student Member
Associate
Discounted Associate
Professional Member
Discounted Professional Member
Self-employed Member
Retired Member
Overseas Member

QUALIFICATION/EXAMINATIONS
BA (Hons)
PG Dip
MSc

DESIGNATORY LETTERS
MBAOT

OPTICIANS (DISPENSING)

Dispensing opticians must be registered with the General Optical Council (GOC, 41 Harley Street, London W1G 8DJ; e-mail: goc@optical.org; website: www.optical.org). The GOC publishes registers of all optometrists, dispensing opticians, student opticians, and optical businesses that are qualified and fit to practise, train or carry on business (www.optical.org/en/utilities/online-registers.cfm).

Qualification takes three years in total, and can be completed by combining a distance learning course or day release while working as a trainee under the supervision of a qualified and GOC-registered optician. Alternatively students can do a two-year full-time course followed by one year of supervised practice with a qualified and registered optician. The GOC has approved training courses in dispensing optics at the following six institutions in the UK: Anglia Ruskin University, Association of British Dispensing Opticians (ABDO) DLI College, Bradford College, City University, City and Islington College, and Glasgow Caledonian University.

All routes are assessed by final ABDO examinations. On successful completion of training you must register with the GOC in order to practise in the UK. Once qualified, you will need to undertake a minimum amount of continuing education and training to remain on the register.

The approved training course for the contact lens specialty is run by ABDO College and City and Islington College. If you qualify as a dispensing optician and have completed training to fit contact lenses, the University of Bradford offers a career progression course that enables you to graduate with a degree in optometry in one calendar year (Tel: 01274 235520; e-mail: do-optom@bradford.ac.uk).

ENTRY REQUIREMENTS

You will normally need to have five GCSEs (or equivalent) at grades C or above, including English, maths and science. For mature and overseas students, alternative and vocational courses, admission requirements will vary and may be more flexible. For further details contact the admissions tutor at the university you wish to apply to.

Membership of Professional Institutions and Associations

ASSOCIATION OF BRITISH DISPENSING OPTICIANS

199 Gloucester Terrace
London W2 6LD
Tel: 020 7298 5100
Fax: 020 7298 5111
E-mail: general@abdolondon.org.uk
Website: www.abdo.org.uk

The ABDO is the qualifying body for dispensing opticians in the UK. Our aims are to advance the science and art of dispensing optics, to further the education and training of dispensing opticians, and to support and promote the interests of the profession.

MEMBERSHIP
Student Member
Associate Member
Full Member
Fellow (FBDO)

QUALIFICATION/EXAMINATIONS
Certificate in Contact Lens Practice (Level 6)
Diploma in The Assessment & Management of Low Vision (Level 6)
Diploma in Ophthalmic Dispensing (Level 6)
Diploma in Advanced Contact Lens Practice (Level 7)
Diploma in Spectacle Lens Design (Level 7)

DESIGNATORY LETTERS
FBDO

ASSOCIATION OF CONTACT LENS MANUFACTURERS

PO Box 735
Devizes
Wiltshire SN10 3TQ
Tel: 01380 860418
Fax: 01380 860863
E-mail: secgen@aclm.org.uk
Website: www.aclm.org.uk

The ACLM was founded in 1962 to publicize the work of UK contact lens manufacturers, to develop new products and to raise standards. Today we represent the manufacturers of the vast majority of prescription contact lenses and lens care products sold in the UK, and provide a cohesive voice for our members.

MEMBERSHIP
Member

BRITISH CONTACT LENS ASSOCIATION

Walmar House
288/292 Regent Street
London W1B 3AL
Tel: 020 7580 6661
Fax: 020 7580 6669
Website: www.bcla.org.uk

The BCLA is the UK's leading supplier of information and education on contact lenses and the anterior eye, with a membership of around 1,800 in more than 40 countries. Our mission is to promote excellence in the research, manufacture and clinical practice of contact lenses and related areas. Our annual Clinical Conference and Exhibition, the world's largest, attracts more than 1,000 visitors.

MEMBERSHIP
Student Member
Member
Fellow (FBCLA)

QUALIFICATION/EXAMINATIONS
Educational activities include approved Continuing Education and Training courses and evening meetings. For details see the website.

DESIGNATORY LETTERS
FBCLA

OPTOMETRY

Careers in optometry are overseen by the General Optical Council (41 Harley Street, London W1G 8DJ; e-mail: goc@optical.org; website; www.optical.org). You can study for an undergraduate optometry degree from one of nine GOC-approved institutions in the UK: Anglia Ruskin University, Aston University, the University of Bradford, Cardiff University, City University, Glasgow Caledonian University, Plymouth University, the University of Manchester and the University of Ulster.

LENGTH OF COURSE
Usually four years in total (five in Scotland): a full-time three-year (four-year in Scotland) degree course, followed by one year's salaried pre-registration training with a practice under the guidance of a GOC-registered optometrist. This includes a series of assessments, set by the College of Optometrists, throughout the placement.

ENTRY REQUIREMENTS
You will normally need five GCSEs (or equivalent) at grade C or above, one of which should be English;

often maths and physics or double science are also required. You will normally be required to have three A Level passes/approximately 320 UCAS tariff points from the following subjects: physics, biology, chemistry or mathematics. Requirements vary between universities, so be sure to check the university's prospectus and/or consult the relevant admission tutors.

Membership of Professional Institutions and Associations

ASSOCIATION OF OPTOMETRISTS

61 Southwark Street
London SE1 0HL
Tel: 020 7261 9661
Fax: 020 7261 0228
E-mail: postbox@aop.org.uk
Website: www.aop.org.uk

The AOP serves its members by promoting and protecting them, providing them with relevant services, representing and supporting them, enhancing their professional and business effectiveness, and expanding the role of optometry in primary and secondary eyecare.

MEMBERSHIP
Student Member
Honorary Member
Dispensing Associate
Full Member

ORTHOPTICS

Membership of Professional Institutions and Associations

BRITISH AND IRISH ORTHOPTIC SOCIETY

4th Floor
14 Bedford Row
London WC1R 4ED
Tel: 0207 306 1135
E-mail: bios@orthoptics.org.uk
Website: www.orthoptics.org.uk

Orthoptists are AHPs, who diagnose and treat problems with visual development and binocular vision (how the eyes work together as a pair), and eye movement disorders. They are experts in childhood vision screening. Extended roles include stroke, glaucoma, reading difficulties, neurological disorders, low vision.

MEMBERSHIP
Student Members
Members

QUALIFICATION/EXAMINATIONS
Degrees in orthoptics are offered by Liverpool University (www.liv.ac.uk) and Sheffield University (www.sheffield.ac.uk)

OSTEOPATHY AND NATUROPATHY
Membership of Professional Institutions and Associations

BRITISH OSTEOPATHIC ASSOCIATION

3 Park Terrace
Manor Road
Luton
Bedfordshire LU1 3HN
Tel: 01582 488455
Fax: 01582 481533
E-mail: boa@osteopathy.org
Website: www.osteopathy.org

The BOA was formed in 1998 as a result of the merger of the British Osteopathic Association, the Osteopathic Association of Great Britain and the Guild of Osteopaths. We provide opportunities for individual and professional development in osteopathic practice and promote the highest standards of osteopathic education and research.

MEMBERSHIP
Student Member
1st/2nd/3rd/4th Year Graduate Member
Full Member
Overseas Member

PATENT AGENCY
Membership of Professional Institutions and Associations

THE CHARTERED INSTITUTE OF PATENT ATTORNEYS

95 Chancery Lane
London WC2A 1DT
Tel: 020 7405 9450
Fax: 020 7430 0471
E-mail: mail@cipa.org.uk
Website: www.cipa.org.uk

CIPA is the professional, training and examining body for patent attorneys in the UK. From 2010 the IP Regulation Board, an independent body within the CIPA, sets the standards for regulation of the profession. Trainees, all technical graduates, also study for the qualification to practise before the European Patent Office.

MEMBERSHIP
Student Member
Associate
Fellow
Registered Patent Attorney (RPA)
Chartered Patent Attorney (CPA)

QUALIFICATION/EXAMINATIONS
Qualifying examination for registration as a Patent Attorney

DESIGNATORY LETTERS
RPA, CPA

PENSION MANAGEMENT
Membership of Professional Institutions and Associations

THE PENSIONS MANAGEMENT INSTITUTE

PMI House
4–10 Artillery Lane
London E1 7LS
Tel: 020 7247 1452
Fax: 020 7375 0603
E-mail: education@pensions-pmi.org.uk
Website: www.pensions-pmi.org.uk

The Pensions Management Institute is the professional body that promotes standards of excellence and lifetime learning for pensions professionals and trustees through its qualifications, membership and ongoing support services. For further details please visit our website.

MEMBERSHIP
Student Member
Ordinary Member (MPMI)
Associate Member (APMI)
Fellow (FPMI)

QUALIFICATION/EXAMINATIONS
Retirement Provision Certificate (RPC)
Advanced Diploma in Retirement Provision
Qualification in Pensions Administration (QPA)
Diploma in Pension Calculations (DPC)
Qualification in Public Sector Pensions Administration (QPSPA)
Diploma in Member Directed Pension Scheme Administration (MDPSA)
Diploma in International Employee Benefits (Dip. IEB)
The Awards in Pensions Trusteeship

DESIGNATORY LETTERS
MPMI, APMI, FPMI

PERSONNEL MANAGEMENT
Membership of Professional Institutions and Associations

CHARTERED INSTITUTE OF PERSONNEL AND DEVELOPMENT

151 The Broadway
Wimbledon
London SW19 1JQ
Tel: +44(0)20 8612 6208
Fax: +44(0)20 8612 6201
E-mail: membershipenquiry@cipd.co.uk
Website: www.cipd.co.uk

The CIPD is the world's largest Chartered HR and development professional body. With 135,000 members across 120 countries it supports and develops those responsible for the management and development of people within organisations.

MEMBERSHIP
Affiliate member
Student member
Associate member (Assoc CIPD)
Chartered Member (MCIPD)
Chartered Fellow (FCIPD)
Chartered Companion (CCIPD)
Academic member
For further information see; www.cipd.co.uk/membership

QUALIFICATION/EXAMINATIONS
CIPD qualifications are available at three levels:
Level 3 Foundation
Level 5 Intermediate
Level 7 Advanced
In three different sizes:
Awards
Certificates
Diplomas

For more information and to find out where to study CIPD qualifications visit; www.cipd.co.uk/qualifications

DESIGNATORY LETTERS
Assoc CIPD, Chartered MCIPD, Chartered FCIPD, CCIPD

THE INSTITUTE OF CONTINUING PROFESSIONAL DEVELOPMENT

Grosvenor Gardens House
35/37 Grosvenor Gardens
London SW1W 0BS
Tel: 020 7828 1965
Fax: 020 7828 1967
E-mail: info@cpdinstitute.org
Website: www.cpdinstitute.org

The Institute of Continuing Professional Development is part of the Continuing Professional Development Foundation, an educational charitable trust providing high-quality and broad-ranging CPD since 1981. We serve the public interest by helping to raise the effectiveness of professionals through the promotion of CPD as an important and integral element of lifelong learning.

MEMBERSHIP
Member (MInstCPD)
Fellow (FInstCPD)

DESIGNATORY LETTERS
MInstCPD, FInstCPD

UK EMPLOYEE ASSISTANCE PROFESSIONALS ASSOCIATION

PO Box 7966
Wilson
Derby DE1 0XP
E-mail: info@eapa.org.uk
Website: www.eapa.org.uk

The UK Employee Assistance Professionals Association represents the interests of professionals concerned with employee assistance, psychological health and wellbeing in the UK. Members include external and internal EAP providers, purchasers, counsellors, consultants and trainers.

MEMBERSHIP
Individual Member
Associate Member
Organisational Member
Registered External or Internal Provider

PHARMACY
Membership of Professional Institutions and Associations

ROYAL PHARMACEUTICAL SOCIETY OF GREAT BRITAIN

1 Lambeth High Street
London SE1 7JN
Tel: 020 7735 9141
Fax: 020 7735 7629
E-mail: enquiries@rpsgb.org
Website: www.rpsgb.org

The RPSGB, which dates from 1841, is the professional body for pharmacists and pharmacy technicians in England, Scotland and Wales. Our primary objectives are to lead, regulate, develop and represent the profession. We promote advancement of the science and practice of pharmacy, and pharmaceutical education and knowledge, and liaise with government and other bodies in the interests of our members.

MEMBERSHIP
Pharmacy Technician
Member (MRPharmS)
Fellow (FRPharmS)

DESIGNATORY LETTERS
MRPharmS, FRPharmS

THE COLLEGE OF PHARMACY PRACTICE

28 Warwick Row
Coventry CV1 1EY
Tel: 024 762 21359
Fax: 024 765 21110
E-mail: info@collpharm.org.uk
Website: www.collpharm.org.uk

The College of Pharmacy Practice, set up in 1981 by the Pharmaceutical Society of Great Britain, is an organization of pharmacists who share the aim of promoting and maintaining a high standard of pharmacy practice. Its mission is to promote professional and personal development through education, examination, practice and research, benefiting both patients and healthcare provision.

MEMBERSHIP
Student Member
Associate (ACPP)
Member (MCPP)
Fellow (FCPP)
Member Emeritus

DESIGNATORY LETTERS
ACPP, MCPP, FCPP

THE PHARMACEUTICAL SOCIETY OF NORTHERN IRELAND

73 University Street
Belfast BT7 1HL
Tel: 028 9032 6927
Fax: 028 9043 9919
Website: www.psni.org.uk

The Pharmaceutical Society of Northern Ireland, founded in 1925, is the regulatory and professional body for pharmacists in Northern Ireland. It maintains a register of more than 2,000 pharmacists and over 500 pharmacy premises, and sets and promotes the standards for pharmacists' admission to and remaining on the register, thereby protecting public safety.

MEMBERSHIP
Trainee
Member

QUALIFICATION/EXAMINATIONS
Registration Examination

PHOTOGRAPHY
Membership of Professional Institutions and Associations

ASSOCIATION OF PHOTOGRAPHERS (AOP)

81 Leonard Street
London EC2A 4QS
Tel: 020 7739 6669
Fax: 020 7739 8707
E-mail: general@aophoto.co.uk
Website: www.the-aop.org

The AOP was founded in 1968 to promote the highest standards throughout the industry and to improve the rights of all professional photographers based in the UK. Our membership currently comprises 1,800 photographers and photographic assistants, and we are supported by photographers' agents, printers, and manufacturers and suppliers of photographic equipment.

MEMBERSHIP
Student Member
Assistant Member
Provisional Member
Photographer (full) Member
Agent Member
College Member
Affiliated Company

BRITISH INSTITUTE OF PROFESSIONAL PHOTOGRAPHY

The Coach House
The Firs, High Street
Whitchurch
Aylesbury
Buckinghamshire HP22 4SJ
Tel: 01296 642020
Fax: 01296 641553
E-mail: info@bipp.com
Website: www.bipp.com

The BIPP is the qualifying body for professional photographers in the UK. We provide support, training and qualifications for photographers across all types of photography, and organize a number of regional activities and events. A not-for-profit organization, we ensure that professional standards are met and maintained.

MEMBERSHIP
Open to full- or part-time professional photographers. Join as a Qualifying member (maximum of 1 year) and work towards gaining a professional qualification. Student membership is also available.

QUALIFICATION/EXAMINATIONS
Three tiers of qualification:
Licentiateship (LBIPP)
Associateship (ABIPP)
Fellowship (FBIPP)
Full details of the qualifications criteria can be found at www.bipp.com

DESIGNATORY LETTERS
LBIPP, ABIPP, FBIPP

MASTER PHOTOGRAPHERS ASSOCIATION

Jubilee House
1 Chancery Lane
Darlington
Co Durham DL1 5QP
Tel: 01325 356555
Fax: 01325 357813
E-mail: general@mpauk.com
Website: www.mpauk.com

The MPA was founded in 1952 and is now the UK's only organization for FT, qualified professional photographers. We have more than 2,000 members, who enjoy a range of benefits, including education, qualifications, informative regional meetings, business building promotions and marketing support, and abide by the Association's Code of Conduct.

MEMBERSHIP
Licentiate (LMPA)
Associate (AMPA)
Fellow (FMPA)

QUALIFICATION/EXAMINATIONS
The Diploma in Photographic Practice (DipPP) is recognised by SkillSet, as a benchmark competence mapped to the Photo Imaging National Standards: it is available to all qualified members and is an assessment process of professional photographic business and personal skills.

DESIGNATORY LETTERS
LMPA, AMPA, FMPA, DipPP

THE ROYAL PHOTOGRAPHIC SOCIETY

Fenton House
122 Wells Road
Bath BA2 3AH
Tel: 01225 325733
Fax: 01225 448688
E-mail: reception@rps.org
Website: www.rps.org

The RPS, which dates from 1853, is an educational charity whose aim is to promote the art and science of photography. Membership is open to anyone and we provide information, training and advice, hold workshops on a variety of photographic topics and stage three major touring exhibitions, as well as a monthly exhibition of members' work at our headquarters in Bath.

MEMBERSHIP
Student Member
Member
Licentiate (LRPS)
Associate (ARPS)
Fellow (FRPS)

QUALIFICATION/EXAMINATIONS
Qualified Imaging Scientist and Licentiate (QIS LRPS)
Graduate Imaging Scientist and Associate (GIS ARPS)
Accredited Imaging Scientist and Associate (AIS ARPS)
Accredited Senior Imaging Scientist and Fellow (ASIS FRPS)

DESIGNATORY LETTERS
LRPS, ARPS, FRPS

PHYSICS
Membership of Professional Institutions and Associations

INSTITUTE OF PHYSICS AND ENGINEERING IN MEDICINE

Fairmount House
230 Tadcaster Road
York YO24 1ES
Tel: 01904 610821
Fax: 01904 612279
E-mail: office@ipem.org.uk
Website: www.ipem.ac.uk

The IPEM is dedicated to bringing together physical science, engineering and clinical professionals in academia, healthcare services and industry to share knowledge, advance science and technology, and inform and educate the public, with the purpose of improving the understanding, detection and treatment of disease and the management of patients.

MEMBERSHIP
Student Member
Affiliate
Associate
Medical Member (MedMIPEM)
Medical Fellow (MedFIPEM)
Incorporated Member (IIPEM)
Corporate Member (MIPEM)
Fellow (FIPEM)
Overseas Affiliate
Company Member

DESIGNATORY LETTERS
MedMIPEM, MedFIPEM, IIPEM, MIPEM, FIPEM

Physics

THE INSTITUTE OF PHYSICS

76 Portland Place
London W1B 1NT
Tel: 020 7470 4800
Fax: 020 7470 4848
E-mail: physics@iop.org
Website: www.iop.org

The IOP is a scientific charity devoted to increasing the practice, understanding and application of physics. We have a worldwide membership of over 36,000 and are a leading communicator of physics-related science to all audiences, from specialists through to government and the general public. Our publishing company, IOP Publishing, is a world leader in scientific publishing and the electronic dissemination of physics.

MEMBERSHIP
Student Member
Affiliate
Associate Member (AMInstP)
Member (MInstP)
Fellow (FInstP)
Chartered Physicist (CPhys)

DESIGNATORY LETTERS
AMInstP, MInstP, FInstP, CPhys

PHYSIOTHERAPY
Membership of Professional Institutions and Associations

THE CHARTERED SOCIETY OF PHYSIOTHERAPY

14 Bedford Row
London WC1R 4ED
Tel: 0207 306 6666
Fax: 0207 306 6611
E-mail: enquiries@csp.org.uk
Website: www.csp.org.uk

The CSP is the professional, educational and trade union body for the UK's 52,000 chartered physiotherapists, physiotherapy students and assistants. In order to become a member of the CSP it is necessary to have undertaken a qualification recognized by the Health and Care Professions Council (HCPC) – see; www.hcpc-uk.org.

MEMBERSHIP
Student Member
Associate
Member (MCSP)
Fellow (FCSP)

DESIGNATORY LETTERS
MCSP, FCSP

PLASTICS AND RUBBER
Membership of Professional Institutions and Associations

LONDON METROPOLITAN POLYMER CENTRE

London Metropolitan University
166–220 Holloway Road
London N7 8DB
Tel: 020 7133 2248
Fax: 020 7133 2184
E-mail: polymers@londonmet.ac.uk
Website: www.londonmet.ac.uk/depts/polymers/

The London Metropolitan Polymer Centre is a leading UK centre for education, research and consultancy in polymer engineering, science and technology. We have a comprehensive range of modern equipment for polymer processing, testing, characterization, etc, offer courses from technician to postgraduate level, and work closely with industry, contributing to its continuing technical and commercial success.

QUALIFICATION/EXAMINATIONS
NC in Polymer Technology
HNC in Polymer Engineering
HND in Polymer Science and Engineering
BEng in Polymer Engineering
BSc in Sports Product Design
MSc in Manufacture and Design for Polymer Products
MSc in Plastics Product Design
MSc in Plastics Product Design with Management
MSc in Plastics Product Design with Marketing
MSc in Polymer Science and Engineering
MRes in Polymer Technology

PLUMBING
Membership of Professional Institutions and Associations

CHARTERED INSTITUTE OF PLUMBING AND HEATING ENGINEERING

64 Station Lane
Hornchurch
Essex RM12 6NB
Tel: 01708 472791
Fax: 01708 448987
E-mail: linfo@ciphe.org.uk
Website: www.ciphe.org.uk

The CIPHE, founded in 1906, is the professional body for the UK plumbing and heating industry. Our membership of around 12,000 is made up of individuals from a wide range of backgrounds and includes consultants, specifiers, designers, public health engineers, lecturers, trainers, trainees and practitioners, as well as manufacturers and distributors.

MEMBERSHIP
Trainee
Affiliate
Companion (CompCIPHE)
Associate (ACIPHE)
Member (MCIPHE)
Fellow (FCIPHE)

QUALIFICATION/EXAMINATIONS
Master Plumber Certificate (awarded jointly with the Worshipful Company of Plumbers and the City & Guilds of London Institute)

Printing

DESIGNATORY LETTERS
CompCIPHE, ACIPHE, MCIPHE, FCIPHE

PRINTING

Membership of Professional Institutions and Associations

PROSKILLS UK

Centurion Court
85b Milton Park
Abingdon
Oxfordshire OX14 4RY
Tel: 01235 833844
E-mail: info@proskills.co.uk
Website: www.proskills.co.uk

Proskills UK is the bridge between employers and government on skills and training. Employer-led representing key industries including, Building Products, Coatings, Furniture, Furnishings & Interiors, Glass & Related Industries, Health and Safety Paper, Printing and Wood industries, which make up a third of UK manufacturing sector. We help to raise the profile of the sector, set the skills standards and qualifications and ensure that the skills and funding system delivers against the current and future needs of the industries.

QUALIFICATION/EXAMINATIONS
Please see the Proskills UK website.

THE INSTITUTE OF PAPER, PRINTING AND PUBLISHING (IP3)

Claremont House
70–72 Alma Road
Windsor
Berks SL4 3EZ
Tel: 0870 330 8625
Fax: 0870 330 8615
E-mail: info@ip3.org.uk
Website: www.ip3.org.uk

IP3 is the professional body representing the interests of individuals within the paper, printing and publishing sector. It was formed in 2005 from the merger of the Institute of Paper, the Institute of Printing and the Institute of Publishing, and brought together more than 2,000 members and a wealth of knowledge.

MEMBERSHIP
Student
Associate (AIP3)
Member (MIP3)
Fellow (FIP3)

QUALIFICATION/EXAMINATIONS
Certificate

DESIGNATORY LETTERS
AIP3, MIP3, FIP3

PROFESSIONAL INVESTIGATION
Membership of Professional Institutions and Associations

THE INSTITUTE OF PROFESSIONAL INVESTIGATORS

Claremont House
70–72 Alma Road
Windsor
Berkshire SL4 3EZ
Tel: 0870 330 8622
Fax: 0870 330 8612
E-mail: admin@ipi.org.uk
Website: www.ipi.org.uk

The IPI was founded in 1976 as a professional body, catering primarily for the work and educational needs of professional investigators of all types and all specializations. We encourage members' CPD and require them to adhere to the Institute's strict code of ethics, and we promote the recognition of professional investigation as a profession by government, legislative bodies and the public.

MEMBERSHIP
Associate
Member (MIPI)
Fellow (FIPI)

QUALIFICATION/EXAMINATIONS
The Institute provides an interactive online Foundation Course for students and others interested in becoming part of the investigative industry; this course also provides a refresher course for those who need to update their specialization and/or interest in other areas of investigative work.

DESIGNATORY LETTERS
MIPI, FIPI

PSYCHOANALYSIS
Membership of Professional Institutions and Associations

THE BRITISH PSYCHOANALYTICAL SOCIETY

Byron House
112a Shirland Road
London W9 2EQ
Tel: 020 7563 5000
Fax: 020 7563 5001
Website: www.psychoanalysis.org.uk

The British Psychoanalytical Society was founded in 1913 and now has 438 members and 46 candidates for membership. Our aims include: to support the development of psychoanalytical knowledge as a general theory of mind, to further the clinical and scientific standards of psychoanalysis, and to train high-quality psychoanalytical professionals in sufficient numbers to develop the profession.

MEMBERSHIP
Associate Member
Full Member

PSYCHOLOGY

Membership of Professional Institutions and Associations

BRITISH PSYCHOLOGICAL SOCIETY

St Andrews House
48 Princess Road East
Leicester LE1 7DR
Tel: 0116 254 9568
Fax: 0116 227 1314
E-mail: enquiries@bps.org.uk
Website: www.bps.org.uk

Psychology is the scientific study of people, the mind and behaviour. The British Psychological Society is the representative body for psychology and psychologists in the UK. We are responsible for the development, promotion and application of psychology for the public good.

MEMBERSHIP
Student Member
Graduate Member (MBPsS)
Associate Fellow (AFBPsS)
Fellow (FBPsS)
Honorary Fellow (HonFBPsS)
Affiliate
Chartered Membership (CPsychol)
Subscriber
e-Subscriber

QUALIFICATION/EXAMINATIONS
Qualification in Educational Psychology (Scotland) (Stage 2)
Qualification in Forensic Psychology (Stage 2) (QFP)
Qualification in Clinical Neuropsychology (QiCN)
Qualification in Counselling Psychology (QCoP)
Qualification in Health Psychology (Stage 2)
Qualification in Occupational Psychology (QOccPsych)
Qualification in Sport & Exercise Psychology (QSEP)

DESIGNATORY LETTERS
MBPsS, AFBPsS, FBPsS, CPsychol, HonMBPsS, HonFBPsS

PSYCHOTHERAPY

Membership of Professional Institutions and Associations

ASSOCIATION OF CHILD PSYCHOTHERAPISTS

120 West Heath Road
London NW3 7TU
Tel: 020 8458 1609
Fax: 020 8458 1482
E-mail: contactus@childpsychotherapy.org.uk
Website: www.childpsychotherapy.org.uk

The ACP is the main professional body for psychoanalytic child and adolescent psychotherapists in the UK. Our members work with children and young people as well as their parents, families and wider networks, treating a wide range of difficulties ranging from problems with sleeping and bed-wetting to eating disorders, self-harm, depression and anxiety.

MEMBERSHIP
Member

BRITISH ASSOCIATION FOR COUNSELLING AND PSYCHOTHERAPY

BACP House
15 St John's Business Park
Lutterworth
Leicestershire LE17 4HB
Tel: 01455 883300
Fax: 01455 550243
E-mail: bacp@bacp.co.uk
Website: www.bacp.co.uk

BACP is the largest and broadest body within the sector and participates in the development of counselling and psychotherapy at an international level. Our work with large and small organizations ranges from advising schools on how to set up a counselling service to assisting the NHS on service provision, working with voluntary agencies and supporting independent practitioners.

MEMBERSHIP
Student Member
Affiliate Member
Associate Member
Member (MBACP)
Accredited Member (MBACP Accred)
Fellow (FBACP)

QUALIFICATION/EXAMINATIONS
We run workshops for members and accredit individual counsellors/psychotherapists, supervisors, counselling services and training courses. For details see our website.

DESIGNATORY LETTERS
MBACP, MBACP (Accred), FBACP

BRITISH ASSOCIATION FOR COUNSELLING AND PSYCHOTHERAPY

15 St John's Business Park
Lutterworth
Leicestershire LE17 4HB
Tel: 01455 883300
Fax: 01455 550243
E-mail: bacp@bacp.co.uk
Website: www.bacp.co.uk

The British Association for Counselling and Psychotherapy welcomes applications from qualified and experienced counsellors who wish to become BACP Accredited. BACP Accreditation as a counsellor offers a direct route to Registration as an independent practitioner with the United Kingdom Register of Counsellors.

MEMBERSHIP
Student
Associate
Member (MBACP)
Fellow (FBACP)

QUALIFICATION/EXAMINATIONS
SEAs Certificate
SEAs Diploma
SEAs Professional Qualification

DESIGNATORY LETTERS
MBACP, MBACP(Accred), FBACP

BRITISH ASSOCIATION FOR THE PERSON CENTRED APPROACH

BAPCA
PO Box 143
Ross-on-Wye
Herefordshire HR9 9AH
Tel: 01989 763863
E-mail: enquires@bapca.org.uk
Website: www.bapca.org.uk

The BAPCA was founded in 1989 as a non-religious, non-profit-making organization with the aim of advancing education in Client-Centred Psychotherapy and Counselling and the Person-Centred Approach through its publications and website, and cooperation with other national and international organizations with similar goals.

MEMBERSHIP
Individual Member
Joint Member
International Member
Institutional Member

BRITISH ASSOCIATION OF PSYCHOTHERAPISTS

37 Mapesbury Road
London NW2 4HJ
Tel: 020 8452 9823
Fax: 020 8452 5182
E-mail: mail@bap-psychotherapy.org
Website: www.bap-psychotherapy.org

The BAP is one of the longest established and largest independent providers of Jungian analytic and psychoanalytic psychotherapy for adults and children in the UK. We have been training psychoanalytic and Jungian psychotherapists for nearly 60 years, and our members work in the NHS, the corporate and voluntary sectors and as private practitioners.

MEMBERSHIP
Member

QUALIFICATION/EXAMINATIONS
Certificate/Diploma/MSc in Psychodynamics of Human Development (jointly with Birkbeck College, University of London)
DPsych in Child and Adolescent Psychotherapy (jointly with Birkbeck College, University of London)

CAMBRIDGE COLLEGE OF HYPNOTHERAPY

24 Milton Road
Impington
Cambridge CB24 9NF
Tel: 01223 235127
E-mail: j.teague@ntlworld.com
Website: www.hypnotherapytraining.org.uk

The CCH offers training to become a professional hypnotherapist. The course is accredited by the NCH, HA, APHP, NGH and NRAH. No formal qualifications are required to enrol on the course. What is required is a willingness to learn, a sense of humour and a genuine compassion and liking for people from all paths in life. This can be a very rewarding new or second career or a supplement to your current work / lifestyle. In addition to the College Diploma, it is possible to gain the HPD (Hypnotherapy Practitioner

Diploma) which is awarded by ncfe and also possible to gain a Diploma awarded by the National Guild of Hypnotists in the USA. The HPD is at NVQ level 4/5 and has transferable credits of 45 for a first year degree with the Open University.

MEMBERSHIP
RSM, HA, NCH, NRAH, NSHP, APHP, HS

QUALIFICATION/EXAMINATIONS
Diploma in Hypnotherapy

DESIGNATORY LETTERS
DipTHP

NATIONAL COLLEGE OF HYPNOSIS AND PSYCHOTHERAPY

PO Box 5779
Loughborough
Leicestershire LE12 5ZF
Tel: 0845 257 8735
E-mail: enquiries@nchp,org,uk
Website: www.hypnotherapyuk.net

The NCHP is a not-for-profit organization founded in 1977 and now offers accredited hypnotherapy training, hypnosis training and psychotherapy training at weekends in Leeds, Leicester, Liverpool, London, Manchester, Newcastle, Oxford, Glasgow and South Wales. We also provide a programme of 1- and 2-day workshops and seminars, and (where appropriate) distance-learning courses.

QUALIFICATION/EXAMINATIONS
Foundation Course
Certificate in Hypno-Psychotherapy (CHP(NC))
Diploma in Hypno-Psychotherapy (DHP(NC))
Advanced Diploma in Hypno-Psychotherapy (ADHP(NC))
European Certificate of Clinical Hypnosis (through the European Association for Hypno-Psychotherapy)
Hypnotherapy Practitioner Diploma

NATIONAL COUNCIL OF PSYCHOTHERAPISTS

PO Box 7219
Heanor
Derbyshire DE75 9AG
Tel: 08452 306072
Fax: 01773 711031
E-mail: ncphq@btinternet.com
Website: www.ncphq.co.uk

The National Council is a registering and accrediting body for psychotherapists, counsellors and coaches within the UK and also, through the International Council, the rest of the world.

Members can join the Council regardless of which discipline and where they completed their training.

MEMBERSHIP
Affiliate (ANCP)
Licentiate (LNCP)
Full Member (MNCP)
Fellow (FNCP)

DESIGNATORY LETTERS
ANCP, LNCP, MNCP, FNCP

THE FOUNDATION FOR PSYCHOTHERAPY AND COUNSELLING

Tel: 020 7378 2090
E-mail: office@thefoundation-uk.org
Website: www.thefoundation-uk.org

The Foundation for Psychotherapy and Counselling was formed during the 1970s as the graduate body of WPF Therapy (the largest charitable provider of counselling and psychotherapy in England) and now has some 700 fully trained and qualified members, most of whom are in private practice.

MEMBERSHIP
Member

THE NATIONAL REGISTER OF HYPNOTHERAPISTS AND PSYCHOTHERAPISTS

1st Floor
18 Carr Road
Nelson
Lancashire BB9 7JS
Tel: 01282 716839
E-mail: admin@nrhp.co.uk
Website: www.nrhp.co.uk

NRHP (est 1985) – a professional association of qualified hypno-psychotherapists who trained with a UKCP-accredited training organisation. Members are required to adhere to a code of ethics and carry appropriate insurance. We publish a Directory of Practitioners and offer a public referral service via our website and office. Member of the UKCP.

MEMBERSHIP
Student
Associate 1 (NRHP(Assoc 1))
Associate 2 (NRHP(Assoc 2))
Associate 3 (NRHP(Assoc 3))
Full Member (MNRHP)
Fellow (FNRHP)

DESIGNATORY LETTERS
NRHP(Assoc 1), NRHP(Assoc 2), NRHP(Assoc 3), MNRHP, FNRHP

UK COUNCIL FOR PSYCHOTHERAPY

2nd Floor Edward House
2 Wakley Street
London EC1V 7LT
Tel: 020 7014 9955
Fax: 020 7014 9977
E-mail: info@ukcp.org.uk
Website: www.psychotherapy.org.uk

The UK Council for Psychotherapy (UKCP) is recognised as the leading professional body for the education, training and accreditation of psychotherapists and psychotherapeutic counsellors. We represent 75 training and accrediting organisations and over 7,500 individual therapists – working privately or in public health organisations – offering a wide variety of psychotherapeutic approaches or modalities. UKCP exists to uphold the highest standards in psychotherapy. Our national register of psychotherapists and psychotherapeutic counsellors lists those practitioner members who meet exacting standards and training requirements. As part of our commitment to protecting the public, we work to improve access to psychological therapies, to support and disseminate research, to improve standards and to respond effectively to complaints against our members.

PUBLIC ADMINISTRATION
Membership of Professional Institutions and Associations

THE INSTITUTE OF PUBLIC SECTOR MANAGEMENT

45 Cherry Tree Road
Axminster
Devon EX13 5GG
Tel: 01297 35423
Fax: 01297 35423
E-mail: info@ipsm.org.uk
Website: www.ipsm.org.uk

The IPSM is the only membership body exclusively dedicated to managers working in the public, voluntary and not-for-profit sectors. We encourage the sharing of knowledge, skills and experience between our members, provide advice and support ourselves, and as a campaigning body seek to raise public awareness and respect for public services and the role of the manager in those services.

MEMBERSHIP
Student Member
Individual (Full) Member (MIPSM)
Fellow (FIPSM)
Corporate Member

PURCHASING AND SUPPLY
Membership of Professional Institutions and Associations

THE CHARTERED INSTITUTE OF PURCHASING & SUPPLY

Easton House
Easton on the Hill
Stamford
Lincolnshire PE9 3NZ
Tel: 01780 756777
Fax: 01780 751610
E-mail: info@cips.org
Website: www.cips.org

The Chartered Institute of Purchasing & Supply (CIPS) is the world's largest procurement and supply professional organisation. It is the worldwide centre of excellence on purchasing and supply management issues. CIPS has a global community of over 88,000 in 150 different countries, including senior business people, high-ranking civil servants and leading academics. The activities of purchasing and supply chain professionals have a major impact on the profitability and efficiency of all types of organisation and CIPS offers corporate solutions packages to improve business profitability.

MEMBERSHIP
Student Member
Affiliate
Certificate Member
Diploma Member
Associate Member
Full Member (MCIPS)
Fellow (FCIPS)

QUALIFICATION/EXAMINATIONS
Please see website; www.cips.org

DESIGNATORY LETTERS
MCIPS, FCIPS

QUALITY ASSURANCE
Membership of Professional Institutions and Associations

THE CHARTERED QUALITY INSTITUTE

12 Grosvenor Crescent
London SW1X 7EE
Tel: 020 7245 6722
Fax: 020 7245 6788
E-mail: info@thecqi.org
Website: www.thecqi.org

The CQI is the chartered body for quality management professionals. Established in 1919, we gained a Royal Charter in 2006 and became the CQI shortly afterwards. Our vision is to place quality at the heart of every organization; we promote the benefits of quality management to industry, disseminate quality knowledge and resources, provide qualifications and training, and assess quality competence.

MEMBERSHIP
Student
Associate Member (ACQI)
Member, Chartered Quality Professional (MCQI, CQP)
Fellow, Chartered Quality Professional (FCQI, CQP)
Company Member

QUALIFICATION/EXAMINATIONS
Certificate in Quality
Diploma in Quality

DESIGNATORY LETTERS
MCQI, CQP; FCQI, CQP

RADIOGRAPHY
Membership of Professional Institutions and Associations

THE SOCIETY OF RADIOGRAPHERS

207 Providence Square
Mill Street
London SE1 2EW
Tel: 020 7740 7200
Fax: 020 7740 7204
E-mail: info@sor.org
Website: www.sor.org

The Society of Radiographers, founded in 1920, represents diagnostic and therapeutic radiographers in the UK. Associated professionals working in medical imaging, radiation therapy and oncology are also welcome. It is responsible for their professional, educational, public and workplace interests. Together with the College of Radiographers, our charitable subsidiary, our efforts are directed towards education, research and other activities in support of the science and practice of radiography.

MEMBERSHIP
We have a range of membership options, including student, associate professional, healthcare support worker and assistant practitioner, retired and international membership options.

RETAIL
Membership of Professional Institutions and Associations

IGD

Grange Lane
Letchmore Heath
Watford
Hertfordshire WD25 8GD
Tel: 01923 857141
Fax: 01923 852531
E-mail: igd@igd.com
Website: www.igd.com

IGD (the Institute of Grocery Distribution) was formed in 1972 from the merger of the Institute of Chartered Grocers and the Institute of Food Distribution. We provide information and practical training to the industry and now have more than 700 corporate members, covering a broad spectrum of companies and organizations across the world.

MEMBERSHIP
Corporate Member

QUALIFICATION/EXAMINATIONS
PG Cert in Food & Grocery Industry Management (validated by the University of Edinburgh)

INSTITUTE OF MASTERS OF WINE

2/3 Philpot Lane
London EC3M 8AN
Tel: 020 7621 2830
Fax: 020 7929 2302
Website: www.mastersofwine.org

The Institute of Masters of Wine is a membership body that represents the interests of its members (Masters of Wine), administers the MW Examination, and runs an education programme in preparation for the examination. We also hold a number of events throughout the year, including seminars and tastings, master classes, discussions, and, every 4 years, a symposium, most of which are open to the public.

MEMBERSHIP
Master of Wine (MW)

QUALIFICATION/EXAMINATIONS
Master of Wine Examination

DESIGNATORY LETTERS
MW

Retail

MEAT TRAINING COUNCIL

PO Box 141
Winterhill House
Snowdon Drive
Milton Keynes MK6 1YY
Tel: 01908 231062
Fax: 01908 231063
E-mail: info@meattraining.org.uk
Website: www.meattraining.org.uk

The MTC is a registered charity, limited by guarantee, working for, and with, the UK meat industry. We provide information about jobs, careers and the qualifications required to work in the red meat and poultry sector of the food business. Professional membership is administered by the Worshipful Company of Butchers via its Guild of Freemen. The qualifications awarding body is now the Food and Drink Qualifications Awarding Body (FDQ Ltd) (www.fdq.org.uk).

MEMBERSHIP
Affiliate (AffInstM)
Associate (AInstM)
Graduate Member (GMInstM)

QUALIFICATION/EXAMINATIONS
Please see the Meat Training Council's website.

DESIGNATORY LETTERS
AffInstM, AInstM, GMInstM

THE BRITISH ANTIQUE DEALERS' ASSOCIATION

20 Rutland Gate
London SW7 1BD
Tel: 020 7589 4128
Fax: 020 7581 9083
E-mail: info@bada.org
Website: www.bada.org

BADA, which was founded in 1918, is the trade association for antique dealers in Britain. Our vetted members are elected for their high business standards and expertise, and adhere to a strict code of practice; we provide safeguards for members of the public who deal with our members, including independent arbitration if a dispute arises.

MEMBERSHIP
Member

THE GUILD OF ARCHITECTURAL IRONMONGERS

8 Stepney Green
London E1 3JU
Tel: 020 7790 3431
Fax: 020 7790 8517
E-mail: info@gai.org.uk
Website: www.gai.org.uk

The GAI represents the interests of architectural ironmongers and manufacturers of architectural ironmongery. We develop, promote and protect standards of integrity and excellence, and encourage academic study relating to the industry, operating an Institute for individual members to facilitate their continuous professional development. We liaise with various bodies on matters affecting the industry.

Retail

MEMBERSHIP
Affiliate Member
Associate Member
Full Member
Registered Architectural Ironmonger (Reg AI)

QUALIFICATION/EXAMINATIONS
The GAI provides a 3-year incremental training programme. Students are examined each year and must pass each year in turn before progressing to the next. A Certificate is awarded to successful students each year, culminating in the GAI Diploma (Dip GAI) on successful completion of year 3.

DESIGNATORY LETTERS
Reg AI

THE INSTITUTE OF BUILDERS MERCHANTS

Touchwood
Oak View Rise
Harlow Wood
Mansfield
Nottinghamshire NG18 4UT
Tel: 01623 427693
E-mail: admin@instbm.co.uk
Website: www.instbm.co.uk

To improve through seminars and website articles, the technical and general knowledge of persons engaged in builders' merchants; to verify management training courses with providers; to acknowledge personal achievements and award diplomas, certificates and other distinctions; to encourage the need for knowledge, integrity and efficiency in the builders' merchants industry.

MEMBERSHIP
Student
Associate
Member
Fellow
Corporate Supporter

QUALIFICATION/EXAMINATIONS
University Degree
The Institute of Builders Merchants Business Studies Course
The Builders Merchants Federation Diploma in Merchanting
Higher National Certificate (HNC) in Business Studies
Higher National Diploma (HND) in Business Studies
NVQ Level 4
Company management programmes as approved by the Board of Governors

THE SOCIETY OF SHOE FITTERS

c/o The Anchorage
28 Admirals Walk
Hingham
Norfolk NR9 4JL
Tel: 01953 851171
Fax: 01953 851190
E-mail: secretary@shoefitters-uk.org
Website: www.shoefitters-uk.org

The Society of Shoe Fitters is a not-for-profit organization started in 1959, set up to assist the trade and public. We disseminate shoe fitting/footwear knowledge to the trade via courses/examination, and endeavour to help the public with shoe fitting advice via our website, leaflets and helpline.

MEMBERSHIP
Student Member
Associate Member
Member (MSSF)
Fellow (FSSF)
Associate Member (corporate membership)

QUALIFICATION/EXAMINATIONS
One-day on-site courses – certificate only

Five- or 10-month course leading to membership qualification
Entrance Examination and Entrance Application for experienced shoe fitters leading to qualification

DESIGNATORY LETTERS
MSSF, FSSF

SECRETARIAL AND OFFICE WORK
Membership of Professional Institutions and Associations

INSTITUTE OF PROFESSIONAL ADMINISTRATORS

6 Graphite Square
Vauxhall Walk
London SE11 5EE
Tel: 020 7091 2606
Fax: 020 7091 7340
E-mail: info@inprad.org
Website: www.inprad.org

The IPA was founded in 1957 as the Institute of Qualified Professional Secretaries and is today the leading membership body for administration and office professionals. We provide our members with information, advice and guidance on suitable training and development to advance their career as well as a CPD scheme designed to meet their individual needs.

MEMBERSHIP
Student Member
Affiliate (AffIPA)
Member (MIPA)
Fellow (FIPA)
Corporate Member

DESIGNATORY LETTERS
AffIPA, MIPA, FIPA

SECURITY
Membership of Professional Institutions and Associations

THE SECURITY INSTITUTE

1 The Courtyard
Caldecote
Warwickshire CV10 0AS
E-mail: info@security-institute.org
Website: www.security-institute.org

The Institute promotes professionalism in the security world and encourages a proper understanding of the value of the security function by management. The Institute has declared its intention to progress towards chartered status. Membership of the Institute is now recognized as an employment prerequisite by many companies and government departments.

MEMBERSHIP
Affiliate/Student

Graduate
Associate
Member
Fellow (FSyI)

QUALIFICATION/EXAMINATIONS
Certificate in Security Management
Diploma in Security Management

DESIGNATORY LETTERS
FSyI

SOCIAL WORK AND PROBATION

SOCIAL WORK

The General Social Care Council (GSCC) was responsible for regulating and supporting social work education and training in England. As part of a review of arm's length bodies (ALBs) in July 2010, the Government announced its intention to close the GSCC and transfer its regulatory functions to the Health Professions Council. To reflect this new remit, the HPC's name has changed to the Health and Care Professions Council (HCPC). This change is contained within the Health and Social Care Act (2012). The GSCC closed on 31 July 2012 and the HCPC became the new regulator from 1 August 2012.

The HCPC accredits universities that offer social work qualifications at both qualifying and post-qualifying levels, and quality-assures all social work courses. In 2003, professional qualifying training for social workers in the United Kingdom changed from the diploma in social work (DipSW) to a degree in social work. To find HCPC-approved degree courses visit http:/ www.hcpc-uk.org/education/programmes/register

For further details, contact The Health and Care Professions Council, Park House, 184 Kennington Park Road, London SE11 4BU; Tel: 0845 300 6184; Fax: 020 7820 9684; e-mail: education@hcpc-uk.org; website; www.hcpc-uk.org

For information about social work training in Scotland, contact Scottish Social Services Council, Compass House, 11 Riverside Drive, Dundee DD1 4NY; Tel: 0845 6030 891; e-mail: enquiries@sssc.uk.com; website; www.sssc.uk.com

For information about social work training in Wales, contact Care Council for Wales, South Gate House, Wood Street, Cardiff CF10 1EW; Tel: 0300 3033 444; e-mail: info@ccwales.org.uk; website; www.ccwales.org.uk

For information about social work training in Northern Ireland, contact Northern Ireland Social Care Council, 7th Floor, Millennium House, 19–25 Great Victoria Street, Belfast BT2 7AQ; Tel: 0289 0417 600; e-mail: info@niscc.hscni.net; website; www.niscc.info.

Membership of Professional Institutions and Associations

THE BRITISH ASSOCIATION OF SOCIAL WORKERS

16 Kent Street
Birmingham B5 6RD
Tel: 0121 6223911
Fax: 0121 6224860
Website: www.basw.co.uk

The BASW is the largest professional association representing social work and social workers in the UK. Whether you are qualified or not, experienced or just entering the profession, we are here to help, support, advise and campaign on your behalf.

MEMBERSHIP
Student Member
Affiliate
Member (4 categories)
Retired Member
Overseas Member

SOCIOLOGY
Membership of Professional Institutions and Associations

BRITISH SOCIOLOGICAL ASSOCIATION

Bailey Suite, Palatine House
Belmont Business Park
Belmont
Durham DH1 1TW
Tel: 0191 383 0839
Fax: 0191 383 0782
E-mail: enquiries@britsoc.org.uk
Website: www.britsoc.co.uk

The BSA was founded in 1951 to promote sociology in the UK. Our members include researchers, teachers, students and practitioners in a variety of fields. We provide a network of communication to all who are concerned with the promotion and use of sociology and sociological research.

SPEECH AND LANGUAGE THERAPY
Membership of Professional Institutions and Associations

ROYAL COLLEGE OF SPEECH AND LANGUAGE THERAPISTS

2 White Hart Yard
London SE1 1NX
Tel: 020 7378 1200
Fax: 020 7378 7254
E-mail: postmaster@rcslt.org
Website: www.rcslt.org

The RCSLT is the professional body for speech and language therapists and support workers. We set, promote and maintain high standards in education, clinical practice and ethical conduct. Our national campaigning work aims to improve services for people with speech, language, communication and swallowing needs and to influence health, education and social care policies.

MEMBERSHIP
Student Member
Newly Qualified Member
Full Member
Fellow (FRCSLT)
Honorary Fellow (Hon FRCSLT)

DESIGNATORY LETTERS
FRCSLT, Hon FRCSLT

SPORTS SCIENCE
Membership of Professional Institutions and Associations

LONDON SCHOOL OF SPORTS MASSAGE

28 Station Parade
Willesden Green
London NW2 4NX
Tel: 020 8452 8855
Fax: 020 8452 4524
E-mail: admin@lssm.com
Website: www.lssm.com

The LSSM, founded in 1989, was the first to provide specialist training in Sport & Remedial Massage. We offer vocational training for those who want to develop a professional career in massage therapy and were instrumental in setting up the Institute of Sport & Remedial Massage (ISRM), which is the professional body promoting our needs and aspirations as clinical therapists.

MEMBERSHIP
Member

QUALIFICATION/EXAMINATIONS
Introductory Massage Workshop
Professional Diploma in Clinical Sport & Remedial Massage Therapy (BTEC Level 5)

STATISTICS
Membership of Professional Institutions and Associations

THE ROYAL STATISTICAL SOCIETY

12 Errol Street
London EC1Y 8LX
Tel: 020 7638 8998
Fax: 020 7614 3905
E-mail: rss@rss.org.uk
Website: www.rss.org.uk

The RSS is the learned society and professional body for statistics and statisticians in the UK. We have over 7,000 members worldwide, and are active in a wide range of areas both directly and indirectly relating to the study and application of statistics.

MEMBERSHIP
Student Member
Fellow
Graduate Statistician (GradStat)
Chartered Statistician (CStat)

QUALIFICATION/EXAMINATIONS
Ordinary Certificate in Statistics
Higher Certificate in Statistics
Graduate Diploma in Statistics

DESIGNATORY LETTERS
GradStat, CStat

STOCKBROKING AND SECURITIES
Membership of Professional Institutions and Associations

CFA SOCIETY OF THE UK

2nd Floor
135 Canon Street
London EC4N 5BP
Tel: 020 7280 9620
Fax: 020 7280 9636
E-mail: info@cfauk.org
Website: www.cfauk.org

The CFA Society of the UK was formerly the UK Society of Investment Professionals (UKSIP) and was renamed in 2007. Our aim is to promote the development of the investment profession in the UK through the promotion of the highest standards of ethical behaviour and the provision of education, professional development, information, career support and advocacy to our members.

MEMBERSHIP
IMC Member
Candidate Member
Affiliate Member
Regular Member

QUALIFICATION/EXAMINATIONS
Investment Management Certificate (IMC)

THE CHARTERED INSTITUTE FOR SECURITIES & INVESTMENT

8 Eastcheap
London EC3M 1AE
Tel: 020 7645 0600
Fax: 020 7645 0601
Website: www.cisi.org.uk

The Chartered Institute for Securities & Investment is the largest professional body for practitioners in stockbroking, derivatives markets, investment management, corporate finance, operations and related activities, having over 44,000 members.

MEMBERSHIP
Student Member
Affiliate
Associate (ACSI)
Member (MCSI)
Chartered Member (Ch. MCSI)
Fellow (FCSI)
Chartered Fellow (Ch. FCSI)

QUALIFICATION/EXAMINATIONS
Introduction to Investment
Islamic Finance Qualification
IT in Investment Operations
Risk in Financial Services
Combating Financial Crime
Global Financial Compliance
Investment Operations Certificate (IOC) also known as Investment Administration Qualification (IAQ)
Certificate in Corporate Finance
Certificate in Investments
Certificate in Investment Management (CertIM)
Certificate in Private Client Investment Advice & Management
International Certificate in Wealth Management
Investment Advice Diploma
Advanced Certificate in Global Securities Operations
Advanced Certificate in Operational Risk
Diploma in Investment Compliance
Diploma in Investment Operations
CISI Diploma
CISI Masters in Wealth Management

DESIGNATORY LETTERS
ACSI, MCSI, Ch. MCSI, FCSI, Ch.FCSI

SURGICAL, DENTAL AND CARDIOLOGICAL TECHNICIANS
Membership of Professional Institutions and Associations

THE BRITISH INSTITUTE OF DENTAL AND SURGICAL TECHNOLOGISTS

4 Thompson Green
Shipley
West Yorkshire BD17 7PR
Tel: 0845 644 3726
E-mail: secretary@bidst.org
Website: www.bidst.org

The BIDST has been established for over 70 years and exists to provide a vehicle for the continuing education of technicians within the spheres of dental and surgical technology. It is our aim to make membership of the Institute an aspiration for all technicians, raising standards and portraying an image of professionalism which professional technicians deserve.

MEMBERSHIP
Student Associate
Associate
Licentiate (LBIDST)
Life Member
Fellow (FBIDST)

DESIGNATORY LETTERS
LBIDST, FBIDST

SURVEYING
Membership of Professional Institutions and Associations

ASSOCIATION OF BUILDING ENGINEERS

Lutyens House
Billing Brook Road
Weston Favell
Northampton NN3 8NW
Tel: 0845 126 1058
Fax: 01604 784220
E-mail: building.engineers@abe.org.uk
Website: www.abe.org.uk

The ABE is the professional body for those specializing in the technology of building and the management processes by which buildings are designed, constructed, renewed and maintained. Our objectives are to promote and advance the planning, design, construction, maintenance and repair of the built environment; to maintain a high standard of professional practice; and to encourage co-operation between professionals.

MEMBERSHIP
Student
Technician
Associate Member (ABEng)
Graduate Member (GradBEng)
Member (MBEng)
Fellow (FBEng)
Honorary Fellow (HonFBEng)

QUALIFICATION/EXAMINATIONS
Edexcel Level 3 NVQ Diploma in Construction Contracting Operations (QCF) Edexcel Level 6 NVQ Diploma in Construction Contracting Operations Management (QCF) Edexcel Level 7 NVQ Diploma in Construction Senior Management (QCF)

DESIGNATORY LETTERS
ABEng, GradBEng, MBEng, FBEng

SWIMMING INSTRUCTION
Membership of Professional Institutions and Associations

THE SWIMMING TEACHERS' ASSOCIATION

Anchor House
Birch Street
Walsall
West Midlands WS2 8HZ
Tel: 01922 645097
Fax: 01922 720628
E-mail: sta@sta.co.uk
Website: www.sta.co.uk

The STA is dedicated to the preservation of human life by the teaching of swimming, lifesaving and survival techniques to as many people as possible, both in the UK and internationally. We offer a range of specialist training programmes and qualifications, which are used in more than 25 countries worldwide, and liaise with other organizations concerned with swimming teaching and water safety.

MEMBERSHIP
Junior Member
Associate Member (ASTA)
Qualified Member (MSTA)
Corporate Member

QUALIFICATION/EXAMINATIONS
STA Certificate in Teaching Swimming – Beginners
STA Certificate in Teaching Swimming – Full
STA Certificate in Teaching Swimming – Primary Teacher
STA Certificate in Aquatic Teaching – Baby & Pre-School
STA Certificate in Aquatic Teaching – Special Needs (Teacher)
STA Foundation Certificate in Swimming Pool and Spa Water Treatment
STA Certificate in Swimming Pool and Spa Water Treatment
STA Certificate for the National Rescue Standard – Pool Lifeguard
STA Certificate for the National Rescue Standard – Pool Attendant
STA Certificate for the National Rescue Standard – Poolside Helper
STA Award in Emergency First Aid at Work
STA Award in Emergency First Aid for Sport

DESIGNATORY LETTERS
ASTA, MSTA

TAXATION
Membership of Professional Institutions and Associations

SOCIETY OF TRUST & ESTATE PRACTITIONERS

Artillery House (South)
11–19 Artillery Row
London SW1P 1RT
Tel: +44 (0)20 7340 0500
Fax: +44 (0)20 7340 0501
E-mail: step@step.org
Website: www.step.org

The Society of Trust and Estate Practitioners (STEP) is a unique professional body providing members with a local, national and international learning and business network focusing on the responsible stewardship of assets today and across the generations.

MEMBERSHIP
Full members of STEP are the most experienced and senior practitioners in the field of trusts and estates.

QUALIFICATION/EXAMINATIONS
STEP Diplomas and Foundation Certificates are recognized as essential qualifications and TEP's are sought after by employers. A portfolio of courses has been designed to enhance your career. STEP qualifications include the STEP Diploma for England & Wales (Trusts and Estates), STEP Diploma for Ireland, STEP Diploma for Scotland, STEP Diploma in International Trust Management, STEP Certificate for Financial Services (Trusts and Estate Planning) and many more.

DESIGNATORY LETTERS
TEP

THE ASSOCIATION OF TAXATION TECHNICIANS

1st Floor
Artillery House
11–19 Artillery Row
London SW1P 1RT
Tel: 0844 251 0830
Fax: 0844 251 0831
E-mail: info@att.org.uk
Website: www.att.org.uk

The ATT was founded in 1989 in recognition of the increasing demand for tax services and the development of tax practice as a professional activity in its own right. Our primary aim is to provide an appropriate qualification for individuals who undertake such work, and we now have more than 10,500 members, affiliates and registered students.

MEMBERSHIP
Student
Affiliate
Member

QUALIFICATION/EXAMINATIONS
Certificate of Competency in Business Compliance
Certificate of Competency in Business Taxation and Accounting Principles

DESIGNATORY LETTERS
ATT

THE CHARTERED INSTITUTE OF TAXATION

First Floor
11–19 Artillery Row
London SW1P 1RT
Tel: 020 7340 0550
Fax: 0844 579 6701
E-mail: post@tax.org.uk
Website: www.tax.org.uk

The CIOT, which dates from 1930, is the professional body for Chartered Tax Advisers and has 14,300 members. Our aims are to promote education in and the study of the administration and practice of taxation, and to achieve a better, more efficient, tax system for all affected by it – taxpayers, advisers and the authorities.

MEMBERSHIP
Associate (CTA or ATII)
Fellow (CTA or FTII)

QUALIFICATION/EXAMINATIONS
Chartered Tax Adviser (CTA) examination
Advanced Diploma in International Taxation (ADIT)

DESIGNATORY LETTERS
CTA, ATII, FTII

Taxation

THE INSTITUTE OF INDIRECT TAXATION

The Stables
Station Road West
Oxted
Surrey RH8 9EE
Tel: 01883 730658
Fax: 01883 717778
E-mail: enquiries@theiit.org.uk
Website: www.theiit.org.uk

The Institute was founded in 1991 to establish a professional body of indirect tax practitioners to regulate and support its members. Membership is worldwide and includes barristers, solicitors, accountants, sole practitioners and tax specialists in commerce, the professions and government. The Institute is a member of the Confederation Fiscale Europeenne.

MEMBERSHIP
Student
Affiliate
Associate (AIIT)
Honorary Associate (AIIT(Hon))
Fellow (FIIT)
Honorary Fellow (FIIT(Hon))

QUALIFICATION/EXAMINATIONS
Associate Examination
VAT Compliance Diploma (IIT (Dip))

DESIGNATORY LETTERS
AIIT, AIIT (Hon), FIIT, FIIT (Hon)

TAXI DRIVERS
Membership of Professional Institutions and Associations

TAXI DRIVERS (LONDON)

Cab drivers and cab proprietors in the Metropolitan Police District and City of London are licensed by an Assistant Commissioner of the Metropolitan Police, through the Public Carriage Office at 15 Penton Street, Islington N1 9PU. A cab driver's licence is valid for 3 years and a cab proprietor's licence for 1 year.

TEACHING/EDUCATION

Initial qualifications in the UK
Qualified Teacher Status
To obtain a teaching appointment as a qualified teacher in maintained schools in England and Wales, it is necessary to have Qualified Teacher Status (QTS). To be qualified, teachers must have satisfactorily completed an approved course of initial teacher training (ITT), and to be able to teach in maintained schools in England must have successfully completed their induction period (there are similar arrangements for teaching in Scotland, Wales and Northern Ireland).
Teacher training courses
Initial teacher training courses in England and Wales are provided by accredited training providers mainly through university departments of education. Courses available include Bachelor of Arts or Bachelor of Science with QTS, Bachelor of Education (BEd) for undergraduates, and Postgraduate Certificates of Education (PGCEs) for graduates.

Undergraduate training courses generally take three or four years full time, or four to six years part time. However, if you have undergraduate credits from previous study you may be able to complete a course in two years. A PGCE generally lasts one year full time, or up to two years part time.

There are also some employment-based routes into teaching. The School Direct Programme allows schools to recruit trainees with the expectation that they will go on to work in the school or group of schools in which they have been trained, though there is no guarantee of employment. There are more than 100 schools offering places. Courses generally last for one year full time, starting from September 2012.

From September 2013, School Direct will be offering the School Direct Training Programme and the School Direct Training Programme (salaried). Following the closure of the Graduate Teacher Programme (GTP), the School Direct Training Programme (salaried) will be open to graduates with three or more years' career experience. Trainees will be employed as unqualified teachers with a salary subsidised by the Teaching Agency. Trainees on a School Direct course will have to pay tuition fees to cover the cost of the course, but home and EU trainees will be eligible for a tuition fee loan to cover these costs. For more information, see Teaching Agency, School Direct (www.education.gov.uk).

Teach First is a programme enabling graduates to spend two years working in challenging secondary and primary schools in seven regions: East Midlands, Kent and Medway, London, North East, North West, West Midlands, and Yorkshire and the Humber. The programme enables trainees to qualify as a teacher while also completing leadership training.

The qualification of Professional Graduate Diploma in Education (PGDE) is a one-year postgraduate degree course leading to registration as a primary or secondary school teacher in Scotland (see www.teachinginscotland.com).

The Postgraduate Certificate of Education course, approved by the Department of Education Northern Ireland, leads to recognition as a school teacher in Northern Ireland (see www.deni.gov.uk).

Qualifications for admission to training

Higher education institutions offering undergraduate ITT courses will set admissions criteria: typically two good A levels (or equivalent qualifications). Entrants to PGCE and other graduate training courses will require a relevant UK Bachelor's degree or a recognized equivalent and be expected to demonstrate a standard equivalent to GCSE grade C in English and mathematics, and additionally a standard equivalent to GCSE grade C in a science subject for those wishing to train to teach primary school children. Trainees who have undertaken their initial teacher training in England must pass professional skills tests in numeracy and literacy. Anyone applying for an ITT course that starts after 1 July 2013 will be required to have passed the skills tests before starting the course. These tests cover core skills that teachers need in their jobs and QTS cannot be awarded until they are passed. If you are undertaking initial teacher training in Wales, you are not required to complete the skills tests in order to be awarded QTS.

The Teaching Agency

The Teaching Agency is a new executive agency of the Department for Education (DfE). It is the body responsible for the following activities in England:
- the award of Qualified Teacher Status (QTS);
- the issue of induction certificates;
- hearing induction appeals;
- the regulation of the teaching profession.

There is no requirement to register with the new Teaching Agency and no registration fee.

For information about the Teaching Agency, visit www.education.gov.uk/. Visit www.education.gov.uk/teachregister or call 0800 389 2500 for queries relating to becoming a teacher, initial teacher training, recruitment opportunities or provision of relevant training.

General Teaching Councils

General Teaching Councils exist in Wales (GTCW), Scotland (GTCS) and Northern Ireland (GTCNI). These councils hold registers of qualified teachers and also act as disciplinary bodies. You can find out more from their respective websites: GTCW; www.gtcw.org.uk; GTCS; www.gtcs.org.uk; GTCNI; www.gtcni.org.uk.

Applications

Applications for undergraduate courses are made through the University and Colleges Admission Services (UCAS) and postgraduate applications through the Graduate Teacher Training Registry (GTTR). You cannot apply for courses in Northern Ireland through GTTR, but must visit the Department for Education in Northern Ireland's website for information about these courses (www.deni.gov.uk). You can find out more about training to teach from the following websites: GTTR; www.gttr.ac.uk; UCAS; www.ucas.ac.uk; the Teaching Agency; www.education.gov.uk/get-into-teaching.

TECHNICAL COMMUNICATIONS
Membership of Professional Institutions and Associations

THE INSTITUTE OF SCIENTIFIC AND TECHNICAL COMMUNICATORS (ISTC LTD)

Airport House
Purley Way
Croydon CR0 0XZ
Tel: 020 8253 4506
Fax: 020 8253 4510
E-mail: istc@istc.org.uk
Website: www.istc.org.uk

The ISTC is a non-profit-making organization and the largest UK body representing professional communicators and information designers. Our aims include improving standards of scientific and technical communication, promoting scientific and technical communication as a career, supporting our members, and consulting, cooperating and collaborating with other bodies that share out ideals.

MEMBERSHIP
Student
Associate
Junior
Member (MISTC)
Fellow (FISTC)
Business Affiliate

DESIGNATORY LETTERS
MISTC, FISTC

TEXTILES
Membership of Professional Institutions and Associations

THE TEXTILE INSTITUTE

1st Floor St James' Buildings
79 Oxford Street
Manchester M1 6FQ
Tel: 0161 2371188
Fax: 0161 2361991
E-mail: tiihq@textileinst.org.uk
Website: www.textileinstitute.org

The Textile Institute covers all disciplines – from technology and production to design, development and marketing – relating to fibres, fabrics, clothing, footwear, and interior and technical textiles.

MEMBERSHIP
Student
Individual
Licentiate (LTI)
Associate (CText ATI)
Fellow (CText FTI)
Companion
Honorary Fellow
Corporate

DESIGNATORY LETTERS
LTI, CText ATI, CText FTI

TIMBER TECHNOLOGY
Membership of Professional Institutions and Associations

WOOD TECHNOLOGY SOCIETY

The Boilerhouse
Springfield Business Park
Caunt Road
Grantham
Lincs NG31 7FZ
Tel: 01476-513880
Fax: 01476-513899
E-mail: emily.drury@iom3.org
Website: www.iom3.org/content/wood-technology

The Wood Technology Society (IWSc – a Division of the Institute of Materials, Minerals and Mining), formerly the Institute of Wood Science, is the professional body for the timber and allied industries. We promote and encourage a better understanding of timber, wood-based materials and associated timber processes, and are the UK examining body, awarding qualifications at Foundation, Certificate and Diploma level.

MEMBERSHIP
Student Member
Affiliate Member
Technician (TIWSc)
Licentiate (LIWSc)
Member (MIWSc)
Fellow (FIWSc)
Corporate Member

QUALIFICATION/EXAMINATIONS
Timber Studies Award (Foundation course)
Certificate
Diploma

DESIGNATORY LETTERS
TIWSc, LIWSc, MIWSc, FIWSc

TOWN AND COUNTRY PLANNING
Membership of Professional Institutions and Associations

ROYAL TOWN PLANNING INSTITUTE

41 Botolph Lane
London EC3R 8DL
Tel: 020 7929 9494
E-mail: membership@rtpi.org.uk
Website: www.rtpi.org.uk

The RTPI is the largest professional institute for planners in Europe, with over 22,000 members. As well as promoting spatial planning, we develop and shape policy affecting the built environment, work to raise professional standards and support members through continuous education, training and development.

MEMBERSHIP
Student Member
Licentiate Member
Associate Member
Legal Associate Member (LARTPI)
Technical Member (TechRTPI)
Retired Member
Honorary Member (HonMRTPI)
Chartered Member (MRTPI)
Chartered Fellow (FRTPI)

QUALIFICATION/EXAMINATIONS
Please see www.rtpi.org.uk/item/178/23/5/3 for a list of accredited training providers

DESIGNATORY LETTERS
LARTPI, TechRTPI, HonMRTPI, MRTPI, FRTPI

TRADING STANDARDS
Membership of Professional Institutions and Associations

THE TRADING STANDARDS INSTITUTE

1 Sylvan Court
Sylvan Way
Southfields Business Park
Basildon
Essex SS15 6TH
Tel: 0845 608 9400
Fax: 0845 608 9425
E-mail: institute@tsi.org.uk
Website: www.tradingstandards.gov.uk

The TSI, formed in 1881, is a not-for-profit membership association representing trading standards professionals in both the public and private sectors in the UK and overseas. TSI encourages honest enterprise and business, and helps safeguard the economic, environmental, health and social well-being of consumers.

MEMBERSHIP
Student Member
Affiliate Member
Associate Member (ATSI)
Full Member (MTSI)
Fellow (FTSI)
Corporate Affiliate

QUALIFICATION/EXAMINATIONS
The Trading Standards Qualification Framework consists of:
Certificate of Competence
Foundation Certificate in Consumer Affairs and Trading Standards
Core Skills Certificate in Consumer Affairs and Trading StandardsModule Certificate in Consumer Affairs and Trading Standards
Diploma in Consumer Affairs and Trading Standards
Higher Diploma in Consumer Affairs and Trading Standards

DESIGNATORY LETTERS
ATSI, MTSI, FTSI

TRANSPORT
Membership of Professional Institutions and Associations

INSTITUTE OF TRANSPORT ADMINISTRATION

The Old Studio
25 Greenfield Road
Westoning
Bedfordshire MK45 5JD
Tel: 01525 634940
Fax: 01525 750016
E-mail: director@iota.org.uk
Website: www.iota.org.uk

The primary aim of IoTA is to broaden and improve the knowledge, skills and experience of its members in the practice of efficient road, rail, air and sea transport. We are one of the few professional bodies still recognized within the terms of the Road Traffic 1968 (Statutory Instrument 78), wherein it is permitted to proffer qualified opinion as to the professional competence of its members. IoTA is seeking awarding organisation status for its Transport Managers Certificate of Professional Competence.

MEMBERSHIP
Student (StInstTA)
Associate (AInstTA)
Honorary Member
Associate Member (AMInstTA)
Member (MInstTA)
Fellow (FInstTA)
Patron Scheme for Companies

DESIGNATORY LETTERS
StInstTA, AInstTA, AMInstTA, MInstTA, FInstTA

THE INSTITUTE OF TRAFFIC ACCIDENT INVESTIGATORS

Column House
London Road
Shrewsbury
Shropshire SY2 6NN
Tel: 08456 212066
Fax: 08456 212077
E-mail: gensec@itai.org
Website: www.itai.org

The Institute provides a means of communication, education, representation and regulation in the field of Traffic Accident Investigation. Our main aim is to provide a forum for spreading knowledge and enhancing expertise among those engaged in the discipline. Members include police officers, lecturers in higher education and private practitioners.

MEMBERSHIP
Affiliate
Associate (AITAI)
Member (MITAI)

DESIGNATORY LETTERS
AITAI, MITAI

TRAVEL AND TOURISM
Membership of Professional Institutions and Associations

CONFEDERATION OF TOURISM AND HOSPITALITY

37 Duke Street
London W1U 1LN
Tel: 020 7258 9850
Fax: 020 7258 9869
E-mail: info@cthawards.com
Website: www.cthawards.com

The Confederation of Tourism and Hospitality is an awarding body approved by Ofqual, and registered on the QCA's National Qualifications Framework. We were established in 1982 to provide recognized standards of management and vocational training appropriate to the needs of the hotel and travel industries, via our syllabuses, examinations and awards.

MEMBERSHIP
Student Member
Associate Member (AMCTH)
Professional Member (PMCTH)
Fellow (FCTH)

QUALIFICATION/EXAMINATIONS
Diploma in Hospitality and Tourism Management
Diploma in Hotel Management
Diploma in Hotel and Casino Management
Diploma in Tourism Management
Diploma in Travel Agency Management
Advanced Diploma in Hotel and Event Management
Advanced Diploma in Tourism Management
Advanced Diploma in Travel Agency Management
Graduate Diploma in Hospitality and Tourism Management
Postgraduate Diploma in Hotel Management

DESIGNATORY LETTERS
AMCTH, PMCTH, FCTH

INSTITUTE OF TRAVEL AND TOURISM

PO Box 217
Ware
Hertfordshire SG12 8WY
Tel: 0844 4995 653
Fax: 0844 4995 654
E-mail: enquiries@itt.co.uk
Website: www.itt.co.uk

The ITT, founded in 1956, is a professional membership body for individuals employed in the travel and tourism industry. We provide support and guidance for our members throughout their career and offer them CPD and training to maintain standards for the benefit of the industry as a whole.

MEMBERSHIP
Student Member
Introductory Member
Affiliate Member
Member
Member (MInstTT)
Fellow
Fellow (FInstTT)
University/College Member
Group Member
Corporate Member

DESIGNATORY LETTERS
MInstTT, FInstTT

THE TOURISM MANAGEMENT INSTITUTE

c/o Hon Secretary, Dr Cathy Guthrie, FTMI, FTS
18 Cuninghill Avenue
Inverurie
Aberdeenshire AB51 3TZ
Tel: 01467 620769
E-mail: secretary@tmi.org.uk
Website: www.tmi.org.uk

Part of the Tourism Society, TMI is the professional body for tourism destination managers. Its network of 250+ members shares information via website, conferences, e-mails and newsletters. Committed to excellence, the TMI CPD programme aims to support destination management professionals through its events, Knowledge Bank and course recognition scheme.

MEMBERSHIP
Student
Associate (ATMI)
Member (MTMI)
Fellow (FTMI)

DESIGNATORY LETTERS
ATMI, MTMI, FTMI

THE TOURISM SOCIETY

Trinity Court
34 West Street
Sutton
Surrey SM1 1SH
Tel: 0208 661 4636
Fax: 0208 661 4637
E-mail: admin@tourismsociety.org
Website: www.tourismsociety.org

The Tourism Society, founded in 1977, is the professional membership body for people working in all sectors of tourism. We strive to drive up standards of professionalism and act as an advocate of tourism to the government and the public and private sectors, and liaise with other tourism professionals worldwide. We also provide advice, support and networking opportunities to our 1,200 or so members.

MEMBERSHIP
Student
Full Member (MTS)
Fellow (FTS)
Overseas/Retired Member
Group Member
Corporate Member

DESIGNATORY LETTERS
MTS, FTS

VETERINARY SCIENCE
Membership of Professional Institutions and Associations

BRITISH VETERINARY ASSOCIATION

7 Mansfield Street
London W1G 9NQ
Tel: 020 7636 6541
Fax: 020 7908 6349
E-mail: bvahq@bva.co.uk
Website: www.bva.co.uk

The BVA is the representative body for the veterinary profession in the UK and has more than 11,500 members. We promote and support the interests of our members and the animals under their care, liaise with the government and are the leading provider of veterinary information to the media and general public.

MEMBERSHIP
Student Member
Associate Member
Full Member
Overseas Member
Organizational Member

SOCIETY OF PRACTISING VETERINARY SURGEONS

The Governor's House
Cape Road
Warwick CV34 5DJ
Tel: 01926 410454
Fax: 01926 411350
E-mail: office@spvs.org.uk
Website: www.spvs.org.uk

The SPVS was founded in 1933 with the aim of promoting the interests of veterinary surgeons in private practice. We are a non-territorial division of the British Veterinary Association. Our remit is to advise on all aspects of managing the business of a clinical veterinary practice, and we hold one-day, weekend and week-long courses and an annual congress.

MEMBERSHIP
Student Member
Associate Member
Full Member
Retired Member

THE ROYAL COLLEGE OF VETERINARY SURGEONS

Belgravia House
62–64 Horseferry Road
London SW1P 2AF
Tel: 020 7222 2001
Fax: 020 7222 2004
E-mail: info@rcvs.org.uk
Website: www.rcvs.org.uk

The RCVS is the regulatory body for veterinary surgeons in the UK. Its role is to safeguard the health and welfare of animals committed to veterinary care, through the regulation of the educational, ethical and clinical standards of the veterinary profession, and to act as an impartial source of informed opinion on relevant veterinary issues.

MEMBERSHIP
Member (MRCVS)
Fellow (FRCVS)

QUALIFICATION/EXAMINATIONS
Certificate in Advanced Veterinary Practice (CertAVP)
Diploma (various titles, eg Small Animal Surgery; Animal Welfare Science Ethics & Law; Equine Internal Medicine; Cattle Health & Production etc)
RCVS Recognised Specialist
Diploma in Advanced Veterinary Nursing
Diploma of Fellowship (FRCVS)

DESIGNATORY LETTERS
MRCVS, FRCVS

WASTES MANAGEMENT
Membership of Professional Institutions and Associations

CHARTERED INSTITUTION OF WASTES MANAGEMENT

9 Saxon Court
St Peter's Gardens
Marefair
Northampton NN1 1SX
Tel: 01604 620426
Fax: 01604 621339
E-mail: education@ciwm.co.uk
Website: www.ciwm.co.uk

The CIWM represents more than 7,000 waste management professionals – predominantly in the UK but also overseas. We promote education, training and research in the scientific, technical and practical aspects of waste management for the safeguarding of the environment, and set and strive to maintain high standards for individuals working in the waste management industry.

MEMBERSHIP
Student Member
Technician Member (TechMCIWM)
Associate Member (AssocMCIWM)
Graduate Member (GradMCIWM)
Licentiate (LCIWM)
Member (MCIWM)
Fellow (FCIWM)
Affiliated Organization

QUALIFICATION/EXAMINATIONS
CIWM Training Services specializes in developing and providing waste management training for individuals & organizations. Each year we organize more than 70 courses. For details see the website.

DESIGNATORY LETTERS
TechMCIWM, AssocMCIWM, GradMCIWM, LCIWM, MCIWM, FCIWM

WATCH AND CLOCK MAKING AND REPAIRING
Membership of Professional Institutions and Associations

THE BRITISH HOROLOGICAL INSTITUTE LIMITED

Upton Hall
Upton
Newark
Nottinghamshire NG23 5TE
Tel: 01636 813795
Fax: 01636 812258
E-mail: clock@bhi.co.uk
Website: www.bhi.co.uk

The BHI, which was formed in 1858 to promote horology, is a professional body with about 3,000 members worldwide. We provide education and specialist training, set recognized standards of excellence in workmanship and professional conduct, and support our members in their work, making, repairing and servicing clocks and watches.

MEMBERSHIP
Associate
Member (MBHI)
Fellow (FBHI)

QUALIFICATION/EXAMINATIONS
Certificate in Clock and Watch Servicing (Level 2) – final registration January 2012
Certificate in the Repair, Restoration and Conservation of Clocks/Watches (Level 3) – anticipated final registration, January 2012
Diploma in Clock and Watch Servicing (Level 3)
Diploma in the Servicing and Repair of Clocks / Watches (Level 4) – awaiting confirmation of accreditation – August 2011
Diploma in the Repair, Restoration and Conservation of Clocks / Watches (Level 5) – awaiting confirmation of accreditation – August 2011

DESIGNATORY LETTERS
MBHI, FBHI

WELDING
Membership of Professional Institutions and Associations

THE WELDING INSTITUTE

Granta Park
Great Abington
Cambridge CB21 6AL
Tel: 01223 899000
Fax: 01223 894219
E-mail: professional@twi.co.uk
Website: www.twiprofessional.com

The Welding Institute is the engineering institution for welding and joining professionals. We are committed to promoting the importance of welding/materials joining technology, given its importance as a key industrial technology governing the reliability and safety of many products, and to the advancement of education, training and CPD for our members.

MEMBERSHIP
Graduate (GradWeldI)
Technician (TechWeldI)
Senior Associate (SenAWeldI)
Incorporated Member (IncMWeldI)
Member (MWeldI)
Senior Member (SenMWeldI)
Fellow (FWeldI)
Honorary Fellow (HonFWeldI)
Engineering Technician (EngTech)
Incorporated Engineer (IEng)
Chartered Engineer (CEng)

QUALIFICATION/EXAMINATIONS
Certificate in Welding and Joining Technology for Students in Materials and Engineering

DESIGNATORY LETTERS
GradWeldI, TechWeldI, SenAWeldI, IncMWeldI, MWeldI, SenMWeldI, FWeldI, HonFWeldI, EngTech, IEng, CEng

WELFARE
Membership of Professional Institutions and Associations

INSTITUTE OF WELFARE

PO Box 5570
Stourbridge DY8 9BA
Tel: 0800 0 32 37 25
E-mail: info@instituteofwelfare.co.uk
Website: www.instituteofwelfare.co.uk

The Institute of Welfare was founded in 1945 and exists to promote the highest possible standards in the delivery of welfare to those who need it. We make representations to government, undertake research on welfare issues, encourage and facilitate the exchange of information, and provide opportunities for those engaged in welfare work to pursue CPD.

MEMBERSHIP
Affiliate Member
Member (MIW)
Fellow (FIW)
Companion (CIW)

DESIGNATORY LETTERS
MIW, FIW, CIW

Part 6

Bodies Accrediting Independent Institutions

THE BRITISH ACCREDITATION COUNCIL FOR INDEPENDENT FURTHER AND HIGHER EDUCATION (BAC)

BAC is a registered charity that was established in 1984 to act as the national accrediting body for independent further and higher education. It is independent both of government and of the colleges it accredits.

A college that is accredited by BAC undergoes a thorough inspection every four years, with an interim visit after two years. Until 2000, BAC accreditation was only available to colleges in the United Kingdom, but there are now accredited colleges in 11 countries around the world: Bulgaria, the Czech Republic, France, Germany, Greece, Hungary, India, Lebanon, Mauritius, South Africa and Switzerland. At present BAC accredits or approves 365 colleges in the United Kingdom and 30 overseas. Lists of accredited colleges are published each year; full details can be viewed on the BAC website.

BAC maintains close links with all the major bodies concerned with the maintenance of standards in British education, including The British Council, Open and Distance Learning Quality Council (ODL QC), the Council of Validating Universities (CVU), National Recognition Information Centre (UK NARIC), the Quality Assurance Agency for Higher Education (QAA), Association of Colleges (AoC), GuildHE and the United Kingdom Council for International Student Affairs (UKCISA).

Accreditation by BAC is recognized by the UK Border Agency (UKBA) of the Home Office as a qualifying requirement for institutions to enrol visa students.

Further details of the work of the BAC and a current list of accredited institutions may be obtained from The Chief Executive, BAC, 7th Floor, 76 Shoe Lane, London EC4A 3JB; Tel: 0300 330 1400; Fax: 0300 330 1401; e-mail: info@the-bac.org; website: www.the-bac.org

THE BRITISH COUNCIL

The British Council runs the Accreditation UK scheme in partnership with English UK for the inspection and accreditation of organizations that provide courses in English as a Foreign Language (EFL) in Britain. One of its aims is to promote accredited UK English Language Teaching (ELT) through the British Council's network of overseas offices.

Under the terms of the scheme, institutions are inspected rigorously every four years in the areas of management, resources and environment, teaching and learning, and welfare and student services. The scheme also includes a system of random spot-checking. The management and policy of the scheme are conducted by an independent board while a separate independent committee reviews inspectors' reports.

The majority of recognized schools are also members of English UK, which insists on British Council accreditation as a criterion for membership. In addition, all English UK members, of which there are around 450, are required to abide by the Association's Code of Practice and Regulations. English UK exists to raise the high standards of its members even further through conferences, training courses and publications. The association also represents the interests of members and students to government bodies, and promotes international student mobility through membership of the UK Border Agency User Panel.

Further information on the Accreditation UK scheme may be obtained from the Accreditation Unit, British Council, Bridgewater House, 58 Whitworth Street, Manchester M1 6BB; Tel: 0161 9577 692; e-mail: accreditation.unit@britishcouncil.org; website: www. britishcouncil.org/accreditation. Further information on English UK may be obtained from English UK, 219 St John Street, London EC1V 4LY; Tel: 020 7608 7960; Fax: 020 7608 7961; e-mail: info@englishuk.com; website: www.englishuk.com.

THE OPEN AND DISTANCE LEARNING QUALITY COUNCIL (ODLQC)

ODL QC was established in 1968 as the Council for the Accreditation of Correspondence Colleges, a joint initiative of the then Labour government and representatives of the sector. It is the principal accrediting body for a wide variety of providers of open and distance learning in the UK, from commercial colleges to professional and public-sector institutions. Now independent, it nevertheless continues to have the informal support of government.

ODL QC promotes quality by:

- establishing standards of education and training in open and distance learning;
- recognizing good quality provision, wherever it occurs;
- supporting and protecting the interests of learners;
- encouraging the improvement of existing methods and the development of new ones;
- linking open and distance learning with other forms of education and training;
- promoting wider recognition of the value of open and distance learning.

Accreditation includes a rigorous assessment of educational provision, covering materials, tutorial support, publicity, contractual arrangements with learners and general administrative procedures, each of which is measured against the Council's published benchmark standards. If accredited, the provider is monitored on a regular basis and reassessed at least once every three years.

The Council promotes those colleges that it accredits, which are by definition quality providers of ODL, and acts as honest broker in matching accredited colleges to potential markets. A list of courses offered by accredited providers is circulated widely, both in the UK and abroad, and is included on the Council's website, www.odlqc.org.uk. The Council also seeks to protect the interests of learners by promoting the importance of accreditation, and by offering advice and support directly to learners. At the same time, knowledge of good practice is disseminated more widely, and quality encouraged wherever open and distance learning occurs.

The Council consists of members nominated by professional and public bodies involved in education, as well as representatives of accredited providers, and has strong links with other bodies in the sector, both in the UK and abroad.

All enquiries should be addressed to ODL QC, 79 Barnfield Wood Road, Beckenham, Kent BR3 6ST; e-mail: info@odlqc.org.uk; website: www.odlqc.org.uk.

THE COUNCIL FOR INDEPENDENT EDUCATION (CIFE)

CIFE was founded in 1973 to promote strict adherence by independent sixth-form and tutorial colleges to the highest standards of academic and professional integrity. All member colleges must be accredited by the British Accreditation Council for Independent Further and Higher Education (BAC), and/or the Independent Schools Inspectorate (ISI). CIFE colleges all undergo regular inspection by the Department for Education. Candidate membership is available for up to three years for colleges that are seeking BAC or ISI accreditation and otherwise satisfy CIFE's exacting membership criteria. All colleges must also abide by stringent codes of conduct and practice; the character and presentation of their published exam results are subject to regulation, and the accuracy of the information must be validated by BAC as academic auditor to CIFE. Full members are subject to re-inspection by their accrediting bodies. There are 18 colleges in full or candidate membership of CIFE at present, spread throughout England but with concentrations in London, Oxford and Cambridge.

CIFE colleges offer a wide range of GCSE, A and AS level courses. In addition, some CIFE colleges offer English language tuition for students from overseas, and degree-level tuition. A number of the colleges offer summer holiday academic courses, and most of them also provide A level and GCSE revision courses during the Christmas and/or Easter holidays. Further information on CIFE may be obtained from the CIFE website: www.cife.org.uk; Tel: 020 8767 8666; e-mail: enquiries@cife.org.uk.

Part 7

Study Associations and the 'Learned Societies'

Study associations consist of people who wish to increase their knowledge of a particular subject or range of subjects; they may be professionals or amateurs. Some associations consist almost entirely of specialists (eg the Royal Statistical Society); others (eg the Royal Geographical Society and the Zoological Society of London) have a more general membership. The learned societies usually have two grades of membership: fellows or members. Some also admit group members (such as schools or libraries), known as corporate members, and junior associate, corresponding and overseas members, who pay lower subscriptions. Some also elect honorary fellows or members. The members of some societies may use designatory letters, but this does not mean that the holder is 'qualified' in the same sense as a doctor or a chartered accountant.

Membership of some learned societies is by election, and is commonly accepted as distinguishing the candidate by admission to an exclusive group. Candidates may be selected in respect of pre-eminence in their subject or in the public service. The chief associations of this type are the Royal Society (founded 1660 and granted Royal Charters in 1662 and 1663), the Royal Academy of Arts (founded 1768) and the British Academy (granted the Royal Charter in 1902).

The Royal Society was established to improve 'natural knowledge' and is mainly concerned with pure and applied science and technology. Election to Fellowship (FRS) is regarded as one of the highest distinctions. The society elects Fellows, Foreign Members and Royal Fellows (www.royalsociety.org). The Royal Academy was established to cultivate and improve the arts of painting, sculpture and architecture. There are two main grades of membership: Academicians (RA), including Senior Academicians, and Associates (ARA); there are also a small number of Honorary Academicians (www.royalacademy.org.uk). The British Academy is the UK's national academy for the humanities and the social sciences. It is the counterpart to the Royal Society that exists to serve the natural sciences. The Academy has Fellows (FBA), Corresponding Fellows and a small number of Honorary Fellows. www.britac.ac.uk

A list of learned societies and study associations can be found below.

OCCUPATIONAL ASSOCIATIONS

The occupational associations do not qualify practitioners but organize them. Some coordinate the activities of specialists and others promote the individual and collective interests of professionals working in a wider area. Both types also seek to safeguard the public interest and to offer an educational service to their members. The latter type of association is especially numerous among teachers, who have over 20 associations (eg the National Union of Teachers (NUT), the Educational Institute of Scotland (EIS), NASWUT (the National Association of Schoolmasters/Union of Women Teachers) and the National Association of Head Teachers (NAHT), and is represented in the medical profession by the British Medical Association.

LIST OF STUDY ASSOCIATIONS AND LEARNED SOCIETIES

This list largely excludes qualifying bodies, which are covered in Part 5. The date on the left is that of foundation or adoption of title.

Agriculture and related subjects

1926	Agricultural Economics Society	1839	Royal Agricultural Society of England
1952	British Agricultural History Society	1882	Royal Forestry Society of England, Wales and N Ireland
1945	British Grassland Society		
1944	British Society of Animal Science	1784	Royal Highland and Agricultural Society of Scotland
1947	British Society of Soil Science		
1921	Commonwealth Forestry Association	1804	Royal Horticultural Society
1927	Herb Society of Great Britain	1854	Royal Scottish Forestry Society
1925	Institute of Chartered Foresters	1904	Royal Welsh Agricultural Society
1938	Institution of Agricultural Engineers	1943	Society of Dairy Technology
1947	International Fertiliser Society	1945	The Soil Association

Anthropology and related subjects

1963	African Studies Association of the UK	1972	Japan Foundation
1979	Association for the Study of Modern and Contemporary France	1891	Japan Society
		1843	Royal Anthropological Institute of Great Britain and Ireland
1982	Association for the Study of Modern Italy		
		1823	Royal Asiatic Society of Great Britain and Ireland
1946	Association of Social Anthropologists of the UK and Commonwealth		
		1868	Royal Commonwealth Society
1985	British Association for Irish Studies	1901	Royal Society for Asian Affairs
1974	British Association for Japanese Studies	1936	Saltire Society
		1977	Society for Caribbean Studies
1972	British Association for South Asian Studies	1964	Society for Latin American Studies
		1969	Society for Libyan Studies
1961	British Institute of Persian Studies	1983	Society for the Promotion of Byzantine Studies
1973	British Society for Middle Eastern Studies		
		1879	Society for the Promotion of Hellenic Studies
1981	European Association for Jewish Studies		
		1910	Society for the Promotion of Roman Studies
1878	Folklore Society		
1943	Hispanic and Luso Brazilian Council	1969	University Association for Contemporary European Studies
1974	International Association for the Study of German Politics		
		1892	Viking Society for Northern Research

Archaeology and related subjects

1924	Ancient Monuments Society	1882	Egypt Exploration Society
1979	Association for Environmental Archaeology	1855	London and Middlesex Archaeological Society
1843	British Archaeological Association	1865	Palestine Exploration Fund
1996	British Epigraphy Society	1908	Prehistoric Society
1948	British Institute at Ankara	1843	Royal Archaeological Institute
1846	Cambrian Archaeological Association	1967	Society for Post-Medieval Archaeology
1944	Council for British Archaeology		
1838	Eccleriological Society		

Art and Design

1974	Association of Art Historians	1754	Royal Society for the Encouragement of Arts, Manufactures and Commerce
1910	Contemporary Art Society		
1915	Design and Industries Association		
1950	International Institute for Conservation of Historic and Artistic Works	1904	Royal Society of British Sculptors
		1904	Royal Society of Marine Artists
		1895	Royal Society of Miniature Painters, Sculptors and Gravers
1888	National Society for Education in Art and Design	1884	Royal Society of Painter/Printmakers
		1891	Royal Society of Portrait Painters
1899	Pastel Society	1804	Royal Watercolours Society
1768	Royal Academy of Arts	1919	Society of Graphic Fine Art
1814	Royal Birmingham Society of Artists	1952	Society of Portrait Sculptors
1883	Royal Institute of Oil-Painters	1952	United Society of Artists
1831	Royal Institute of Painters in Watercolours	1955	William Morris Society
1826	Royal Scottish Academy of Art and Architecture		

Biology and related subjects

1936	Association for the Study of Animal Behaviour	1931	Society for Applied Microbiology
		1911	The Biochemical Society
1904	Association of Applied Biologists	1913	The British Ecological Society
1968	Biomedical Engineering Society	1896	The British Mycological Society
1836	Botanical Society of Scotland	1858	The British Ornithologists' Union
1836	Botanical Society of the British Isles	1959	The British Society for Cell Biology
1896	British Bryological Society	1933	The British Trust for Ornithology
1929	Freshwater Biological Association	1937	The Systematics Association
1889	Marine Biological Association	1826	Zoological Society of London
1833	Royal Entomological Society		

Chemistry

1918	Oil and Colour Chemists' Association	1897	Society of Leather Technologists and Chemists
1980	Royal Society of Chemistry		
1881	Society of Chemical Industry		

Economics, Statistics and related subjects

1992	Association of Business Schools	1955	Institute of Economic Affairs
1927	Economic History Society	1902	Royal Economic Society
2003	Economic Research Institute of Northern Ireland	1834	Royal Statistical Society
		1897	Scottish Economic Society

Engineering and related subjects

1847	Architectural Association	1997	Institute of Ergonomics and Human Factors
1966	Concrete Society		
1946	Faculty of Building	1976	Royal Academy of Engineering
1978	Institute of Concrete Technology	1866	Royal Aeronautical Society

Year	Society
1916	Royal Incorporation of Architects in Scotland
1860	Royal Institution of Naval Architects
1916	Society of Automotive Engineers
1958	Society of Environmental Engineers
2003	The Energy Institute
1899	Town and Country Planning Association

Geography, Geology and related subjects

Year	Society
1963	British Cartographic Society
1949	British Geotechnical Society
1940	British Society of Rheology
1968	Council for Environmental Education
1923	English Place-Name Society
1931	Gemmological Association of Great Britain
1893	Geographical Association
1807	Geological Society of London
1858	Geologists Association
1846	Hakluyt Society
1971	Institution of Environmental Sciences
1876	Mineralogical Society of Great Britain and Ireland
1847	Palaeontographical Society
1957	Paleontological Association
1830	Royal Geographical Society
1997	Royal Institute of Navigation
1884	Royal Scottish Geographical Society

History and related subjects

Year	Society
1902	British Academy
1952	British Agricultural History Society
1888	British Record Society
1932	British Records Association
1947	British Society for the History of Science
1988	Centre for Metropolitan History
1864	Early English Texts Society
1964	Furniture History Society
1869	Harleian Society
1885	Huguenot Society of Great Britain and Ireland
1961	Institute of Heraldic and Genealogical Studies
1921	Institute of Historical Research
1893	Jewish Historical Society of England
1964	London Record Society
2000	Museums, Libraries and Archives Council
1920	Newcomen Society for the Study of the History of Engineering and Technology
1921	Oriental Ceramic Society
1868	Royal Historical Society
1836	Royal Numismatic Society
1869	Royal Philatelic Society, London
1953	Scottish Genealogy Society
1886	Scottish History Society
1897	Scottish Record Society
1976	Social History Society
1921	Society for Army Historical Research
1910	Society for Nautical Research
1967	Society for Renaissance Studies
1970	Society for the Social History of Medicine
1707	Society of Antiquaries of London
1780	Society of Antiquaries of Scotland
1956	Society of Architectural Historians in Great Britain
1947	Society of Archivists
1911	Society of Genealogists
1906	The Historical Association
1958	Victorian Society

Languages

Year	Society
1883	Alliance Française
1891	An Comunn Gaidhealach
1981	Association for French Language Studies
1932	Association for German Studies in Great Britain and Ireland
1990	Association for Language Learning
1910	Chartered Institute of Linguists
1991	Instituto Cervantes

1964	National Association for the Teaching of English	1993	University Council of Modern Languages
2003	National Centre for Languages	1988	Women in German Studies

Law

1958	British Institute of International and Comparative Law	1949	Law Society of Scotland
1972	Intellectual Property Bar Association	1920	Royal Institute of International Affairs
1922	Law Society of Northern Ireland	1965	Scottish Law Commission
		1887	Selden Society

Literature and Arts

1959	Academi – Yr Academi Gymreig	1906	English Association
1973	Alliance of Literary Societies	1886	Francis Bacon Society Inc
1969	Art Libraries Society	1960	H. G. Wells Society
1970	Association for Scottish Literary Studies	1997	Historical Novel Society
		1973	Joseph Conrad Society
1989	Association of Independent Libraries	1997	Leeds Philosophical and Literary Society
1892	Bibliographical Society		
1992	British Association for Information and Library Education and Research	1906	Malone Society
		1781	Manchester Literary and Philosophical Society
1975	British Comparative Literature Association	1995	Philip Larkin Society
		1842	Philological Society
1933	British Film Institute	1909	Poetry Society
1960	British Society of Aesthetics	1820	Royal Society of Literature
1893	Bronte Society	1884	Society of Authors
1949	Cambridge Bibliographical Society	2004	Society of College, National and University Libraries
1935	Charles Lamb Society		
1904	Classical Association	1984	Standing Conference for the Arts and Social Sciences
1902	Dickens Fellowship		
1890	Edinburgh Bibliographical Society	1968	Thomas Hardy Society

Management

1986	British Academy of Management

Mathematics and Physics

1924	Astronomical Society of Edinburgh	1930	Institution of Electronics
1890	British Astronomical Association	1871	Mathematical Association
1966	British Biophysical Society	1820	Royal Astronomical Society
1927	British Institute of Radiology	1850	Royal Meteorological Society
1933	British Interplanetary Society		

Medicine (including Psychology)

1887	Anatomical Society of GB and Ireland	1913	British Psychoanalytical Society
1957	Association for Child and Adolescent Mental Health	1901	British Psychological Society
		1948	British Society for Allergy and Clinical Immunology
1957	Association for the Study of Medical Education	1962	British Society for Clinical Cytology
1932	Association of Anaesthetists of GB and Ireland	1937	British Society of Gastroenterology
		1960	British Society for Haematology
1933	Association of British Neurologists	1947	British Society for Research on Ageing
1953	Association of Clinical Biochemistry	1945	British Thoracic Society
1927	Association of Clinical Pathologists	1947	Ergonomics Society
1920	Association of Surgeons of GB and Ireland	1946	Experimental Psychology Society
		1950	Faculty of Homeopathy
1959	British Academy for Forensic Science	1959	Forensic Science Society
2003	British Association for Sexual Health and HIV	1819	Hunterian Society
		1969	Institute of Occupational Medicine
1977	British Association of Clinical Anatomists	1964	Institute of Pharmacy Management
		1773	Medical Society of London
1950	British Association of Forensic Medicine	1901	Medico-Legal Society
		1941	Nutrition Society
1962	British Association of Oral Surgeons	1906	Pathological Society of Great Britain and Ireland
1943	British Association of Otolaryngologists		
		1875	Royal Environmental Health Institute of Scotland
1954	British Association of Paediatric Surgeons		
		1734	Royal Medical Society
1973	British Association of Surgical Oncology	1931	Royal Pharmaceutical Society of Great Britain
1945	British Association of Urological Surgeons	2008	Royal Society for Public Health
		1805	Royal Society of Medicine
1934	British Diabetic Association	1907	Royal Society of Tropical Medicine and Hygiene
1948	British Geriatrics Society		
1832	British Medical Association	1946	Society for Endocrinology
1950	British Neuropathological Society	1950	Society for Reproduction and Fertility
1953	British Occupational Hygiene Society	1884	Society for the Study of Addiction
1965	British Orthodontic Society	1926	Society of British Neurological Surgeons
1918	British Orthopaedic Association		
1925	British Osteopathic Association		

Music

1977	Alkan Society	1882	Incorporated Society of Musicians
1979	British Music Society	1888	Plainsong and Medieval Music Society
1971	Chopin Society	1874	Royal Musical Association
1932	English Folk Dance and Song Society	1955	Welsh Music Guild

Philosophy

1880	Aristotelian Society	1984	British Society for the History of Philosophy
2003	British Philosophical Association		
		1819	Cambridge Philosophical Society

1990	Friedrich Nietzsche Society	1913	Philosophical Society of England
1979	Hegel Society of Great Britain	1925	Royal Institute of Philosophy
1781	Manchester Literary and Philosophical Society	1802	Royal Philosophical Society of Glasgow

Politics

1975	British International Studies Association	1987	Institute of Welsh Affairs
1951	David Davies Memorial Institute of International Studies	1974	International Association for the Study of German Politics
1884	Electoral Reform Society	1950	Political Studies Association
1945	Federal Trust for Education and Research	1868	Royal Commonwealth Society
		1920	Royal Institute of International Affairs

Science general

1924	Association for Informational Management	1960	British Society for the Philosophy of Science
1831	British Science Association	1799	Royal Institution of Great Britain
1956	British Society for the History of Science	1660	Royal Society
		1783	Royal Society of Edinburgh

Theology and Religious Studies

1908	Baptist Historical Society	1981	European Association for Jewish Studies
1954	British Association for the Study of Religions	1903	Friends Historical Society
1904	Canterbury and York Society	1972	United Reformed Church History Society
1904	Catholic Record Society	1893	Wesley Historical Society
1961	Ecclesiastical History Society		

General Index

General Index

Note: In addition to the abbreviations listed at the beginning of the book, the following are used throughout the index; FE – Further Education; HE – Higher Education. Universities are listed under locations eg: Aberdeen, University of

Aberdeen, University of 35
Abertay, Dundee, University of 37
Aberystwyth University 37
ABRSM (Associated Board of the Royal Schools of Music) 404
The Academy of Executives & Administrators 275
The Academy of Experts 367
The Academy of Multi-Skills 275
Accountancy
    Association of Accounting Technicians 249
    Association of Charity Independent Examiners 249
    The Association of Chartered Certified Accountants 253
    The Association of Corporate Treasurers 253
    The Association of International Accountants 254
    Chartered Institute of Internal Auditors 250
    The Chartered Institute of Public Finance and Accountancy 254
    CIMA – The Chartered Institute of Management Accountants 250
    ICAEW (The Institute of Chartered Accountants in England and Wales) 251
    ICAS (Institute of Chartered Accountants of Scotland) 251
    The Institute of Certified Bookkeepers 255
    Institute of Financial Accountants 252
    International Association of Book-keepers 252
Acoustics
    Institute of Acoustics 255
Advertising and Public Relations
    Chartered Institute of Public Relations 256
    Institute of Practitioners in Advertising 257
    Institute of Promotional Marketing 257
    London School of Public Relations 258
Agriculture and Horticulture
    Institute of Horticulture 258
    The Royal Botanic Garden Edinburgh 259
    Royal Horticultural Society 259
Ambulance Service Institute 260
Ambulance Service
    Ambulance Service Institute 260

Anglia Ruskin University 38
Arbitration
    The Chartered Institute of Arbitrators 260
The Arboricultural Association 332
Archaeology
    The Institute for Archaeologists 261
Architects Registration Board 261
Architecture
    Architects Registration Board 261
    Chartered Institute of Architectural Technologists (CIAT) 262
    Royal Institute of British Architects 262
Art and Design
    British Association of Art Therapists 263
    British Association of Paintings Conservator-Restorers 263
    The Chartered Society of Designers 264
    D&AD (British Design & Art Direction) 264
    The Index of Professional Master Designers 265
    Society of Designer Craftsmen (SDC) 264
Ashridge 40
Askham Bryan College 123
Association for Project Management 370
Association of Accounting Technicians 249
Association of Average Adjusters 352
Association of British Dispensing Opticians 409
Association of Building Engineers 439
The Association of Business Executives 378
Association of Business Recovery Professionals (R3) 274
Association of Certified Commercial Diplomats (ACCD) 371
Association of Charity Independent Examiners 249
The Association of Chartered Certified Accountants 253
Association of Child Psychotherapists 424
Association of Computer Professionals 295
Association of Contact Lens Manufacturers 411
The Association of Corporate Treasurers 253
Association of Cost Engineers 317
The Association of International Accountants 254

General Index

Association of Medical Secretaries, Practice Managers, Administrators and Receptionists 391
Association of Optometrists 411
Association of Photographers (AOP) 417
Association of Principal Fire Officers 315
The Association of Taxation Technicians 441
Association of Therapy Lecturers 268
Aston University 40
Astronomy and Space Science
 The British Interplanetary Society 265
AUA 372
Aviation
 The Guild of Air Pilots and Air Navigators 266
 The Guild of Air Traffic Control Officers 266
Bangor University 42
Banking
 The Chartered Institute of Bankers in Scotland 267
 ifs School of Finance 267
Baptist Union of Scotland 284
Bath Spa University 45
Bath, University of 44
Beauty Therapy and Beauty Culture
 Association of Therapy Lecturers 268
 British Association of Beauty Therapy and Cosmetology Ltd 268
 British Institute and Association of Electrolysis Ltd 269
 Federation of Holistic Therapists 269
 ITEC 270
Bedfordshire, University of 46
The Benesh Institute 300
BII 277
Biological Sciences
 Institute of Biomedical Science 270
 Society of Biology 271
Birmingham City University 52
Birmingham, University of 49
Bishop Burton College 112
Bishop Grosseteste University College 54
Blackpool and The Fylde College 119
Bournemouth University 54
Bradford College 56
Bradford, University of 55
Brewing
 Institute of Brewing & Distilling 271

Brighton, University of 56
Bristol Baptist College 284
Bristol, University of 58
The British (Theatrical) Arts 305
British Agricultural and Garden Machinery Association 308
British and Irish Orthoptic Society 412
The British Antique Dealers' Association 432
British Association for Counselling and Psychotherapy 425
British Association for the Person Centred Approach 426
British Association of Art Therapists 263
British Association of Beauty Therapy and Cosmetology Ltd 268
British Association of Dental Nurses 302
British Association of Occupational Therapists 409
British Association of Paintings Conservator-Restorers 263
British Association of Psychotherapists 426
The British Association of Social Workers 435
British Ballet Organization 299
British Chiropody and Podiatry Association 281
British Computer Society 295
British Contact Lens Association 411
The British Dental Association 301
The British Dietetic Association 303
The British Horological Institute Limited 452
The British Horse Society 347
British Institute and Association of Electrolysis Ltd 269
British Institute of Cleaning Science 292
The British Institute of Dental and Surgical Technologists 439
The British Institute of Embalmers 306
British Institute of Facilities Management 372
The British Institute of Non-Destructive Testing 408
British Institute of Professional Photography 418
British International Freight Association (BIFA) 334
The British Interplanetary Society 265
British Kinematograph Sound and Television Society (BKSTS) 291
British Medical Acupuncture Society 386
British Occupational Hygiene Society – Faculty of Occupational Hygiene 343
British Osteopathic Association 413
The British Psychoanalytical Society 423

474

British Psychological Society   424
British Safety Council   349
British Society of Dental Hygiene and Therapy   301
British Society of Scientific Glassblowers   341
British Sociological Association   436
British Veterinary Association   450
Brunel University   62
Buckingham, University of   63
Buckinghamshire New University   64
Building
    The Chartered Institute of Building   272
    Institute of Asphalt Technology   272
    The Institute of Carpenters   273
    The Institute of Clerks of Works and Construction Inspectorate of Great Britain Inc   273
Business Management Association   373
Business Studies
    The Academy of Executives & Administrators   275
    The Academy of Multi-Skills   275
    Association of Business Recovery Professionals (R3)   274
    The Faculty of Secretaries and Administrators (1930) with The Association of Corporate Secretaries   276
    Institute of Assessors and Internal Verifiers   274
    The Institute of Chartered Secretaries and Administrators   276
The Cambridge Academy of Management   379
Cambridge College of Hypnotherapy   426
Cambridge International College   67
Cambridge, University of   64
Canterbury Christ Church University   67
Cardiff Metropolitan University   71
Cardiff University   69
Catering and Institutional Management
    BII   277
    Confederation of Tourism and Hospitality   278
    Guild of International Professional Toastmasters   278
    Institute of Hospitality   279
Central Lancashire, University of   73
CFA Society of the UK   438
The Chartered Institute for Securities & Investment   438
The Chartered Institute of Arbitrators   260

Chartered Institute of Architectural Technologists (CIAT)   262
The Chartered Institute of Bankers in Scotland   267
The Chartered Institute of Building   272
Chartered Institute of Environmental Health   344
The Chartered Institute of Housing   348
Chartered Institute of Internal Auditors   250
The Chartered Institute of Journalists   355
Chartered Institute of Library and Information Professionals   370
The Chartered Institute of Linguists   359
The Chartered Institute of Logistics and Transport (UK)   303
The Chartered Institute of Loss Adjusters   353
The Chartered Institute of Marketing   383
The Chartered Institute of Patent Attorneys   413
Chartered Institute of Personnel and Development   414
Chartered Institute of Plumbing and Heating Engineering   421
The Chartered Institute of Public Finance and Accountancy   254
Chartered Institute of Public Relations   256
The Chartered Institute of Purchasing & Supply   429
The Chartered Institute of Taxation   441
The Chartered Institution of Building Services Engineers   311
The Chartered Institution of Highways and Transportation   327
Chartered Institution of Wastes Management   451
The Chartered Institution of Water and Environmental Management   314
The Chartered Insurance Institute   353
The Chartered Management Institute   379
The Chartered Quality Institute   430
The Chartered Society of Designers   264
The Chartered Society of Physiotherapy   420
Chemistry
    The Oil and Colour Chemists' Association   280
    The Royal Society of Chemistry   280
    Society of Cosmetic Scientists   279
Chester, University of   74
Chichester, University of   76
Chief Fire Officers' Association   316
Chiropody
    British Chiropody and Podiatry Association   281

General Index

The Institute of Chiropodists and Podiatrists 281
The Society of Chiropodists and Podiatrists 282
Chiropractic
    McTimoney Chiropractic Association 282
    Scottish Chiropractic Association 283
    United Chiropractic Association 283
The Church in Wales 290
The Church of England 285
The Church of Scotland 285
The Churches
    Baptist Union of Scotland 284
    Bristol Baptist College 284
    The Church in Wales 290
    The Church of England 285
    The Church of Scotland 285
    The Methodist Church 286
    Methodist Church in Ireland 285
    The Moravian Church in Great Britain and Ireland 286
    The Presbyterian Church in Ireland 287
    The Presbyterian Church of Wales 287
    The Roman Catholic Church 287
    The Salvation Army 288
    The Scottish Episcopal Church 288
    The Scottish United Reformed and Congregational College 288
    The Unitarian and Free Christian Churches 289
    United Free Church of Scotland 290
    The United Reformed Church 289
    The Wesleyan Reform Union 290
CIMA – The Chartered Institute of Management Accountants 250
Cinema, Film and Television
    British Kinematograph Sound and Television Society (BKSTS) 291
    The London Film School 291
    The National Film and Television School 292
City College Norwich 91
City of Sunderland College 216
City University London 76
Cleaning, Laundry and Dry Cleaning
    British Institute of Cleaning Science 292
    The Guild of Cleaners and Launderers 293
Clinical Dental Technicians Association 302
Colchester Institute 40
The College of Estate Management 356

College of Operating Department Practitioners 391
The College of Pharmacy Practice 416
College of the Resurrection 123
Colour Technology
    Painting and Decorating Association 293
    The Society of Dyers and Colourists 294
Communications and Media
    The Picture Research Association 294
Computing and Information Technology
    Association of Computer Professionals 295
    British Computer Society 295
    Institute for the Management of Information Systems 296
    Institution of Analysts and Programmers 296
Confederation of Tourism and Hospitality 278
Confederation of Tourism and Hospitality 448
Council for Awards in Children's Care and Education 408
Council for Licensed Conveyancers 360
Counselling Ltd 297
Counselling
    Counselling Ltd 297
    Counsellors and Psychotherapists in Primary Care 297
    CSCT Counselling Training 298
Counsellors and Psychotherapists in Primary Care 297
Coventry University 79
Cranfield University 80
Cranmer Hall, St John's College 88
Credit Management
    Institute of Credit Management 298
CSCT Counselling Training 298
Cumbria, University of 81
D&AD (British Design & Art Direction) 264
Dancing
    The Benesh Institute 300
    British Ballet Organization 299
    Imperial Society of Teachers of Dancing 299
    International Dance Teachers' Association Limited 300
De Montford University 82
Dental Technologists Association 302
Dentistry
    British Association of Dental Nurses 302
    The British Dental Association 301

British Society of Dental Hygiene and
    Therapy 301
  Clinical Dental Technicians Association 302
  Dental Technologists Association 302
  General Dental Council 301
Derby, University of 83
Dietetics
  The British Dietetic Association 303
Diplomatic Academy of Europe and the
    Atlantic 373
Distribution
  The Chartered Institute of Logistics and
    Transport (UK) 303
Diving Certificates 304
Diving
  Diving Certificates 304
Doncaster College 112
Dramatic and Performing Arts
  The British (Theatrical) Arts 305
  Equity 304
  National Council for Drama Training 305
Driving Instructors
  Register of Approved Driving Instructors 305
Dundee, University of 84
Durham University 87
East Anglia, University of 89
East Lancashire Institute of Higher Education at
    Blackburn College 54
East London, University of 138
East Riding College 129
Edge Hill University 119
Edinburgh College of Art 95
Edinburgh Mathematical Society 388
Edinburgh Napier University 94
Edinburgh, The University of 91
Embalming
  The British Institute of Embalmers 306
  International Examinations Board of
    Embalmers 306
Employment and Careers Services
  The Institute of Career Guidance 307
  Recruitment and Employment
    Confederation 307
Energy Institute 313
The Engineering Council 318
Engineering Design
  The Institution of Engineering Designers 329

Engineering, Aeronautical
  Royal Aeronautical Society 308
Engineering, Agricultural
  British Agricultural and Garden Machinery
    Association 308
  The Institution of Agricultural Engineers 309
Engineering, Automobile
  Institute of Automotive Engineer Assessors 309
  The Institute of the Motor Industry 310
  Society of Automotive Engineers 310
Engineering, Building Services
  The Chartered Institution of Building Services
    Engineers 311
Engineering, Chemical
  The Institution of Chemical Engineers 311
Engineering, Civil
  Institution of Civil Engineers 312
Engineering, Electrical, Electronic and Manufacturing
  The Institution of Engineering and
    Technology 313
  Institution of Lighting Professionals 312
Engineering, Energy
  Energy Institute 313
Engineering, Environmental
  The Chartered Institution of Water and
    Environmental Management 314
  Institute of Environmental Management and
    Assessment 314
  The Society of Environmental Engineers 315
Engineering, Fire
  Association of Principal Fire Officers 315
  Chief Fire Officers' Association 316
  The Institution of Fire Engineers 316
Engineering, Gas
  The Institution of Gas Engineers and
    Managers 317
Engineering, General
  Association of Cost Engineers 317
  The Engineering Council 318
  Institute of Measurement and Control 318
  The Institution of British Engineers 319
  SEMTA – The Sector Skills Council for Science,
    Engineering and Manufacturing
    Technologies 318
  Women's Engineering Society 319
Engineering, Marine

General Index

The Institute of Marine Engineering, Science and Technology 320
Engineering, Mechanical
    Institution of Mechanical Engineers 321
Engineering, Mining
    Institute of Explosives Engineers 322
    The Institute of Materials, Minerals and Mining (IOM^3) 322
    The Institute of Quarrying 323
Engineering, Nuclear
    The Nuclear Institute 323
Engineering, Production
    The Institute of Operations Management 324
Engineering, Refractories
    Institute of Refractories Engineering 324
Engineering, Refrigeration
    The Institute of Refrigeration 325
Engineering, Road, Rail and Transport
    The Chartered Institution of Highways and Transportation 327
    Institute of Highway Engineers 325
    Institution of Railway Signal Engineers 326
    Society of Operations Engineers 326
Engineering, Sheet Metal
    Institute of Sheet Metal Engineering 327
Engineering, Structural
    The Institution of Structural Engineers 328
Engineering, Water
    Institute of Water 328
Environmental Sciences
    Institute of Ecology and Environmental Management 329
Equity 304
Ergonomics Society 344
Essex, University of 95
Exeter, University of 97
Export
    The Institute of Export 330
The Faculty and Institute of Actuaries 354
Faculty of Professional Business and Technical Management 374
The Faculty of Secretaries and Administrators (1930) with The Association of Corporate Secretaries 276
Farnborough College of Technology 218
Federation of Holistic Therapists 269

The Federation of Royal Colleges of Physicians of the United Kingdom 394
Fisheries Management
    Institute of Fisheries Management 330
Flooring Industry Training Association 336
Floristry
    Society of Floristry Ltd 331
Food Science and Nutrition
    Institute of Food Science and Technology 331
Forestry and Arboriculture
    The Arboricultural Association 332
    Institute of Chartered Foresters 332
    The Royal Forestry Society 333
The Foundation for Psychotherapy and Counselling 428
Foundry Technology and Pattern Making
    The Institute of Cast Metals Engineers 333
Freight Forwarding
    British International Freight Association (BIFA) 334
Fundraising
    Institute of Fundraising 334
Funeral Directing, Burial and Cremation Administration
    The Institute of Burial and Cremation Administration 336
    National Association of Funeral Directors 335
    National Association of Memorial Masons 335
Furnishing and Furniture
    Flooring Industry Training Association 336
    National Institute of Carpet and Floorlayers 337
The Gemmological Association of Great Britain 337
Gemmology and Jewellery
    The Gemmological Association of Great Britain 337
    The National Association of Goldsmiths 338
Genealogy
    The Heraldry Society 339
    The Institute of Heraldic and Genealogical Studies 339
    Society of Genealogists 338
General Dental Council 301
Geography
    Royal Geographical Society (with The Institute of British Geographers) 340
The Geological Society 340
Geology

The Geological Society   340
Glamorgan, University of   99
Glasgow Caledonian University   102
The Glasgow School of Art   103
Glasgow, University of   100
Glass Technology
   British Society of Scientific Glassblowers   341
   Society of Glass Technology   341
Gloucestershire, University of   103
The Greek Institute   359
Greenwich, University of   104
Grimsby Institute/University Centre   105
The Guild of Air Pilots and Air Navigators   266
The Guild of Air Traffic Control Officers   266
The Guild of Architectural Ironmongers   432
The Guild of Cleaners and Launderers   293
The Guild of Hairdressers   342
Guild of International Professional Toastmasters   278
Guildhall School of Music & Drama   78
Habia   342
Hairdressing
   The Guild of Hairdressers   342
   Habia   342
Harper Adams University College   106
Health & Safety Executive Approved Mining Qualifications   350
Health and Health Services
   British Occupational Hygiene Society – Faculty of Occupational Hygiene   343
   Chartered Institute of Environmental Health   344
   Ergonomics Society   344
   Institute of Health Promotion and Education   345
   Institute of Health Records and Information Management   345
   Institute of Healthcare Engineering and Estate Management   346
   Institute of Healthcare Management   346
   The Royal Society for Public Health   347
The Heraldry Society   339
Heriot-Watt University   106
Hertfordshire Regional College   109
Hertfordshire, University of   107
Horses and Horse Riding
   The British Horse Society   347
Housing
   The Chartered Institute of Housing   348
Huddersfield, The University of   109
Hull College   129
Hull, University of   110
ICAEW (The Institute of Chartered Accountants in England and Wales)   251
ICAS (Institute of Chartered Accountants of Scotland)   251
ifs School of Finance   267
IGD   431
Imperial College, London   112
Imperial Society of Teachers of Dancing   299
Incorporated Society of Musicians   405
Incorporated Society of Organ Builders   405
The Index of Professional Master Designers   265
Indexing
   Society of Indexers   348
Industrial Safety
   British Safety Council   349
   Health & Safety Executive Approved Mining Qualifications   350
   The Institution of Occupational Safety and Health   352
   International Institute of Risk and Safety Management   350
   NEBOSH (The National Examination Board in Occupational Safety and Health)   351
The Institute for Archaeologists   261
Institute for Sport, Parks and Leisure   368
Institute for the Management of Information Systems   296
Institute of Acoustics   255
Institute of Administrative Management   374
Institute of Asphalt Technology   272
Institute of Assessors and Internal Verifiers   274
Institute of Automotive Engineer Assessors   309
Institute of Biomedical Science   270
Institute of Brewing & Distilling   271
The Institute of Builders Merchants   433
The Institute of Burial and Cremation Administration   336
Institute of Business Consulting   375
The Institute of Career Guidance   307
The Institute of Carpenters   273
The Institute of Cast Metals Engineers   333
The Institute of Certified Bookkeepers   255

General Index

Institute of Chartered Foresters   332
The Institute of Chartered Secretaries and Administrators   276
The Institute of Chiropodists and Podiatrists   281
The Institute of Clerks of Works and Construction Inspectorate of Great Britain Inc   273
The Institute of Clinical Research   395
The Institute of Commercial Management   380
The Institute of Continuing Professional Development   415
Institute of Corrosion   401
Institute of Credit Management   298
The Institute of Direct Marketing   384
Institute of Directors   375
Institute of Ecology and Environmental Management   329
Institute of Environmental Management and Assessment   314
Institute of Explosives Engineers   322
The Institute of Export   330
Institute of Financial Accountants   252
Institute of Fisheries Management   330
Institute of Food Science and Technology   331
Institute of Fundraising   334
Institute of Groundsmanship   369
Institute of Health Promotion and Education   345
Institute of Health Records and Information Management   345
Institute of Healthcare Engineering and Estate Management   346
Institute of Healthcare Management   346
The Institute of Heraldic and Genealogical Studies   339
Institute of Highway Engineers   325
Institute of Horticulture   258
Institute of Hospitality   279
The Institute of Indirect Taxation   442
Institute of Leadership & Management   376
The Institute of Legal Cashiers and Administrators (ILCA)   368
Institute of Legal Executives   367
Institute of Management Services   377
The Institute of Management Specialists   380
The Institute of Manufacturing   381
The Institute of Marine Engineering, Science and Technology   320
Institute of Martial Arts and Sciences   386

Institute of Masters of Wine   431
The Institute of Materials, Minerals and Mining (IOM^3)   322
The Institute of Mathematics and its Applications   389
Institute of Measurement and Control   318
The Institute of Metal Finishing   402
The Institute of Operations Management   324
The Institute of Paper, Printing and Publishing (IP3)   422
Institute of Physics and Engineering in Medicine   419
The Institute of Physics   420
Institute of Practitioners in Advertising   257
Institute of Professional Administrators   434
The Institute of Professional Investigators   423
Institute of Promotional Marketing   257
The Institute of Public Sector Management   429
The Institute of Quarrying   323
Institute of Refractories Engineering   324
The Institute of Refrigeration   325
The Institute of Revenues, Rating and Valuation   356
The Institute of Sales and Marketing Management   384
The Institute of Scientific and Technical Communicators (ISTC LTD)   444
Institute of Sheet Metal Engineering   327
Institute of Sport and Recreation Management (ISRM)   369
The Institute of the Motor Industry   310
The Institute of Traffic Accident Investigators   447
Institute of Translation & Interpreting   358
Institute of Transport Administration   447
Institute of Travel and Tourism   448
Institute of Value Management   377
Institute of Water   328
Institute of Welfare   453
The Institution of Agricultural Engineers   309
Institution of Analysts and Programmers   296
The Institution of British Engineers   319
The Institution of Chemical Engineers   311
Institution of Civil Engineers   312
The Institution of Engineering and Technology   313
The Institution of Engineering Designers   329
The Institution of Fire Engineers   316
The Institution of Gas Engineers and Managers   317
Institution of Lighting Professionals   312

General Index

Institution of Mechanical Engineers   321
The Institution of Occupational Safety and
    Health   352
Institution of Railway Signal Engineers   326
The Institution of Structural Engineers   328
Insurance and Actuarial Work
    Association of Average Adjusters   352
    The Chartered Institute of Loss Adjusters   353
    The Chartered Insurance Institute   353
    The Faculty and Institute of Actuaries   354
International Association of Book-keepers   252
International Dance Teachers' Association
    Limited   300
International Examinations Board of
    Embalmers   306
International Institute of Risk and Safety
    Management   350
International Professional Managers
    Association   378
ITEC   270
Journalism
    The Chartered Institute of Journalists   355
    National Council for the Training of
        Journalists   354
Keele University   113
Kent, University of   114
Kingston University   116
Laban   78
Lancaster University   117
Land and Property
    The College of Estate Management   356
    The Institute of Revenues, Rating and
        Valuation   356
    The National Federation of Property
        Professionals   357
    The Property Consultants Society   357
    RICS (Royal Institution of Chartered
        Surveyors)   355
Landscape Architecture
    Landscape Institute   358
Landscape Institute   358
Languages, Linguistics and Translation
    The Chartered Institute of Linguists   359
    The Greek Institute   359
    Institute of Translation & Interpreting   358
The Law Society of Scotland   366
Law

The Academy of Experts   367
Council for Licensed Conveyancers   360
The Institute of Legal Cashiers and
    Administrators (ILCA)   368
Institute of Legal Executives   367
The Law Society of Scotland   366
LCSP Register of Remedial Masseurs and
    Manipulative Therapists   387
Leeds College of Art   123
Leeds College of Music   123
Leeds Metropolitan University   124
Leeds Trinity University College   123
Leeds, University of   120
Leicester, University of   126
Leisure and Recreation Management
    Institute for Sport, Parks and Leisure   368
    Institute of Groundsmanship   369
    Institute of Sport and Recreation Management
        (ISRM)   369
Librarianship and Information Work
    Chartered Institute of Library and Information
        Professionals   370
Lincoln, University of   128
Liverpool Hope University   132
Liverpool John Moores University   132
Liverpool, University of   130
London Centre of Marketing   382
London Contemporary Dance School   134
The London Film School   291
London Metropolitan Polymer Centre   421
London Metropolitan University   135
The London School of Osteopathy   136
London School of Public Relations   258
London School of Sports Massage   437
London South Bank University   137
London, University of
    Birkbeck, University of   140
    Courtauld Institute of Art, University of   141
    Goldsmiths, University of   141
    Heythrop College, University of   142
    Institute in Paris, University of   142
    Institute of Education, University of   142
    King's College London, University of   143
    London School of Economics & Political Science,
        University of   145
    London School of Jewish Studies,
        University of   145

481

General Index

    Queen Mary, University of   145
    Royal Holloway, University of   147
    Royal Veterinary College, University of   148
    School of Oriental and African Studies, University of   149
    The School of Pharmacy, University of   149
    University College London (UCL), University of   150
Loughborough, University of   153
Management
    Association for Project Management   370
    The Association of Business Executives   378
    Association of Certified Commercial Diplomats (ACCD)   371
    AUA   372
    British Institute of Facilities Management   372
    Business Management Association   373
    The Cambridge Academy of Management   379
    The Chartered Management Institute   379
    Diplomatic Academy of Europe and the Atlantic   373
    Faculty of Professional Business and Technical Management   374
    Institute of Administrative Management   374
    Institute of Business Consulting   375
    The Institute of Commercial Management   380
    Institute of Directors   375
    Institute of Leadership & Management   376
    Institute of Management Services   377
    The Institute of Management Specialists   380
    Institute of Value Management   377
    International Professional Managers Association   378
    The Society of Business Practitioners   381
Managing and Marketing Sales Association Examination Board   382
Manchester Metropolitan University   158
Manchester, University of   155
Manufacturing
    The Institute of Manufacturing   381
Marketing and Sales
    The Chartered Institute of Marketing   383
    The Institute of Direct Marketing   384
    The Institute of Sales and Marketing Management   384
    London Centre of Marketing   382
    Managing and Marketing Sales Association Examination Board   382
    MRS (The Market Research Society)   383
    The Society of Sales & Marketing   385
Martial Arts
    Institute of Martial Arts and Sciences   386
Massage and Allied Therapies
    British Medical Acupuncture Society   386
    LCSP Register of Remedial Masseurs and Manipulative Therapists   387
    Northern Institute of Massage Ltd   387
    Society of Homeopaths   388
Master Photographers Association   418
The Mathematical Association   389
Mathematics
    Edinburgh Mathematical Society   388
    The Institute of Mathematics and its Applications   389
    The Mathematical Association   389
McTimoney Chiropractic Association   282
Meat Training Council   432
Medical Herbalism
    The National Institute of Medical Herbalists   390
Medical Secretaries
    Association of Medical Secretaries, Practice Managers, Administrators and Receptionists   391
Medicine
    College of Operating Department Practitioners   391
    The Federation of Royal Colleges of Physicians of the United Kingdom   394
    The Institute of Clinical Research   395
    The Royal College of Anaesthetists   395
    Royal College of General Practitioners   392
    Royal College of Obstetricians and Gynaecologists   393
    The Royal College of Pathologists   396
    The Royal College of Physicians and Surgeons of Glasgow   396
    The Royal College of Physicians of Edinburgh   397
    The Royal College of Physicians of London   397
    The Royal College of Psychiatrists   399
    The Royal College of Radiologists   399

General Index

The Royal College of Surgeons of
    Edinburgh   400
The Royal College of Surgeons of England   400
Royal Society of Medicine   393
The Society of Apothecaries of London   400
Met Office College   402
Metallurgy
    Institute of Corrosion   401
    The Institute of Metal Finishing   402
Meteorology and Climatology
    Met Office College   402
    Royal Meteorological Society   403
Methodist Church in Ireland   285
The Methodist Church   286
Microscopy
    The Royal Microscopical Society   403
Middlesex University   160
The Moravian Church in Great Britain and
    Ireland   286
MRS (The Market Research Society)   383
Museum and Related Work
    Museums Association   404
Museums Association   404
Music
    ABRSM (Associated Board of the Royal Schools
    of Music)   404
Musical Instrument Technology
    Incorporated Society of Organ Builders   405
    Pianoforte Tuners' Association   406
Music
    Incorporated Society of Musicians   405
National Association of Funeral Directors   335
The National Association of Goldsmiths   338
National Association of Memorial Masons   335
National College of Hypnosis and
    Psychotherapy   427
National Council for Drama Training   305
National Council for the Training of Journalists   354
National Council of Psychotherapists   427
The National Federation of Property
    Professionals   357
The National Film and Television School   292
National Institute of Carpet and Floorlayers   337
The National Institute of Medical Herbalists   390
The National Register of Hypnotherapists and
    Psychotherapists   428
The Nautical Institute   407

Naval Architecture
    The Royal Institution of Naval Architects   406
Navigation, Seamanship and Marine Qualifications
    The Nautical Institute   407
    The Royal Institute of Navigation   407
NEBOSH (The National Examination Board in
    Occupational Safety and Health)   351
NESCOT (North East Surrey College of
    Technology)   219
New College Durham   88
Newcastle upon Tyne, University of   162
Newman University College   127
Non-destructive Testing
    The British Institute of Non-Destructive
    Testing   408
The Nordoff-Robbins Music Therapy Centre   78
North Hertfordshire College   109
North Lindsey College   129
Northampton, University of   165
Northern Institute of Massage Ltd   387
Northern School of Contemporary Dance   124
Northumbria at Newcastle, University of   167
Nottingham Trent University   173
Nottingham, University of   169
The Nuclear Institute   323
Nursery Nursing
    Council for Awards in Children's Care and
    Education   408
The Nursing & Midwifery Council   409
Nursing and Midwifery
    The Nursing & Midwifery Council   409
Oaklands College   109
Occupational Therapy
    British Association of Occupational
    Therapists   409
The Oil and Colour Chemists' Association   280
The Open University   177
Opticians (Dispensing)
    Association of British Dispensing Opticians   409
    Association of Contact Lens Manufacturers   411
    British Contact Lens Association   411
Optometry
    Association of Optometrists   411
Orthoptics
    British and Irish Orthoptic Society   412
Osteopathy and Naturopathy
    British Osteopathic Association   413

483

General Index

Otley College   91
Oxford Brookes University   182
Oxford, University of   178
Painting and Decorating Association   293
Patent Agency
   The Chartered Institute of Patent Attorneys   413
Pension Management
   The Pensions Management Institute   414
The Pensions Management Institute   414
Personnel Management
   Chartered Institute of Personnel and Development   414
   The Institute of Continuing Professional Development   415
   UK Employee Assistance Professionals Association   415
The Pharmaceutical Society of Northern Ireland   417
Pharmacy
   The College of Pharmacy Practice   416
   The Pharmaceutical Society of Northern Ireland   417
   Royal Pharmaceutical Society of Great Britain   416
Photography
   Association of Photographers (AOP)   417
   British Institute of Professional Photography   418
   Master Photographers Association   418
   The Royal Photographic Society   419
Physics
   The Institute of Physics   420
   Institute of Physics and Engineering in Medicine   419
Physiotherapy
   The Chartered Society of Physiotherapy   420
Pianoforte Tuners' Association   406
The Picture Research Association   294
Plastics and Rubber
   London Metropolitan Polymer Centre   421
Plumbing
   Chartered Institute of Plumbing and Heating Engineering   421
Plymouth, University of   184
Portsmouth, University of   186
The Presbyterian Church in Ireland   287
The Presbyterian Church of Wales   287
Printing

The Institute of Paper, Printing and Publishing (IP3)   422
Proskills UK   422
Professional Investigation
   The Institute of Professional Investigators   423
The Property Consultants Society   357
Proskills UK   422
Psychoanalysis
   The British Psychoanalytical Society   423
Psychology
   British Psychological Society   424
Psychotherapy
   Association of Child Psychotherapists   424
   British Association for Counselling and Psychotherapy   425
   British Association for the Person Centred Approach   426
   British Association of Psychotherapists   426
   Cambridge College of Hypnotherapy   426
   The Foundation for Psychotherapy and Counselling   428
   National College of Hypnosis and Psychotherapy   427
   National Council of Psychotherapists   427
   The National Register of Hypnotherapists and Psychotherapists   428
   UK Council for Psychotherapy   428
Public Administration
   The Institute of Public Sector Management   429
Purchasing and Supply
   The Chartered Institute of Purchasing & Supply   429
Quality Assurance
   The Chartered Quality Institute   430
Queen Margaret University College   189
The Queen's University of Belfast   47
Radiography
   The Society of Radiographers   430
Reading, University of   189
Recruitment and Employment Confederation   307
Register of Approved Driving Instructors   305
Retail
   The British Antique Dealers' Association   432
   The Guild of Architectural Ironmongers   432
   IGD   431
   The Institute of Builders Merchants   433
   Institute of Masters of Wine   431

General Index

Meat Training Council 432
The Society of Shoe Fitters 433
RICS (Royal Institution of Chartered Surveyors) 355
Riverside College, Halton 198
Robert Gordon University 191
Roehampton University 192
The Roman Catholic Church 287
Royal Academy of Dance 89
Royal Academy of Dramatic Art 193
Royal Aeronautical Society 308
Royal Agricultural College 194
Royal Ballet School 194
The Royal Botanic Garden Edinburgh 259
The Royal College of Anaesthetists 395
Royal College of Art 194
Royal College of General Practitioners 392
Royal College of Music 194
Royal College of Obstetricians and Gynaecologists 393
The Royal College of Organists 195
The Royal College of Pathologists 396
The Royal College of Physicians and Surgeons of Glasgow 396
The Royal College of Physicians of Edinburgh 397
The Royal College of Physicians of London 397
The Royal College of Psychiatrists 399
The Royal College of Radiologists 399
Royal College of Speech and Language Therapists 436
The Royal College of Surgeons of Edinburgh 400
The Royal College of Surgeons of England 400
The Royal College of Veterinary Surgeons 451
Royal Conservatoire of Scotland 195
The Royal Forestry Society 333
Royal Geographical Society (with The Institute of British Geographers) 340
Royal Horticultural Society 259
Royal Institute of British Architects 262
The Royal Institute of Navigation 407
The Royal Institution of Naval Architects 406
Royal Meteorological Society 403
The Royal Microscopical Society 403
Royal Northern College of Music 195
Royal Pharmaceutical Society of Great Britain 416
The Royal Photographic Society 419
The Royal Society for Public Health 347
The Royal Society of Chemistry 280
Royal Society of Medicine 393
The Royal Statistical Society 437
Royal Town Planning Institute 445
Salford, University of 197
The Salvation Army 288
School of Education, Selly Oak 52
School of Psychotherapy & Counselling Psychology at Regent's College 78
Scottish Chiropractic Association 283
The Scottish Episcopal Church 288
The Scottish United Reformed and Congregational College 288
Secretarial and Office Work
Institute of Professional Administrators 434
The Security Institute 434
Security
The Security Institute 434
SEMTA – The Sector Skills Council for Science, Engineering and Manufacturing Technologies 318
Sheffield Hallam University 203
Sheffield, University of 199
Social Work and Probation
The British Association of Social Workers 435
The Society of Apothecaries of London 400
Society of Automotive Engineers 310
Society of Biology 271
The Society of Business Practitioners 381
The Society of Chiropodists and Podiatrists 282
Society of Cosmetic Scientists 279
Society of Designer Craftsmen (SDC) 264
The Society of Dyers and Colourists 294
The Society of Environmental Engineers 315
Society of Floristry Ltd 331
Society of Genealogists 338
Society of Glass Technology 341
Society of Homeopaths 388
Society of Indexers 348
Society of Operations Engineers 326
Society of Practising Veterinary Surgeons 450
The Society of Radiographers 430
The Society of Sales & Marketing 385
The Society of Shoe Fitters 433
Society of Trust & Estate Practitioners 440
Sociology
British Sociological Association 436
South Devon College 186

Southampton Solent University   175
Southampton, University of   206
Speech and Language Therapy
    Royal College of Speech and Language
        Therapists   436
Sports Science
    London School of Sports Massage   437
St Andrews, University of   195
St Mary's College   219
Staffordshire University   209
Statistics
    The Royal Statistical Society   437
Stirling, University of   210
Stockbroking and Securities
    CFA Society of the UK   438
    The Chartered Institute for Securities &
        Investment   438
Stockport College   212
Strathclyde, University of   212
Sunderland, University of   215
Surgical, Dental and Cardiological Technicians
    The British Institute of Dental and Surgical
        Technologists   439
Surrey, University of   216
Surveying
    Association of Building Engineers   439
Sussex, University of   219
Swansea University   222
Swimming Instruction
    The Swimming Teachers' Association   440
The Swimming Teachers' Association   440
Taxation
    The Association of Taxation Technicians   441
    The Chartered Institute of Taxation   441
    The Institute of Indirect Taxation   442
    Society of Trust & Estate Practitioners   440
Taxi Drivers (London)   442
Taxi Drivers
    Taxi Drivers (London)   442
Teaching/Education
    442
Technical Communications
    The Institute of Scientific and Technical
        Communicators (ISTC LTD)   444
Teesside, University of   223
The Textile Institute   444
Textiles

The Textile Institute   444
the Arts London, University of   134
the West of England, Bristol, University of   60
Timber Technology
    Wood Technology Society   445
The Tourism Management Institute   449
The Tourism Society   449
Town and Country Planning
    Royal Town Planning Institute   445
The Trading Standards Institute   446
Trading Standards
    The Trading Standards Institute   446
Transport
    The Institute of Traffic Accident
        Investigators   447
    Institute of Transport Administration   447
Travel and Tourism
    Confederation of Tourism and Hospitality   448
    Institute of Travel and Tourism   448
    The Tourism Management Institute   449
    The Tourism Society   449
Trinity College London   224
Truro & Penwith College   186
UCP Marjon-University College Plymouth St Mark &
    St John   98
UK Council for Psychotherapy   428
UK Employee Assistance Professionals
    Association   415
Ulster, University of   225
The Unitarian and Free Christian Churches   289
United Chiropractic Association   283
United Free Church of Scotland   290
The United Reformed Church   289
University Campus Suffolk   214
University Centre Barnsley   44
University Centre Doncaster   84
University College Birmingham   52
University College Falmouth (Inc Dartington College
    of Arts)   99
University College Worcester   240
University for the Creative Arts   81
Ushaw College   89
Veterinary Science
    British Veterinary Association   450
    The Royal College of Veterinary Surgeons   451
    Society of Practising Veterinary Surgeons   450
Wales, University of

Glyndwr University 227
Newport 229
Swansea Metropolitan University 230
Trinity Saint David 231
Warwick, University of 233
Wastes Management
    Chartered Institution of Wastes
        Management 451
Watch and Clock Making and Repairing
    The British Horological Institute Limited 452
The Welding Institute 453
Welding
    The Welding Institute 453
Welfare
    Institute of Welfare 453
The Wesleyan Reform Union 290
West Herts College 109
West London, University of 139
West of Scotland, University of 235
Westminster, The University of 236
Winchester, The University of 237
Wolverhampton, University of 238
Women's Engineering Society 319
Wood Technology Society 445
Writtle College 97
York St John University 124
York, University of 241
Yorkshire Coast College 243